America's National [Parks] For Dummies, 2nd Edition

W9-BUF-383

The Best of America's National Parks

Acadia National Park (Chapter 9)

Best vista: Sunrise or sunset from Cadillac Mountain
Notable wildlife: Whales, harbor seals
Most unique experience: Climbing Precipice Trail
Top attraction: Park Loop Road
Best time to visit: Late summer, fall

Arches National Park (Chapter 10)

Best vista: Petrified Dunes Viewpoint
Notable wildlife: Desert bighorn sheep, western collared lizards
Most unique experience: Touring Fiery Furnace
Top attraction: Delicate Arch
Best time to visit: October through May

Cape Cod National Seashore (Chapter 11)

Best vista: From any beach
Notable wildlife: Whales, shorebirds
Most unique experience: Whale-watching
Top attraction: Coast Guard and Nauset Light Beaches, Provincetown
Best time to visit: Summer, early fall

Death Valley National Park (Chapter 12)

Best vista: From atop Dante's View
Notable wildlife: Mules, desert bighorn sheep
Most unique experience: Standing 282 feet *below* sea level
Top attraction: Scotty's Castle
Best time to visit: November through March

Grand Canyon National Park (Chapter 13)

Best vista: Sunset from Lipan Point
Notable wildlife: Condors, ringtail cats, Grand Canyon pink rattlesnakes
Most unique experience: Mule ride into the canyon
Top attraction: South Rim
Best time to visit: Spring, fall

Grand Teton National Park (Chapter 14)

Best vista: Oxbow Bend
Notable wildlife: Elk, moose, bison, wolves, and pronghorn antelope
Most unique experience: Standing atop the Grand Teton
Top attraction: Teton Range
Best time to visit: Late summer

Great Smoky Mountains National Park (Chapter 15)

Best vista: From atop Clingmans Dome
Notable wildlife: Black bears, giant salamanders
Most unique experience: Tubing in one of the rivers
Top attraction: Cades Cove
Best time to visit: Spring, fall

Mammoth Cave National Park (Chapter 16)

Best vista: Frozen Niagara
Notable wildlife: Turkeys
Most unique experience: Wild Cave Tour
Top attraction: Mammoth Cave
Best time to visit: Spring, early fall

Mount Rainier National Park (Chapter 17)

Best vista: Emmons Glacier from Sunrise
Notable wildlife: Mountain goats
Most unique experience: Walking on a glacier in summer
Top attraction: Mount Rainier
Best time to visit: Late summer, fall

For Dummies: Bestselling Book Series for Beginners

BESTSELLING
BOOK SERIES

America's National Parks For Dummies, 2nd Edition

Cheat Sheet

Olympic National Park (Chapter 18)

Best vista: Hurricane Ridge
Notable wildlife: Harbor seals, Roosevelt Elk
Most unique experience: Visiting the beach, a rain forest, and a snowfield in one day
Top attraction: Hoh Rain Forest
Best time to visit: Summer

Sequoia and Kings Canyon National Parks (Chapter 19)

Best vista: From atop Moro Rock
Notable wildlife: Black bears
Most unique experience: Standing next to General Sherman Tree
Top attraction: Giant Forest
Best time to visit: Summer

Yellowstone National Park (Chapter 20)

Best vista: Upper Geyser Basin from Observation Point
Notable wildlife: Wolves, grizzly bears, bison
Most unique experience: Watching wildlife in Lamar Valley
Top attraction: Old Faithful geyser
Best time to visit: Early summer, fall

Yosemite National Park (Chapter 21)

Best vista: From atop Glacier Point
Notable wildlife: Black bears
Most unique experience: Hiking to the top of Half Dome
Top attraction: Yosemite Valley
Best time to visit: Early summer

Zion National Park (Chapter 22)

Best vista: From Angel's Landing
Notable wildlife: Mountain lions
Most unique experience: Hiking The Narrows
Top attraction: Zion Canyon
Best time to visit: Spring, early fall

Top Ten Rules for a Safe and Fun Trip

1. Park animals are wild, not part of a petting zoo, so keep your distance.
2. Make sure that the only souvenirs you take out of a park are pictures or items you buy in a gift shop.
3. Pack plenty of film and extra batteries for your camera.
4. Pack plenty of sunscreen, and don't be bashful about using it.
5. Waterfalls can be awfully slippery, so don't try to climb them or get too close to the edge.
6. When visiting parks inhabited by bears, don't leave any food in your car or in your tent.
7. Pack rain gear — even if you don't expect rain on your trip.
8. Be careful where you put your hands when you're hiking — you never know when you might disturb a snake or spider.
9. Don't drink water from a lake or stream unless you treat or filter it first.
10. When traveling to a park at a higher elevation, ease into your vacation by taking it easy and acclimating on the first day.

For Dummies: Bestselling Book Series for Beginners

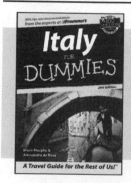

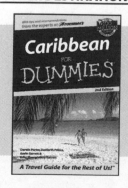
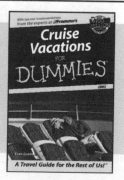

America's National Parks

FOR

DUMMIES®

2ND EDITION

by Kurt Repanshek

WILEY

Wiley Publishing, Inc.

America's National Parks For Dummies,® 2nd Edition

Published by
Wiley Publishing, Inc.
909 Third Avenue
New York, NY 10022
www.wiley.com

Copyright © 2003 by Wiley Publishing, Inc., Indianapolis, Indiana

Published simultaneously in Canada

For general information on our other products and services or to obtain technical support, please contact our Customer Care Department within the U.S. at 800-762-2974, outside the U.S. at 317-572-3993, or fax 317-572-4002.

Wiley also publishes its books in a variety of electronic formats. Some content that appears in print may not be available in electronic books.

Library of Congress Cataloging-in-Publication Data:

Library of Congress Control Number: 2002114833

ISBN: 0-7645-5493-X

ISSN: 1531-751X

Manufactured in the United States of America

10 9 8 7 6 5 4 3 2 1

2B/RR/QS/QT/IN

WILEY is a trademark of Wiley Publishing, Inc.

About the Author

Kurt Repanshek, a misplaced Easterner, has been roaming the Rocky Mountains since 1985, when he arrived in Wyoming as state correspondent for The Associated Press. A freelance writer now based in Park City, Utah, he has managed to find his way to the top of the Grand Teton; paddled portions of the Green, Colorado, and Middle Fork of the Salmon rivers, as well as Yellowstone's Shoshone and Yellowstone lakes; and cross-country skied in the pre-dawn cold to catch sunrise on the North Rim of the Grand Canyon, all in the pursuit of stories. He is the author of *Hidden Utah* and *Hidden Salt Lake City & Beyond* (both from Ulysses Press), and his work has appeared in *Audubon, Sunset, National Geographic Traveler,* and *Hemispheres,* among other publications.

Dedication

To my sons, Jesse and Sean, that they'll always share my curiosity to see what lies behind the next mountain.

Author's Acknowledgments

Believe it or not, books are not as easy to cobble together as they are to read. I'm thankful to my wife, Marcelle, for her belief that I'm a somewhat decent writer. I'd also be remiss if I didn't acknowledge her remarkable tolerance every time she heard that I still had "just one more" park to visit in the name of research. Kudos go to my editor, Lisa Torrance, a never-ending source of encouraging words and wise suggestions. Countless other folks came to my assistance time and again whenever I ran into dead-ends. Specifically, for their time, patience, and efforts, I'd like to thank David Barna and his communications staff at National Park Service headquarters in Washington, D.C., and the communications staff and various rangers at Acadia National Park, Cape Cod National Seashore, Death Valley National Park, Grand Canyon National Park, Grand Teton National Park, Great Smoky Mountains National Park, Mammoth Cave National Park, Mount Rainier National Park, Olympic National Park, Sequoia/Kings Canyon National Parks, Yellowstone National Park, Yosemite National Park, and Zion National Park. Finally, a big "thank you" to those many behind-the-scenes folks in the parks who ran down lodging, trail, and sightseeing information at a moment's notice.

Publisher's Acknowledgments

We're proud of this book; please send us your comments through our Dummies online registration form located at www.dummies.com/register/.

Some of the people who helped bring this book to market include the following:

Editorial

Editors: Linda Brandon, Project Editor; Lisa Torrance, Senior Editor

Copy Editor: Linda Brandon

Cartographer: Elizabeth Puhl

Senior Photo Editor: Richard Fox

Front Cover Photo: © Dan Sherwood/ Tony Stone Images

Back Cover Photo: © Art Wolfe/ Tony Stone Images

Cartoons: Rich Tennant, www.the5thwave.com

Production

Project Coordinator: Nancee Reeves

Layout and Graphics: Carrie Foster, Joyce Haughey, LeAndra Johnson, Michael Kruzil, Jacque Schneider, Julie Trippetti

Proofreaders: John Bitter, David Faust, Andy Hollandbeck, TECHBOOKS Production Services

Indexer: TECHBOOKS Production Services

Special Help

Michelle Hacker

Publishing and Editorial for Consumer Dummies

Diane Graves Steele, Vice President and Publisher, Consumer Dummies

Joyce Pepple, Acquisitions Director, Consumer Dummies

Kristin A. Cocks, Product Development Director, Consumer Dummies

Michael Spring, Vice President and Publisher, Travel

Brice Gosnell, Publishing Director, Travel

Suzanne Jannetta, Editorial Director, Travel

Publishing for Technology Dummies

Andy Cummings, Vice President and Publisher, Dummies Technology/General User

Composition Services

Gerry Fahey, Vice President of Production Services

Debbie Stailey, Director of Composition Services

Contents at a Glance

Maps at a Glance

Table of Contents

Introduction

· ·

Y ou've managed to carve some time out of your hectic schedule to visit one of America's national parks. That's great! You'll see some of the most breathtaking scenery in America, and you'll glimpse wildlife ranging from wolves, bears, elk, and moose to bald eagles and great blue herons. Plus, depending on which park you visit, you may discover something interesting about America's cultural history. Stop by Yellowstone, the nation's first national park, and you can even find out how the whole park movement began.

What makes a trip to a national park so wonderful? For starters, the parks give you a chance to flee the rat race and unwind in gorgeous settings. America's national park system is more diverse than any other park system in the world. You can stroll the seashore at Olympic National Park in Washington or Cape Cod National Seashore in Massachusetts, climb (or just admire) craggy mountains in Grand Teton National Park in Wyoming, or go underground into the world's largest cave network at Mammoth Cave National Park in Kentucky. At Arizona's Grand Canyon National Park, you can marvel at the largest canyon on Earth, and at Utah's aptly named Arches National Park, you can hike among the planet's largest collection of rock arches. California and Nevada share Death Valley National Park, the lowest and hottest spot in the Western Hemisphere, whereas Tennessee and North Carolina share Great Smoky Mountains National Park, a realm of forests and misty mountains.

These attractions are just a few of your park options. In the year 2002, the national park system included 380 sites — parks, monuments, historical sites, recreation areas, battlefields, military parks, lakeshores, seashores, scenic rivers, and trails — scattered across America. Even the White House is part of the national park system, but unlike the sites described in this book, you can't spend the night at 1600 Pennsylvania Avenue unless you're an incredibly big political donor or a friend of the Prez.

So much diversity, so little vacation time. With the breadth of the national park system (no chance of developing a "been there, done that" attitude), you need guidance to decide which park is for you, when to go, and what to see when you reach your destination. This book is designed to anticipate your questions and point out the not-so-obvious factors in a cut-to-the-chase format.

About This Book

America's National Parks For Dummies, 2nd Edition, is designed to guide you through the park system and show you what it offers. This book isn't like a novel, which you must read from beginning to end in order to stay on top of the plot. Instead, you can simply jump to the chapter about the park that interests you and then move on.

This book isn't an encyclopedia, either. My goal is to whet your interest in the park system with a solid look at 15 of its crown jewels. I also help you choose the park and plan the vacation that's right for you.

Just as early explorers in Yellowstone returned to the East Coast with maps of their newly discovered wonderland, I assembled a map of this book, which my editor calls a table of contents. Use this map judiciously. If you're already a road warrior and you know how to find accommodations, you probably can skip Chapter 6. On the other hand, if you've never been to a national park and are concerned about hiking through forests with mountain lions (but no tigers) and bears, oh my, turn to Chapter 8 for some tips on surviving — and enjoying — your park trip.

Conventions Used in This Book

All the individual park chapters contain the same types of information — top attractions, when to go, how to get there, where to stay, where to eat, and so on — in the same order. This format allows you to open the book to any chapter and access the information that you need quickly and easily.

How was I able to squeeze so many words into this book? By abbreviating a few of them to free up space. (A really shrewd editor didn't hurt, either.) Throughout the book, I include abbreviations for commonly accepted credit cards in listings for hotels, restaurants, and attractions. Take a look at the following list for an explanation of each abbreviation:

AE	American Express
CB	Carte Blanche
DC	Diners Club
DISC	Discover Card
MC	MasterCard
V	Visa

I also include the following abbreviations for amenities in the hotel listings:

A/C	Air-conditioning
TEL	Telephone
TV	Television

I divide the hotels into two categories — my personal favorites and the runner-ups. Those in the second category don't quite make my preferred list but still get my hearty seal of approval. If you can't get a room at one of my favorites or if your preferences differ from mine, don't be shy about considering the runner-up hotels — their amenities and service make all these accommodations good choices to consider as you determine where to rest your head at night.

I also include some general pricing information to help you decide where to unpack your bags or refuel for another day of hiking. I use a system of dollar signs to show a range of costs for one night in a hotel (rates are based on double occupancy during high season) or one meal at a restaurant (including appetizer, entree, and dessert but not tip or alcohol). The dollar signs correspond to the following price ranges:

Cost	Hotel	Restaurant
$	$50 and under	$10 and under
$$	$51–$100	$11–$20
$$$	$101–$150	$21 –$26
$$$$	$151–$200	$27–$35
$$$$$	$201 and more	$ 36 and more

Please be advised that travel information is subject to change at any time — this advice is especially true of prices. I therefore suggest that you write or call ahead for confirmation when making your travel plans. The author, editors, and publisher cannot be held responsible for the experiences of readers while traveling. However, your safety is important, so I encourage you to stay alert and be aware of your surroundings. Keep a close eye on cameras, purses, and wallets — all favorite targets of thieves and pickpockets.

Foolish Assumptions

While writing this book, I made the following assumptions about you and what your needs may be as a traveler:

 ✔ You may be an inexperienced traveler looking for guidance when determining whether to take a trip (or how to plan one) to America's national parks.

 ✔ You may be an experienced traveler who hasn't explored America's national parks and wants expert advice when you finally get a chance to enjoy one.

 ✔ You're not looking for a book that provides all the available information about America's national parks or that lists every available hotel, restaurant, or attraction. Instead, you're looking for a book that focuses on the places that will give you the best or most unique park experience.

If you fit any of these criteria, *America's National Parks For Dummies, 2nd Edition*, gives you the information you're looking for!

How This Book Is Organized

Vacations are precious and often too short. They're certainly too short to spend flipping through a guidebook trying to figure out how and where to relax. As a result, this book is user-friendly and organized in a logical fashion. The book includes four parts; each one covers a major aspect of your trip. The parts are further broken down into chapters that delve into the nitty-gritty of trip planning or the highlights of each park.

Part 1: Getting Started

Why visit a national park? What makes them special? Which park should you visit? The chapters in this part answer these questions. I touch on the diversity of the national park system, explain some of your vacation options, and tell you when parks are the most (and least) crowded. Deciding which park is best for you and your family is the tricky part. The subtle and not-so-subtle differences between the parks can determine which one is right for you. Although I quickly fell in love with Yellowstone's geysers and wildlife, Yellowstone may not appeal to you at all. Therefore, I get specific and explain, for example, why Kings Canyon National Park is a great choice if you're a backcountry nut, but not the best choice if you're hauling three young kids with you. I also address what kind of weather to expect and how to plan a budget.

Part 11: Ironing Out the Details

Getting from Point A to Point B has always been a problem for me, usually because I like to detour to Points C and D along the way. Fortunately, in this book, I don't take the alternate route. In this part, I describe how you can get to the parks and find your way around after you arrive. (You can determine how much meandering you want to do.) This section also details the best and easiest ways to book accommodations. I also touch on how to cope with money while you travel. Finally, I sprinkle in some helpful hints on how to survive your park experience (a national park is considerably less tame than an amusement park), and I offer some pointers on what things to toss in your suitcase.

Part III: Exploring America's National Parks

In Chapters 9 through 22, you get the lowdown on 15 of America's best parks — all of which are crowd pleasers and worthy of your attention. Each park chapter begins with the must-see attractions. Then I give you the scoop on what you need to do before you get to the park and how to manage your time after you arrive (whether you can stay one day or a few). I even introduce you to each park's wild kingdom, reveal the best spots for memorable photographs, and let you in on a few safety issues. Read these chapters so you'll know what to expect when you drive through the entrance gates and can explore the park on your own with confidence.

Part IV: The Part of Tens

Do you need ten reasons to visit a national park? I give plenty of justification in this part. Turn to Chapter 23 where I sum up ten incredible national park vistas, to Chapter 24 where I reveal why a national park vacation beats a trip to [insert the name of your nearest man-made, woefully expensive amusement park], or to Chapter 25 where I point out ten ways to enjoy a national park on the cheap.

At the back of the book, I include an Appendix, which *Dragnet's* Joe Friday would love because it deals in just the facts. This Quick Concierge begins with an A–Z directory of phone numbers and other practical information that you may need when you're in the parks, including emergency telephone numbers, safety tips, and ATM network numbers. Then, to help you with your planning, I provide a rundown of handy toll-free numbers and Web sites for airlines, park concessionaires, and rental car agencies. Finally, I direct you to other useful information sources, such as local Web sites, newspapers and magazines, and tourist information centers.

I also include a bunch of worksheets to make your travel planning easier; among other things, you can determine your travel budget and keep track of your preferred hotels. You can easily find these worksheets because they're printed on yellow paper.

Icons Used in This Book

In the margins throughout this book, you find little doodles called *icons* (I figured Post-its wouldn't last forever). They point out helpful (and sometimes money-saving) tips to consider before leaving home and while you're on the road. Here's how to decipher them:

 This book is entirely devoted to giving you useful advice, but this symbol lets you know when to pay attention if you want to make the most of your time and energy.

 Watch for this icon to identify annoying or potentially dangerous situations, such as traffic jams, crowded outlooks, and unsafe conditions.

 Parks are kid-friendly by their very nature. Still, I use this icon to point out hotels, restaurants, and activities that are particularly attractive to kids and families.

 This baby alerts you to money-saving tips and/or great deals.

 Helpful rangers can make recommendations that guide you toward a great park experience. Look for this symbol to discover spectacular views, wonderful hikes, and not-to-be-missed activities.

Where to Go From Here

To Yellowstone. Or Yosemite. Or maybe Cape Cod National Seashore. Or any other park mentioned in this book. (I guarantee that you won't be disappointed.) The following pages resemble a great long-distance hike — you never know what's around the next bend in the trail. So throw on a backpack, take a swig of water, and get ready to explore the national parks!

Part I
Getting Started

The 5th Wave   By Rich Tennant

"Yes sir, our backcountry orientation programs are held at the Footblister Visitor Center, the Lostwallet Ranger Station or the Cantreadacompass Information Pavilion."

In this part . . .

You've finally decided to take a national park vacation. Great! You won't be sorry. But you need a game plan. Which park do you want to visit? When should you visit? And how do you get there? You're probably also curious about the costs involved in visiting a national park and whether the kids will enjoy the trip. Maybe you need to know how accessible parks are for the mobility impaired or if parks are a good destination for solo travelers. In this part, I help answer all these questions and more.

Chapter 1

Discovering the National Parks

· ·

In This Chapter

▶ Introducing the eastern and western parks

▶ Stretching your buck

▶ Checking out your many lodging options

▶ Touching on highlights: Trails, animals, rangers, and more

· ·

As a boy growing up in New Jersey (insert your favorite "Joizy" joke here), I discovered the national parks in *National Geographic* magazine. While flipping through an issue fresh from the mailbox, I stumbled across a story about this guy who spent his winters in Yellowstone National Park shoveling snow off the roofs of cabins so they wouldn't collapse under the weight. Totally cool, I thought, a guy who gets paid to live in a cabin surrounded by forests, lakes, and animals in some place called Wyoming. No cars, no congestion, no smog. At the time, I was only 10 or 11 years old — too young to sign on for this type of life — but the image stuck with me.

Years passed — okay, a couple decades — before I made my first trip to Yellowstone, and I wasn't disappointed. The environment that I read about so many years earlier came to life in steam-shrouded geyser basins, bison- and elk-packed meadows, and endless miles of trails through dense forests and along lake shores. Sure, by the time I reached the park (1985), annual visitation was in the low millions, not the hundreds of thousands from my childhood days. But at 2.2 million acres, Yellowstone is big enough to handle the crowds.

After my first night at the atmosphere-laden Old Faithful Inn, I was hooked on Yellowstone specifically and national parks in general. Through the years, I've explored national parks from coast to coast, and although Yellowstone remains my favorite, countless parks are close seconds.

Heading East for History, West for Wilderness

All parks aren't created equal. You see, the national parks movement didn't begin until most of the eastern half of the country was thoroughly tamed, settled, and politically subdivided. As a result, the eastern parks are rich in America's cultural history — you know, George Washington slept here, there, and over there. Highlights include **Acadia National Park** in Maine, which served as the inspiration for a 19th-century group of artists and writers called the *rusticators* (see Chapter 9), and **Cape Cod National Seashore** in Massachusetts, which is rich in maritime history (see Chapter 11). At **Great Smoky Mountains National Park,** straddling the North Carolina–Tennessee border, log cabins built in the 19th century provide insight into the hearty folks who moved to the area so they could own their own land (see Chapter 15).

The western parks, on the other hand, preserved the country's magnificent and spectacular wild side. In the rugged backcountry of **Grand Teton, Yellowstone,** and **Yosemite national parks,** vistas remain unchanged from when mountain men and explorers first saw them in the early 19th century (see Chapters 14, 20, and 21, respectively). The same is true of **Arches** and **Zion national parks,** which boast stunning red-rock landscapes (see Chapters 10 and 22, respectively). **Sequoia National Park** is a shrine to tall trees, whereas its neighbor, the more rugged **Kings Canyon National Park,** boasts granite domes and outcrops, shimmering high-country lakes, and dense forests (see Chapter 19 for both parks).

That's not to say that eastern parks don't present spectacular landscapes, or that western parks don't recount pages of cultural history. In fact, stand atop Acadia's Cadillac Mountain any time of year, and you can enjoy spectacular views of Frenchman Bay. (Get to the peak early in the morning between October and March and be the first in the United States to see the sun rise.) As for culture out West, at Yellowstone's Albright Visitor Center, you can find out about 19th-century painter Thomas Moran, whose sketches and paintings of the region helped sway Congress to make Yellowstone the country's — and the world's! — first national park.

Saving Money: A Bargain at Twice the Price

My friends think that I'm financially obsessed. If that means saving a buck when I can, I plead guilty. Maybe my thriftiness is why I love national parks. A national park vacation is one of the best entertainment bargains around. Where else can $10 or $20 get you — and everyone else in your car, truck, or motor home — admission to someplace fun not just for one day but an entire week? (Okay, Jersey may be free, but I said *fun*.)

A $20 fee covers the whole family's weeklong admission to **Yellowstone National Park,** where you can see the world's most magnificent collection of hot springs, geysers, and *fumaroles* (holes leaking volcanic vapors), or you can stand in Lamar Valley and watch hundreds of elk and bison mill about trying to protect their newborn calves from packs of wolves and grizzlies (see Chapter 20). The same $20 gets you into **Grand Teton National Park,** 50 miles to the south, where you can explore craggy peaks and the world-famous Oxbow Bend on the Snake River (see Chapter 14).

In **Olympic National Park,** a $10 entrance fee not only provides access to a temperate rainforest but also allows you to gaze at the Pacific Ocean from the park's pristine beaches (see Chapter 18). You can also drive up to Hurricane Ridge and look south at the snow-capped Olympic Mountains or gaze north into the Strait of Juan de Fuca.

For similarly low fees, you can experience **Grand Canyon National Park** ($20 per car), where you can gape at extraordinary views from the rim or floor of the canyon (see Chapter 13); **Mammoth Cave National Park** (free entry for the park; cave tours beginning at $2 for children and $4 for adults), where you can take a ranger-led tour and descend into the most expansive cave system on Earth (see Chapter 16); or **Mount Rainier National Park** ($10 per car), which is dominated by a slumbering, snow-capped volcano and ringed with excellent hiking trails (see Chapter 17).

See what I mean about the parks being a bargain? And I haven't even touched on what you and your kids can discover in the parks' museums or on hikes and walks together — just some of the bonuses included in your admission fee.

If you turn into a regular parkie, you can whittle down the cost of admission through the purchase of an annual National Parks Pass for $50. The pass gets you into as many parks as you can jam into a one-year period. See Chapter 8 for more details.

Bunking Inside or Outside

The national parks offer several lodging options ranging from luxury digs to rustic campsites. A stay in **The Ahwahnee Hotel** in Yosemite is like a stay in a European palace, thanks to its cavernous and elegant dining and reading rooms (see Chapter 21). The **Lake Yellowstone Hotel** resembles a page out of the 1920s, with its Sun Room full of wicker furniture overlooking Yellowstone Lake and with the prim, white-shirted waitstaff in the dining room (see Chapter 20). The **El Tovar** in the Grand Canyon is a sort-of hybrid between a Swiss chalet and a Norwegian villa (see Chapter 13). You can expect to pay $100, $200, or even $300 or more per night at these places.

If you're not looking for elegance, you can find **rustic cabins** in Yellowstone and **canvas tent cabins** in Yosemite for $50 to 55 a night. For considerably less (from free up to about $20 a night), you can stay in one of the parks' developed campgrounds. An outstanding facility, Yosemite's **North Pines Campground** is located along the Merced River in an idyllic setting on the valley floor. Another notable spot is Grand Teton's **Jenny Lake Campground,** which boasts a forest setting near Jenny Lake with huge boulders and knockout views of the Tetons (see Chapter 14).

Taking a Walk on the Wild Side

Ever feel the need to get away from the mundane concerns of day-to-day life? Who hasn't? You can quickly cut loose by heading down a national park trail. How far you trek — 1 mile or 10 miles or even 50 miles — is up to you. What's important is that you get out of your car and go!

You may be tired (and perhaps even a little bit dusty or sweaty) when you return to the trailhead, but in return for your effort, I promise that you'll also feel mentally refreshed. All you need to do is enjoy your walk, look at the mountains, gulp in the fresh air, and stretch your legs.

If you hike the **Mist Trail** to the top of Nevada Falls in Yosemite National Park, you'll enjoy some spectacular views of the Yosemite Valley (see Chapter 21). If you don't wear rain gear, however, the plummeting Merced River will soak you with its mist. Of course, you won't mind the spray if the temperature outside is 90 degrees.

In Great Smoky Mountains National Park, you can hike portions of the country's oldest recreational trail — the **Appalachian Trail** — and gain an appreciation for hardwood hollows, fresh mountain streams, and succulent berries in season (see Chapter 15). Although Cape Cod National Seashore doesn't offer as many well-defined trails as its forested counterparts, you can walk for mile after mile on **sandy beaches** (see Chapter 11). Bring a fishing pole, and you may even catch your dinner before turning back.

Spotting Bears and Bison: Nature's Open-air Zoos

National parks host animals — lots of animals — and some creatures are incredibly easy to spot. In fact, I've seen so many **elk and bison** in

Yellowstone that I no longer stop on the road to gaze at these guys. (But I wish that all the folks who park in the middle of the road to watch the elk dawdle 10 feet away from their cars would let me pass.) My standards are higher these days; I now scan the meadows and hillsides for grizzlies and wolves.

Because so many animals live in national parks, they should be considered open-air zoos, although you definitely need to remember at all times that these animals are wild. Western parks like Yellowstone, Yosemite, and Sequoia/Kings Canyon are full of **bears** — grizzlies and black bears in Yellowstone and black bears in the other two parks. Along the coast of Cape Cod, you can spot **whales** and, occasionally, **porpoises.** And in Great Smoky Mountains National Park, the forests are full of **turkeys** (the birds, not the hikers) and even **wild hogs.**

When you reach the park of your choice, ask a ranger for the best spot to see animals. Meanwhile, keep these tips in mind: In Yellowstone, the Lamar Valley in late spring is zoo central with **wolves, grizzlies, bison,** and **elk;** in Great Smoky Mountains National Park, Cades Cove around sundown in summer and fall is a magnet for **black bears** and **white-tailed deer;** and if you find yourself in Olympic National Park, look for **seals** around the *sea stacks* (a kind of rock formation) just off the shoreline.

Profiting from Your Park Ranger's Wisdom

One of the best ways to brush up on your national park trivia is to spend some time with a ranger (but not because you're illegally parked or guilty of feeding bears). For years, rangers have offered campfire programs and hikes that explore an aspect of their parks' wildlife or geology or history, and these programs continue in full swing today.

Visit **Yellowstone,** and you're sure to find a program on geysers and hot springs (see Chapter 20). Travel to **Death Valley,** and you see rangers, dressed in period costume at Scotty's Castle, recounting a bit of the park's intriguing human history (see Chapter 12). At **Mount Rainier National Park,** you shouldn't have to look too far to find a program that delves into the park's volcanology (see Chapter 17). In **Mammoth Cave National Park,** rangers take you underground — for a price — to show off their subterranean park. In general, though, ranger programs are free for the asking (see Chapter 16).

Unfortunately, most parks offer ranger programs only during the high season, which, in all but Death Valley, occurs during the summer months.

Chapter 2

Choosing a Park and Deciding When to Go

*H*ow do you decide which park is right for you? Tossing a coin is one method, but not necessarily one that ensures a great vacation. In this chapter, I give you some guidance for making this decision. I ask a few questions to get you started and then give you a rundown of each park's strong points — and pitfalls. I help you add up your likes, dislikes, and goals into one lump sum to determine which park is best for you. But if you're like me, one park won't sate your soul. So at the end of the chapter, I recommend a few loop trips that can get you to more than one.

Deciding What You Want from a National Park

Okay, now you get to answer some questions. Truthfully. If you take a little time to consider your preferences and options, you can identify exactly how, and where, to spend your ideal national park vacation.

Are you looking for an **active vacation,** one that works your body by climbing mountains, rafting rivers, hiking through forests, or kayaking in an ocean? Outfitters at Grand Teton National Park and Mount Rainier National Park offer mountaineering classes that may culminate in an assault on one of these mountains. At Acadia National Park or Cape Cod National Seashore, you can find out how to paddle a sea kayak; from Acadia, you can even embark on a multiday adventure along the coast. A great way to see the Grand Canyon is aboard a raft during a wet and wild trip down the Colorado River. And in just about any national park, you can plan a weeklong backpacking trip into the woods.

Do you want a **relaxing trip** rather than a workout? Then pack the beach umbrella and a quart of sun block and head for Cape Cod National Seashore, where you can listen to the Atlantic Ocean's pounding surf while relaxing in a beach chair. (Later, you can head to Cape Cod Bay to enjoy the sunset.) Acadia National Park also offers wonderful ocean views as well as quaint and colorful fishing communities perfect for afternoon strolls. At Olympic National Park, you can rent a cabin along Lake Crescent and do nothing but enjoy the view or head over to Sol Duc Hot Springs Resort for a refreshing soak in the warm waters.

Do you want an **educational getaway,** where you can find out about America's cultural or military heritage? Check out Great Smoky Mountains National Park, with its mid-19th-century buildings and working gristmills. Mammoth Cave National Park is renowned for its underground trails, but above ground, the park holds family and community cemeteries that date back 150 years and more. The cemeteries, and few remaining churches, tell tales of the people who settled this part of the country. The 19th-century's whaling industry put Cape Cod on the map, and today, you can get a flavor of the time period in museums and historic houses. Yosemite National Park offers a wonderful glimpse into its cultural past through a pioneer cemetery and a living history exhibit on the Ahwahneeche, a tribe that once inhabited the Yosemite Valley. For more information on educational programs or research opportunities at the parks featured in this book, see Chapter 4.

Are you looking for the best place for a **family vacation** that doesn't break the bank? I can't think of a park that isn't a wonderful experience for kids of all ages. See Chapter 4 for my park recommendations and for tips on traveling with families.

Do you need to plan a **wheelchair-accessible trip**? Would you or anyone in your group have a difficult time walking down (and back up) 300 stairs into Mammoth Cave National Park or roaming through Olympic National Park's Hoh Rain Forest? Then see Chapter 4 for my park recommendations and tips for travelers with special needs.

Flipping through Park Snapshots

Knowing that America's national park system comes pretty darn close to offering something for everyone doesn't make choosing which park to visit any easier. So, in this section, I provide a few snapshots. Breeze through these 30-second previews and get a feel for each park — both what's good and not so good.

Acadia National Park (Maine)

One of the park system's surf-splashed jewels, Acadia is great for wildlife lovers. You can find beavers in the ponds, harbor seals and harbor porpoises off the coast, and foxes running through the forests. Not a bad start. Now toss in white-tailed deer, coyotes, minke whales, and a half-dozen varieties of salamanders.

You want scenery? The waters of the Atlantic Ocean explode upon crashing into Acadia's rugged coastline. Left behind by long-forgotten glaciers, rocky beaches give way to thick pine forests that hide freshwater ponds and surround granite domes rising above the woods. Want a classic photograph? Snap a shot of the Bass Harbor Lighthouse in the fog.

Mount Desert Island is home to most of Acadia, which also sprawls onto a nearby peninsula and even some islands. Quaint fishing towns surround the park, and the town of Bar Harbor, also located on the island, offers enough inns, motels, B&Bs, and restaurants to keep you happy.

Park pros

- Bald mountains back a ruggedly beautiful seascape.

- Quiet carriage paths ramble through Acadia's forests.

- This park boasts the East Coast's only *fjord* — a narrow inlet bordered by steep cliffs.

Park cons

- Acadia doesn't offer stately national park lodges.

- Winter shuts down most of the park's activities.

- Crowds can be substantial in summer, when most of the 3 million-plus visitors show up.

Arches National Park (Utah)

In a state with five national parks, visitors often overlook Arches. And I can't quite figure out why. No greater collection of rock arches exists on Earth. You can find big arches, tiny arches, arches about to give way to gravity, and arches under construction. You can also see classic red-rock vistas. In late afternoon, the landscape seems to catch fire in the sweeping rays of the setting sun.

Thanks to southern Utah's relatively mild winters, Arches is a true four-season park. Although summer draws the biggest crowds, you may opt for one of the other, more temperature-friendly, seasons. Come in late fall or anytime in the winter, and you're likely to have most of the park to yourself.

Arches is also kid-friendly. Youngsters stay happy for hours by climbing up into rock windows or playing in vast sandboxes created by sandstone erosion.

Park pros

- ✔ Visit Arches to see fantastic rock formations.

- ✔ Find more rock arches than anywhere else on Earth.

- ✔ You can see the park's highlights in one day.

Park cons

- ✔ The park can be brutally hot in summer.

- ✔ Arches has no in-park lodging and only one (relatively small) campground.

- ✔ Restaurants and accommodations in nearby Moab can be pricey.

Cape Cod National Seashore (Massachusetts)

Surf, sun, and sand succinctly sum up Cape Cod National Seashore. Want more? Toss in biking, whale-watching, and swimming in warm, freshwater ponds. Still not convinced? How 'bout sunset strolls along Cape Cod Bay, clam bakes on the beach, and surf fishing?

Maritime history flows through the park, thanks to the 19th-century whalers who made Cape Cod's ports some of the richest in the world. This park had a dastardly side to its maritime history, too, and in Provincetown, you can explore a great museum chronicling one of the East Coast's most notorious pirates, Black Sam Bellamy.

Like Acadia, its northern neighbor, Cape Cod National Seashore doesn't have lodges within its boundaries. But in the many towns that dot Cape Cod itself, you can find all measures of accommodations and eateries.

Park pros

- ✔ You can wander beach after beach after beach.

- ✔ Restaurants serve some of the freshest seafood around, virtually from port to plate.

- ✔ Activities abound: You can bike on miles of trails, swim in freshwater ponds, or discover the Cape's rich history.

Park cons

- ✔ The Cape's midsummer crowds can be suffocating.

- ✔ When the rain falls, the crowds move almost in unison from the beach to the shops.

- ✔ Winters drastically reduce park activities.

Death Valley National Park (California/Nevada)

If you like hot weather, the hottest place in the Western Hemisphere is Death Valley National Park. But the beauty of this desert playground is that the weather isn't intolerably hot 365 days of the year. You can visit in summer if you think that enduring the heat is like some red badge of courage (which it literally will be, if you forget your sun block). Or come in the winter months (November through March) when temperatures are comfortable enough for you to spend all day exploring the park and its otherworldly landscape.

If you enjoy stately national park lodges, book a room (if you can afford the rate) at the Furnace Creek Inn. This Death Valley resort is truly an elegant desert oasis complete with palm groves and a watering hole, which happens to be a wonderful swimming pool. Western history lives on in Scotty's Castle, a shrine to a once-upon-a-time cowboy who proved that living off someone else's largesse is easier than working for your own. (For the story on Scott's ill-gotten gains, see Chapter 12.)

Kids enjoy this park. They can play in its sand dunes, search for desert pupfish, or avoid the heat in a swimming pool.

Park pros

- ✔ Death Valley is the Western Hemisphere's lowest spot.

- ✔ The bleak, otherworldly landscape is intriguing.

- ✔ The valley becomes delightful when winter rains produce wild-flower blooms.

Park cons

- ✔ The park is as hot as the proverbial firecracker in the middle of summer.

- ✔ The valley offers few accommodations from which to choose.

- ✔ The landscape is dry and dusty.

Grand Canyon National Park (Arizona)

Stand on either side of the enormous Grand Canyon and the landscape unfolds in dramatic earthen layers. Explore the canyon's floor and discover towering waterfalls that nourish hanging gardens.

Although the focus of this park is a hole in the ground, the Grand Canyon offers more than opportunities to gape. You find mule rides, raft trips, hiking paths, and, of course, gorgeous views galore. The two rims of the canyon have distinct personalities, too. The higher North Rim (with an average elevation of 8,000 feet) is cooler, less crowded, and more remote than the more popular South Rim, which features more tourist facilities, easier access, and a longer season.

Park pros

- ✔ Encounter dramatic vistas of one of the world's most startling landscapes.

- ✔ The canyon floor is wet and wild, thanks to the rollicking Colorado River.

- ✔ Numerous activities test your limits above and below the Grand Canyon's rim.

Park cons

- ✔ The canyon bottom turns into a convection oven in midsummer.

- ✔ Getting from one rim to the other rim is a long, inconvenient process.

- ✔ The South Rim is very crowded in July and August.

Grand Teton National Park (Wyoming)

America's Matterhorn towers over the national park that anchors Wyoming's western border. If you're looking for wildlife, come to Grand Teton. Drive (or float) through this park and you encounter moose, bison, elk, antelope, and the occasional black bear. If you hike into the backcountry, you may even see a grizzly bear. Plus, bald eagles and osprey perch in the trees, otters frolic in the waters of the Snake River, and wolves (that have migrated down from Yellowstone National Park) lope through the park.

But the park features more than just wildlife. You also find world-class mountain climbing in the Tetons, numerous boating opportunities (such as power boats on Jackson Lake and drift boats, rafts, kayaks, and canoes on Snake River and other lakes), and a portal into the Old West. The Tetons' craggy, snow-capped peaks reflect the rising and setting suns. Lakes cupped at the bottom of mountains mirror the peaks. And the Snake River, with its oxbow bends, attracts wildlife. You definitely won't have to work hard to compose your photographs at Grand Teton.

The nearby town of Jackson isn't officially part of the park, but it definitely hangs its hat on the Tetons. If you ever grow weary of the park's natural resources, head to town for a slice of the Old West.

Park pros

✔ Grand Teton is wildlife central.

✔ Mountain climbers can scale the purple mountains' majesty.

✔ You can paddle along alpine lakes and explore rivers with world-class trout fisheries.

Park cons

✔ Winter can be grueling in terms of the weather and a lack of things to do.

✔ If you stay in Jackson, driving back and forth to the park puts a lot of miles on your rig.

✔ Flat-landers may need a day or two to acclimate to the elevation.

Great Smoky Mountains National Park (North Carolina/Tennessee)

If you're a Baby Boomer who grew up watching the TV show *Walton's Mountain,* the landscape of the Great Smoky Mountains may seem familiar to you. Cascading mountain streams cut the rumpled Appalachian Range, and backwoods lore oozes out of old homesteads in Cades Cove and Big Cataloochee. You may half expect to encounter moonshine stills in the hills.

The heavily wooded park is rich not only in cultural history but in wildlife, too. Black bears, white-tailed deer, and salamanders are the main wildlife attractions — in fact, this park is known as the salamander capital of the world. You can also see resident river otters, bobcats, wild hogs (which you want to avoid because of their irascible demeanor), ruffed grouse, golden eagles, and two species of fox. Plus, the park service started returning elk to the park in January 2001.

The Smokies can be difficult to negotiate by car because of the overall lack of roads. However, long-distance hikers enjoy the park because of the Appalachian Trail, which passes through from north to south, reaching its high point atop Clingman's Dome. Fall is definitely the high season thanks to the colorful forests, but spring and summer are delightful, too.

Park pros

- ✔ An array of wildlife lives in the Smoky Mountains.

- ✔ The park has a rich cultural history, whether you call the early residents hillbillies or pioneers.

- ✔ Countless miles of hiking trails, including a section of the Appalachian Trail, cross the park.

Park cons

- ✔ In-park lodging isn't available, aside from one lodge that is accessible only on foot.

- ✔ Gateway towns of Gatlinburg, Pigeon Forge, and Cherokee, with their touristy roadside attractions, appear tacky to some tastes.

- ✔ The Great Smokey Mountains is the most crowded park in the national park system.

Mammoth Cave National Park (Kentucky)

Big dark hole — a pretty good description of the park that rambles for 350 miles or so beneath the rolling Kentucky landscape. But Mammoth Cave, created by underground streams that continue to dissolve new passages, is much more than a hole in the ground. Some sections of the cave are truly beautiful, with delicate crystalline formations that took hundreds, if not thousands, of years to form. Other sections are spooky, because mile after mile of tight passages lead to . . . who knows where?

Human history is recorded in this underground netherworld. Over the years, the park has recovered ancient Native American artifacts and preserved soot graffiti that early explorers painted on the ceilings with smoky candles long before Kilroy was born. Above ground, the park is a cultural reservoir with well-preserved churches and dozens of cemeteries, some of which hold the remains of settlers born in the 18th century.

Park pros

- ✔ Mammoth Cave is the world's largest cave system.

- ✔ Intriguing Native American history enlivens the cave experience.

- ✔ The cave's atmosphere is constant in winter and summer.

Park cons

- ✔ The park's accommodations are limited in number and appeal.

- ✔ The caves aren't recommended for claustrophobics.

- ✔ In midsummer, the above-ground humidity can be stifling.

Mount Rainier National Park (Washington)

You never really lose sight of the snow-capped volcano during your visit at Mount Rainer. Rising to 14,410 feet, the mountain *is* the park; everything revolves around it, from the hiking trails and the glaciers to the lodges, which offer wonderful views of the peak. If you like to hike, this park was made for you. You can work your way around the base of the mountain on the Wonderland Trail or take shorter hikes to glacial snouts, lookout towers, and even the snowy summit.

Highlights of the southern flank include Paradise, the site of the atmospheric Paradise Inn, an extensive visitor center, and a resident glacier. Not to be overlooked is Sunrise on the mountain's eastern slopes, a hub of hiking activity and the highest point on the mountain that can be reached by car.

The lack of park roads makes navigation difficult, especially if you need to travel from Point A to Point B. And plenty of intriguing spots discourage a windshield tour of Mount Rainier — you'll want to stop your car so you can get out and look around.

Park pros

- ✔ More than 20 glaciers surround Mount Rainer.
- ✔ You can hike trails through dense forests and wildflower meadows.
- ✔ The beautiful and historic Paradise Inn is a great lodging option.

Park cons

- ✔ Winters can be incredibly brutal, restricting the park to only the most hearty travelers.
- ✔ Summer weekends, which draw throngs from nearby Seattle and Tacoma, make Paradise hard to reach.
- ✔ A lack of roads makes navigating the mountain difficult and time-consuming.

Olympic National Park (Washington)

Where else can you interrupt a seaside vacation for an afternoon trip to a snowfield? Or end a rainforest hike with a dip in a swimming pool fed by hot springs? Talk about a park with diversity.

Olympic National Park is a crowd pleaser in many ways. At this park, you can ski, hike, boat, fish, and comb the beach or explore hot springs, waterfalls, and dense rainforests. If you're lucky (and a bit persistent), you can spot a wealth of wildlife, such as Roosevelt elk, deer, sea otters, seals, sea lions, black bears, eagles, and osprey. And don't forget the huge, slimy Banana Slugs that crawl through the Hoh Rain Forest.

Although road access is limited, Olympic offers enough interesting nooks that you don't need to travel all over the park to stay busy (or amazed).

Park pros

- ✔ Olympic is a three-in-one park with seashore, rainforest, and glaciers.
- ✔ Impressive *sea stacks* (cool rock outcrops) rise above offshore waves.
- ✔ Great hiking possibilities abound.

Park cons

- ✔ Foggy, wet weather can dampen a park vacation.
- ✔ In-park lodging is very limited.
- ✔ Winter rains can shut down trails and roads.

Sequoia/Kings Canyon National Parks (California)

Although these two parks are joined at the waist like Siamese twins and share a common administration, they have distinctly different personalities. Most folks are familiar only with Sequoia because of its famous trees; as a result, Kings Canyon National Park is wonderfully uncrowded.

Wilderness lovers can roam spacious Kings Canyon, a ruggedly beautiful and thoughtfully underdeveloped park. Its off-the-beaten path location encourages back-to-earth vacations and discourages rampant commercialism. You may huff and puff your way into its high backcountry, but once you get there, you can cruise the High Sierra terrain in near solitude.

On the other hand, Sequoia isn't overdeveloped, but most of the park's visitors are drawn to the protected tall trees. This limits human intrusion on the park's backcountry — a fact that benefits the environment and means you can enjoy the backcountry scenery with a dose of solitude.

Park pros

- ✔ Really, really, really big trees fill Sequoia.
- ✔ The beautiful High Sierra landscape dazzles visitors who make the effort to trek into the backcountry.
- ✔ Kings Canyon is an uncrowded beauty.

Park cons

✔ Kings Canyon is hard to get to during the summer months and is closed to vehicular traffic during the winter months.

✔ Both parks have limited lodging options.

✔ The parks don't have eastern entrances.

Yellowstone National Park (Wyoming/Idaho/Montana)

Long known as the crown jewel of the national park system, Yellowstone easily justifies the label. In 1872, this 2.2-million-acre preserve became the world's first national park and jumpstarted the national parks movement not only in America but also around the globe.

Thermal features (such as geysers), the Grand Canyon of the Yellowstone, and Yellowstone Lake are just some of the park's awe-inspiring highlights. The rustic charm of the Old Faithful Inn never fails to astonish. And I haven't even mentioned the park's wild kingdom — the most complete animal habitat in the United States. Yellowstone has been referred to as North America's Serengeti because of its diverse wildlife population, including elk, bison, moose, grizzly and black bears, wolves, mountain lions, and bald eagles. If you had visited Yellowstone in 1750, you would have found the same wildlife species that live in the park today.

The park also boasts diverse lodging options. You can pamper yourself with a stay at the charming Lake Yellowstone Hotel, go low budget in one of the bare-bones cabins surrounding Roosevelt Lodge, or hoist your house on your back and head off into the forest.

Park pros

✔ The world's first national park, Yellowstone is a leader in the national parks movement.

✔ Yellowstone features the world's largest collection of geysers, hot springs, and *fumaroles* (holes leaking volcanic vapors).

✔ This wild kingdom is crawling with wolves, grizzlies, bison, moose, elk, and more.

Park cons

✔ Some park cabins are horribly run down.

✔ Stretches of the Grand Loop road network are woefully dilapidated.

✔ Crowds descend in summer.

Yosemite National Park (California)

Ansel Adams made a career out of photographing the waterfalls, forests, and granite outcrops of Yosemite National Park. You probably can't duplicate his work, but you can enjoy the park's wonders as much as he did.

The great natural scenery by itself captivates the young ones, whereas the Merced River is the perfect place to float on a hot summer day for kids of all ages. Staying in one of the park's canvas tent cabins is a real kid-pleaser, too.

The park's collection of hiking trails has only one downfall: You're so busy staring at the surrounding landscape that you risk losing your footing.

Park pros

- ✔ Cliffs, domes, and waterfalls make for outstanding scenery.
- ✔ The Ahwahnee Hotel is arguably the park system's most beautiful lodge.
- ✔ Great backcountry trails lead to solitude.

Park cons

- ✔ The Yosemite Valley floor can be crowded during summer months.
- ✔ Summer's end and low rainfall greatly temper the fury of the park's waterfalls.
- ✔ You need to plan far ahead to land a room in the more-popular lodges.

Zion National Park (Utah)

Five national parks are crammed into southern Utah, and Zion is the kingpin of them all. Oh, Canyonlands may be more rugged, Arches more sculpted, Bryce Canyon home to more *hoodoos* (a cool rock outcrop), and Capitol Reef more sprawling, but Zion is the patriarch — and not just because it's the oldest.

Driving down into and riding through Zion Canyon is a humbling experience because of the canyon walls that tower over you.

A hike along The Narrows is a trek that you'll never forget. Few other parks offer water-filled riverbeds for hiking trails, and I can't think of any other park that features a 16-mile-long slot canyon that in places is 2,000 feet deep. Other hikes, short and long, lead to hanging gardens in secluded grottos or peaks overlooking the valley. Zion has many wonders.

Park pros

- ✔ Red-rock scenery dazzles the eye.
- ✔ The mild winters of southwestern Utah make this park a four-season wonder.
- ✔ You can hike amid incredible slot canyons and towering cliffs.

Park cons

- ✔ The park offers limited in-park lodging.
- ✔ Hot, low-humidity summer weather discourages exploration.
- ✔ Navigating the entire park is tough due to its sprawling terrain and few roads.

Scheduling Your Trip

Most families' hands are tied when deciding the right time to take a vacation — they usually go in summer because school is out. But I don't want to discourage summer vacations; in fact, most parks are fabulous in the summertime. (Death Valley is an exception. Although the park is truly interesting, you won't appreciate it in mid-August when the temperature is 120 degrees or more.) However, summer does bring the most crowds, the highest lodging rates (except in Death Valley), and the most difficult-to-find accommodations. But I can tell you how to work around these woes.

To get a room at one of the more-popular lodges in summer, reserve at least three to four months in advance of your trip — six months is even better. By booking way ahead of time, you can almost pick from the available accommodations.

In summer, you can avoid most crowds by refusing to move with the pack. Many park visitors like to sleep til around 8 a.m. and then enjoy a leisurely breakfast before beginning to explore around 10 a.m. If you rise soon after the sun and take off by 7 a.m., you can enjoy a few hours of solitude. This plan works on the other end of the day, too. Because most people return to their rooms around 5 p.m., you can schedule a late dinner and head to the places that you didn't see in the morning.

If you can travel any time during the year, seriously consider spring, fall, and even winter excursions.

Spring and fall are spectacular seasons in national parks. Spring is a time of renewal, a time when forests and meadows come colorfully to life. But for most parks, spring is also mud season; melting snows and spring rains make backcountry trails generally mucky and, in some cases, temporarily closed. (Exceptions are southwestern and southern parks.) Still, temperatures aren't bad (aside from the occasional fluke snowstorm in some parts of the country) and crowds are minimal. In many parks, high-season rates don't kick in until Memorial Day, so spring trips benefit cost-conscious visitors. Fall is even better than spring: Crowds shrink, forests dip into their Technicolor wardrobe, temperatures are mild, and lodging rates decline.

If you get cold feet shuffling across your bedroom floor, standing outside in 20-below-zero temperatures in February waiting for Old Faithful to erupt may not be for you. But if you enjoy the season, winter can make for a peaceful escape thanks to the lack of crowds (except in Death Valley). Yosemite, best known for its waterfalls and majestic granite domes, is shamefully overlooked as a winter destination; you can find not only great cross-country skiing but also a small downhill-ski area. Yellowstone is also a magical winter destination, a place where the Northern Lights occasionally dance in the night skies and where winter storms leave bison shrouded in ice and snow.

You don't need a full week to enjoy a national park getaway. You can experience a satisfying trip in just a few days, particularly if you go in the middle of the week when most park traffic is reduced from the congestion of the weekends.

Visiting More Than One

In some parts of the country, you can hit two or more national parks during one trip. To do this, you need to budget a little more time (and money) and perhaps be a little more punctual than usual. (I once hit four parks in one week, but that was overdoing it.) Some of the trips are obvious and easy, whereas others require the careful planning of a military assault. I give you several options.

Geysers and grands

Even the park service realizes that **Yellowstone** and **Grand Teton** national parks belong in the same trip. Why else would they charge you one fee that provides access to both places? And even though these two parks are next-door neighbors, you get two entirely different experiences. Grand Teton has a relaxed Western style with its rail fences, grazing cattle, and log cabins. Yellowstone contains so many animals that you may feel as if you're on a wildlife safari. (Many people debate whether Yellowstone is famous for its wildlife or its geysers. After you visit the park, let me know what you think.)

Red rock wonders

Referred to as the Grand Circle, the parks certainly present a wide circle if you visit the **Grand Canyon** and Utah's five national parks — **Arches, Bryce Canyon, Canyonlands, Capitol Reef,** and **Zion** — in one swing. You can visit them all, but not in less than two weeks. My suggestion is to cut the trip in half. Visit the Grand Canyon, Zion, Bryce, and Capitol Reef or the Grand Canyon, Canyonlands, and Arches. Whichever combination you choose, count on seeing lots of stunning, red-rock landscapes.

I include Arches, Bryce, Grand Canyon, and Zion in this book. For details on Capitol Reef and Canyonlands, you may want to pick up a copy of *Frommer's National Parks of the American West* (Wiley).

California on a budget

California boasts more national parks — eight, in fact — than any other state in the Lower 48: **Channel Islands, Death Valley, Joshua Tree, Kings Canyon, Lassen Volcanic, Redwood, Sequoia, and Yosemite.** But although these parks are contained within the same state border, you can't visit all of them — nor would you want to — in a single vacation. Death Valley may look close to Sequoia on a map, but a good seven-hour drive separates them (no roads cross the eastern ridge of the High Sierra). On the plus side, Sequoia and Kings Canyon share a common border, so you can think of them as one park. And because only 200 miles separates Sequoia/Kings Canyon and Yosemite, tackling these three parks on one trip is very doable.

Washington two-step

A drive of about four hours separates **Olympic** and **Mount Rainier** national parks in Washington state, so you can reasonably hit these two in one trip. The contrast in landscapes — Olympic with its seacoast and rainforests and Mount Rainier with its snow-shrouded volcano — is incredible to see. The crowds provide another contrast; although Mount Rainier's visitors pack the park's main destinations and roads in summer, the crowds at Olympic are wonderfully dispersed.

Chapter 3

Preparing Your Budget

. . . .

In This Chapter

▶ Estimating your total costs

▶ Revealing hidden charges

▶ Cutting costs for the frugal traveler

. . . .

Y ou don't have to return home from your trip to a mailbox jammed with unexpected vacation bills. If you take a little time to plan your expenses, you can avoid surprises and control costs. In this chapter, I show you how to tally your vacation charges and minimize the total.

Adding up the Elements

Projecting exactly how much you'll spend is difficult, if not impossible. But you can develop fairly sound parameters for your budget by running through your trip in your mind (with a pencil, paper, and calculator nearby to run the tally, of course).

Where to start? How 'bout with getting to the park of your choice — mentally speaking, that is. Calculate your transportation costs from your home to your hotel (or campsite). Then jot down your lodging and estimated meal costs. Next, add park entry fees and, finally, include the cost of any activities you want to do, such as cave tours, horseback riding, or whale-watching.

The following sections help you gather the appropriate figures for your balance sheet. You can also use the budget worksheet at the back of this book. (Whether you pay any attention to the final estimate is strictly up to you.) Because some costs vary depending on your destination, you need to turn to the appropriate park chapter (Chapters 9–22) for figures on admission, lodging, dining, and activity costs.

Transportation

Travel represents a big chunk of your total vacation expenses, but if you fly, the cost is easy to identify and may be paid far in advance (unless you float the cost on your credit card). If you rent a car, add the rental fee and the cost of gasoline to your expenses. Make sure that you get a car-rental package that includes unlimited mileage. For a rental car or your own car (if you drive to the park), approximate gas expenses by dividing your estimated mileage by the car's miles per gallon. Then multiply the resulting figure by the cost of gasoline. Voila! Transportation component solved. See Chapter 5 for details on flying to the park of your choice and for ways to minimize rental-car fees.

Need a hand with approximating gas expenses? You can determine mileage to the park from your home or the car-rental agency (if you have the agency's address) by using an online program at www.map quest.com. Simply click on Driving Directions, input your starting location and final destination, and then watch as a total distance in miles is calculated for you. To that number, add any additional mileage you think you'll put on the car while you're in the park. For miles per gallon, assume that you'll get around 25 miles per gallon with a rental car. As far as gas prices go, your guess is as good as mine.

Lodging

As with transportation, your lodging expense is pretty easy to calculate. (How big or small the price depends on you.) Top-of-the-line accommodations in such parks as Yellowstone, Yosemite, and Grand Canyon cost $150 or more per night. However, you can stay on-the-cheap for almost half as much if you go during low season, or even between high and low seasons. (For most parks, winter is low season and summer is high season. The exception is Death Valley, where the seasons are reversed.) The National Park Service holds a great deal of control over lodging prices for properties inside park borders, so prices are kept reasonably low. But no such control exists at parks that lack in-park accommodations: in this book, Acadia, Arches, Cape Cod, and Great Smoky Mountains. (Great Smoky Mountains does offer limited in-park accommodations in the form of a hike-in lodge.) See Chapter 6 for specifics about lodging categories and costs.

If you plan to stay in one of the parks' developed campgrounds, expect to pay anywhere between nothing and $20 a night.

Dining

Like lodging expenses, dining costs are extremely variable. If you insist on a four-course dinner with wine, you pay for it. Conversely, many parks feature relatively inexpensive cafeterias and restaurants where you can save substantial bucks. You won't find fast-food chains inside the national parks, but they offer equivalents, so don't fear that you'll pay through the nose for every meal. What you find on menus varies from park to park — Rocky Mountain parks almost always serve trout and steaks, coastal parks land lots of seafood, and every park seems to offer some sort of local dish.

Throughout this book, I use dollar signs to indicate the price range of each restaurant that I recommend. The dollar signs are based on the cost of one meal at dinner (including appetizer, main course, and desert — not alcohol or tip) and represent the following price ranges:

$	$10 and under
$$	$11–$19
$$$	$20–$26
$$$$	$27–$35
$$$$$	$36 and more

When estimating meal costs, exclude the cost of breakfast if you're staying at a hotel outside of the park that includes breakfast in its rates. (The only in-park hotel to include breakfast in its rates is Jenny Lake Lodge in Grand Teton National Park.)

Either inside the parks or in one of the gateway communities surrounding them, you can find grocery stores where you can stock up on food. Loading up on picnic items will save you substantial sums on lunches. If you camp, you can save even more money by cooking your own meals.

What things cost in Yellowstone National Park

Double room (with bath) at Old Faithful Inn: $91–$159

Double room (with lake view) at Lake Yellowstone Hotel: $155–$160

Dinner for two at the Old Faithful Inn restaurant, without drinks, tax, or tip: $65

Dinner for two at Lake Yellowstone Hotel restaurant, without drinks, tax, or tip: $72

Pint of Old Faithful Ale in Old Faithful Inn's Bear Pit Lounge: $3.75

Glass of Chardonnay in the Lake Yellowstone Hotel's Sun Room: $5.25

Chuckwagon dinner at Roosevelt Lodge for family of four: $104

Stagecoach ride for family of four: $26.50

> # What things cost in Olympic National Park
>
> Double room (with fireplace) at the Lake Quinault Lodge: $180
>
> Cabin for four (with fireplace and kitchen) at Kalaloch Lodge: $204
>
> Dinner for two at Lake Quinault Lodge: $90
>
> Dinner for two at Kalaloch Lodge: $78
>
> Swimming passes for four at Sol Duc Hot Springs: $35–$40

Park fees

National parks are a bargain. For a $10 to $20 entrance fee, everyone in your car gains access to the park for a week. See Chapter 8 for more information on park fees and for details on the National Park Pass. For discounts for senior citizens and the disabled, see Chapter 4.

Most attractions are free after you enter a national park. You can look into the Grand Canyon, watch Old Faithful spout, or walk across the salt pan at Badwater in Death Valley — all free of cost. However, you may have to pay for a few attractions, such as cave tours in Mammoth Cave and Sequoia and some ranger programs, notably snowshoeing at Mount Rainier or visiting one of Acadia's island outposts.

Activities and tours

What money you save by not paying to view attractions can quickly — frightfully quickly, actually — be spent on activities, such as wild river trips in the Grand Canyon or Grand Teton; lazy river floats in Yosemite; and climbing expeditions in Grand Teton, Yosemite, and Mount Rainier. For instance, a 2001 guided climb to the top of the Grand Teton ran $815 per person, including the cost of two days of climbing school. A Grand Canyon river trip runs roughly $200 a day per person, making a weeklong sojourn costly. Many parks also feature concessionaires that provide other activities; for example, you can go horseback riding in Great Smoky Mountains National Park for $15 an hour, on average. Not as expensive, but a cost nonetheless, are the fishing licenses that you need to buy in some parks. (See the "Fast Facts" section at the end of each park chapter for fishing license fees.)

Shopping

National parks and shopping don't normally appear in the same sentence, but gift shops carry more than just film and guidebooks. Some carry wonderful artworks, and others natty attire. You can nickel-and-dime yourself into debt on coffee cups, framed posters, and paperweights, or you can shoot a week's paycheck on a beautiful oil painting of the Tetons. Are you a compulsive buyer? If so, you may want to give your credit cards to a more tight-fisted traveling companion.

Nightlife

Watching sunsets, counting stars, and listening to the wind riffle through the trees can all be yours at no charge. In many parks, nightlife consists of sitting around a campfire listening to a ranger program (for free), sitting in front of a roaring fire in your lodge (free), or listening to the waves crash on the beach (also free). Local musicians strum the evening away in the lodge lounges at some parks (for example, string quartets and pianists entertain in Lake Yellowstone Hotel), and these offerings are free as well. (Are you picking up any trends yet?) Your biggest nightlife bill will likely come from quaffing after-dinner drinks in the lodge lounge.

Keeping a Lid on Hidden Expenses

Because the national parks are geared toward families and bargain travelers, you encounter fewer hidden costs than you would in a resort area or big city. Lodging and meal rates are straightforward and generally reasonable, thanks to park service management.

About the only wild card in calculating your lodging expenses is **local taxes,** which vary from state to state and even from county to county. For parks that have only one rate, I give you the percentage in the "Fast Facts" sections of the park chapters. For parks that have more than one rate (and I let you know which ones do), you should call the lodging directly to find out which rate applies.

One cost that you may overlook is **tipping.** If the service is very good in an upscale restaurant (for example, Furnace Creek Inn in Death Valley, The Ahwahnee Hotel in Yosemite, or the El Tovar in Grand Canyon), the servers will expect 20%. In more relaxed settings, 15% is standard for decent service, 10% sends a message that the service is lacking, and 20% is for good service and manna from heaven.

Many national parks hire college students in the summer to clean rooms and cabins, and tipping them isn't out of the question. How much you tip depends on your generosity — and the cleanliness of the room — but $5 a day isn't unreasonable. In some park hotels, you may also come across bellmen anxious to tote your bags to your room. A dollar or two per bag is sufficient; more cash is appropriate if they give you a tip to a secret hiking trail or backcountry lake.

You should also tip those who give you professional guidance. I have no qualms about laying a substantial tip on a guide who safely herds me to the top of the Grand Teton and back down. The same goes for river guides and horse wranglers. In watching out for the safety of neophytes and making sure that everyone has a good experience, they more than earn their keep.

Cutting Costs

By now, you've probably figured out that parks are a great bargain. Even still, you can save more money if you follow these suggestions:

- ✔ **Travel off-season when lodging prices are cheapest.** For most parks, the off-season means the winter months. For Death Valley, the summer months are off-season.

- ✔ **Pack picnic lunches**. If you're going to be hiking a lot, you can munch your lunch along the trail.

- ✔ **Travel midweek.** If you can travel on a Tuesday, Wednesday, or Thursday, you may find cheaper flights to your destination. When you ask about airfares, ask if you can get a cheaper rate by flying on a different day.

- ✔ **Shop the Web for airfares, rental cars, and park lodging.** Someone is usually running some sort of Internet special that will save you money. See Chapter 5 and the Appendix for the Web site addresses of airlines, car-rental agencies, park concessionaires, and Internet travel sites.

- ✔ **Join organizations that provide travel discounts to members.** Are you a card-carrying AAA member (see Chapter 5)? How 'bout AARP (see Chapter 4)? Or some other group that has arranged for savings on car rentals, plane tickets, hotel rooms, or meals? Don't be bashful about inquiring about available discounts when planning your trip; the savings may make another night affordable.

- ✔ **Share facilities.** Don't mind walking down the hall to a communal bathroom/shower house? You can save quite a bit by reserving rooms (or a tent cabin in Yosemite) without bathrooms.

- ✔ **Buy (or bring) a cheap, disposable cooler for drinks.** The cost will be quickly offset if you buy large bottles of water and six-packs of soft drinks at a grocery store rather than at more expensive vendors in the parks.

- ✔ **Buy (or bring) a cheap, disposable cooler for picnic lunches.** I've enjoyed many wonderful lunches — perhaps with cheese, smoked salmon, lunch meats, veggies, or fruit — out in the open overlooking some spectacular setting for half the cost of a sit-down lunch. If you're really thrifty, you can do the same for dinner. (Frugal folks, with space issues in their cars, may want to combine suggestions 7 and 8 and buy one big cooler.)

✔ **Park it and ride.** A growing number of parks have installed shuttle systems to move people to the most popular sites. Not only do these systems get you to most, if not all, of the places you want to see, they also save you precious gasoline money — and spare your nerves from tense parking-spot searches.

✔ **If you can't park it, at least avoid a gas-guzzler.** Your pocket (and the environment) will appreciate it.

Chapter 4

Planning Ahead for Special Travel Needs

. . . .

In This Chapter

▶ Traveling with tots and teens

▶ Making age work (and pay) for you

▶ Rising above disabilities

▶ Going it alone

▶ Traveling with gay (and lesbian) abandon

▶ Exploring special interests in field courses

. . . .

*I*f you have special needs, interests, or concerns that affect your travel plans — almost everyone does — this chapter is for you. I may not be able to address all your questions on a particular topic, but I can direct you to some additional information sources.

Bringing the Brood: Advice for Families

The prospect of visiting a national park excites most kids. With a little advance planning and by taking advantage of the parks' many kid-friendly activities, you can hold onto their attention once you arrive. In this section, I let you know which parks offer activities and attractions that appeal to most kids, and I suggest resources to check out for additional information. I also share tips to make the most of your family time together.

Just for kids

You find top-notch children's activities at almost all the national parks. **Yosemite National Park** offers a wide variety of kid-friendly stuff, such as floating down the Merced River in a raft or swimming in one of the valley's pools. At **Olympic National Park,** kids can explore the Hoh Rain Forest and, in early summer, have a snowball fight atop Hurricane Ridge. At **Sequoia National Park,** kids like to walk among the towering trees, which makes them feel like they've entered the Land of the Giants. In the East, **Great Smoky Mountains National Park** features meandering rivers perfect for floating the afternoon away in an inner tube. And what kid can't stay happy on the beach at **Cape Cod National Seashore?** Throughout this book, I use the Kid Friendly icon to point out these recreations and other kid-pleasing activities.

All parks offer special programs for children. One of the most popular is the **Junior Ranger Program,** which uses puzzles and games to teach kids about their surroundings. As a part of the program, kids occasionally perform some public service — such as collecting trash — for which they receive a Junior Ranger badge. Park rangers also conduct kid-friendly campfire programs addressing such topics as wildlife or geology.

Are your kids older? Are you looking for ways to restore family bonds with a world-weary teenager? Consider a joint climb of the **Grand Teton,** a backcountry adventure into **Kings Canyon,** or a wild cave tour at **Mammoth Cave National Park.** (When I crawled on my belly through sections of Mammoth Cave, I noticed that the teens in my group were having just as much fun as I was.)

Where to find information

You can find information about kids' programs in each **national park newspaper,** which is available at the entrance station, at the visitor center, and often in advance by mail. (See the "Fast Facts" section of each chapter for contact information.) You can also find information online at the **National Park Service Web site,** www.nps.gov.

John Bigley and Paris Permenter mix kids and national parks in *National Parks With Kids* (Open Road Publishing, 1999), available at most major bookstores or via the Internet at Amazon.com. This book covers park service properties in every state and focuses on kid-friendly activities and programs. Frommer's *Family Vacations in the National Parks* (Wiley) is another good resource.

The Family Travel Times newsletter, *Travel With Your Children* (☎ **888-822-4388** or 212-477-5524; Internet: www.familytravel times.com), is published six times a year and offers good general information as well as destination-specific articles. One-year subscriptions cost $39; get one online, by phone, or by snail mail.

Some quick travel-with-kids tips

About to explore a national park with a car full of kids? Here are some tips to increase their enjoyment and comfort while on the road.

In advance of your trip:

✔ **Pack "security blankets."** Take along some of your youngest kids' favorite books and toys, even if they add bulk to your luggage. Going to unfamiliar places can be hard on even the most outgoing youngsters, and security blankets of all sorts will help.

✔ **Read up on the park.** Take your children to the library to study up on the national park that about to visit. They can become experts on wildlife and natural attractions before you leave home. Net-literate kids can dial up www.nps.gov/interp/learn.htm to delve into the natural and cultural resources of the park system.

✔ **Prepare for the sun.** Take steps to ward off the hot sun that beams down on most parks — pack sunscreen or sun block, hats, and sunglasses.

✔ **Get car safety seats.** If your kids are small, be sure to arrange with the car rental companies for child safety seats.

After you arrive at the park:

✔ **Pick up Junior Ranger Program materials.** You can get these materials from a visitor center. They usually include crossword puzzles and other games pertaining to the park.

✔ **Buy snacks.** Don't forget to stock up on snacks to combat energy lows and car sickness.

✔ **Watch your children.** Keep a tight rein on young children near overlooks; around rivers, lakes, and beaches; on snowfields; in Yellowstone's geothermal basins; and near wild animals. (No matter how cuddly bison look, they are *definitely* not tame.)

✔ **Don't push your kids to have fun.** Realize the energy limits of your children — don't try to hit every attraction in one day or go too far on hikes. Gear activities to your child's age, physical condition, and attention span.

Taking Advantage of Age: Tips for the Mature Traveler

National parks are not just for the young. Or middle-aged. Or even the old. They're for everyone. Parks don't go out of their way any more for seniors than they do for youngsters; tourists of all ages are welcomed pretty much equally. One exception is entrance fees. The **Golden Age Passport** serves as a lifetime entrance pass for its holders 62 and older. The pass is available for a one-time fee of $10. You can buy this pass only at a National Park Service entrance area. Be sure to bring proof of age and U.S. citizenship or permanent residency. Like the National Park

Pass (see Chapter 8), this pass admits free of charge the pass holder and any accompanying passengers in a personal vehicle. What's more, the Golden Age Passport provides a 50% discount on federal use fees charged for facilities and services, such as camping, swimming, parking, boat launching, and tours. This does not include park lodging or fees charged by concessionaires.

Most major domestic airlines, including American, United, Continental, US Airways, and TWA, also offer discount programs for senior travelers; be sure to ask whenever you book a flight. See the Appendix for the airlines' toll-free numbers.

Not yet 60 years old? You can still reap the benefits of maturity. One of them is membership in the **American Association of Retired Persons, or AARP** (601 E St. NW, Washington, DC 20049; ☎ **800-424-3410** or 202-434-AARP; Internet: www.aarp.org). Yes, first-wave baby boomers, you need to be only 50 years old to join. For just $10 a year, you can get discounts on package tours, airfares, car rentals, and hotels — to mention only the travel-related items.

The Mature Traveler, a monthly newsletter on senior travel, is another valuable resource, available by subscription for $30 a year. For an information packet on the newsletter, send a postcard with your name and address to Mature Traveler, P.O. Box 1579, Sacramento, CA, 95852, or e-mail your information to maturetravel@mindspring.com. Mature Traveler (www.thematuretraveler.com) also publishes *The Book of Deals* ($9.95), a collection of more than 1,000 senior discounts on airlines, lodging, tours, and attractions around the country You get a copy of this book with a subscription to the newsletter, or you can buy it alone by calling ☎ **800-460-6676.**

Maupin Tour (☎ **800-255-4266;** Internet: www.maupintour.com) offers general-interest bus tours, which often include national parks, suitable for older travelers. The "50 or Better" division of **GORPtravel** (☎ **877-440-GORP;** Internet: www.gorp.com) offers park excursions for active, older travelers who want to fish, hike, or canoe their way through the parks.

Accessing the Parks: Resources for Travelers with Disabilities

A disability shouldn't stop anybody from traveling. Although people with disabilities won't be able to travel everywhere in a national park, more options and resources are available than ever before.

Even though national parks, by their very nature, feature wide expanses of forests, meadows, mountains, and canyons, they are still accessible to the handicapped. Visit a park's Web site (see the "Fast Facts" section of each park chapter for the address), and you find a rundown on its accessibility. In Yellowstone, for instance, wheelchair-accessible boardwalks wind through most of the geyser basins, and the park even offers accessible campsites. At Acadia National Park, a paved walkway leads to the upper viewing area of Thunder Hole. In Grand Canyon National Park, wheelchairs are available for temporary day use at no charge, and several of the interpretive ranger programs are wheelchair accessible.

The **Golden Access Passport,** a lifetime entry pass into the national parks and monuments, is available free of charge to any U.S. citizen or permanent resident (regardless of age) who has been medically certified as disabled or blind; all you need to do is go to one of the parks or monuments with proof of disability status to be issued a pass on the spot. The Golden Access Passport admits free of charge the pass holder and any accompanying passengers in a personal vehicle. This pass also provides a 50% discount on fees for park services and facilities, not including lodging or fees charged by concessionaires.

Nationwide resources

Access-Able Travel Source (www.access-able.com) is a comprehensive database of travel agents who specialize in disabled travel; this source is also a clearinghouse for information about accessible destinations around the world.

Travelers with various disabilities can also obtain customized itineraries from **Access Adventures** (☎ 716-889-9096).

A World of Options, a 658-page book of resources for disabled travelers, covers everything from biking trips to scuba outfitters. The book costs $35 and is available from Mobility International USA, P.O. Box 10767, Eugene, OR 97440 (☎ 541-343-1284, voice and TTY; Internet: www.miusa.org).

Flying Wheels Travel (☎ 800-535-6790; Internet: www.flyingwheel stravel.com) offers escorted tours and cruises that emphasize sports and private tours in minivans with lifts.

Many of the major car-rental companies now offer hand-controlled cars for disabled drivers. Avis can provide such a vehicle at any of its locations in the United States with 48-hour advance notice; Hertz requires between 24 and 72 hours in advance at most of its locations. **Wheelchair Getaways** (☎ 800-642-2042 or 859-873-4973; Internet: www.wheelchair-getaways.com) rents specialized vans with wheelchair lifts and other features for the disabled in more than 35 states.

Vision-impaired travelers should contact the **American Foundation for the Blind,** 11 Penn Plaza, Suite 300, New York, NY 10001 (☎ 800-232-5463; Internet: www.afb.org), for information on traveling with Seeing Eye dogs.

National park resources

If you're curious about accessibility in a particular park, call the park directly or go to its Web site. (See the "Fast Facts" section of each park chapter for its telephone number and Web-site address.) Every national park Web site, which is linked to the National Park Service site at www.nps.gov, provides a section on accessibility.

Going Solo: Advice for Singles

You may be independent minded but not independently wealthy. Hotels and packages that offer discounts for singles are rarer than original come-on lines at pick-up bars. If you don't want to shell out for a room for two, consider finding someone to share costs through the **Travel Companion Exchange,** P.O. Box 833, Amityville, NY 11701 (☎ 631-454-0880; Internet: www.travelcompanions.com).

If you join Travel Companion Exchange, you get a newsletter that lists profiles and travel interests of other members. Spot someone who seems compatible, and the organization enables you to contact them directly, so you can get to know them before deciding to take up closer quarters.

This company makes no restrictions. If you want to travel with someone of the opposite gender, it's nobody's business but your own. On the other hand, even though it has a Web site, this organization is careful to make sure that members have genuine mailing addresses (as opposed to, say, an e-mail address in prison). The company often corresponds with its members via the U.S. mail for this purpose.

The thick, 20-plus page newsletter, published six times a year, also offers other types of travel information for singles, including safety tips. If you're not looking for a roomie, you can subscribe to the publication alone for $48 a year.

Stepping Out: Resources for Gays and Lesbians

A top travel information resource is **Out & About Online** (☎ 800-929-2268 or 415-644-8044; Internet: www.outandabout.com), which has a comprehensive list of travel agents catering to gays and lesbians, a calendar of gay travel events, and links to other useful Web sites and health resources. The monthly newsletter ($49 per year for a regular subscription; $99 for unlimited access to all back issues online) features articles about specific destinations and events. Previously published articles, including one about planning a trip to the national parks, are available for purchase on the site.

Learning Outside the Classroom: Educational Programs

Psst! Want to know how to visit just about any national park at any time of year and not only avoid crowds but also gain insights unavailable to other visitors? Take part in a field course or research program. These activities are organized by the parks themselves or by private groups. Participation takes you off the beaten path into the park's backcountry, where you can study landscape or wildlife or even work on perfecting your brush strokes or paddle strokes. I spent three days one summer in Yellowstone attending a symposium on the park's burgeoning wolf population. Not only did we hear from the wildlife biologists and rangers who oversaw the wolf recovery program, but we also went into the field with hopes of spotting some of the packs. (We didn't spot any, by the way. But now, following the reintroduction effort, the wolf population is thriving.)

Most of the parks offer some kind of educational programming. Go to the parks' Web sites (via www.nps.gov) to learn about specific courses and schedules. You can also track down private organizations that invite travelers — for a price — to help with research. Although these options aren't always publicized, you may find information about them on the parks' Web sites or through visitor centers. Still, some programs are advertised in national magazines, such as *National Geographic Traveler* and *Outside*.

The educational programs can get pricey, running up to more than $300 per person depending on length. But they offer a wealth of knowledge, get you away from the crowds and into some beautiful locations, and introduce you to new friends. They are also very popular, so if you're interested, January is a good time to check with the associations for a catalog of their upcoming summer programs.

The following information gives you an idea of their diversity:

✔ The list of programs offered by the **Yellowstone Association Institute** (P.O. Box 117, Yellowstone National Park, WY 82190; ☎ 307-344-2294; Internet: http://yellowstoneassociation.org) is incredibly broad, ranging from courses on wildlife and geology to courses on photography, nature writing, and wilderness first aid. In about a third of these courses, you can earn college credit. You can also line up lodging in one of the log cabins at the institute's headquarters at the historic **Buffalo Ranch** in the Lamar Valley.

✔ The **Grand Canyon Field Institute** (P.O. Box 399, Grand Canyon, AZ 86023; ☎ **800-858-2808, ext 7035,** 928-638-2485; Internet: www.grandcanyon.org/fieldinstitute) runs a similar program, with classes in human history, wilderness studies, natural history, photography, and the arts. In the **Advanced Wilderness Studies Workshops,** you get a chance to move through the park's backcountry without the benefit of a human trail under your feet. You find out how to follow wash beds and game trails, tossed in with a little scrambling up and over geologic impediments.

✔ The **Yosemite Association** (P.O. Box 230, El Portal, CA 95318; ☎ **209-379-2646;** Internet: www.yosemite.org) operates in the same fashion as the previous program, offering backpacking treks, birding hikes, art programs, family day hikes, and natural history and photography courses in the park.

Part II
Ironing Out the Details

The 5th Wave   By Rich Tennant

"Be patient everyone. This will just take a minute."

In this part . . .

Whoever said "Getting there is half the fun" didn't have to stick to a budget. And because getting there can be expensive, this section not only contains helpful information on how to get to the park of your choice, but I also suggest how to save some money along the way. You find helpful tips on getting good deals on airfares and car rentals, the ins and outs of escorted and packaged tours, and a primer on the types of accommodations you can expect to find. Finally, I toss in odds and ends on everything from what to pack to how to survive (with a smile) your national park experience.

Chapter 5

Getting to the Parks and Getting Around

*F*iguring out how to plan your national park vacation is one of the toughest — and earliest — decisions you need to make about your trip. Only you can decide whether you want to make your own plans (with my assistance, of course), let someone else call the shots, or devise a combination strategy.

Consulting a Travel Agent: A Good Idea?

You may never have thought about working as a travel agent, but by the time you finish this book, you'll be qualified to arrange most, if not all, of your travel needs. Still, I realize that some of you don't have the time or inclination to arrange every logistical aspect of your trip. You want someone to make the calls, run down the pricing, and even haggle a bit, and then call you back with the itinerary and bottom-line cost. Finding a great travel agent comes in handy.

In a lot of ways, a good travel agent is like a good mechanic or plumber: hard to find, but invaluable once you've located the right one. The best way to find a good travel agent is by word of mouth.

To get the most out of a travel agent, do a little homework. Read up on your destination (you've already made a sound decision by buying this book) and choose some accommodations and attractions that appeal to you. If you have Internet access, check prices on the Web to get a sense of ballpark figures. Then take this guidebook and Web information to the travel agent and ask him or her to make the arrangements for you. Because travel agents have access to more resources than even the most complete Web travel sites, they often can obtain better prices than you can get on your own. And agents can issue your tickets and vouchers right on the spot. If they can't get you into the hotel of your choice, they can recommend an alternative, and you can look for an objective review in this guidebook.

Some travel agents work on commission. The good news is that you don't pay the commission — the airlines, accommodations, and tour companies do. The bad news is that unscrupulous travel agents will try to persuade you to book the vacations that nab them the most money in commissions. But in recent years, more and more airlines and resorts have begun to limit or eliminate these commissions altogether. As a result, some travel agents now charge customers for their services.

If you opt to place your trip in an agent's hands, ask the agent if he or she works with a park concessionaire on lodging or focuses on motels or hotels in gateway communities just outside the park. (Some agents prefer to work with nonpark properties because they receive a higher commission.) This information will help you choose an agent that's right for you.

Weighing the Benefits of Organized Tours

When you think of escorted or package tours, you may picture being herded to overrated, touristy sights with a busload of fellow travelers. Think again, my friends. Times — and tours — have changed.

Even though an **escorted tour** does, in fact, involve an escort, the trip doesn't need to be dull — or even tame. Escorted tours range from cushy bus trips, in which you sit back and let the driver worry about the traffic, to adventures that may include cycling tours of national parks or trekking in the Grand Canyon — activities for which most travelers can use a bit of guidance. You travel with a group, which may be just the thing if you're single and want company. In general, your costs are taken care of when you arrive at your destination, but you still need to cover the airfare.

Unlike escorted tours, **package tours** generally package costs rather than people. Although some companies do bundle every aspect of your trip (including tours to various sights), most companies deal only with selected aspects that allow you to get good deals by putting together an airfare and hotel arrangement or, say, an airfare and greens fee package. Most packages tend to give you a lot of leeway while saving you a chunk of money.

How do you find these deals? I suggest some strategies in the next two sections of this chapter. If the tour operations that I mention don't offer deals suited to your departure point, check with a local travel agent. They generally know best how to put together deals that depart from your area.

Joining an escorted tour

Some people love escorted tours. The tour company takes care of all the details and tells you what to expect at each leg of your journey. You know your major costs up front, and in the case of tame tours (which don't include adventure travel), you won't encounter many surprises. Escorted tours can take you to the maximum number of sights in the minimum amount of time with the least amount of hassle. One problem, though, is that you and your tour guide may differ on which attractions to see and how long to spend at each one.

If you decide to go with an escorted tour, think strongly about purchasing travel insurance, especially if the tour operator asks you to pay up front. But don't buy insurance from the tour operator! If the operator doesn't fulfill its obligation to provide you with the vacation you've paid for, you can't assume the operator will fulfill its insurance obligations. Get travel insurance through an independent agency (see Chapter 8).

Along with finding out whether you need to put down a deposit and when final payment is due, ask a few questions when choosing to buy an escorted tour:

1. **What is the cancellation policy?** Can the operator cancel the trip if it doesn't get enough people? How late can you cancel if you are unable to go? Do you get a refund if you cancel? If they cancel?

2. **How jam-packed is the schedule?** Does the tour operator try to fit 25 hours into a 24-hour day, or will you have ample time to shop or to relax by the pool? If getting up at 7 a.m. every day and not returning to your hotel until 6 or 7 p.m. at night sounds like a grind, certain escorted tours may not be for you.

3. **How big is the group?** The smaller the group, the less time you spend waiting for people to get on and off the bus. Tour operators may be evasive about this, because they may not know the exact size of the group until everybody has made their reservations. But they should be able to give you a rough estimate.

4. **Do you have a minimum group size?** Some tour operators require a minimum group size and may cancel a tour if they don't book enough people. Find out what the quota is and how close they are to reaching it. Again, tour operators may be evasive in their answers, but the information may help you select a tour that's sure to happen.

5. **What exactly is included?** Don't assume anything. You may have to pay to get yourself to and from the airport. A box lunch may be included in an excursion, but drinks may cost extra. Also, beer may be included but not wine.

6. **How much flexibility do you have?** Can you opt out of certain activities, or does the bus leave once a day, with no exceptions? Are all your meals planned in advance? Can you choose your entree at dinner, or does everybody get the same chicken cutlet?

When it comes to escort tours in national parks, you can choose from a small handful of well-established companies, each with a different emphasis. I recommend the following:

✔ **Backroads** (☎ 800-GO-ACTIVE or 510-527-1555; Internet: www. backroads.com), a company that has been leading trips since 1979, is a good choice for travelers who can't decide whether to bike, hike, or combine a variety of activities during a park visit. Among the offerings is a six-day biking, walking, and sea-kayaking tour along Penobscot Bay and Acadia National Park. The price of $1,998 per person includes shuttle support, guides, bikes and kayaks, food (except for one dinner), and accommodations, but not airfare. Prices are based on double occupancy; an extra fee is usually charged for single occupancy.

✔ **GORPtravel** (☎ 877-440-GORP; Internet: www.gorp.com) also focuses on adventure travel. One of its trips is a seven-day winter wildlife viewing safari into Yellowstone and Grand Teton national parks ($2,095 per person, including transportation from Jackson, Wyoming; participation in wildlife research projects; guidance from a wildlife specialist; six nights lodging; and most meals) and a six-day hiking trip through parts of Yosemite, Kings Canyon, and Sequoia national parks ($1495 per person, including all meals, accommodations, park fees, support vehicle, and guides). For both trips, airfare is extra and prices are based on double occupancy.

Also see Chapter 4 for descriptions of field-study packages offered in many of the national parks.

Picking a peck of package tours

For lots of destinations, package tours can be a smart way to go. A package that includes airfare, hotel, and transportation to and from the airport generally costs less than the hotel alone if you book the room yourself. Buying a package tour is kind of like buying your garbage bags at a buy-in-bulk store — except the tour operator is the one who actually buys the 1,000-count box of garbage bags and resells them 10 at a time at a cost that undercuts the local supermarket.

Package tours can come in as many varieties as the garbage bags, too. Some offer a better class of hotels, and some offer the same hotels for lower prices. Some offer flights on scheduled airlines, whereas others book charters. In some packages, your choice of accommodations and travel days may be limited. Some tours let you choose between escorted vacations and independent vacations; others allow you to add on just a few excursions or escorted day trips (also at discounted prices) without booking an entirely escorted tour. The bottom line: The variations are nearly limitless; the more research you do, the more likely you're going to discover the right package for you.

One package tour source is the **American Automobile Association** (call ☎ **407-444-7000** for the phone number of your local club or check online at www.aaa.com). Known as AAA ("Triple A"), this group occasionally packages tours to destinations around the country. One trip runs through Grand Teton and Yellowstone national parks; the tour starts in Salt Lake City and ends ten days later in South Dakota.

AAA members can also receive (for free) the association's "Guide To" maps and travel planners for a select number of national parks. These materials feature information on park history, flora, and fauna. Nonmembers can purchase these guides at large chain bookstores. If you're a member, AAA offices will also be more than happy to arrange your lodging, airfare, and car-rental needs if you tell them where you want to go and how long you want to stay. If you're driving, as a bonus they can compile a "Triptik" booklet with succinct directions to the park and the sights you want to see.

Some **park concessionaires** also offer package tours — which isn't much of a surprise in the one-stop shopping world. Check out their individual Web sites for activity offerings and lodging options. Then call them directly to lock in your reservations. See the Appendix for concessionaire Web sites and telephone numbers.

Being Your Own Travel Agent

You may want to make all your travel arrangements yourself, whether you're an independent soul or you're into spontaneity and don't pre-arrange anything outside of what's absolutely essential (like your flight). Whatever the reason, I'm happy to supply you with some basic contact information to help you make the necessary arrangements. If you have a computer and any familiarity with the Web, you can arrange your own accommodations, airline tickets, and car rental with surprisingly little hassle in amazingly short time.

Booking your room

Curious about the lodging possibilities in each park? Dial up www.nps.gov on your computer and go to the park of your choice. On each park's opening Web page, you find a link to its lodges that includes phone numbers and, in some cases, an online reservations page. Some national park concessionaires provide their own Web sites (see the Appendix for these), where you can get a rundown on rooms, find out about availability and pricing, and occasionally stumble upon Internet specials that can save you money. For more information about booking your accommodations, see Chapter 6.

Flying to the parks

Most parks, by their nature, are off the beaten path. But don't worry: None of them is very difficult to access. Even though Grand Teton National Park resides in sparsely populated Wyoming, it may be the country's most accessible park thanks to the nearby Jackson Hole Airport. Of the 15 parks described in this book, Arches and Death Valley national parks win the prize for being the farthest away from a major airport. Arches is 125 miles from the airport at Grand Junction, Colorado; Death Valley is 140 miles away from the Las Vegas Airport. For information about which airport is closest to the park that interests you, see the "Getting There" section of each park's chapter.

Getting the best airfare

Competition among the major U.S. airlines is unlike that of any other industry. Every airline offers virtually the same product — a coach seat is a coach seat is a coach seat — but prices can vary by hundreds of dollars.

Business travelers, who need the flexibility to buy their tickets at the last minute and change their itinerary at a moment's notice (and still want to get home before the weekend), pay the premium rate, known as the full fare. But if you can book your ticket far in advance; stay over Saturday night; or travel on a Tuesday, Wednesday, or Thursday, you can qualify for the least expensive price — usually a fraction of the full fare. On most flights, even the shortest hops within the United States, the full fare is close to $1,000 or more, but a ticket purchased 7 or 14 days in advance is closer to $200 or $300. Obviously, planning ahead pays off.

The airlines also periodically hold sales, in which they lower the prices on their most popular routes. These fares have advance purchase requirements and date-of-travel restrictions, but you can't beat the prices. As you plan your vacation, keep your eyes open for these sales, which tend to take place in seasons of low travel volume. You almost never see a sale around the peak summer vacation months (July and August) or around Thanksgiving or Christmas, when many people fly regardless of the price of the fare.

Consolidators, also known as *bucket shops,* buy seats in bulk from the airlines and then sell them back to the public. Their prices are much better than the fares offered from the airlines and are often lower than your travel agent's price. You can find consolidator ads in the travel section of your Sunday newspaper in small boxes at the bottom of the page. Some of the most reliable include **Cheap Tickets** (☎ **888-922-8849**; Internet: www.cheaptickets.com), which also offers discounts on car rentals and hotel rooms; **Travac Tours & Charters** (☎ **800-TRAV-800**; Internet: www.thetravelsite.com); and **FlyCheap** (☎ **800-FLY-INTERNET**; Internet:www.1800flycheap.com), which requires you to provide a lot of information about yourself before you can find out very much about them.

Buying your ticket online

Another way to find the cheapest fare is to scour the Internet. What computers do best is search through millions of pieces of data and return information in rank order. The number of virtual travel agents on the Internet has increased exponentially in recent years.

Checking all the travel booking sites would be impossible, but a few of the more respected (and more comprehensive) ones are **Frommers** (www.frommers.com), **Travelocity** (www.travelocity.com), **Expedia** (www.expedia.com), and **Orbitz** (www.orbitz.com). Each has its own little quirks, but all provide variations of the same service. Just enter the dates you want to fly and the cities you want to visit, and the computer looks for the lowest fares. Several other features have become standard to these sites: the ability to check flights at different times or dates in hopes of finding a cheaper fare; e-mail alerts when fares drop on a route you specified; and a database of last-minute deals that advertises super-cheap vacation packages or airfares for those who can get away at a moment's notice.

Great last-minute deals are also available directly from the airlines themselves through a free e-mail service called E-savers. Each week, the airline sends you a list of discounted flights, usually scheduled to leave the upcoming Friday or Saturday and return the following Monday or Tuesday. You can sign up for all the major airlines at once by logging on to **Smarter Living** (www.smarterliving.com). **Orbitz** (www.orbitz.com), a ticketing service run by the major airlines, is another good resource. Finally, you can search each airline's Web site (see the Appendix for these addresses) for bargains. These sites offer schedules, flight booking, and information on late-breaking bargains.

Renting a car

Unless you drive your own vehicle to the park of your choice, you need to rent a car. What kind of car should you choose? You definitely won't need any high-performance wheels, because park roads are not conducive to speeds over 45 mph. For years, I've been traveling in trusty Subaru wagons — they're economical, reliable, hold all the gear I need, and come in all-wheel-drive. (That's not an endorsement, mind you, but an example of the type of rig that works.) Outside of winter months, you're not likely to need four-wheel-drive. But I do heartily recommend a rig with decent ground clearance — just in case you decide to venture a bit off the beaten path and down a washboard-weary dirt road. Look for a station wagon or SUV that gets reasonable gas mileage and has enough space to hold your luggage and gear.

Finding the best deal

Car-rental rates vary even more than airline fares. The price depends on the size of the car, the length of time you keep it, where and when you pick it up and drop it off, where you take it, and a host of other factors. The following list gives you some factors to keep in mind.

- ✔ **Calculate your mileage before choosing a package**. If you have to drive a long way from the airport to the park and if you plan to do a lot of driving within the park, you'll want a rental package with unlimited mileage.

- ✔ **Weekend rates may be lower than weekday rates.** If you're keeping the car five or more days, a weekly rate may be cheaper than the daily rate. Ask if the rate for pickup on Friday morning is the same as the rate for pickup on Thursday night.

- ✔ **Some companies assess a drop-off charge.** You may be charged a fee if you don't return the car to the same location where you picked it up. National Car Rental is one of the few companies that doesn't charge this fee.

- ✔ **Find out whether age is an issue.** Many car-rental companies add on a fee for drivers under 25 — or don't rent to them at all.

- ✔ **If you see an advertised price in your local newspaper, be sure to ask for the specified rate.** If not, you may be charged the standard (higher) rate. Don't forget to mention membership in AAA, AARP, and trade unions. These affiliations usually entitle you to discounts ranging from 5% to 30%.

- ✔ **Check your frequent-flyer accounts.** Not only are your favorite (or at least most-used) airlines likely to send you discount coupons, but most car rentals add at least 500 miles to your frequent-flyer account.

- ✔ As with other aspects of planning your trip, using the Internet can make comparison shopping for a car rental much easier. All the major booking sites — **Frommers** (www.frommers.com), **Travelocity** (www.travelocity.com), **Expedia** (www.expedia.com), **Orbitz** (www.orbitz.com), and **Smarter Living** (www.smarterliving.com), for example — have search engines that can dig up discounted car-rental rates. Just enter the size of the car you want, the pickup and return dates, and location, and the server returns a price. You can even make the reservation through any of these sites.

Adding up the charges

On top of the standard rental prices, other optional charges apply to most car rentals (and some not-so-optional charges, such as taxes). The **Collision Damage Waiver** (CDW), which requires you to pay for damage to the car in a collision, is covered by many credit card companies as well as your own auto policy. Check with your credit card company, or your insurance agent, before you leave so you can avoid paying this hefty fee (as much as $15 a day).

The car-rental companies also offer additional **liability insurance** (if you harm others in an accident), **personal accident insurance** (if you harm yourself or your passengers), and **personal effects insurance** (if your luggage is stolen from your car). Your insurance policy on your car at home probably covers most of these unlikely occurrences. However, if your own insurance doesn't cover you for rentals or if you don't have auto insurance, definitely consider the additional coverage. Unless you're toting around the Hope diamond — and you don't want to leave it in your car trunk, anyway — you can probably skip the personal effects insurance. But driving around without liability or personal accident coverage is never a good idea. Even if you're a good driver, other people may not be, and liability claims can be complicated.

Some companies also offer **refueling packages,** in which you pay for your initial full tank of gas up front and can return the car with an empty gas tank. The prices can be competitive with local gas prices, but you don't get credit for any gas remaining in the tank. If you reject this option, you pay only for the gas you use, but you have to return the car with a full tank or face charges of $3 to $4 a gallon for any shortfall. In my experience, gas prices in the refueling packages are at the high end. So I usually forego the refueling package and allow plenty of time for refueling en route to the car-rental return. However, if you usually run late and if stopping at a refueling stop may cause you to miss your plane, you're a perfect candidate for the fuel-purchase option.

Chapter 6

Booking Your Accommodations

· ·

In This Chapter

▶ Running down the options

▶ Reserving the bunk of your choice

▶ Strategizing for last-minute lodgings

▶ Roughing it: Campgrounds and the backcountry

· ·

*P*lanning a trip to a national park can be a surprisingly daunting task when you consider the logistics of finding a place to bed down for the night. Many of the best accommodations are fully booked several months, even a year, in advance. While the park chapters get into the specifics of each lodge and campground, this chapter helps you choose the right accommodation type for your needs and budget.

Finding the Right Room

National parks are scattered from sea to shining sea, in remote places, and along sandy beaches. As you can imagine, the range of quality of rooms in each park is mind-boggling. In Yosemite, for example, the dizzying variety of accommodations ranges from three-sided *housekeeping units* (which are tossed together with three canvas walls, a double-layer of canvas for the roof, and a slab of cold concrete that greets you in the morning) to the six-story Ahwahnee Hotel that has catered to royalty.

Because the spread of park accommodations is so vast, about the only standard amenities that I'll vouch for are beds and lights (which may be candles or electric bulbs). Some rooms include air-conditioning, and some provide wood stoves to fight off the frost. Telephones and televisions are not standard amenities.

But if you step outside of a park, you find a world where good beds, air-conditioning/heating, phones, and televisions are standard in most hotels and motels. And in some of the fancier spots, you also find hot tubs and fireplaces — some B&Bs have both!

As wide-ranging as the accommodations in and around the parks are, so are their nightly rates, which can range from $40 to $350. Of course, setting affects price as well as amenities. (An Old Faithful Inn room facing the Old Faithful geyser, for example, is more expensive than one not facing the geyser.) To guide you through the maze of pricing options, I give each accommodation in this book a dollar sign rating from $ to $$$$$. The number of dollar signs is based on the *rack rate* — the maximum rate a hotel charges for a room — per night for two people in a double room during high season, which is summer in all parks except Death Valley. The dollar signs represent the following price ranges:

$	$50 and under
$$	$51–$100
$$$	$101–$150
$$$$	$151–$200
$$$$$	More than $200

Now about that rack rate: Although all the hotels in this book charge rack rates, those hotels outside the park are more flexible. These places are happy to charge you the rack rate, but you usually don't have to pay it — hardly anyone does. The best way to avoid paying the rack rate is surprisingly simple: Ask for a cheaper or discounted rate. Make sure to mention membership in AAA, AARP, frequent flyer programs, or any other corporate rewards programs you can think of. You may be pleasantly surprised by the discount you receive. For the in-park hotels, you should ask about off-season deals when you call and look for Internet specials on the Web. A little bit of digging can save you dollars.

Fit for royalty, presidents, and actors

In-park accommodations are generally modest throughout the national park system, but some places are exceptions. If price is no object, head to **The Ahwahnee Hotel** in Yosemite (see Chapter 21) or **Lake Yellowstone Hotel** in Yellowstone (see Chapter 20). Both are located in spectacular settings — the Ahwahnee not far from Yosemite Fall and Lake Yellowstone Hotel on the shores of Yellowstone Lake — and both have suites suitable for kings, queens, and presidents (not to mention Hollywood royalty such as Clint Eastwood, who has stayed at the Ahwahnee). In my middle-class opinion, these hotels epitomize "national park stateliness." They're elegant, dignified, and a heckuva way to end a weeklong trek in the backcountry. Compared to the rest of the options in these two parks, these accommodations are very, very nice. I'm talking thick comforters (atop king- or queen-sized beds) to ward off evening chills, plush carpeting, and handsomely tiled bathrooms. Telephones are standard, but televisions are not. (You didn't come to a national park to watch the soaps, did you?) Both feature well-appointed public spaces, and the Ahwahnee boasts an outdoor pool. Suites at these hotels are priced in the very expensive range ($$$$$), while standard doubles are priced in the expensive category ($$$$).

A new wave of park motels

An accommodations revolution is slowly moving through the park system. Park Service officials, well aware of the need for lodging upgrades, demanded that concessionaires make a bigger investment in the parks' infrastructure than they had in the past. As a result, concessionaires replaced the 1960s-era buildings with several new lodgings that are cleaner, roomier, and more comfortable. **Dunraven Lodge** and the **Snow Lodge** in Yellowstone (Chapter 21), for example, use rustic pine furniture and artful lamps to lend a woodsy atmosphere to the rooms. Although the rooms at **Wuksachi Lodge** (opened in 1999) in Sequoia (Chapter 19) are nothing to rave about, the main lodge, with its cedar and stone construction, blends nicely with the surrounding park. Of course, you pay in the higher range ($$$$) for these abodes, and you still may not have a television in your room.

Motels and other roadside fare

When the World War II generation rebounded from the war and began to pencil vacations into their summers, roadside America responded with motels. These places weren't fancy, but they were clean and offered basic amenities such as beds, telephones, and televisions. Best of all, they were economical. These chain-style hotels sprouted up in the national parks in the 1960s, and they're still common today in almost every park. In the moderate to expensive range ($$$–$$$$), park motels are generally clean and comfortable. Some have televisions and telephones; some have neither.

National park rustic: Do you want that with or without running water?

At some national parks, roughing it doesn't necessarily mean sleeping under the stars or in a tent. Visit Yosemite and Yellowstone, and you can really curb your spending by staying in tent cabins — four walls and a roof of canvas over a concrete slab — or in aging (although not always gracefully) cabins where wood stoves provide the heat and where communal bathhouses only a short walk away contain showers and toilets.

Yosemite's tent cabins are long on romance but short on comfort (Chapter 21). These candle-lit cabins provide cots and a few heavy wool blankets to defend you from any cold air that the woodstove can't combat. Some cabins at Yellowstone's Roosevelt Lodge and Old Faithful can probably qualify as national historic sites because they're so old (Chapter 20). They're also stark, tiny, and tend to hold dirt better than lodge rooms.

Mammoth Cave National Park also offers cabins. In my opinion, the ones with plumbing, heating, and phones are the best lodging bet, whereas other cabins are equipped with only a ceiling fan to circulate the thick summer air (Chapter 16). Rates for these types of accommodations range from very inexpensive ($) to moderate ($$$), and although you may not expect it, they tend to be fairly high in demand. You can have your meals, which are not included in the prices, at lodges, restaurants, or hotels, usually a short walk away.

On the outside: B&Bs and pricier abodes

Some parks don't have lodges within their borders. Visit any of these parks, and you'll stay in a tent, motel, hotel, or bed-and-breakfast in one of the gateway communities. These places come in more sizes, shapes, styles, and prices than space allows to describe. You can find sumptuous B&Bs with fireplaces and hot tubs in their rooms and with manicured gardens where you can enjoy your breakfast. Palatial estates that date to the early 1900s have been turned into inns near Acadia National Park (Chapter 9). Outside Mount Rainier's Nisqually Entrance, you can even stay in a deluxe tree house with running water (Chapter 17). Naturally, gateway communities are packed with chain properties (see the Appendix for a list of toll-free telephone numbers). These accommodations offer little in the name of ambience but are usually clean, comfortable enough for a multiday stay, and reasonably priced.

Among the extent of accommodations outside the parks, prices range from inexpensive ($) to very expensive ($$$$$). At any of the bed-and-breakfasts that I recommend in this book, you can expect a full breakfast and, in some cases, an afternoon snack.

Nabbing Bunks at Popular Lodgings

Even though national parks don't advertise on television, people know that they exist. Park lodgings are usually in high demand because of limited offerings and, in the case of the northern parks, short seasons. If you want to stay at a park lodging, you need to plan ahead. For summer vacations, reserve at least three to four months in advance of your trip — six months is even better. For the most popular lodges — Yosemite's Ahwahnee Hotel (Chapter 21), Yellowstone's Old Faithful Inn (Chapter 20), and the Grand Canyon's El Tovar (Chapter 13) — you need to call earlier than six months ahead. In fact, in Yosemite, you need to start dialing a year in advance. In the individual park chapters, I give you the lowdown (and share a few tricks) on how to get the room of your dreams.

 Also keep in mind that not all parks experience the same busy seasons; I give reservation guidelines in each park chapter. While December and January are very slow in Sequoia, these months are bustling in Death Valley (see Chapter 2 for more details on the seasons).

Private companies also run lodges inside national parks. Some of these concessionaires operate in more than one park. **Xanterra Parks & Resorts,** for instance, oversees lodges in Yellowstone, Grand Canyon, Death Valley, and Zion national parks, as well as in Everglades and Bryce Canyon. Big companies such as this one (and even some of the smaller ones) provide their own Web sites where you can check out the accommodations, inquire about availability and pricing, and even lock in a room. See the Appendix for a list of these concessionaires and their Web site addresses.

 In addition to using this book, you can find out more about the national park lodgings on the **National Park Service** Web site at www.nps.gov. Links to individual parks let you know which concessionaires to call for in-park reservations and what towns offer out-of-park lodgings.

Making Reservations at the Last Minute

I'm a procrastinator — a darn good one, too (just ask my editor). So I understand how you can forget about making a room reservation until a month before your scheduled vacation. Frankly, the odds aren't good that you can land a room in Yosemite in August if you wait until July to call. But hey, it can happen.

 How, you wonder? Well, every now and again tour *wholesalers* — commercial folks who book tours (see Chapter 5) — fail to sell out trips and are forced to cancel large blocks of their reserved rooms. These releases typically occur 21 to 30 days in advance of their bookings, so try calling the park's reservation desk during this time window to find out if they've received any cancellations. Sometimes, you can find a vacancy even if a wholesaler hasn't relinquished any of its rooms. Astute folks (such as the ones reading this book) who make reservations months in advance sometimes need to cancel at the last minute — and voilà! — a room opens up.

Another way to find a vacancy — either when you're booking in advance or at the last minute — is to inquire about Tuesday and Wednesday night possibilities because most folks stretch their weekends by booking the more popular Thursday and Friday nights.

In a pinch, you may want to check out some of the hotel booking sites on the Internet. Although these sites don't give you access to in-park accommodations (see the Appendix for a list of park concessionaires that do), you may be able to get a room in one of the gateway towns outside the parks. A few of the sites worth surfing are the following:

✔ **All Hotels on the Web** (www.all-hotels.com). Although the name is something of a misnomer, the site does provide tens of thousands of listings throughout the world. Bear in mind that each hotel has paid a small fee (of $25 and up) to be listed, so the site is less an objective list and more like a book of online brochures.

✔ **hoteldiscount!com** (www.180096hotel.com). This site lists bargain room rates at hotels in more than 50 U.S. and international cities. The cool thing is that hoteldiscount!com prebooks blocks of rooms, so it sometimes offers discount rates on hotel rooms that are otherwise sold out.

✔ **InnSite** (www.innsite.com). This extensive directory of B&Bs has listings in all 50 U.S. states and in more than 50 countries around the globe. Find an inn at your destination, see pictures of the rooms, and check prices and availability. InnSite includes a B&B listing only if the proprietor has submitted one (getting an inn listed is free). The innkeepers write their own descriptions, and many listings link to the inn's own Web sites. B&B fans can also check the **Bed and Breakfast Channel** (www.bedandbreakfast.com).

✔ **TravelWeb** (www.travelweb.com). Listing more than 26,000 hotels in 170 countries, TravelWeb focuses mostly on chains (the upper and lower ends), and you can book almost 90% of these rooms online. TravelWeb's Click-It Weekends, updated each Monday, offers weekend deals at many leading hotel chains.

Pitching Your Tent or Parking Your RV

At last count, 25,700 campsites at 548 campgrounds are located in 77 areas of the national park system. If you're after one of these campsites, you can chase it down via telephone, by mail, in person at the park, or over the Internet. The **National Park Reservation Service (NPRS)** maintains the reservation system and operates a Web site (http://reservations.nps.gov) where you can find campground listings and make a reservation.

You can also make park reservations over the phone by calling NPRS at ☎ 800-365-2267 (800-530-9796 TTY and 301-722-1257 for international calls). Yosemite, due to its popularity, has its own phone number (☎ 800-436-7275). You can pay for your reservation with Visa, MasterCard, or Discover, or by check or money order. However, if you want to make a phone reservation and pay by check or money order, you need to call at least 21 days in advance of your arrival, and NPRS must receive your check within 7 days of making your reservation. Don't dally!

If you want to mail in your payment or make a campsite reservation by mail, the address is NPRS, P.O. Box 1600, Cumberland, MD 21501. If you're replying by overnight letter, the address is NPRS, 3 Commerce Drive, Cumberland, MD 21502. On your mail-in application, which must be received 21 days before your arrival, be sure to list the following information:

1. Your name, address, and telephone number.

2. The name of the park and specific campground.

3. Your arrival and departure dates.

4. The number of persons in your party.

5. Whether you're hauling an RV or plan to pitch a tent.

6. Your method of payment (VISA, MC, DC, personal check, or money order). If paying by credit card, include the card number and expiration date; checks should be made out to the National Park Service.

7. Any pass holder discounts you can claim (Golden Age or Golden Access).

8. Whether you're bringing a pet.

Thanks to the park reservation system, you can now book a campsite up to five months before you actually arrive in the park. For example, for all parks except Yosemite, if you call on January 5, you can make a reservation for dates as late as June 4; if you call on February 5, you can make a reservation for dates as late as July 4; and so on.

For Yosemite, beginning on the 15th of each month, you can make a reservation for up to five months in advance. So if you call on January 15, you can schedule an arrival for June 14; on February 15, you can schedule an arrival for July 14, and so on.

When you call to book your campsite, make sure to ask your reservation agent for park-specific restrictions, such as the one that places a maximum of two reservations per customer for the same dates in the same park. A good idea is to make several choices before you call (or list alternatives on the mail-in application) in case your first choice is booked solid. Also, if you need a wheelchair-accessible site, mention that when making a reservation.

Keep in mind that not all campgrounds are open year-round. Also, not all campgrounds charge a fee. Some provide running water, some don't. In the individual park chapters, I point out the specifics of each campground. A final word of caution: Some parks periodically change which campgrounds are open seasonally and which ones are open year-round. If in doubt, double check.

Gambling for Backcountry Permits

Even though all parks require you to pick up a permit before you head off into the backcountry, some places are so popular that you have to enter a lottery or go through a permit process to win a chance to visit them. Why? Because officials restrict access to a specific number of campsites to protect the backcountry from overuse. Yellowstone and the Grand Canyon use this system. Yellowstone's Shoshone Lake is the most sought after backcountry attraction, and on April 1 of each year, park officials conduct a lottery to see who wins a campsite reservation. After this date, any available campsite reservations are issued on a first-come, first-served basis.

Yellowstone is a pretty big place, though. If you can't obtain a permit for a specific piece of backcountry, chances are, you can head someplace else in the park.

The demand for the High Sierra backcountry tent camps in Yosemite and Sequoia national parks, which are available from late June to Labor Day, is ridiculously high. Applications for the camps are accepted between October 15 and November 30, and winners are notified by the end of the following March. See the Yosemite and Sequoia chapters (Chapters 21 and 19, respectively) for information on how to obtain an application.

Chapter 7

Managing Your Money

- -

- -

*I*f you've read Chapters 1 through 6, you probably know what type of park vacation fits into your budget. Now you can think about how much money — and in what form — you want to take with you. Plus, you need an action plan in case you lose (or someone steals) your wallet. No one likes to think of such nightmares, but if you're prepared for the worst, you can survive any turn of events.

Considering Cash or Credit

Paying cash or credit is a capitalist's quandary, one that, come vacation time, can cause many people to lose sleep. Do you follow a pay-as-you-go philosophy, cramming your wallet with big bills, and chance having your cash lost or stolen? Or should you reach for the plastic and hope the bill that greets you at home doesn't bankrupt you? Some folks carry little cash and prefer instead to test their credit card limit — and their self-restraint. Others hate plastic and prefer cash, traveler's checks, and conservatism. The approach you take depends on what makes you comfortable. But keep in mind that you'll be spending more money than you usually spend on a daily basis, so you'll need to have access to more of the green stuff. Plus, if your mind slips into vacation mode, you may not be as vigilant of your personal belongings as you are when you're on your own turf.

Carrying cash

If you generally like to pay for all your day-to-day expenses with cash to keep from melting your credit card, you don't need to abandon this practice on vacation. Just don't leave your wallet in your room or on the dashboard of your car while you're touring the park. If you've grown accustomed to carrying small amounts of cash and refilling at ATMs, these ubiquitous machines now infiltrate the park system. (If you can't find an ATM inside a park, you'll find one in a gateway community.)

Toting traveler's checks

Traveler's checks are something of an anachronism from the days when people wrote personal checks instead of going to an ATM. Because traveler's checks can be replaced if lost or stolen, they are a sound alternative to filling your wallet with cash at the beginning of a trip. I haven't used traveler's checks for 25 years. But if they make you feel safer, go for it. Cerebral nirvana, however achieved, is crucial to any vacation.

You can get traveler's checks at almost any bank. **American Express** offers checks in denominations of $20, $50, $100, $500, and $1,000. You pay a service charge ranging from 1% to 4%, though AAA members can obtain checks without a fee at most AAA offices. You can also get American Express traveler's checks over the phone by calling ☎ 800-221-7282. **Visa** (☎ 800-221-2426) also offers traveler's checks at Citibank locations across the country and at several other banks. The service charge ranges from 1.5% to 2%; checks come in denominations of $50, $100, $500, and $1,000. **MasterCard** has its hand in the traveler's check market, too. Call ☎ 800-223-9920 for a location near you.

Frequenting ATMs

These days, far more people use ATMs than traveler's checks. Most cities have handy 24-hour cash machines linked to a national network that almost always includes your bank at home. **Cirrus** (☎ 800-424-7787; Internet: www.mastercard.com) and **Plus** (☎ 800-843-7587; Internet: www.vias.com) are the two most popular networks; check the back of your ATM card to see which network your bank belongs to. The 800 numbers and Web sites will give you specific locations of ATMs where you can withdraw money while on vacation. You can periodically use the machines to withdraw just the money you need for a couple days to eliminate the insecurity of carrying around a large stash of cash. Of course, many ATMs are little money managers (or dictators, depending on how you look at them) that impose limits on your spending by allowing you to withdraw only a certain amount of money — say, a maximum of $200 — per day.

One important reminder before you go ATM crazy: Many banks charge (or inflict) a fee ranging from 50¢ to $3 whenever a nonaccount holder uses their ATMs. Your own bank may also charge you a fee for using an ATM that's not one of their branch locations. In other words, you may get charged twice for the same transaction, so reverting to the traveler's check policy may be cheaper. To decide which method is right for you, call your bank and ask if they have branches or ATM outlets near the national park that you'll be visiting.

Doting on debit cards

Another way of working with your money — as opposed to the theoretical money of credit cards — is by using a debit card. You can use a debit card with a major credit card logo anywhere that accepts the credit card. The difference is that the money comes directly out of your checking account. As long as you record all your debit-card purchases, just as you would check purchases, debit cards are a great way to go. Not only do you not need to carry cash, but also the receipts provide a convenient record of all your travel expenses.

Charging ahead with credit cards

Credit cards are a good and a bad thing. They afford the advantages of a debit card — they're accepted in most places, you don't need to carry cash, and you receive receipts of all your purchases — and one important disadvantage: They allow you to spend money that you don't have. You can charge as much as your credit limit will allow (which may relate little to your actual financial resources). With a credit card, you can indulge in more impulse buying than with any other form of payment.

But they also have an important advantage. If you suddenly need extra cash, a credit card comes in handy. You can get cash advances off your credit card at any ATM if you know your *personal identification number* (PIN) number. If you've forgotten it or didn't even know you had one, call the phone number on the back of your credit card and ask the bank to send the PIN to you. Your new number should arrive in five to seven business days, although some banks will give it to you over the phone if you tell them your mother's maiden name or some other security clearance.

Personally, I would never get a cash advance from my credit card except in emergency situations. Interest rates for cash advances are often significantly higher than rates for credit-card purchases. More importantly, you start paying interest on the advance the minute you receive the cash. On an airline-affiliated credit card, a cash advance does not earn frequent-flyer miles.

Coping with Loss or Theft

Sometimes, no matter how careful you are, you can lose your wallet. Although far from being the greatest thing that can happen to you, this mishap is not the end of the world, either (although it may seem like it). In fact, if you don't let your emotions take over, your loss may only put a small crimp in your trip.

Although national parks are in most ways immune from big-city ills, occasionally thieves break into cars. You can save yourself some grief by making sure not to leave any valuables in sight in your rig. Also, if at all possible, park in a well-lit area and close to pedestrian traffic areas, such as in front of visitor centers or lodges.

So what happens if your belongings somehow escape? Take a deep breath and get to a phone. Almost every credit card company provides an emergency 800 number that you can call if your wallet or purse is lost or stolen. They may be able to wire you a cash advance off your credit card immediately; in many places, they can get you an emergency credit card within a day or two. The issuing bank's 800 number is usually on the back of the credit card, but that doesn't help much if your card is gone. Write down the number before you leave for your trip and keep it in a safe place (um, not your wallet or purse).

The U.S. emergency numbers for the most popular credit cards are as follows:

- ✔ American Express, ☎ 800-221-7282
- ✔ Citicorp Visa, ☎ 800-645-6556
- ✔ MasterCard, ☎ 800-307-7309

If you opt to carry traveler's checks, keep a record of their serial numbers — in the same, separate place in which you keep your emergency credit card number — so you can handle this emergency, too.

If your wallet is stolen, you've probably seen the last of it, and the police won't likely recover it for you. However, after you realize that your wallet is gone and you've canceled your credit cards, call the local police to report the incident. You're likely to need the police report number for credit card and insurance purposes later.

Finally, although perhaps not much of a solace at the time, federal law restricts your liability for unauthorized charges if your card is stolen and you immediately report the incident; you generally won't be required to pay more than $50. Fraud protection also includes debit cards. Check with your bank for the specific limits.

Chapter 8

Taking Care of the Remaining Details

*O*kay, so you've made the big decisions about your national park vacation; you've figured out when, where, and how you want to go. In this chapter, you get to consider the last picky details and important safety measures that can make or break your trip.

Packing for the Parks

If you're like me, packing for a national park visit involves taking an inventory of your toys — cross-country skis or snowshoes for the winter excursion to Grand Teton or Mount Rainier, the canoe for the journey to Yellowstone, and the hiking stick for just about every park. What you haul depends on what activities you plan to do. When I climbed the Grand Teton, I packed heavy mountaineering gear to get me to the top of the Grand, as well as shorts, T-shirts, and sandals for touring the lower elevations after I returned.

If you're not spending time in the higher elevations, your **summer** packing list for most parks should include a couple pairs of comfortable hiking shorts, T-shirts (preferably some synthetic ones, not cotton tees that leave you shivering once they're soaked with sweat), a good rain jacket or a water-resistant shell parka, hiking boots, socks, a wide-brimmed hat, a fanny pack, and water bottles. You may also want some nice jeans or a pair or two of slacks and casual shirts for dining out, as well as a light sweater or sweatshirt for cool evenings.

Summer gear checklist

- ❏ Hiking T-shirts
- ❏ Walking stick
- ❏ Backpack
- ❏ Hiking boots
- ❏ Sunglasses
- ❏ Topographical maps
- ❏ Hiking shorts
- ❏ Fanny pack/day pack
- ❏ Compass
- ❏ Dress shirts
- ❏ Sunscreen or block

- ❏ Sleeping bag*
- ❏ Dress slacks
- ❏ First-aid kit
- ❏ Sleeping pad*
- ❏ Dress shoes
- ❏ Binoculars
- ❏ Cooking gear*
- ❏ Light sweater/ sweatshirt
- ❏ Camera/film
- ❏ Tent*

- ❏ Jeans
- ❏ Water bottles/ hydration system
- ❏ Water filter*
- ❏ Sneakers
- ❏ Insect repellent
- ❏ Bear spray**
- ❏ Broad-brimmed hat
- ❏ Guidebooks
- ❏ Rain gear
- ❏ Bird book

*for camping   **for parks with black and/or grizzly bears

When devising your packing list, remember that dealing with temperature changes is easier if you dress in layers. You can fend off the coldest summer weather with shirt layers, a fleece jacket, a water-resistant shell, and a hat. Layers can usually combat the chilly nights in the Rockies or High Sierra, too. If you plan to backpack, a good summer sleeping bag works in the East and Southwest, although you may want a three-season bag for the Rockies and High Sierra.

What do you stuff in your suitcase for a **winter** trip? Again, you want to dress in layers regardless of where you're headed so you're suited for Arctic blasts as well as unseasonable warm spells that tend to show up at least once each winter. In addition, polypropylene underwear is a must for dealing with snow and cold because the material dries quickly and, unlike cotton, doesn't hold moisture next to your skin. Wool shirts, sweaters, and pants are good, and so is fleece outerwear. Your final layer should be water-repellent or waterproof. Of course, don't forget a good warm hat and gloves or mittens. A nice pair of warm, weather-resistant boots will ensure that your feet don't suffer.

For a variety of reasons, I recommend a hiking stick for almost every park. The best sticks ease the burden on your knees during downhill stretches. If you find yourself fording a stream, a walking stick will go a long way to keep you upright. In some parks, you may encounter a copperhead snake or a rattlesnake. I don't recommend prodding these fellas, but if one is in the middle of the trail and won't scoot, a nice long walking stick is great for shooing 'em on.

Winter gear checklist

- ❏ Shell parka
- ❏ Walking stick
- ❏ Backpack
- ❏ Down/synthetic vest
- ❏ Sunglasses
- ❏ Topographical maps
- ❏ Gloves
- ❏ Fanny pack/day pack
- ❏ Compass
- ❏ Hiking boots
- ❏ Sunscreen or block

- ❏ Gaiters
- ❏ Thermal underwear
- ❏ First-aid kit
- ❏ Tent*
- ❏ Sweater
- ❏ Binoculars
- ❏ Cooking gear*
- ❏ Fleece pants
- ❏ Camera/film
- ❏ Sleeping pad*
- ❏ Shell pants

- ❏ Water bottles/ hydration system
- ❏ Water filter*
- ❏ Snowshoes
- ❏ Guidebooks
- ❏ Sleeping bag*
- ❏ Extra shoes
- ❏ Bird book
- ❏ Broad-brimmed hat
- ❏ Cross-country skis/ poles

*for camping

First-aid kits are must-haves, even if you don't plan to go far into the great outdoors. You never know if you'll pick up a splinter, cut a finger, or gash a knee. A good first-aid kit contains tweezers, butterfly and other adhesive bandages, sterile gauze pads, adhesive tape, an antibiotic ointment, children and adult pain relievers, alcohol pads, a knife, and scissors. And don't forget wrapping bandages in case someone turns an ankle, as well as different medicines to combat upset stomachs, motion sickness, minor allergic reactions, and skin rashes.

You can buy some pretty decent prepackaged first-aid kits at your local outdoor goods store for around $40. They carry all the things you need — some kits even contain instruction manuals for treating injuries and wounds.

When packing for your trip, use the summer and winter gear checklists in this chapter.

Traveling with Spot or Fluffy

National parks allow pets, but if you really love your pet, leave him or her at home. Park regulations require that pets be restrained at all times, and many parks prohibit pets from going on trails or entering the backcountry. So while you're out on a half-day hike, Spot sits panting in your car as the heat slowly rises.

In parks with predators, such as Yellowstone where wolves, grizzly bears, and mountain lions roam, if your faithful friend somehow escapes his leash and darts into the woods, he can quickly become some critter's appetizer.

If leaving your pet at home isn't an option, consider boarding him or her at a kennel in your own town or in one of the parks' gateway communities, which usually offer them. To find out about an individual park's pet policy, call ahead (see the Appendix for the individual park numbers) or check the park's Web site at www.nps.gov.

Paying Fees and Getting Permits

The national parks are an incredible bargain when you consider what you get for your **entrance fee,** which ranges from $10 to $20 per car in most cases and can even be free — notably at Mammoth Cave and Great Smoky Mountains national parks. If you want to visit several parks in a year, you can stretch your buck even farther by purchasing a **National Park Pass.** This $50 pass covers admission to any national park that charges an entry fee. The pass is good for one year, and you can use it as many times as you like. All the folks riding in your car when you arrive at the entrance station get in free as well. The pass even works if you're traveling in some other manner, say by bicycle or on foot. You can buy this pass at any National Park Service entry station or by sending a check for $53.95 to the National Parks Foundation, Attn: Parks Pass, P.O. Box 34108, Washington, D.C., 20043-4108. You also can purchase the pass, or renew your existing one, through the Park Service's Web site, www.nps.gov. Got questions? Call 1-888-GO-PARKS.

The national parks also offer passes that include **discounts** for travelers over 62 and for the disabled. See Chapter 4 for information on the Golden Age Passport or Golden Access Passport, respectively.

Although the entrance fees cover most of the national parks' attractions, you do need a **permit** for some activities. For instance, if you plan to canoe in Yellowstone, you need to buy a $5 permit, which is good for seven days (see Chapter 20 for information on where to buy this permit). If you want to fish in any of the parks, you need a park permit or a state fishing license; see the "Fast Facts" section at the end of the individual park chapters for information on fishing requirements.

All the parks require you to pick up a **backcountry permit** for overnight backcountry travel. (Unless noted otherwise in this book, you don't need a permit for day hikes.) In almost all cases, you must buy the permit. The fees, which are nominal, go toward mitigating any impact that travel has on these areas. To determine the cost of a backcountry permit at the park you're going to visit, call ahead (see the

Appendix for the individual park numbers) or check the National Park Service Web site at www.nps.gov. For more information on obtaining backcountry permits, see Chapter 6.

Buying Travel and Medical Insurance

Having insurance is kind of like carrying around an umbrella; if you carry it, you won't need it. However, buying insurance can be expensive. So should you or shouldn't you?

Of the three primary kinds of travel insurance — trip cancellation, medical, and lost luggage — the only one I recommend is **trip cancellation insurance,** which comes in three types: one, in the event that you pre-pay for a tour that gets cancelled and you can't get your money back; two, when you or someone in your family gets sick or dies, and you can't travel (but beware that you may not be covered for a pre-existing condition); and three, when bad weather makes travel impossible. **Medical and lost luggage insurance** don't make sense for most travelers. Your existing health insurance should cover you if you get sick while on vacation (although if you belong to an HMO, check to see whether you are fully covered when away from home). Homeowner's insurance policies cover stolen luggage if they include off-premises theft. Check your existing policies before you buy any additional coverage. The airlines are responsible for $2,500 on domestic flights if they lose your luggage; if you carry anything more valuable than that, keep it in your carry-on bag.

Some credit cards (American Express and certain gold and platinum Visa and MasterCards, for example) offer **automatic flight insurance** against death or dismemberment in case of an airplane crash. If you feel you need still more insurance, try one of the companies in the following list. But don't pay for more insurance than you need. For example, if you only need trip cancellation insurance, don't buy coverage for lost or stolen property. Trip cancellation insurance costs approximately 6% to 8% of the total value of your vacation. You can get any kind of travel insurance from the reputable travel insurance companies in the following list:

- ✔ **Access America** (☎ 800-284-8300; Internet www.access america.com)

- ✔ **Travel Guard International** (☎ 800-826-1300; Internet www.travelguard.com)

- ✔ **Travel Insured International** (☎ 800-243-3174; Internet www.travelinsured.com)

- ✔ **Travelex Insurance Services** (☎ 800-228-9792; Internet www.travelex-insurance.com)

Finding Medical Care in the Parks

Illness cannot only ruin your vacation, but it can be scary. Finding a doctor that you trust isn't always easy when you're away from home. The best defense against illness is a good offense: Bring all your medications with you, as well as a prescription for more if you worry that you'll run out. Also be sure to carry your identification card with you. In addition, see "Packing for the Parks" earlier in this chapter for my recommendations for a reliable first-aid kit.

If you have health insurance, check with your provider to find out the extent of your coverage outside of your home area. And if your existing policy won't be sufficient, get more medical insurance for comprehensive coverage (see the list of issuers in the preceding section). If you suffer from a chronic illness, talk to your doctor before taking the trip. For illnesses such as epilepsy, diabetes, or a heart condition, wearing a **Medic Alert identification tag** will immediately alert any doctor to your condition and give him or her access to your medical records through Medic Alert's 24-hour hotline. Membership is $35, with a $20 annual renewal fee. Contact the Medic Alert Foundation, 2323 Colorado Ave., Turlock, CA 95382 (☎ **800-432-5378**; Internet: www.medicalert.org).

Within the national parks, you find gift shops and general stores stocked with over-the-counter medicines and first-aid items. For more serious injuries, some parks provide clinics within their borders, or you can find hospitals in nearby towns. The "Fast Facts" section at the end of each park chapter includes the locations of the nearest pharmacies and hospitals.

Surviving Your Park Visit

National parks are gorgeous places, but they're also wild places. Surprisingly, many folks swarm into them with the bizarre notion that all the animals are cuddly and the landscape is safe. Although much of the landscape is safe, certain areas require caution. Despite the best efforts by park officials and guidebooks like this one to convince park visitors that they have to be careful, a surprising number of people wind up in a predicament — lost in the woods, stuck on a mountainside, or fallen into a canyon — that requires rangers to come to their rescue. In 2001, more than 4,400 people were the subject of search-and-rescue operations carried out throughout the park system. Even though rangers are ready, skilled, and equipped to rescue you, everyone would be better off if they didn't have to. And about those animals? Well, they may be cute, but they're definitely not tame.

In the following sections, I outline some simple measures you can take to ensure that you joyfully survive your national park trip.

Walking with care

No one plans to get hurt on vacation, but accidents happen. Release a bunch of people into the woods on a daylong hike, and I'll lay you odds that someone will return with a twisted ankle or muscle strain. You can take the following precautions to make sure that you're not the injured person:

- ✓ **Properly prepare for your hike.** Do you own good, sturdy, comfortable hiking boots that are adequately broken in? Are you carrying enough water to sate your thirst from start to finish? What about rain gear? Sure, the weather may look great when you hit the trailhead at 8 a.m., but in the Rockies by noon, thunderheads can form, and they can drench you by 2 p.m. In case the clouds do stay away, pack a good hat, sunscreen, and sunglasses. A hot sun can inflict a world of pain on your body if you're not prepared to ward it off.

- ✓ **Pack some munchies.** Put fruit, granola bars, or candy into your fanny pack or backpack for a burst of energy somewhere down the trail.

- ✓ **Know your limitations.** Everything is relative when it comes to hiking trails. A moderate trail to one person may be strenuous to another and easy to a third. A hike that takes the average person four hours can take another person two hours or even six. Distances can be incredibly deceiving, too. Although the map indicates 6 miles, the ups and downs of the landscape can make the distance feel twice as long. If you feel the trail is getting the better of you, don't be embarrassed to turn around and head back to your car with plans for tackling the route again some other day.

Filtering your drinking water

Sadly, you probably won't find a stream during your travels that isn't contaminated with a parasite from feces called *giardia lablia,* which causes chronic diarrhea. Giardia can remain in your system for years if untreated. Symptoms usually arise a week to ten days after exposure and last one to three weeks, but they can return repeatedly.

You contract this nasty bug by drinking from contaminated streams and lakes without first treating, filtering, or boiling the water. You can treat the water with tablets, but these leave an aftertaste that some (including this guy) don't care for. Boiling is effective, but the method leaves you with hot water and isn't always practical, especially on a hot summer day. The best option is to use a filter. Reliable filters, which range from $70 to $140 at an outdoor goods store, may seem costly at first, but consider the alternative.

Also, be sure that your children know not to swallow water while swimming. If someone does come down with diarrhea a month or so after your outdoor trip, ask your doctor for a giardiasis stool test. Several prescription medicines are available to treat the symptoms.

Getting too hot, too cold, or too high

Spending any amount of time in a national park involves exposure to the elements — rain, sleet, snow, or simply sunshine. If you're not prepared, you can quickly fall victim to one of five serious conditions.

- **Heat exhaustion:** A threat in parks like Death Valley, Arches, Grand Canyon, and Zion (places where the summer temperatures routinely surpass the century mark), this condition strikes if you sweat too much in a short period of time and wind up dehydrating. Under severe conditions, you can lose 1 to 2 liters of water per hour. Your body normally runs through 2 or 3 quarts of water a day, and in the desert, you need to drink four times that amount to ensure proper hydration. If you lose just 2% of the water in your body, you can suffer weakness, headaches, and nausea. You may stop thinking clearly or may become irritable.

  How can you identify heat exhaustion? A pale face, nausea, cool and moist skin, a headache, and cramps are all symptoms. If your urine is dark yellow, you're becoming dehydrated. Avoid heat exhaustion by drinking lots of water and by pacing yourself during the hottest parts of the day. Wear a wide-brimmed hat in the Southwest and even in mountainous areas where the atmosphere is thin. If you fall victim to heat exhaustion, drink water, eat high-energy foods, and find a place in the shade to rest and cool down.

  (If you think you're immune to heat exhaustion, the next time you visit the Phantom Ranch or Indian Garden in the Grand Canyon, ask the rangers about their experiences. They treat up to 20 cases of heat exhaustion a day during the summer.)

- **Heatstroke:** This condition is another heat-related one that can be life-threatening. Heatstroke short-circuits your body's ability to regulate its temperature. Symptoms include a flushed face, hot but dry skin, high temperature, and confusion. In extreme cases, you can lose consciousness, and if untreated, you can die. If you see someone with these symptoms, immediately take them to a shady place and cool them down with water while someone goes for help.

- **Hyponatremia:** This little-heard-of condition can arise if you drink too much water. The high water volume drastically reduces the sodium level in your bloodstream through sweating. Symptoms range from nausea and vomiting to frequent urination and mental confusion. The obvious treatment is to eat salty foods and, in extreme cases when the victim loses alertness, seek medical attention.

✔ **Hypothermia:** Your body may cool too much, usually from swimming in a frigid alpine lake or being soaked to the skin in cold weather. Many people no doubt have faced mild cases of hypothermia. Symptoms include starting to shiver uncontrollably or losing some muscle control. Treat this condition by getting the victim out of the cold elements and having them put on warm clothing, drink warm liquids, and, in severe cases, share a sleeping bag with someone.

✔ **Altitude sickness:** If you go from sea level to 8,000 feet or higher, you may experience altitude sickness. This problem is most common at elevations above 10,000 feet, where the body needs to gradually adjust to getting less oxygen in each breath. However, even if you don't plan to climb the Grand Teton, which tops out at 13,770 feet, I recommend that you take a day or two to get acclimated to a higher elevation park before launching into a 10-mile hike.

How do you know if you're experiencing trouble with the altitude? Headaches, insomnia, general sluggishness, and nosebleeds are all signs that your body is struggling with the elevation. Usually, these symptoms disappear after a couple of days. If they don't, consider seeing a doctor.

Minding furry beasts and creepy crawlies

Upon arriving in Yellowstone, you're almost immediately greeted by bison, grazing contentedly in a meadow. You think, "What a great picture!" So you park your car and hop out, armed with your 35mm or video camera. Unfortunately, you don't have a telephoto or zoom lens. "Heck," you say, looking at these seemingly docile creatures, "I can get a little closer." So you do. Then a little more. And a bit more. When finally, this big, shaggy, 2,000-pound bison is fed up with your advances and charges. Not only do you miss the picture, but you're whisked to the park hospital to have your leg stitched up where the bison gored you. (True, a nice memento of your trip, but probably not what you had in mind.)

Can't happen to you? Well, animals injure people every year in Yellowstone, despite warnings to keep tourists away from bison, elk, and other park inhabitants. The odds of you encountering one of the more deadly critters diminish in proportion to their nastiness. In other words, you may see a black bear before you see a grizzly, and a grizzly before you see a mountain lion. And you probably won't see a mountain lion.

Legally, you're prohibited from getting within 100 yards of bears or 25 yards of other wildlife or nesting birds. Logically, you should keep at least the required distance from the animals if you want to ensure that the memories you take away from your trip are positive ones. Be especially careful when a young animal is around since that's when its momma is even more concerned about humans than usual.

In the following sections, I give you my general advice on how to avoid or handle run-ins with the parks' furry and even creepy crawly populations.

Black bears

These animals are highly common in Sequoia, Yosemite, Great Smoky Mountains, and Grand Teton. The bears who live out West tend to be bigger, stronger, and generally more obnoxious than their eastern kin. When you enter Sequoia and Yosemite, rangers tell you how many parked cars have been torn open like sardine cans by hungry black bears that sniffed an empty potato chip bag from 50 yards. At Sequoia's Lodgepole Campground, the rangers not only keep a running total of attacks on parked cars, but they also display some impressive pictures showing the damage.

For the most part, bears are driven by food. So if you're camping out West, be sure to clean every chip bag, apple core, and even gum wrapper from your rig or tent before you call it a night. Also, make sure to change your clothes after cooking dinner (and put the clothes somewhere other than in your tent) so you don't go to bed smelling like a hotdog or hamburger. Take advantage of the parks' bear-proof boxes for storing food. One night when I pulled into Tuolumne Meadows Campground, a black bear came trotting out of the woods and inspected each and every bear box in sight, only to pad away disappointedly because he couldn't get into them.

Eastern bears, a bit smaller and weaker, don't have a reputation for destroying cars, and you're encouraged to use your vehicle to store food.

In the highly unlikely event that a black bear — East or West — pops into your tent while you're sleeping or approaches you on the trail, reach for a weapon (sticks, stones, flashlights, and pepper spray all work), not your camera. Don't play dead, because black bears approach humans when they're hungry. If you curl up in a ball, the bear may think that you're tossing in the towel and view you as the main course.

Deer ticks

The deer tick, a very small cousin to the wood tick, causes Lyme disease, a disturbing malady named after a town in Connecticut, the site of its discovery. The early symptoms of this disease resemble the signs of the flu, but you also get a bull's eye-looking rash — a dead ringer for the culprit. If overlooked, Lyme disease can attack the nervous system and cause heart abnormalities.

Keeping Lyme disease at arm's length is pretty easy. For starters, you need to be on the lookout for deer ticks especially in California, the Northeast (particularly on Cape Cod), and the Pacific Northwest. What should you do if you find yourself in these parts of the country? Try to avoid hiking through tall grasses or brushy areas. If you do plan on going into the outback, use a good insect repellent with DEET, and apply it to your arms and legs. After your hike, inspect yourself meticulously; if necessary, ask a friend to search your scalp and the other parts of your body that elude your own eyes. A Lyme disease vaccine does exist, but the vaccination process requires several injections over a year to create immunity. I wouldn't go this route unless I expected to frequently spend time in tick habitat.

If you find a tick, remove it with tweezers by pulling directly outward without squeezing the parasite's body, an action that can inject more bacteria into your bloodstream. Dab the bite with alcohol to help disinfect the wound, and save the tick in a jar to determine later if it is a deer tick. If you're close to a medical facility, see a doctor to handle the extraction; if not, remove the tick yourself and go for testing and treatment as soon as possible, taking the tick with you.

Grizzly bears

The only park in this book where you may encounter a grizzly bear is Yellowstone — and I visited Yellowstone for a dozen years before I saw one about 2 miles away from me. Although grizzlies routinely begged from cars and fed from the park's garbage pits in the 1940s and 1950s, stringent bear management policies in the 1960s returned the park's grizzlies to their wilder nature by convincing them that the backcountry (not the campgrounds) was their territory. Today, you can go into the Lamar Valley or the Hayden Valley and, with a good spotting scope or binoculars, safely see grizzlies in their native landscape doing what grizzlies do in the wild.

Be particularly careful when you go for a hike in the spring or early summer. In Yellowstone in springtime, carcasses of elk and bison that failed to survive the winter litter the park. These remains are grizzly magnets. After a long winter's snooze, grizzlies are famished. Once they find a carcass, they often munch on it for days. If you come upon a carcass during a hike, you may not only disturb a bear dining on it, but you may also be perceived as competition for the meat and find yourself in a fight.

In the backcountry, the odds of confronting a grizzly increases, but they're not as high as you may think. Keeping a clean camp (by storing all food on the bear poles that the park service has erected at many designated backcountry campsites) and hiking loudly in groups of two or more further reduces the odds of encountering a grizzly. If you do come upon one while hiking, stop, speak softly to it, and slowly back away. If the bear charges, drop to the ground, fold your knees into your stomach, and wrap your arms around your head. While the bear may swat you with its paws or bite your back, most grizzly attacks occur because they feel threatened. Subtract the threat — playing dead takes guts, but it usually does the trick — and the bear skedaddles off into the woods.

Bear repellent, also known as pepper spray, is gaining more popularity these days as a great way for getting a charging grizzly bear to reverse its course. I carry some myself, although I hope that I never have to use it. The thought of standing my ground in the face of a charging grizzly, waiting for it to come within 5 to 6 yards so I can direct the spray into its face, is not a pleasant one.

Mountain lions

Mountain lions (also known as pumas and cougars) live in Arches, Death Valley, Grand Canyon, Grand Teton, Mount Rainier, Olympic, Sequoia/Kings Canyon, Yellowstone, Yosemite, and Zion national parks. Confronting one of these big cats is scary, but, fortunately, you'll probably never see one. If you come upon one and it doesn't bolt in the opposite direction, stand your ground and throw rocks, sticks, backpacks, or whatever you can heft in its direction. Also try to make yourself seem as big as possible by holding your arms, or even your pack, over your head. If the cat still attacks, fight it as tenaciously as you can. When hiking on remote trails, stay in groups, make noise, and don't let young children lag behind or dart ahead of the group.

Snakes, spiders, and scorpions

Other nasties in parks are poisonous snakes and spiders and, in the Southwest, scorpions. Your best defense is to keep your eyes open, to never put your hand someplace that you can't see (such as when climbing), and, in the East, to be alert around stone fences and wood piles.

If bitten by a snake, remain calm. Symptoms quickly follow, starting with a funny taste in your mouth. Snake-bite kits (the ones that include a razor and a suction cup) are no longer recommended. You can often inflict more damage trying to get the venom out with one of these kits than by seeking medical attention. If you or someone in your party is bit on the hand or arm, keep the limb below the heart while heading to the doctor. Carry anyone who has been bitten on the leg or foot.

Spider bites can be nasty, depending on which spider does the biting. Bites from black widows and brown recluse spiders need medical attention. While not typically fatal, they can cause damage to the skin surrounding the bite, and may cause infection. Chances are, though, that you won't see the culprit that bit you. In these cases, play it safe and visit the nearest clinic for precautionary treatment.

Scorpion bites can be painful, but they're rarely deadly. To help ease the pain, apply an ice pack to the bite. You should also seek medical attention in the off-chance that your bite came from one of the more harmful species.

Being wary of national wonders

Pounding surf, rugged cliffs, or glistening glaciers — the landscape of the national parks is spectacular but potentially hazardous. Keep safety in mind when exploring the wonders of your chosen park.

✔ **Cliffs:** In Yellowstone, trails that lead to observation points of the Grand Canyon of the Yellowstone River leave little room for error, and in early spring, fall, and winter storms can leave the cliffs slippery with ice and snow. In the Grand Canyon, five people fell to their deaths in 1998. Use caution whenever you approach the rim. Don't think you can dart beyond a guardrail for a quick picture and then safely return. Propping yourself atop that guardrail for a picture is never a good idea.

✔ **Glaciers:** You may encounter glaciers on the higher elevations of Mount Rainier. You don't face any risk of being run over by these slow-moving rivers of ice, but if you find yourself in the wrong place — specifically, below the snout (front section) of the glacier — you can be bopped on the head by a chunk of ice, boulder, or other debris.

✔ **Ocean beaches:** In the Pacific Northwest, rivers running to the sea often carry logs that work their way down the coast before coming ashore with the waves. Obviously, you need to watch out for these objects, which will make short work of you if a wave crashes one into your body. In Olympic National Park, you'll see warning signs on your way down to the beaches but no lifeguards caution you at the water's edge, so be extremely careful if you venture into the surf.

Something to beware of on the East and West Coasts are tricky undercurrents, known as *rip tides*. These currents can be incredibly powerful, particularly around the full moon, and they can yank you out to sea. Also, in Olympic and Acadia, rocky shorelines and outcrops of rocks pose dangers, as does the incredibly cold ocean water. Even though rock scrambling is great fun, a misplaced step can send you into the ocean or onto more rocks. Also, if you decide to leapfrog into the water on rock formations, keep an eye on the tide, which can quickly change and leave you marooned far from shore.

✔ **Ocean waves:** You'd hate for an unnecessary bout of seasickness to ruin your trip to Acadia, Olympic, or Cape Cod. You can avoid this problem by taking motion-sickness tablets before your trip. A downside is that these tablets may make you sleepy.

What should you do if you feel seasickness coming on? Head for an open deck for fresh air and keep your eyes on the horizon until the feeling passes.

✔ **Snowfields:** Sometimes, you can't predict where trouble will surface during your stay in a park. Take Mount Rainier, for instance. Because the park sports year-round snowfields, you and your kids may naturally be drawn to sliding across the snow and waging war with snowballs, in the name of good cold fun. But if you're out for a hike, pay particular attention to your footing when crossing snowfields, especially if the slope is steep. Stopping a downhill slide can be difficult in these conditions, and you don't want to slide headfirst into a rock.

✔ **Thermal features:** Yellowstone's thermal features never cease to amaze me. Year after year, I return to the park in large part to stare into these steaming aquamarine pools. Every now and then, I see the bleached bones of some unfortunate animal that slipped into a spring and was quickly poached. When you and your kids are touring the geyser basins, keep in mind that they are called "hot" springs. These unforgiving waters are near boiling point or even higher. Sadly, many people and pets have fatally fallen into the springs over the years. Don't join the list. Stay on the boardwalks that wind through the geyser basins, keep your children under control and your pets, if you bring them, on their leashes.

The backcountry doesn't have boardwalks to keep you a safe distance from the thermal features. Use common sense and double your distance when you approach these features.

✔ **Waterfalls:** Water can pose a problem even when you're hundreds of miles from the coast. In many parks, waterfalls are gorgeous to look at and tantalizing (to some visitors) to climb. Some folks even stand on the brink of a fall. But the routes up waterfalls are always steep and often slippery. Yosemite has a long history of people tumbling off the top of Nevada Falls. Don't add to this history.

Part III
Exploring America's National Parks

In this part . . .

One of the beauties of the national park system is its diversity. Most folks can find one park that fits them like a glove in terms of things to do, places to stay, and sights to see. After you read this part, I bet you'll have at least one, and maybe a half dozen, parks that you can't wait to visit. In the following chapters, you find out everything you need to know about 15 of the country's best national parks, from what to see and what to do to where to eat and sleep. I even give you the blueprint for a great day in the park of your choice, with some extra ideas tossed in if you have more than one day to visit.

Chapter 9

Acadia National Park

• •

In This Chapter

▶ Introducing a seaside wonder

▶ Planning your visit to the park

▶ Enjoying the outdoors and escaping the rain

▶ Finding the best sleeps and eats

• •

*T*his surf-flecked jewel is one of the smallest parks in the national park system, but its natural beauty is immense. Acadia National Park packs a lot into its 46,784 acres. The rocky beaches, thick pine forests, placid lakes, and easily scaled mountains make this park one of the country's most scenic and popular — 3 million fans flock to the park each year.

You can hike the dramatic grounds of this ocean-wrapped treasure or relax in a charming fishing village, where boats leave port every day just as they did more than a century ago. You can also escape from the crowds entirely to experience the park's many moods in solitude; Acadia is joyful and exuberant when the sun shines, introspective when fog rolls in, and sullen when storms lash its shores.

Acadia takes up much of Maine's **Mount Desert Island** (called MDI by locals), part of a point on the mainland called **Schoodic Peninsula,** and a smaller island to the southwest, **Isle au Haut.** MDI, surrounded by the Atlantic Ocean, includes most of the park's attractions, although less is definitely more along this ruggedly beautiful convergence of mountain and sea. In addition to the spectacular natural sights, you find only a handful of quaint towns.

MDI was once a stodgy retreat for East Coast blue bloods — the Rockefellers, Morgans, Fords, Vanderbilts, Carnegies, and Astors, to name a few — who summered on the island in the late 1800s. They came from New York, Philadelphia, and Boston to enjoy the cool weather, and they built expansive and expensive homes, which they called "cottages."

But then a funny thing happened. Others began to discover MDI. Worried that development would overrun the wild coastal areas, many of the island's affluent residents donated 6,000 acres to the federal government for a park. In 1916, President Woodrow Wilson designated the area a national monument.

Thanks to the wealthy dwellers' foresight, Acadia provides visitors with a handsome land and seascape unlike anything else in the national park system. Sure, Cape Cod National Seashore is surrounded by the Atlantic Ocean and boasts pristine beaches, but Acadia claims a raw, wild side that Cape Cod lacks. Acadia's rugged personality comes from its mix of mountains and cobblestone beaches. Plus, rainy days on Cape Cod drive most visitors indoors to antique stores, theaters, and museums. At Acadia, stormy days invite you to watch the waves explode on the granite cliffs and coves, or they draw you inland, where you can stroll amid mist-shrouded pines, hardwood forests, and idyllic ponds.

Although you can see Acadia's highlights in one day, most visitors spend three to four days in the park. Acadia is a three-season park (excluding winter), with summer being the most popular time to visit. (If you do come in summer, try to visit in the middle to late August, when the human and black fly populations are less dense than in June and July.) Both spring and fall are nice times to visit; however, I prefer fall when the park bursts with color as hardwoods blaze orange and red against a backdrop of green pines and an emerald ocean. Choose to visit during winter if you're in search of solitude and cold weather — average daytime highs are in the mid-30s and nighttime temperatures sometimes drop below zero.

Must-see Attractions

At Mount Desert Island, big things come in small packages — clichéd but true. Spend any time on the island, and you quickly realize that Acadia National Park is packed with eye-catching scenery. What follows is a best-of-the-best list of stops to include in your itinerary:

- ✔ **Cadillac Mountain:** At just 1,530 feet tall (puny by Rocky Mountain standards), this peak catches the first sunlight in the country from early October to early March. And if you can't get up early enough to make your way to the summit for this eye-opener, a trip later in the day gives you an incredible view of the surrounding island and Frenchman Bay with its dozens of outlying islands.

- ✔ **The Carriage Roads:** A legacy of the island's wealthy, early 20th-century residents, these roads run for 45 miles throughout the eastern half of the park. They offer a wonderfully relaxing way to tour Acadia by bicycle in the summer and by cross-country skis in the winter.

- ✔ **Echo Lake:** Sure, you can dive into the ocean at Sand Beach. But with its water temperature usually at a bracing 55 degrees, why not save the coastline for walking and head inland to Echo Lake for swimming?

- ✔ **Somes Sound:** This sound, New England's only fjord, nearly cuts Mount Desert Island in half. You get killer views of this 5-mile-long watery crack from Sargent Drive or, if you enjoy a good walk, from the 681-foot summit of Acadia Mountain.

- ✔ **Thunder Hole:** At high tide and during storms, the Atlantic Ocean audibly explodes in this narrow rocky chasm found off Ocean Drive. If you don't mind a drenching, you can walk down to an overlook that's virtually on top of the hole. (If you prefer to remain dry, you can stand on a nearby platform.)

Getting There

Anchored in the Atlantic Ocean off the coast of Maine, Acadia National Park is located off the beaten path. Boston, six hours by car (264 miles) to the south, is the closest metropolitan area. Still, you can get to the park in a variety of ways: by driving, by flying to Bar Harbor airport, or by taking a shuttle bus from Boston or from Bangor, Maine, 41 miles from Acadia.

If you visit Mount Desert Island between late June and Labor Day, you really don't need a vehicle. The Island Explorer shuttle bus system offers seven routes across the Island that pass hotels, bed-and-breakfasts, campgrounds, trails, and beaches. (See "Getting around," later in this chapter, for more details.)

Driving in

If you drive from Boston, head north on Interstate 95 for 225 miles to Bangor, Maine. Next, head east on Route 1A for 28 miles to Ellsworth; then take Route 3 for a mere 13 miles down to Mount Desert Island. Looking at a road map, you may think you can make better time from Boston by veering off I-95 at Brunswick and heading up the coast on Route 1. But this meandering route is much slower, particularly in the summer months when tourist traffic swells along the coast.

Flying in

You can fly to the park via the **U.S. Airways Express,** which in the summer months offers five daily flights from Boston to Hancock County-Bar Harbor Airport. The rest of the year, they offer four daily flights Monday through Friday and three flights on Saturday. When you arrive at the airport, which is 12 miles west of Bar Harbor on Mount Desert Island, you can rent a car from **Budget** or **Hertz** (see the

Appendix for the toll-free numbers of the car-rental agencies and the airline) or ride one of the free **Island Explorer** shuttle buses into Bar Harbor. (See "Getting around," later in this chapter.) These propane-powered buses, which operate from late June through early September, stop every hour at the airport between 9:15 a.m. and 9:15 p.m. They deliver passengers to the five private campgrounds between the airport and Bar Harbor. If you plan to utilize these buses, be aware that they lack luggage compartments. As a result, you may not find room for your bags on the bus if you arrive at the airport in the morning along with most of the folks who fly to Bar Harbor. To avoid this dilemma, arrive in the afternoon when fewer people use the service. (When you depart from Acadia, reverse this timetable, and leave in the morning.)

Vermont Transit (☎ **207-945-3000** in Bangor) can bus you to Bar Harbor from Bangor or Boston from May through October. Although the ride from Bangor is only $10.25 one-way ($19.25 round-trip), the ride from Boston costs $42.50 one-way, $82 round-trip.

Planning Ahead

You want a great room with an ocean view during your visit to Acadia? Then start arranging your vacation early. Right around the middle of January is a good time to make reservations for a summer or early fall visit. If you wait too long, you'll be left with the dregs or nothing at all. During the high season (summer and early fall), you can't arrive on the island and expect to get a room. The entire island may be booked, in which case your only recourse is to retreat to the mainland.

Near the park are a wide variety of lodging possibilities, including upscale hotels and inns, cute bed-and-breakfast establishments, and cottages. Some of these places may give you sticker shock ($500 a night!), but don't panic. You can also find reasonably priced accommodations. Inside Acadia, the only accommodations come in the form of two campgrounds. I give you the lowdown on your whole range of choices in "Where to Stay," later in this chapter.

For general information about the park, you can write Acadia National Park, P.O. Box 177, Bar Harbor, ME 04609-0177; call ☎ **207-288-3338** (voice/TTY); or check the Internet at www.nps.gov/acad/.

Learning the Lay of the Land

Acadia National Park can be sliced into three pieces: the 110-square-mile **Mount Desert Island,** which makes up the bulk of Acadia's acreage and attractions; **Isle au Haut,** a largely undeveloped island with hiking trails and a rocky coastline; and **Schoodic Peninsula,** a granitic promontory that juts out into the Atlantic and the only part of the park on the mainland.

Acadia National Park

Mount Desert Island includes five towns. **Bar Harbor,** the island's largest town and main hub of activity, will likely be the base of operations during your stay. Even if you camp, you may head to this town to dine, rent a bike, or board a boat for a whale-watching cruise. The other four towns (in clockwise order around the island from Bar Harbor) are **Seal Harbor, Northeast Harbor, Southwest Harbor** (the largest after Bar Harbor), and **Bass Harbor.** The island is divided in half by Somes Sound, a fjord more than 5 miles long. The eastern side of the park has the most attractions, including Bar Harbor, Cadillac Mountain, carriage roads, botanical gardens, and a public shoreline. Less of the western side belongs to the park, but the area is still worth a visit for its pretty lakes and quiet spots.

Mount Desert Island is located at the end of Route 3, some 13 miles east of Ellsworth, Maine. Route 3 runs across the bridge and around the eastern side of the island. You can follow this route to the main visitor center in Hulls Cove (see "Finding information," later in this chapter) and then on to Bar Harbor or Seal Harbor. From the bridge, you can also head south on Route 102, which circles the western side of the island and passes through Southwest Harbor. In the southern part of this loop, 102A connects the road to Bass Harbor, near the much-photographed Bass Harbor Lighthouse. To get to Northeast Harbor from the bridge, take Route 102 to Route 198 to Route 3.

The 27-mile-long **Park Loop Road** circles the eastern section of the park and is bordered by Somes Sound on the west and the Atlantic Ocean on the east. The park's main drag, this scenic loop passes some of Acadia's major attractions, as well as a fee station. (See "Paying fees," later in this chapter.)

The underpasses on Park Loop Road are 11 feet, 8 inches tall. If you haul a trailer or drive an RV that exceeds this height, you need to take an alternative route, probably Route 3.

Forty-five miles of **carriage roads** meander around the eastern half of Mount Desert Island between Hulls Cove Visitor Center and the forests just west of Jordan Pond. Cars are not allowed on these roads, which are popular for biking. Maps of the carriage roads are available at the park's visitor and information centers. (See the next section.)

Arriving in the Park

Given Acadia's relatively small size compared to other national parks, getting your bearings and getting around the park are fairly simple.

Finding information

While crossing Mount Desert Narrows on Route 3 from the mainland, you can stop at **Mount Desert Island Information Center** at Thompson Island (☎ 207-288-3411). This center is open from mid-May to mid-October, 10 a.m. to 6 p.m. But **Hulls Cove Visitor Center,** at the northern end of Park Loop Road just off Route 3 in Hulls Cove, is a much more complete facility in terms of orienting you to the park. You can view the 15-minute *Gift of Acadia,* which gives you the lowdown on the park's history and highlights. (If you have kids, you can pick up some activity books and a booklet on the park's Junior Ranger Program.) The visitor center, which greets upwards of 8,000 folks a day during the busy summer season, is open from mid-April through June, 8 a.m. to 4:30 p.m., and from July through August, 8 a.m. to 6 p.m. Hours vary from September through October, and the center is closed November through mid-April.

For information on Acadia, call the park's administrative headquarters at ☎ 207-288-3338.

Paying fees

Acadia charges entrance fees at a station on Park Loop Road, 1 mile north of Sand Beach. Vehicles are $10 for 7 days; $20 for a year. See Chapter 8 for information on the National Park Pass and Chapter 4 for information on Golden Age and Golden Access passports

Getting around

Although the distances aren't great, traffic is slow on these winding roads. Plan your days to spend as much time as you can in one area. Cars aren't allowed on the carriage roads, so you need a bike, a horse, or walking shoes to get to some ponds. Roads connect to all major sites.

If you want someone else to do the driving, hop aboard one of the free **Island Explorer** shuttle buses (☎ 207-667-5796). From late June through Labor Day, these buses run from the Hancock County Airport to Bar Harbor and throughout the eastern half of Mount Desert Island. They can drop you at a campground, in downtown Bar Harbor, at Sand Beach, Jordan Pond, or Southwest Harbor. All the shuttles have bike racks.

Remembering Safety

Acadia National Park is a ruggedly beautiful place. However, be careful not to become so enthralled with the landscape that you fail to take some common-sense safety precautions. With all the sun and sea, first don't hesitate to smear on some sun block or sunscreen before setting out for a day of sightseeing. And for the mountains? Watch your footing — and on the Precipice Trail and other trails with rungs and ladders, watch your handholds — while hiking or climbing. Along the coastline, the picturesque cobblestone beaches can also be slippery, particularly when they're wet or covered with seaweed. Finally, always be alert when near the surf, but take particular care of yourself and your kids when you view Thunder Hole up close or roam on the rock outcrops on Schoodic Peninsula — waves in both places have knocked folks into the sea.

For additional tips on how to ensure a safe park visit, see Chapter 8.

Enjoying the Park

What follows are my suggestions for how best to enjoy Acadia. I go
over the top attractions, suggest a few hikes, and provide a one-day
itinerary for those with limited time. I also mention notable ranger programs, ways to keep active, and where to go when it rains.

Exploring the top attractions

Far and away, most tourists head to Mount Desert Island. They come
for the island's quaint inns and fine restaurants, to meander Park Loop
Road with occasional stops to play in the surf or enjoy the warmer
ponds, and to climb to the top of Cadillac Mountain by foot or by car.

Bar Harbor
Mount Desert Island

Bar Harbor is the park's active hub, with restaurants, lodgings, shops,
and museums. You can get a good feel for the town, and discover restaurants and shops along the way, by strolling four principle streets: **West,
Main, Cottage, and Mount Desert streets.** West Street, the first one that
you encounter when arriving from the north via Route 3, is known for its
many mansions that date to the turn of the 20th century. Today, some of
these aristocratic homes are inns and bed-and-breakfasts, whereas
others remain private residences. The wharf at the bottom of West Street
is home to all manner of boats, such as fishing boats, private schooners,
and day-excursion ships.

Cottage Street (the place to play) boasts shops that rent bikes, canoes,
sea kayaks, and more. You can find guides who show you how to climb or
paddle or take you on a whale- or puffin-watching excursion. Restaurants
and shops crowd Main Street, and Mount Desert Street is home to Bar
Harbor's national historic district and has several inns in older homes.

Bar Harbor is on Route 3 on the eastern side of Mount Desert Island.

Bass Harbor Head Lighthouse
Mount Desert Island

Overseeing the southern-most tip of Mount Desert Island is the historic
Bass Harbor Head Lighthouse, one of the most photographed places on
Maine's coast. Since 1858, this 32-foot lighthouse with its distinctive red
lenses has marked the entrance to Blue Hill Bay and alerted captains to
Bass Harbor Bar at the eastern entrance to Bass Harbor. You can walk
down the wooden stairs to the rocks below the lighthouse, where you'll
hear the carillons of the channel buoy just offshore and, if Poseidon is
willing, spy some harbor seals.

Kids enjoy the lighthouse because of the tidal pools along the rocky shore. At low tide, they're a great place to search for sea urchins and starfish.

The lighthouse is a short ride south of the town of Bass Harbor on Route 102A.

Cadillac Mountain
Mount Desert Island

Cadillac Mountain is the tallest mountain on the Atlantic Coast between Maine and Brazil. If you have plenty of energy, hike one of the many trails to the summit, such as the 4½-mile round-trip North Ridge Trail; the hike to the top takes roughly an hour. The North Ridge Trail is moderate in difficulty and accessible from the North Ridge Cadillac parking area. You can also drive to the top of the mountain and stroll along a ⅓-mile loop trail. The granitic summit is devoid of trees, making the views spectacular in all directions.

To drive to the top of the mountain, take a spur off the Park Loop Road, just south of the Cadillac Mountain entrance and west of Bar Harbor.

Echo Lake
Mount Desert Island

Echo Lake is the only lake in the park where you're allowed to swim. It's warmer than the ocean and has a lifeguard-patrolled beach. A small network of trails winds out from the beach on the southern tip of the lake. On the east side of the lake is the trailhead to Acadia Mountain, which offers great views of Echo Lake as well as Somes Sound. Swimming isn't allowed in any of the island's other lakes and ponds (because they're municipal water sources), so the beach can be crowded when the weather turns hot.

The lake is on the west side of the island off Route 102.

Isle au Haut

Don't mind roughing it? Then Isle au Haut is for you. Surrounded by the Atlantic and southwest of Mount Desert Island, you can savor this place in solitude. The 2,000 undeveloped park acres are reachable only by a mailboat that crosses 8 miles of open water from Stonington, 70 miles by car from Bar Harbor. On the island, you can hike 18 miles of trails through wooded hills and along the rocky shoreline.

The island includes a small village, a ranger station, and the Duck Harbor Campground, which has five, three-sided lean-tos. (See "Where to Stay," later in this chapter.) Most folks who come for the day bring their own lunch, although you can buy picnic fixings at the general store. The only lodging option are the four guestrooms at the **Keeper's House** (P.O. Box 26, Isle Au Haut, ME 04645; ☎ **207-367-2261;** Internet: www.keepershouse.com), where candles and oil lamps, not electricity, illuminate the nights. This quaint yet expensive spot ($300 and up per night per couple, meals included), built to house the keeper of the Robinson Point Lighthouse, is perfect for a romantic getaway.

You can't bring your car or truck to the island, and bikes are discouraged because only 4 miles of road are paved (bikes are not allowed on the hiking trails). You can, however, bring your canoe or sea kayak.

Isle-Au-Haut Company (☎ 207-367-5193; Internet: www.isleauhaut.com*) operates the mailboat from Stonington to Duck Harbor and Town Landing. (To get from Bar Harbor to Stonington, take Route 3 to Route 172 to Route 15.) The boat ride takes 45-minutes to an hour. Two to four boats a day depart year-round Mon–Sat, except postal holidays. One-way fares are $14 for adults, $6.50 for passengers under 12. Bikes are $7 one-way; kayaks are $12 one-way for the first 10 feet; then $2 for each additional foot. Schedules and fares are likely to change; call to confirm information.*

Park Loop Road
Mount Desert Island

You can easily spend an entire day exploring the sights on this 27-mile road. After entering Park Loop Road at the entrance to Cadillac Mountain, you can head south or east. The southbound route carries two-way traffic to Seal Harbor. This scenic eastern stretch is a one-way route that follows the shoreline from Sand Beach around the southeast corner of the island to the northern tip of Seal Harbor. Just north of Sand Beach is the fee station.

Heading east brings you first to the **Wild Gardens of Acadia** (open year-round; free admission), where you can see a representative cross section of the island's vegetation. The native plantings include wildflowers (such as lupines, goldenrod, and fireweed) and shrubs (including bearberry, blueberry, and chokeberry). Next along the road at Sieur de Monts Springs is the **Nature Center** (open from June to late September; free admission), where you can find out about the role of fire in the park, about the quality of the park's air and water, or about the latest wildlife sightings. Then you come upon the **Abbe Museum** near Sieur de Monts Springs (open mid-May to mid-October; admission $2 adult, $.50 kids; ☎ 207-288-3519), a great resource that details the Native Americans who once called the island home. You can view prehistoric pottery, trading beads, and a birch-bark canoe. You can also watch native artists at work.

Park Loop Road then bends south and begins to parallel the coastline, passing **Sand Beach,** a beautiful, crescent-shaped spit of sand rimmed by pine trees. During the summer, lifeguards oversee the beach, although the ocean water is a bit too cold for me to enjoy. Less than a mile south is **Thunder Hole.** The name stems from the booming sound that the surf makes at high tides and during storms when waves crash into the rocky crevice. (For a hike to Thunder Hole, see the Ocean Trail information in "Taking a hike," later in this chapter.) About a mile past Thunder Hole is

Otter Cliff, with its hiking trail that offers breathtaking views out to sea. This spot is also good for peering into tide pools in search of marine life — a practice the locals call *tide pooling.* But remember to be careful on the slippery rocks and watch out for any waves that may be rolling in.

The 2-mile stretch between Sand Beach and Otter Cliff is the likely spot for traffic jams on the loop road. To avoid the crowds, go early in the morning or late in the afternoon. This stretch is busiest between 10 a.m. and 2 p.m.

After Otter Cliff, Park Loop Road darts north toward **Jordan Pond.** I can still remember eating flaky popovers served with oodles of strawberry jam at the Jordan Pond House when I was a kid. (See "Where to Eat," later in this chapter.) To help kids burn off their sugar-induced energy, walk the trails (see the Jordan Pond Shore Trail in "Taking a hike," later in this chapter) and let them explore **The Bubbles,** an interesting collection of granitic mounds near the pond's northern end.

Continue to follow the road north to **Eagle Lake,** which nearly completes the loop and returns you to where you began.

Park Loop Road runs 27 miles around the southeastern corner of Mount Desert Island.

Schoodic Peninsula

If you want to leave the crowds behind, visit Schoodic Peninsula. Two-thousand park acres occupy this promontory where the main attraction is watching the fury of the Atlantic Ocean slam into the coast. You can stroll along windswept Schoodic Point and enjoy magnificent views of Frenchman Bay and distant Mount Desert Island. Gulls, cormorants, and other shorebirds wheel in the winds and fish the tidal pools for their meals. Blocks of granite, striped with volcanic intrusions of basalt, stand in the relentless surf. The park maintains a 7-mile-long, one-way road that winds counterclockwise around the peninsula, as well as a short trail that climbs to the top of 440-foot-tall Schoodic Head. The peninsula also has a ranger station and a picnic area.

Schoodic Peninsula is 46 miles northeast of Mount Desert Island. Take Route 1 east from Ellsworth and then go south on Route 186.

Somes Sound
Mount Desert Island

Nearly splitting Mount Desert Island in half, the 5-mile-long Somes Sound is the only fjord on the East Coast. Actually, geologists debate whether this 168-foot-deep crack of salt water is truly a fjord in the Norwegian fashion. Because the sound isn't very deep, some people call it a *fjard,* which is much smaller. Regardless, this body of water is a sight to see because the mountains climb steeply up from its shoreline. If you take a boat out on the waters, you may be rewarded by spotting an inquisitive harbor seal. The best trail for viewing the sound is Acadia Mountain (see the next section, "Taking a hike").

To see Somes Sound by car, follow Sargent Drive, which runs north along the eastern shore from Northeast Harbor and hooks into Route 3.

Taking a hike

For centuries, hikers have trekked back and forth across Mount Desert Island. As a result, you don't need to look far for a good walk. Native Americans were the first to blaze paths across the island, but in the mid-1800s, a group of Americans now known as the *rusticators* — artists who flocked to the island for inspiration — built upon the trail base.

Today, you find 120 miles of trails winding almost everywhere in Acadia, from along the coast and through the park's interior to the cliff sides of Champlain Mountain. Stop by the Hulls Cove Visitor Center for a chart outlining the hikes (see "Finding information," earlier in this chapter.) I give you descriptions of the island's best trails in the following sections.

Capturing Acadia on film

National parks are open-air photo studios with many incredible vistas to record with your camera. No exception to this rule, Acadia offers several photo ops.

When fog shrouds the park, you can capture wave-pounded rocky shorelines and anchored lobster boats as well as red beacons that cut through the soupy mist as they shoot out from lighthouses. **Bass Harbor** and **Southwest Harbor** are good spots to photograph lobster boats at anchor. If your camera has a long lens (300 mm at least), you can usually catch the boats in the water off Otter Cliff and Little Hunters Beach. The **Bass Harbor Head Lighthouse**, meanwhile, is one of the most photographed lighthouses on the East Coast.

You can find wave-pounded settings along **Otter Cliff** and at **Ship Harbor**, southeast of Bass Harbor. A short foot trail off Route 102A leads to Ship Harbor; the trail is marked on the park map and by a sign along the road. Another great setting for pounding surf is the **Schoodic Peninsula**, a 35-mile drive from Ellsworth on the mainland.

If you want some help improving your camera skills, join a Kodak representative during the summer months for some free lessons. These programs range from morning and afternoon photo walks to discovering which parts of the park provide the most alluring settings. A sunset class even meets atop Cadillac Mountain several days a week. Check the park newspaper, the *Beaver Log,* to find out where and when these classes are held.

Acadia Mountain

Two amazing things enhance the hike up Acadia Mountain: The view is breathtaking, and you're likely to find solitude. Due to its relative remoteness and lack of development, people unfairly regard Mount Desert Island's western side as an ugly stepsister to the eastern half. The gorgeous Acadia Mountain path weaves through forests of birches and pines before crossing rocky ledges. From the top, you get an incredible view of the East Coast's only fjord, Somes Sound; to the south, you can watch fishing boats and yachts in Southwest Harbor.

Distance: 2 miles round-trip. Level: Strenuous. Access: Acadia Mountain parking area along Route 102, 3 miles south of Somesville.

Dorr Mountain

The trek up Dorr Mountain (also known as the Dorr Ladder Trail) begins with a series of stone steps that climb along the mountain's granitic base and then passes through some crevasses before finally ascending a series of ladders anchored in the rock face. From the summit of this 1,270-foot mountain, you get beautiful views to the east and south.

Distance: 4¾ miles round-trip. Level: Moderate to strenuous. Access: Canon Brook parking area off Route 3.

Great Meadow Loop

This gentle path connects downtown Bar Harbor to the park's trail network. Near the junction of Spring Street and Cromwell Harbor Road, the trail heads south for about a mile to the Park Loop Road, where it connects with the Jessup Trail. From there, the distance is only about a mile to Sieur de Monts Spring. Returning to town, you can either retrace your steps or continue along the loop as it swings north to the Cromwell Harbor Road and back into Bar Harbor.

Distance: 2 miles round-trip. Level: Easy. Access: Spring Street and Cromwell Harbor Road.

Jordan Pond Shore Trail

The hike along Jordan Pond's edge includes some rocky sections, but overall the path is hiker-friendly. Jordan Pond Shore Trail heads northward from the parking area on the eastern shore of the pond. The return trip on the western shore follows a carriage road. Near the north end, take some time to inspect the oddly symmetrical granite mounds known as The Bubbles.

Distance: 3¼ miles round-trip. Level: Easy. Access: Jordan Pond overflow parking area.

Ocean Trail

What would a trip to the beach be without a hike along the shore? Ocean Trail hugs the shoreline and takes you across Sand Beach and sea cliffs. About halfway along the trail, you come across a rocky gorge in the shoreline called Thunder Hole; at high tides and during storms, waves sound like thunder as they slam into it. A viewing area places you right above the gorge, so be prepared to get soaked if you go out for a look.

Distance: 3 miles round-trip. Level: Easy. Access: Sand Beach or Otter Cliff parking areas.

Precipice Trail

As a young boy, I vaguely recall climbing Precipice Trail to the top of 1,058-foot Champlain Mountain. For reasons that escape me, my dad carried our miniature poodle to the very top (something you don't want to duplicate). But the climb to the summit (by way of iron-rung ladders and footpaths) is invigorating, and the views of the Atlantic Ocean and Frenchman Bay are awesome. You must scale some exposed cliffs and work your way along ledges, so this hike isn't for the frail or for folks who fear heights. If you make the climb, keep an eye out for peregrine falcons that nest on the mountain.

Precipice Trail is usually closed in spring and summer to protect nesting peregrine falcons. You can still reach the summit via the 2½-mile Champlain Mountain Trail, also called the Beachcroft Trail. (The trailhead is at the north end of a pond called The Tarn on Route 3.) This route scales the mountain's eastern flanks over rocky, open slopes. From Champlain Mountain Trail, you may find yourself stopping frequently to peer over your shoulder at Frenchman Bay.

Distance: Just over 1½ miles round-trip. Level: Moderate to strenuous. Access: Precipice parking area.

One-day wonder

Those with limited time are in luck because you can navigate Acadia's highlights in one day. (For more information on the sights in this section, see "Exploring the top attractions," earlier in this chapter, unless noted otherwise.)

Start at the **Hulls Cove Visitor Center.** (See "Finding information," earlier in this chapter.) Then head south on **Park Loop Road,** past the entrance road to Cadillac Mountain, and on down the eastern edge of the park. Make sure to stop at the **Schooner Head Overlook** for a beautiful view of the Atlantic Ocean, tiny Egg Rock with its lighthouse, and the many other islands that dot Frenchman Bay.

Spotting wildlife, big and small

Growing up with regular visits to New Jersey's sandy shores, I wasn't prepared for the summer when we headed north to Acadia National Park. Oh, the park had plenty of beach, but certainly not the kind of beach with which I was familiar. Instead of smooth, sandy beaches, Mount Desert Island's coast is mostly rocky with small spits of sand. In the tidal pools among the boulders, I discovered the park's rich marine life of spiny **sea urchins, northern starfish,** and **mollusks.** Today, you and your children can discover these same sea creatures and more. You can even spot **whales** or **seals** on one of the island's many cruises. (See "Keeping active" and "Ranger programs," later in this chapter.)

Acadia is also a wildlife haven. The inland forests, ponds, and lakes host hundreds of animal species ranging from **coyotes, red fox,** and **deer** to **porcupines, northern flying squirrels,** and **river otters.**

Because the park is located where the northern and temperate zones overlap, the park attracts thousands of migratory birds, of which nearly 300 species have been sighted. **Great blue and green herons, American black ducks,** and **green-winged teals** are commonly spotted on Thompson Island and at Bass Harbor Marsh. **Bald eagles** frequently appear in Acadia, and so do **eider ducks** (which are prized for their down) and several species of **woodpeckers.** Whereas you may have a hard time spying **puffins** in Olympic National Park on the West Coast, since they tend to keep to themselves on off-shore islands, you can visit the puffins' nesting grounds in the Petit Manan National Wildlife Refuge (Internet: http://petitmanan.fws.gov) located north of the park along U.S. 1 near Milridge.

You can also find **peregrine falcons** nesting on some of the park's rocky cliffs between late March and early August. While you can't climb the Precipice Trail during nesting season, rangers and volunteers set up spotting scopes at the trail's parking lot so you can gaze at the raptors.

About a mile past the overlook, you reach **Thunder Hole.** This rocky gorge on the coast is a great stop for the whole family, although kids may get the biggest kick out of walking to the end of the overlook to get soaked by the spray of waves that crash into the hole. Be careful, though, as waves can be powerful enough to knock you off the overlook.

Less than a mile south of Thunder Hole is the trailhead for the hike to **Gorham Mountain,** which is a moderate trek for young ones. Only a mile long from the parking lot to the mountaintop, this entire hike takes about 30 to 45 minutes and gives kids a sense of accomplishment when they reach the 525-foot summit and gaze out into the Atlantic. From the top, not only can you see Cadillac Mountain to the north but also Otter Cliff to the south and Sand Beach to the east. If you visit during August, spend some time munching on the ripening blueberries that grow along the trail.

If you're interested in a more-demanding hike, try the Beehive Trail that leads to the top of a 520-foot mountain called "The Beehive." The trailhead for this ⅘-mile round-trip hike is just north of the Sand Beach Parking Area.

On the other hand, if you want to cram as much as possible into your day, after passing Little Hunters Beach on Park Loop Road, get back on Route 3, head through Seal Harbor, and continue on to Northeast Harbor where you can get on **Sargent Drive.** This country road takes you along the edge of **Somes Sound** and offers tremendous views. At the northern tip of the sound, bear left on Route 198, which links with Route 102 in 1 mile. Take 102 south about 5 miles to Southwest Harbor where, if you're a lover of lobster, you need to stop at Beal's Lobster Pier for lunch. (See "Where to Eat," later in this chapter.)

After lunch, continue south on 102 to the quaint fishing village of **Bass Harbor** and, just below it, **Bass Harbor Head Lighthouse,** one of the most picturesque spots on the Maine coast.

On your return to Bar Harbor, retrace your route to the junction of Routes 198 and 3 and turn right at the light onto Route 233 instead of heading south on Route 3. This shortcut takes you past park headquarters, beyond the north end of **Eagle Lake,** and to the entrance to **Cadillac Mountain.** If you still have energy and the sun won't set for a few hours, trek to the top of Cadillac; the view of Frenchman Bay and all of Mount Desert Island is definitely worth the effort. Feel like you need more of a challenge? Then skip Cadillac and head to the **Precipice Trail** or the Beehive Trail, depending on the season, (see "Taking a hike," earlier in this chapter). By the time you reach the summit at either of these mountains, you'll definitely be ready to return to your room in Bar Harbor and enjoy a nice, relaxing dinner.

Ranger programs

Acadia's rangers always seem to involve visitors in activities. Sure, they offer campfire talks and nature walks just like their peers in other parks, but these rangers also stand ready to take you to sea.

You can take a cruise with rangers during the summer months. The **Islesford Historical Cruise** (☎ 207-276-5352) takes three hours and makes a stop at the Cranberry Islands, where you can find out about Mount Desert Island's seafaring heritage at the Islesford Historical Museum (admission $17 adults, $10 ages 12 and under).

Acadia's rangers don't limit their attentions to the sea, however. They offer a number of programs that include the following activities:

✔ **Bird-watching:** If you're a birder, look for nesting peregrine falcons on the rocky ledges of Champlain Mountain. During the summer months (up through mid-August), ask a ranger or park volunteer to help you find one of these fast birds by guiding you toward a few spotting scopes on the Precipice Trailhead. (See "Taking a hike," earlier in this chapter.)

✔ **History hikes:** Some ranger hikes delve into the park's rich cultural history. They depart from the Parkman Mountain parking area several times a week. (Check with the visitor center or park newspaper for times and days.) These hikes cover 2 miles while the rangers expound on the history of the park's carriage roads and stone bridges.

✔ **Tidal pool tours:** Kids love the "Life Between the Tides" tour that the rangers give daily throughout the summer months. For reservations, visit the Hulls Cove Visitor Center (see "Finding information," earlier in this chapter) or call ☎ **207-288-5262.** During this 2½-hour journey for kids of all ages, rangers explore the tidal pools along Acadia's rocky shores. Participants get the chance to examine a sea urchin and maybe even spot a harbor seal.

✔ **Storytelling hikes:** If your kids love stories as much as mine do, make reservations (☎ **207-288-5262**) to join one of the afternoon "Tell Me A Story" hikes. This program is designed for kids 8 and younger and isn't likely to bore them. During the 90-minute program, a ranger leads you and your children on a short, ½-mile walk and recounts a story that touches on the park's natural side.

Keeping active

You can enjoy the beauty of Acadia in numerous ways. If you prefer to take in the scenery while you're on the go, try one of the following activities (also see "Taking a hike" earlier in this chapter).

✔ **Biking:** Acadia is one of the best biking parks in the country. You can peddle along the many carriage roads without worrying about cars. Bike rentals are available at **Acadia Bike and Coastal Kayaking Tours** (48 Cottage St., Bar Harbo; ☎ **800-526-8615** outside of Maine or 207- 288-9605) and **Bar Harbor Bicycle Shop** (141 Cottage St., Bar Harbor; ☎ **207-288-3886**). Rates are between $17 and $32 a day, depending on the type of bike you rent, with discounts for multiple-day or weeklong rentals. For a guide to the carriage roads, pick up a park service map at the visitor center in Hulls Cove. (See "Finding information," earlier in this chapter.)

✔ **Canoeing:** The calm waters of Mount Desert Island's lakes and ponds are perfect for beginning canoeists. If you paddle early in the morning or during the evening, you just may spot some of the park's wildlife, such as white-tailed deer or raccoons. Canoe rentals are available at **Acadia Outfitters** (106 Cottage St., Bar Harbor; ☎ **207-288-8118**) and **Acadia Bike and Coastal Kayaking Tours** (48 Cottage St., Bar Harbor; ☎ **800-526-8615** or 207-288-9605).

✔ **Fishing:** Acadia features freshwater and saltwater fishing. You need a nonresident fishing license for freshwater angling. (See "Fast Facts: Acadia," at the end of this chapter, for details on getting a license.) Saltwater fishing doesn't require a permit.

✔ **Mountain climbing:** Aspiring climbers can get expert advice on the sport from **Acadia Mountain Guides Climbing School** (198 Main St., Bar Harbor; ☎ **888-232-9559** or **207-288-8186;** Internet: www.acadiamountainguides.com) or the **Atlantic Climbing School** (24 Cottage St., Bar Harbor; ☎ **207-288-2521**). These outfitters work with novice as well as expert climbers and coach them on the park's granite cliffs.

✔ **Sea kayaking:** Frenchman Bay is one of the most popular sea-kayaking destinations on the East Coast. Sea kayaks are much more stable than the smaller kayaks used to negotiate whitewater rivers, so you probably don't need any experience before shoving off in these two-person boats. Outfitters who can help you master this sport include **Acadia Outfitters** (106 Cottage St., Bar Harbor; ☎ **207-288-8118**), **Acadia Bike and Coastal Kayaking Tours** (48 Cottage St., Bar Harbor; ☎ **800-526-8615** or 207-288-9605), **Island Adventures Sea Kayaking** (141 Cottage St., Bar Harbor; ☎ **800-824-2453** or 207-288-3886), or **National Park Sea Kayak Tours** (39 Cottage St., Bar Harbor; ☎ **800-347-0940** or 207-288-0342).

✔ **Swimming:** During the summer months, lifeguards patrol Echo Lake and Sand Beach.

✔ **Whale-watching:** You can take to the high seas in search of humpbacks, finbacks, and other whale species. **Bar Harbor Whale Watching Company** (☎ **800-942-5374** or 207-288-2386; Internet: www.whalesrus.com) sails from Harbor Place next to the Town Pier on whale-watching cruises ($39 adults, $25 ages 6–14, $8 ages 5 and under) or combined whale-watching and puffin-watching trips ($43 adults, $25 ages 6–14, $8 ages 5 and under).

Escaping the rain

Although I enjoy watching storms roll ashore (Thunder Hole is a dramatic vantage point), I realize that this diversion isn't for everyone, especially for families with young children. If you're looking for rainy-day activities, pay a visit to the **Mount Desert Island Biological Laboratory** (Route 3, Salisbury Cove; ☎ **207-288-3605** or 207-288-5195), where you can see dogfish sharks and other marine animals up close, or the **Oceanarium Lobster Museum** (Route 3, Bar Harbor; ☎ **207-288-5005** or 207-244-7330). The oceanarium features a salt marsh, a working lobster hatchery, and the Maine Lobster Museum — the main attraction.

Where to Stay

Mount Desert Island offers accommodations ranging from modest tent sites to elegant hotels. However, none of the lodges are in the park itself. The following section gives you a sample of the best offerings.

Top lodgings

Acadia Hotel

$$$–$$$$ **Bar Harbor**

The Acadia Hotel, overlooking the Village Green in downtown Bar Harbor, offers easy access to all in-town activities. This handsome, simple home, dating from 1884, features a wraparound porch and attractive guest rooms decorated in a pleasant floral motif. The rooms vary widely in size and amenities; two have whirlpools, and one has a kitchenette. Why stay in the heart of Bar Harbor? You're close to cruises and shops renting bikes and boats, and restaurants are never far away. However, you won't enjoy the same peace and quiet that you find in some of the island's other towns.

20 Mt. Desert St. ☎ *888-876-2463 or 207-288-5721. Internet:* www.acadia hotel.com. *11 units. A/C TV. Rack rates: July 1–Sept 3 $100–$160 double; Sept 4– June 29 $55–$130 double. MC, V.*

Bar Harbor Inn

$$$–$$$$$ **Bar Harbor**

Situated on shady waterfront grounds just a minute's stroll from downtown and a mile from the park, Bar Harbor Inn offers convenience as well as gracious charm. The main shingled inn, dating from the turn of the century, evokes a settled, old-money feel with its elegant lobby and semicircular dining room with ocean views. The guest rooms, located in the main inn and two additional structures, are more contemporary. Guest rooms in the Oceanfront building (remodeled in 1999) and the Main Inn offer spectacular views of the bay, and many rooms include private balconies; the less expensive Newport building, constructed in 1994, lacks views but adds comfort. Bar Harbor Inn offers attractive packages in the spring and fall.

Newport Drive (just off Agamont Park). ☎ *800-248-3351 or 207-288-3351. Internet:* www.barharborinn.com. *153 units. A/C TEL. Rack rates vary monthly, but fall roughly into these ranges: May 17–Oct 12 $109–$319, Oct 13–May 16 $75–$225. Rates include Continental breakfast. Closed Dec to late March. AE, DISC, MC, V.*

Balance Rock Inn
$$$$$ Bar Harbor

Want to imagine life as a Rockefeller or Astor? Then stay at the Balance Rock Inn. Built in 1903, this mansion is an architecturally elaborate affair of gray shingles and colorful trim. The common rooms are expansive yet comfortable. Serious loungers enjoy the front covered patio with its green wicker furniture and recessed bar. The inn's view — across a wonderful pool; down a long, verdant lawn framed by hardwoods; and to the rich, blue waters of Frenchman Bay — is among the best in Maine. The rooms are wonderfully appointed, and many include whirlpool baths or fireplaces.

21 Albert Meadow (off Main Street at Butterfield's grocery). ☎ *800-753-0494 or 207-288-2610. Internet:* www.balancerockinn.com. *23 units. A/C TV TEL. Rack rates: July 20–Aug 22, July 4th, and Columbus Day $255–$625 double; rest of the year $125–$595 double. All rates include Continental breakfast. Closed Nov to early May. AE, DISC, MC.*

Claremont Hotel
$$$$–$$$$$ Southwest Harbor

To get a feel for New England Yankeedom, stay at Claremont Hotel, a nearly 120-year-old graceful inn overlooking Somes Sound. The country-side seems to sweep inside the hotel, where you find fireplaces and a library with rockers and jigsaw puzzles in various stages of completion. The hotel serves meals in seaside rooms overlooking the water. Room rates may seem a bit high for the smallish rooms, but some include break-fast and dinner; be sure to ask what meal plan is available when you make reservations. Cottages, set in the woods or with views of the sound, come in a variety of bedroom layouts and feature woodstoves or fireplaces, and kitchenettes. The Claremont also operates two guest houses with B&B-style accommodations.

20 Claremont Rd. (Call for directions.) ☎ *800-244-5036 for reservations. Fax: 207-244-3512. Internet:* www.acadia.net/claremont. *24 rooms, 13 cottages, 2 guest houses with a total of 7 rooms. TEL. Rack rates: Double in Claremont Hotel or guest houses mid-July to Labor Day $165–$235, off-season from $115; cottages per night mid-July to Labor Day $170–$240, off-season $125–$175. Cottages require a 3-night minumum stay. Some rates include breakfast and dinner. Closed mid-Oct to early June. No credit cards.*

Inn at Southwest
$$$–$$$$ Southwest Harbor

The hospitable and elegant Inn at Southwest has a decidedly turn-of-the-century air but is restrained on the frills. The guest rooms, named after Maine lighthouses, are furnished with contemporary and antique furni-ture. All rooms feature ceiling fans and down comforters. One of the most pleasant rooms is Blue Hill Bay on the third floor, which includes a large bath, a sturdy oak bed and bureau, and glimpses of the scenic harbor. Breakfasts offer ample reason to rise and shine, featuring specialities such as vanilla Belgian waffles with raspberry sauce and crab bake.

371 Main St. ☎ 207-244-3835. Internet: www.innatsouthwest.com. 7 units. Rack rates: Summer to early fall $110–$185 double, off-season $75–$135. All rates include breakfast. Closed Nov–Apr. DISC, MC, V.

Runner-up lodgings

Anchorage Motel

$–$$ **Bar Harbor** Shops, restaurants, and the waterfront are close to this inexpensive motel. *51 Mount Desert St. ☎ 800-336-3959 or 207-288-3959.*

Bar Harbor Quality Inn

$$–$$$$ **Bar Harbor** A short walk from downtown Bar Harbor and a mile to the park, this motel offers kitchenettes, laundry facilities, and a heated pool. *Route 3 and Mount Desert St. ☎ 800-282-5403 or 207-288-5403. Internet: www.acadia.net/quality.*

The Ledgelawn Inn

$$–$$$$$ **Bar Harbor** Just as nice but less expensive than its sister property, the Balanced Rock Inn, the Ledgelawn offers 33 rooms, many of which include working fireplaces. *66 Mount Desert St. ☎ 800-274-5334 or 207-288-4596. Internet: www.barharborvacations.com. Closed Nov–April.*

The Villager

$$–$$$ **Bar Harbor** No frills, just clean, tidy rooms with a heated swimming pool outside and restaurants nearby. *207 Main St. ☎ 207-288-3211. Internet: www.acadia.net/villager.*

Campgrounds

Acadia National Park offers only two campgrounds — Blackwoods and Seawall — but between them, they include more than 500 sites. A few shelters are also available on Isle au Haut, and you can find about a dozen private campgrounds scattered about Mount Desert Island.

Blackwoods Campground
Near Bar Harbor

From an aesthetic viewpoint, Blackwoods Campground is the best in the park. Its heavily wooded sites provide a measure of privacy, and you're not far from Seal Harbor. However, due to its size and location, this campground sees more traffic than Seawall Campground.

From April through November, the campground offers picnic tables, fire rings, restrooms with cold running water, dump stations, and an amphitheater for ranger talks that are offered from mid-June into mid-October. RVs no longer than 35 feet can park in the designated sites, which don't include utility hookups. Off-season amenities include chemical toilets, hand-pumped water, fire rings, and picnic tables.

Route 3, 5 miles south of Bar Harbor. ☎ 800-365-2267. More than 300 sites. Rates: May–Oct $20 per night, reservations required; Nov–April $10 per night, no reservation needed, during this period the water is turned off.

Duck Harbor Campground
Isle au Haut

The island offers five lean-to shelters, which can accommodate six people each. Nearby amenities include picnic tables, fire rings, chemical toilets, and hand-pumped water.

Duck Harbor, Isle au Haut. ☎ 207-288-3338. 5 lean-tos. Rate: $25 total for three to five nights. Mail-in reservations required. Open May 15–Oct 14. Send reservation request to Acadia National Park, Isle au Haut Reservations, P.O. Box 177, Bar Harbor, ME 04609. The reservation requests must be accompanied by a $25 fee and be postmarked no earlier than April 1 for the coming season. Reservations sent before this date will be returned.

Seawall Campground
Near Southwest Harbor

If you don't want the large town feel of Blackwoods Campground, head to Seawall, which is also wooded. Seawall is near a cobbled beach and seaside nature trails. You can also swim at Echo Lake, about 6 miles away.

From late spring to early fall, the campground offers picnic tables, fire rings, restrooms with cold running water, dump stations, and amphitheaters for ranger talks. RVs no longer than 35 feet can park in the designated sites, which don't include utility hookups. Sites are assigned on a first-come, first-served basis, so arrive early in the day to get one.

Route 102A, 4 miles south of Southwest Harbor. No reservations. More than 200 sites. Rates: $20 a night (accessible by car); $14 a night (requires a short walk). Closed Sept 30 to late May.

Where to Eat

Mealtime in Acadia National Park means seafood, lobsters, more seafood, and (believe it or not) a full menu of other tantalizing possibilities. Bar

Harbor is the focal point for the park's culinary delights, but you can find many wonderful restaurants elsewhere on Mount Desert Island.

124 Cottage Street Restaurant

$$–$$$$ **Bar Harbor**   **SEAFOOD/AMERICAN**

Along with plenty of lobster, the menu of this picturesque restaurant, located on Bar Harbor's main drag, offers steaks, chicken dishes, and vegetarian fare. The salad bar is a good starter for any meal — and may be a meal in itself for some travelers. Entrees range from fresh Maine crab baked with three cheeses and fresh asparagus to Mussels Fra Diablo (mussels sauteed in a spicy marinara sauce), Lobster chowder, and grilled swordfish. The setting is almost as delicious as the menu, with huge maple trees and plenty of flowering plants.

124 Cottage St. ☎ *207-288-4383. Reservations recommended. Main Courses: $12.95–$29.95. MC, V. Open: Daily 5–9:30 p.m; closed Nov–May.*

Beal's Lobster Pier

$$$ **Southwest Harbor**   **SEAFOOD**

Lobsters, lobster bibs, and bowls of butter await at this dockside eatery with just-off-the-boat seafood. After you've selected a lobster from one of Beal's tanks on the pier, you eat it on covered picnic tables with a front-row view of Southwest Harbor. If the weather is questionable, though, plan on heading somewhere else because the tables aren't sheltered from the elements. You can sample Beal's seafood before you take your park trip; they ship lobsters across the country year-round.

Clark Point Road. ☎ *207-244-3202 or 800-245-7178. Cooked lobsters range from $7.55–$9.75 per pound; sides extra. AE, DISC, MC, V. Open: Daily 9 a.m.–8 p.m.; closed mid-Oct to April.*

Jordan Pond House

$$–$$$$ **Near Seal Harbor**   **AMERICAN**

Although tea and delicious popovers served with strawberry jam are a daily highlight at Jordan Pond House, which dates from the 1800s, lunches and dinners (lobster and fish dishes as well as prime rib) are also on the menu. You can't go wrong with the lobster stew or the Maine crab cakes. Kids of all ages love the rich, homemade ice cream. The setting alongside Jordan Pond is hard to beat.

Park Loop Road. ☎ *207-276-3316. Reservations recommended for lunch, tea, and dinner. Main courses: $10–$18 lunch; $7.25 afternoon tea; $14–$20 dinner. AE, DISC, MC, V. Open: Daily 11:30 a.m.–8 p.m. (until 9 p.m. July–Aug); closed Late Oct to mid- May.*

Rupununi

$$$–$$$$ Bar Harbor AMERICAN

Settling on which of Mount Desert Island's restaurants offers the freshest seafood is tough, but this self-described "American Bar and Grill" (whose name Rupununi derives from a South American river, by the way) is in the running for most complete menu. You find not only fresh lobster and clams here but also prime rib, filet mignon, venison, buffalo, and even wild boar. Choosing a drink is tougher than choosing dinner, thanks to a selection of more than 60 beers and more than 40 whiskeys. When you make your reservation, be sure to ask for a table on the patio if the weather's nice. Jazz musicians serenade the diners on Sunday evenings.

119 Main St. ☎ 207-288-2886. Reservations suggested. Main courses: $4.95–$17 lunch; $8.95–$22 dinner. AE, DISC, MC, V. Open: Daily 11 a.m.–1 a.m.; closed Nov to mid-Apr.

Fast Facts: Acadia

Area Code

☎ 207.

ATM

Located in banks found in all MDI towns.

Emergency

Call ☎ 911 island-wide; ☎ 207-288-3369 within the park.

Fees

$10 per vehicle per week; $5 per motorcycle.

Fishing License

No license needed for saltwater fishing; freshwater license required for Maine residents 16 and older and for nonresidents 12 and older. Resident licenses are $19, plus the agent's fee; nonresidents for one week are $34 for adults, plus the agent's fee, and $7 for ages 12 to15, plus agent's fee.

Hospitals/Clinics

Mount Desert Island Hospital, 10 Wayman Ln., Bar Harbor; ☎ 207-288-5081.

Information

Acadia National Park, P.O. Box 177, Bar Harbor, ME 04609-0177; ☎ 207-288-3338 voice and TTY.

Lost and Found

☎ 207-288-3360.

Pharmacies

Rite Aid Pharmacies, 38 Cottage St., Bar Harbor; ☎ 207-288-2222.

Post Office

55 Cottage St., Bar Harbor; ☎ 207-288-3122.

Road Conditions and Weather

☎ 207-288-3338. Note: This is a general number.

Taxes

7% for lodging and meals.

Time Zone

Eastern standard time.

Web Site

www.nps.gov/acad.

Chapter 10

Arches National Park

• •

In This Chapter

▶ Introducing a redrock wonder

▶ Planning your visit to the park

▶ Enjoying the natural highlights

▶ Heading to Moab for the best sleeps and eats

• •

Among Utah's five national parks (a total that only California and Alaska can surpass), Arches National Park is often lost in the shuffle. Why? Well, this park lacks the towering cliffs and slot canyons of Zion, isn't chock-full of whimsical rock formations like Bryce Canyon, can't match the mountainous formations of Capitol Reef, and doesn't feature the swallow-the-world canyons of Canyonlands.

Because fewer than one million people visit the park each year, you may wonder why Arches is a national park. Stop wondering. What Arches does have, you can't find anywhere else in the world. Within the park's 76,519 dry and dusty acres in southeastern Utah, you find an otherworldly landscape of rock arches, windows, spires, pinnacles, and keenly balanced rocks that somehow manage to thumb their collective noses at gravity's ever-constant pull. According to last count, the park features more than 2,000 officially recognized stone arches. But with gravity at work, a new arch can fall into place at any time due to erosion of the park's rock walls. Conversely, an existing arch, weary from standing against time, can simply crumble off the list.

But Arches is more than an art gallery of rocks. If you look past the arches, windows, and balanced rocks, you see a wild and pure desertscape. At first glance, the land seems inhospitable, but if you look closer, you may spot lizards, snakes, ravens, mule deer, foxes, and — in season — gorgeous blooms of wild flowers. And with all the open countryside and sandstone, the sun paints Arches more than parks that are heavily forested. Early morning and late afternoon sun rays glisten on the sandstone cliffs and arches and even on the sandy earth. When the rays change their angle, the red, yellow, and orange hues of the landscape change, too.

Finding fins in the landscape

Rock *fins* (humpback rock formations) that jut up from the landscape are just as imposing as the arches, but not quite as obvious. The results of erosion, fins are the precursors to arches. Over the centuries, erosion has carved archways and windows into these upright sheets of rock. Wherever you see an arch, a fin previously stood.

You can easily see the park's highlights in one day; however, photographers may need two days in order to capture the late afternoon lighting in two particularly photogenic spots, Delicate Arch and Fiery Furnace.

With the park's high desert climate, you can visit Arches any time of year, although many restaurants in Moab are closed from December through February. Summer is the park's busiest season and the hottest — temperatures frequently surpass 100 degrees in June, July, and August. I like to visit Arches during the fall. By mid-October, the summer crowds have waned, and the weather is somewhat cooler — daily highs average 77 degrees. Winter can also be wonderful. Even though the mercury drops below freezing at night, daytime highs are routinely in the 40s and 50s, which are great temperatures for hiking — the best way to explore the park.

Must-see Attractions

In a park that boasts the world's largest collection of rock arches, you don't have to hunt far to find them. In this sandstone playground, arches of all sizes and curious shapes abound. You also find intriguing rock mazes and short but worthwhile trails. So where do you head after entering the park? I suggest checking out the following sites:

- ✔ **Delicate Arch:** The image of this arch decorates Utah's license plates, but the real thing is much more impressive. Although you can drive to a viewpoint to glimpse Delicate Arch, the hiking trail provides a more dramatic perspective. Plus, a photograph of you or your family posing under the arch is a classic.

- ✔ **Devils Garden:** Located on the north end of the park, this area features an easy trail that leads to Landscape Arch. Along the trail, you encounter six more arches and Fin Canyon, a sprawling maze of sandstone fins.

- ✔ **Fiery Furnace:** This labyrinth of sandstone fins features so many colorful twists and turns that park officials want you to enter with a ranger so you can find your way out.

Name that rock

Arches National Park features arches, windows, and natural bridges. What's the difference between these structures? Arches are formed when erosion, usually without the aid of rushing water, cuts holes in large rock spans (called *fins*). Natural bridges are the result of stream erosion in rock faces. Windows are just small arches. You usually find these gaps, which may resemble the windows in your house, high off the ground.

✔ **Park Avenue Trail:** This easy hike takes you past incredible stone monoliths. Talk about being overpowered by your surroundings.

✔ **The Windows:** No need to expend a lot of sweat to see a great collection of arches and windows (see this chapter's "Name that rock" sidebar for details on these structures). Short walks from a parking lot lead to the various attractions in The Windows, including North and South Windows, Turret Arch, Double Arch, and Cove of Caves.

Getting There

Arches is a park that requires a little extra effort to reach, but the visit is worth the inconvenience.

Driving in

If you're driving, U.S. 191 runs north and south past Arches. From the north, take Interstate 70 across central Utah to Crescent Junction and then head south on U.S. 191 to the park entrance. From the south, U.S. 191 connects with U.S. 160 in northeastern Arizona. Once you cross the border into Utah, you're 128 miles south of the park.

Flying in

Moab's air service seems to change annually. At last check, **Great Lakes Aviation** (☎ 800-554-5111; Internet www.greatlakesav.com) was using twin, turbo-prop aircraft to fly to Canyonlands Field near Moab (which is just 5 miles south of the park on U.S. 191) from Denver, Phoenix, or Page, Arizona. From the airport, you need to rent a car to drive to the park. **Thrifty** and **Budget** have offices in Moab and will deliver a car to the airport.

The nearest major commercial airport to Arches is **Walker Field** (☎ 970-244-9100) in Grand Junction, Colorado — 125 miles from the park. **America West Express, Delta/Skywest, Mesa Airlines,** and

United Express all fly to Walker Field. Once you arrive, you must rent a car and drive to the park. **Avis, Hertz, National,** and **Thrifty** all rent cars at the airport, whereas **Budget** and **Enterprise** operate nearby and provide a shuttle to/from the airport.

See the Appendix for the toll-free numbers of car-rental agencies and airlines mentioned in this section.

Busing or training in

Greyhound (☎ 800-229-9424; Internet: www.greyhound.com) can drop you off at Crescent Junction, which is north of Moab and 27 miles from the park. Then you can arrange to take a regional shuttle, **Bighorn Express** (☎ 888-655-7433; Internet: www.bighornexpress.com), to Moab for $24 one-way, but you must call ahead for reservations. You can also catch the Bighorn Express in Salt Lake City; the bus makes one trip per day to Moab at a cost of $49 one-way and $98 round-trip. From Moab, you want to rent a car to visit the park. (See the preceding "Flying in" section for information on rental car agencies in Moab.)

Want to ride the rails? The closest **Amtrak** station (☎ 800-USA-RAIL; Internet: www.amtrak.com) is at Grand Junction, Colorado. If you choose this route, you need to rent a car to visit the park. (See the preceding "Flying in" section for information on rental car agencies in Grand Junction.)

Planning Ahead

Moab has drawn tourists for a long time. First they came to see the colorful redrock landscape, and then they discovered the nearby whitewater rafting, and more recently, they went nuts over mountain biking opportunities. The upside of visiting Moab is that the small town caters to tourists; the downside is that the motels are often booked. The *No Vacancy* signs have been known to burn out, so you must plan ahead if you want to secure a room.

If you plan to come during the busy summer and early fall months, be sure to book a motel room at least three months in advance of your trip because Moab's motels fill up quickly. Sorrel River Ranch and Sunflower Hill Bed & Breakfast are two noteworthy places in high demand (see "Where to Stay," later in this chapter, for more information).

For general information about the park in advance of your trip, write Superintendent, Arches National Park, P.O. Box 907, Moab, UT 84532-0907; call ☎ 435-719-2299 or 435-719-2319 (TTY); or check the Internet at www.nps.gov/arch.

Arches National Park

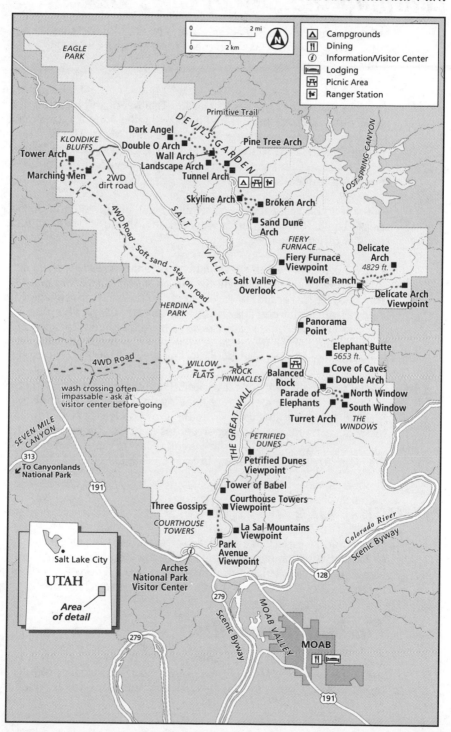

Campgrounds
Dining
Information/Visitor Center
Lodging
Picnic Area
Ranger Station

EAGLE PARK

0   2 mi
0   2 km

DEVILS GARDEN

Primitive Trail

Dark Angel
Double O Arch   Pine Tree Arch
Wall Arch
Landscape Arch
KLONDIKE BLUFFS
Tower Arch   Tunnel Arch
Marching Men   2WD dirt road

4WD Road - Soft sand - stay on road

LOST SPRING CANYON

SALT VALLEY

Skyline Arch   Broken Arch

Sand Dune Arch

FIERY FURNACE   Delicate Arch
Fiery Furnace Viewpoint   4829 ft.

HERDINA PARK   Salt Valley Overlook   Wolfe Ranch
Delicate Arch Viewpoint

Panorama Point

4WD Road   WILLOW FLATS   ROCK PINNACLES

wash crossing often impassable - ask at visitor center before going

Elephant Butte
5653 ft.
Cove of Caves
Balanced Rock   Double Arch
Parade of Elephants   North Window
South Window
Turret Arch   THE WINDOWS

THE GREAT WALL

SEVEN MILE CANYON

313
To Canyonlands National Park
191

PETRIFIED DUNES

Petrified Dunes Viewpoint

Tower of Babel
Courthouse Towers Viewpoint

Three Gossips

COURTHOUSE TOWERS

La Sal Mountains Viewpoint

Park Avenue Viewpoint

Colorado River Scenic Byway

Salt Lake City

UTAH

Area of detail

Arches National Park Visitor Center

279

Scenic Byway

MOAB VALLEY

128

MOAB

279

191

Learning the Lay of the Land

Although covering 76,519 acres, Arches National Park is laid out in a rather straightforward fashion thanks to a natural clustering of the major arches and windows.

The park has one visitor center. Arches' main road, which runs from the visitor center to the Devils Garden Trailhead (the location of the park's only campground), is just under 18 miles long. Off this main artery run three major spurs: the 2½-mile-long leg to The Windows, a 2¼-mile-long branch to the Delicate Arch Trailhead and the Delicate Arch Viewpoint, and the 7¾-mile-long Salt Valley road to the relatively remote Klondike Bluffs area.

All the roads, except for the Salt Valley road, are paved and in good shape. The Salt Valley road is unpaved and, therefore, slower going than the other roads.

A road for four-wheel-drive vehicles runs 9 miles northwest from near Balanced Rock to Klondike Bluffs, but park officials recommend that this route be traversed only from north to the south because of steep, sandy pitches that can mire rigs going the other way. The park's other four-wheel-drive route scampers west from Balanced Rock to U.S. 191, but this road can be impassable when wet. For more information on four-wheeling in the park, see "Keeping active," later in this chapter.

Even if you're driving your favorite SUV, you may want to think twice and check with a ranger before heading down one of the backcountry roads. SUVs don't always provide the ground clearance needed in the rocky desert, and some tricky stretches may require off-road experience. You don't need to go four-wheeling in Arches anyway, because all the main attractions are along the paved roads.

Arriving in the Park

You shouldn't experience any trouble navigating through Arches, thanks to its relatively compact size and simple road network. From the visitor center just off U.S. 191 to the campground at Devils Garden, crisscrossing the bulk of the park won't take you longer than 30 minutes.

Finding information

The **Arches National Park Visitor Center** (☎ 435-719-2200), just inside the entrance gate off U.S. 191 and 5 miles north of Moab, provides maps, brochures, and other information. The center is open year-round from

8 a.m. to 4:30 p.m. A museum tells you all that you need to know about arch formation and other features of the park, and you can go to a short orientation program in the auditorium.

Paying fees

Entry for up to seven days costs $10 per private vehicle or $5 per person on foot or bicycle. See Chapter 8 for information on the National Park Pass and Chapter 4 for the lowdown on Golden Age and Golden Access Passports.

Getting around

Basically, you need a car in Arches, because the park doesn't provide its own transportation system. You can also get around by bicycle, but bikes are allowed only on the main road and not in the backcountry. (See "Keeping active" for more information on biking in the park.)

You can see many of the park's most famous rock formations through your car's windshield, but by all means, get out of the car and walk around. You can walk short distances to a number of viewpoints or stretch your legs on longer hikes (see "Taking a hike," later in this chapter). The main road is easy to navigate, even for RVs, but parking at some viewpoints is limited. Please be considerate and leave trailers at the visitor center parking lot or in the campground.

Remembering Safety

For your own safety, keep in mind the following precautions while touring Arches National Park:

- ✔ **Use your senses — all of them.** When hiking around arches, keep your ears open for any popping or cracking sounds — noises that signal a rock fall. If you hear such sounds, get out from under the arch immediately and then look up to see if anything is falling. Don't stop to look up while you're under the arch, because a falling rock is one natural phenomenon that you want to see from a distance.

- ✔ **Keep an eye on the weather.** Thunderstorms can build quickly in the spring and summer months. Because of the miles of open space and few trees, you make a pretty good impression of a lightning rod. Sudden storms can also generate flash floods, so if you're in the backcountry, never camp in a *dry wash* (a dry stream bed) and never try to cross one during flood conditions.

> ✔ **Drink plenty of water.** In the hotter months (such as July when the temperature usually reaches 100 degrees during the day), drink plenty of water and keep an eye on your traveling companions. With the intense sunlight, high temperatures, low humidity, and lack of shade, the park can be like an oven. If you're not drinking enough water, you can quickly succomb to heat exhaustion or heatstroke. During a summer visit, try to drink at least a gallon of water per day in the park, and do your friends a favor by making sure that they drink frequently, too.
>
> ✔ **Know your limits.** If you're a climber, don't climb higher than your level of skill allows. Park rangers rescue many climbers who have worked their way up rock faces only to realize that they can't get back down. A few unfortunate ones have fallen and suffered broken bones.

For additional tips on how to ensure a safe visit to a national park, see Chapter 8.

Enjoying the Park

With its lack of vegetation and fairly flat landscape, Arches National Park is extremely user-friendly for seeing the sights. Although hiking is the best way to get perspective on the size of the park's arches and other formations, you don't need to hike to see many of the major attractions, which are visible from the park's roadways.

Exploring the top attractions

For information on hikes to each of these attractions, see the "Taking a hike" section later in this chapter.

Courthouse Towers

Minutes past the park entrance lies a towering collection of pillars; as you walk among them, they impart the same type of claustrophobia that you get when you walk along a narrow street with tall buildings on either side. Instead of glass and steel, however, these skyscrapers are made of rock. In the southwestern corner of the park, the Courthouse Towers evokes a sense of nobility, too, because one rock formation clearly visible from the Park Avenue Trailhead bears a striking resemblance to Queen Nefertiti. Use your imagination while strolling along the mile-long trail that runs from the Park Avenue Trailhead to the Courthouse Towers Viewpoint. Although you may come up with some noteworthy descriptions of your own, the park calls some of these formations Three Gossips, Organ Rock, and Courthouse Towers.

The viewpoints and trailheads for Courthouse Towers are just north of the visitor center on the main road.

Delicate Arch

Whether you think that Delicate Arch looks like a pair of bloomers or a cowboy's chaps doesn't matter; what matters is that you see the formation up close. The image on Utah's commemorative license plates doesn't do justice to the arch. Hiking the 1½-mile trail that winds across slick rock and along a narrow shelf of rock is worth the effort. When you slip around the last corner — stepping onto the sandstone rim of an ancient sinkhole — and see Delicate Arch, you'll understand what I mean. Make sure that you pack water, wear a hat, and avoid this hike at midday in the middle of summer.

The turnoff for Delicate Arch is 11¾ miles north of the visitor center.

Devils Garden

This rumpled area of canyons, fins, and arches anchors the northern end of the park's main road. At Devils Garden, you find the only campground in the park as well as eight major arches, including Landscape and Double O. Make sure that you have plenty of time to explore this area. You can spend a couple hours just on the hike to and from Landscape Arch, Wall Arch, Pine Tree Arch, and Tunnel Arch. If you're not in a rush, toss in longer walks to Double O Arch or the Primitive Trail, but if you're afraid of heights, you may want to avoid these hikes because a stretch of trail runs across the spine of a fin.

You can find the trail through Devils Garden at the end of the park's main road.

Capturing Arches on film

For shutterbugs, timing is everything — a rule that definitely applies in Arches National Park. Two of the most photogenic attractions, **Fiery Furnace** and **Delicate Arch,** are best photographed in the late afternoon because the low angle of the sun's rays seems to add depth to the formations, igniting their redrock features. Plus, in late spring and early summer, if your timing is right and the weather cooperates, you can get a great picture of Delicate Arch with the snow-capped La Sal Mountains in the background.

But you can't be in two places at the same time. You can view Fiery Furnace by signing up for the afternoon guided tour (which is the best way to see it), but you likely won't be finished in time to make the hike to Delicate Arch before the sun slips beneath the horizon. I recommend taking the Fiery Furnace tour, which winds through incredible passages and is more of a hands-on experience than standing in front of Delicate Arch.

The early morning provides the best light for photographing many of the park's other formations.

Fiery Furnace

The name of this twisting maze of rock doesn't come from the heat, but from the glowing reds, oranges, and pinks that flare across the sandstone fins in the rays of the setting sun. On hot days, the fins actually provide shade, which makes this furnace feel cooler than the rest of the park. See "Ranger programs," later in this chapter, for information on the afternoon guided tour — the best way to see the area.

The Fiery Furnace Viewpoint, accessible by car, is located off the main park road.

The Windows

The easiest and quickest way to appreciate the park's features is to head to The Windows. This attraction is worth a visit because of the size of the windows, the rock scrambling you can do, and the closeness of several unusual formations. You can easily see the North and South Windows from the parking lot; however, you should definitely hike through the area to gain a better perspective on their size. Both windows, as well as Turret Arch and Double Arch, are less than a quarter-mile from the parking lot. You can easily spend a half day in this area if you leave the well-trodden trail. Not to be missed is the Parade of Elephants formation and its associated arch. A primitive trail also winds behind and below the North and South Windows and features placards that describe the surrounding plants and cacti.

The turnoff to The Windows is 9¼ miles north of the visitors center on the main road.

Taking a hike

In light of Arches' heated temperatures, most hikes in the park are short. The longest hike, Devils Garden Trail (which includes the Primitive Trail), is only 7¼ miles from start to finish; the rest are 4 miles or less. With film-gobbling redrock scenery scattered throughout the park, who cares about racking up miles on the trail? You don't need to go far to be impressed by the landscape.

Before I offer some examples of sure-to-please walks, please heed some words of wisdom: Pack at least a quart of water (preferably two) per person, wear a hat with a wide brim, and slather on the sun block before you set foot on the trail.

Broken Arch Trail

Passing through sand dunes and across slick rock, Broken Arch is a good place to look for Western gopher snakes. These yellow snakes with black patches aren't poisonous, but they coil and shake their tails like rattlesnakes to scare off predators.

Distance: 2-mile loop trail from the campground in Devils Garden to the arch. Level: Easy to moderate. Access: Across from campsite 40.

Delicate Arch Trail

The hike to Delicate Arch seems intimidating when you first leave the parking lot. During the busy season, the folks hiking up the trail resemble a line of ants plodding across the red rock. Don't worry, just get in line and follow the path to the top. The first ½ mile takes you across a wide slab of rock with a well-defined trail. If you think that you may not be going the right way, look for the *cairns* (piles of rocks that indicate the trail's direction). Just before you get to the arch, you wander through a rock outcrop and scoot along a ledge for about 200 yards. (Don't worry, the ledge is wide enough to soothe your nerves.) At the end of the ledge, you stroll out onto a sprawling rock basin to face Delicate Arch.

Even though this hike is fairly short, it can be brutal if the temperature is in the 90s or higher. Most of the trail is fully exposed on a sandstone ridge, which is why you don't want to hike to Delicate Arch in the middle of the day. Setting out at 5 p.m. or even 6 p.m. in summer or early fall is perfect. Plus, around this time of day, the sun gets into position for some great photographs of the arch.

On your way to the arch, after you cross the footbridge that spans Salt Wash just beyond Wolfe Ranch, look for a path that leads north about 100 to 200 yards to the nearby cliffs, where you can find a panel of horse **petroglyphs** painted by Ute Indians.

Distance: 3 miles round-trip. Level: Moderate to strenuous in the heat. Access: Wolfe Ranch parking area.

Primitive Trail from Double O to Landscape Arch

Don't let the word *primitive* scare you away from this hike, which is the best one in the park in my opinion. This 2¼-mile-long loop passes and climbs towering rock fins while weaving through some of the park's heavier vegetation and in and out of sandy washes. To reach the loop, hike past Landscape Arch to Double O Arch on the trail from the Devils Garden Trailhead. Beyond Landscape Arch, the trail narrows substantially and, at times, can be located only by following *cairns,* little stacks of rocks that denote the trail's direction. Shortly before you reach Double O, the trail climbs onto the spine of one of the fins — the experience is fun, the views are great, but the drop is dangerous, so be careful. When you climb down off the fin, before heading on to Double O, take a minute to stroll to your right to see Black Arch down below in Fin Canyon. The view is worth the five-minute side trip.

At Double O Arch, you come upon the northern end of the Primitive Trail and a spur that leads to Dark Angel, a dark sandstone spire. Unfortunately, Dark Angel isn't as imposing or impressive as its name implies. Skip it and take the loop trail, which circles back to the south and connects with the main trail near Landscape Arch. Along the way, you see stunted and gnarled pinion and juniper trees; yuccas that more than double their height in May and June when they sprout tall shafts of cream-colored flowers;

pretty red springtime displays of scarlet gilia that lure hummingbirds; spike-laden blackbrush; and scores of sagebrush that lend their pungent yet aromatic scent to the air after rains.

I don't recommend the Primitive Trail for novice hikers or ones with trepidations about heights. Plus, the trail is rugged in places and can be difficult to follow along the fins. However, this path is the one to take if you like adventure and want to escape the crowds.

Distance: 7¼ miles round-trip from the parking lot at the Devils Garden Trailhead to Double O Arch and back via the Primitive Trail. Level: Difficult. Access: Devils Garden parking area.

Fiery Furnace Area

This tall maze of red- and salmon-colored sandstone fins is the park's most colorful hike. However, the area doesn't feature marked trails. Before, many hikers got lost and/or trampled fragile soils and rare plants; so now, to hike Fiery Furnace, you must obtain a $2 permit at the visitor center and watch a video about minimum impact. I recommend that you join one of the excellent ranger-led hikes for which you don't need to buy a permit, but you do have to pay a small fee (see "Ranger programs," later in this chapter). The absolute best time for this hike is in the late afternoon at sunset — the rays appear to set the rocks on fire.

Distance: 2 miles round-trip. Level: Moderate to difficult. Access: Fiery Furnace parking area.

Landscape Arch Trail

Although the trail to this arch is crowded during the high season, this spindly rim of rock is one of the park's classics. With its 306-foot span, Landscape Arch may be the world's largest freestanding arch. A mostly flat, gravel trail winds through rock canyons to the arch. For the best picture of the arch, stop at the viewpoint in front of and just below the arch. This angle allows you to get not only the entire arch in your viewfinder but also a slice of blue sky.

Distance: 2 miles round-trip. Level: Easy. Access: Devils Garden parking area.

Park Avenue Trail

Although you won't closely encounter any arches along Park Avenue Trail, you pass interesting towering walls of sandstone. You can see the notable formations — Courthouse Towers, Tower of Babel, Three Gossips, and Organ Rock — from your car while driving in or out of the park, but on Park Avenue Trail, you can get down to the bases of these incredible giants. The trail winds through scattered groves of juniper, single-leaf ash, blackbrush, and, in spring, wildflowers that brighten the way. The one problem with this hike is that you have to backtrack to return to your car, unless you travel in a group and can arrange a shuttle with cars at either end. If not, try starting out at Courthouse Towers so you get the steep part out of the way first and end the walk going downhill.

Distance: 1 mile one way. Level: Easy. Access: Park Avenue or Courthouse Towers parking areas.

Sand Dune Arch Trail

The hike to Sand Dune Arch is great for kids. The trail is easy, and kids enjoy the giant sandbox beneath the arch. Surrounding the arch are fins of rock where you can flee the sun and relax while the kids play.

Distance: Just under ½ mile. Level: Easy. Access: Broken Arch/Sand Dune Arch parking area.

The Windows Trail

Kids enjoy this trail because they can scurry up onto rocks and into windows, although you don't want kids to get too carried away because the trail doesn't include railings to contain them. This hike leads to three arches — the North and South Windows and the Turret Arch. A gentle path leads to your first stop, which is in front of North Window; the South Window is just around the corner. To the west (behind you) is Turret Arch. A primitive, 1¼-mile trail begins on the south side of South Window and winds down onto the desert floor for a short distance before circling back up to the parking lot. (This route is interesting for its short botanical course on high desert vegetation but is not a must.) After you visit the Windows and Turret Arch, head to the north side of the parking area to find the short, less-than-½-mile trail to Double Arch.

Distance: 1 mile round-trip. Distance: Easy. Access: Windows parking area.

One-day wonder

Because of the size and layout of Arches National Park, you can easily see the highlights in one day. For more information on the attractions in the following itinerary, see "Exploring the top attractions" and "Taking a hike" earlier in this chapter.

Start your day around 8 a.m. Make sure to pack a picnic lunch and a cooler full of drinks. To ensure that you drink enough water throughout the day, buy a case of bottled water when you're in Moab and stash it in the trunk of your car. Then gauge your intake by the number of empty bottles that accumulate.

First, stop at the park's **visitor center,** which isn't the most elaborate in the park system but does offer a decent interpretation of the park's geology. You can pick up a hiking guide, make any last-minute restroom stops, and top off your water bottles or buy water. I recommend that you sign up for the afternoon tour of Fiery Furnace at this time (see "Ranger programs," later in this chapter, for information on this tour).

Just north of the visitor center, stop at **Park Avenue.** You don't need to hike the trail, but from the viewpoint, get a good look at the rock outcrop on the left rim that resembles the profile of Queen Nefertiti. Get back in your car and continue up the road to **Balanced Rock,** which sits precariously on its slowly eroding pedestal. Don't hike the Balanced Rock Trail, either; the sight of this balancing act is impressive even from the viewpoint.

Back on the road, head north from Balanced Rock and take the first right. Drive 2½ miles to **The Windows.** Follow The Windows Trail mentioned in the "Taking a hike" section. Climbing up into the windows and gazing across the rockscape no doubt duplicates an age-old ritual and also makes for an interesting photo opportunity.

Get back in your rig and return to the main road. If you did not sign up for the afternoon tour of Fiery Furnace, head north along the main road to **Devils Garden.** If you did sign up for the tour, make a quick stop at the **Delicate Arch** viewpoint to ogle this upright loop of rock before proceeding to Devils Garden. (Those who did not sign up for the tour will have plenty of time to return here in the late afternoon.)

By this point you're no doubt ready for lunch. You find some picnic tables, running water, and restrooms in Devils Garden.

Following lunch and after quenching your thirst, top off your water bottles at the water fountain at the trailhead and then start down the **Devils Garden Trail.** You want to reach Landscape Arch, which is about ¾ miles down the trail. If you're not running too late, are a strong hiker, and aren't traveling with anyone who will slow you down, push on past Landscape Arch to Double O Arch, another 1¼ miles down the trail. If heights bother you, you may want to skip this section, because part of the trail runs along the top of a rock fin. While retracing your steps on the way back to the parking lot, the short (less than a ½ mile) side trails to Pine Tree and Tunnel Arches are easy and worth taking.

Once back in your car, head back south on the main road towards Fiery Furnace. If you're traveling with kids (or simply want to see as many of the park's arches as possible), stop at **Sand Dune Arch,** found just over 1 mile south of the Devils Garden parking lot.

If you signed up, the **Fiery Furnace** tour is your next stop. If you decided to pass on the tour, make the hike to Delicate Arch if the weather isn't too hot. In either case, make sure that your water bottles are full before you leave the trailhead.

Following your final hike through Fiery Furnace or to Delicate Arch, call it a day — return to your lodging and enjoy a relaxing dinner.

If you have more time

Klondike Bluffs, in the park's northwestern corner, is worth exploring if you have more time. You can come to this place to flee the crowds — and to test the stability of your vehicle. To get to Klondike Bluffs, take the washboard-weary dirt road off the main road near Sand Dune Arch. The dirt road runs 7¾ miles through the Salt Valley to the Klondike Bluffs Road turnoff. Check the road conditions before traveling because runoff from thunderstorms can create problems. Also be careful not to drive off the road — soft sand along the shoulders can strand your rig. And finally, don't take the left turn just before the Klondike Bluffs Road unless you're in a four-wheel-drive vehicle (see "Keeping active," later in this chapter, for information on this four-wheel-drive road).

From the Klondike Bluffs parking area, you can take a round-trip hike just under 2½ miles past two notable formations. The first is **Marching Men** — a collection of stone spires that resemble soldiers to some creative minds. The second, visible from the top of a sand dune, is **Tower Arch,** a gigantic opening in the rock wall. Near its bottom on the right side is an inscription left in 1922 by Alex Ringhoffer, a gentleman who explored this area and is credited with lobbying for the designation of Arches as a national park.

Ranger programs

This relatively small park, with its similarly sized small staff, offers only a few ranger programs. One that I heartily recommend is the ranger-led tour of **Fiery Furnace** (see "Exploring the top attractions," earlier in this chapter). Rangers offer insights into natural history, vegetation, and geology; for example, they point out the difference between an arch and a bridge. The 2-mile hike takes 2½ to 3 hours and occurs twice a day between March and October. You must sign up for this tour in advance at the visitor center and pay a fee ($6 adults, $3 ages 6–12 and ages 62 or more).

Between early April and late October, rangers lead daily, one-hour hikes at various locations in the park, so check with the visitor center for times and locations. During this same period, rangers also give nightly talks at the amphitheater at Devils Garden. Although topics vary from season to season, one of the more interesting talks delves into the geology that produced Arches; another examines the mysterious disappearance in 1934 of Everett Ruess, a young artist who vanished in southern Utah's canyon country. Film buffs enjoy *Nature Framed: Canyon Country Through Hollywood's Lens,* which touches on many of the Westerns and other movies filmed in this part of Utah.

For kids, make sure that you pick up information on the Junior Ranger Program (see Chapter 4) at the visitor center.

Spotting the local wildlife

You may be surprised at the number of animals that live in the park's seemingly harsh environment. Bird-watchers have spied 273 bird species, including seasonal and year-round residents as well as migrants, in the park. Closer to ground level, 65 types of mammals, 22 reptile species, 9 types of amphibians, and 8 fish species make Arches their home. Where are they? Well, they're smart. The mammals and most reptiles lay low during the heat of the day and reserve their travels for the evenings and early mornings.

The biggest animals you're likely to see are the big-eared **mule deer.** They're highly visible in the Devils Garden area. Not so obvious are the **mountain lions** and **coyotes** that consider the park home (and consider mule deer, black-tailed jackrabbits, and desert cottontails their dinner). You probably won't see either lions or coyotes, but if you camp out in the park and have a little luck, you may hear coyotes yipping and howling in the night.

Desert bighorn sheep also live in this arid corner of Utah. The best place to look for them is on the cliffs created by the Moab Fault to the west of the visitor center.

Lizards are fairly common in the park. The western whiptail, which totes a tail twice the length of its body, is the most common. Photographers prefer to spot the western collared lizard, which has a bright-green body with a black collar.

The park also houses a few **poisonous critters** — rattlesnakes, scorpions, and black widow spiders. So keep a close eye on your kids and tell them not to put their hands into nooks and crannies or atop ledges that they can't see.

Although you may see wildlife in most areas of the park around dawn and before sundown, the Devils Garden Trail and its Primitive Trail offer the best odds for sighting wildlife thanks to their distance from roads and traffic. Of course, anywhere in the park, you may spot a **golden eagle** or **redtail hawk** circling overhead in search of a meal.

Keeping active

If you want to work up a sweat while taking in the scenery, consider one of the following activities. (Unless indicated otherwise, all outfitters are located in Moab, zip code 84532.)

✔ **Biking:** You can bike the scenic drive through the park; however, keep in mind that this almost 18-mile dead-end road is narrow and winding in spots and can be crowded with motor vehicles during the summer. Mountain bikers can also tackle one of several four-wheel-drive roads (see "Four-wheeling," later in this section). But keep in mind that bikes are prohibited on all trails and off-road in the backcountry. Cyclists can get information as well as rent or repair bikes at **Rim Cyclery,** 94 W. 100 North (☎ **800-304-8219** or

435-259-5333; Internet: www.rimcyclery.com), and **Poison Spider Bicycle Shop,** 497 Main St. (☎ **800-635-1792** or 435-259-7882; Internet: www.poisonspiderbicycles.com). Bike rentals start around $32 per day.

✔ **Canoeing/kayaking/rafting:** Although Arches doesn't include any bodies of water, the Colorado River follows the park's boundary along its southeast edge, and river-running is a wonderful change of pace from hiking over the park's dry, rocky terrain. You can rent a canoe, kayak, or raft from **Canyon Voyages,** 211 N. Main St., Box 416 (☎ **800-733-6007** or 435-259-6007; Internet: www.canyon voyages.com). Rentals begin at $30 for a half day. Canyon Voyages also offers guided river trips.

✔ **Four-wheeling:** For an antidote to your daily car commute, drive one of the park's two four-wheel-drive roads — but check first with rangers on possible road closures and conditions that make roads impassable. The more interesting of the two routes is the one from Klondike Bluffs to Willow Flats, which is best driven from north to south because of soft sand on steep grades. To access the road, turn west off the main park road 1 mile south of Devils Garden Trailhead; follow the road up through the Salt Valley 7¾ miles to the turnoff for Klondike Bluffs. The next 10¾ miles, which head into high desert terrain, are strictly for four-wheelers. The route passes drifting sane dunes, the redrock Marching Men formation, and Eye of the Whale Arch. The road ends at the Balanced Rock parking area. Four-wheel-drive vehicles are available for rent from **Slickrock 4X4 Rentals,** 2251 South Hwy. 191 (☎ **888-238-5337,** or 435-259-5678; Internet: www.moab-utah.com/jeep), beginning at $135 per day, and from **Farabee Adventures,** 401 North Main (☎ **888-806-5337**; Internet: www.moab-utah.com/farabee).

✔ **Rock climbing:** Unless you plan an overnight expedition, you can climb in Arches without a permit; however, you have to follow a few rules. For instance, you can't use a motorized drill to set an anchor. You also can't climb on any arch that is identified on current U.S. Geological Survey topographical maps. If you use chalk while climbing, its color must blend in with the rock, which is mostly buff or reddish. Climbers also are encouraged to use dull-colored webbing if they plan to leave any behind, and they should access climbing routes via established trails, across slickrock, or by sandy washes. You can get climbing guides at the visitor center (see "Finding information," earlier in this chapter) for a leg up on where to climb.

Where to Stay

Arches doesn't offer any lodging within the park unless you're toting a tent. But Moab, just 5 miles south on U.S. 191, overflows with lodging possibilities, ranging from roadside motels to quaint B&Bs.

Top lodgings

Aarchway Inn

$$ Moab

You can find this motel on the south side of the Colorado River when you cross the bridge on the way to Moab. Although lacking uniqueness, most of the large rooms feature two queen-size beds. All the rooms come with small refrigerators and microwave ovens so you can store and warm up snacks in your room. You also find barbecue grills in the courtyard and an outdoor pool great for dips after a long day in the park. If you're toting bikes, you can keep them in the inn's storage room.

1551 North U.S. 191. ☎ *800-341-9359 or 435-259-2599. Fax: 435-259-2270. Internet:* http://moab-utah.com/aarchway/inn.html. *90 rooms, 7 suites. A/C TV TEL. Rack rates: March–Oct $95 double, $120–$150 suite; Nov–April rates lower. Rates include Continental breakfast. AE, DISC, MC, V.*

Cali Cochitta Bed & Breakfast

$$–$$$ Moab

Although this quaint B&B is relatively new, having opened in 2000, the adobe brick house is not. Dating to the 1870s, the historic building no doubt has stories held deep within its walls. Guests can choose from three guest rooms, a suite, or cottage. Each comes with its own bathroom, queen-size beds, and cable TV if you lack the strength to head out to the park. You also find a hot tub on the property, as well as bike storage and, if you absolutely can't live without the Internet, modem hookups. As for the B&B's name, it means "House of Dreams" in Aztec.

110 South 200 East. ☎ *888-429-8112 or 435-259-4961. Internet:* www.moabdream inn.com. *5 units. A/C TV. Rack rates: March–Oct $89–$110 double, $130 suite, and $150 cottage; Nov–April $69–$90 double, $110 suite, and $130 cottage. DISC, MC, V.*

Sorrel River Ranch

$$$$$ Moab

This growing inn places you in the middle of some of southeastern Utah's famous redrock countryside. The ranch also offers probably the best lodging that you can find in the area — at a price. The Colorado River flows on the north side of the ranch, and towering buttes and canyon cliffs fill the other compass directions. The large guest rooms feature plush furniture, a small kitchen area with microwave and mini-refrigerator, and Southwestern-influenced decor. From the covered porches outside, you can watch herons in the Colorado River or see the sun cast fiery rays on the redrock landscape in the evenings. The River Grill provides daylong meal service, and the 4,300-square-foot lodge offers a place to retreat for a cool drink and a chat in front of a roaring fire. The ranch also features a swimming pool and hot tub.

Highway 128 (17 miles northeast of Moab). ☎ *877-359-2715 or 435-259-4642. Internet:* www.sorrelriver.com. *33 units. A/C TV TEL. Rack rates: $199–$360 double. Ask about summer specials. AE, DISC, MC, V.*

Sunflower Hill Bed & Breakfast Inn

$$$–$$$$ Moab

This picturesque spot is the nicest place to stay in town. The best flower gardens in Moab grace the lawns surrounding this B&B, located just three blocks off Main Street on a quiet dead-end street. The rooms are elegant and include use of an outdoor hot tub. A picnic table and grill are at your disposal, so you don't have to eat out every night during your stay. You can prepare for a day in the park with their breakfast of homemade breads and granola, fresh fruits, and a hot entree, such as Belgian waffles.

185 North 300 East. ☎ *800-MOAB-SUN or 435-259-2974. Fax: 435-259-3065. Internet:* http://sunflowerhill.com. *12 units. A/C TV. Rack rates: March–Oct and holidays $139–$199 double; Nov–Feb $89–$139 double, $20 each additional person (up to 2). Rates include full breakfast. DISC, MC, V*

Runner-up lodgings

Comfort Suites

$$–$$$ Moab   Near the heart of downtown, this chain motel is dutifully reliable, if unremarkable, with large suites, a refreshing pool, and a suitable exercise room if you didn't get enough of a workout in the park. *800 South Main St.* ☎ *800-228-5150 or 435-259-5252. Internet:* www.moab-utah.com/comfortsuites.

The Gonzo Inn

$$$–$$$$ Moab   Hunter S. Thompson would feel at home at this bright, eclectically colored inn with 43 rooms and suites. Just off Main Street, the inn offers rooms with fireplaces, vaulted ceilings, and jetted tubs. *100 West 200 South.* ☎ *800-791-4044. Internet:* www.gonzoinn.com.

Moab Best Western Greenwell Inn

$$–$$$ Moab   In the heart of downtown, this 72-room inn comes complete with a restaurant, pool, and fitness center. *105 South Main St.* ☎ *800-528-1234 or 435-259-6151. Internet:* www.moab-utah.com/bestwesternmoab.

Redstone Inn

$$ Moab   Five miles south of Arches on the northern edge of Moab, the Redstone is not only inexpensive but also puts together packages involving white-water rafting, four-wheeling, or horseback riding. *535 South Main St.* ☎ *800-772-1972 or 435-259-3500. Internet:* www.moabredstone.com.

Campgrounds

The **Devils Garden Campground,** located just past Fiery Furnace, is the only campground in Arches. Facilities are limited to restrooms within walking distance. The campground offers 52 sites on a first-come, first-serve basis at $10 a night. But before you rush to the campground, you need to preregister for a site at the visitor center between 7:30 a.m. and 8 a.m.; after 8 a.m., register at the entrance station. Preregistration guarantees you a site; however, you need to then head to the campground to pick it out from what's available. Sites fill early during the high seasons, which are late spring and fall. If you're traveling in a group of ten or more, you can reserve a site by writing the park at Reservations Office, Arches National Park, 2282 South West Resource Blvd., Moab, UT 84532. They begin accepting reservations on January 2 for the coming year.

The park's water system is turned off from November through mid-March to keep the lines from freezing. So you need to bring water if you camp during this period. Year-round, you also need to bring your own wood if you want a campfire because wood gathering in the park is prohibited. You must also carry out all trash, even cigarette butts.

Although you can backpack anywhere in the park, trails and campsites aren't marked, so you should know how to read a topographical map and be good with a compass before you head out. Streams are non-existent, so you need to tote all your water, too. Plus, backcountry overnight hikers must get a free permit from the visitor center.

Where to Eat

You won't find any restaurants in the park, so head to Moab for your meals. Don't be discouraged by the many restaurants that call themselves cafes. This eclectic town offers a variety of eating possibilities, ranging from brewpubs with pizza and burgers to multicourse spreads comparable to the ones found in ritzy New York City eateries. While many Moab restaurants shut down during the winter slow season, other eateries are ready and willing to provide you with three meals a day

Center Café and Market
$$$$ Moab CONTEMPORARY AMERICAN

This eatery constantly ranks among Utah's top restaurants. The Center Café serves up innovative game, vegetarian, seafood, and pasta dishes. On the menu, you find such varied offerings as grilled Black Angus tenderloin with creamy polenta and gorgonzola, Maine Lump meat crab cakes with fresh tomato coulis and citrus crème fraîche, and cedar planked salmon with applewood bacon-shallot crust and roasted garlic white beans. The cafe's new location comes complete with an adobe-walled patio out back, as well as a deli that offers a wide array of imported cheeses, house-smoked salmon, and other goodies for a picnic in the park.

60 North 100 West. ☎ *435-259-4295. Reservations recommended. Main courses: $14–$32. DISC, MC, V. Open: Daily 5:30–10 p.m. Closed Dec–Jan.*

Eddie McStiff's Restaurant and Microbrewery
$–$$ Moab   AMERICAN/ITALIAN

You find a baker's dozen of brews to wash down the pizzas, burgers, ribs, and steaks that keep the locals happy at Utah's oldest legal brewery. There are specials every night, but do you really need one with a menu that offers 22 pizza toppings, ten different pasta entrees, and smoked dinners ranging from Jack Daniels Beef Short Ribs to a hickory smoked salmon dish? Kids are welcome here, as evidenced by their own menu.

57 South Main St. ☎ *435-259-2337. Main courses: $7–$15. AE, DISC, MC, V. Open: Daily 5 p.m. to midnight.*

Jailhouse Café
$–$$ Moab   BREAKFAST

The best breakfast in Moab is served in this renovated jailhouse or on its covered patio. From the Jailhouse Chorizo Scramble (three eggs scrambled with seasoned potatoes and chorizo sausage and topped with sour cream and fresh salsa) to the Old-fashioned ginger pancakes with Dutch apple butter, this place serves an overwhelming breakfast. You won't leave hungry, and you may be able to skip lunch.

101 North Main St. ☎ *435-259-3900. Main courses: $ 4.95–$7.95. MC, V. Open: Daily 7 a.m. to noon. Closed Nov to early March.*

Slickrock Café
$–$$ Moab   AMERICAN/SOUTHWESTERN

Innovative courses, great atmosphere, central location, and cold drinks — What else can you want? This reliable restaurant features some of Utah's best microbrews on tap, and the menu is diverse and tasty but not the epitome of fine dining. The lunch menu features the usual burgers and sandwiches, but you can also enjoy a delicious chicken breast sandwich with a Southwestern marinade. For dinner, try the center-cut pork loin with a red and green pepper sauce with cilantro and tequila.

5 North Main St. ☎ *435-259-8004. Main courses: $4.25–$7.50 breakfast; $6.25–$8.25 lunch; $8.75–$14.75 dinner. AE, MC, V. Open: Daily 7 a.m.–10 p.m. Closed Dec–Feb.*

Fast Facts: Arches

Area Code
☎ 435.

ATM
Located in most banks and at City Market, 425 South Main St., Moab.

Emergency
☎ 911.

Fees
$10 per vehicle per week; $5 per person on foot or bicycle.

Fishing License
No fishing in the park.

Hospitals/Clinics
Allen Memorial Hospital, 719 West 400 North, Moab; ☎ 435-259-7191.

Information
Superintendent, Arches National Park, P.O. Box 907, Moab, UT 84532-0907; ☎ 435-719-2299 or 435-719-2319 (TTY).

Lost and Found
Arches Visitor Center; ☎ 435-719-2200.

Pharmacies
Walker Drug, 290 South Main St., Moab (☎ 435-259-5959); and City Market, 425 South Main St., Moab.

Post Office
50 East 100 North, Moab.

Road Conditions and Weather
☎ 800-492-2400.

Taxes
12.25% lodging in Moab, 9% lodging outside the city; 8.75% meals.

Time Zone
Mountain standard time.

Web Site
www.nps.gov/arch.

Chapter 11

Cape Cod National Seashore

. . . .

In This Chapter

▶ Introducing the seashore

▶ Planning your assault on the cape

▶ Exploring the cape's natural and manmade wonders

▶ Finding the best hotels, cottages, and restaurants

. . . .

*W*ith a well-placed phone call or the right Internet address, you can order a canned clambake to savor anywhere in the United States — probably anywhere in the world for that matter. But the 5-gallon cans that are crammed with clams, lobsters, and corn-on-the-cob and are packed in moist seaweed don't contain a gust of the salty, humid air that you find only on the coast.

Dangling in the Atlantic on a 70-mile-long spit of sand off the Massachusetts coast, the Cape Cod National Seashore wraps sun, surf, sand, and humid breezes (not to mention clams and lobsters) into one neat, tidy package — which is tied up with congestion. After all, this area is the Northeast, and Cape Cod is the greatest beach magnet around: More than 4.8 million folks head to the national seashore every year.

A trip to the beach is supposed to be an ordeal, right? You spend hours in a car inching along behind thousands of other tourists heading to the same place, and you spend even more time after you arrive searching for a parking spot. Then you haul your sand chairs, blanket, beach umbrella, and cooler down to the beach, where you waste another 30 minutes looking for the perfect 10-square-foot patch of sand that's close, but not too close, to the high-tide line.

Yes, this ordeal is all part of the Cape Cod National Seashore experience. Accept it. When you glance at a map and see the cape's location (within a relatively short drive of Boston), you'll understand why this park isn't a remote wilderness like Yellowstone, Olympic, or Death Valley national parks. This 40-mile-long sandbox is largely an urban creature, complete with towns, villages, people, and automobiles.

But with more than 43,000 acres, the Cape Cod National Seashore offers plenty of room for you to get away from the hustle. You can explore mile after idyllic mile of mostly deserted beaches, sand dunes on the cape's north and south ends, and marshlands perfect for canoeing. You can tour historic lighthouses that guided whaling ships to the cape's safe harbors and swim in freshwater ponds — I call them small lakes. You can stand on windswept bluffs and gaze out to sea in the same way that 19th-century wives did when waiting for their whaling husbands to return home. Perhaps best of all, after a day on the beach, you can stroll through quaint coastal towns and then settle down for a meal of seafood brought ashore the same afternoon.

Don't complain about the midday traffic jams. Think instead about how wonderful a lobster dinner with an appetizer of littleneck clams will taste because the seafood comes fresh from the ocean, not from a can.

Plan to spend two days minimum at Cape Cod National Seashore so you can pass one day at a beach and another exploring Provincetown and elsewhere.

There's no two ways about it — Cape Cod is most enjoyable during the height of summer when the weather is warmest and the water refreshing. Of course, the cape is also the most crowded during this season. If you're adept at negotiating heavy traffic and don't mind crowds, July and August are definitely the months for a visit. Fall can also be enjoyable. September and October attract fewer crowds than does the height of summer. Plus, the water — in freshwater ponds and in the Atlantic — is still warm enough for swimming. Overall, fall weather is warmer and dryer than spring. Winters on the cape can be brutal; many seasonal businesses in Eastham and Provincetown close at this time.

Must-see Attractions

Cape Cod National Seashore is more than a one-stop vacation. Each beach has its own personality; the park has century-old maritime attractions to check out; and the quaint, colorful towns are fun to explore. I won't tell you where to begin, but you may want to add the following places to your to-do list:

- **Coast Guard Beach:** This beach is one of the best on the seashore. Native Americans lived here more than 5,000 years ago, and on November 9, 1620, a group of religious refugees known as Pilgrims landed here on the first stop of their New World tour.

- **Fort Hill area:** Two towering whale jawbones frame a 19th-century clapboard home built by Captain Edward Penniman, who went to sea as an 11-year-old cook and became a captain at the age of 29. Behind the home is a fine nature trail with a view of the Atlantic Ocean.

✔ **Provincetown:** Anchoring the tip of the cape, this eclectic, artsy town features wonderful restaurants and curious shops. Provincetown is the launching point for many whale-watching cruises and is also the most crowded town on the cape in the middle of summer.

✔ **Race Point:** This spot on the cape's northern end boasts a great beach (particularly good for swimmers and shell collectors) and a good museum that traces the history of the U.S. Lifesaving Service.

✔ **Salt Pond and Nauset Marsh:** At Salt Pond, you find the park's best visitor center with loads of books and exhibits on the cape's maritime history. You can also view a short film about local geology. Nearby is the actual Salt Pond (a 40-foot-deep kettle hole created by the glaciers that sculpted the cape) and Nauset Marsh, which has a walking trail.

At press time, the Salt Pond Visitor Center was scheduled to be closed for a period of 12 to 16 months beginning in October 2002. A temporary facility will be available in the vicinity during this time.

Getting There

I have good news and bad news about getting to Cape Cod National Seashore. The good news is that one main road leads onto the cape and one main road traverses the cape. However, the bad news is that one main road leads onto the cape and one main road traverses the cape. (Secondary routes do funnel onto the cape and down its length, but these routes are narrow and easily become congested.)

If you drive on or off the cape during summer weekends (particularly on holidays), you'll be mired in a traffic jam measured in miles. Lots of miles. Fifteen-mile-long backups have occurred during the July 4th weekend. You can get the latest traffic updates, as well as tips on avoiding congestion and construction, by calling **SmarTraveler** (☎ **617-374-1234;** Internet: www.smartraveler.com). This service also provides updates on parking logistics at the lots that serve the island ferries.

Driving in

Now that the warnings are out of the way, if you drive to the seashore from Boston, head for Massachusetts 3, which leads to the Sagamore Bridge that crosses the Cape Cod Canal at Sagamore. After you cross this towering suspension bridge, you can choose between taking Route 6 and Route 6A. Both roadways lead in the same direction — towards Provincetown — but they're a world apart in terms of getting from point A to point B.

Route 6 starts out as a divided, well-maintained, four-lane expressway that runs to the middle of the cape near Orleans, where it briefly turns into a two-laner before resuming life as a four-lane highway that runs on to Provincetown. **Route 6A,** known locally as Old King's Highway, is dotted with traffic lights and fraught with nips and tucks that force you to putter along from Bourne to Orleans.

Routes 6 and 6A merge at Orleans into **Route 6,** which easily and quickly bogs down in traffic. I wish I could tell you how to avoid this mess, but this route is the only route up the cape.

If you drive from Providence, Rhode Island, take Interstate 95 to Route 25 and then cross the canal at Buzzards Bay via the Bourne Bridge. When you reach Bourne, you can either continue on **Route 28** (which runs south to Hyannis Port, veers back to the east and along the cape, and then arrives at Orleans and merges with 6 and 6A) or enter the Bourne Rotary and follow the signs to Route 6 on the east side of the Sagamore Bridge.

Figure on spending two hours driving from either Boston or Providence to Hyannis, and about seven hours from New York City. After you cross onto the cape, plan on spending another 1 to 1½ hours (depending on the traffic) to reach Provincetown.

You first access the national seashore at Orleans, where Beach Road leads to Orleans Beach. North of Orleans, you find seashore access off Route 6 in the towns of Eastham, Wellfleet, Truro, and Provincetown.

Flying in

You do have alternatives to driving to Cape Cod. From Boston's Logan International Airport, you can fly into Hyannis and Provincetown. In the New York City area, you can fly from LaGuardia or Newark Airports to Hyannis.

Airlines that serve Logan, LaGuardia, and Newark include **American, Continental, Delta, Northwest, United,** and **U.S. Airways.** Some of these airlines have local agreements with commuter lines, such as **Cape Air** (☎ 800-352-0714) and **Colgan Air** (☎ 800-428-4322), which offer connections to Provincetown and Hyannis's Barnstable Municipal Airport. Rental car agencies at the Hyannis Airport include **Avis, Hertz, Enterprise, Budget,** and **National.** Rental car agencies aren't available at the Provincetown Airport. See the Appendix for the toll-free numbers of the airlines and rental-car agencies.

Busing in

You can also bus your way onto the cape. **Bonanza Bus Lines** (☎ 888-751-8800 or 401-751-8800; Internet: www.bonanzabus.com) can get you from Boston's Logan Airport to Bourne, Falmouth, and Woods Hole.

Cape Cod National Seashore

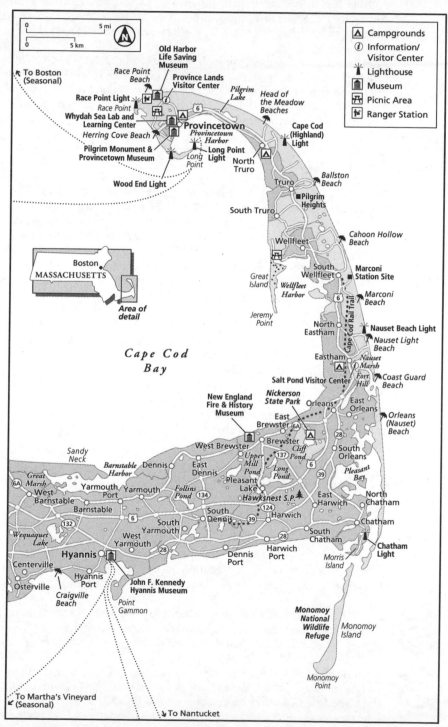

These towns are far from the national seashore, so you need to take another bus to your final destination. **The Cape Cod Regional Transit Authority** (☎ 800-352-7155; Internet: www.capecodtransit.org) runs buses year-round all over the cape. All buses provide bike racks.

Another bus company, **Plymouth & Brockton** (☎ 508- 746-0378; Internet: www.p-b.com), provides bus service from Logan to Hyannis via the Sagamore Bridge. On the cape, this company offers service to Yarmouth, Barnstable, Dennis, Harwich, Orleans, Eastham, Truro, Wellfleet, and Provincetown.

Boating in

Interested in a slower, more relaxing mode of transportation? Then take a ferry. **Bay State Cruises** (☎ 617-748-1428; Internet: www.baystatecruisecompany.com) offers daily round-trip express service from Boston to Provincetown from late May through mid-October. Round-trip fares for the 90-minute trip are $49 for adults and children ($29 one-way). A three-hour ferry runs on weekends from Memorial Day through Labor Day; round-trip fares are $30 per person ($15 one way). **Cape Cod Cruises** (☎ 800-242-2469 or 508-747-2400; Internet: www.provincetownferry.com) runs across Cape Cod Bay from Plymouth to Provincetown in about 90 minutes. These boats operate from late May into mid-September at a cost of $28 round-trip and $18 one-way. (The one-way fare isn't available in July and August.) **Boston Harbor Cruises** (☎ 877-733-9425 or 617-227-4321; Internet: www.bostonharborcruises.com) also serves Provincetown from Boston daily from Memorial Day weekend into October. Adult rates are $49 for a round-trip ($28 one-way), seniors and students cost $39 ($21 one-way), while kids under 12 cost $35 ($19 one-way).

Planning Ahead

How soon you need to start planning a trip to Cape Cod National Seashore depends on where you plan to stay. Interested in renting a house or cottage? I advise that you start making inquiring phone calls in January. (Keep in mind that some properties won't be available no matter how early you call, because many families return year after year to the same places, making them unavailable to others.)

Even though rental prices may initially put you off — a week at a small cottage can easily cost $1,000 or more — remember that you'll save money by eating in the rental as opposed to going out for every meal.

To find out what's available, check with local real estate agencies. (See "Where to Stay," later in this chapter, for listings.) You can also contact the **Cape Cod Chamber of Commerce** (☎ 888-332-2732 or 508-862-0700; Internet: www.capecodchamber.org). The Chamber of Commerce Web site lists information on house and cottage rentals, as well as camp-grounds and motels.

With motels and hotels, you can usually find a room a month or less in advance of your visit, although the room may not be as picturesque as you'd hoped. For the best selection, call early.

For general information about the seashore, write to Cape Cod National Seashore, 99 Marconi Station Site Rd., Wellfleet, MA 02667; or check the Internet at www.nps.gov/caco.

Learning the Lay of the Land

As you can see from the map in this chapter, Cape Cod resembles an arm trying to flex its biceps. Cape Cod National Seashore runs for 40 miles in a relatively thin swath from the "elbow" of the arm to the "fist." For the most part, the national seashore hugs the eastern coastline of the cape, although it crosses to the western side at Wellfleet and Provincetown.

From Orleans at midcape to Provincetown, the main access along the length of the national seashore is **Route 6.** You may come to dislike this narrow, congested highway, which is the only way to get from Nauset Beach in the south to Race Point in the north unless you walk along the beaches.

A series of **side roads** leads to the seashore's beaches off Route 6 between Eastham and Provincetown. Driveways hidden by trees and curves can make driving on these narrow, twisting creatures a challenge, so drive slowly and carefully when you're heading down one of them.

This seaside playground also has **off-road access.** Dune buggies and other off-road rigs that can handle sand have miles of beaches in the Truro-Provincetown area to play on. You need to buy a permit before you head off into the sand; seven-day ($40) and seasonal ($65) passes are available at the **Off-Road Permit Station** (☎ 508-487-3698) next to the Race Point Ranger Station in Provincetown between mid-April and mid-November. A limited number of permits are available, so don't wait until the last minute to get one. For information on permits, driving conditions, campgrounds, and any closures, call the permit station.

Cape Cod is very bike-friendly. The main artery of the Cape's bike system is the **Cape Cod Rail Trail,** which runs 26 miles between Dennis and Wellfleet. Along this route, the level trail passes many side roads that lead to the coast and Cape Cod Bay. You can even cobble together a 100-mile ride from Provincetown to the Charles River Bike Path in Boston via the trail and back roads. If you ride, keep in mind that children 12 and under must wear a helmet in Massachusetts — a good idea is that you always wear one, too.

Shifting sands

Once upon a time, Great Island was an island. Back in 1831, however, sands moved by the ocean connected the island to the mainland (near Wellfleet). Although the area's beauty alone is worth a visit, Great Island's history as a whaling outpost is equally interesting. In 1970, an archaeological dig discovered the foundations of an early 18th-century building, the Smith Tavern. A side trail takes you past the site, but no remains are visible today. (For details on this hike, see Great Island Trail under "Taking a hike," later in this chapter.)

The Park Service controls six beaches on the seashore — Coast Guard, Nauset Light, Marconi, Head of the Meadow, Race Point, and Herring Cove. Thanks to its out-of-the-way location, the **Head of the Meadow Beach** is probably the least visited of them all. **Marconi Beach** also offers some solitude. **Race Point Beach,** on the other hand, sees a lot of traffic thanks to its location close to Provincetown. **Coast Guard Beach** and **Nauset Light Beach** vie for the honor of busiest beach on the national seashore. All the beaches are wonderful spots for spending a morning or afternoon, but **Herring Cove Beach** is good for people who prefer calmer waters because waves on the bay side of the cape are more tranquil than the rollers tossed by the Atlantic onto the eastern shore. The water is also warmer on the bay side, and when the tide is out, the exposed mud flats are fun places for young kids to explore.

Arriving at the Seashore

Whether you arrive on Cape Cod by land, sea, or air, you'll want to get your national seashore bearings. So where do you head for information and maps? Read on.

Finding information

The seashore includes two visitor centers. For guidance on what's happening during your visit, stop by either facility to pick up the park's annual newspaper.

The **Salt Pond Visitor Center** (☎ 508-255-3421) is the park's main visitor center. Just off the Doane Road in Eastham, the visitor center is open daily (except Christmas) from 9 a.m. to 4:30 p.m., with longer summer hours. You can view short orientation films that touch on the cape's geology and whaling history, Henry David Thoreau's days on the cape, and Guglielmo Marconi's pioneer wireless radio station. The center also features a well-stocked bookstore and a museum that touches on the cape's natural and cultural history.

Set atop a dune roughly 100 feet above sea level, the **Province Lands Visitor Center** (☎ 508-487-1256) offers nice views of the surrounding dunes and the Atlantic Ocean from its 360-degree observation deck. The center is open daily from May through October, 9 a.m. to 5 p.m., and is located along Race Point Road in Provincetown. You can pick up a variety of park brochures and permits, and you can see the same movies that are shown at the Salt Pond center. You can also check out a good exhibit that details the Pilgrims' arrival in the New World.

For advance information, send a stamped, self-addressed, business-sized envelope to Superintendent, Cape Cod National Seashore, 99 Marconi Site Rd., Wellfleet, MA 02667, or call ☎ **508-349-3785.** You can also check the Internet at www.nps.gov/caco.

Paying fees

The Park Service collects **entrance fees** for beaches inside the national seashore from late June through early September when lifeguards are on duty, as well as on weekends and holidays from Memorial Day to late June and again from Labor Day through Columbus Day. Fees are $10 per vehicle per day; $3 per pedestrian or cyclist per day; and $30 for a seasonal pass, which provides access for one vehicle for an entire season. Of course, if you own a park pass, you don't have to pay the entrance fee; see Chapter 8 for information on the National Park Pass and Chapter 4 for the lowdown on Golden Age and Golden Access Passports.

Off-road vehicle permits are available for use on Cape Cod National Seashore's off-road driving corridor. (See "Learning the Lay of the Land," earlier in this chapter.) A seven-day permit costs $40 and a permit for mid-April through mid-November costs $65. Self-contained recreational vehicles may obtain a permit that allows for overnight stays for $110 from mid-April through mid-November. All permits are obtained through the Race Point Ranger Station in Provincetown. (See "Finding information," earlier in this chapter.)

Many beaches outside the park system are controlled by towns and open only to town residents and their guests, so ask your hosts if they own a **beach pass** that you can display on your vehicle.

Getting around

You can choose from a few options for getting around the cape. You can stick to the main roads with a car or, if you drive an SUV and purchase an off-road vehicle permit, you can explore the driving corridor along the cape's western beaches. Cyclists can take advantage of the 26-mile Cape Cod Rail Trail. For information on all these routes, see "Learning the Lay of the Land," earlier in this chapter.

You can also bus your way around the cape. **The Cape Cod Regional Transit Authority** (☎ **800-352-7155;** Internet: www.capecodtransit. org) runs buses year-round all over the cape. All buses provide bike racks. Another company, **Plymouth & Brockton** (☎ **508-746-0378;** Internet: www.p-b.com), provides service to Yarmouth, Barnstable, Dennis, Harwich, Orleans, Eastham, Truro, Wellfleet, and Provincetown.

Remembering Safety

Odds are, the worst injury that you'll incur during a vacation to the national seashore is a bad sunburn. Follow my tips for avoiding sunburn and these other problems:

- **Slather on the sunscreen.** A good sunscreen with a high SPF is the best defense again sunburn. Don't think that a single layer applied early in the day will work for the next 12 hours. Even products that claim to be waterproof should be reapplied after swimming. You especially need to pay attention to children in this regard, because they probably won't remind you to re-coat them after a swim.

- **Be aware of deer ticks.** The cape has tiny, pin-sized deer ticks, which can transmit Lyme disease. For information on how to avoid these critters, or deal with them if you find one, see Chapter 8.

- **Watch out for poison ivy.** This shiny, green three-leafed cluster is ubiquitous and potent. If you so much as brush past poison ivy, the plant's oil is likely to give you an itchy rash. Also, clothing that collects the oil during hikes can transmit it to your skin. If you think that you've been in contact with the plant, wash with soap immediately to keep any remaining oil from spreading. Calamine lotion, which is readily available over the counter at all pharmacies, helps sooth the itching.

For additional tips on how to ensure a safe visit to a national park, see Chapter 8.

Enjoying the Seashore

Cape Cod National Seashore is a rich mixture of two environments — one natural and one manmade. To make the most of your visit, take advantage of both worlds by exploring the coastline with its beaches, dunes, and marshes as well as the quaint fishing villages.

Unless you plan strategically, you find that life practically stands still on Cape Cod anytime between Memorial Day and Labor Day. If you visit on the Fourth of July and need to get somewhere in five minutes, accept the fact that you're going to be late. You can get around the summer crowds, though, if you travel to your day's destination by 9 a.m. and head back home during midafternoon.

Cell phone pioneer

Near South Wellfleet, one stretch of barren, windswept bluff overlooking the Atlantic Ocean is the famous site where Italian Guglielmo Marconi, in 1903, transmitted the first wireless communication between the United States and Europe. The message, sent January 18, 1903, by Morse code, was from President Theodore Roosevelt to King Edward VII of England. Marconi's station was dismantled in 1917, but in its place is an observation platform with views of the ocean and Cape Cod Bay. The bluff is due east of the park headquarters, 6 miles north of the Salt Pond Visitor Center, off Route 6. Signs point the way from Route 6. To get to the site, take the Atlantic White Cedar Swamp Trail listed under "Taking a hike," later in this chapter.

Exploring the top attractions

Coast Guard Beach

Coming to the seashore to swim? Then Coast Guard Beach should definitely be one of your stops. With nice sandy beaches, windswept dunes, and bracing water, this beach is one of the best on the national seashore for swimming. Lifeguards patrol the waters throughout the busy summer season. And don't worry about getting sandy, because the beach provides showers and restrooms. But you don't have to swim; many folks simply like to hike up and down this beach to admire the setting. History buffs can revel in the historic Coast Guard Station.

The beach's small parking lot is reserved for handicapped visitors during the summer months. Other beach-goers must park at the Little Creek parking area where you can ride a free shuttle bus to the beach. Although the shuttle may sound inconvenient, the buses run frequently and the ride is short.

Coast Guard Beach is near the Salt Pond Visitor Center in Eastham.

Fort Hill area

You can find a mix of maritime history and seashore wilderness in the Fort Hill area. The stately Captain Penniman House (built in the French Second Empire style for all you architectural buffs) with its whale jawbone arch is the area's most prominent structure, but the captain wasn't the first person to call this part of the cape home. Native Americans lived in the area for thousands of years, and Pilgrims settled in the area in 1644. Beyond the Penniman House, interpretive trails wind through open fields and white cedar, red maple, and oak forests to the edge of Nauset Marsh and a view of the Atlantic. (See Fort Hill Trail/Red Maple Swamp Trail under "Taking a hike," later in this chapter.) If you're curious about the name Fort Hill, you're not alone; historians aren't exactly sure how it came about.

The Fort Hill area is in Eastham just off Route 6 about a mile north of the Orleans–Eastham rotary.

Lighthouses

The cape's legacy as a whaling and fishing port includes the six lighthouses that overlook the ocean between Chatham and Race Point. If you have some nautical blood in your veins or even if you're a land lubber, you may want to visit each of the lighthouses. From the bottom of the cape to the top, the lighthouses include Chatham Light, which dates from 1878; Nauset Beach Light; Highland Light, an active tower on the sea cliffs near Truro since 1798; Race Point Light, which requires a good walk several miles down Race Point Beach to reach it; and Wood End and Long Point lights, both in Provincetown Bay on an island accessible by an hourly boat from MacMillan Wharf.

Provincetown

Provincetown, without a doubt, is the most colorful town on Cape Cod. Thanks to its narrow, crooked streets, the town is also the most crowded — especially on weekends when Bostonians come over for the day. A long-time artistic community, Provincetown is chock-full of art galleries, restaurants, and gift shops. Head to **MacMillan Wharf** if you're interested in taking a whale-watching cruise or looking for a fishing boat (see "Keeping active," later in this chapter) or if you want to see artifacts salvaged from the pirate ship *Whydah* (see "Escaping the rain," later in this chapter).

Before the artists arrived, Provincetown was a whaling community that originated in the early 1700s. By 1880, the tiny community was the richest town (per capita) in Massachusetts and the third largest whaling port in the world. Today, you can look back into the town's maritime past at the **Pilgrim Monument & Provincetown Museum.** (See "Escaping the rain," later in this chapter, for details.)

Provincetown is off Route 6 at the northern end of the cape.

Shipwreck central

Despite the cape's many lighthouses, more than 3,000 recorded shipwrecks have occurred off Cape Cod. The first noted one in this long history was the *Sparrowhawk* wreck in 1626. The shallow *shoals* (sandbars, basically) that lie several hundred yards off the cape are the cause of these wrecks. In 1786, the situation prompted the organization of the Massachusetts Humane Society to provide rescue teams. Among the society's early accomplishments was the construction of a series of huts along the outer cape for sheltering crews. Later, the society added lifeboat stations and surfboats that were used to rescue crews from the sea.

Race Point

Wonderful for swimming, the beach at Race Point provides a great vantage point for watching sunsets and spotting whales in the spring. Race Point also features a visitor center (see "Finding information," earlier in this chapter) and the **Old Harbor Life Saving Station,** built in Chatham in 1897. The U.S. Coast Guard ran the station until it was decommissioned in 1944; the station was moved to its present location in 1977. Highlights include rescue equipment dating from the turn of the century and a rescue boat used a half-century ago. You can also see a re-enactment of the *breeches buoy system,* a suspension system employed to haul people off ships (in what looks like a cut-off pair of pants) that were stranded in the surf. Consult the park's newspaper for the station's hours, which tend to fluctuate.

Race Point is off Route 6 at the northern end of the cape.

Salt Pond and Nauset Marsh

The Salt Pond area is visitor central. You can find the best visitor center on the national seashore, hiking trails along the marsh, and the Nauset Bike Trail that winds down to Coast Guard Beach. The 1½-mile Fort Hill Trail (see "Taking a hike," later in this chapter) roams along the pond's shore and an edge of Nauset Marsh, and the kid-friendly, ¼-mile Buttonbush Trail tests kids' senses. Along this paved loop, you find interpretive panels (which also feature Braille characters) that discuss the plants and wildlife found on the trail. If you spend time at Salt Pond, you discover that the pond isn't really a pond at all, but rather a tidal basin that rises and falls twice a day as tides flow through Nauset Marsh. Birdlovers know that Salt Pond lures various species of ducks, Great Blue Herons, and Snowy Egrets.

The visitor center and trail access is north of downtown Eastham off Route 6.

Taking a hike

For stretching your legs, you can find mile after mile of secluded beach — on the ocean and bay sides — and a few designated trails.

Atlantic White Cedar Swamp Trail

This trail is historically significant as well as scenic. The path leads you into a stand of White Cedar (prized by Native Americans for building canoes) and to the Marconi Station Site (see the "Cell phone pioneer" sidebar, earlier in this chapter). A stretch of boardwalk keeps you above the deep peat bogs.

Distance: 1¼ miles. Level: Easy. Access: Marconi Station Site.

Capturing the seashore on film

Carrying a camera with you? Make sure that you bring plenty of film because Cape Cod National Seashore and its surrounding towns offer oodles of photo opportunities. If wildlife is what you're after, you can find feathered subjects waiting in Nauset Marsh next to the Salt Pond Visitor Center. The cape's lighthouses, of course, make wonderful images (particularly because they stay still for the camera!). Visit a fishing port to find charming architecture as well as colorful boats. I like to head to the Chatham docks in late afternoon when the fishing boats return with their catches; the swarming seagulls looking to steal a bite are great subjects.

For artsy beach shots, head to the parabolic dunes area east of Provincetown. I took one of my best shots of the cape on the Fourth of July. After an afternoon whale-watching cruise, we returned to port near sundown and stayed on the boat to watch the fireworks explode over Provincetown. The resulting pictures — the sunset coming down on P-town and the fireworks — were outstanding.

Beech Forest Trail

This trail on the cape's northern tip rolls up and down through a beech forest. Along the way, you pass a small pond and dunes that are slowly but surely enveloping a section of the forest. This area is great for youngsters to burn off some energy.

Distance: 1 mile. Level: Easy. Access: In Provincetown, turn right at the light on Race Point Road and head a ½ mile to the Beech Forest parking lot.

Fort Hill Trail/Red Maple Swamp Trail

The 1½-mile Fort Hill loop trail that begins behind the Captain Penniman House winds through red cedar and along Nauset Marsh to Skiff Hill. Along the trail, you have good views of the marsh and Atlantic Ocean beaches, and you even come across an old Indian sharpening stone. Birders love this trail because the marsh is a favorite of great blue herons and egrets. Connected to the Fort Hill Trail is a ½-mile boardwalk loop, the Red Maple Swamp Trail, which is one of my favorites and one that kids enjoy. You can look for frogs, turtles, woodpeckers, and catbirds. Remember to apply your bug repellent because the mosquitoes are ravenous.

Distance: 2 miles. Level: Easy. Access: Penniman House, Fort Hill Rd. off Route 6 in Eastham.

Great Island Trail

The longest hike on the seashore, the Great Island Trail provides refuge from the crowds and shows off the seashore's version of wilderness. From the parking lot, the trail winds its way through marsh and woods and across soft beach sand, tidal flats, and dunes. The walk traces the outer edge of the Wellfleet Harbor and ambles along sandy stretches between the elevated areas of Great Island and Great Beach Hill; the higher elevations offer you great views through the pitch pine forest of Cape Cod Bay. At one point, a side trail (which hooks back up with the main path) passes a site where a tavern once stood in the late 1600s and early 1700s.

If you embark on this hike, plan on at least three hours and make sure to take water and sunscreen. And if you plan to trek to the tip of Jeremy Point, check with a park ranger to make sure that the tide is on the way out because this part of the island becomes submerged at high tide. If the tide is coming in, hike at least out to Great Beach Hill, where you get great views of the slowly submerging point as well as Cape Cod Bay and Wellfleet Harbor.

Near the trailhead is a picnic ground, so you can hike early in the morning with plans for lunch on your return.

Distance: 8 miles round-trip. Level: Moderate due to soft sand. Access: Beach parking lot off Chequessett Neck Road in Wellfleet.

One-day wonder

As nasty as the traffic flow and parking can be on the cape, you really don't want to frustrate yourself by making an all-encompassing sweep of the national seashore in one day. Still, you can follow a relatively easy path that uncorks the essence of Cape Cod National Seashore. (Unless otherwise noted, see "Exploring the top attractions," earlier in this chapter, for information on the attractions in this section.)

Start early — by 8:30 a.m. at least. Pack a picnic lunch and head to the Little Creek parking area to catch the free shuttle to **Coast Guard Beach** east of Eastham. By arriving early, you can select a great spot on the beach instead of having to search far and wide for an opening in the beach blanket maze that begins to build by midmorning.

Several hours at the beach should give you plenty of time for a swim or two in the surf and some time to construct a sand castle. Shortly before noon, head 14 miles north to **Great Island** off the Chequessett Neck Road west of Wellfleet, a picturesque town noted for its art galleries. Enjoy a picnic lunch near the trailhead of Great Island Trail.

After lunch (and perhaps after a stroll through some of the art galleries in Wellfleet), return to Route 6 and head 4½ miles north to Truro, where you want to turn right onto North Pamet Road for a 1½-mile ride to the **Pamet Area Bearberry Hill Overlook.** Long ago, this area was part of a large cranberry operation that was abandoned in the 1950s. From the overlook, you enjoy great views of the Atlantic Ocean and the Pamet Valley.

Spotting the local wildlife

Despite the somewhat urban setting, Cape Cod and the national seashore harbor an incredibly diverse number of animals that creep, crawl, swim, and flutter.

The cape has numerous **forest animals.** Raccoon, skunk, red fox, and even coyote prowl throughout the pine forests. Weasels, river otters, and mink live in the area, too. Rabbits — New England cottontails and the snowshoe hare — run rampant over the cape. And enough white-tailed deer live on Cape Cod for some people to justify a fall hunting season.

Thanks to its location along the Atlantic flyway and to numerous marshes, wetlands, and freshwater ponds, Cape Cod is a magnet for **migratory birds.** If you spent a season counting them, you'd wind up with more than 350 species and thousands and thousands of individuals. The biggest bird turnout begins in midsummer, when adult shorebirds (such as terns and sandpipers) migrate to the cape for a few months. By the time October and November roll around, hawks and waterfowl are added to the mix. You can spot birds throughout the year ranging from herons, egrets, osprey, and terns to songbirds, ducks, snow geese, avocets, and endangered piping plovers. See "Keeping active" in this chapter for information on birding locations.

Regular visitors to the seashore include **harbor and grey seals,** but they mostly turn up in the winter months. These furry creatures, which sometimes arrive as early as September or October, can often be seen at low tide just off shore. A good spot to spy them is the tip of Nauset Spit along Coast Guard Beach. Better yet, make a trip to Monomoy Island in late winter, when thousands of harbor seals often turn up for a break from Maine's rougher coastal weather. (See "Keeping active" in this chapter for information on cruises to Monomoy Island, which is also a popular spot for bird-watching.)

At Provincetown's MacMillan Wharf, you can board a boat for a whale-watching cruise to Stellwagen Bank — one of my family's favorite destinations. This relatively shallow spot in the Atlantic north of Provincetown attracts **whales** who come to Stellwagen Bank to feast on schooling fishes. Seeing whales come up for air near the side of your boat is an experience you won't soon forget. (I wonder about the ice water that must have flowed through the veins of the 19th-century whalers who hunted these leviathans from rowboats lowered from their ships.) On these trips, you can spot humpback, minke, and finback whales. Right whales, one of the world's most endangered whale species, also show up from time to time. See "Keeping active" in this chapter for information on whale-watching cruises.

Next, head to **Race Point,** the northernmost part of the Cape. The 13-mile drive north from Truro along Route 6 is particularly beautiful, as dunes rim the road. To the west of Route 6, tidy cottages are backed by Cape Cod Bay, and to the east is Pilgrim Lake, ringed by even bigger sand dunes. In Race Point, you can stroll the beach looking for intriguing shells and surf-polished stones, walk through the Beech Forest, and visit the Old Harbor Life Saving Museum. In spring, you can scan the Atlantic with hopes of spying migrating whales.

By now, you've had quite a full day and no doubt are ready for dinner, either back in your cottage or at one of the cape's great lobster houses.

Ranger programs

Cape Cod National Seashore offers so many ranger-led activities during the summer that choosing one is difficult. You can fish the surf during a two-hour class offered at Coast Guard Beach (meet at the guard station), or you can harvest some of the bay's clams during a demonstration at the Salt Pond Visitor Center. History buffs can sign up for a tour of the Captain Edward Penniman House at Fort Hill. These programs are just a few of the many options available.

Keep in mind that ranger programs are offered only from mid-May to Columbus Day in October. And because the programs rotate through-out the season and from year to year, the programs in this section may not be available during your visit. To find out what's happening when you're at the seashore, pick up a copy of the park newspaper at one of the visitor centers. (See "Finding information," earlier in this chapter, for locations.) Also keep in mind that some programs, such as canoe trips, require advance reservations and fees.

If you have kids, make sure to pick up information on the Junior Ranger Program (see Chapter 4) at the visitor center.

Some of the best ranger programs at the national seashore include:

- ✔ **Canoeing Nauset Marsh:** This program is one of my favorites. You must sign up in advance at the Salt Pond Visitor Center for this two-hour tour. The tours are popular, so take advantage of the seven-day advance reservations. (The tours are also buggy, so be sure to bring some insect repellent along.) The cost is $20 adult, $12 ages 6 to 12; 5 and under are not allowed on the trip.

- ✔ **Art in the Dunes:** If you're an art buff, sign up at the Province Lands Visitor Center for this program. Participants hike across the dunes to meet an artist-in-residence. You can pick up helpful tips for dealing with lighting conditions while appreciating the natural environment that has made the northern end of the cape a magnet for artists.

- ✔ **A retro-rescue:** Ongoing for more than two decades, this Cape Cod classic reenacts an historic surf rescue at Race Point Beach below the Province Lands Visitor Center. The hour-long program is set in 1902 and shows how the U.S. Livesaving Service used now-antique equipment to rescue ships and people.

✔ **Exploring history:** You can take a walking tour that explores Provincetown's history and some of its notable residents, such as playwright Eugene O'Neill, who wrote some of his works at his home at Peaked Hill Bars, a converted Coast Guard Station. Call the **Pilgrim Monument & Provincetown Museum** (☎ 508-487-1310) for details and reservations. Tickets cost $5 per person, young or old.

✔ **End of a perfect day:** This 90-minute-long program at Herring Cove Beach features a campfire on the beach and, of course, a setting sun over Cape Cod Bay. At Nauset Light Beach and Ballston Beach in Truro, rangers hold campfire talks about the natural and historic resources of the cape. *Warning:* Rangers have been known to burst into song.

Keeping active

Whether your preferences for an active vacation include working up a sweat on a bike or at the beach, you can probably find your desired activity on Cape Cod. For many of your equipment needs, aside from bike rentals, check out the **Goose Hummock Outdoor Center** (☎ 508-255-2620 or 508-255-0455) on Route 6A in Orleans. This outfitter can prepare you for just about anything, including canoeing, kayaking, and fishing. Activities that you may want to try on the cape include:

✔ **Beachcombing:** The national seashore includes six developed beaches: Coast Guard Beach, Nauset Light Beach, Marconi Beach, Head of the Meadow Beach, Race Point Beach, and Herring Cove Beach. Each one offers lifeguard supervision during the summer season as well as changing facilities, restrooms, and cold showers. To avoid the crowds — Coast Guard and Nauset Light Beaches are the busiest — head to the beach early in the morning or late in the afternoon (say around 3 p.m.). See "Learning the Lay of the Land," earlier in this chapter, for some information on the individual beaches.

✔ **Biking:** Three designated bike trails, ranging in difficulty and length, meander through sections of the national seashore. The just over 1½-mile **Nauset Trail** is a handy option for getting to the beach without worrying about scrambling for a parking spot. This course runs through pine and oak forests from the Salt Pond Visitor Center to Coast Guard Beach. Another ride, the **Province Lands Bike Trail,** is a hilly 5-mile loop that passes through hardwood forests and near freshwater ponds from the time it starts and ends at the Province Lands Visitor Center. This route is the seashore's most enjoyable ride, with spurs running to Herring Cove Beach (just over 1 mile, one-way), Race Point Beach (½ mile, one-way) and Bennett Pond (¼ mile, one-way). You can easily spend a morning or afternoon on this trail. The third option is the **Head of the Meadow Trail,** 2 relatively flat miles one-way along an old road bed between Pilgrim Lake and Head of the Meadow Beach. You have to pay a fee to leave your car at Head of the Meadow Beach, so park at High Head, just south of Pilgram Lake along Route 6, on the other end of the trail. High Head doesn't charge a parking fee, but space is limited, so arrive early in the morning or late in the afternoon.

If you're intested in a longer ride, check out the 26-mile **Cape Cod Rail Trail.** (See "Learning the Lay of the Land," earlier in this chapter, for information.)

If you want to ride but left your bike at home, go to one of the rental shops on the cape. In Provincetown, you can rent bikes at **Arnold's** (☎ 508-487-0844), **Galeforce Bike Rentals** (☎ 508-487-4849), **Nelson's Bike Rental** (☎ 508-487-8849), or **Provincetown Bikes** (☎ 508-487-8735). In Eastham, try **Idle Times Bike Rental** (☎ 508-255-8281) or **Little Capistrano Bike Shop** (☎ 508-255-6515). In the Wellfleet area, try **Black Duck Sport Shop** (☎ 508-349-9801) or another location of **Idle Times Bike Rental** (☎ 508-349-9161).

When riding your bike, wear a helmet. In Massachusetts, children 12 and under must wear one, and you want to be a good example for your kids, right?

✔ **Bird-watching:** Good spots for bird-watching on the cape include the Beech Forest Trail, Fort Hill Overlook, Nauset Marsh, and Sandwich's Great Marsh, and all the beaches. To keep track of your sightings, pick up a bird list at one of the visitor centers. (See "Finding information," earlier in this chapter, for center locations.) You can also join the Wellfleet Bay Wildlife chapter of the **National Audubon Society** (☎ 508-349-2615) on a summer bird-watching trip to Monomoy Island, a 2,750-acre spit of land located south of Chatham (and accessible only by boat) that teems with bird life. The tour, which starts with a 10-minute boat ride from Chatham, runs 3 hours and costs $35.

✔ **Fruit picking:** You and your kids can spend an hour or so picking fruit at one of the "pick your own" farms scattered about the cape. At **Tony Andrews Farm** (☎ 508-548-5257) in East Falmouth, the kids can pick strawberries while you work on the beans and tomatoes. Over in Barnstable Village, blueberries are the crop of choice at **Blueberry Hill Farm** (☎ 508-362-3781).

✔ **Whale-watching:** Join a trip that includes a naturalist from the **Center for Coastal Studies** (☎ 508-487-3622, Internet: www. coastalstudies.org). This Provincetown-based organization conducts long-term whale studies. Having one of their representatives on your boat is invaluable in terms of whale identification (they can distinguish not only species but individual whales). Their representatives work with **Dolphin Fleet** (☎ 800-826-9300 or 508-349-1900; Internet: www.whalewatch.com), one of the companies that head to Stellwagen Bank for three to four-hour whale-spotting cruises. The **Portugese Princess** (☎ 800-442-3188 or

508-487-2651; Internet: www.princesswhalewatch.com) also heads to Stellwagen Bank. These companies offer competitive pricing (usually around $20 for adults, free for kids under 7).

Escaping the rain

What do you do when it rains on Cape Cod, as it almost certainly will sometime during your vacation? Head indoors, of course. Scattered throughout Cape Cod you find quaint towns with quaint shops, museums, and, if you're really out of ideas, movie theaters.

Cape Cod tells a few pirate tales. At a small wharf-side museum in Provincetown, you can learn about the *Whydah,* a ship commanded by Sam Bellamy that sank off the cape in 1717 during a storm. Discovered in 1984, the shipwreck has given up more than 100,000 artifacts, including coins ("pieces of eight"), gold jewelry made in Africa, weapons, and nautical instruments. Many of these items are on display at **Expedition Whydah Sea Lab and Learning Center,** 16 MacMillan Wharf, Provincetown (☎ **877-WHYDAH1** or 508-487- 8899; Internet: www.whydah.com). Open daily from 10 a.m. to 7 p.m. during summer and early fall, weekends only in winter. Admission is $8 adults, $6 ages 6 to 12, and free ages 5 and under.

The **Pilgrim Monument & Provincetown Museum,** High Pole Hill (☎ **508-487-1310;** Internet: www.pilgrim-monument.org), traces the town's history with curious exhibits on such items as clay pipes found by beachcombers, souvenir snow domes, and antique aquarium ornaments. The museum also peeks into the life and writings of Eugene O'Neill, one of America's best-known playwrights, who lived in Provincetown. To find the museum, look across the Provincetown skyline for the 252-foot-tall Pilgrim Monument — you can't miss it. Open daily April through November, from 9 a.m. to 5 p.m. Admission is $6 for adults, $3 for ages 4 to 12, and free ages 3 and under.

Rain or shine, **antique hunters** flock to the Old King's Highway (Route 6A) between Orleans and Sandwich. While the going is decidedly slow on this meandering two-lane country road, shoppers find numerous stores selling everything from fine French antiques to 20th-century kitsch.

Where to Stay

Unlike many other national parks, Cape Cod National Seashore doesn't have lodging within its borders. You can find a place to stay in one of the cape's countless motels, hotels, or bed-and-breakfasts. Or you can crack open your piggy bank and rent a cottage or house. The diverse choices range from historic inns to run-of-the-mill motels. Whatever your preference, make sure to call months in advance of your visit. Calling in January for a summer visit isn't too early.

Top lodgings

Best Western Tides Beachfront

$$–$$$$$ **Provincetown**

Chain motels are usually reliable. With a great location away from the hubbub of Provincetown and right on Cape Cod Bay, this Best Western is no exception. Some of the rooms in the complex, which is situated on six acres, open right onto the 600-foot-wide beach. If you're not up for a swim in the salty bay, try the motel's pool. You also find a small restaurant for breakfast or lunch on the grounds. When making reservations, make sure to mention whether you're traveling with kids because ground-floor rooms are reserved for families.

837 Commercial St. ☎ *800-528-1234 or 508-487-1045. Internet:* www.bestwestern. com/tidesbeachfrontmotorinn. *64 rooms. A/C TV TEL. Rack rates: $79–$269 double; $199–$319 family units; $20–$50 extra adult; kids under 18 free. AE, CB, DC, DISC, MC, V. Closed mid-Oct to mid-May.*

Captain Freeman Inn

$$$–$$$$$ **Brewster**

Off-the-beaten-path, Brewster offers a slower, more bucolic experience than many of the towns clustered along Route 6; the town is a wonderful retreat after a day of battling crowds. The Captain Freeman Inn makes the extra few minutes it takes you to get to the seashore worth it. The "luxury" rooms come complete with a fireplace, private porch, and hot tub for two. And I can't forget the four-poster queen-size bed, TV/VCR, telephone with answering machine, and refrigerator stocked daily with refreshments. Regular double rooms are pretty nice, too. Each has a sitting area, canopy bed, and antique and Victorian-reproduction furniture. Delicious breakfasts are served in the elegant parlor or out on a screened porch overlooking a solar-heated pool and a lawn ready for an afternoon of croquet or badminton. Plus, Cape Cod Bay is just a short walk away. Stay during the off-season and participate in one of the inn's cooking schools.

15 Breakwater Rd. ☎ *800-843-4664 or 508-896-7481. Fax: 508-896-5618. Internet:* www. captainfreemaninn.com. *14 rooms. A/C TV TEL. Rack rates: June–Oct $150–$220 double; Nov–May $130–$190 double; $30 for third person. Rates include gourmet breakfast and loaner bicycles. No smoking. No children under 10. AE, MC, V.*

Chatham Town House Inn

$$$–$$$$$ **Chatham**

Nestled on two acres in the heart of the charming fishing village of Chatham, this spot commands a high price — but you won't be disappointed. The rooms are large and well-appointed, most with queen-size beds. Rooms with king beds also boast balconies. A buffet-style Continental breakfast comes with your room, as does a pool and Jacuzzi.

The property is a short walk from beaches, restaurants, shopping, and Friday night band concerts. For longer stays, you can rent one of two cottages — small houses, really — that sleep four and have kitchen and laundry facilities, even fireplaces.

11 Library Lane. ☎ *800-242-2180 or 508-945-2180. Internet:* www.chathamtown house.com. *23 rooms, 2 cottages. A/C, TV, TEL. Rack rates: $135–$350 double; $400–$450 cottage. Rates include breakfast. AE, CB, DC, DISC, MC, V.*

The Even'tide Motel & Cottages
$$–$$$ **South Wellfleet**

If you're bringing your entire family along, this retreat is the place to stay. The owners know how to treat families. Rooms are neat and clean and fairly attractive. Rooms come in four arrangements — with a queen bed, with a double and twin bed, with two double beds in a two-room suite, or as an efficiency. You find a small play area in the courtyard and a huge (and heated) indoor swimming pool for rainy days when you don't want to go outdoors. Although the highway runs by the front of the motel, you can head out the back door and walk onto the national seashore. A forest trail leads three-quarters of a mile to Marconi Beach. The cottages are set in the woods right by the Cape Cod Rail Trail.

Route 6 (mileage marker 98). ☎ *508-349-3410. Fax: 508-349-7804. Internet:* www.eventidemotel.com. *31 rooms, 8 cottages. A/C TV TEL. Rack rates: $59–$140 double, $15 extra adult, $8 extra child; cottages $650–$1175 weekly, $90 extra child or adult. AE, DC, DISC, MC, V. Closed late Oct to March.*

Kadee's Gray Elephant
$$$ **Orleans**

Elegant? No. Comfortable? Very much so. And the location in the heart of Orleans is charming. The price is reasonable, too, but with only six rooms, this old farmhouse fills quickly. Each room is whimsically decorated with bright paintings, stencils, and quilts. Not only do they welcome children here, but they also feature a miniature golf course on the premises. Kadee's Lobster and Clam Bar, a well-worn spot on the premises, is a great, reliable place for dinner. Nauset Beach is close to the inn — about 1½ miles down the road.

216 Main St. ☎ *508-255-7608. Fax: 508-240-2976. 6 rooms. A/C TV . Rack rates: $110–$130 double; $750 weekly. $25 for cot in room; cribs free. No smoking. MC, V.*

Kalmar Village
$$$–$$$$$ **North Truro**

Life moves at a slightly slower pace in this village of white cottages and green lawns just south of Provincetown. You can spend the evenings barbecuing and socializing with your neighbors while your kids build sand castles on the private beach or splash in the outdoor pool. The efficiencies rent by the night, whereas the cozy, 1950s-style cottages, which accommodate four or six people, rent by the week during the high season. The efficiences have kitchenettes with a microwave and cooktop stove, while the cottages have full kitchens. On the downside, the village doesn't get much shade, but you can always head into the bay or the pool to escape the heat.

674 Shore Rd. (Route 6A). ☎ *508-487-0585, call 617-247-0211 in winter. Internet:* www.kalmarvillage.com. *15 efficiencies, 40 cottages. TV; A/C in some. Rack rates: Efficiencies $750 double weekly, $75 extra child or adult, cribs free; cottages $1200–$1500 weekly, $120 extra child or adult. DISC, MC, V. Closed Nov to early May.*

Runner-up lodgings

Blue Dolphin Inn

$$–$$$$ **North Eastham** This inexpensive motel doesn't have a waterfront, but it's centrally located and has a swimming pool, shuffleboard, and access to the Cape Cod Rail Trail. *Route 6 East (6 miles north of the Orleans Rotary).* ☎ *508-255-1159 or 800-654-0504. Internet:* www.bluedolphincapecod.com.

Blue Sea Motor Inn

$$–$$$$ **North Truro** A short ride from both Provincetown and the national seashore, this budget-minded motel offers rooms as well as efficiency units and an indoor heated pool. *696 Shore Rd. (Route 61).* ☎ *508-487-1041 or 888-768-7666. Internet:* www.blueseamotorinn.com.

Chatham Highlander Motel

$$–$$$ **Chatham** The Highlander is set on a knoll on the edge of town. The rooms are clean and comfortable, while outside on the motel's 3 acres are two heated pools and colorful gardens. *946 Main St.* ☎ *508-945-9038. Internet:* www.realmass.com/highlander.

Pilgrim Colony Inn

$$$–$$$$ **North Truro** On the dune-surrounded outskirts of North Truro, and just a short ride from Provincetown, this beachfront inn with six cottages is a surprising find. *670 Shore Rd.* ☎ *508-349-8072 or 866-349-RENT. Internet:* www.pilgrimcolony.com.

Top cottages and houses

Growing up in New Jersey meant that I spent two weeks every summer on the coast in a house we'd rent just blocks from the ocean. The traditional way to organize a Cape Cod vacation is to rent a place of your own for a week or two. You can settle in and get comfortable and relax on your own dining schedule with meals prepared when you want them. You can rent a cottage in a compound, a house or cottage off by itself, or even a home where the resident family is away on their own vacation.

However, these propositions can be pricey. Prices are highest close to the mainland, near town centers, or on the beach. Keep in mind that rentals in Orleans are generally less expensive than the ones in Chatham, and if you head farther north, the prices are less than in Orleans. Not surprisingly, places within walking distance of a beach are the most expensive. You may luck out and find a small, rustic cottage for $600 a week, or you may need to pony up $1,500 a week for a modern house.

You must start early in your search for a cottage or house, preferably in January for a summer vacation. By the end of March, pickings are pretty slim. Develop an idea of what lodgings you want and how much you can afford to spend. For cottages at motels, you can call directly and reserve with a credit card, but real estate agents handle most cottage and house rentals. To explore your options, contact one of the following sources:

✔ **Cape Cod Chamber of Commerce:** 307 Main St., Suite 2, P.O. Box 790, Hyannis, MA 02601. ☎ **888-332-2732** or 508-862-0700. Internet: `www.capecodchamber.org`.

✔ **Cape Cod Realty:** P.O. Box 719, Wellfleet, MA 02667. ☎ **800-545-7670** or 508-349-2245. Internet: `www.capecodrealty.net`.

✔ **Duarte/Downey Real Estate Agency:** 12 Truro Center Rd., P.O. Box 2016, Truro, MA 02666. ☎ **508-349-7588.** Internet: `www.ddre.com`.

Remember: Whoever is the most flexible finds the best bargain. Absolutely nothing is wrong with staying in a place that has bare-board walls and requires a short bike ride to the beach. In fact, this lodging is more Cape Cod-ish than a ritzy condo.

If an owner or agent requests references — a common practice — give them one from a previous vacation rental. You may also be required to pay a large deposit up front, or even the whole rental amount (by check), just to make a reservation.

Before you go, find out exactly what linens, kitchen items, and so on are included. Plan all your meals in advance so you can make one major shopping trip when you arrive on the cape. (You won't find any large grocery stores between Orleans and Provincetown.) Inventory any problems in writing when you arrive at the rental and again before you leave to make sure that you don't get charged for someone else's damage.

Campgrounds

Images of driftwood fires flickering on the beach while you're bedding down under the stars are romantic. But unfortunately, you can only imagine these images on the national seashore because camping is prohibited in the park. However, you can find a good number of private campgrounds nestled in pine forests a bit farther inland. I give my recommendations in the following section, but for a complete list, call the Cape Cod Chamber of Commerce (☎ 888-332-2732 or 508-862-0700).

Among your camping possibilities is **Nickerson State Park** (☎ 508-896-3491), located along 6A in Brewster. At 1,900 acres, this state park is the largest and nicest one on the cape because of the many ponds scattered within its boundaries. The park boasts 420 campsites nestled amid towering white pines and clumped in seven groups scattered about the ponds, so you won't get claustrophobic. You can both swim and sail in the ponds. Plus, the Cape Cod Rail Trail runs through the park. (See "Learning the Lay of the Land," earlier in this chapter for more on this.) Sites cost $12 for Massachusetts residents and $15 for non-residents. In summer, the park provides flush toilets, showers, and a dump station. Spots are hard to come by, even with a reservation system that allows you to reserve as early as six months ahead of your arrival. Reservations are accepted by phone (☎ 877-422-6762) or through the Internet (www.reserveamerica.com).

In the Eastham area, your choices include **Atlantic Oaks Campground** (☎ 508-255-1437) with its 100 tent and RV sites. Near Provincetown, you find **Dunes' Edge Campground** (☎ 508-487-9815; Internet: www.dunesedge.com) with its 100 sites. These campgrounds are much more expensive than the state park because they are privately owned. Atlantic Oaks charges from $24 to $32 a night for sites without hookups, $32 to $45 with hookups. Dunes' Edge costs you $34 for a site with water and electricity and $28 for a tent site. If you're not planning to move up and down the cape, Dunes' Edge may be your best bet among all the campgrounds listed in this section because of its location next to the Province Lands area within easy biking distance of Route 6. The sites are situated among scrub pine and small oaks along the hilly side of a stabilized dune.

At North Truro, you can pitch your tent at **North of Highland Camping Area** (☎ 508-487-1191; Internet: www.capecodcamping.com) for $20. Hot showers, a recreation building, laundry, and a store support the 237 campsites. The national seashore surrounds the campground on all sides, and a short walk brings you to Meadow Beach. The most natural setting of all the campgrounds, this campsite is a prized location that requires you to reserve a spot well in advance of your arrival.

Where to Eat

So much seafood, so little time. Seafood doesn't get much fresher anywhere but the cape, where the fishing boats unload their catches each afternoon and, in some cases, shuttle them right off to the restaurants. Do you want your traditional lobster feed with bowls of butter, long bibs, and corn-on-the-cob? You got it. Do you prefer fine dining where the cooks do the dirty work with the lobsters? You can get that, too. No doubt, you'll find your own favorite eatery during one of your many trips up and down Routes 6 and 6A, but here's a good sampler to get you drooling.

Bubala's by the Bay

$$–$$$ Provincetown   ECLECTIC

This place is great for lunch or dinner after you've been milling about Provincetown. With its bright yellow paint job and Picassoesque wall murals, you may think that you've brought the town's in-your-face audacity inside with you. The food is both serious and sensibly priced. Show up for breakfast and try the buttermilk waffles with real maple syrup. At lunchtime, the burgers, focaccia sandwiches, fajitas, and Cajun calamari are all reliable. If you stop in for dinner, the menu reflects the catch of the day. Try the Rum and Pepper Painted Cod with mango salsa, black beans, and basmati rice. You won't regret it.

183 Commercial St. (in the West End). ☎ *508-487-0773. Internet:* www.bubalas. com. *Reservations recommended. Main courses: $6.95–$25.95. AE, DISC, MC, V. Open: May–Oct daily 8 a.m.–1 a.m. Closed Nov–Apr.*

Captain Linnell House

$$–$$$$ Orleans   AMERICAN

This eatery is not the place to take the kiddies, but if you and your significant other want a wonderfully romantic evening, this place is great. The mansion that houses the restaurant was built in 1854 and has an exterior like something you'd expect to see in the Deep South, not Yankee New England. But appearances are deceiving; inside you find a traditional New England menu with dependable service. Chef/owner William Conway's lobster bisque, bolstered with bourbon, is the kind that lingers in your memory. If you can arrive before 5:30 p.m., this wonderful soup, as well as the dessert, is free. The best view is from the garden room.

137 Skaket Beach Rd. (about 1 mile NW of Route 6A). ☎ *508-255-3400; Internet:* www.linnell.com. *Reservations recommended. Main courses: $19–$30. AE, MC, V. Open: Daily 5–9 p.m.*

Kadee's Lobster & Clam Bar

$–$$$$ East Orleans   SEAFOOD

Although you can't see or hear the ocean or Cape Cod Bay from this shanty, you never doubt that you're at the beach. When the sun's out, the brightly colored umbrellas pop up on the patio; as soon as the chilly sea-born fog rolls in, a curtained awning drops down. The tables can be packed close together, leaving little elbow room, but you come to eat, not dance. Kadee's classic chowders and stews or healthy seafood kabob take the chill off. You also find a raw bar with oysters, clams, and shrimp.

Due to Kadee's huge following, and the lack of a reservation system, expect to wait if you show up during the dinner hour.

212 Main St. ☎ 508-255-6184. Reservations not accepted. Main courses: $8.50–$28. MC, V. Open: Late Memorial Day to Labor Day, Mon–Thur 5 p.m.–9 p.m.; Fri–Sun noon to 9 p.m. Closed early Sept to late May.

Land Ho!
$–$$$ Orleans   SEAFOOD/AMERICAN

If you're on the move with little time or money for a full-blown, multicourse meal, head to this eatery. This rough-and-tumble restaurant (known affectionately as "the Ho" by locals) features seafood, steaks, fast service, and reasonable prices. Along with the daily offerings of fried flounder, broiled scallops, and BBQ pork ribs, you find a daily special, which may be surf and turf, a cajun shrimp appetizer, or fried clams and oysters.

38 Main St. ☎ 508-255-5165; Internet: www.land-ho.com. *Reservations not accepted. Main courses: $ 6.25–$25. AE, DISC, MC, V. Open: Mon–Sat 11:30 a.m. to midnight., Sun noon to midnight.*

Scargo Café
$$–$$$ Dennis   SEAFOOD/INTERNATIONAL

If you wander south of the national seashore — or need a meal stop while driving onto the cape — this place serves up some great food. A former captain's house, the cafe offers a wide variety of dishes, from the ubiquitous surf-and-turf and grilled lamb loins served with mint jelly to the unusual Wildcat Chicken, a sautéed chicken dish featuring sausage, mushrooms, and raisins, all flambéed with apricot brandy. If you love shrimp, you can't miss with the Shrimp Aegean, sautéed jumbo Gulf shrimp with fresh vegetables in a lobster sauce over angel hair pasta and topped with feta cheese.

799 Main St. (Route 6A). ☎ 508-385-8200; Internet: www.scargocafe.com. *Reservations required for parties of 6 or more. Main courses: $13.50–$23. AE, DISC, MC, V. Open: Mid-June to mid-Sept, daily 11 a.m.–11 p.m. Closed late Sept to early June.*

Fast Facts: Cape Cod

Area Code
☎ 508.

ATM
Located in banks and major grocery stores.

Emergency
☎ 911.

Fees
$10 a day per vehicle for entrance to beaches; $3 per day on foot to beaches.

Fishing License

No license needed for saltwater fishing. Non-resident freshwater fishing license required: $37.50 for the season, $23.50 for three days, $11.50 for anglers ages 15 to 17.

Hospitals/Clinics

Cape Cod Hospital, 27 Park St., Hyannis; ☎ 508-771-1800. Outer Cape Health Services, 49 Harry Kemp Way, Provincetown (☎ 508-487-9395), or Route 6, Wellfleet (☎ 508-349-3131).

Information

Cape Cod National Seashore Headquarters, 99 Marconi Station Site Rd., Wellfleet, MA 02667; ☎ 508-349-3785.

Pharmacies

Adams Pharmacy, 254 Commercial St., Provincetown; ☎ 508-487-0069.

The CVS Pharmacy chain has locations throughout the cape; call ☎ 800-746-7287 for directions to the nearest one.

Post Office

211 Commercial St., Provincetown; ☎ 800-275-8777.

Taxes

9.7% lodging.

Time Zone

Eastern standard time.

Weather Conditions

☎ 508-255-8500.

Web Site

www.nps.gov/caco.

Chapter 12

Death Valley National Park

· ·

In This Chapter

▶ Introducing a hot winter getaway

▶ Planning your vacation

▶ Making your way to the valley's highlights

▶ Finding the best meals and beds

· ·

*L*et's get it out of the way right from the start: Death Valley National Park is hot in the summer. Despite the dry heat, this place broils in July and August. Death Valley boasts the highest mean temperature readings on Earth. Average highs in the summer top 110 degrees. (On July 10, 1913, the temperature boiled to a record 134 degrees.) What else would you expect from the lowest place in the Western Hemisphere?

Badwater, a roadside stop in the valley, is a mind-boggling 282 feet *below* sea level. Wrapped by the Panamint Range to the west and the Funeral Mountains and Black Mountains to the east, Death Valley in the summer is a frying pan that challenges the existence of anyone or anything that crawls into it.

This park is hot even in the shade. With summer temperatures frequently eclipsing 120 degrees, you definitely need some shade, and a gallon or two of water. Automakers actually seek out this heat during the dead of summer to see whether their latest models can function when the road tar flows like maple syrup. And because park officials know that not everyone's car, truck, or RV can handle the park's intense baking, they kindly locate tanks of radiator water near the top of the park's few hills so you can cool off your rig when you arrive.

You can avoid this oven-like experience by traveling to Death Valley in December and January, when the daily highs struggle to reach 65 degrees and wildflowers color the landscape. But if you avoid the park during the summer months, you miss the essence of Death Valley. Ask any Europeans you meet in the park (and you meet plenty of them in June, July, or August) why they come during the summer. They may tell you that they want to sizzle in this frying pan so they can gloat to their friends that they survived Death Valley at its worst. Think of a summer trek into the valley as a badge of courage.

But don't go solely for the dry heat (which supposedly has some therapeutic effects for people with asthma). Although Death Valley looks inhospitable, the park is rich in geology, human history, and — believe it or not — wildlife.

Stand in the middle of this 3.4-million-acre park, and you're surrounded by a surreal landscape painted in varying shades of gray, buff, yellow, and red. You find towering sand dunes constantly shifted by the winds, fractured plates of white salt pan blinding in the bright sun, and mile after mile of gently rolling sagebrush flats. Beyond the valley's sunken floor, mostly barren mountain ranges riddled by erosion tower the valley on all sides like the walls of a convection oven. Near the park's northern border, a 500-foot-deep crater, Ubehebe, serves as a bowl-shaped calling card of Death Valley's volcanic past.

While you travel the park, take time to soak up the intriguing human sagas that left their marks on the landscape. The most dramatic story is the tale of the '49ers — groups of pioneers who struggled to cross the valley floor on their way to California's gold fields in the mid-1800s. One of these groups gave the valley its harsh name, even though only one of its members died during the trek. These pioneers actually crossed the valley in the winter, when the temperatures are relatively mild.

Over the years, other miners drifted in and out of the valley searching futilely for gold and silver. In the crumbling ghost towns that dot the park, you hear sordid tales of hardscrabble miners who hoped to redeem their lives by finding the mother lode. A man named Death Valley Scotty struck rich, but not with pick and shovel. A slick-talking eccentric, he mined the pockets of Easterners blinded by tales of the golden mother lode that he promised to share with them.

Death Valley's name is certainly intimidating but tells a great story. To get the most out of your visit to Death Valley, plan to stay at least two days.

A work in progress

Death Valley has been slowly dropping for thousands of years, and the valley is still falling at a rate of roughly 6 inches a century. At the same time, wind and water erosion are chiseling away at the surrounding mountains. As a result, rubble in the form of sand dunes and sprawling *alluvial fans* (spreading beds of rock, gravel, and dirt washed downhill and deposited at the mouth of canyons) spill onto the valley floor. The dunes near Stovepipe Wells Village are a great display of how powerful erosion can be.

Must-see Attractions

All of Death Valley seems to lie before your eyes when you top the Panamint or Amargosa Ranges on your way to the park. Of course, that's only a mirage. In its 3.4 million acres, the park hides more than a few surprises for visitors. While you're poking into its nooks and crannies, be sure to visit these highlights:

- ✔ **Badwater:** This stop is a can't-miss photo op, thanks to the "Badwater, Elevation −282 FT" sign, the brackish spring waters, and the crusty and fractured salt beds in the background.

- ✔ **Dantes View:** Telescope Peak, the highest point in Death Valley, may offer a more-stunning view, but Dantes View is the best vantage point reached by car. At 5,475 feet above sea level, the air makes this spot cooler than the valley floor, too.

- ✔ **Furnace Creek Inn:** This historic inn, which dates to 1927 when it opened as a private corporate retreat, is planted on a hillside and nurtured by a spring that also sustains the groves of 1,800 imported date palm trees. Don't overlook the swimming pool.

- ✔ **Sand Dunes:** The park features several dune fields. The most accessible field is near Stovepipe Wells Village in the center of Death Valley. A moonlight stroll across these dunes is something to talk about.

- ✔ **Scotty's Castle:** Located near the park's northeastern corner, this Moorish castle was built by a Chicago millionaire who came to Death Valley to invest in a gold mine and wound up building an opulent "winter" home in his friend's name.

- ✔ **Zabriskie Point:** This outlook, 4½ miles southeast of the Furnace Creek Visitor's Center, offers not only a view of present-day Death Valley but also a glimpse into its past. The erosion-riddled mounds were laid down millions of years ago as volcanic deposits.

Getting There

Not surprisingly for such an inhospitable place, Death Valley is not easy to reach. There are no direct flights to the park, unless you fly your own plane or hire a charter to one of the private runways at Furnace Creek or Stovepipe Wells Village. Short of that, plan on a long drive to Death Valley.

Driving in

Coming from the West, U.S. Route 395 connects with Route 178 (near Ridgecrest) and Highway 190 (near Olancha). Both Route 178 and Highway 190 lead into the park. On the east side, U.S. Route 95 intersects with Route 267 at Scotty's Junction, Route 374 at Beatty, and Route 373 at Lathrop Wells. Furnace Creek, the heart of the park, is five hours and 310 miles from Los Angeles via Baker or Lone Pine and 285 miles via Trona. Bakersfield is 236 miles away.

From Las Vegas, Death Valley is about two hours and 140 miles via Death Valley Junction. The distance is not great, but the ride can get monotonous. Don't fall prey to the tedium. Watching for jets from the Indian Springs or Nellis Air Force bases as they head out to their practice bombing ranges just north of U.S. Route 95 is one way to stay alert.

Flying in

The nearest commercial airport is **McCarran International Airport** in Las Vegas, 140 miles away. The following airlines have regularly scheduled flights into Las Vegas; some of these are regional carriers, so they may not all fly from your point of origin: **Air Canada, Alaska Airlines, America West, American/American Eagle, American Trans Air, Continental, Delta/Skywest, Frontier, Midwest Express, Northwest, Southwest, Sun Country, United,** and **US Airways.** See the Appendix for their toll-free numbers.

At the Las Vegas airport, you need to rent a car to travel to the park. Some of the car-rental agencies represented at the airport include: **Avis, Budget, Dollar, Hertz,** and **National.** See the Appendix for their toll-free numbers.

Planning Ahead

You kinda need to think in reverse when planning a visit to Death Valley National Park. This park is crowded when most other parks are empty. Death Valley's busy season runs from February through mid-April when the temperature is relatively cool. November can also be busy. While December and January (outside of the holidays) are the slowest months, and therefore the easiest for making lodging reservations, the hot months of June, July, and August are also fairly slow.

If you want to stay at **Furnace Creek Inn** during high season, make reservations at least three months in advance. During the heat of summer, though, a week's leeway is usually enough time to get a room. See "Where to Stay" later in the chapter for descriptions of this hotel and others mentioned in this section.

From May through October, the **Furnace Creek Inn** offers substantial discounts — price reductions of $85 to $140 per night. But if you don't consider a $140 discount off a $350-per-night room to be much of a bargain, then stay at the **Furnace Creek Ranch** (cabins are available during the summer months for $105 a night), **Stovepipe Wells** ($58–$104 for a double room year-round), **Panamint Springs Resort** ($65–$79 for a double year-round), or one of the campgrounds.

Death Valley National Park

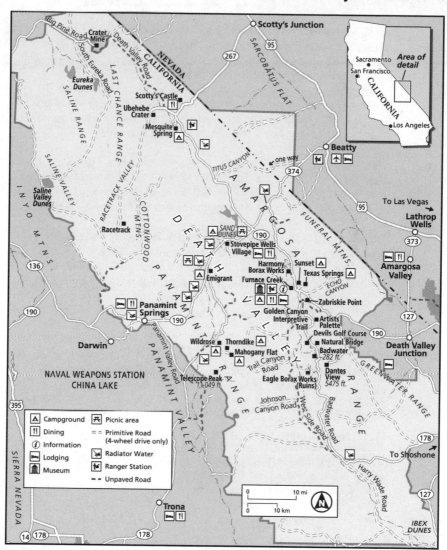

If you plan a trip to the park between mid-October and mid-April and want to stay at one of the campgrounds, you can make a reservation for a spot at the **Furnace Creek Campground** and group sites at **Texas Springs Campground** up to five months in advance of your trip by calling ☎ **800-365-2267**. The rest of the campgrounds fill on a first-come, first-served basis.

For general information in advance of your trip, write Death Valley National Park, P.O. Box 579, Death Valley, CA 92328-0579; call ☎ **760-786-3200**; or check the park's Web site: www.nps.gov/deva.

Learning the Lay of the Land

In a place with such a colorful mining history, it's fitting that Death Valley's paved roads — Highway 190 and Routes 267, 374, and 178 — resemble a treasure map: They slash across the park much like a gigantic X, coming together just east of Stovepipe Wells Village. Unfortunately, you won't find a pot of gold at this intersection — or a handy circular route connecting all the highlights. If you want to see all of the park's main attractions, you have to backtrack at least a time or two to go out and back from your base of operations.

Route 267 runs north from the intersection to the Titus Canyon road, the Mesquite Spring Campground, Scotty's Castle, and Ubehebe Crater. **Route 374** juts off to the northeast up Mud Canyon and past Hell's Gate and Daylight Pass before leaving the park and running to Beatty, Nevada.

Running south from the intersection is **Highway 190,** which snakes 19 miles to **Furnace Creek,** the best place to base a visit to Death Valley because of its central location and accommodations. You find the park headquarters, the visitor center, a museum, gift shops, restaurants, a service station, a convenience store, and even a golf course. The lavish Furnace Creek Inn, nestled in a grove of palm trees, is across the highway.

From Furnace Creek you can head south on **Route 178,** which drains down to Badwater (the lowest spot in the Western Hemisphere at 282 feet below sea level) before beginning a slow rise to the ghost site of Ashford Mill. Then the road swings east and up into the Black Mountains, through 3,315-foot Salsberry Pass, and out of the park.

Running parallel to 178 for 40 miles through the middle of Death Valley and along the foot of the Panamint Range is the unpaved **West Side Road,** which leads past the ruins of the Eagle Borax Works, one of the valley's old mining operations. Several four-wheel-drive roads head west into the mountains from this road. (See "If you have more time," later in this chapter, for information on off-road routes.)

Meanwhile, **Highway 190** cuts east from Furnace Creek and passes Zabriskie Point after 4½ miles. Another 5½ miles down the road, 190 divides. At this intersection, you can continue east and leave the park via 190, or turn south and head down a spur road 13 miles back up into the Black Mountains and Dantes View.

Going west from the junction of the four roads, Highway 190 passes a parking area for Death Valley Sand Dunes (22 miles from Furnace Creek), Stovepipe Wells Village (24 miles), and Panamint Springs (60 miles) before leaving the park.

Stovepipe Wells Village is the other major community in Death Valley. Although its accommodations are not as nice as the ones at Furnace Creek, Stovepipe Wells Village is nevertheless an adequate way station with a lodge, restaurant, gas station, convenience store, campground, and ranger station.

Panamint Springs is near the park's western border on Highway 190. Definitely not as fancy as Furnace Creek, Panamint Springs does offer a comfortable motel, a restaurant, a service station, a campground and RV park, and showers.

Between Panamint Springs and Stovepipe Wells Village is a spur road that darts to the south from Highway 190. This road leads 21 miles to the Wildrose Campground and the trailhead for a hike up Telescope Peak.

Arriving in the Park

Where do you head and what do you do when you first arrive in Death Valley? The information in this section helps you get your bearings.

Finding information

Located in the center of the park on Highway 190, the **Furnace Creek Visitor Center** offers museum exhibits, an information desk, and a bookstore. The center is open daily from 8 a.m. to 6 p.m.

Paying fees

Entry for up to seven days costs $10 per private vehicle. A $20 Death Valley Park Pass is good for one year's entrance to the park. See Chapter 8 for information on the National Park Pass and Chapter 4 for the lowdown on Golden Age and Golden Access passports.

Getting around

How do you tour this sprawling park? In an air-conditioned vehicle with plenty of water to stave off dehydration, with a map pinpointing the tanks of emergency radiator water, and by returning to a room reserved near a swimming pool at day's end. The park does not have public transportation. Plus, given the heat (and risk of dehydration), I advise against touring the park by bike.

Remembering Safety

In summer, take precautions for you and your car against Death Valley's intense heat. For yourself, pack a **case of bottled water** so you can easily grab a drink when you need one. For your car, tote a **gallon of water** or two so you can top off your rig's radiator when you need to if you're not in the general vicinity of one of the park service's water tanks.

Also, invest in some good **sunscreen or sunblock.** Death Valley is a hot place, and the brilliant salt pan on the valley floor reflects a lot of sunshine.

Besides the drive to Dantes View, you really won't encounter any steep grades. But when the temperature is above 100 degrees, you don't need much of a hill to overwork your **engine's radiator.** If you do notice your temperature gauge beginning to head for the red zone, shut off your air-conditioner. True, you'll miss the blasts of cool air, but living with the windows open for 10 to 15 minutes while your radiator simmers down is a lot better than sitting on the side of the road trying to fix a busted radiator hose. If turning off the air-conditioner doesn't do the trick, try pulling over and turning the heater on full blast. If that doesn't work, turn off your rig for a while and admire the landscape.

Death Valley's **abandoned mines** are mysterious and intriguing, but stay out of them. Their roof supports could collapse at any time, and their shafts may be filled with poisonous air.

Before you head out on that four-wheel-drive adventure into the back-country, make sure you have a map of the park and check at the visitor center or a ranger station for the park's *Morning Report.* These reports provide the day's weather forecast and alert you to impassable roads. Even though Death Valley's scenery is certainly captivating, your eyes shouldn't wander too far from the road while you're driving. The number one cause of death in the park is single-vehicle accidents that occur because motorists drift off the road onto soft, sandy shoulders. (When drivers whip the wheel around to steer their rigs back onto the road, the vehicles can roll.)

For additional tips on how to ensure a safe park visit, see Chapter 8.

Enjoying the Park

Is Death Valley truly inhospitable? On its face, perhaps. But if you take the time to explore the park, you come to appreciate its many nuances. The key to enjoying a summer visit is to lay low during the heat of the day and explore the park during the early morning and evening hours.

Exploring the top attractions

Badwater

At the roadside turnoff at Badwater is one of the park's best photo ops — the "Badwater, Elevation –282 FT" sign. However, in the years ahead, the sign may read –283 FT. The valley floor is a victim of fault-block geology, in which the surrounding mountains rise as the valley floor sinks — in this case, at a rate of roughly 6 inches per century.

From the turnoff, you can walk due west past the sign and onto salt flats. The way the surface of these flats is fractured into plates by the brutal heat is an interesting sight — and a warning that you shouldn't dally too long. But before leaving the turnoff, look high up on the rock cliff across the road for the sign denoting sea level.

 If you're thirsty enough to sample the water in Badwater, you'll find out how the place got its name. Saltier than the ocean, a sip of the water won't kill you, but it won't slake your thirst, either.

Badwater is south of Furnace Creek about 18 miles on Route 178.

Dantes View

You gain a lot of elevation heading to this 5,475-foot summit, and one of the park service's trusty radiator water tanks waits near the top in case your rig wasn't ready for the climb. From the overlook on top, you can clearly see how Death Valley's rimming mountain ranges prevent any stream outlet to the sea. That's why any minerals and salts washed into the valley by storms stay in the area and accumulate. On the valley floor, the greatest accumulations stand out clearly as a snow-white layering of salt pan.

From the overlook, you can look up more than a mile to see 11,049-foot Telescope Peak atop the Panamint Range directly to the west. You can look down more than a mile to see the lowest point in the Western Hemisphere. And you can see the Grapevine Mountains to the north, the Funeral Mountains to the east, and the Greenwater Range to the south.

You may be tempted to spend all day at Dantes View because the temperature typically is 25 degrees cooler than the temperature you find below at Badwater.

 If you're driving a motorhome longer than 25 feet or hauling a trailer that extends your rig by 25 feet or more, you won't be able to travel to the top of the spur road due to some tight curves. You can drop off your trailer at a parking lot about halfway to the top.

To reach Dantes View, head east on Highway 190 from Furnace Creek for 16 miles; turn right onto the spur road to the viewpoint and go another 13 miles.

Sand Dunes

One of five dune complexes in the park, the Sand Dunes is the easiest to reach, with access available along Highway 190 just 2 miles east of Stovepipe Wells Village. Standing 120 feet tall in places, these dunes roam back and forth as the winds blow. Interesting patterns are swirled into the sand by vegetation that is pushed back and forth by the breezes, which makes for intriguing photos. (For a walk in this area, see Sand Dunes under "Taking a hike," later in this chapter.)

Access to the Sand Dunes can be found 2 miles east of Stovepipe Wells Village on Highway 190.

Scotty's Castle

"Summer home" isn't an accurate description of this palatial mansion, but that's what it was to Chicago owner Albert Johnson, who built the castle in 1922. The castle contains a tiled courtyard, a streaming indoor waterfall opposite a fireplace in the living room, and a music conservatory with a massive pipe organ taking up one wall. Walter Scott, a schemer adept at convincing gullible investors to give him money, boasted that he built the castle for himself with gold mined from shafts beneath the structure. Johnson contributed to the story by telling inquiring reporters who trekked to the castle that he was merely Scotty's banker. (For more information on Scotty and Johnson, see the sidebar "The tale of Death Valley Scotty.")

You easily can spend two or three hours at Scotty's Castle. Before or after the 50-minute castle tour, which I recommend that you take, roam the grounds to inspect the sprawling (but unfinished) swimming pool, stand before the clock tower, visit the stables, and pay your respects at Scotty's grave. The grounds are free to roam; during high season, rangers give tours of them. You also find a gift shop and snack bar, as well as a gas station nearby.

From the junction of Highway 190 and Route 374 just east of Stovepipe Wells Village, head north for 33 miles to the intersection with Route 267. Turn right onto 267 and drive 3 miles up Grapevine Canyon to Scotty's Castle. ☎ *760-786-2392. Open: Castle grounds and picnic areas open free to the public 7 a.m.–6 p.m. Tours: Daily 9 a.m.– 5 p.m. on the hour (last tour starts at 5 p.m.). Tour admission: $8.*

Ubehebe Crater

Nine miles west of Scotty's Castle is a 500-foot-deep hole in the ground known as Ubehebe Crater. The recession was blasted into existence during a volcanic period about 1,000 years ago when eruptions fueled by ground water mixing with molten rock tossed rocks and cinders across a 6-square-mile area. You won't find any steam venting from the ½-mile-wide crater today, but you can walk to its lip and stare down into its bowels. Although the main crater is right next to the parking area, you can take a ½-mile walk to the right (around the rim) to inspect two other, smaller craters.

From the junction of Highway 190 and Route 374 just east of Stovepipe Wells Village, head north for 33 miles to the intersection with Route 267. Turn left and drive 5 miles.

Zabriskie Point

Zabriskie Point, just east of Furnace Creek, is a snapshot of the West's renowned painted deserts. The colorful, fingered landscape at this spot once was a mishmash of sediments on a lake floor: sand, mud, and a little volcanic ash. Over millions of years, the sediments were compressed into rock, the waters evaporated, and seismic activity buckled and tilted the landscape. Winds and rains then took over the task of carving the landscape, which makes a great early morning photograph.

The roadside turnoff for Zabriskie Point is 4¾ miles east of the Furnace Creek Visitors Center on Highway 190.

The tale of Death Valley Scotty

Walter Scott is Death Valley's most intriguing character. Raised in the comparatively cool bluegrass state of Kentucky, Scott fled home and headed to Nevada because (if for no other reason) his brother worked on a ranch there. The cowboy life suited Scott. He became good enough that, in 1890, he joined the *Buffalo Bill Cody Wild West Show* and toured the world for 12 years. Maybe Cody's showmanship rubbed off on Scott, or maybe he simply was determined to lead a life of leisure, but near the end of his *Wild West Show* career Scott learned how to swindle wealthy businessmen with tales of a secret gold mine in Death Valley that could make them all rich beyond their wildest dreams.

With that pitch, and their money, Scott transformed himself into Death Valley Scotty, an eccentric desert rat who never actually struck it rich by digging in the ground, but who always had money to spend, thanks to his gullible investors.

All good things usually come to an end, and Scotty met his match in the early 1900s when one of his marks, Albert Johnson, followed up his investment in Scotty's "mine" with a personal visit to Death Valley to inspect the diggings. After several days of leading Johnson around the valley on horseback and hoping that the Chicago insurance tycoon would grow weary under the unrelenting sun and heat and return home, Scotty realized his scheme had been uncovered.

Surprisingly, Johnson, whose health and strength improved in the dry heat and from the horseback rides, didn't turn his back on Scotty. Instead, he returned each winter over the next decade to explore the valley with Scotty. Then, in the 1920s, Johnson dipped deeply into his personal holdings to build a lavish winter retreat in Grapevine Canyon near the northern end of Death Valley. Here, with a reliable and plentiful spring, Johnson spent $2 million (a sizeable sum in 1922 dollars) to erect what is known as "Scotty's Castle."

Capturing Death Valley on film

Death Valley, with its surreal landscape, is a photographer's dreamscape. Head out with a cameraful of film during the morning or late afternoon, and you'll have a hard time not taking a good picture. Some of the best spots for sunrise photos are the sand dunes, Zabriskie Point, Dantes View, and Badwater. Sunset shots also pick up a lot of the desert's color; good spots to aim your camera at this time of day include Artists Palette, Zabriskie Point, and the Furnace Creek campgrounds with their groves of palm trees. No matter what the time of day is, a shot of the "Badwater, Elevation –282 FT" sign with the salt flats in the background is a classic. Much of Death Valley's landscape appears so out of this world that you can enjoy experimenting with your camera and the lighting conditions. When the famed landscape photographer Ansel Adams visited Death Valley, he often parked his rig near Stovepipe Wells Village and slept on its roof, where he had a camera platform measuring 5 feet by 9 feet.

Taking a hike

Most people are intimidated to hike in Death Valley. But if you schedule your visit for one of the cooler times of year or if you start early in the morning and concentrate on shorter treks, the valley rewards you with its hidden vistas. The valley has few truly long-range hikes but dozens of shorter hikes well worth the effort — and sweat.

Before heading out, remember to carry plenty of water and to keep an eye out for storm clouds that could produce flash floods.

Golden Canyon Interpretive Trail

You can choose from two ways to explore this colorful canyon that sprawls beneath Zabriskie Point: Into or out of the canyon. I encourage you to take the route into the canyon — the more dramatic direction and one that corresponds with an interpretive trail map that you can pick up at the Furnace Creek Visitor Center. The path, which used to have a paved road until a winter storm in 1976 washed it out, passes through spectacularly colorful scenery. The Red Cathedral — a formation named for the iron oxides that stain its hillsides — is located to your left about a ½ mile beyond the last numbered trail marker along the interpretive trail. For a longer hike, stay on the main trail for another 2 miles, and you find yourself at Zabriskie Point.

Distance: 2 miles round-trip (without the extra hike to Red Cathedral). Level: Easy. Access: Trailhead is at the Golden Canyon parking area 2 miles south of the Furnace Creek Inn on Badwater Road.

Mosaic Canyon

This interesting trail leads through a twisting canyon of buff and tan marble and a conglomerate of black and grey stream gravels — all highly polished over time by runoff waters that punish the canyon walls with their rocky slurry. Although the first mile of the trail is easy, the higher you go, the more difficult the hike becomes. You have to scramble across some slickrock, and take special care when climbing up dry waterfalls because they're easier to go up than down. You can occasionally see bighorn sheep in this area.

Disance: 4 miles round-trip. Level: Easy. Access: Mosaic Canyon parking area, 2 miles from Stovepipe Wells Village.

Natural Bridge Canyon

Rock arches and natural bridges are common in southern Utah and northern Arizona, but you probably don't associate them with Death Valley. Nevertheless, you find one near the head of a narrow canyon through which this trail passes. The natural bridge, about 50 feet high, spans the canyon three-tenths of a mile from the trailhead. Just beyond the bridge, the trail ends at the bottom of a dry waterfall. Although not as interesting as the Golden Canyon Interpretive Trail, this is a good short walk.

Distance: 1 mile round-trip. Level: Moderate. Access: Natural Bridge parking area, 1½ miles off Badwater Road, 13¼ miles south of Furnace Creek.

Sand Dunes

Plenty of beach and not a wave in sight! This area is a great place to spend a few hours. Although this sprawling dunefield doesn't have a defined trail, it has dunes and more dunes to scamper up and glide down. Kids love sliding on the sand and searching for animal tracks. For an unusual and somewhat cooler trek, visit the dunes under a full moon.

Distance: 4 miles round-trip. Level: Easy. Access: Sand Dunes parking area, 2 miles east of Stovepipe Wells Village off Highway 190.

Telescope Peak Trail

The highest point in Death Valley (at 11,049 feet) is not easily reached, and this trek is not for inexperienced hikers. That said, if you do make the summit in the summer months, you'll enjoy the much cooler air. When winter arrives, however, *crampons* (iron spikes for your shoes) and ice axes are recommended. From the trailhead, you gain 3,000 feet in elevation on the way to the summit. You encounter bristlecone pine trees, some of the oldest living organisms on earth, near the 10,000-foot level. From the summit, you can see the lowest point in the Lower 48 — Badwater — as well as the highest point, Mount Whitney, at 14,494 feet.

Distance: 14 miles round-trip. Level: Strenuous. Access: Mahogany Flat Campground, which is at the end of the upper Wildrose Canyon Road. High-clearance four-wheel-drive vehicles are necessary to negotiate the last 1½ miles of road.

One-day wonder

Scotty's Castle, Death Valley Sand Dunes, Zabriskie Point, Dantes View, Badwater, and Ubehebe Crater — they're the must-see highlights of a Death Valley trip. With nearly 200 miles of asphalt between you and these attractions (assuming you stay at Furnace Creek), visiting them all makes for a long, but not intolerable, day. This itinerary shows you how to execute this ambitious itinerary. Unless otherwise noted, see "Enjoying the park," earlier in this chapter, for description of attractions in this section.

The key to getting the most out of Death Valley — and out of any national park, for that matter — is to get an early start on the day. With Death Valley's heat, getting out early is particularly important. If possible, eat breakfast at Furnace Creek and get on the road by 7 a.m. The sun is still low enough to coax the most color out of the landscape, you may be able to see wildlife on the move, and you won't find many other people on the roads. Plus, the stillness at this time of day is intoxicating.

From the junction just below the Furnace Creek Inn, begin by heading 3½ miles down Highway 190 to **Zabriskie Point.** The colorful landscape in the early morning light makes for a great photograph.

Continue along 190 in the same direction; Dantes View is 19½ miles from Zabriskie Point. (When you come to a fork in the road, be sure to bear right rather than following 190 out of the park.) In addition to the great vista from **Dantes View,** you can enjoy the cooler temperatures, which are often 25 degrees cooler than on the valley floor. In the middle of the summer, that alone is enough of a reason to drive to this mountaintop.

You need to backtrack to Furnace Creek to reach **Badwater,** which you can see from Dantes View. From Furnace Creek, head south 17 miles on Route 178. If you make this trip in the middle of summer, you will feel the heat in Badwater. But braving the heat is worth the cool experience of being 282 feet *below* sea level and walking across Death Valley's fractured salt-pan floor.

After exploring the area and taking the requisite pictures to document your visit, turn back north for the 71-mile drive to **Scotty's Castle,** which takes about 90 minutes. In Furnace Creek, take 190 north to Route 267 north. Sure, it's a long drive. But although Scotty's Castle is somewhat out of the way, this site is not to be missed.

Depending on the time, you may want to stop for lunch in Furnace Creek. If you do, I recommend that you go to **Furnace Creek Ranch** (see "Where to Eat" later in this chapter). Or you can head up to

Scotty's Castle, buy your tickets for the tour, and eat lunch at the snack bar while waiting for your tour to come up.

On the way to Scotty's Castle, just north of Stovepipe Wells Village on 267, look for the roadside sign that notes how long the wait is for a tour. If you're visiting in the winter months and don't have to wait, stop at **Death Valley Sand Dunes** and **Ubehebe Crater** so you can see them before the daylight wanes. (In winter, if you do have to wait, go directly to the castle to pick up your tickets; otherwise, you may not get on a tour.) In the summer months, when the sun rises early and provides light even at 8:30 p.m., take the castle tour first and stop at the crater and the Sand Dunes on your way back.

During the hot summer months, you may want to spread this trip over 1½ or even 2 days. I'd spend one day traveling to Scotty's Castle, Ubehebe Crater, and the Sand Dunes, and start out the next morning to Zabriskie Point, Dantes View, and Badwater. Depending on how fast you're moving, on one of the two days squeeze in a stop at the **Furnace Creek Visitor Center** to cool off and to visit the museum. The visitor center does a great job of chronicling the valley's fascinating mining background, as well as touching on the cultural highlights.

The 2-mile hike along the **Golden Canyon Interpretive Trail,** which is just 2 miles south of the Furnace Creek Inn, may also be a good addition to your second day. Try to fit this hike in your schedule late in the afternoon, when the setting sun's rays coax the most color out of the canyon.

If you have more time

The **Harmony Borax Works,** just 2 miles north of Furnace Creek, gives you a glimpse of the valley's hard-working past. This mining operation proved more profitable than efforts to bore gold and silver out of the surrounding mountains. The raw borax, known as ulexite cottonball borax, was collected in the alkali flats west of Harmony by Chinese laborers who hauled it to Harmony for processing. The borax was loaded onto wagons, each pulled by 18 mules and two horses, and hauled 165 miles west to a train station at Mojave, California.

Today, all that remains are the alkali flats, the ruins of the processing mill, and a haul wagon. But standing before the ruins and realizing the conditions that the laborers endured may give you a new appreciation for hard work.

Artists Palette is a colorful addition to the photographic record of your Death Valley trip, if you can catch the late-afternoon sun igniting this hillside. Located on Artist Drive, which is 9½ miles south of Furnace Creek, a rumpled hillside midway along the drive constitutes the palette. Infused with volcanic sediments containing iron salts, mica, and manganese, the hillside shimmers under the setting sun with hues of reds, grays, blues, pinks, and yellows.

Finding local wildlife and vegetation

Imagining that much of anything lives in Death Valley is hard. At first glance, your eyes won't detect any living thing when they pan across this apparent wasteland, because you're likely searching in the middle of the day when critters are hiding in some relatively cool place. But as you become more discerning, you begin to see things. Come out before the sun rises or in the waning evening, and you're likely to spot one of the valley's critters.

Not too many years ago, **burros** trotting around the park were not uncommon sights. Those hoofers were descendants of the animals brought into the region by miners in the late 1800s to haul their gear. Once fairly visible in the Panamint Valley between Stovepipe Wells Village and Panamint Springs, the burros were rounded up and moved out of the park by the National Park Service because they weren't native to Death Valley.

These days, if you're determined you can spot **desert bighorn sheep.** These recluses prefer rocky hillsides — look for them near Mosaic Canyon — and their dull grey coats provide the perfect camouflage.

The park also has **coyotes,** the consummate beggars. You're likely to run into them near a developed area, such as Furnace Creek or Stovepipe Wells Village. They stand in the middle of the road with hopes that you'll stop and toss them a bite to eat. Don't feed them, but slow down because a number of coyotes have been hit by cars.

If you're patient, you can even find life around the park's sand dunes. **Kangaroo rats, lizards, sidewinder rattlesnakes, coyotes,** and the **kit fox** are among the animals that call the dunes home. If you're quiet and crafty, you may spot one of these guys in the dunes at night. Bring a flashlight to help you find your way, but cover its lens with red cellophane so the light won't spook the animals.

The valley's most unusual residents are **desert pupfish** that live, somehow, in salty marshes along Salt Creek just 10 miles south of Stovepipe Wells Village on Highway 190. Ancestors of these fish lived in the sprawling freshwater lake that once filled the bottom of Death Valley. As the lake slowly evaporated, the waters became saltier and saltier, and the pupfish managed to adapt quickly enough to stay alive. As the lake eventually separated into smaller, distinct pools, pupfish in each pool evolved to tolerate their respective environments. The Salt Creek pupfish endure water temperatures that fluctuate from more than 100 degrees in the summer to near freezing in the winter.

Death Valley's **wildflowers** have learned to cope with minimal water. It's hard to believe, but more than 1,000 plant species grow in the valley. Most of these flowers simply remain dormant until quenching rainstorms tell them that it's time to awaken, blossom, and go to seed. The alluvial fans that spill out of the mountains are perfect seedbeds for the park's flowers, and after a wet winter or spring, you see scores of sunflowers creep across the fans.

Other species that grow in the valley include **evening primrose, orange globemallow,** and 13 varieties of **cacti.** A species that appears dead even when it's alive is **desert holly,** which has evolved to be able to pull nourishment from salt water. The salt forms crystals on the holly leaves, and the result is a shimmering, crusty leaf.

If you have a good four-wheel-drive rig, head to the park's northwest corner and the **Racetrack.** Riddling Death Valley are old dirt roads leading to and from abandoned mining communities and into the mountains. You must take one of these roads to reach this attraction — no doubt, one of the oddest in Death Valley. The Racetrack is a dry lake bed across which rocks mysteriously slide, pushed possibly by the howling winds. Unless you're incredibly patient for weeks on end, you never actually see them move. Instead, you're left to ponder their tracks that zigzag across the ground. To get to the Racetrack, head north on Route 267 to Ubehebe Crater (38 miles from the 190/374 junction near Stovepipe Wells Village), and then drive 27 miles south on a dirt road.

Another four-wheel-drive destination is **Echo Canyon,** site of Needles Eye, a natural arch. For directions and current road conditions, track down a ranger at the Furnace Creek Visitor Center or another ranger station. If you plan to stay overnight in the backcountry, pick up a backcountry camping permit, too.

Ranger programs

Because summers are the hottest time of the year in Death Valley, and mostly non-English–speaking Europeans come to visit, ranger programs go on a siesta this time of year. But from mid-October into April, there's quite a bit going on, such as nightly ranger sessions in the Furnace Creek Visitor Center on everything from Death Valley's geology to human history. Pick up a weekly schedule of programs at the visitor center to find out what's happening during your visit. And if you have little ones, don't forget to pick up information on the Junior Ranger Program (see Chapter 4 for information).

The best show — and one that's offered year-round — is at **Scotty's Castle,** an attraction that's one part museum and one part theater. The theatrics come to life through Park Service employees who dress in 1920s garb and infiltrate tour groups to inquire about Death Valley Scotty. Be ready for these interruptions, because the actors may question your opinion on whether a gold mine is deep beneath the castle's floors. For information on visiting Scotty's Castle, see "Exploring the top attractions," earlier in this chapter.

Escaping the heat

What do you do if the heat begins to bake your brain? Head indoors. **Scotty's Castle** is a great place to hide from the sun. (See "Exploring the top attractions," earlier in this chapter.) The castle is not air-conditioned, but its interior is cooler than the air outside. Plus, the castle is set in something like an oasis in Grapevine Canyon, and after your tour you can relax with ice cream under the palm trees. Another place to avoid the sun is the **Borax Museum** at the Furnace Creek

Visitor Center (see "Arriving in the Park," earlier in this chapter). Inside, you find exhibits that trace the valley's checkered mining history plus a steam locomotive, antique stagecoaches, and mining tools. If you stay at the **Furnace Creek Inn,** escape the sun for a few minutes by venturing from the lower parking lot through a passageway in the inn's basement that leads to elevators that haul guests to the upper floors. Several illuminated "windows" in this passageway display interesting mining artifacts. The best way to deal with the heat is to go swimming, which is possible if you stay at the Furnace Creek Ranch, the Furnace Creek Inn, or Stovepipe Wells Village.

Where to Stay

If you're not going to camp out, you have four lodging choices in the park. If price is no object, get a room at the Furnace Creek Inn, which is located in the heart of Death Valley at the junction of Highway 190 and Route 178. Rich architecture, a tropical setting, fine dining, and a refreshing swimming pool make the inn a luxurious base camp to return to after a day of exploring. A less expensive option that shares the inn's central location is the Furnace Creek Ranch just to the west across 190. Your third option is Stovepipe Wells Village to the northwest of Furnace Creek. All three properties are run by **Xanterra Parks & Resorts** (☎ **303-297-2757;** Internet: `www.xanterra.com`). With one call to Xanterra, you can check on availability at all three places and make a reservation. Your fourth option is Panamint Springs Resort, although its location near the park's western border is far removed from Death Valley's heart.

Lodging in the park

Furnace Creek Inn
$$$$$ **Furnace Creek**

Think of a desert oasis, and you get a hint of the setting. This Mission-style inn is surrounded by groves of date palm trees. Springs not only keep the trees and surrounding gardens thriving, but a warm spring fills the swimming pool. Although swimming in 85-degree water may seem ridiculous in a place as hot as Death Valley, the pool feels refreshing when the air temperature is around 100 or more.

The rooms are on the small side when you consider today's newest accommodations. But they're comfortable and have a warm atmosphere (no pun intended) thanks to the Mission design. Ceiling fans aid air-conditioners that can struggle during the summer. Are the rooms worth several hundred dollars a night? Probably not. But your options aren't the greatest, either, and this inn offers the best atmosphere in the park. Although the winter rates are hefty, a summer visit saves you money as off-season rates drop significantly. Whenever you go, ask for a room facing the gardens. The view from the small balcony outside your room is tropical, and the paths that wind down to the pool are perfect for an evening stroll.

If you're not exhausted by the day's heat, you can take to the inn's four lighted tennis courts when things cool down a bit at night.

Highway 190. ☎ *760-786-2361 or Internet:* www.furnacecreekresort.com *for reservations. 66 rooms, including 2 suites. A/C TV TEL. Rack rates: Mid-Oct to mid-May $235–$365 double; mid-May to mid-Oct $155–$225 double. AE, DC, DISC, MC, V.*

Furnace Creek Ranch

$$$–$$$$ Furnace Creek

The pace here is more laid back than at the Furnace Creek Inn across the highway. Rooms have more of a motel feel, and with a general store, three restaurants, a saloon, and a museum on the property, you get the sense that you're staying in a small village. For the budget-minded, this is the place to stay. Kids love cooling off in the pool, and if you brought your clubs, the 18-hole golf course will torment you as its setting at 214 feet below sea level takes some zing out of your Pings. Rooms are a bit cheaper during the off-season (summer), but not much. The cabins are single-story duplex units; they're efficient — two double beds, a shower — but that's about it.

Highway 190. ☎ *760-786-2345. Internet:* www.furnacecreekresort.com. *224 rooms. A/C TV TEL. Rack rates: Nov 28–30 and Dec 24–31 $117–$169; the rest of the year $105–$159 double. AE, DC, DISC, MC, V.*

Panamint Springs Resort

$$–$$$ Panamint Springs

If you come to Death Valley from points west, this is a good place to stop. The resort is located near the western border of the park, 48 miles east of Lone Pine, California, and 31 miles west of Stovepipe Wells Village. You won't find many frills, but you do find a gorgeous, laid-back setting; decent food; and ready access to nearby ghost towns, abandoned mines, and even a waterfall. The views aren't too shabby, either, as you can see sand dunes off in the Panamint Valley and the Panamint Range. The place is even pet friendly. The rooms are clean but plain. The one cottage may not look like much, with its tin roof and walls, but inside are two bedrooms, a full bath, and a living room with the only color TV in a hotel this side of Death Valley.

Highway 190. ☎ *775-482-7680 for reservations. Fax: 775-482-7682. Internet:* www.deathvalley.com. *14 rooms, 1 cottage, 26 tent sites, 42 RV sites. A/C. Rack rates: $65–$79 double; $139 cottage; $12 tent sites, $25 RV sites with full hookups (12 available); $15 RV sites with water only (30 available). DISC, MC, V.*

Stovepipe Wells Village
$$-$$$ **Stovepipe Wells Village**

If the best deal, not location or atmosphere, determines where you stay in Death Valley, this is the place, 23 miles northwest of Furnace Creek. The plain rooms are uninspiring and look like the ones in a run-of-the-mill, roadside motel, but the price is right. You find a general store, restaurant, and saloon, and the Death Valley Dunes are a 10-minute walk away.

Highway 190. ☎ *760-786-2387 for reservations. 83 rooms. TV and TEL in some rooms; A/C in all rooms. Rack rates: $58–$104 double. AE, DC, DISC, MC, V.*

Lodging outside the park

Being so far removed, Death Valley has few nearby accommodations to which you can retreat in an effort to save money. At Beatty, Nevada, 41 miles northeast of Furnace Creek, you find a small handful of uninspiring motels. To the southeast, Death Valley Junction offers the **Amargosa Hotel** (☎ 760-852-4441) with 14 air-conditioned rooms. Still, this hotel is 30 miles from Furnace Creek.

Looking west, the closest "big" little towns are Lone Pine (104 miles) and Ridgecrest (123 miles); the pickings are a bit better, but the ride is much longer.

Campgrounds

If you really want to experience Death Valley 24 hours a day, camp out during your visit. During the summer months, in which hot breezes offer little relief, you may soon wish that you'd sprung for an air-conditioned room. Still, camping is an inexpensive way to stay in the park, and some campgrounds are at relatively high elevations where the temperature actually cools off at night.

Although ten campgrounds are scattered throughout Death Valley, only half (**Furnace Creek, Emigrant, Mesquite Spring, Wildrose,** and the privately owned **Panamint Springs**) are open year-round. The seasonal closures are the Park Service's way of telling you that camping out in the open is really too hot at certain times of the year.

The **Furnace Creek, Texas Spring,** and **Sunset campgrounds** are the park's most popular. You can make advance reservations for Furnace Creek and two group sites at Texas Springs, but only for dates between October 15 and April 15 (see the following listings for telephone numbers). Besides these dates, the campsites are first-come, first-served. The busiest periods are in early November and in spring, although once Easter has passed business dips.

Here's a rundown of your camping options (all the prices given are per night):

- ✔ **Emigrant Campground:** Nine miles south of Stovepipe Wells Village along Highway 190, this year-round campground is free and has 10 tent sites as well as drinking water, picnic tables, and flush toilets. Fires are prohibited.

- ✔ **Furnace Creek Campground:** Here you find the most picturesque campground — and the lowest, at 196 feet below sea level. 136 campsites ($16) are adjacent to the ranch's palm groves. The year-round facility has flush toilets and drinking water, but you need to walk to the ranch for a shower, which costs a small fee. With a pool and restaurants nearby, this is my favorite campground. Reserve a site as much as six months in advance by calling ☎ **800-365-2267.**

- ✔ **Mesquite Spring Campground:** This campground, 3 miles south of Scotty's Castle off Route 267, is the farthest one north in Death Valley. Open year-round, the facility offers 30 sites ($10), flush toilets, fire rings, an RV dump station, and drinking water.

- ✔ **Panamint Springs Resort:** Thirty-one miles west of Stovepipe Wells Village on Highway 190, this campground has 26 tent sites ($10). Twelve RV sites ($ 25) provide full utility hookups for recreational vehicles while 30 other RV sites ($12) just have water hookups. Resort amenities include flush toilets, showers, and drinking water. The campground is open year-round. For more information, call (☎ **775-482-7680**).

- ✔ **Stovepipe Wells Village:** If you don't mind camping in a crowd, try this 190-site campground ($10). This campground provides flush toilets and drinking water, and for a fee, you can use shower facilities. Due to the summertime heat, the campground is open only from October to April. Fires are not allowed.

- ✔ **Sunset Campground:** If you want crowds, come to this campground ¼ mile east of the Furnace Creek Ranch. With 1,000 sites, Sunset is the park's biggest campground. Your $10 per night camping fee gets you a space and access to flush toilets and drinking water, but showers are extra and fires are prohibited. This campground is open October to April.

- ✔ **Texas Spring Campground:** This campground is in the same area as Sunset Campground. Its 92 sites ($12) and two group areas, which run $40 a night, are available from October to April. (Call ☎ **760-786-3247** for group reservations.) As with Sunset, you find flush toilets, picnic tables, and drinking water here, but showers cost extra.

- ✔ **Wildrose Campground:** If you go 30 miles south of Stovepipe Wells Village on the Trona-Wildrose Road, you find this campground and its 23 free sites. Open year-round, the campground provides water, picnic tables, fire rings, and pit toilets.

✔ **Primitive Campgrounds:** Two campgrounds offer the coolest nights in Death Valley thanks to their location at 8,133 feet, but you need a four-wheel-drive vehicle to access them. Located 37 miles and 38 miles south of Stovepipe Wells Village, respectively, are **Thorndike Campground** (six primitive sites, free, open March through November) and **Mahogany Flat Campground** (ten primitive sites, free, open March through November). Both campgrounds provide pit toilets, picnic tables, and fire rings, but no water.

Where to Eat

Maybe it's the relief that comes from escaping the heat inside an air-conditioned restaurant, but this park's food is a pleasant surprise. Don't get your expectations up, however; the dining's not on a par with that of Yosemite or Cape Cod. But the food is pretty good and only woefully pricey if you dine at the Furnace Creek Inn. The menus carry pretty much what you may expect in a national park — grill items and eggs for breakfast; burgers and sandwiches for lunch; and beef, poultry, pastas, and seafood or trout for dinner.

Forty Niner Café
$–$$ **Furnace Creek   AMERICAN**

Down the hill from the Furnace Creek Inn, this hole-in-the-wall cafe with its ever-present pitchers of ice water offers a wide menu, both price-wise and selection-wise. Breakfasts are simple but filling, as you find out if you try the Denver omelet, which comes with a large side of hash browns and toast. You can fill yourself up for lunch or dinner with a taco salad; for dinner, you can get a bit more serious with an 8-ounce New York steak accompanied by veggies and fries. You also can choose from chicken and trout dishes, as well as lasagna or other pastas.

Highway 190. ☎ *760-786-2345. Main courses: $6–$8.75 breakfast; $7.25–$14 lunch; $8.50–$17.95 dinner. AE, DC, DISC, MC. V. Open: Daily 7 a.m.–9 p.m.*

Furnace Creek Inn Dining Room
$$$–$$$$ **Furnace Creek   AMERICAN**

If you feel like dressing up and spending big bucks on a meal, this is the only place to do it in the park. In fact, during the high season, men are encouraged to wear jackets during dinner. The view out the windows is fantastic, but although the dinner entrees are enticing, the prices may dampen your appetite. The least expensive dinner entrée (at $22) is grilled vegetable stew served with a wheat risotto. The most expensive is the Southwestern grill, which essentially is a sampler of beef, chicken breast, and shrimp, all prepared with interesting salsas and marinades. At $32, this meal is definitely pricey, but at least you feel like you've tried three different entrées. This is not the place to haul a large family, but if you can splurge one night, the experience is memorable, particularly when the sun is going down.

Highway 190. ☎ 760-786-2345. Reservations recommended. Main courses: $4.75–$12.50 breakfast; $8–$14 lunch; $22–$32 dinner. AE, DC, DISC, MC, V. Open: Daily 7–10:30 a.m., 11:30 a.m.–2:30 p.m., and 5:30–9 p.m. (until 9:30 Fri–Sat).

Panamint Springs

$$–$$$ **Panamint Springs** **AMERICAN**

Once upon a time, this sleepy resort on the park's western border was hailed for its burgers and beer, and not much more. More recently, though, the menu has become a bit more diverse, with a variety of barbecued items grilled outside on the porch. Steaks — 16-ounce ribeyes and 10-ounce filets — naturally lead the way, but you can also choose from lasagna, chili, spaghetti, and homemade soups.

Highway 190. ☎ 775-482-7680. Main courses: $4–$10 breakfast; $4 –$11 lunch; $10.95–$22.95 dinner. DISC, MC, V. Open: 7 a.m.–10 p.m.

Stovepipe Wells Village

$$–$$$ **Stovepipe Wells Village** **AMERICAN**

Looking like a cross between a camp dining room and a relaxed cafe, this restaurant offers little ambience. Breakfast options also resemble camp dining room fare — eggs, eggs and steak, French toast, and biscuits and gravy — and lunches are of the short-order-grill variety, with burgers and sandwiches. Dinners don't get much more elaborate, with steaks, seafood, a chicken dish, and liver and onions leading the way.

Highway 190. ☎ 760-786-2387. Main courses: $3.50–$8.95 breakfast; $5.95–$10 lunch; $9.95–$21.95 dinner. AE, DC, DISC, MC, V. Open: Daily 7 a.m.–2 p.m., 5:30–9 p.m.

Wrangler Steakhouse

$$$$$ **Furnace Creek** **AMERICAN**

Located next to the Forty Niner Café, the only reason to opt for this steakhouse is to gorge yourself on one of the all-you-can-eat buffets (offered for breakfast 6–9 a.m. and lunch 11 a.m.–2 p.m.). Otherwise, your meal can get pretty pricey; entrees start at $21 for half a chicken and run up to $29 for a T-bone steak. The size of the servings isn't bad, but if you're going to pay these prices, why not head up the hill to the inn, put on a jacket, and shell out just a few more dollars for a more enjoyable dining experience? If you show up for the breakfast buffet, expect to find fruit, a salad bar, eggs, bacon, waffles, and French toast. Lunchtime brings out three hot entrees, such as fried chicken or lasagna, as well as a soup and salad bar.

Highway 190. ☎ 760-786-2345. Reservations recommended. Main courses: $8.50 breakfast buffet; $9.75 lunch buffet; $21–$29 dinner. AE, DC, DISC, MC, V. Open: 6–9 a.m., 11 a.m.–2 p.m.; 6:30–9:30 p.m. (Early bird special 5–6 p.m.)

Fast Facts: Death Valley

Area Code

☎ 760.

ATM

Inside the Furnace Creek Ranch registration office and the Stovepipe Wells Village motel.

Emergency

☎ 760-786-2330.

Fees

$10 per vehicle per week.

Hospitals/Clinics

None in the park. Beatty (Nevada) Health Clinic, ☎ 775-553-2208.

Information

Death Valley National Park, P.O. Box 579, Death Valley, CA 92328-0579; ☎ 760-786-3200.

Lost and Found

☎ 760-786-2331.

Post Office

Furnace Creek Ranch complex; ☎ 760-786-2223.

Road Conditions

California, ☎ 800-427-7623; Nevada, ☎ 776-793-1313.

Taxes

9% hotel, 7.75% meals.

Time Zone

Pacific standard time.

Web Site

www.nps.gov/deva.

Chapter 13

Grand Canyon National Park

● ●

In This Chapter

▶ Discovering the grand gorge

▶ Planning your vacation — and avoiding the crowds

▶ Exploring the highlights from rim to rim

▶ Finding the best lodging and restaurants

● ●

*W*elcome to one of the biggest, deepest, and most interesting showcases of erosion in the world. Yes, this chapter is all about that illustrious hole in the ground — the Grand Canyon.

You can see thousands of spectacular canyons around the United States — Hell's Canyon in Idaho, Kings Canyon in California, and the Grand Canyon of the Yellowstone in Wyoming, to name a few. But none is quite as magnificent, as colorful, or as big as the one near the northern Arizona border. Nothing else exists like the Grand Canyon. When you stand on either the South or North rims, you look out across a mile-deep abyss, 18 miles wide in places. This rocky gorge is stunning, both in its display of the power of erosion and in its intricate, delicately carved layers, ridges, and promontories of rock.

The Grand Canyon is a mesmerizing combination of multihued ridges, cliffs, pinnacles, and side canyons unlike any other. You can explore the park in an afternoon by following one of the many hiking trails or by spending a couple weeks negotiating the Colorado River as it continues to gnaw at the bedrock on the canyon floor. But this is the one park in the country where you can just stand in one place — preferably Point Sublime or the more accessible Hopi Point — and admire the park's ruggedly beautiful essence. At sunset at Point Sublime, the fiery sky melds with the glowing, red- and gold-colored walls of rock. The deep and sprawling canyon, aglow from these atmospheric fireworks, provides a humbling setting.

 You can see the South Rim's highlights in one day. If you also want to hike and visit the North Rim, plan to spend at least four days in the park — one at the South Rim, one hiking, one driving to the North Rim, and one touring the North Rim.

What gouged the gorge?

The waters of the Green and Colorado rivers run downhill from west-central Wyoming and central Colorado before merging in Utah and continuing into Arizona, where the rivers carved the Grand Canyon. Over the last 6 million years, the Colorado River did a masterful job of slicing through the rock landscape that took nearly 2 billion years to form. Along the way, the river laid bare an incredible record of North American geology. While steadily and relentlessly washing bits and pieces of rock, dirt, sand, and silt downstream to the Gulf of California, the river created a 277-mile-long canyon that's chock-full of breathtaking views in all directions. (By the way, this 277-mile length is measured in "river miles," beginning at Lees Ferry near Page, Arizona, and ending at the Grand Wash Cliffs near the Arizona/Nevada border.)

For most national parks, I staunchly recommend fall visits, and I follow this rule with the Grand Canyon. After all, crowds are usually down, temperatures are more reasonable, and forest colors can be stunning. Summer isn't a bad season either, but the park is most overrun with tourists during June, July, and August, and temperatures on the canyon floor can exceed 100 degrees. (If you don't plan to hike into the canyon, temperature isn't really an issue — in summer, the South Rim has average highs in the 80s, whereas the North Rim reaches the 70s.) Winter is a good time to visit if you want to avoid crowds on the South Rim. Winter hits the North Rim so hard, though, that it closes to traffic from late October through mid-May.

Must-see Attractions

When you arrive at Grand Canyon National Park, the biggest attraction — the hole in the ground — is incredibly obvious. But don't overlook what else the park has to offer. The following little cheat sheet can save you some time figuring out where to go and what to see:

- **Canyon View Information Plaza:** Accessed by the park's shuttle bus system, the plaza has exhibits on the park's geology, history, and wildlife, and a selection of trail guides and maps.

- **Desert View Drive:** Along this drive, you see great canyon panoramas from such overlooks as Grand View and Moran points. Lipan Point offers the best sunset pictures.

- **Tusayan Ruins:** To some people, the low lines of foundation stones that remain at this site near the South Rim are nothing more than rocks. But these rocks are the lasting mark of an ancestral Puebloan community that flourished 800 years ago. The ruins, and a nearby museum, offer the park's best cultural display.

✔ **Watchtower:** Modern man imitated prehistoric man by building this stone tower, located on the Desert View Drive. The tower houses a nice Native American art collection and a great observation deck.

✔ **North Rim:** A refuge from the crowds, the "other" rim has stunning vistas and thick conifer forests with great hiking trails. The higher elevation translates into cooler summers.

✔ **Point Imperial:** The highest point on the North Rim, reaching 8,803 feet, Point Imperial offers the best view of the canyon's northeastern corner. This is *the* spot for great sunrise photographs.

Getting There

Reaching the Grand Canyon takes effort, especially if you plan to visit the North Rim. Nonetheless, several modes of transport can get you there.

Geologic layer cake

Think a canyon is nothing more than a V-shaped gouge in the earth? Think again. The Grand Canyon is a myriad collection of canyons cut by the Colorado River and its tributaries. The maze-like formation is the result of different types of rock layers that erode at different rates in different ways. This geologic wonder has at least 13 different layers of rock. From top to bottom, these layers represent roughly 2 billion years of the Earth's history (give or take a few millennia), or roughly half the world's geologic history. Capping these layers is Kaibab Limestone, a fossil-rich, buff-colored layer of rock that holds the rim in place by resisting erosion. Descending beneath the limestone, in order, are the Toroweap formation, Coconino Sandstone, Hermit Shale, the Supai Group, the Surprise Canyon formation, Redwall Limestone, Temple Butte Limestone, Muav Limestone, Bright Angel Shale, Tapeats Sandstone, Zoraster Grante, and, finally, Vishnu Schist.

Study these layers (or talk to someone who makes a living as a geologist) and you discover that they chronicle a history of rivers, oceans, volcanoes, and mountains possibly as tall as today's Himalayas. You also discover that this layer cake is missing some ingredients. One gap in the chronology, known as the "Great Unconformity," represents an estimated 1 billion years of missing geology. As for the canyon's colorful outer frosting, these hues are the result of a wonderful mix of mineral deposits. One of the more common minerals is iron, which is responsible for the reds, oranges, yellows, and even greens.

Grand Canyon National Park

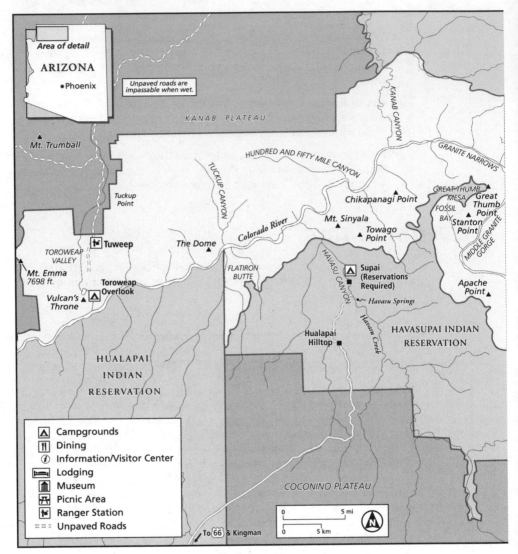

Area of detail

ARIZONA

•Phoenix

Unpaved roads are impassable when wet.

KANAB PLATEAU

KANAB CANYON

GRANITE NARROWS

▲ Mt. Trumball

HUNDRED AND FIFTY MILE CANYON

TUCKUP CANYON

Tuckup Point

Chikapanagi Point

GREAT THUMB MESA

Great Thumb Point ▲

FOSSIL BAY

Stanton Point ▲

Mt. Sinyala ▲

Towago Point ▲

Colorado River

The Dome ▲

⛺ Tuweep

TOROWEAP VALLEY

Mt. Emma 7698 ft. ▲

FLATIRON BUTTE

HAVASU CANYON

▲ Supai (Reservations Required)

MIDDLE GRANITE GORGE

Apache Point ▲

Toroweap Overlook

Havasu Springs

Vulcan's Throne ▲

Hualapai Hilltop ■

Havasu Creek

HAVASUPAI INDIAN RESERVATION

HUALAPAI

INDIAN

RESERVATION

⛺ Campgrounds
🍴 Dining
ⓘ Information/Visitor Center
🛏 Lodging
🏛 Museum
🔭 Picnic Area
⛺ Ranger Station
=== Unpaved Roads

COCONINO PLATEAU

0   5 mi
0   5 km

To (66) & Kingman

Driving in

Most people drive to the Grand Canyon from one of the region's airports. Grand Canyon Village on the South Rim is 80 miles north of Flagstaff, Arizona (the region's largest city), via U.S. Route 180, and 59 miles north of Williams, Arizona, via Highway 64. The closest town to the park is Tusayan, Arizona, 1 mile beyond the south entrance on Highway 64.

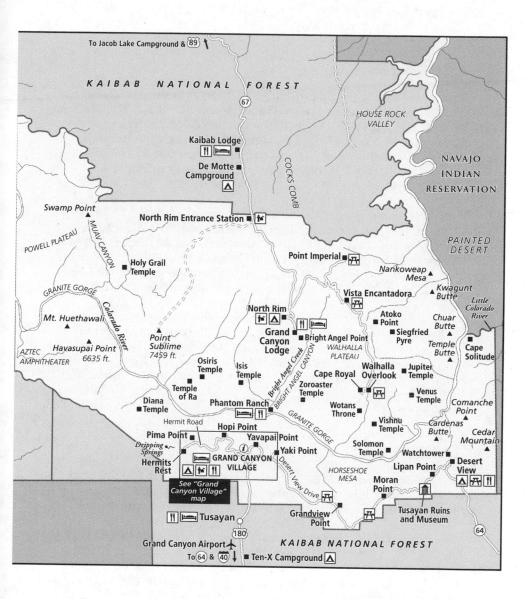

An alternative to driving all the way to Grand Canyon Village is to leave your car in Williams or Tusayan. From these towns, you can take a train or shuttle bus, respectively, to the village. See the following sections, "Flying in" and "Training in," to find out more about these options. See also the "Transportation travails" sidebar in this chapter to find out about changes tentatively set to take effect in 2004, after which traffic restrictions are likely on the South Rim.

The North Rim is closest to Kanab, Utah, 78 miles to the northwest via Arizona 67 and U.S. Route 89A.

Flying in

If you plan to fly to the park, the biggest runways in the general vicinity are **Phoenix/Sky Harbor International Airport** (☎ 602-273-3300), which is 220 miles from the South Rim, and **McCarran International Airport** (☎ 702-261-5743) in Las Vegas, which is 263 miles from the North Rim. **America West Express** has daily jet service between Phoenix/Sky Harbor International Airport and **Flagstaff Pulliam Airport** (☎ 928-556-1234), which is 80 miles from the South Rim.

If you don't mind smaller airports, **Eagle Canyon Charter** (☎ 702-736-1182, ext 153) and **Scenic Airlines** (☎ 800-634-6801 or 702-638-3200) can fly you from Las Vegas to **Grand Canyon National Airport** (☎ 928-638-2446) in Tusayan, 1 mile south of Grand Canyon Village, on one of their daily flights. Scenic and Eagle Canyon both fly out of **North Las Vegas Airport** (☎ 702-261-3800) as well as McCarran International.

Most of the major rental car agencies have offices at the Phoenix/Sky Harbor International Airport and McCarran International Airport in Las Vegas; see the Appendix for contact information. **Hertz, Budget, Avis,** and **National** rent cars at Flagstaff Pulliam Airport, and **Enterprise** rents cars at Tusayan during the high season. You can also take a shuttle from Tusayan to the Grand Canyon Village; see "Busing in," later in this chapter, for details.

Training in

Even rail fans have ways to get to the park. **Amtrak** (☎ 800-872-7245 or 928-774-8679; Internet: www.amtrak.com) runs into downtown Flagstaff. **Budget** has a car-rental office two blocks from the station.

You can also ride the **Historic Grand Canyon Railway** (☎ 800-843-8724; Internet: www.thetrain.com), which makes daily runs linking Williams, Arizona, and Grand Canyon Village. A vintage steam engine or 1950 diesel lugs the train 65 miles, leaving Williams in the morning and returning late in the afternoon.

Busing in

From Tusayan, you can take one of the hourly shuttles to Grand Canyon Village offered by **Grand Canyon Coaches** (☎ 520-638-0821; Internet: www.grandcanyoncoaches.com). The shuttles operate from March through October and link five stops in Tusayan to the village. Using the shuttle is a great way to avoid parking problems inside the park. The adult fare is $4; ages 16 and under ride free.

Planning Ahead

Not surprisingly, with a park of Grand Canyon's stature, you have to make plans early. Make reservations as far in advance as possible — even two years in advance — for each activity you plan to do, including mule rides, backcountry hikes, river trips, lodging, and camping. For help in sorting out your trip, contact the park for a Trip Planner by mail (Trip Planner, P.O. Box 129, Grand Canyon, AZ 86023), phone (☎ 928-638-7888), or Internet (www.nps.gov/grca). You can request a Backcountry Trip Planner by writing to Backcountry Office, Grand Canyon National Park, P.O. Box 129, Grand Canyon, AZ 86023.

One company — **Xanterra Parks & Resorts** (14001 E. Eliff, Aurora, CO 80014; ☎ 303-297-2757; Internet: www.xanterra.com) — oversees all the lodging in the park under the auspices of Grand Canyon National Park Lodges. Through their telephone number or Web site, you can make reservations up to 23 months in advance. As a general rule, if you have your heart set on visiting during a holiday period or in fall or spring, you should call 20 to 23 months in advance. However, even at some of the park's most popular hotels, such as the El Tovar, you can sometimes get a reservation within a month's time because of cancellations — good news for those who can't conceive of planning so far in advance.

For me, one of the best places to spend a night in the park is in a tent or under the stars. Camping brings you one step closer to the park's essence. The Grand Canyon has four campgrounds, two of which require reservations during some seasons. You can call ☎ 1-800-365-CAMP, or log on to the park's Web site at www.reservations.nps.gov, to make reservations at the Mather and North Rim Campgrounds. The Mather Campground is open year-round, and I strongly recommend reservations for visits between mid-March and November 1. If you're serious about planning, you can make these reservations up to five months in advance of your visit. From December to March, however, Mather sites are assigned on a first-come, first-served basis. The North Rim Campground, meanwhile, is open only from mid-May to late October, and again I recommend reservations, although sometimes you can stumble upon last-minute vacancies. For information on all the campgrounds, see "Where to Stay," later in this chapter.

Learning the Lay of the Land

Grand Canyon is a fairly straightforward park in terms of layout. Flanking the main attraction — the incredibly large, colorful, and jagged chasm — are two rims that offer fantastic views. The South Rim boasts the most manmade attractions and facilities (and some darn impressive views), but the North Rim offers cooler temperatures, thick forests, and relative solitude (as well as, of course, some darn impressive views).

Grand Canyon Village

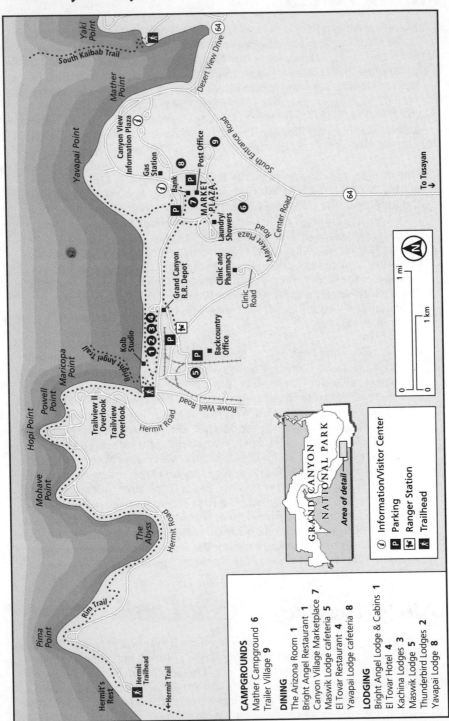

CAMPGROUNDS
Mather Campground **6**
Trailer Village **9**

DINING
The Arizona Room **1**
Bright Angel Restaurant **1**
Canyon Village Marketplace **7**
Maswik Lodge cafeteria **5**
El Tovar Restaurant **4**
Yavapai Lodge cafeteria **8**

LODGING
Bright Angel Lodge & Cabins **1**
El Tovar Hotel **4**
Kachina Lodges **3**
Maswik Lodge **5**
Thunderbird Lodges **2**
Yavapai Lodge **8**

Information/Visitor Center
P Parking
Ranger Station
Trailhead

GRAND CANYON
NATIONAL PARK
Area of detail

You're probably not going to visit both rims during the same trip. Why not? For starters, an easily traveled route does not exist between Point A (the South Rim) and Point B (the North Rim). Going from rim to rim by auto entails a highway odyssey of about 220 miles (one-way) that takes about five hours. Sure, you can hike down into the canyon and up the other side. But doing so is impractical unless you plan to make such a trek the focus of your trip: A hike from one side to the other covers 21 miles via the North and South Kaibab Trails, a trek that usually takes three days each way.

The park covers more than 1.2 million acres, but has relatively few roads and developed areas. The **South Rim** is the main travel corridor for Grand Canyon visitors. The air is not as cool as on the North Rim, and the trees aren't as tightly packed together, but the views are more numerous and, in some minds, more incredible. Unlike the North Rim overlooks, some of those at the South Rim take in the Colorado River. **Grand Canyon Village** lends a sense of community to this rim, with its lodgings, visitor center, ranger station, restaurants, gift shops, sprawling campgrounds, and picnic grounds (see the Grand Canyon Village map, in this chapter).

During July and August, the South Rim can seem like Grand Central Station at rush hour. You can avoid this madness by visiting during another time of year. If you do visit in the summer, arrive at the park before 10:00 a.m. or after 2:00 p.m. in order to avoid the lines at the entrance gates and the parking problems. You can also leave your car in Tusayan or Williams and take a shuttle or train to the South Rim (see "Getting There," earlier in this chapter).

You negotiate the South Rim along two roads — Hermit Road and Desert View Drive, both of which have several overlooks. (See "Enjoying the top attractions," later in this chapter, for details on the overlooks.) **Desert View Drive** starts in the village and runs 25 miles to the east, whereas **Hermit Road** starts in the village and travels 8 miles west to the Hermits Rest Overlook. A public highway, Desert View Drive is open year-round to motorists, but private vehicles can't stop at the Yaki Overlook and the South Kaibab Trailhead during high season (Mar–Nov), a ban park officials might make year-round. Hermit Road is closed to private vehicles during high season but open to them from December through February. During closures, you must take a free park shuttle to visit the outlooks. (See "Getting around," later in this chapter, for information on shuttles.)

Looking for a slower pace than the hustle and bustle of the South Rim? Then head to the **North Rim,** which you can access via U.S. Route 89A and Highway 67. At an average elevation of 8,000 feet — 1,000 feet higher than the South Rim — this rim is incredibly lush (especially in contrast to the South Rim and Inner Gorge). Ponderosa pine, spruce, fir, pockets of aspen, groves of gambel oak, and stands of juniper and pinyon fill the area. Much of the rim is accessible only to the most determined travelers. Roads are few, requiring anyone who wants to go beyond the Cape Royal, Point Imperial, and Point Sublime Overlooks, or the Grand Canyon Lodge (the rim's only hotel), to do so by foot, horse, or mule. In winter, you can add cross-country skis to the mix. (See "Keeping active," later in this chapter, for information on horse, mule, and ski excursions.)

Transportation travails

If you like traffic jams, make the South Rim your first stop in Grand Canyon. Every year, an estimated 1.5 million private vehicles and another 30,000 tour buses converge on this side of the park. Smog blurs the views, and not enough parking lots are available to handle the traffic, so at the height of summer, you often encounter lines of rigs parked along the road. Not only are they ugly, but they're also dangerous for visitors and deadly for roadside vegetation.

The National Park Service isn't ignoring the problem. In 1995, officials agreed that they had to change the way people visit the Grand Canyon's South Rim. The park has free shuttle buses available, but that is just a start. One day you won't be able to drive yourself onto the South Rim. Instead, to see the park's beauty from the south side, you'll have to catch a shuttle bus or a light-rail train.

Fall 2000 saw the opening of the **Canyon View Information Plaza** (CVIP) near Mather Point. For now, this location is primarily an orientation center. However, when the Park Service implements a mass-transit system, CVIP will be the nerve center for tourist traffic on the South Rim. Here you'll find a bookstore and even bicycle rentals. Currently, you can reach CVIP via the park's shuttle bus system or by walking a ¾-mile, paved trail from Market Plaza.

If a light-rail system is built, you'll be kindly asked to park your car at the South Rim gateway community of Tusayan and ride the train into the park. One spur will run to CVIP, where shuttle buses, powered by electricity or natural gas, very likely will haul you to Hermits Rest, Yaki Point, Desert View, and locations within Grand Canyon Village. A second spur likely will run to the Village Transit Center, a second transportation hub near Maswik Lodge. If the light-rail system is deemed unnecessary, a shuttle-bus system likely will haul the bulk of the South Rim's visitors.

If you choose not to ride the rail or shuttle, you can rent a bike and pedal your heart out along the slowly expanding Greenway trail that is designed to parallel the transit system from Hermits Rest to Desert View and south to Tusayan. The first section of the Greenway opened in the fall of 2001 and runs 2 miles from CVIP to the train depot. Another section, from CVIP to Tusayan, was expected to be under construction by mid-2003

If you have lodging reservations in the park, you'll park at designated parking areas, where you'll take the transit system to reach your accommodations on the South Rim. Campers will be able to drive to their campground.

For more details and updates on the transit system, as well as information on the decisions behind it, visit the park's Web site, www.nps.gov/grca/transit.

The only other road into the park is a dirt route that runs to the **Toroweap Valley** on the western edge of the park. Follow this road, and you gain access to a campground, the Toroweap Overlook, and Vulcans Throne, a volcanic cone. Another dirt route drops south from U.S. Route 89A and bisects **House Rock Valley** near the northeastern tip of the park. This road doesn't go into the park, but it leads to the South Canyon Trail, which heads into the park and toward the Colorado River.

Arriving in the Park

When you arrive at the North or South rims, you need to pay an entrance fee and get your bearings. This section explains how to do both, as well as how to get around the park.

Finding information

Upon entering the park on the South or North rims, you receive a copy of the free park newspaper, *The Guide.* This useful publication contains information on ranger activities, a map and schedule for the park's free shuttle buses, and general information on the park.

After you pass through the **South Rim** entrance station and park your car, catch one of the shuttle buses to the **Canyon View Information Plaza** (☎ 928-638-7888), about 1,000 feet from the canyon's rim. Here you can orient yourself to the park, get any questions answered, find activity schedules, pick up brochures, and browse a bookstore. Hours are 8 a.m. to 5 p.m. every day; open longer during the summer season.

The **North Rim** has a small visitor center near the Grand Canyon Lodge with a small bookstore and information desk.

Paying fees

Admission to Grand Canyon National Park costs $20 per private vehicle and $10 for travelers on foot or bicycle. Your receipt is good for a week and provides access to both rims. See Chapter 8 for information on the National Parks Pass and Chapter 4 for the lowdown on Golden Age and Golden Access passports.

Although you can make day hikes into the canyon without a permit, if you plan to stay overnight in the backcountry, you need to obtain a $10 permit and also pay a $5 per night per person user impact fee. You can obtain a camping permit four months in advance of your planned stay. To get a permit, see "Planning Ahead," earlier in this chapter, for information about requesting a Backcountry Trip Planner.

Getting around

After you get to Grand Canyon Village, you don't need a car to enjoy the sights. In fact, you can't use your car during high season to visit some viewpoints; from March through November, cars are prohibited on Hermit Road and cannot stop at Yaki Point on Desert View Drive.

The park's **free shuttle buses** can get you where you want to go on the South Rim. One bus laps Grand Canyon Village, another traverses Hermit Road, and a third runs along Desert View Drive to Yaki Point and the South Kaibab Trailhead. During high season, shuttles run daily, about every 15 to 20 minutes, from an hour before sunrise to an hour after sunset. The Grand Canyon Village shuttle runs from March through April and from October through November until 10 p.m., from May through September until 11 p.m., and from December through February until 9 p.m. In the off-season the Desert View shuttle runs until an hour after sunset. The Hermit Road shuttle does not operate during December, January, and February. The Kaibab shuttle runs year-round from an hour before sunrise to an hour after sunset.

You can catch the shuttles in a lodge parking lot; in parking lots A, B, C, D, or E; or at any of the drop-off points along the routes. (You receive directions to the parking lots at the entrance station.) For information and schedules, call **Bright Angel Transportation Desk** (☎ 928-638-3283). You can also pick up a shuttle map and schedule at the Canyon View Information Plaza.

You can also board one of the sightseeing buses run by the **Fred Harvey Transportation Company** (☎ 928-638-2822). These tours depart mornings and afternoons from Bright Angel, Maswik, and Yuavapai lodges. Rates are $16 per person for a Hermit Road tour (two hours); $28 for a Desert View Drive tour (four hours); and $33 for a combination of the two. Children under age 16 are free when traveling with an adult. Tickets are available at the transportation desks at the three departure points. This company also operates a 24-hour taxi service.

For hikers who travel from one rim to the other, the best way to get back to your car is aboard the **Trans-Canyon Shuttle** (☎ 928-638-2820), which runs a bus each day, in each direction, from mid-May through mid-October. The 220-mile trip takes about 4½ hours each way and costs $65 per person one-way, $110 round-trip. A reservation deposit is required. The shuttle travels between Bright Angel Lodge on the South Rim and Grand Canyon Lodge on the North Rim. You can also arrange to be picked up at a campground or trailhead on the North Rim.

Remembering Safety

If you stand on one of the canyon overlooks, you'll likely notice that a fall off the ledge would bring a nasty ending to your vacation. So no matter how badly you want a slightly different photograph, do not leap over the railings that keep you a safe distance from the canyon's lip. A slip or stumble could be your last.

The park is home to poisonous critters like scorpions and the Grand Canyon rattlesnake, so be careful where you put your hands when scrambling in rocky areas. Think twice about putting your hand in a spot you can't see.

If you plan to hike, read through the safety tips at the beginning of the "Taking a hike" section, later in this chapter. For additional tips on how to ensure a safe visit to a national park, see Chapter 8.

Enjoying the Park

Spend any time in Grand Canyon National Park and you quickly realize that three distinct areas exist in its borders: the North Rim, the Inner Gorge, and the South Rim. Spend a little more time and you discover that these three areas can be further dissected into side canyons, smaller plateaus, and a collection of overlooks — all worthy of exploration.

How do you want to explore the canyon? Does strapping a 40-pound pack on your back and disappearing below the rim for several days appeal to you? Are you interested in joining one of the mule trips that head down to the Phantom Ranch, a great base from which to investigate the river and the side canyons? Or would joining one of the scenic plane or helicopter flights that jog back and forth over the canyon every day, giving passengers a bird's eye view of the park, be more appealing?

Options, options, and more options. In this section, I introduce the top attractions and tell you how best to enjoy them.

Exploring the top attractions

Desert View Drive
South Rim

From Grand Canyon Village, Desert View Drive takes you to six great overlooks. One of the best, **Yaki Point,** offers views of some of the Grand Canyon's more renowned rock monuments — Vishnu Temple, Zoroaster Temple, and Wotan's Throne. Another overlook, **Moran Point,** is named after Thomas Moran, the landscape painter who helped put Yellowstone

National Park on the map before journeying to Grand Canyon with Major John Wesley Powell. This overlook offers the best view of the tilting block of rock known as The Sinking Ship. You can spot the "ship" by looking southwest at the rocks level with the South Rim. The ship seems to be submerged in the horizontal layers of Coronado Butte.

If you can't leave the canyon without a killer sunset photo, head to **Lipan Point,** arguably the best spot on the South Rim for watching the setting sun — and for glimpsing the Colorado River. Almost straight below you at this point, the Colorado River makes a long, lazy S-curve. Just downstream of the curve you can see where the river cuts into the Vishnu Schist, one of the oldest rock layers in the canyon, and enters the steep-walled Inner Gorge. **Desert View,** the eastern-most overlook on Desert View Drive, also offers spectacular views into the eastern arm of the canyon.

Near Desert View overlook is the **Watchtower,** an impressive 70-foot stone structure designed by architect Mary Colter in 1932. You can climb a narrow stairway to an enclosed observation deck on the tower's top. Traditional Native American art, including many images seen on rocks in the Southwest, decorate the walls. The most impressive work is by Hopi artist Fred Kabotie, whose depiction of the Snake Legend, the story of the first person to have floated down the Colorado River, graces the Watchtower's Hopi Room. The Watchtower is open from 7:30 a.m. to 7:00 p.m. in summer and 9:00 a.m. to 5:00 p.m. in winter.

Just before Lipan Point on the drive is **Tusayan Ruinand Museum,** a must-see if you have any interest in America's ancient cultures. The 14-room, stone-walled structure dates to 1185 and has been traced to ancestors of today's Pueblos. You can take a self-guided walk through the ruins, which are little more than stone foundations. Still, interpretive signs along the way do a good job bringing the place to life. Nearby is the Tusayan Museum, which traces the lives of the region's Native Americans through displays of jewelry, clothing, and tools. This free museum is open from 9:00 a.m. to 5:00 p.m.

Desert View Drive starts at Grand Canyon Village and runs east for 25 miles.

Hermit Road
South Rim

Hop on one of the shuttle buses that ply the 8-mile-long Hermit Road during the summer season (see "Getting around," earlier in this chapter), and you come upon, among other lookouts, Powell Memorial, Hopi Point, and Mohave Point. **Powell Memorial** is a tribute to Major John Wesley Powell, an explorer who led the first successful navigation of the Colorado River through the canyon in 1869. **Hopi Point** is the best place on the West Rim to take in a sunset. From **Mohave Point,** you can spot some of the Colorado River's best rapids, including Hermit Rapids, Granite Rapids, and Salt Creek Rapids. **Hermits Rest,** a rock shelter designed to look as if some reclusive mountain man had built it, marks the end of the road. Built in 1914 to serve as a resting spot for tourists heading below the rim to Hermit Camp, this building still caters to travelers. You can relax in front of the fireplace or buy a snack to munch on before moving on.

Hermit Rd. starts at Grand Canyon Village and runs west for 8 miles.

Inner Gorge

In the middle of the Grand Canyon is a relatively narrow, 1,000-foot-deep channel known as the Inner Gorge. At the bottom of this gorge, hidden from most viewpoints on the North and South rims, the Colorado River's often-muddy waters flow. The canyon floor offers you another incredible view: the look up. The towering canyon walls are so impressive — and so jagged, fluted, and riddled from erosion — that you risk a sore neck from gazing upwards at them. Springs gush from numerous spots along the river corridor, creating waterfalls that quench wildlife and vegetation. (Before quenching your own thirst, make sure that you treat the water.) **Vasey's Paradise** is one of the more memorable gushers, pouring out of the north canyon wall in Marble Canyon and nourishing a thick bed of vegetation in the otherwise arid landscape.

River-bottom travelers see some of the park's best prehistoric ruins. At Nankoweap, near river mile 52, ruins used for grain storage are tucked under an alcove high on a canyon wall.

The canyon floor has one hotel, Phantom Ranch. See "Where to Stay," later in this chapter, for information on this accomodation.

You can access the bottom of the Grand Canyon by foot, raft, or mule. See "Taking a hike" for information on walks and "Keeping active" for raft or mule trips. Both sections appear later in this chapter.

North Rim

The North Rim's overall lack of crowds — relative to the South Rim, that is — results from the remoteness of this side of the canyon. The rim's major overlooks are at Bright Angel Point, Cape Royal, Point Imperial, and Point Sublime; all offer dazzling views of the Grand Canyon and its many side canyons. The hub of activity on the rim is **Grand Canyon Lodge,** a beautiful hotel that practically melds with the landscape, thanks to its green roof shingles, rugged log beams, and limestone exterior that matches the rim's Kaibab limestone. (See "Where to Stay," later in this chapter, for information on the lodge.) A short walk from the lodge is **Bright Angel Point,** which offers great views of a side canyon and the South Rim. Hardy travelers pause only briefly at this point before heading down the North Kaibab Trail, which starts 1½ miles from Grand Canyon Lodge and winds its way through Bright Angel Canyon to the Phantom Ranch nearly 6,000 feet below.

The best view at the North Rim is from the lip of **Cape Royal,** 23 miles from the lodge on Cape Royal Drive off Highway 67. Here the Grand Canyon plunges abruptly away from the rim. Although you can't immediately see the river, a short hike leads to a view through Angels Window, an eroded hole in a rock wall, which takes in the lower canyon and a tiny stretch of the Colorado River. Nearby are the **Walhalla Ruins,** once part of an Anasazi community, and **Roosevelt Point,** a small promontory on Cape Royal Drive that offers a view of where the Little Colorado River gorge and the Grand Canyon meet.

Point Imperial, the highest point on the North Rim at 8,803 feet, stands at the end of a 3-mile-long spur road running east from Cape Royal Drive. Although the point can become crowded in summer — when its picnic ground is a magnet — the view is worth sharing. The overlook faces east, drawing your eyes not only down into the depths of the canyon but also out across to **Mount Hayden,** a spindly spire somehow still standing on the edge of the canyon. Beyond and below Mount Hayden is the **Marble Platform** (a desolate-looking plain that geologists consider to be the top section of the Grand Canyon) and the Painted Desert. The hump that appears on the northeastern horizon is southeastern Utah's Navajo Mountain.

After the isolated Toroweap Overlook, the most remote North Rim overlook accessible by vehicle is **Point Sublime,** which lies west of Grand Canyon Lodge and which you reach by a rugged, bouncy road off Highway 67 that sedans should avoid. If you arrive at the point in late afternoon, you find intoxicating sunsets that seemingly spray a cascade of colors across the canyon walls. Because the overlook is off the beaten path, this viewpoint (which induces vertigo if you venture to its lip) is not overrun with tourists.

You can reach the North Rim via U.S. Route 89A and Highway 67.

Yavapai Point
South Rim

This point has a neat historic observation station on the canyon rim. Inside, a bank of windows lets you gaze down into the canyon. As a bonus, a long interpretative panel beneath the windows helps you identify many of the landmarks in the central portion of the canyon, including such formations as **Zoroaster Temple, Isis Temple,** and **Buddha Temple.** Also visible from the point is the **Kaibab Suspension Bridge.** A new geology exhibit is planned for the observation station in 2003 or 2004.

Yavapai Point is about 1 mile east of the visitor center in Grand Canyon Village.

Capturing the Grand Canyon on film

The canyon provides countless good areas to take pictures, but some spots are definitely better than others. If you're striving for that definitive Grand Canyon sunset, try shooting from the Hopi, Mojave, or Pima points located along Hermit Road on the South Rim. Or focus your camera from Lipan Point and Desert View Overlook on Desert View Drive. If you're an early riser and prefer sunrise shots, try Mather, Yaki, Yavapai, and Lipan points on the South Rim. On the North Rim, Bright Angel Point, Point Sublime, and Cape Royal are good for sunsets and sunrises. To find out how early you need to get up for sunrise or how late in the evening the sun will set, check the park's newspaper, *The Guide.* To get some ideas on specific shots to take, visit the Kolb Studio in Grand Canyon Village. The Kolb brothers, early canyon photographers, used this building as their studio. Inside you find a good bookstore and photography exhibits.

Taking a hike

Grand Canyon National Park offers an interesting variety of hiking trails, from incredibly steep, knee-pounding trails that plunge deep into the canyon to some relatively level walks through cool, shaded pine forests and along the rims. The bottom line is that you can sweat as much or as little as you want and still see some incredible views of the park.

Remember the following points before you head off down the trail:

- **Gravity is both your friend and your enemy.** If you hike below the rim, gravity works for you and makes the walk somewhat easy. However, save some strength for the return hike uphill, when gravity is no longer your best buddy.

- **Timing is everything.** If you plan to hike into the canyon and back out the same day, budget one-third of your time to hike down into the canyon, and two-thirds to climb back out. Do *not* think that you can hike down to the Colorado River and back to one of the rims in one day. The terrain and conditions make this trek pretty close to impossible.

- **Water is good.** Lots of water is very good. The temperature may not feel so hot while you're walking along the rim or when you first start down into the canyon. But trust me, the lower you go, the more rugged the terrain becomes, and the higher the thermostat climbs. Remember that, while you're enjoying 75-degree weather on the top of the North Rim, the temperature way down below at Phantom Ranch can easily be 105 degrees! If you're visiting from either coast, you soon realize how the dry air can suck the moisture out of your body. So after you decide on a hike, but before you set foot down the trail, make sure that you pack at least two quarts of water (preferably more) for every eight hours of hiking.

✔ **Pack some shade.** Wear a wide-brimmed hat and maybe even a neckerchief to shade your neck. Bringing a full tube of sun block is a good idea, too.

✔ **Energize yourself.** If you plan to go on an overnight hike, you need to give nutrition some serious thought. But even if you're planning on a relatively short hike, say a couple miles, granola bars or some fruit are great to snack on when you reach the halfway point.

Overnight access to the park's backcountry is controlled through a permit system, so if you don't plan ahead, you can arrive ready to head off on a multiday hike only to discover that no permits are available. (See "Paying fees," earlier in this chapter, for permit costs.) The park does employ a waiting list for this sort of situation, but in spring, summer, and fall you can wind up waiting two or three days for a permit. To get on the list, show up in person at the Backcountry Office, where you receive a number. To stay on the waiting list, you have to show up at the office at 8 a.m. every morning until your number is called. Although cancellations don't always happen, the office some-times sets aside a spot or two at the Bright Angel Campground or Cottonwood Campground for people on the list.

Finally, during the summer months, rangers recommend that overnight backpackers avoid hiking during the middle of the day because of high temperatures. So, begin trips, hike to new campsites within the canyon, or make your return to one of the rims either before 7 a.m. or after 4 p.m.

With these details out of the way, here's a look at some reliable hiking options in the park.

Bright Angel Trail

This trail has existed for quite a while. Both Native Americans and early settlers recognized this trail as a good route down into the canyon. Not only do you get to enjoy some shade along the way, but this place is the wettest on the South Rim, so finding water isn't usually a problem.

However, some words of caution to consider: Although this trail is very popular, it's also the scene of many rescues, because folks forget that it's a long, steep way back to the top. The hike to Indian Garden alone drops more than 3,000 feet. Mule trips head down into the canyon via this route and leave deposits along the way, so watch your footing. Also, the trail can be crowded at times. If you're into winter hiking, the upper section of this trail can be very icy, so pack some instep crampons.

If you're just heading out for a day hike, follow the trail as it zigzags below Grand Canyon Village to Mile-and-a-Half-Mile House or Three-Mile House. At each location, you find shade, an emergency phone, and water when in season, which is usually from late-April through mid-October. (Weather can shorten or extend the season.)

If you head on down below Three-Mile House, you find yourself on a steep descent to a picnic area near the spring at Indian Garden. This setting is almost like an oasis, with lush vegetation and towering cottonwood trees. It's a great place to be, but if you're not experienced with drastic elevation changes, the heat, or the dry air, don't make this destination your first hike in the park.

Distance (one-way): Just over 4½ miles to Indian Garden, 7¾ miles to Colorado River, 9¼ miles to Bright Angel Campground. Level: Moderate. Access: Trailhead is just west of Kolb Studio, near Grand Canyon Village.

Grandview Trail

This hike to Horseshoe Mesa tests your lungs and your knees, but it rewards you with a visit to a turn-of-the-20th-century mine site, not to mention great views. You definitely need to pack water on this trek, because you won't find any along the way. Also, take care on the steep, cobblestone ramps on the trail, because they become awfully slippery during rain or snow. Depending on your physical condition and the weather, the round-trip hike can take as little as 4 hours or as many as 11 because the trail drops 2,600 feet on the way to Horseshoe Mesa. After you arrive there, take time to examine the remains of Pete Barry's copper mine, but don't enter the actual shafts. By the way, this trail dates to the 1890s, when crews used dynamite to blast ledges into the canyon walls for the path.

If you find on your way down into the canyon that you're not as physically prepared for this hike as you thought, a good turnaround point is the Coconino Saddle rock formation, which is just a ¾-mile from the trailhead. Atop the saddle, you find some trees for shade, as well as great views of Hance and Grapevine canyons.

This trail connects with the 95-mile-long Tonto Trail, which many use to piece together numerous loop hikes with other South Rim trails.

Distance: 6 miles round-trip. Level: Difficult. Access: Grandview Point, 12 miles east of Grand Canyon Village on Desert View Drive.

North Kaibab Trail

This trail is a great way to get down into the canyon for a variety of reasons. First, you won't encounter as many hikers as you would on the South Kaibab Trail. Second, the trail winds through thick, pine forests at the head of Roaring Springs Canyon. Finally, this trail is much kinder to day hikers than the Bright Angel and South Kaibab trails.

Don't overlook the fact that this trail is much longer, and steeper, than its South Rim counterpart. Still, it's a great place for a hike. From the trailhead, the trail winds down a series of switchbacks into Roaring Springs Canyon. The first major landmark to watch for is **Supai Tunnel,** which is just 2¾ miles from the trailhead. This spot is a great stopping place for day hikers. You find a seasonal water source, shade, and restrooms. From here, the trail drops in relatively gradual switchbacks through the Supai Group, a 300-million-year-old rock layer about 1,000 feet thick and then crosses a bridge over a creek bed. Past the bridge, the creek plummets. The trail then follows the south wall of Roaring Springs Canyon on ledges above Redwall Cliffs.

A spire of Redwall Limestone known as "The Needle" marks the point where the trail begins its descent of the Redwall. You begin to hear Roaring Springs, the water source for both rims, just above the confluence of Bright Angel and Roaring Springs Canyons. A short (¼ mile) spur trail runs to the springs.

Distance (one-way): 2¾ miles to Supai Tunnel, 4¾ miles to Roaring Springs, 6¾ miles to Cottonwood Campground, 14½ miles to the Colorado River. Level: Moderate to strenuous. Access: On the North Rim entrance road, 2 miles north of Grand Canyon Lodge.

South Kaibab Trail

Steep and shadeless, this trail pretty much dives down into the Grand Canyon. Starting at Yaki Point, the trail drops 3,514 feet along the 7 miles it takes to reach Bright Angel Campground. Thanks to the trail's path along ridgelines, you enjoy spectacular views into the canyon from start to finish. Roughly 4½ miles from the trailhead lies a junction with the Tonto Trail, which runs 95 miles along the lower canyon, tying into many other trails and so giving you many options for crafting your own loop hikes. Because the South Kaibab Trail lacks shade, many hikers follow it to Bright Angel Campground and then return to the South Rim via the Bright Angel Trail.

Distance (one-way): 1½ miles to Cedar Ridge, 4½ miles to Tonto Trail Junction, 7 miles to Bright Angel Campground. Level: Moderate to strenuous. Access: On the Yaki Point access road, although shuttles run from Backcountry Information Center to the trailhead.

Rim Trails

If you don't have time to head down into the canyon or if you just don't like steep hikes, a walk along the South Rim is a great way to view the canyon. In the village area, the walking (along paved trails) is easy, and you pass some historic buildings. Along Hermit Road, the pavement turns to dirt just west of Maricopa Point. In both areas, the views into the canyon are wonderful.

How far you go is up to you. You can hike for 15 minutes or all day, as the Rim Trail runs from Hermit Rest to the first overlook on Desert View Drive, a distance of 13 to 14 miles. If you hike along the West Rim Trail, you have the option of catching a shuttle bus back to the village at the Abyss, which is about halfway to Hermits Rest.

The drawback for rim trails: In high season, you won't be hiking alone.

Distance: Varies. Level: Easy. Access: Any viewpoint in Grand Canyon Village or along Hermit Road.

One-day wonder

Seeing the Grand Canyon in one day requires a South Rim visit. After all, some of the best, and most accessible, overlooks are on the south side of the canyon, and the most accommodations are there, too. Fortunately, the roads on the South Rim do not run on endlessly toward the horizon. Compared to Yellowstone, Acadia, and the Great Smoky Mountains, the South Rim is really very condensed. Unless otherwise noted, for information on the attractions in this itinerary, see "Exploring the top attractions," earlier in this chapter.

Start your day by stopping at the park's **main visitor center** in the Canyon View Information Plaza (see "Finding information," earlier in this chapter). Here you can gorge yourself on park information, including which hiking trails are open and which aren't. You can also buy just about all the maps and guidebooks you need to survive the park.

From Grand Canyon Village, head east toward the **Desert View Drive,** stopping at Yavapai Point. If the timing works, stick around for a ranger talk on the canyon's geologic history at the Yavapai Observation Station. (The ranger schedule changes seasonally; consult your park newspaper.)

Next, head east to Grandview Point, and if the weather isn't too hot, head down the Grandview Trail. How far you go depends on how you want to spend the bulk of your day. If you prefer to spend the day hiking, by all means follow the trail to **Horseshoe Mesa** (see the "Taking a hike" section). This 6-mile round-trip hike offers a glimpse of the canyon's mining history. Depending on your physical condition, this hike takes between 4 and 11 hours. (If it's particularly hot, count on the latter figure.) If the weather's too hot or if you're simply not up for this sort of hike, just take in the view from the point. Now, if you want to sample the trail, head down about a ¾ mile to Coconino Saddle, a relatively flat, shady spot with killer views perfect for a picnic lunch. After lunch, head back to the rim.

From Grandview Point, continue east towards Desert View with a plan to stop just west of Lipan Point at **Tusayan Ruin and Museum.** Here you get a great primer on the ancestral Puebloans who lived in the region.

On the way to Desert View, make a mental note to stop at **Lipan Point** on your way back to Grand Canyon Village. This overlook is arguably the most impressive in the park, and if you arrive near sunset on a haze-free day, the views are spectacular.

At Desert View, the highlight is the **Watchtower,** which has been designed in the image of ancient towers, such as the ones that still stand at Hovenweep National Monument in southeastern Utah. Climb to the observation deck and let the views wash over you.

After your stop at Desert View, head back to Grand Canyon Village, planning, of course, to stop at Lipan Point and fire off a couple frames of film before retreating to the village for dinner and maybe a rim walk.

If you have more time

Beyond the North and South rims, you need to work to get to some of the canyon's more isolated points. If you're on the north side of the canyon, a day trip into the **Toroweap Valley** is worthwhile, even though the access road is dirt, rough in places, and offers no services. Not only can you see Vulcans Throne, a volcanic cone left over from the canyon's pubescent period, but from the Toroweap Overlook, you can stare 3,000 feet down to the river bottom. Easy to spot is Lava Falls, one of the Colorado River's more famous (and perhaps meanest) rapids. To get to Toroweap, head south 55 miles on one of the dirt roads leading from Route 389 just west of Fredonia at Pipe Spring National Monument. The roads are impassable when wet.

Ranger programs

Throughout the park's high season — mid-March through October — if you can't keep yourself busy with things to do, the rangers can help you out with their daily agendas of interpretive programs. You can always find hikes, walks, and discussions about the park's geology, as well as programs that delve into Grand Canyon's human history. These programs often change from year to year, so I won't give you a specific rundown of daily programs, because some may be discontinued. To find out what's offered, scan the park's newspaper, _The Guide,_ or ask for information at one of the visitor centers.

If you have little ones, don't forget to pick up information on the Junior Ranger Program at one of the visitor centers (see Chapter 4 for details).

Spotting the local wildlife

Although you may consider the Grand Canyon a pretty inhospitable place — and you'll likely think so if you stay at the Phantom Ranch in mid-July when the temperature soars above 100 degrees — quite a few animals live here.

Visitors most frequently spot **mule deer**. These fellas can adapt to just about any habitat. To get your mule deer fix, look for them browsing on the bushes and grass around Grand Canyon Village. Harder to spy are the **desert bighorn sheep** that reside inside the canyon, usually on remote slopes. However, from time to time, you may come across one on a trail.

Of course, where prey exists, predators exist, and the Grand Canyon is no exception. Lurking about are **coyotes, bobcats,** and even a few **mountain lions.**

Along the South Rim, a cute, furry mammal called the **Abert squirrel** feasts on seeds. A North Rim cousin is the **Kaibab squirrel,** a funny-looking rodent with tasseled ears that stand up like mule ears. Other small creatures include **ringtails,** which are relatives of the raccoon. Found down along the river, ringtails typically don't show themselves during the day. At night, they head out in search of food, and they have been known to raid campsites.

If you get down into the canyon, either by raft or trail, you're likely to come across lizards and possibly snakes, including the **Grand Canyon pink rattlesnake.** The **chuckwalla** is a lizard that loves to bake under the sun. However, if the chuckwalla feels threatened, it crams its body into a crack in the rock and puffs up its abdomen so it can't be pulled out. A real neat creature is the **collared lizard,** which has a black band around its neck. The canyon also has **scorpions,** but you probably won't see one unless you go looking for it.

The canyon cliffs naturally make wonderful nesting areas for birds, and more than 300 species have been spotted in the park. The most visible hawk is the **red-tail hawk,** which you often see turning lazy circles on the air currents. **Golden eagles** also nest in the canyon. You may not see a **canyon wren,** but you'll surely hear its sweet song if you hike down into the canyon.

If you keep your eyes to the sky and are lucky, you may see a **condor.** Beginning in 1996, biologists made several releases of these big birds in an area about 30 miles north of the park. These guys seem to be doing well in the wild, and from time to time, they make a swing down to the park to see whether they can scrounge up a meal. Just remember, though, that these big birds are an endangered species, and park rules prohibit you from getting within 300 feet of a condor that has landed.

Keeping active

Want to get another perspective on the canyon? Try one of the popular mule rides or even a rafting trip along the Colorado River. If you prefer a bird's eye view, consider flying over the canyon in a plane or helicopter.

Mule rides

Mule rides into the canyon leave from both the South and the North rims. Those from the North Rim are only day rides — with one option as short as an hour — and those from the South Rim are longer and include day trips and overnight trips with stays at Phantom Ranch.

The rides can be grueling. Most people's legs aren't used to bending around the wide belly of a mule, and the saddles aren't soft. Along with the pounding, the canyon can be scorching, and breaks are few. Because the rides are strenuous for both riders and mules, the wranglers strictly adhere to the following requirements: You must weigh less than 200 pounds, be at least 4 feet 7 inches tall, speak and understand basic English, and not be visibly pregnant. If the wranglers think that you weigh too much, they won't hesitate to pull out a scale.

South Rim mule rides begin at 8 a.m. (9 a.m. in winter) every morning at a corral west of Bright Angel Lodge. You can almost hear the jangling nerves of the riders as they contemplate the prospect of descending narrow trails above steep cliffs on animals hardly famous for their intelligence. Although the mules walk close to the edges and have been rumored to back off the trails, accidents are rare, especially among riders who follow the wrangler's instructions.

You have two options for mule rides from the South Rim:

- ✔ **A day trip to Plateau Point:** This trip is the more grueling of the two mule rides. It travels down the Bright Angel Trail to Indian Garden and then follows the Plateau Point Trail across the Tonto Platform to an overlook of the Colorado River. Having descended more than 3,000 vertical feet, the riders return on the same trails. This 12-mile round-trip ride, which breaks for lunch at Indian Garden, returns to the rim in the middle or late afternoon. The cost of this trip is $126.88, which includes lunch.

- ✔ **An overnight trip with lodging at Phantom Ranch:** Going down, riders follow the Bright Angel Trail to the river and then head east on the River Trail before finally crossing the river via the Kaibab Suspension Bridge. Coming back, they use the South Kaibab Trail. The 9½-mile descent takes 5½ hours; the 8-mile climb out is an hour shorter. One- and two-night packages are available at Phantom Ranch (see "Where to Stay," later in this chapter). The one-night package costs $342.59 for one person, $610.72 for two people, and $279.30 for each additional person. The two-night trip, offered only during the winter months, costs $480.14 for one person, $811.36 for two people, and $353.55 for each additional person. Meals are included for all overnight trips.

Despite their arduous nature, these trips are wildly popular and fill up months in advance. For advance reservations, call ☎ **303-297-2757.**

For reservations in the next four days (in case last-minute cancellations), call the **Bright Angel Transportation Desk** at ☎ 928-638-2631, ext. 6015. If you arrive without reservations, you can put your name on a waiting list by going to the desk in person.

A small, family-run outfit, Grand Canyon Trail Rides, offers four types of mule rides on the **North Rim.** Open to ages 6 and up, the **easiest ride** goes 1 mile along the rim on the Ken Patrick Trail before returning. This 1-hour ride costs $20 per person. Two **half-day rides,** for those at least 8 years old and costing $45 per person each, are also available. One stays on the rim, following the Ken Patrick and Uncle Jim Trails to a canyon viewpoint; the other descends 2 miles into the canyon on the North Kaibab Trail, turning back at Supai Tunnel. The **all-day ride,** which includes lunch, travels 5 miles on the North Kaibab Trail to Roaring Springs before turning back. Cost for the all-day ride is $95; riders must be at least 12 years old. No one over 200 pounds is allowed on the canyon rides; for the rim rides, the weight limit is 220. All riders must speak English.

The mule rides on the North Rim tend to fill up later than the rides on the South Rim. To sign up, visit the Grand Canyon Trail Rides desk (open daily 7 a.m.–6 p.m.) at Grand Canyon Lodge, or call ☎ 928-638-9875. The off-season number is ☎ 435-679-8665. Credit cards are not accepted.

White-water and smooth-water rafting

The world-class rapids that lure countless numbers of boaters to the Grand Canyon are constantly changing. Simple rises and falls in the river flow can affect the punch of a rapid, and rockfalls or storm debris can create new rapids or wash away existing ones. Crystal Rapid, for example, rose in 1966 as storms sent slurries of rock and mud into the Colorado River near the mouth of Crystal Creek and altered the river bottom.

If you are intrigued by this white water or are looking for a sure-fire way to cool off in the middle of summer, sign on for a white-water trip. Commercial raft trips inside the park generally last from 3 to 14 days and must be booked about a year in advance. Costs for these commercial trips run about $200 a day. This fee buys you transportation, guides who know which rapids you can run right down the middle and which ones you can "sneak" around, food, portable toilets, much of your camping gear, and access to parts of the Inner Gorge that are hard, if not impossible, to reach any other way. Some of these places, such as Mooney Falls, are among the most beautiful on Earth.

All the companies operating in the Grand Canyon are experienced and run excellent trips, subject to the whims of the Colorado River and the storms that move through the canyon. Most trips begin at Lees Ferry, Arizona, but the endpoints vary. Some companies allow for partial trips by picking up or dropping off passengers at various points in the canyon (most often Phantom Ranch). The companies also differ on what makes a trip special. For example, some allow for plenty of day hiking; others don't. Because the trips vary greatly, consider the following important factors before planning your trip:

- **Motorized versus nonmotorized trips:** Motorized trips are fastest, often covering the 277 miles from Lees Ferry to Pierce Ferry (Lake Mead) in 6 days, compared to as many as 19 days for nonmotorized trips. The motorized trips use wide pontoon boats that almost never capsize, making them slightly safer than the nonmotorized trips. Also, moving about on these solid-framed boats is easier than on oar or paddle boats, a plus for people who lack mobility. Because of the speed of the trips, however, you have less time for hiking or resting in camp. If motorized trips are for you, consider using the companies **Aramark-Wilderness Adventures** (☎ 800-992-8022 or 928-645-3296) or **Western River Expeditions** (☎ 800-453-7450 or 801-942-6669).

If you enjoy exploring and want to bask in the canyon's beauty, I strongly recommend nonmotorized trips, even if you end up seeing half the canyon rather than all of it. A motorless raft quietly glides close to the water's pace, giving passengers time to observe subtle, enticing patterns — swirls of water in eddies; the play of shadows and light as the sun moves across rock layers; and the opening, unfolding, and gradual closing of each side canyon. Without motors running, the sounds of the water and canyon wrens provide a dreamlike backdrop to the journey.

- **Oar boats versus paddle boats:** These are two types of nonmotorized boats. Oar boats are wooden *dories* (flat-bottomed boats with high sides) or rubber rafts, each of which holds six passengers and a guide who does most or all of the rowing. If a guide is highly skilled, the passengers on an oar-powered trip have an excellent chance of floating the entire river without taking a life-threatening swim in the rapids. (Don't let this scenario scare you away from paddle trips. I tell you where to find skilled guides in the next paragraph.)

In a paddle boat, six passengers paddle, assisted by a guide who instructs them and helps steer. This experience is ideal for fit people who want to be involved at all times. However, because of the inexperience of the participants, these trips can be more risky than others. And paddling can become burdensome during the long, slow-water stretches, especially when a head wind blows. **Canyon Explorations** (☎ 800-654-0723 or 928-774-4559) and **Outdoors Unlimited** (☎ 800-637-7238 or 928-526-4546) both have excellent reputations for paddle trips.

If an oar-powered trip appeals to you, try the company known as **Oars** (☎ 800-346-6277 or 209-736-2924), which has some of the most experienced guides on the river. During the busiest months, Oars assures quality service by sending six crew members out with each group of 16 passengers — providing one of the best crew-to-client ratios on the river. Oars also offers paddle trips. However, to ensure that each group of paddlers meshes, the company accepts paddle boat reservations only by the boatload (six).

✔ **The season:** Commerical trips run year-round, but the main season is May through September. In April, cacti bloom in the lower canyon, splashing bright colors across the hillsides, and the river is relatively uncrowded. However, cold weather — even snow — can occasionally make an April trip a test of the spirit. In May, the weather is usually splendid, but the river is at its most crowded. June and July can be oppressively hot. In late July and August, monsoons break the heat and generate waterfalls all along the river, but they also soak rafters. From September 16 to December 15, motorized rigs are banned from the river, so the canyon is quiet. Cold weather keeps most people off the river from January through April.

The following partial list of river companies permitted to float through the canyon provides basic tour information. For more vendors, check the park's Trip Planner.

✔ **Aramark-Wilderness River Adventures** (P.O. Box 717, Page, AZ 86040; ☎ **800-992-8022** or 928-645-3296) offers both motorized and oar-powered excursions. Trip lengths vary from 4 to 14 days.

✔ **Arizona Raft Adventures** (4050-F E. Huntington Dr., Flagstaff AZ 86004; ☎ **800-786-7238** or 928-526-8200) offers motorized, oar-powered, and paddle trips. Excursions last from 6 to 14 days.

✔ **Canyon Explorations** (P.O. Box 310, Flagstaff, AZ 86003; ☎ **800-654-0723** or 928-774-4559; Fax: 928-774-4655) offers oar-powered and paddle trips with lengths varying from 6 to 16 days.

✔ **Grand Canyon Expeditions Co.** (P.O. Box O, Kanab, UT 84741; ☎ **800-544-2691** or 435-644-2691) offers both motorized and oar-powered trips with trip lengths ranging from 8 to 16 days.

✔ **Hatch River Expeditions** (P.O. Box 1200, Vernal, UT 84078; ☎ **800-433-8966** or 435-789-3813) offers motorized trips with lengths varying from 4 to 14 days.

✔ **Oars** (P.O. Box 67, 2687 S. Hwy. 49, Angels Camp CA 95222; ☎ **800-346-6277** or 209-736- 2924) became the first outfitter to run oar-powered trips through the Grand Canyon in 1969. Today, they offer trips in oar-powered wooden dories as well as paddle-powered rafts.

✔ **Outdoors Unlimited** (6900 Townsend Winona Rd., Flagstaff, AZ 86004; ☎ **800-637-7238** or 928-526-4546) offers oar-powered and paddle trips with trip lengths ranging from 5 to 13 days.

✔ **Western River Expeditions** (7258 Racquet Club Dr., Salt Lake City, UT 84121; ☎ **800-453-7450** or 801-942-6669) offers motorized and oar-powered trips with trip lengths varying from 3 to 12 days.

One and two-day trips through the westernmost part of Grand Canyon are available through **Hualapai River Runners** (P.O. Box 538, Peach Springs, AZ 86434; ☎ **888-255-9550** or 928-769-2210). These motorized trips begin with rapids in the lower Granite Gorge of the Grand Canyon and end on Lake Mead. Rates are $250 per person.

Overflights

For a bird's eye view of the canyon, consider a plane or helicopter tour. Several companies, leaving from Grand Canyon National Park Airport in Tusayan, offer scenic trips over the giant hole.

This type of touring is controversial. With more then 250,000 people flying out of Tusayan alone every year, the flights, which generate a great deal of noise in parts of the park, have become a politically charged issue. Many people claim that the planes and helicopters create noise pollution in what should be a pristine wilderness area. Whether or not these tours will be discontinued is anyone's guess.

For the time being, though, you can fly over the canyon by plane with **Air Grand Canyon/Sky Eye Tours** (☎ **800-247-4726** or 928-638-2686; Internet: www.airgrandcanyon.com), or **Grand Canyon Airlines** (☎ **800-528-2413** or 928-638-2407; Internet: www.grandcanyon airlines.com). Prices range from $75 to $90 ($45–$49 for children under 12) for a 50- to 60-minute flight, including the airspace fee.

You can also whirl through the air in a helicopter with **Kenai Grand Canyon Helicopters** (☎ **800-541-4537** or 928-638-2764; Internet: www.flykenai.com), **AirStar Helicopters** (☎ **800-962-3869** or 928-638-2622; Internet: www.airstar.com), and **Papillon Grand Canyon Helicopters** (☎ **800-528-2418** or 928-638-2419; Internet: www.papillon.com). Tours run from around $100 for a 25- to 30-minute flight and $165 for a 40- to 45-minute flight to $436 for a seven-hour tour; not all tours offer lower children's rates.

Escaping the rain

What do you do when it rains in the park? Well, in the height of summer, you may enjoy the cool drenching. Any other time of year, you no doubt want to head for shelter.

The **Kolb Studio** (☎ **928-638-2771**) in Grand Canyon Village is one good option. The Grand Canyon Association sponsors a rotating series of art exhibits in this historic studio. A fun, but somewhat short, time can be spent watching the latest big-screen production at the **Grand Canyon IMAX Theater** (☎ **928-638-2203**) located just south of the park's South Rim entrance on Highway 64. A recent 34-minute show, "Grand Canyon — The Hidden Secrets," touched on the park's Native American history, as well as treks into the park by Spanish explorers and by Major John Wesley Powell. The **Yavapai Observation Station,** a great place to seek shelter during a cloudburst, provides good views into the canyon and a geological primer on the hole in the ground. If you're near the east end of Desert View Drive when the rains come, stop at the **Watchtower** (☎ **928-638-2736**), where you find Native American artworks on display. Finally, if you haven't gotten your share of souvenirs, head to the **Hopi House** (☎ **928-638-2631,** ext. 6383), in Grand Canyon Village, which vends a wealth of Native American arts and crafts.

Where to Stay

Thanks to the logistical marvel that one concessionaire — **Xanterra Parks & Resorts** (☎ **888-297-2757** or 303-297-2757; Internet: www.grandcanyonlodges.com) — oversees all the lodging in the park, one easy phone call enables you to make a room reservation in the Grand Canyon. You can also check their Web site for discounted rates. AE, MC, DISC, and V are accepted for rooms.

The following listings for the park hotels don't include individual phone numbers or addresses. A single telephone number (☎ **928-638-2631**) is good for all South Rim properties. The Grand Canyon Lodge, the elegant grand dame on the North Rim, has its own telephone number (☎ **928-638-2611**). Don't worry about not being able to find your hotel. When you enter the park, you receive a map pinpointing the location of each one.

Lodging at the South Rim

Bright Angel Lodge & Cabins
$$–$$$$$ **Grand Canyon Village**

This hotel is budget central in the Grand Canyon. You find a bed with a roof overhead for as little as $59 a night. Of course, you can pay more than that if you prefer more amenities. For $59, you get a "hiker" room with only a single bed, a desk, and a sink. Two long buildings adjacent to the Bright Angel Lodge house these dormitory-style rooms, the least expensive in the park.

From that base unit, your options escalate as do the prices. Some rooms have double beds and a toilet, but no shower, while others contain a bed, toilet, and tub but no shower. More comfortable, and charming, accommodations are the cabins that stand along the canyon's rim and feature fireplaces, two bedrooms, and a bathroom. Understandably, the cabins often are booked a year in advance. The cabins, which have one or two queen-sized beds, were renovated in 2000 and have new furniture, draperies, and tile floors.

37 rooms (6 with sink only, 13 with sink and toilet, 18 with bath); 55 cabin rooms. TVs in cabins. Rack rates: $59–$71 double, some with shared bath; cabins $84–$244.

El Tovar Hotel
$$$–$$$$$ Grand Canyon Village

It's pricy, but the El Tovar is the most luxurious accommodation in the park. After a hot day of hiking below the rim, most visitors are delighted to return to one of these rooms. The hotel was built in 1905 — out of Oregon pine logs — and designed to accommodate tourists riding to the canyon on the Santa Fe Railroad. The El Tovar is an architectural cross between a Norwegian villa and a Swiss chalet and bears a strong resemblance to old European hunting lodges. Located just a stone's throw from the canyon's South Rim, the building casts a long shadow across the Grand Canyon Village at sundown. Inside you find moose and elk heads hanging on varnished walls and copper chandeliers casting light. The cool, dark spaces are a dramatic contrast to the warmer, pueblo buildings you find elsewhere in the park. The upstairs offers a nice, private sitting area (reserved for guests) and rooms with classic American furnishings. The hotel offers room service that will turn down your beds at night, if you desire. About half of the suites are non-smoking.

66 rooms, 12 suites. A/C, TV, TEL. Rack rates: $127–$289 double; $204–$289 suite.

Maswik Lodge
$$–$$$ Grand Canyon Village

Set in a ponderosa pine forest, this lodge offers a different, cooler perspective than most other Grand Canyon properties. Most of the guest rooms are in the two-story wood-and-stone buildings known as Maswik North and South. The rooms in Maswik North have nice furnishings, queen-size beds, and new carpet; many also have balconies overlooking the pine forest. The rooms in Maswik South are five years older, a bit smaller, and have less pristine views, but they also cost about $40 less per night.

Next to Maswik North are several cabins. Each cabin has two double beds and a shower. Because of their proximity to the road and to festive off-duty employees, these cabins can be noisy. If you stay in one of these, bring a flashlight because the grounds are dark at night.

250 rooms, 28 cabins. TV, TEL. Rack rates: $66 cabin; $79 double in Maswik South; $121 double in Maswik North.

Thunderbird and Kachina Lodges
$$$ Grand Canyon Village

These lodges are the newest in the park, but given that they resemble 1960s-era college dormitories, they're not the most gorgeous. They have flat roofs, decorative concrete panels, and metal staircases on the exterior; inside are concrete steps, tile floors, and brick walls. Rooms are pleasant enough, with Southwestern-style furnishings and windows as wide as the rooms themselves. Although Xanterra (the concessionaire that runs all lodging in the park) refuses to guarantee a canyon view, in both lodges most of the upstairs rooms on the more expensive "canyon side" have at least a partial view of the canyon. Check-in for the Thunderbird is at the Bright Angel Lodge; for the Kachina, it's at the El Tovar.

55 rooms at Thunderbird, 49 rooms at Kachina. A/C, TV, TEL. Rack rates: $119 double (park side), $129 double (canyon side).

Yavapai Lodge
$$–$$$ Grand Canyon Village

This lodge is the largest in the canyon. Although the lodge is a mile away from the Grand Canyon Village's historic district, the location is conveniently close to a bank, Canyon Village Marketplace, and the park's visitor center. The A-frame lodge was built in the early 1970s and has a large cafeteria and gift shop. Its rooms are housed in ten single-story buildings known as Yavapai West and six two-story wood buildings known as Yavapai East. Most rooms in Yavapai West have cinder block walls, and all are compact. Yavapai East's rooms are larger and many have good forest views, which make them worth the extra $15 per night. Because the parking lots were built to accommodate tour buses, they are larger than at other lodges. The gravel paths connecting the buildings are dark at night, so don't forget your flashlight.

358 rooms. TV, TEL. Rack rates: $93 double (Yavapai West), $129 double (Yavapai East).

Lodging inside the canyon

Phantom Ranch
$–$$ Grand Canyon floor

Staying at the Phantom Ranch takes some effort because no road leads to the front door. You have to hike, ride a mule, or float down the Colorado River to get here. Despite the remote location and so-so rooms, the ranch's rooms often sell out far in advance. To reserve a spot, call as early as possible, as much as 20 to 23 months in advance. If you arrive at the park without a reservation, call the Bright Angel Transportation Desk (☎ 928-638-2631, ext. 6015) for information about openings in the next four days due to cancellations.

The ranch's nine cabins are a treat during the summer. Architect Mary Colter, who also designed Watchtower, designed four of them (the ones with the most stone in the walls) using rocks from the nearby Bright

Angel Creek. Connected by dirt footpaths, they stand, natural and elegant, alongside picnic tables and under the shade of cottonwood trees. Inside each cabin, you find a desk, a concrete floor, and four to ten bunk beds, as well as a toilet and sink. A shower house for guests is nearby.

Most of the Phantom Ranch was completed in the 1920s and 1930s; however, four ten-person dorms, each with its own bathing facilities, were added in the early 1980s. Used mostly by hikers, these dorms are ideal for individuals and small groups looking for a place to bed down; larger groups are better served by reserving cabins, which provide both privacy and a lower per-person cost.

For information on mule rides to Phantom Ranch, see the "Keeping active" section, earlier in this chapter.

½ mile north of the Colorado River on the North Kaibab Trail. 7 four-person cabins, 2 cabins for up to ten people each, 4 dorms for up to ten people each. Rates: $28 dorm bed; $74 cabin (for 2 people, $10.50 each additional person).

Lodging at the North Rim

Grand Canyon Lodge
$$–$$$ **North Rim**

Architecture and landscape come together at this lodge, which blends into its surroundings with its exterior walls of Kaibab limestone and log beams similar to the trunks of the nearby pines. Just past the lobby and into the Sun Room, you face the canyon's grandeur through towering picture windows.

Outside, row after row of cabins surround the lodge. All the cabins have bathrooms, but they're definitely not all alike. The Western Cabins and Rim Cabins are the most luxurious, complete with wicker furniture, bathtubs, and small vanity rooms. The Rim Cabins, which cost $10 more per night than the Western Cabins, perch on the lip of Bright Angel Canyon and are usually booked as much as two years in advance.

Your more rustic choices are the Pioneer and Frontier Cabins on the rim of Transept Canyon. They have walls and ceilings of exposed logs, upright gas heaters, and showers instead of tubs. The Frontier Cabins have one guest room with a double bed and twin bed; the Pioneer Cabins have two guest rooms, one with a double and a twin and the other with two twins. If you stay in a Frontier or Pioneer Cabin, be sure to ask when you check in for one that overlooks Transept Canyon.

You also find a few motel rooms at this location, but they're nothing to write home about.

201 cabin and motel rooms. TEL. Rack rates: $112 double Rim Cabin; $102 Western Cabin; $99 Pioneer Cabin; $87 Frontier Cabin; $87 motel room.

Runner-up lodgings

The following properties cluster together on Highway 64 in Tusayan, Arizona (only 1 mile from the south entrance to the park). They do not have specific addresses.

Best Western Grand Canyon Squire Inn

$$–$$$ **Tusayan** You won't be lodging in the park, but at least you have two restaurants, a bowling alley, video arcade, billiards inside, and pool and tennis court outside. *Highway 64, Tusayan.* ☎ *800-622-6966 or 928-638-2631. Internet:* www.grandcanyonsquire.com.

Grand Hotel

$$$–$$$$ **Tusayan** This knock-off of a national park lodge takes you to the Old West with its heavy timbers, antler chandeliers, and Native American craftworks. Southwestern cuisine in the restaurant and Western entertainment in the lounge complement the setting. *Highway 64, Tusayan.* ☎ *888-63-GRAND or 928-638-3333. Internet:* www.gcanyon.com.

Holiday Inn Express Hotel and Suites

$$–$$$$$ **Tusayan** This place offers rooms in two flavors: Generic double or family-friendly suite (with microwaves, fridges, and VCRs). *Highway 64, Tusayan.* ☎ *888-473-2269 or 928-638-3000. Internet:* www.gcanyon.com/holiday.htm.

Campgrounds

The park has four developed campgrounds. Each offers its own unique style, from sites surrounded by pinyon and juniper trees or old-growth ponderosa pines to an RV park that you should avoid if all you're hauling is a tent. For my advice on making reservations in the campgrounds, see the "Planning Ahead" section earlier in this chapter.

Camping at the South Rim

Desert View Campground
South Rim

If you agree that there's nothing quite like falling asleep to the sound of yipping coyotes, this place is the one for you. Far enough away from Grand Canyon Village to be shielded from its noise and lights, this campground is cool and breezy and just a short walk from the Desert View Overlook. The tent sites are set amid pinyon and juniper groves, adding a wonderful dash of fragrance to your dreams. One problem with this location is that the nearest shower is 25 miles away, in the village. During the high season, this first-come, first-served tent city often fills up by noon.

25 miles east of Grand Canyon Village on Highway 64. No phone, no advance reservations. 50 sites. Rates: $10 per site. Open: Mid-May to mid-Oct.

Mather Campground
South Rim

Given its size and proximity to Grand Canyon Village, you may think this campground would be a loud, crowded tent town, but it's really not that bad thanks to good spacing of the sites and the surrounding pinyon and juniper trees. Of course, for every rule there's an exception, and in this case, you definitely want to avoid sites 150 through 171 on the Juniper Loop because they are way too close to the park's entrance road. Also, although you probably want to be near the showers, which are in the Camper Services Building, you don't want to be so close that you find yourself counting the hundreds of happy campers tramping by.

This campground fills up quickly during high season. If you arrive without a reservation, check at the campground entrance for any unclaimed sites.

Near Grand Canyon Village on the South Rim. ☎ 800-365-2267 advance reservations, 301-722-1257 from outside the U.S. 319 sites, 4 group sites. No hookups. Rates: $15 mid-March to Nov, $10 Dec to early March. Open: Year-round.

Trailer Village
South Rim

If you don't have your own RV to shut out the rest of the campground, you don't want to be at this campground; the sites are very close to each other, and the vegetation is vanishing. If you stay here, take time to scout the campground before settling on a site. At the end of the numbered drives, you find some sites with grass, shade trees, and one neighbor-free side. The showers are roughly a ½-mile away from the sites.

East of Grand Canyon Village, adjacent to the Mather Campground. ☎ 303-297-2757 for advance reservations or 928-638-2631, ext. 6035 for same day reservations and questions. Fax: 928-638-9247. 84 full hookups. Rates: $24 for two people per site, $2 each additional person over 16. Open: Year-round.

Camping at the North Rim

North Rim Campground
North Rim

This campground vies for the most picturesque in the park. (The Desert View campground is also a contender for this award.) Towering old-growth ponderosa pine trees shade the sites set along Transept Canyon.

From here you can walk 1½ miles down the Transept Trail to reach Grand Canyon Lodge, and the North Rim General Store is close to the campground. The best sites are those on the rim; they're an extra $5, but the canyon view's worth the cost. Showers are nearby, too, although you have to pay $1.25 for five minutes of water.

This place fills quickly and stays full. To obtain a site, make a reservation up to five months in advance of your arrival.

44 miles south of Jacob Lake on Highway 67. ☎ *800-365-2267 advance reservations or 928-638-2151. 83 sites, 4 group sites. No hookups. Rates: $15 per site; $4 for tent only (no vehicle). Open: May 15–Oct. 15.*

Where to Eat

When mealtime rolls around, the Grand Canyon offers several restaurant options. You can find meals for the most austere budget, as well as fare suitable for an elegant evening out. In addition to the places listed in this section, the Maswik and Yavapai lodges have cafeterias in the $ to $$ range that serve three meals at day.

Restaurants at the South Rim

The Arizona Room
$$–$$$$ Grand Canyon Village   AMERICAN

If you dine here, you don't have to miss dinner to watch the sunset. You get great canyon views through the long windows. If you want to jockey to be first in line when this restaurant opens at 4:30 p.m., you can snag the seats with the best views. If you decide to watch the sunset and then head here, you may find yourself at the end of an hour-long waiting list. Although the service could be quicker, at least you're not rushed through your meal. You have plenty of time to choose from the wine list or order an appetizer — the fried jalapeno and chipolte chicken poppers are a good, and spicy, choice. Entrees include hand-cut steaks and prime rib, chicken, trout, and a daily vegetarian special.

At Bright Angel Lodge. ☎ *928-638-2631. Reservations not accepted. Main courses: $16–$21. AE, DC, DISC, MC, V. Open: Daily 4:30–10 p.m.*

Bright Angel Restaurant
$–$$ Grand Canyon Village   AMERICAN

If you're looking for a decent family restaurant in the park, this spot is good. The burgers and patty melts are tasty, and so are some of the Southwestern dishes. If you're hauling kids around, you won't have to worry much about their behavior. The games on the kid's menu should distract the small fries until the French fries arrive. Still, the food at the Maswik and Yavapai cafeterias is just as good, and it's cheaper.

Located in Bright Angel Lodge. ☎ 928-638-2631. Reservations not accepted. Main courses: $2.50–$7.40 breakfast; $6.70–$11 lunch and dinner. AE, DC, DISC, MC, V. Open: Daily 6:30–10:45 a.m. and 11:15 a.m.–10 p.m.

Canyon Village Marketplace
$ Grand Canyon Village   AMERICAN/MEXICAN

Many Park Service employees dash into this cafeteria for lunch. You can sit in a corner booth, read the paper, and watch the parade of tourists. Settle for a quick hot dog or a fried chicken basket, or go lighter and healthier with the walnut chicken salad, albacore tuna salad, or one of the other made-to-order salads or sandwiches. If you love Mexican food, look for the green chili burritos on Wednesdays and Thursdays.

In Canyon Village Marketplace. ☎ 928-638-2262. Main courses: $4–$6. AE DC DISC MC V. Open: Summer daily 7 a.m.–8:30 p.m.

Desert View Trading Post
$ Desert View   FAST FOOD

This fast-food joint is pretty much what you'd expect. There are no frills, but you can get a sandwich, hot dog, or burger to tide you over until you get back to the village. The breakfast offerings include eggs and French toast.

At Desert View, 25 miles east of Grand Canyon Village on Highway 64. ☎ 928-638-2360. Main courses: $1.40–$2.85 breakfast; $1.75–$3.05 lunch. No credit cards. Open: Summer 8 a.m.–6 p.m.; rest of the year 9 a.m.–5 p.m.

El Tovar Restaurant
$–$$$$$ Grand Canyon Village   CONTINENTAL

This restaurant has established a nearly century-old tradition of fine food and good value, which isn't about to change soon. The dining room reflects this commitment with its walls of Oregon pine graced with murals depicting the ritual dances of four Indian tribes. Atop the restaurant's fine linen tablecloths, fresh flowers catch light from the windows.

At dinner, a Southwestern influence spices the Continental cuisine. Appetizers include Mozzarella roulades of prosciutto and basil pesto and Clesan-Du-Klish, which is Native American Blue Corn Tamales with roasted red pepper coulis and charbroiled corn salsa. For the main course, meat-eaters will enjoy the flame-broiled peppercorn crusted filet mignon with roasted garlic sauce and gorgonzola mashed potatoes. You also find intriguing seafood and vegetarian dishes, such as broiled portabello Napoleon with a vanilla thyme risotto.

The El Tovar accepts reservations for dinner only, but is open for breakfast and lunch as well. If you're traveling on a budget, consider dining here during non-dinner hours, when you can get the same high-quality food for just a few dollars more than you'd spend at the other canyon eateries.

In the El Tovar Lodge. ☎ *928-638-2631, ext. 6432. Reservations recommended for dinner. Main courses: $4.25–$10.50 breakfast; $8.75–$15 lunch; $17–$25 dinner. AE, DC, DISC, MC, V. Open: Daily 6:30–11 a.m., 11:30 a.m.–2 p.m., and 5–10 p.m.*

A restaurant inside the canyon

Phantom Ranch
$$$–$$$$$ Inside the canyon   AMERICAN

Even if you don't snag a room at the Phantom Ranch, you can still eat here. And by the time you arrive from your trek down into the canyon, just about anything will taste good. Every evening, the ranch offers two options: a steak dinner at 5 p.m. and a hearty beef stew at 6:30 p.m. The vegetarian plate at both meals consists of side dishes, such as vegetables, cornbread, and salad. With any dinner, the dessert is chocolate cake.

The family style, all-you-can-eat breakfasts are excellent, as heaping platters of eggs, bacon, and pancakes make their way up and down the long blue tables. The only disappointment is the sack lunch, whose simple contents (bagel, summer sausage, juice, apple, peanuts, raisins, and cookies) don't seem worth the price. You may as well stash similar munchies in your pack before heading into the canyon.

Because the ranch can accommodate a fixed number of diners for each meal, hikers and mule riders must reserve meals ahead of time through Xanterra or at the Bright Angel Transportation Desk. As a last resort, inquire upon arrival at Phantom Ranch to see whether any meals remain. Up until 4 p.m., you can do so in the canteen itself. After 4 p.m., ask at a side window behind the canteen. Between 8 a.m. and 4 p.m. and from 8 p.m. to 10 p.m., anyone is allowed in the canteen, which has snacks, soda, beer, and wine.

Inside the canyon, ½-mile north of the Colorado River on the North Kaibab Trail. To order meals more than four days in advance, call ☎ *303-297-2757; to order meals in the next four days, contact the Bright Angel Transportation Desk at 928-638-2631, ext. 6015. Main courses: $15 breakfast; $7.50 box lunch; $20 stew dinner; $30 steak dinner. AE, DC, DISC, MC, V.*

Restaurants at the North Rim

Café on the Rim
$–$$ North Rim   AMERICAN

This snack bar serves the best pizza on the North Rim — actually, the only pizza on the North Rim. This spot also churns out burgers, premade salads, and breakfasts. If all you desire is a cup of coffee and a muffin, stop by the saloon, where an espresso bar operates daily from 5 a.m. to 9:30 a.m.

In the east wing of Grand Canyon Lodge. ☎ 928-638-2611. Main courses: $1.75–$4.95 breakfast; $2.95–$7.95 lunch; $5.95–$9.95 dinner; $12–$18 whole pizza. Open: Mid-May to mid-Oct 7 a.m.–9 p.m.

Grand Canyon Lodge Dining Room
$$$–$$$$ North Rim   CONTINENTAL

Long banks of west- and south-facing windows provide views of Transept Canyon and help warm this room, while the high ceiling absorbs the clamor of diners. Although expecting gourmet dining in a place as remote as the North Rim is unreasonable, the food is nearly as satisfying as the surroundings. A long-time favorite, and quite tasty too, is the Pasta Lydia — fresh asparagus and potatoes tossed in pesto sauce with bowtie pasta. Heartier eaters will like the Apple Cider Pork Medallions. You also find interesting preparations of steaks, prime rib, fish, poultry, and excellent desserts on the menu. Lunch offerings include a variety of salads, sandwiches, and burgers.

At Grand Canyon Lodge. ☎ 928-638-2611, ext. 160. Reservations required for dinner, not accepted for breakfast or lunch. Main courses: $4.25–$8 breakfast; $4.75–$9.50 lunch; $14–$23 dinner. AE, DC, DISC, MC, V. Open: Mid-May to mid-Oct daily 6:30–10 a.m., 11:30 a.m.–2:30 p.m., and 4:45–9:30 p.m.

Fast Facts: Grand Canyon

Area Code
☎ 928.

ATM
On the South Rim at the bank in Grand Canyon Village; in Tusayan at the Imax Theater. The North Rim does not have an ATM.

Emergency
☎ 911 or 9-911 from lodging rooms.

Fees
$20 per vehicle per week; $10 for those on foot per week; $10 backcountry permit fee; $5 per person per night backcountry impact fee.

Fishing License
Arizona license required.

Hospitals/Clinics

Grand Canyon Walk-in Clinic, 1 Clinic Rd, southeast of Grand Canyon Village.

Information

Grand Canyon National Park, P.O. Box 129, Grand Canyon, AZ 86023; ☎ 928-638-7888.

Lost and Found

☎ 928-638-7888.

Pharmacies

None, but the clinic (see "Hospitals/Clinics" above) has some medicines.

Post Office

Grand Canyon Village.

Road Conditions and Weather

☎ 928-638-7888.

Taxes

6.3% lodging and restaurants.

Time Zone

Mountain standard time; Arizona does not observe daylight saving time.

Web Site

www.nps.gov/grca.

Chapter 14

Grand Teton National Park

• •

In This Chapter

▶ Admiring "the Grand"

▶ Planning your assault on the park

▶ Exploring the mountains and lakes

▶ Finding the best sleeps and eats

• •

Although the United States may have bigger mountains, and even ranges that are longer and older, nothing is more rugged and picturesque than Wyoming's Teton Range.

True, the craggy, battleship-gray Grand Teton (known simply as "the Grand") tops out at *only* 13,770 feet, whereas some Rocky Mountain peaks surpass 14,000 feet. But to understand the magnificence of this park, you must consider the setting. The Grand ratchets almost 7,000 vertical feet straight up from the Jackson Hole valley floor, and without any foothills to temper the rise, its 13,770 feet are in-your-face impressive. Plus, the peaks and surrounding terrain have been clawed, carved, and sculpted by several periods of glaciation that left behind some sparkling lakes. This all adds up to a beautiful, remarkable setting that demands attention, encourages recreation, and pays off in satisfaction.

The Grand offers several world-class climbs. Some climbers tackle the mountain on their own, and others climb under the guidance of Jackson's two resident climbing outfitters, Exum Mountain Guides and Jackson Hole Mountain Guides. (See "Keeping active," later in this chapter, for information on these companies.) But a trip to Grand Teton isn't wasted if you can't climb the Grand. Just looking at these peaks justifies a trip to western Wyoming.

Grand Teton National Park is more than just mountains. You find lakes of all sizes, from the sisterly trio of Jenny, Leigh, and String that graces the front of the Tetons to Jackson Lake — a natural glacial-lake, enlarged in 1906 by a dam, where you can rent a motorboat for an afternoon of fishing or a canoe for a leisurely paddle.

Grand Teton National Park

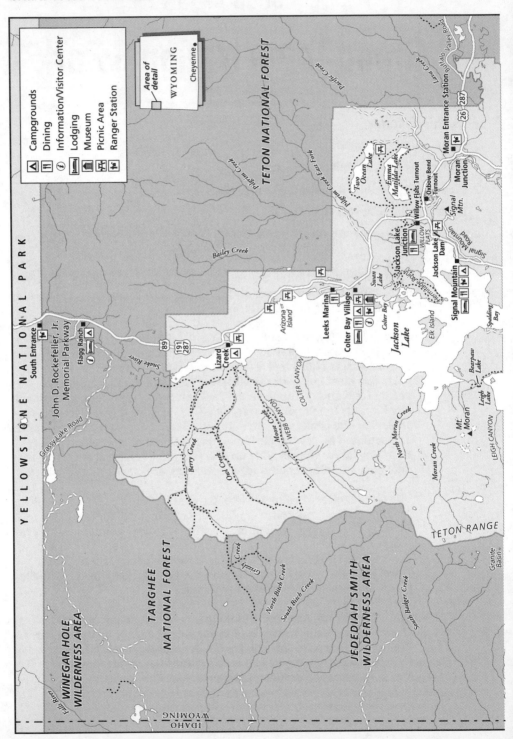

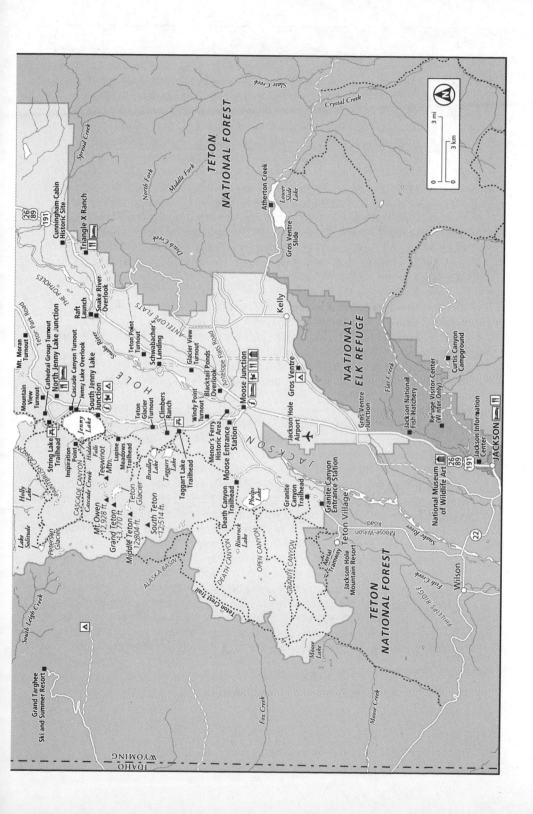

The three *what?*

Early 19th-century French-Canadian fur trappers provided the name for Grand Teton National Park. After stumbling too long in the wilderness before arriving in Jackson Hole, they thought the three central peaks bore some semblance to a woman's anatomy and thus named them *le trois tetons* — the three breasts.

East of Jenny, Leigh, and String lakes are rolling sagebrush flats (favorites with pronghorn antelope) that surround U.S. Route 26/89/191 as the highway travels, north to south, the length of the park. Paralleling the road to the west is the trout-filled Snake River, which braids its way from Jackson Lake Dam 27 miles through the park before adding some punch for white-water enthusiasts in the stretch that runs south of Jackson.

You find swathes of thick evergreen forest in Grand Teton, steep canyons gnawed into the landscape by cascading streams that run flush with melting snow in spring, and lush meadows colored by wildflowers in late June. In 1998, the arrival of wolves from Yellowstone to the north added a dash more wildness to the park, fleshing out a menagerie that already included bison, elk, moose, coyotes, mountain lions, and grizzly bears.

With its mix of landscape and accommodations, Grand Teton is both a rugged and comfortable park, one where you can test your outdoors skills or relax with a book in the afternoon shadow of America's Matterhorn. The Old West is kept alive by ranchers who graze cattle inside the park, by the nearby town of Jackson lined with wooden boardwalks, and by the coyote yips and wolf howls in the cool evening air.

Grand Teton is a year-round playground, although some seasons are definitely better than others. Summer weather is wonderful, with daily highs roaming between the mid-70s and the high-80s; however, most of the park's 4.1 million yearly visitors show up during this season. The crowds taper off during fall, my favorite season in the park. During autumn, aspens flutter in their golden glory, the evenings' crispness is intoxicating, and animals are more visible as they prepare for winter. Although winter can be brutally cold and snowy, the season provides great opportunities for cross-country skiing and snowshoeing. Because of late-season snowfalls and mud, spring is about the worst time for a visit.

Plan to spend at least two to three days in Grand Teton National Park.

Must-see Attractions

With Grand Teton and its sister peaks visible from just about everywhere in the park, you really don't have to work hard to appreciate the gorgeous landscape. Trust me, though, in addition to the mountains you'll definitely want to see some other attractions during your visit. I won't reveal them all, because part of the enjoyment of visiting a national park is discovery and exploring. But here's a good list to get you started:

- ✔ **Cunningham Cabin Historic Site:** This rustic cabin built by Pierce Cunningham in 1890 is the oldest pioneer cabin still standing in the park. Pierce knew a good view when he saw one. Stopping here really gives you an idea of what roughing it meant to early settlers.

- ✔ **Grand Teton:** You can't miss this attraction. Just look for the highest knob on the western skyline. You can climb the mountain if you're in decent shape.

- ✔ **Jenny Lake:** One of the park's idyllic lakes, this shimmering jewel is perfect for an afternoon paddle or hike. The park's premier lodge, also named Jenny Lake, is nestled in a grove of conifers not far from the lake shore.

- ✔ **Oxbow Bend:** This series of bends in the Snake River is a great place to view the Tetons as well as wildlife; swans, geese, and pelicans drift on the waters in the mornings and afternoons. Look for bald eagles and osprey that roost in the trees along the river and moose that browse the marshy meadows.

- ✔ **Snake River:** Whether you raft it, fish it, or just walk beside it, this river is an American classic.

Getting There

Getting there is half the fun, right? Located on Wyoming's western border, the park is not really a short drive from anywhere. Salt Lake City and Billings, Montana, are each about five hours away, and Cheyenne — Wyoming's capital — is a good seven-hour drive. You don't have to drive — because the park has its own airport — but if you do, know that you'll pass incredibly beautiful countryside along the way.

Flying in

You could argue that this park is the most accessible in the country thanks to the **Jackson Hole Airport** (☎ **307-733-7682**) that lies within the park's boundaries. **American, Continental Express, Northwest,**

Skywest (Delta Connection), and United Express all have flights to and from Jackson Hole Airport. Most of the major car-rental companies have outlets here as well. For toll-free numbers, see the Appendix.

Driving in

If you don't fly, getting to Grand Teton takes a bit longer, but the scenic drive is worth the trip. Arriving from the east, U.S. Route 26/287 leads you up and over Togwotee Pass and to the Moran Entrance Station if you're heading to Jackson Lake Lodge. If you're looking for the Moose Entrance Station, drive 18 miles south of Moran Junction to Moose Junction.

If you drive south from Yellowstone to enter the park, you pass through the John D. Rockefeller Jr. Memorial Parkway — a 37-square-mile swath of land between the two parks that was established in 1972 to honor Rockefeller for his formidable land contributions to the national park system. Although no official entrance station to Grand Teton exists along the park's northern border, Flagg Ranch has an information station.

You can also reach the park from the south through Jackson on U.S. Route 26/89/191, which leads to Moose, Wyoming, and points north.

No public bus service exists between Jackson and the park, and even though Amtrak actually superimposed one of its trains in front of the Tetons for a brochure in the 1980s, no train service exists.

Planning Ahead

To receive park maps and information before your arrival, write to Superintendent, Grand Teton National Park, P.O. Drawer 170, Moose, WY 83012-0170; or call ☎ 307-739-3300 or 307-739-3400 (TTY). You can also check the park Web site at www.nps.gov/grte. For a trip-planning packet, call ☎ 307-739-3600.

If you want to try climbing the Grand, you need to make a reservation with one of the park's two climbing companies several months in advance. See "Keeping active," later in this chapter, for information on climbing.

Even if you don't plan to climb, make plans for your summer trip as early as February or March. Starting at this time virtually assures you a room in the park hotel of your choice, including the most popular lodges, Jackson Lake Lodge or Jenny Lake Lodge.

Although nearby Jackson has more than 4,200 motel rooms, they fill quickly in summer — and fall, too, if bad weather forces hundreds of elk hunters out of the mountains and into warm, dry rooms.

Learning the Lay of the Land

Unless you visit in the dead of winter, one fact you need to accept on a trip to Grand Teton is that you're not going to be alone. Millions of people flock to this park each year, and just about every one of them is interested in seeing the same handful of attractions that you want to see.

The lack of roads makes avoiding the crowds difficult. **U.S. Route 26/89/191** is the main north-south artery through the park, and the more narrow and meandering **Teton Park Road** runs parallel to this highway, sandwiched between it and the Tetons. The U.S. highway remains open year-round, but the Teton Park Road closes November 1 and doesn't reopen until May 1.

U.S. Route 26/89/191 is the best route through the park if you're in a rush, whereas Teton Park Road offers a much slower pace with more interesting views and pullouts and many trailheads. From its northern end at Jackson Lake Junction to its southern terminus at Moose, the Teton Park Road moseys along, much like the Snake River. The road leads you past the southeastern arm of Jackson Lake, the Signal Mountain Lodge complex, String and Jenny lakes, and Jenny Lake Lodge. Just north of the Moose Visitor Center, the road passes the Menor's Ferry Historic Site, famous for the ferry service used to cross the Snake River.

North of Jackson Lake Junction, U.S. Route 89/191/287 runs towards Yellowstone, passing Jackson Lake Lodge and Colter Bay Village before entering the John D. Rockefeller Jr. Memorial Parkway.

One of the park's scenic back roads is the **Moose-Wilson Road,** which is sort of a shortcut to Moose if you're coming into the park from Idaho or if you want to go from Moose to a restaurant at Teton Village without making the roundabout trek through Jackson. I say "sort of a shortcut" because you shouldn't expect to make up any time on this 9-mile-long route that twists, turns, and bounces its way through the forests. It's sometimes closed by snows and never open to trucks, trailers, or motor homes. But if you're not in a rush, this scenic route offers opportunities to spot moose and black bears and escape the hordes. Head into the park this way from Teton Village and you receive park information at the new **Granite Canyon Entrance Station** about 2 miles north of Teton Village.

Another oft-overlooked backroad is the **Antelope Flats-Kelly-Gros Ventre loop.** Travel this road along the "quiet" east side of the park and you stand a good chance of spotting bison, pronghorn antelope, migrating elk in spring and fall, and moose in fall and winter. This route also takes you past historic Mormon Row homesteads and classic rustic barns, and allows you to enjoy the vast, sweeping views of the Teton Range. It's also a great place to bike thanks to minimal auto traffic.

As you move north and south across the park, you come upon three areas chock-full of visitor services. Near the park's southern tip lies **Moose,** home to park headquarters with its sprawling visitor center, museum, and bookstore. Nearby is a small cluster of businesses that includes a liquor store, grocery, restaurant, and outdoor gear shop where you can rent bikes, boats, and climbing gear. Farther north near the park's midsection lies **Jackson Lake Lodge,** where you not only have lodging options but also restaurants, a handful of gift shops, a gas station, and even a medical clinic. A short drive north of the lodge lies **Colter Bay Village** with its lodging, campground, restaurants, grocery, gift shops, picnic area, and marina where you can launch boating excursions or sign on for a scenic lake cruise or an evening dinner cruise. The village also has an engaging museum that features artifacts and artworks of various American Indian tribes. If you ever find yourself in need of a civilization fix, head south to **Jackson.** This eclectic mountain town has great restaurants, a variety of hotels and motels, gift shops, and boutiques. If you show up during the height of the summer season, head to the Town Square for the nightly Old-West style shoot-outs, complete with damsels in distress, good guys, and bad guys.

Arriving in the Park

There's a good chance that you'll enter the park before you even realize it, because the main highway — U.S. Route 26/89/191 — runs north and south through the park with the entrance stations located off this main road. Whether you come from the north, south, or east, however, you're never really far from a visitor center where you can get your bearings.

Finding information

Grand Teton National Park has three visitor centers. The **Moose Visitor Center** (☎ 307-739-3399) is a ½ mile west of Moose Junction at the southern end of the park. As the park headquarters, it offers exhibits on geology and natural history, a bookstore, and audiovisual programs. You can check into the schedule of ranger programs and pick up maps and permits for boating and backcountry trips. This center is the only one open year-round. From mid-September to mid-June, hours are 8 a.m. to 5 p.m., and from mid-June through mid-September, hours are 8 a.m. to 7 p.m.

The **Jenny Lake Visitor Center** (☎ 307-739-3392) at South Jenny Lake has maps, publications, and a geology exhibit. The center is open from mid-June to mid-September, 8 a.m. to 7 p.m.

The **Colter Bay Visitor Center** (☎ 307-739-3594), the northernmost of the park's visitor centers, provides permits, information, audiovisual programs, and a bookstore. You can take part in ranger-led activities here or hike along the lakeshore. You can also explore the on-site **Indian**

Arts Museum (hours: mid-May to mid-June 8 a.m.–5 p.m., mid-June to early Sept 8 a.m.–8 p.m., and early Sept to Oct 1 8 a.m.–5 p.m.).

Finally, the **Flagg Ranch Resort** complex has an information station approximately 5 miles north of the park's northern boundary.

Paying fees

U.S. Route 26/89/191 does not have park gates, so the views are free as you pass through the park on this route. When you enter park entrance stations near Moose or Moran junctions, you pay the park fee of $20 per vehicle, $10 per hiker or biker, or $15 per motorcycle. All fees are good for a seven-day stay. If you expect to visit Yellowstone, too, the admission fee is good for both parks. Annual permits for Grand Teton and Yellowstone national parks are also available for $40.

See Chapter 8 for information on the National Park Pass and Chapter 4 for the lowdown on Golden Age and Golden Access passports.

Getting around

The park does not have a public transportation system, so you need a car to get around.

With the exception of the Antelope Flats-Kelly-Gros Ventre loop, this park isn't great for road bikers because paved roads have narrow shoulders and are crowded with RVs and other vehicles.

Remembering Safety

While taking in the many sights of Grand Teton National Park, keep the following precautions in mind:

- **Prepare for the high elevation.** Even the lowest parts of the park are more than a mile above sea level, which can leave you gasping for breath if you're coming from the lowlands and jump right into cycling, hiking, paddling, skiing, or climbing without acclimating to the park's thinner air.

- **Watch out for bears.** You also need to be aware of the park's resident grizzly and black bears. The grizzly bear population is small, but black bears abound in the park. Before you head out on a hike, check with rangers for any reports of recent bear activity. On the trail, I recommend hiking in groups of two to four people and talking or singing loudly so you don't surprise any wildlife lurking just around the next bend. Carrying bear pepper spray in an easily accessible location is also a good idea.

✔ **Be wary of other beasts.** The park also has bison, moose, and elk. They may look cuddly, but their horns and antlers are not merely ornamental, so keep your distance. Moose are also highly adept at stomping anything they don't like, and even though they look ungainly, they're surprisingly quick and agile.

✔ **Look out for your fellow tourist.** Paying attention to your fellow park visitors while tooling down the roads, particularly the Teton Park Road, is always a good idea. Often people become so caught up with the scenery that they actually forget to look where they're going — a recipe for disaster on this curvy, busy road. Also, if you're driving, watch out for cyclists, and if you're pedaling, watch out for motorists.

✔ **Swim with caution.** Do you plan to head to one of the lakes for a dip? It's a great way to cool off during the summer heat. But you won't find any lifeguards in the park, so be careful.

For additional tips for a safe national park visit, see Chapter 8.

Enjoying the Park

No matter why you've come to Grand Teton, you won't have trouble filling your days. After touching on the park's highlights and hikes in this section, I give you a strategy for maneuvering around and a rundown of the park's best programs and activities.

If you come to Grand Teton in the summer, expect the park to be crowded. To negotiate around these crowds, think like a "parkie." Visit prime attractions early or late in the day, head north to Lizard Creek for a campsite instead of joining the masses at Colter Bay, hike into Death Canyon instead of up Cascade or Garnet Canyons, and paddle Leigh Lake instead of Jenny Lake.

Exploring the top attractions

Cunningham Cabin Historic Site

Pierce Cunningham built this well-weathered and slowly slumping cabin in 1890 to hold down his claim to the 160 acres he received from the government for $10 through the Homestead Act of 1862. When you visit, imagine enduring a winter of below-zero overnight temperatures and drifting snows in this shack. A ¾-mile self-guided hike offers some insight into the park's ranching history.

The cabin is located 5½ miles south of Moran Junction on U.S. Route 26/89/191. Free and open at all times.

Jenny Lake

Grand Teton National Park is a classic piece of America's alpine high-country, with jagged peaks, fragrant pine forests, beautiful lakes, and an elevation of nearly 7,000 feet. Located at the base of the Grand Tetons, Jenny Lake is one of the markers left behind by the glaciers that sculpted the mountains and their valleys. As the ice retreated, the melting water filled in a basin carved by the glaciers.

Jenny Lake is a tourist magnet. But unlike other spots in the park, you have a variety of activities to choose from here. You can take the shuttle boat across the lake and vanish up a trail into the mountains, spend a morning or afternoon hiking around the lake, try your hand at fishing, or rent a canoe or kayak from **Dornans** (☎ 307-733-2415) in Moose and paddle away from the crowds.

For $5 one-way or $7 round-trip adult fares, a shuttle boat operated by **Jenny Lake Boating** (☎ 307-734-9227) can ferry you from the East Shore Boat Dock to the West Shore Boat Dock. From early June through the third week of September, the ferry operates daily, departing about every 20 minutes between 8 a.m. and 6 p.m.

Hikes, both the easy variety and those that lead deep into the park's backcountry, start and end at Jenny Lake, making it possible for you to spend a few hours or a week or more on the trail. For my recommended hikes, see Cascade Canyon Loop, Hidden Falls/Inspiration Point, and Jenny Lake Loop in the "Taking a hike" section.

You can minimize your association with crowds by arriving early in the morning to watch the sun's first rays ignite the mountains, or come late in the afternoon when most folks are heading out of the park. At either time, press on up the trail past Inspiration Point, and you leave most other tourists behind.

Jenny Lake is on Teton Park Road 8 miles north of Moose and 12 miles south of Jackson Lake Junction.

Menor's Ferry Historic Area

The Menor's Ferry Historic Area has a self-guided trail that leads you to the site where Bill Menor began his ferry business in 1894. Kids like the free ride across the Snake River on a replica of his ferry.

The nearby **Chapel of the Transfiguration** is a log cabin built in 1925 by settlers who didn't want to make the long ride into Jackson every Sunday for church. Today, the chapel offers Episcopalian services during the summer months.

If walls could talk, **Maud Noble's Cabin** near Menor's Ferry would tell the story of how Grand Teton became a national park. Maud Noble took over the ferry business from Bill Menor in 1918. In 1923, a group of Jackson residents — determined to preserve the land that sprawls beneath the Tetons — gathered at the cabin to talk with Horace Albright, the superintendent of Yellowstone National Park, about creating some sort of federal preserve. The land would be, they said, a "museum on the hoof." Today, the cabin contains some interesting reproductions of photos taken early in the valley's history, including some of the Teton Range taken by William Henry Jackson, a prominent 19th-century explorer photographer.

The Menor's Ferry Historic Area is located a ¼ mile north of the Moose Entrance Station on Teton Park Road.

Oxbow Bend

A great place to go in search of wildlife (and priceless beauty) is Oxbow Bend just 3 miles west of Moran Junction. On just about any spring, summer, or early fall day you can spot white pelicans, trumpeter swans, geese, ducks, bald eagles, ospreys, and other birds on or around the river. Moose also occasionally appear in the river bottom meadows, and river otters cavort along stretches of the riverbank.

The main road has a pullover for picture taking and gazing, but you can get closer to the river and its wildlife by taking the Cattleman's Bridge Road. This dirt road, found nearly a ¼-mile north of the Oxbow Bend Turnout, runs south for 1 mile to a parking area where you can get out and walk along the river or try your luck with a fishing pole.

Even better, rent a canoe to float along the 5-mile stretch of river that runs from below Jackson Lake Dam to Pacific Creek. (See "Keeping active," later in this chapter, for canoe rental information.) The water flows lazily and the wildlife gets in your face.

 If you do wander along Oxbow Bend during the summer months, be prepared to slather on bug repellent because the mosquitoes can be voracious.

Few people head to the trails that wrap Emma Matilda and Two Ocean lakes found due north of Oxbow Bend. (See Two Ocean Lake Trail in "Taking a hike," later in this chapter, for my recommended hike.) As a result, you find solitude here, not to mention two beautiful lakes and the wildlife they draw. If you head to this area, keep in mind that this is prime grizzly habitat (perhaps explaining why few people hike here). Make lots of noise while hiking (singing is good) so you don't surprise any bears. As a precaution carry, and know how to use, bear pepper spray. You can drive to the picnic area on the edge of Two Ocean Lake by taking the Pacific Creek Road just north of the Moran Entrance Station.

Oxbow Bend is 5 miles north of the Moran Entrance Station on U.S. Route 89/191/287.

Capturing the park on film

If you consider yourself even the most marginal of photographers, you have to stop at **Oxbow Bend.** This stretch of the Snake River is likely the most photographed setting in the park, thanks to the river's meanders and the background of Mount Moran and the rest of the Tetons. In the early morning hours when the waters are calm, you can get great shots of Mount Moran's reflection in the river.

Taking a hike

With 200 miles of maintained trails, the biggest problem you face in Grand Teton is trying to decide where to hike. When you first glance at the steep mountains, you'll probably guess that most hikes here involve some hills. The park does seem to have more than its share of uphill treks, but other trails are available that won't exhaust you in the first ¼ mile.

Two of the hikes in this section, Cascade Canyon Loop and Hidden Falls/Inspiration Point, begin at the West Shore Boat Dock on Jenny Lake. To reach the boat dock, hike the Jenny Lake Loop Trail or take a shuttle boat from the East Shore Boat Dock. **Jenny Lake Boating** (☎ **307-734-9227**) operates the shuttle from early June through the third week of September; the boat runs daily, departing about every 20 minutes between 8:00 a.m. and 6 p.m. If you have early dinner reservations, watch your time carefully. Shuttle boats back to the East Shore are in high demand late in the afternoon, and a 45-minute wait is not unheard of. Either get in line early or plan time to hike back via the Jenny Lake Loop Trail.

If you plan to head into the backcountry overnight, you have to obtain a permit for $15 and reserve a campsite. Visit the nearest visitor's center to make these arrangements.

For tips on how to hike safely, see "Remember Safety," earlier in this chapter.

Cascade Canyon Loop

This hike is a great way to get away for two to three days. The trail starts out from Jenny Lake's west boat dock with a steep uphill trek that grinds 7¼ miles up Cascade Canyon before reaching Lake Solitude on the way to the Paintbrush Divide and Holly Lake. When you reach Holly Lake, you've traveled 10¼ miles, but at this point, the grade works with you, because you're heading downhill most of the time.

Not only does this overnight hike feature fantastic scenery, but moose and black bears frequent the area so you may see some wildlife. Keep your eyes open early in the hike, because moose like to browse in the ponds that form along Cascade Creek as it comes down the canyon.

Distance: 19¼ miles. Level: Moderate to strenuous with an elevation change of 3,845 feet. Access: West Shore Boat Dock on Jenny Lake.

Hidden Falls/Inspiration Point

This trail is probably the busiest hiking corridor in Grand Teton. Not only do shuttle boats haul people to the West Shore Boat Dock, where these trails begin, but climbing schools practice on the rock walls that rim Cascade Canyon. Crowds notwithstanding, Hidden Falls is beautiful, and from Inspiration Point, you get a great view back across Jenny Lake to the eastern side of Jackson Hole and the Gros Ventre Mountains. If you think climbing appeals to you, watching the classes work on rappeling and climbing will either convince you to take a class or dash the thought from your mind.

Hidden Falls is less than a ½ mile from the boat dock, and Inspiration Point lies just a ½ mile further up the trail. But I do mean *up* — the trail gets pretty steep.

Enough rock slabs and boulders line this trail to keep kids busy; they scramble over them and don't realize how much effort they're exerting.

Distance: 5¾ miles round-trip or 1¾ miles round-trip via shuttle boat access. Level: Moderate. Access: You can take the shuttle boat across Jenny Lake to these trails or follow the Jenny Lake Loop to the West Shore Boat Dock.

Jenny Lake Loop

This mostly level trail, which winds around the lake close to the shore-line, provides a nice hike for families. The setting is great, with the lake wrapped by a thick forest and the Tetons towering over the western shore. The downside is that this is one of the more popular trails in the park. If you have really young children and prefer a shorter hike, you can take a shuttle boat across the lake to the West Shore Boat Dock and then walk back to the east shore. This trail also connects with hikes up into Cascade Canyon (described earlier in this section) and to String and Leigh lakes to the north.

Distance: Just over 6½ miles round-trip. Level: Easy. Access: The trailhead is at the East Shore Boat Dock.

Two Ocean Lake Trail

This hike on the east side of U.S. Route 89/191/287 gives you a taste of the backcountry without the need for a long hike. Because few people stray from the mountains, you're likely to enjoy a little solitude. The trail loops around the lake, so the direction you head from the trailhead doesn't matter. The route passes through conifer forests on the south shore and aspen groves and meadows along the north shore. In the early summer, you can spot swans and ducks in a bay at the lake's north end, or maybe even spy beavers — or at least their handiwork. In June, the meadows blossom with wild geraniums, lupine, and mountain asters.

If you prefer a longer hike, you can make a 13-mile loop around both Two Ocean Lake and nearby Emma Matilda Lake. A bonus of this hike is a moderate climb to Grand View Point, which, at 7,327 feet, gives you a nice panoramic view of the two lakes as well as Jackson Lake to the west. Another treat is to canoe Two Ocean Lake. (For canoe rental information, see "Keeping active," later in this chapter.) This is bear country, so check with rangers before you head out to ask whether any bruins have been spotted around the lake, and be sure to make noise as you hike.

Distance: 6½ miles round-trip. Level: Easy. Access: Two Ocean Lake Trailhead on Two Ocean Lake Road.

Willow Flats Trail

This great trail through wildlife habitat often provides glimpses of moose, great blue herons, and other waterfowl or wading birds. Views of Mount Moran and the rest of the Teton Range are priceless. A good daylong adventure is to hike from Jackson Lake Lodge to Colter Bay, where you can stop for lunch, and then backtrack to the lodge for dinner.

Distance: 8½ miles round-trip. Level: Easy. Access: The trailhead is at Jackson Lake Lodge.

One-day wonder

Just by driving along U.S. Route 26/89/191, you see the focal point of Grand Teton National Park — the Teton Range. But if you don't get off that highway, you cheat yourself and your family by failing to get a feel for this beautiful land, something you can begin to do in just a day with this itinerary. (Unless otherwise noted, for information on the attractions in this section, see "Exploring the top attractions," earlier in this chapter.)

If you're staying at Jackson Lake Lodge or Signal Mountain Lodge, a good place to start a daylong loop tour is at Jackson Lake Junction. (If you're staying in Jackson, start midloop at Moose.) From Jackson Lake Lodge, drive just 1 mile east from the junction on U.S. Route 89/191/287 to the **Oxbow Bend Turnout,** where you can look for moose in the river bottom and then gaze west at Mount Moran with Skillet Glacier seemingly hanging on its flanks.

From Oxbow Bend, continue southeast on the highway to Moran Junction. (In the fall, watch the woods and flats on either side of the highway for wildlife.) At that junction, turn right and head south on U.S. Route 26/89/191 for 5½ miles until you reach the **Cunningham Cabin Historic Site** on your right.

After exploring the cabin, continue about 4 miles south on the highway until you arrive at the **Snake River Overlook,** the spot where renowned landscape photographer Ansel Adams took a dramatic black-and-white photo of the Tetons in 1942. Although not as interesting as the view of the Tetons, the view of the braided Snake River below has its own merits.

As you get back on the highway and head south toward Moose, you pass three more turnouts, but they offer pretty much the same view as the one you saw at the Snake River Overlook.

The **Moose Visitor Center,** located just west of U.S. Route 26/89/191 on Teton Park Road, is a good place to supplement your literature on the park. (My library on national parks grows substantially after each trip, because I have a hard time turning my back on books about wildlife, early settlers, or geology.) Nearby is **Moose Village,** where you find **Dornans** (☎ 307-733-2415) — a jack-of-all-trades family business that offers accommodations, restaurants, a grocery store, a gift shop, sports equipment rentals, fishing shop, and chuckwagon cookouts, among other things. Some items can get pricey (particularly the libations in the package store), so you may want to shop in Jackson instead.

A ¼ mile past the park's Moose Entrance Station, you come upon **Menor's Ferry,** the **Maud Noble Cabin,** and the **Chapel of the Transfiguration.** Unless you're a serious historian, or have children who'd be interested in seeing the ferry cross the river (the ferry operates during the summer months if the river isn't too high), you can skip these attractions and continue north toward Jenny Lake.

Jenny Lake is a great lunch setting, whether you shuttle across the lake, hike around the water to Cascade Canyon, or simply find a spot along the shore not far from the parking area. On the same side of the lake as the visitor center is **Exum Mountain Guides,** so if you're curious about climbing, stop by and inquire about their classes. (See "Keeping active," later in this section, for information on climbing.) If you visit during the height of summer, you're likely to be confronted by crowds along the lakeshore, but just the same, head across or around the lake to Cascade Canyon and take a short hike to Inspiration Point. The view of Jenny Lake below is great. You pass Hidden Falls along the way, and if you're curious about climbing, you can watch classes at work on the canyon's rock faces.

If the crowds are too suffocating, head just north of Jenny Lake to **String** and **Leigh lakes,** two perfect spots for canoeing, swimming, fishing, and simply relaxing. An easy 3½-mile trail curls around String Lake, which has the park's best swimming, because its waters are only 10 feet deep and the warmest in the park. Leigh Lake, a 1-mile hike north of String Lake, has the park's best beaches.

From these two lakes, follow Teton Park Road north, arriving after 9 miles at the **Signal Mountain Lodge complex** with its lodgings, restaurants, stores, and marina. From here, you're just 3 miles from Jackson Lake Junction.

If you have more time

Just 2½ miles north of Jackson on U.S. Route 26/89/191 is the **National Elk Refuge** (☎ 307-733-9212). Although thousands of elk crowd the refuge in winter, the best time to visit, spring, summer, and fall are excellent times for spotting birds and waterfowl. The refuge sprawls across 23,754 acres of land covered by various degrees of meadows, sagebrush flats, thin stands of timber, and rocky outcrops. The Gros Ventre River traces the refuge's northern boundary, and Flat Creek slices through its middle.

Elk typically spend the months from November into April on the refuge; the rest of the year, they scoot off into the high country for cooler weather and lush vegetation. When the snows of autumn begin to fall, the elk descend en masse on the refuge, and by midwinter, 7,000 to 8,000 animals live off the feed tossed out by the local U.S. Fish and Wildlife Service.

In winter, you can sign on for a 45-minute **horse-drawn sleigh ride** ($12 for adults; $8 for kids ages 6–12, free for 5 and under) through the refuge. During early-winter trips, you may come across bulls tangling their antlers in battles intended to determine a mating hierarchy and impress the cows. You may also glimpse the wolves that follow the elk to the refuge.

When spring rolls around, Boy Scouts from Jackson scour the refuge for antlers shed by the elk. Then, on the third Saturday in May, Jackson's Town Square takes on a carnival atmosphere when it's overrun by thousands of tourists and antler buyers (who sell the antlers for their reputed medicinal qualities) as the scouts stage their **annual elk antler auction.** Stacks of antlers, collected by the scouts and by private collectors, fill the streets bordering the square. As an auctioneer encourages onlookers to raise their price for the antlers, young scouts heft them high overhead so all can see. Eighty percent of the money raised goes to buy more feed for the refuge, and the scouts keep the rest for administrative costs.

Spotting the local wildlife

Before **wolves** returned to the scene, Grand Teton National Park was best known for its moose, elk, bison, and pronghorn antelope. But in 1998, wolves wandered down from Yellowstone and discovered the National Elk Refuge, which thousands of elk call home during the winter months. That was all the wolves needed to know. In recent winters, as many as three wolf packs have been spotted on the refuge in search of a meal. One pack even set up a den in the northeastern corner of the park not far from Moran Junction, but they retain a low profile. Your best bet for spotting wolves is to tour the elk refuge in winter.

Grizzly bears also are showing up with increasing frequency in the park. The area near Lower Slide Lake just east of Kelly has proven popular with the bruins, although backcountry travelers may also see them throughout northern parts of Grand Teton.

Black bears also inhabit the park and are more visible than grizzlies. Unfortunately, some have associated people with food, so make sure to clean up after picnics and keep an eye out while hiking. Black bears occasionally turn up in the Jenny Lake area, and in August, you may catch a glimpse of one in the woods near Signal Mountain because they're drawn to the area for the ripening huckleberries.

Moose are year-round park residents. You can often see them browsing in the ponds along the Moose-Wilson Road. Willow Flats, a big marshy area between Jackson Lake Lodge and Jackson Lake, is a great place to look for moose early in the morning and in the evenings, as is nearby Oxbow Bend. Sometimes you can find them browsing in the pools formed by Cascade Creek as it falls out of the Tetons on the way to Jenny Lake.

Grand Teton does not have as many **bison** as Yellowstone, but a fair number exist, and they're pretty visible. In June, you can often spot cows and their calves in the grasslands along the Antelope Flats Road north of the town of Kelly and east of Mormon Row. They also graze in the sagebrush meadows between Signal Mountain and North Jenny Lake Junction.

The animal responsible for generating the initial interest in Jackson Hole back in the early 19th century still abounds in the park today. These days, **beavers** continue to ply the park's rivers, creeks, and lakes, building their dams and lodges. If you spend any time along the river and creek bottoms, you'll see their stick-built dams and lodges and the gnawed tree stumps they left behind. Oxbow Bend is a reliable area for seeing beavers, or at least their work.

You can also find **river otters** along the Snake River near Oxbow Bend. These critters like to frolic and will ham it up for you, as long as you don't get too close. On a float through Oxbow Bend, my wife and I came across a family of five otters who posed until we ran out of film.

Oxbow Bend is a great place to spot some of the park's wildlife. In addition to the moose, **elk,** and **mule deer** you may see in the marshy bottom lands along the river, waterfowl usually crowds the river in the mornings and late afternoons. You can see **American white pelicans, Canada Goose, a variety of ducks,** and possibly even **Great Blue Herons** wading along the shore in search of minnows.

If you're lucky during your visit, you may see one of the park's rarer birds — the **trumpeter swan.** These big birds can measure 6 feet long from the tip of their black bills to the end of their white tails. In recent years, a pair of the swans has been nesting in Christian Pond just east of Jackson Lake Lodge. You can't get within 300 feet of the nesting site because the pond is off-limits to give the swans some privacy, but with a good pair of binoculars, you can watch these elegant birds from the Christian Pond Trail. (If you plan to hike along the trail in May or June, check with rangers to see whether any bear activity has been reported in this area. Note, too, that the resident mosquitoes are ravenous in summer.)

Ranger programs

Grand Teton's rangers always seem to be getting out and about in the park — and inviting the public along. They lead hikes to Inspiration Point above Jenny Lake each summer morning from early June through September. Other ranger-led offerings include talks about Teton geologic history, cultural history, fire ecology, and wildflower walks.

A great summer afternoon hike with an educational, as well as scenic, payoff is the **String Lake Stroll.** This 2-mile-long easy hike along the shores of String Lake passes through a section of forest that burned in 1999. Joining a ranger-led hike, you can discover the important role fire has in maintaining a healthy ecosystem. These 2½-hour hikes start from the String Lake Trailhead just northwest of Jenny Lake Lodge. For details on any ranger-led activities, consult the park's newspaper, *Teewinot,* or inquire at a visitor center for a schedule.

A great trip for kids and adults alike is the **Fire and Ice Cruise** that sets sail on Jackson Lake several times a day. During these 90-minute excursions, a ranger explains how glaciers helped sculpt the park and how forest fires impact the ecosystem. If this activity sounds interesting to you, check with the **Colter Bay Marina** (☎ **800-628-9988**) for ticket prices and tour times.

In addition to these programs, campfire talks and evening-slide shows take place throughout the park. Check the park's newspaper or bulletin boards in the visitor centers and campgrounds for times and topics.

Most national parks offer Junior Ranger Programs as a way to get kids interested in parks, but Grand Teton has what's known as the **Young Naturalist Program.** Kids receive a newsletter discussing the park's wildlife, geology, and human history and a related worksheet with questions. After a youngster completes the worksheet (with your help if necessary) and participates in two ranger programs, he or she receives a special patch. You can sign up your kids (ages 8–12) at the Moose, Jenny Lake, or Colter Bay visitor centers. The programs are free, but a $1 donation is suggested for the patch.

Keeping active

In Grand Teton National Park, you can pursue a variety of activities, some of which, such as boating, canoeing, and fishing, require permits, licenses, or registration. Special regulations may also apply, so check the park's Web site at www.nps.gov/grte in advance or stop at one of the visitor centers for complete information.

✔ **Boating:** Many of the park's front-country lakes are perfect for canoeing and kayaking. The Snake River below Jackson is known for its white-water rafting, and the stretch of the river that flows through the park is great for experienced canoeists or rafters. Boat and canoe rentals are available at Colter Bay Village through **Grand Teton Lodging Company** (☎ **800-628-9988**) and at Signal Mountain through **Signal Mountain Lodge** (☎ **307-543-2831**) for use on Jackson Lake. You can also rent boats for use on park lakes in Moose at **Dornans** (☎ **307-733-3307**).

Human-powered vessels are permitted on Phelps, Jackson, Jenny, Emma Matilda, Two Ocean, Taggart, Bradley, Bearpaw, Leigh, and String lakes. Motorized boats are allowed only on Phelps, Jackson, and Jenny lakes, but on Jenny Lake, the motor can't be more than ten horsepower. Only muscle-powered rafts, canoes, dories, and kayaks are allowed on the Snake River within the park. No boats are allowed on Pacific Creek or the Gros Ventre River.

If you bring your own boat, you must register it. For nonmotorized craft, the registration fee is $5 for seven days or $10 for a year; for motorized boats, the fee is $10 for seven days and $20 for an annual permit. You can pay these fees at any visitor center.

✔ **Climbing:** Climbing to the top of Grand Teton is not as far-fetched as you may think. Each year, thousands of people, many who have never climbed before, set out from Lupine Meadows in a bid to conquer the Grand. I consider the trek more of a long, strenuous hike than a technical climb.

The easiest way to the top is with one of the park's two climbing companies: **Exum Mountain Guides, Inc.** (☎ **307-733-2297**; Internet: www.exumguides.com; P.O. Box 56, Moose, WY 83012) or **Jackson Hole Mountain Guides** (☎ **800-239-7642**, 307-733-4979; Internet: www.jhmg.com; P.O. Box 7477, Jackson, WY 83001). They typically require you to enroll in a two-day climbing school conducted in the park before attempting the summit. The cost depends on the route and your experience level. With Exum, figure $600 for one person ($460 per person for two people) to climb the Grand via the Owen-Spalding Route. The Exum Route runs $600 for one person ($460 per person for two people). On top of that, if you're a rank novice, two days of climbing school cost $215 per person. Jackson Hole Mountain Guides is a bit cheaper; its Grand climb, which includes climbing school, runs $640 per person for two people.

To climb the Grand, you need to make reservations several months in advance. If you have a particular window during the summer for the climb, make sure to call early in the year because reservations fill quickly. Middle to late August usually offers the best climbing weather, whereas in late June and early July, you're likely to encounter snow that can hamper or even cancel a climb.

Speaking of snow, make sure you call the climbing company several days before you arrive to check the weather conditions. I climbed the Grand in mid-July and was confronted by midwinter snow conditions that necessitated not only an ice axe and *crampons* (shoe spikes) but also waterproof shell gloves, water-resistant pants, a shell jacket, and warmer layers that I usually don't pack for a summer vacation.

If you live at a substantially lower elevation, you may want to arrive in the park as much as a week before your scheduled climb so your body can get used to the altitude. Acclimating makes the climb to almost 14,000 feet easier, and quickens the recovery time afterward.

✔ **Fishing:** The lakes and streams of Grand Teton are popular fishing destinations, loaded with lively cutthroat trout, whitefish, and mackinaw (lake) trout in Jackson, Jenny, and Phelps lakes. To angle in the park, you need a Wyoming state fishing license, and you have to check creel limits, which vary from year to year and place to place. Tackle and fishing licenses are available at Colter Bay Village and Signal Mountain.

✔ **Horseback Riding: Grand Teton Lodge Company** (☎ **800-628-9988;** Internet: www.gtlc.com) offers tours from stables at Colter Bay Village and Jackson Lake Lodge. Choices are one- and two-hour guided trail rides daily aboard well-broken, tame animals. An experienced rider may find these tours too tame; wranglers refer to them as "nose and tail" tours.

✔ **Skiing:** You can ski flat or steep in Grand Teton; the two hazards to watch out for are hypothermia and avalanches. Know your limitations and make sure you're properly equipped. Check with local rangers and guides for trails that match your ability. For downhill skiing contact **Snow King Resort** (☎ **800-522-7669**) and **Jackson Hole Ski Resort** (☎ **307-733-2292;** Internet: www.jacksonhole.com); both have rental facilities on the premises. For cross-country skis and snowshoe rentals, visit outdoor equipment shops in Jackson or stop at Dornans in Moose.

Escaping the rain

A great rainy day spot is the **National Museum of Wildlife Art** (☎ **800-313-9553** or 307-733-5771; Internet: www.wildlifeart.org), 2½ miles north of Jackson on Highway 26/89/191 across from the National Elk Refuge. The museum arguably houses the country's best collection of wildlife art, from bronzes to oil paintings to watercolors. You gain a keen appreciation of the West's ruggedness and beauty through the artworks displayed in the museum's 51,000 square feet. Among the 2,000 art pieces are original works by 19th-century masters Albert Bierstadt, Charles M. Russell, and John James Audubon. The museum is open every day of the year, except Christmas and Thanksgiving, from 8 a.m. to 5 p.m. in summer and from 9 a.m. to 5 p.m. the rest of the year (1 p.m.–5 p.m. Sundays in spring and fall). The cost is $6 for adults, $5 for students and seniors, and $14 for families. You can grab a bite to eat on the property at the Rising Sage restaurant.

Where to Stay

The park provides a cornucopia of accommodations, ranging from shorefront cottages and rustic log cabins to elegant log lodges and even motel-style rooms. Prices run the gamut, too. The park properties have in-room telephones, but lack televisions and air-conditioning. Nearby Jackson provides options for those who want all the creature comforts.

Lodging in the park

Colter Bay Village Cabins
$–$$$ **Colter Bay Village**

If the park has a central hub of activity, this is it, so don't come here looking for seclusion. On the other hand, if you have a troop of kids, this choice is wonderful, both because of the many things to do in the area and because it's easier on your wallet. The cabins have a rustic flavor and are simply furnished and clean. But not all cabins are created equal. Some feature shower stalls, whereas others share baths. The tent cabins have rough log walls, canvas roofs, wood-burning stoves, double-deck bunk beds, and concrete floors. If that's not rustic enough, you must use communal restroom facilities (showers are available for a fee) and bring your own sleeping bag. The nearby village offers a restaurant, food court, convenience store, service station, and laundry. You also can sign up for a horseback ride.

U.S. Route 89/191/287. ☎ *800-628-9988 or 307-543-3100. Internet:* www.gtlc.com/CBVLod.htm. *274 units. TEL. Rack rates: $34–$129 cabins; $34 tent cabin; $25–$38 RV spots. AE, DISC, MC, V. Open: Mid-May to late Sept.*

Flagg Ranch Resort

$$$ Flagg Ranch

This ain't no ranch, so you don't need to worry about stepping around cow patties on your way to your cabin. But the location is a bit remote, so if you plan to spend most of your time below Jackson Lake, you could do better, location-wise. However, if you want to bounce between Grand Teton and Yellowstone, Flagg Ranch is perfect: The location is 5 miles north of Grand Teton and two miles south of Yellowstone in the John D. Rockefeller Memorial Parkway, a park-like middle ground between the two parks.

You won't be roughing it at this resort. In 1992, an old motel was replaced with 92 log cabins that feature king- or queen-size beds, spacious sitting areas, wall-to-wall carpeting, and bathrooms with tubs and showers. The lodge, built in 1995, features a large stone fireplace (perfect for warming yourself after a wintry excursion), restaurant, bar, gift shop, and convenience store. Open year-round, the Flagg Ranch is perfect for both summer fly-fishing trips and winter ski adventures.

5 miles north of Grand Teton's Northern Boundary on the John D. Rockefeller Jr. Parkway. ☎ *800-443-2311 or 307-543-2861. Fax: 307-543-2356. Internet:* www.flagg ranch.com. *92 cabins. TEL. Rack rates: $139–$145 summer; $99–$110 winter. AE, DISC, MC, V. Open: Year-round.*

Jackson Lake Lodge

$$$–$$$$$ Jackson Lake Junction

For such a beautiful location — a bluff overlooking willow flats and Jackson Lake, with the Tetons just beyond the lake — what were the architects thinking when they dreamed up this concrete edifice? But this lodge compensates in other ways for what it lacks in architecture. From the patio off the backside of the lodge, you can often spot moose and waterfowl on spring, summer, and fall mornings and evenings. If the weather is too chilly, you can get the same view in the lobby through 60-foot-tall windows.

If you book one of the lodge's cottages (preferably one with a lakeside view), you can enjoy a bit more atmosphere and feel as if you've escaped most of the crowds. These motel-style units are clean and comfortable, and they sport small patios where you can enjoy a picnic lunch or dinner while watching the clouds swirl about the Tetons and the sun's rays gleam on the lake. Lodge rooms are spacious, and most come with double beds. Suites have one or two bedrooms. You find formal dining in the lodge's Mural Room and soda fountain-style dining in the Pioneer Grill, which seems to have a 1950s' decor hangover. The Blue Heron lounge across from the Mural Room offers great mountain and lake views and occasional live entertainment, but it can be smoky. The lodge also features a number of upscale clothing and jewelry shops, and boasts a heated pool.

Near junction of US. Route 89/191/287 and Teton Park Road. ☎ *800-628-9988 or 307-543-3100. Internet:* www.gtlc.com/JacLLLod.htm. *348 cottages, 37 rooms. TEL. Rack rates: $124–$225 double; $154–$164 cottage; $394–$564 suite. AE, DISC, MC, V. Open late May to Oct.*

Jenny Lake Lodge
$$$$$ **Jenny Lake**

Nestled — no, make that hidden — in the woods off a curve along a one-way road between Leigh and Jenny lakes, this elegant lodge epitomizes a romantic Rocky Mountain retreat. This place is the one to steal away to for a memorable anniversary weekend; it's not a place to bring the kids. The price alone gets that message across. The lodge with its cracklin' fireplace is the setting for meals and chats, but come bed time, guests retreat to beautiful log cabins topped by pitched shingle roofs and pillared porches. The cabins are comfortably outfitted with log furniture with cowhide upholstery, thick quilts on the beds, generous closet space, and tiled combination baths. Multi-course meals in the lodge are gourmet, and a classical guitarist often accompanies dinners. (Do pack your jackets, guys, as they're strongly encouraged for dinner.) Oh yeah, the rack rate also covers horseback rides or the use of the lodge's bicycles. To ensure a reservation, call a year in advance.

North of Jenny Lake off Teton Park Road. ☎ *800-628-9988 or 307-733-4647. Internet:* www.gtlc.com/JenLLLod.htm. *37 cabins. TEL. Rack rates: $348 single; $429 double; $579–$619 suite. Rates include breakfast, dinner, horseback riding, and bicycles. AE, DISC, MC, V. Open: Late May to Oct.*

Signal Mountain Lodge
$$–$$$$$ **Signal Mountain**

You can hear the lapping waters of Jackson Lake from this small resort, which is tucked away in the woods along the southeastern arm of the lake on the main road that runs from Jenny Lake to Moran Junction. Book a room at this lodge and you're close to the water and hiking trails. Plus, you have Mount Moran with its glacier fields as a background. The accommodations aren't bad, either. You can choose from cabins and one- and two-bedroom bungalows with beach frontage. The log cabins feature handmade pine furniture, electric heat, covered porches, and tiled baths. Some have cobblestone fireplaces (if you want one, ask when making a reservation) as well as kitchenettes with microwave ovens and refrigerators. Within walking distance is the main lodge with its restaurant, coffee shop, small lounge, and gift shop. As far as the lodge's overall location, you're just 30 miles north of Jackson and 25 miles from Yellowstone National Park's South Entrance.

Teton Park Road near junction with US. Route 89/191/287. ☎ *307-543-2831. Fax: 307-543-2569. Internet:* www.signalmtnlodge.com. *79 units. TEL. Rack rates: $95–$225 double. AE, DISC, MC, V. Open: Mid-May to mid-Oct.*

Top lodging outside of the park

Rusty Parrot Lodge
$$$$$ **Jackson**

Although it's billed as a hotel, this lodge two blocks from Jackson's Town Square operates more like a bed-and-breakfast. Breakfasts of fresh fruit, Russian Eggs Benedict with smoked trout, and griddle favorites greet you every morning, and a hot tub waits to welcome you home at night. Dinners are available, but for an additional charge. In between, the library is a good place to retreat if you're not interested in conversation in front of the river-rock fireplace. Or, you can stop at the lodge's Body Sage spa and get a mud or seaweed wrap or facial. For those cold winter nights or fall's early chill, wool blankets and down comforters top the king-size beds made from logs. To secure particular dates, make a reservation at least three months in advance.

175 North Jackson St. ☎ *800-458-2004 or 307-733-2000. Internet:* www.rusty parrot.com. *31 rooms. A/C TV TEL. Rack rates: June–Sept $284–$500 double; Oct–Nov $164–$450 double; Dec–March $264–$500; April–May $164–$450 double. AE, DC, DISC, MC, V.*

Spring Creek Ranch
$$$$–$$$$$ **West of Jackson**

If you don't want to stay in Jackson, and if price is not a problem, this resort huddled atop East Gros Ventre Butte just west of town assures a relaxing, off-the-beaten-path stay during any season. You can't beat the views, either. Set atop the butte, 1,000 feet above the Snake River, the resort and its 1,500 acres offer spectacular panoramas of the Tetons. Deer and moose are frequent visitors to the resort's property, and eagles fly by regularly. Hotel rooms and condo units are available. Guest rooms feature wood-burning fireplaces, Native American floor and wall coverings, refrigerators, and coffee makers. The condo units are sized and furnished for men 6 feet and taller. Studio units have kitchenettes. On the grounds, you find a heated outdoor pool, tennis courts, and a small pond. To ensure a reservation, call a year in advance.

1800 Spirit Dance Rd. ☎ *800-443-6139 or 307-733-8833. Internet:* www.spring creekranch.com. *125 units. AC TV TEL. Rack rates: $150–$250 double; $225–$1,200 condo per night. AE, MC, V.*

Wort Hotel
$$$–$$$$$ **Jackson**

If you stay in Jackson, stay here. It's worth it. The location is in the heart of downtown, less than five minutes from the Town Square. The rooms are spacious and comfortable. Although the building's exterior is Tudor, inside you find Western art and taxidermy. A large fireplace anchors the lobby, and the mezzanine has a small sitting area. All the guest rooms feature "New West" decor — primarily lodgepole furnishings — as well as air-conditioning, tub/shower baths, and thick carpeting. The Governor's Suite boasts a traditional parlor. Although you can find better meals a short walk away, the hotel has a restaurant as well as the Silver Dollar Bar, which features a bar top inlaid with 2,032 silver dollars.

50 N. Glenwood. ☎ *800-322-2727 or 307-733-2190. Fax: 307-733-2067. Internet:* www.worthotel.com. *55 rooms, 5 suites. A/C TV TEL. Rack rates: June–Sept $235–$485 double; Oct–Dec $145–$485 double; Jan–March $190–$485 double. AE, DISC, MC, V. Kids 14 and under stay free.*

Runner-up lodgings

Anglers Inn
$$–$$ **Jackson**   Pine-paneled rooms and log furniture give this place a touch of the West. Flat Creek flows nearby, and downtown Jackson is a five-minute walk away. *265 N. Millward St.* ☎ *800-867-4667 or 307-733-3682. Internet:* www.anglersinn.net.

Days Inn of Jackson Hole
$$–$$$$$ **Jackson**   This property is a good walk from the heart of town, but suites are spacious and equipped with fireplaces. Plus, you get a Continental breakfast. *350 S. Hwy. 89.* ☎ *800-329-7466 or 307-733-0033. Internet:* www.daysinnjacksonhole.com.

Trapper Inn
$$–$$$$ **Jackson**   Just two blocks from the Town Square, the Trapper is a short walk from Jackson's best restaurants and a short drive from the park. *235 N. Cache.* ☎ *888-771-2648 or 307-733-2648. Internet:* www.trapperinn.com.

Virginian Lodge
$–$$$$ **Jackson**   The Old West still resides here, in the form of stuffed and mounted hunting trophies. The rates are reasonable, and you're in the heart of Jackson. *750 W. Broadway.* ☎ *800-262-4999 or 307-733-2792. Internet:* www.virginianlodge.com.

Campgrounds

If you want to commune with the great outdoors, you have several camping options within and around the park.

In the park

Grand Teton National Park has five park-operated campgrounds, which charge $12 a night and operate on a first-come, first-served basis. Four of these offer gorgeous lake settings, whereas the fifth — Gros Ventre — is riverside. The park also has one concessionaire-operated RV campground at Colter Bay.

The most popular campground — thanks to its killer views of the Grand, the embracing pine forest, and the nearby lake — is the **Jenny Lake Campground.** If you're not there to check in by 8 a.m., you probably won't be able to snag one of the 49 tent spots during the busy summer months. The sites are sprinkled amid evergreens and boulders left behind by melting glaciers, and the Tetons tower just above the western shore of the lake.

Signal Mountain Campground and its 86 sites just 12 miles north of Jenny Lake is the next campground to fill, which it usually does by 10 a.m. The sites, scattered among spruce and fir trees on the shore of Jackson Lake, provide awesome views. The nearby amenities — a marina, picnic area, camp store, dump station, and the restaurant at Signal Mountain Lodge — are a big bonus.

The **Colter Bay Campground and Trailer Village** just 6 miles north of Jackson Lake Junction has 310 sites, laundry and shower facilities, and a dump station nearby in Colter Bay Village. The sites, not far from the lakeshore, are big and have easy access if you're towing a trailer or using an RV. The proximity to Colter Bay Village with its public showers, Laundromat, grocery store, stables, restaurant, and visitor center help make this a high-demand campground. By noon most, if not all, of these sites are claimed.

Grand Teton Lodge Company (☎ **800-628-9988** or 307-543-2855) manages a trailer village with 112 sites at Colter Bay. Summer-season (late May to early September) rates range from $34 to $36 depending on the size of your RV.

On a small promontory not far from the northern tip of Jackson Lake is **Lizard Creek Campground.** Although not as developed as the Colter Bay or Signal Mountain campgrounds, Lizard Creek is popular for its quiet, lake-side setting in a spruce and fir forest. The 60 sites often go by 2 p.m.

The **Gros Ventre Campground,** no doubt because of its 360 sites as well as its location away from the lakes and mountains, is the last in the park to fill. Often you can still find space at 6 p.m. The sites are scattered among sagebrush and cottonwoods, and the Gros Ventre River is a short walk away. This campground is not the most picturesque, but if you're running late, you'll likely find a place here.

Outside the park

Beyond the park boundaries, you find the **Wagon Wheel Campground** (☎ 307-733-4588) close to the heart of downtown Jackson. This campground with its 42 sites that go for $42 a night is just five blocks north of the town square. Twelve miles northwest of Jackson and not far from Grand Teton's southwestern corner is the **Teton Village KOA** (☎ 307-733-5354). You find 153 sites here; tent sites run about $30 for two people, $5.50 each additional person 5 and older, and RV sites about $40 for two people. A bonus of this location is nearby Teton Village with its shops, saloons, and restaurants, as well as the Jackson Hole Mountain Resort tram that can haul you to the top of Rendezvous Mountain for some hiking or mountain biking.

Back at the **Flagg Ranch Resort** (☎ 800-443-2311) north of Grand Teton are 97 RV sites ($38 for two people, $2 per additional person) and 74 tent sites ($22 for two people, $2 per additional person). The campground has showers, laundry facilities, a restaurant, and service station.

Finally, the national forests that surround the park have a number of campgrounds where you can pitch your tent. For details on these campgrounds, call the **Bridger-Teton National Forest** in Wyoming (☎ 307-739-5500) or the **Caribou-Targhee National Forest** (☎ 208-524-7500) in Idaho.

Where to Eat

Meals in the park are largely typical national park fare, with steaks, poultry, fish, and pasta dishes presented in American fashion. But head down the road into Jackson and you easily double, and even triple, your dining options. You can find wild game, Italian and Mexican meals, even Greek dishes just a short drive from the park. That said, you definitely won't go hungry if you opt to remain within the park's boundaries.

Restaurants in the park

Chuckwagon Steak and Pasta House
$–$$ **Colter Bay Village** AMERICAN

This restaurant is one of two sit-downs in Colter Bay Village. The Chuckwagon serves three meals a day. Options include breakfasts of scrambled eggs or three-egg Chuckwagon omelettes with ham, mushrooms, green peppers, and onions. Dinner is a buffet with a nightly special. Entrees include New York strip steak, trout, lasagna, pork chops, beef stew, and a vegetarian pasta dish.

Across from the marina and visitor center. No phone. Main courses: $5.25–$8.50 breakfast; $5.25–$8 lunch; $10.50–$16.75 dinner. AE, DISC, MC, V. Open: Daily in summer 6 a.m.–10 p.m.

Flagg Ranch Resort

$–$$$ **Flagg Ranch**   AMERICAN

It's not fine dining on silver and china, but the meals are better than what you get at a typical family restaurant. The menu features the American standards — chicken, fish, and beef in its many incarnations. In winter, the setting becomes cozy with a fireplace roaring. The ambience is down-home as well, both in winter and summer. Although you can't see the Snake River from the dining room, its banks are just a short walk away through the forest.

5 miles north of Grand Teton's Northern Boundary on the John D. Rockefeller Jr. Parkway. ☎ *800-443-2311 or 307-543-2861. Main courses: $5–$7 breakfast; $6–$8 lunch; $10–$25 dinner. AE, DISC, MC, V. Open: Daily 7 a.m.–9 p.m.*

Jenny Lake Lodge

$$$$$ **Jenny Lake**   CONTINENTAL

This lodge serves the best meals in the park — both in terms of cuisine and ambience. The chefs have a long reputation for pleasing not only lodge guests but also U.S. presidents. Dinners are an event, often starting with grilled Portabello mushrooms, spring asparagus wrapped in prosciutto and served with a cracked pepper truffle oil, or chilled lobster salad. Entrees may include whole roasted pheasant, hickory-smoked rack of lamb, or roasted buffalo tenderloin. The desserts are decadent, so leave room. If you stay at the Jenny Lake Lodge, the cost of breakfast and dinner are included in your room rate.

North of Jenny Lake off Teton Park Road. ☎ *307-733-4647. Reservations required. Main courses: $15.50 fixed-price breakfast; $5.95–$10.95 lunch; $47.50 fixed-price dinners. AE, DISC. MC, V. Open: Summer daily 7:30–9a.m., noon –1:30 p.m., 6 p.m.–8p.m.*

John Colter Café Court

$–$$ **Colter Bay Village**   AMERICAN

In keeping with Colter Bay Village's bargain nature, quick and easy are the hallmarks of the eateries here. This sit-down spot, as well as the nearby **Chuckwagon Steak and Pasta House,** are favorites with kids because they don't serve gourmet dishes. You can get three meals a day, but breakfast in the deli is a serve-yourself affair. The lunch and dinner menu includes sandwiches, chicken, pizzas, salads, and soup.

Across from the marina and visitor center. No phone. Main courses: $3.10–$13.25 all-day menu. AE, DISC, MC, V. Open: Summer daily 6:30 a.m.–10 p.m.

The Mural Room

$–$$$ **Jackson Lake Junction**   AMERICAN

The view of Willow Flats, Jackson Lake, and the jagged Tetons through this restaurant's floor-to-ceiling windows is particularly intoxicating at sundown. A major refurbishing of the restaurant resulted in a brand new look for the 2002 season: rough-hewn oak flooring, new seating, and even a new menu with a "Rocky Mountain Chop House" theme. In Jackson Lake Junction, your only other dining options are to make a 76-mile round-trip to Jackson for one of its fine restaurants or to see whether a last-minute cancellation comes up at Jenny Lake Lodge. Dinner items include steaks, chops, fish, and pasta. Specialities include pan-seared duck breast, prime rib of buffalo, and grilled venison sausage.

Jackson Lake Lodge (near junction of US. Route 89/191/287 and Teton Park Road). ☎ *307-543-2811. Reservations recommended. Main courses: $3.50–$8.50 breakfast; $3.70–$9.75 lunch; $16.25–$23 dinner. AE, DISC, MC, V. Open: Summer daily 6 a.m.–10 p.m.*

Peaks Restaurant
$$$$–$$$$$ **Signal Mountain**   **AMERICAN**

This full-service dining room has great views of both Signal Mountain and Jackson Lake. The menu isn't bad either, with daily specials usually of trout or salmon, and regular offerings ranging from elk medallions to New York strip steaks and shrimp scampi. The bar has one of the few televisions in the park, so this place is packed and noisy during the broadcasts of major sporting events. In addition to the main dining room, a coffee shop — the Trapper Grill — serves breakfast and lunch in an informal setting.

Signal Mountain Lodge (Teton Park Road near junction with US. Route 89/191/287). ☎ *307-543-2831. Reservations accepted only on Mother's Day. Main courses: $5–$10 breakfast; $5–$10 lunch; $15–$26 dinner. AE, DISC, MC, V. Open: Summer daily 7–11 a.m., 11 a.m.–5 p.m., and 5:30–10 p.m.*

Pioneer Grill
$–$$ **Jackson Lake Junction**   **AMERICAN**

For no-frills dinners, the Pioneer Grill in Jackson Lake Lodge is the place to go. The atmosphere is 1950s soda fountain, and the entrees are light and inexpensive when compared to those found at the Mural Room up the hall. The grill is open for three meals a day and keeps kids happy with their own menu. Be careful at breakfast: The "cowboy helping" of huckleberry pancakes could leave you too full to move. The nearby Blue Heron lounge is a great place for a drink, and the only place in the lodge with a television.

Near junction of US. Route 89/191/287 and Teton Park Road. ☎ *307-543-2811. Main courses: $2.80–$8.75 breakfast; $5.50–$8 lunch; $9.80–$13 dinner. AE, DISC, MC, V. Open: Summer daily 6 a.m.–10 p.m.*

Restaurants outside the park

Sweetwater Restaurant

$$$$–$$$$$ **Jackson**   NOUVEAU AMERICAN

This turn-of-the-20th-century log home was converted into a restaurant back in 1976, and the locals have never regretted it. Some describe the food as eclectic, others say it's regional with a Greek influence. I just say it's good, very good. The herb-roasted chicken is always reliable, and I can't decide if I like the herb-crusted rack of lamb more than the garlic mashed potatoes served on the side. Rainbow trout also is on the menu, and the chef decides daily how to prepare it.

85 S. King. ☎ *307-733-3553. Reservations recommended. Main courses: $7–$11 lunch; $14.95–32 dinner. AE, DC, DISC, MC, V. Open: 11:30 a.m.– 2:30 p.m.; 6–9:30 p.m.*

Fast Facts: Grand Teton

Area Code
☎ 307.

ATM
Banks in Jackson, Jackson Lake Lodge, Colter Bay Village, Dornans at Moose, and Flagg Ranch have ATMs.

Emergency
☎ 911 or 307-739-3300.

Fees
$20 per car per week (good for entry to both Grand Teton and Yellowstone National parks); $10 per hiker/biker per week; $15 per motorcycle per week.

Fishing License
A Wyoming state license is required, which you can purchase at sporting good stores in Jackson or at park marinas.

Hospitals
Grand Teton Medical Clinic at Jackson Lake Lodge is open mid-May to mid-Oct.; ☎ 307-543-2514. St. John's Hospital in Jackson, ☎ 307-733-3636.

Information
Grand Teton National Park, P.O. Drawer 170, Moose, WY 83012; ☎ 307-739-3300.

Lost and Found
☎ 307-739-3450.

Pharmacies
Found in most major Jackson grocery and discount stores. Also Stone Drug, 830 W. Broadway, Jackson; ☎ 307-733-6222.

Post Office
Branches are located at Moose, Moran, and Kelly, as well as in Jackson.

Road Conditions and Weather
☎ 1-888-996-7623; ☎ 307-739-3611 in winter for park weather conditions.

Taxes
6% for lodging and meals.

Time
Mountain standard time.

Web Site
www.nps.gov/grte.

Chapter 15

Great Smoky Mountains National Park

● ●

In This Chapter

▶ Stepping back in time in this popular park

▶ Planning your trip

▶ Exploring the valleys, trails, and mountain tops

▶ Finding the best hotels and restaurants near park entrances

● ●

*T*en million people visit Great Smoky Mountains National Park each year — that's an impressive endorsement. Of course, that also means there are ten million reasons why you must be as crafty as possible when arranging your visit.

This 521,490-acre park, which straddles the Tennessee–North Carolina border, draws more crowds than the Grand Ole Opry could in a year of Saturday nights headlined by Garth Brooks. Why would anyone want to endure such tourism, the kind that backs up winding mountain roads, lines refreshing streams with inner tube flotillas, and raises dust on backcountry trails? Because Great Smoky has intriguing backwoods history, incredibly diverse woodlands, beautiful smoky mountains, and spectacular fall foliage — that's why.

The park's deep woods *hollows* (small, sheltered valleys) were traditional lands of the Cherokee Nation until the early 1800s, when settlers were lured by the area's rich, fertile soils and forests abundant in elk, deer, bear, and turkeys. Today, the park is a well-preserved open-air museum of early Americana. You find churches, homesteads, and working gristmills as well as corncribs, smokehouses, barns, and farm implements. After touring these sites, you can drift into the mountains to discover the largest virgin stands of forest in the eastern United States, with more than 130 tree species — more than exist in all of Europe. Between the mouth of Abrams Creek, which sits at an elevation of 840 feet, and the forested 6,643-foot summit of Clingmans Dome are five forest types. They range from a temperate rain forest to spruce-fir woodlands — the latter left behind in the upper, cooler elevations by the Ice Age climates.

Fantastic fall

With the possible exception of nearby Shenandoah National Park, no other park is as colorful in the fall as Great Smoky Mountains. Drive the Newfound Gap or Little River roads in autumn, and your eyes feast on a kaleidoscope of color as black cherry, red maple, dogwood, poplar, hickory, and mountain ash trees mix their yellow, scarlet, and red leaves with the crimson of blackberry and blueberry bushes. This vibrant display begins in the park's upper elevations as soon as late August, before slowly trickling downhill into the valleys through October. With fall's warm, usually dry days and cool nights complementing these leafy fireworks, you couldn't ask for a better season for your visit. Of course, beautiful foliage makes October one of the park's busier months, trailing just behind June, July, and August in visitation.

In fall, the forests — which are havens for black, white, and red oaks; yellow and tulip poplars; maples; hickory; beeches; and birches — erupt with dramatic foliage that paints the mountainsides in red, yellow, and crimson. Toss in the spruce, fir, pines, and hemlock and an undergrowth of waxy-green mountain laurels and rhododendrons — along with the mist of "blue smoke" that earned the park its name — and you have a breathtaking landscape.

True, you must be strategic about your visit in order to avoid the hordes — and I tell you how to do just that in this chapter. But the extra effort is worth it. No other park matches Great Smoky's rich mixture of human and natural history in such a colorful and diverse setting.

You'll want to spend at least two days in Great Smoky Mountains National Park. When planning your visit, remember that each season has its pros and cons. Accessibility is best in summer and fall, but crowds are highest during these seasons. Fall also offers moderate temperatures and beautiful foliage. (See this chapter's "Fantastic fall" sidebar for more about autumn.) Offering precious solitude in a picturesque setting, winter is also short on daylight and possibly deep on snow. Winter temperatures in the park's higher elevations can dip to zero and below, but for most of the park, the temperatures are moderate. Late spring erupts with wildflowers, but unpredictable and rainy weather keeps most visitors away in March and April.

Must-see Attractions

Rugged wilderness, cultural reservoir, mountain playground — Great Smoky Mountains National Park is all these things. At roughly a half-million acres, the park is dwarfed by many of its Western cousins. But

Great Smoky Mountains National Park

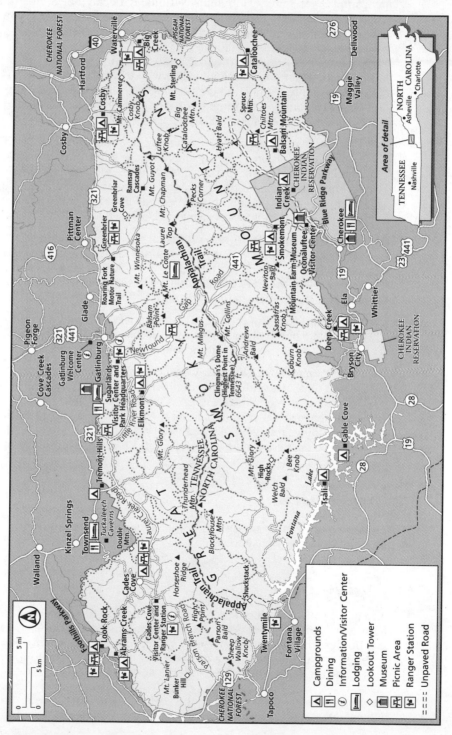

with only one road bisecting the park, and only 384 miles of road in all, navigating Great Smoky Mountains National Park can take some time. While you traverse the roads and hike some of the park's trails, you find rich rewards awaiting you, such as these not-to-miss sites:

- ✔ **Cades Cove:** Arguably the park's most celebrated, and crowded, tourist attraction, this small valley with its historic buildings is the best example of mid-19th-century life in the Smokies. Plus, the valley surrounded by mountains rising 5,500 feet is a good place to spot black bears and turkeys.

- ✔ **Cataloochee:** A lack of crowds makes this valley the smart visitor's Cades Cove, but on a slightly smaller scale in terms of preserved buildings. Hard to get to, the valley requires an 11-mile drive down an unpaved road that threads along the park's eastern edge. But after you arrive, you find preserved buildings and rolling orchards surrounded by mountains rising to 6,000 feet.

- ✔ **Mountain Farm Museum:** Huddled in a meadow outside the Oconaluftee Visitor Center, this outdoor museum captures farm life in the mid-1800s. The park service relocated several buildings from around the park to this area, including a farmhouse, spring-house, smokehouse, and blacksmith shop.

- ✔ **Newfound Gap Road:** True, a 33-mile stretch of road doesn't sound like much of an attraction. But this road, the only one that crosses the entire park, offers some of the prettiest vistas.

- ✔ **The Roaring Fork Motor Nature Trail:** This "trail" is actually a paved road open during the summer months. This oft-overlooked loop route, which starts and ends in Gatlinburg, takes you past a slew of historical sites, including the remains of a village settled about 150 years ago and those of a post–Civil War homestead. You also roll past cascading waterfalls and a handful of trailheads.

Getting There

Straddling the Tennessee–North Carolina border, Great Smoky Mountains is pretty easy to reach.

Flying in

You can fly into McGhee–Tyson Airport just south of Knoxville, Tennessee, and 45 miles northwest of Gatlinburg on the park's northern border. The airport is served by **Delta, United,** and **Northwest,** among others. Most of the major car-rental companies have outlets there. See the Appendix for the toll-free numbers.

There is no direct bus service to the park, but you can ride on a shuttle from the McGhee–Tyson Airport to Gatlinburg; call **Rocky Top Tours**

(☎ **877-315-8687** or 865-429-8687). The cost is $50 per person one-way; $5 for each additional family member.

Driving in

From Knoxville, drive 45 miles to the park's Gatlinburg entrance by taking Interstate 40 east to Route 66 and then U.S. Route 441, which runs south to Gatlinburg, where you're just 2 miles from park head-quarters and the Sugarlands Visitor Center. Coming from the south through North Carolina, take U.S. Route 441 to Cherokee, where you're just 2 miles from the Oconaluftee Visitor Center. From the west, take U.S. Route 129 south to Maryville, Tennessee, and then head back north on U.S. Route 321 to Townsend, Tennessee, and drive into the park's west entrance. From the east, head 40 miles west on I-40 from Asheville, North Carolina, to U.S. Route 19 at Cherokee, where you need to head north on U.S. Route 441 into the park.

Planning Ahead

To obtain information in advance of your trip, write **Great Smoky Mountains National Park,** 107 Park Headquarters Rd., Gatlinburg, TN 37738; call ☎ **865-436-1200;** or check the Web site at www.nps.gov/grsm.

Reserving a room

When planning a trip to Great Smoky Mountains National Park, address lodging first. The park has only one lodge, LeConte Lodge on Mount Le Conte. (The "lodge" consists of ten cabins that have no electricity and no plumbing.) You have to hike to these rustic accommodations, which do not make for the best base camp if you plan to tour the park.

Fortunately, the park's gateway communities — notably Gatlinburg, Tennessee; Cherokee, North Carolina; and Townsend, Tennessee — offer a variety of lodgings. You often need to arrange a stay at LeConte Lodge a year in advance, but the gateway communities have enough rooms to allow you to secure a bed a month or two in advance, generally. Of course, the longer you wait, the less of a selection you have. See "Where to Stay," later in this chapter, for more details on landing a room.

Packing for the park

When packing for your trip, be aware of the weather, which can be pretty wet and raw in the spring and late fall (because 80 inches of rain falls annually, on average, in the park's high country), particularly as you head up to the higher reaches. This moisture comes in many forms — driving sheets of rain dumped by thunderstorms, steady rain, drizzle, and heavy mists — so invest in some good rain gear and sturdy footwear. Naturally, packing warm layers that you can add or subtract, depending on the conditions, is wise.

Learning the Lay of the Land

This park is an island of wilderness surrounded by a sea of humanity, which explains why it's the most visited of all the National Park Service's properties. On truly clear days — which, sadly, are few and far between — you can see into seven states (North Carolina, Tennessee, Georgia, South Carolina, Virginia, Kentucky, and Alabama) from the observation platform atop Clingmans Dome. In less than three hours, residents of Atlanta, Charlotte, Chattanooga, and Greenville — and all the smaller towns in between — can drive to one of the park's 13 entrances.

Look at the park map in this chapter, and you quickly see that the park cannot easily disperse all these folks. Shaped like an oblong blob of jelly, Great Smoky Mountains National Park has only one road, the **Newfound Gap Road,** that fully crosses its girth. This 33-mile-long stretch of blacktop between Gatlinburg, Tennessee, and Cherokee, North Carolina, takes about one hour to traverse if you adhere to the 35-mph speed limit. Because of traffic, the ride becomes longer during the height of summer vacations and the fall foliage season. Just over the park border from Gatlinburg, the road leads you almost immediately to the **Sugarlands Visitor Center** with its exhibits, orientation film, and well-stocked gift shop. If you continue south on the Newfound Gap Road from Sugarlands, you come upon several impressive overlooks and the cutoff to the 7-mile-long **Clingmans Dome Road.** Driving farther south brings you to the **Oconaluftee Visitor Center** and its Mountain Farm Museum on the park's southeastern edge near the Cherokee Indian Reservation.

Your other option from the Sugarlands Visitor Center is to head southwest to **Cades Cove** via **Little River Road** and **Laurel Creek Road.** This beautiful, mountain-rimmed valley is near the western end of the park and reachable year-round by this serpentine route. An **11-mile loop road** winds through the cove, taking you past historic buildings and through farmland and forest glades. During the height of summer and fall, traffic can be bumper-to-bumper, but inspecting the buildings is worth the snail's pace, and the cove is one of the park's best locations for spotting wildlife.

Cades Cove is the park's most popular attraction — and the most crowded. If you visit during June, July, August, or October, instead of sticking to the cove's crowded loop road, take the **Parson Branch Road.** This well-maintained dirt road lures only about 1% of the 800,000 vehicles that enter Cades Cove. The Parson Branch Road connects with U.S. Route 129, the Foothills Parkway, and then U.S. Route 321 back to Gatlinburg.

On the opposite end of the park is **Cataloochee,** a valley as lovely as Cades Cove but much harder to reach — and as a result, less crowded. From Gatlinburg, head north on **U.S. Routes 321/73** to the **Foothills Parkway,** which connects with **Interstate 40.** Travel 25 miles on the interstate before getting off at Exit 20 and then drive 11 miles on the serpentine **Cove Creek Road** to Cataloochee. In all, the ride is 65 miles from Gatlinburg. To get to Cataloochee from Cherokee, take either the **Blue Ridge Parkway** 17½ miles or **U.S. Route 19** 20½ miles northeast to **U.S. Route 276** and then drive 5 miles north to Exit 20 and Cove Creek Road.

The park does have other roads: Some are short stretches of pavement, and others are less-traveled gravel roads.

If you ever feel like you're about to be overcome by traffic jams, watch the shoulder of the road for a small, unobtrusive "Quiet Walkway" sign and pull over. These signs, scattered throughout the park, point to short trails, usually less than a ½-mile in length, that lead you away from the crowds for some peace and quiet. Surprisingly, few folks seem to take advantage of them.

Arriving in the Park

The park's two main entrances are at Gatlinburg on the northern side and Cherokee on the southern side. Visitor centers are near each entrance. In Gatlinburg, you can park your car and ride a shuttle bus.

Finding information

Great Smoky Mountains National Park has three visitor centers run by the park service:

- ✔ **Cades Cove Visitor Center** (no phone) on Cades Cove Loop is open daily in spring through fall from 9 a.m. to 6 p.m. and daily in the winter from 9 a.m. to 4:30 p.m. This center is basically a gift shop with some artifacts.

- ✔ **Oconaluftee Visitor Center** (☎ 828-497-1904) on Newfound Gap Road, 1½ miles from the south entrance, is open daily year-round from 9 a.m. to 5 p.m. This center has a small interpretive area, but the big attraction is the Mountain Farm Museum.

> ✔ **Sugarlands Visitor Center** (☎ 865-436-1291) on Newfound Gap Road, 2 miles from Gatlinburg, is open daily year-round from 8 a.m. to 5 p.m. This is the park's main visitor center. You can pick up self-guiding brochures to the park's nature trails, as well as to Cades Cove, Cataloochee, and the Roaring Fork Motor Nature Trail. You can also find out about the park's flora and fauna through a wonderful exhibit featuring plant cuttings and stuffed animals and fish. An orientation film that runs every 30 minutes provides background on the park's natural and human history.

Paying fees

The Park Service does not charge a fee to enter the park.

Getting around

After you're inside the park, you can ride a bike, travel by vehicle, or utilize the shuttle service that the city of Gatlinburg runs between the **Gatlinburg Welcome Center** (☎ 865-436-0519) on Highway 441 and the Sugarlands Visitor Center, Laurel Falls Trail, and Elkmont Campground. The shuttle runs about every 90 minutes between 11 a.m. and 9 p.m. and costs $2 for the entire circuit, less for shorter rides. The shuttle operates from June through October.

Remembering Safety

To ensure a safe visit to Great Smoky Mountains National Park, keep these points in mind:

> ✔ **Winterize your vehicle.** Winter storms can close the park's main roads or cause them to be icy, so make sure that your rig is prepared for these conditions if you visit during this season. (If you're from farther north, winter in the park's valleys probably won't faze you.)
>
> ✔ **Do not feed the bears.** As with other park animals, no matter how cute you think they look, bears are dangerous. In May 2000, a black bear killed a hiker 2 miles above the Elkmont Campground near the Little River Trail. The first documented fatal bear attack in the park, the killing may have been a fluke, but the incident drives home the point that no one should trifle with bears. Never try to feed a bear. Not only do you stand a chance of being hurt, but if a bear tastes human food, it's difficult, if not impossible, for the bear to return to its natural diet.

For additional safety tips for a national park visit, see Chapter 8.

Enjoying the Park

Touring Cades Cove, climbing to the top of Clingmans Dome, wandering through the Mountain Farm Museum, taking a hike — how do you fit in all these activities? Thoroughly exploring the Smokies may take more than one trip, but you won't regret any of the time you spend here.

Exploring the top attractions

Cades Cove

Great Smoky Mountains National Park is just as much about history as it is about wilderness. Cades Cove is a great place to discover the story of the mountain folk who settled here in 1819 and farmed the land until the 1930s, when the park was created. Today, you can see several well-preserved historic buildings — three churches, some log and plank homes, several barns, and a working gristmill. While you roam about the buildings, try to envision what life must have been like 150 years ago, when wood smoke puffed from the chimneys and the men relaxed before the fire drinking moonshine after a long day's work.

Second only to the cove's historical attractions is the wildlife. This pastoral bowl in the mountains lures numerous birds and animals. Occasionally, you can spot turkeys, coyotes, fox, and bears. Weasels, mink, and spotted and striped skunks also live in the area, and white-tailed deer are almost as numerous as the human visitors.

The cove has an 11-mile-long loop road and several trailheads for striking out into the hills. You can also take a buggy or hay ride on the loop road from April through October and in December; the cost for a buggy ride is $7.50 a person, while hay rides run $6 per person without an accompanying ranger, $8 with a ranger. For reservations or more information, call ☎ **865-448-6286.**

Unfortunately, this place is the most popular in the park. Each year, roughly 800,000 vehicles hauling 2½ million people crowd into this 5,000-acre patch of open space. In mid-October, when tourists come in search of gorgeous foliage, negotiating the loop road can take three hours or more.

To avoid the crowds, don't come to the cove during the busy months of June, July, August, and October. September is a pretty good month for a visit. Sure, you won't see the spectacular colors that abound in October, but crowds won't overrun you, either. If you do visit during the busy months, arrive at the cove early in the morning or late in the afternoon. (But keep in mind that you can't drive the loop road before 10 a.m. on Wednesdays and Saturdays from May through September — see the following paragraph.) You can avoid the brunt of the traffic at these times. Moreover, your odds of seeing wildlife, particularly black bears, are dramatically higher than at midday. Bears particularly are drawn to the cove in August, when cherries in the orchards ripen, and in October, when the acorns ripen.

Finally, a great way to enjoy the loop road and avoid the vehicular traffic jams is to show up with your bike on a Wednesday or Saturday morning between early May and late September. That's when park officials ban automobile traffic before 10 a.m. so cyclists can enjoy the circuit without battling automobiles. If you don't have your own bike, rent one at the **Cades Cove Store** (☎ **865-448-9034**) next to the cove's campground.

Cades Cove is 25 miles west of the Sugarlands Visitor Center via the Little River Road and the Laurel Creek Road.

Cataloochee

Unlike at Cades Cove, you don't have to elbow your way into this valley (also known as Big Cataloochee) to enjoy the views or the historic buildings. I visited in mid-June and practically had the place to myself. But like Cades Cove, Cataloochee features preserved 19th-century buildings and rolling orchards alive with wildlife.

A highlight in the valley is the **Palmer House,** a log cabin of "dog trot" construction in which two separate cabins (later covered with planking) were linked together by a common covered porch that dogs favored on hot summer days. Although the home is musty and creaky, using the narrow old staircase to reach the second-floor bedrooms and seeing how newspapers (circa 1909) were used as insulation on the walls is interesting. You can also view a video featuring some of the valley's descendents giving an oral history of the region.

Other noteworthy buildings in the valley include the **Palmer Chapel,** a Methodist Church; the two-room **Beech Grove Schoolhouse** built in 1901; the relatively elaborate **Caldwell House,** which was built in 1903 with a covered porch on two sides; and the **Woody House,** which you can access via a 1-mile hike through the woods along a creek — the same route folks used 150 years ago.

Wildlife lovers should definitely plan to visit Cataloochee, the home to the newest members of the park's wildlife community. In 2001 the park began a 5-year experiment to reintroduce elk to the Smokies. These 800-pound members of the deer family were wiped out by settlement in the early 1800s. The reintroduced elk are very visible in the Cataloochee meadows, especially in the morning and evening hours.

Cataloochee is far away from other attractions in the park.

From Gatlinburg, take U.S. Route 321 to the northern arm of Foothills Parkway to I-40; drive south to Exit 20; take a right on Cave Creek Road; the 65-mile drive takes about 2 hours. From Cherokee, take U.S. Route 19 to U.S. Route 276; drive north to the junction with I-40; take a left on Cave Creek Road; the 39-mile drive takes 50–60 minutes.

Clingmans Dome

On clear days, a great place to be is atop Clingmans Dome, the park's highest point at 6,643 feet and the third highest summit in the Eastern United States. You can sometimes experience incredible, 100-mile-long views from the top of the 54-foot-tall observation tower, but on many spring and summer days, clouds or mist obscure the view. In fact, most days, you can see no farther than 22 miles, and on some summer days, views are limited to just a dozen miles or even less.

To reach the observation tower, drive to the end of Clingmans Dome Road and then hike up the ½-mile asphalt trail that rises 330 feet in elevation from the parking lot. The observation tower — a concrete spiral that corkscrews up above the treetops — can be interpreted as modern art. From the top, not only do you get a fantastic view of the park, but you also reach the highest point along the Appalachian Trail, which runs along the ridge.

Clingmans Dome Road shuts down on December 1st for the winter season, but the observation platform is open year-round. You can hike or cross-country ski to the top when the road is closed. This sort of off-season jaunt not only guarantees you a much less-crowded trip to the top but also offers gorgeous views — the winter weather is typically much clearer than that of spring and summer — when the surrounding red spruce and Fraser fir forest is nestled under a blanket of snow.

The dome is at the end of 7-mile-long Clingmans Dome Road, off Newfound Gap Road.

Mountain Farm Museum

Just as neat as Cades Cove, but easier to access, is the Mountain Farm Museum adjacent to the Oconaluftee Visitor Center. Open year-round from dawn to dusk, this free open-air museum offers an interesting look into backwoods life through a collection of log buildings taken from throughout the Smoky Mountains. Check out the tools that late 19th-century blacksmiths wielded, stick your head into the smoke house, or inspect the small log cabin that one family once called home. Horses and cattle roam the pasture behind the barn, and chickens roost in the barn's rafters.

The museum is near the southern end of Newfound Gap Road near the Cherokee Indian Reservation.

Roaring Fork Motor Nature Trail

You can leave behind much of the park's vehicular traffic and discover more about the settlers who scraped together a living in these mountains by heading here. This paved road gets you off the beaten path and into dense woods where you drive past some well-worn, but well-preserved, log cabins and gristmills. Every now and then a stream cascades out of the forest, and you may even spy some wildlife. The one-way road rambles beneath a lush forest canopy for 6 miles and is off-limits to buses, trailers, and motor homes, so the traffic is not as sluggish as the traffic in Cades Cove.

You find the **Trillium Gap Trail** along the road, which leads 5¼ miles through the forest and up onto the summit of Mount Le Conte. If you enjoy waterfalls, hike the first 1¼ miles of this trail to the base of Grotto Falls, which cascades 25 feet off a rocky, moss-coated ledge.

The Roaring Fork community set down its roots in the 1830s and 1840s, when the lowlands were getting crowded and when folks went into the mountains in search of land to call their own. You can check out examples of their homes at the **Jim Bales Place,** where a log cabin, corncrib, and barn still stand (although the cabin was moved from elsewhere in the park). Nearby is the **Ephraim Bales Home,** a two-room cabin where Ephraim and Minerva reared nine children. More impressive is **Alfred Reagan Place,** which started out as a log cabin but evolved into a much more substantial home as he covered the logs with planks for a cleaner look. Not far from the house is a mill that Reagan built to grind his neighbors'corn into meal.

The loop is open only in the summer. RVs and trailers aren't allowed.

To access the trail, take Airport Road from downtown Gatlinburg to Cherokee Orchard Road; drive 5 miles to the one-way Roaring Fork Motor Nature Trail. The entire route to and from Gatlinburg is 11 miles.

Taking a hike

More than 800 miles of maintained trails wind through the park, so how are you supposed to choose which ones to walk down? First think about your timetable, your hiking prowess, and whether any kids are involved. Then consider what you want to get out of a hike. Do you want to see some of the park's gorgeous waterfalls or hike a portion of the Appalachian Trail? Is seeing old-growth forest important to you? What about mountaintop views?

To help yourself decide, pick up a copy of the park's *Day Hikes* pamphlet from one of the visitor centers. This pamphlet neatly packages park hikes into categories: Loop Hikes, Waterfall Walks, Hikes to Old-Growth Forests, Hikes with Views, Pleasant Strolls, and Riverside Rambles.

Capturing the Smokies on film

Where should you point your camera in this park? Photo opportunities abound. Students of 19th-century **architecture** will use roll after roll of film in Cades Cove or at the Mountain Farm Museum, whereas **nature** lovers will find spectacular shots along the park's many streams. If you find yourself along the Roaring Fork Motor Nature Trail during, or just after, a rainstorm, head to the Place of a Thousand Drips, where the storm's runoff creates dozens of tiny rivulets streaming through moss-covered boulders. For more spectacular waterfalls, hike to the 80-foot cascade at Rainbow Falls, a 5½-mile round-trip journey from the trailhead at the end of the Cherokee Orchard Road just past the Noah "Bud" Ogle homestead.

A good place for **wildlife** shots is Cades Cove early in the morning or late in the afternoon during the fall harvest, when ripe fruit lures deer and even black bears. If you just want a great shot of the **Smoky Mountains,** go to any of the pullouts on the Newfound Gap Road or hike to Clingmans Dome. For **wildflowers,** scan the meadows and gaps in the forest along the Little River Road, the Roaring Fork Motor Nature Trail, Clingmans Dome Road, and the Balsam Mountain and Heintooga Ridge Roads.

Wherever you take pictures in the park, you'll need a relatively fast film, or a good tripod, due to the low light. If you want assistance with your photography skills, look into one of the photography workshops offered by the park service in the spring and fall. These three-day programs cost $360 and include instruction, meals, and lodging (a pretty good deal, if you ask me).

In the meantime, this section offers a sample of worthy jaunts.

Appalachian Trail

This granddaddy of the national trails network runs 2,100 miles from Georgia to Maine. In Great Smoky Mountains National Park, you find 68 miles of the Appalachian Trial, commonly known as the "AT." These miles approximately follow the Smokies ridgeline. Several places in the park provide access to the AT for a short or long hike. They include trailheads at Newfound Gap, Clingmans Dome, the end of Highway 32 just north of the Big Creek Campground, and Fontana Dam. You can put together a nice 8-mile round-trip hike on the AT by starting at Newfound Gap and hiking north to Charlies Bunion. The elevation gain isn't bad, just 980 feet, and the trail takes you through a spruce-fir forest with showy wildflowers in spring and summer.

Distance: Varies. Level: Moderate. Access: Various points, as noted in the preceding section.

Indian Creek Trail

This relatively flat trail is good if you have young hikers who limit your distance. About ¾ mile down Deep Creek Trail, you encounter Indian Creek Trail. Turn right at the junction, walk another 200 feet or so, and you come upon two waterfalls — Tom Branch, which plunges 75 feet, and Indian Creek, which drops 25 feet. If you retrace your steps back to the trail head, you'll have walked just over 1½ miles. If you continue past the falls, you come upon the aptly named Loop Trail, which wraps back around to Deep Creek Trail and your car. Follow this route, and you'll cover a total of 4 miles.

Distance: Just over 1½ or 4 miles round-trip. Level: Easy. Access: Via Deep Creek Trail, end of Deep Creek Road, just past Deep Creek Campground.

Low Gap Trail

Despite the payoff — Mount Cammerer Lookout, an octagonal 1930s-era stone fire-lookout station unlike any other in the Eastern United States — this hike draws relatively few people, possibly due to its location in the northern half of the park away from Newfound Gap Road. The lookout was built from 1937 to 1939 by Civilian Conservation Corps crews using logs and stones from Mount Cammerer; the structure was restored in 1995. Along with offering a glimpse at firefighting history, the mountain top offers some great views into North Carolina and Tennessee. The trail gains 2,650 feet in elevation along the way to the summit, so plan on a good workout.

Distance: 12 miles round-trip. Level: Moderate to Strenuous. Access: Cosby Campground.

Ramsay Cascades

If you're like me, the taller the waterfall, the better the hike. If that's the case, this hike is the best in the park because Ramsay Cascades, which falls 100 feet, is the park's tallest waterfall. This 4-mile hike to the waterfall gains more than 2,000 feet in elevation. But the trail winds through stands of old-growth hardwood forest, so you enjoy the trees along the way. Just don't think of climbing to the top of the falls — over the years a few folks have tried and have met unpleasant deaths.

Distance: 8 miles round-trip. Level: Difficult. Access: 4¾ miles east of the park's Greenbrier entrance, 6 miles east of Gatlinburg on U.S. Route 321.

Smokemont Loop Trail

If you hate backtracking, as I do, try this loop trail. The stroll through the woods takes you past tumbling mountain streams and offers glimpses of wildflower displays in the late spring and early summer. From the Smokemont Campground, walk to the Bradley Fork Trailhead in D-Loop (the campground contains a number of loops) and follow the trail to the Smokemont Loop Trail.

Distance: 5¾ miles round-trip. Level: Moderate. Access: Smokemont Campground.

One-day wonder

What do you do with just one day in the park? Float in a stream. Climb a mountain. Hike through the woods. Wonder how 19th-century families endured living in the cramped, drafty confines of log cabins. Enjoy the mist from a waterfall. Or, if you visit in winter, try cross-country skiing.

Whatever you decide to do, though, make some tactical decisions before arriving so you don't spend your entire visit idling in traffic. No matter what route you decide to take, start early in the morning. Getting on the road no later than 8 a.m., if possible, is key.

What follows includes my recommendations for seeing the best of the park in one day. (For information on these sights, see "Exploring the top attractions," earlier in this chapter, unless otherwise noted.)

The tour begins in **Gatlinburg.** Not only does this town offer countless lodging, eating, and entertainment options — if you somehow can't find enough to do in the park — but the park's best visitor center is only minutes away.

From Gatlinburg, take the Newfound Gap Road to the **Sugarlands Visitor Center.** Here you can pick up self-guiding brochures to the park's nature trails and to Cades Cove, Cataloochee, and the Roaring Fork Nature Trail.

From the visitor center, drive 25 miles southwest via the Little River and Laurel Creek roads to **Cades Cove,** which contains the park's greatest concentration of historic buildings, including some bare-bones churches with adjoining cemeteries. Although the cove usually is crowded, sitting in the old churches, seeing the old log cabins, walking through their tight quarters, and getting a feel for the rustic conditions the cove's settlers endured (so they could enjoy ownership of their own land) is worth it.

From Cades Cove, backtrack to Newfound Gap Road and head east 21 miles to the **Clingmans Dome** cutoff and then 7 more miles to the parking lot below the observation tower. From the top of the tower, you can, on clear days, get a great view of the surrounding park and into seven states.

After returning to Newfound Gap Road, drive 15 miles east to the Oconaluftee Visitor Center and the **Mountain Farm Museum.** Walk through the museum's mid-1800 buildings for another glimpse into the region's past. You can skip the visitor center, which is nothing special compared to Sugarlands.

Great smoggy mountains

Sadly, since 1948, visibility in Great Smoky Mountains National Park during the summer months has decreased by 80%. Marring the views are fossil-fuel emissions from plants in the Tennessee, Ohio, and Mississippi River Valleys, as well as industries in the Southeast, the Gulf States, and, on rare occasions, even the Northeast. The park service and other federal and state agencies are working to remedy the problem, but it will be a long, long time — if ever — before the park's historic visibility returns.

After touring the farm museum, you'll no doubt be ready to head back to Gatlinburg via Newfound Gap Road in time to enjoy dinner.

If you have more time

If you're adventurous, head to **Little Cataloochee,** which is near Cataloochee, also known as Big Cataloochee (see "Exploring the top attractions" earlier in this chapter). The well-preserved Little Cataloochee Church, still used on occasion, comes complete with a working bell in the belfry. (After entering the church, pull the rope hanging down just inside the front door.) From the church and its somber cemetery, you can hike a mile to the ruins of the Cook Place and Messer Farm, two of the oldest and best-preserved cabins in the park, dating from the 1850s. Although the surrounding farmsteads have grown over, you can see the stone walls that enclosed the fields. Also remaining is the stone foundation of the Messer apple barn. The Dan Cook Cabin was reconstructed in 1999 from materials salvaged from the original cabin.

To get to Little Cataloochee from Gatlinburg, take U.S. Route 321 to the northern arm of Foothills Parkway to Interstate 40 to Cataloochee. (From Cherokee, take U.S. Route 19 to U.S. Route 276 to Cataloochee.) Then drive north along old North Carolina 284, also known locally as the Cataloochee Turnpike, until you see a pullover with a sign for Little Cataloochee. From the pullover, you can hike down an old road 2 miles to the Little Cataloochee Church.

Ranger programs

Walks, talks, and slide shows dominate the ranger-led activities in Great Smoky Mountains National Park. You can tag along for walks as short as a ½ mile or as long as 5 miles.

Rangers lead **nature walks** at Clingmans Dome, the Little Greenbrier School, the Smokemont Campground, and the Sugarlands Visitor Center. For the most part, these walks focus on natural and cultural history. For times and details of the talks offered during your stay, check out the bulletin boards at any of the visitor centers or call ☎ 865-436-0120.

If you don't want to walk and you don't suffer from an allergy to hay, sign up for the **hayrides** that negotiate the 11-mile-long Cades Cove Loop Road. During these rides, the rangers fill you in on the background of the settlement, some of the notable settlers, the history of some of the structures, and the wildlife that call this area home. Ranger-guided rides cost $8. (You can also just go for a hayride for $6.) Call ☎ **865-448-6286** for information.

Rangers offer **evening slide shows** one or more times a week at the Cades Cove, Cosby, Elkmont, and Smokemont campgrounds. The topics rotate frequently but usually touch on the night skies overhead, the park's history, wildlife, and even the air quality problems faced by the park.

If you have kids, make sure to pick up information on the Junior Ranger Program at one of the visitor centers. (See Chapter 4 for information on this program.)

Unfortunately, if you visit during the winter season, you'll have to figure out the park and its natural and cultural history on your own, because rangers do not offer programs during the slow months of November through early April.

Keeping active

Whether on dry land or in flowing rapids, you can enjoy the outdoor beauty of Great Smoky Mountains National Park in the following ways:

- ✔ **Biking:** The park has both paved and unpaved roads for cyclists. The **Nantahala Outdoor Center** (13077 Highway 19 West, Bryson City, NC 28713; ☎ **800-232-7238;** Internet: www.noc.com) rents bikes, offers guided mountain biking outings, and has a full-service bike shop. Bryson City is near the southern end of the park.

- ✔ **Horseback riding:** Most of the park's trails are open to horses. Regularly scheduled day trips are offered by four stables: **Cades Cove Stables** (☎ 865-448-6286); **McCarter Stables** (☎ 865-436-5354), near the Sugarlands Visitor Center; **Smokemont Stables** (☎ 828-497-2373), near the campground of the same name on the North Carolina side; and **Smoky Mountain Riding** (☎ 865-436-5634), a few miles east of Gatlinburg.

- ✔ **Inner Tubing:** Floating down a creek, or "tubing" as its called in this area, is a great way to cool off on a hot day. Many businesses and campgrounds outside the park rent tubes on streams where you can jump right in. Remember to wear a swimsuit and shoes you can get wet, and make sure that kids have life jackets. **Deep Creek Tube Center** (West Deep Creek Road, Bryson City; ☎ 828-488-6055) is a good spot to go to find tubes and water.

Spotting the local wildlife

Long before Great Smoky Mountains became a park, its wild kingdom was very similar to the one found today in Yellowstone. Bison and elk, mountain lions and wolves, and fishers and river otters were all residents. Unfortunately, settlement pressures conspired against the wildlife, and you no longer can find bison, gray wolves, or mountain lions in the park. However, park officials have been working to restore some of the native species to the Great Smoky Mountains. In recent years, the Park Service has returned river otters and peregrine falcons to the park. In January 2001, they began an elk reintroduction program. (The original elk vanished from the area under heavy hunting pressure in the mid-1800s.)

So what animals can you see during a visit? Although **white-tailed deer** numbered only about 30 when the park was established in 1934 and were in danger of being hunted out of existence, today they are plentiful. You also stand a good chance of running across one of the park's **two fox species** — gray and red. **Bobcats** are also fairly common, but you aren't likely to spot one because they're highly reclusive and roam mainly at night. If you want to try your luck, head to Cades Cove.

Populations of **river otters,** the subject of a reintroduction effort launched in 1986, are recovering, and you may be able to see some of these playful critters in Abrams Creek, Little River, Hazel Creek, Fontana Lake, and Lake Cheoah.

Also visible in the park's forests and along its streams are **salamanders.** With more than 30 species of these critters, the park is known as the world's salamander capital. Among the more interesting varieties are Jordan's salamanders, which have red cheeks; marbled salamanders, which are black with white or gray splotches; and hellbenders, which can grow to 2 feet in length. A good place to look for Jordan's salamanders is the Chimneys Picnic Area as well as around Newfound Gap.

In the trees and sky overhead, look for **pileated woodpeckers** and, near water, **belted kingfishers.** Meanwhile, you're more likely to see **Ruffed grouse,** scurrying through the underbrush. In the fall, you may see a **golden eagle** passing overhead.

One animal you hopefully won't see scurrying through the forests is a **wild hog.** These nasty-tempered pigs are descended from hogs that escaped from a game preserve in the 1920s. Equipped with sharp tusks, they can weigh 220 pounds and can be dangerous. Rangers, who are trying to round up the hogs and get them out of the park, estimate their numbers at 500.

If you spend much time in the park during the summer and fall, you'll no doubt spot one of the almost 2,000 **black bears** that live here. The park, in fact, is the largest protected black bear habitat in the Eastern United States. Although they're called "black" bears, their fur can be black, cinnamon, various shades of brown, and even blond. For a four-legged animal, the park's black bears spend a lot of time in the trees. They climb into oaks to hunt for acorns, search for bugs, or raid egg nests. If you're determined to spot one of these bruins, look for them between 6 and 10 a.m. or between 3 and 7 p.m.; bear studies in the park have determined that these are their most active hours. Good spots to look for bears are in Cades Cove and along the Roaring Fork Motor Nature Trail. In the spring and fall, add Newfound Gap Road to these search areas. And if you do see a bear, don't give him food and remember to be careful. These cute animals are dangerous.

Escaping the rain

For more insight into the Native Americans who made the Great Smoky Mountains home, visit the **Museum of the Cherokee Indian** (441 North on Drama Road, Cherokee, NC; ☎ 828-497-3481; Internet: www.cherokeemuseum.org). The museum is open June to mid-September, daily 9 a.m. to 8 p.m., and mid-September to May, daily 9 a.m. to 5 p.m. The cost is $8 for adults and $5 for ages 6 to 12. You can't miss the museum, because out front is a towering redwood sculpture of Sequoyah, a revered tribal chief. Inside, you find tribal artifacts as well as high-tech, interactive displays involving lasers, lighting, and sound effects that recount tribal history and rituals.

If you can't find an indoor activity in Gatlinburg, you must be asleep. The town overflows with theaters, museums, and arcades. Kids enjoy the **Guinness World Records Museum** (631 Parkway, Gatlinburg, TN; ☎ 865-436-9100), which is open from 9 a.m. to 10 p.m. seven days a week. The cost is $9.95 for adults and $5.95 for ages 6 to 12. Displays include the world's most expensive car and the Batmobile.

At the **Ripley's Aquarium of the Smokies** (88 River Rd., Gatlinburg, TN; ☎ 888-240-1358, Internet: www.ripleysmuseumofthesmokies.com), you can explore rain forests, coral reefs, and the oceans of the world. If that's not enough, you also find a Discovery Center and a shark lagoon. Admission runs $15.95 for ages 12 and up, $7.95 for kids. The aquarium is open Sunday through Thursday from 9 a.m. to 9 p.m., and Friday through Saturday from 9 a.m. to 11 p.m.

Where to Stay

Aside from ten campgrounds and the rustic lodge found atop Mount LeConte, no accommodations exist in the park. Fortunately, you can find more than enough lodging options in the gateway towns of Gatlinburg, Cherokee, and Townsend. Gatlinburg alone has more than 90 hotels and motels.

Most hotels and B&Bs feature fireplaces, hot tubs, and wonderful amenities, so make sure to inquire about them before confirming a reservation.

Lodging in the park

LeConte Lodge

$$ **Mount Le Conte**

You can reach this collection of ten rustic log cabins only on foot, and after you arrive, you don't find indoor plumbing, showers, or electricity. Still, for many people, coming here is an annual ritual — one that makes landing a reservation challenging. Open only during the late spring, summer, and early fall, you can make reservations for each season by phone, fax, or e-mail beginning the previous October 1st. In many cases, the coming season is almost entirely booked by the end of the first week of October. Why so popular? Well, the allure of hiking up a mountain to spend a night or two in a rustic cabin appeals to many. Plus, the sunrise and sunset views from Mount LeConte are gorgeous. The nightly rates include dinner, breakfast, and a kerosene lamp to light your room at night. Each heated lodge has a central living room. Water is available from a pump on the grounds.

The Alum Cave Bluffs Trail is one of five trails that lead to the cabins, and although it's the shortest hike, covering just 5 miles, it's also the steepest.

Hike-in on one of five trails: Alum Creek, Rainbow Falls, Trillium Gap, Bullhead, and Boulevard; see the Web site for details. ☎ *865-429-5704. Fax: 865-774-0045. Internet:* www.leconte-lodge.com. *E-mail:* reservations@leconte-lodge.com. *10 cabins total: 7 one-bedroom units (4 cabins sleep 4, 3 cabins sleep 5), 2 3-bedroom units (each sleeps 13), 1 2-bedroom unit (sleeps 10). Rack rates: $82 per person ages 11 or older; $66 for ages 4–10. Rate includes dinner and breakfast, as well as lunch if you stay more than one night. No credit cards.*

Top lodging outside the park

If you're in the Cherokee–North Carolina area, you're near a wide range of longing options, including **Best Western, Days Inn,** and **Quality Inn** (see the Appendix for the toll-free numbers). You find a complete list of Cherokee's hotels online at www.cherokee-nc.com.

Best Western Fabulous Chalet
$$–$$$$ **Gatlinburg**

You're heading to a mountainous national park, so you may as well stay in the mountains, right? At this stylish Best Western with two swimming pools, you do just that: The chalet-style lodge is landscaped into the mountains on the edge of Gatlinburg. Most budgets can be accommodated, because the choices range from standard, motel-style rooms to two- and three-bedroom condos with rock fireplaces and balconies.

310 Cottage Dr. ☎ *800-933-8675 or 865-436-5151. Internet:* www.reaganresorts. com/fabchal.htm. *75 rooms. A/C TEL TV. Rack rates: $60–$170 double. Rates include Continental breakfast. AE, CB, DC, DISC, MC, V.*

Eight Gables Inn
$$$–$$$$$ **Gatlinburg**

Designed as a B&B and built in 1991, this sprawling inn offers accommodations a notch or two higher than the usual B&B. The rooms approach the size of minisuites and all feature private baths. One kid-friendly room has two double beds; call in advance to request it. Downstairs, a classic brick fireplace dominates the Magnolia Tea Room. Breakfasts often feature a variety of breads (banana nut, pumpkin, cranberry, and zucchini), and you can come back for lunch if, for some reason, you're not in the park.

219 North Mountain Trail. ☎ **800-279-5716** _or 865-430-3344. Internet:_ www.eight gables.com. _20 rooms. A/C TEL TV. Rack rates: $149–$249 double; $15 per extra person. DC, DISC, MC, V._

Tennessee Ridge Inn
$$$–$$$$ **Gatlinburg**

Away from the hubbub of downtown Gatlinburg, this three-story bed-and-breakfast that clings to a mountainside is a romantic hideway decidedly not for kids. Couples love the large bedrooms — some with stone fireplaces for cozy evenings — with great views of the surrounding mountains and two-person jetted-tubs for soothing any kinks you picked up in the park. Breakfasts are served in a dining room with gorgeous views of the Smokies through a floor-to-ceiling window.

507 Campbell Lead. ☎ **800-737-7369** _or 865-436-4068. Internet:_ www.tn-ridge. com. _7 rooms. A/C. Rack rates: $119–$159 double. AE, DISC, MC, V._

The Wright Cabins
$$–$$$ **Townsend**

You find these backwoods cabins in Townsend, a quieter community than Gatlinburg located just north of Cades Cove. The cabins are remote, but they're not what you may expect from a Tennessee log cabin. These modern versions are fully equipped with kitchens, dishwashers, washers and dryers, stone fireplaces, and grills — kind of like a home away from home. Most also have Jacuzzi tubs. The Rocky Top cabin, with three bedrooms, two baths, and a loft, is perfect for families, as is the River Bend with its four bedrooms and two baths.

136 Black Mash Hollow Rd. ☎ **865-448-9090.** _Internet:_ www.thewrightcabins. com. _12 cabins. A/C TEL TV. Rack rates: $85–$125 double; $10 per extra person over 18, $5 per extra person under 18. No credit cards._

Runner-up lodgings

Bearskin Lodge on the River
$$–$$$$ **Gatlinburg**   With ten different room layouts (some featuring gas fireplaces and jetted tubs), an outdoor pool, and a lazy river for floating the afternoon away, this year-old lodge makes a great base camp. _840 River Rd._ ☎ **877-795-7546** _or 865-430-4330. Internet:_ www.bearskinlodgeon theriver.com.

Brookside Resort

$–$$$$ **Gatlinburg** Whether you want a standard motel room, a deluxe room, or even a four-bedroom cottage, this resort is one of the most economical and family-friendly places to stay. *463 East Parkway.* ☎ *800-251-9597 or 865-436-5611. Internet:* www.brooksideresort.com.

Clarion Inn & Suites of Gatlinburg

$$–$$$ **Gatlinburg** Whether you go with a regular room or a suite, you get a microwave, refrigerator, and private balcony at your disposal. Spring for a suite and also get a fireplace and hot tub. *1100 Parkway.* ☎ *800-933-0777. Internet:* www.clariongatlinburg.com.

Days Inn & Suites

$–$$$$ **Gatlinburg** In the heart of Gatlinburg, this inn is a short walk away from restaurants and shopping. Kids love to cool off in the pool after a long day in the park. *1109 Parkway.* ☎ *800 637-7846 or 865-436-5811. Internet:* www.daysinnandsuitesgatlinburg.com.

Campgrounds

With 10 million visitors each year, you better believe that Great Smoky Mountains National Park features a lot of campsites. Ten campgrounds in the park offer nearly 1,000 sites in all. They all have running water and flush toilets, but none have hookups for trailers or recreational vehicles.

You can reserve a spot (☎ **800-365-2267** or Internet: www.reservations.nps.gov) at just three of the ten campgrounds: Cades Cove, Elkmont, and Smokemont. The other seven — Abrams Creek, Balsam Mountain, Big Creek, Cataloochee, Cosby, Deep Creek, and Look Rock — operate on something of a free-for-all basis: Arrive early, and you just may luck out and get a spot to flop your tent or park your rig.

Oh yeah, just two of the campgrounds — Cades Cove and Smokemont — are open year-round. The rest open sometime between March and May and stay open into November, except for Balsam Mountain, located at 5,000 feet, which closes its gates at the end of September when the weather turns cold.

Cades Cove (159 sites, $14–$17/night) is a great place to camp. You can navigate the loop road on a bike, and the area has good hiking. The sites aren't exactly private, but the grounds have shade trees, as well as a nearby camp store and covered amphitheater. This area is also one of the better spots in the park for spotting wildlife. **Smokemont** (142 sites, $14–$17/night) is also a good campground thanks to its tall trees and location on the banks of the Bradley Fork of the Oconaluftee River. **Elkmont** (220 sites, $14–$20/night) lies along the Little River between Gatlinburg and Cades Cove.

If you want to get away from the activity in the center of the park, consider **Abrams Creek** (16 sites, $12/night) on the west side of the park off Highway 72/129. This out-of-the-way location has good swimming areas and decent fishing. Locals love this area, in large part because it sidles up against the largest creek in the park, one that's perfect for a lazy afternoon float or a soak on a hot day. In fact, locals have been known to visit the campground at midweek, pick out a site, and set up camp for the weekend. If this campground has a negative strike, it's the elevation. At 840 feet above sea level, Abram's Creek is the lowest spot in the park, and in summer, it can quickly become the hottest.

Cataloochee (27 sites, $12/night) is even more removed from the beaten path, found at the end of an 11-mile, mostly gravel road in the park's northeastern corner. RV campers don't typically head to this campground because of the narrow and winding dirt road leading to it. Also, thanks to the remote location, sites are easy to get midweek, although they can fill quickly on summer weekends. The campground's other pluses include decent wildlife viewing, miles of roads for mountain biking, and historic structures that teach you about the valley's past. Fishing along Cataloochee Creek has a long history, too; in the early 1900s, some of the valley's residents stocked the streams with trout and rented rooms to anglers. Some sites border the creek, so fishing is readily at hand.

Another campground that seems to be ignored, compared to the others, is **Cosby** (157 sites, $14/night), which can handle RVs up to 25 feet in length. The reason people tend to forget about this campground is probably because of its location east of Gatlinburg, far from Newfound Gap Road. Many trails run out of the area, however, so if you like to hike, this area is a good base camp. I recommend the hike that runs up Mount Cammerer to a restored fire lookout.

The smallest campground (12 sites, $12/night) in the park is at **Big Creek** on the southern boundary of the park just above Bryson City, North Carolina. Restricted to tent campers, the sites are a short walk (100–300 feet) from the parking area. Thanks to the somewhat remote location and the limited number of sites, this campground never really feels crowded. Big Creek flows past the campground and offers some nice pools for cooling off in the summer.

When staying at one of these campgrounds, don't forget to keep a clean campsite that won't attract animals, particularly bears. However, these bears are not the brutes that you find in Yosemite or Sequoia national parks, so you can store your food, coolers, and cooking gear inside your car without fear of its doors being peeled open by some muscle-popping bruin.

If you're into **backcountry camping,** you find dozens of places to pitch a tent. The park requires you to stay in one of its 98 designated backcountry tent sites or 16 lean-to sites. Fifty of the tent sites and 11 of the lean-to sites are open to horse packers. Reservations are needed for all of these sites, so plan early and call the backcountry office at ☎ 865-436-1231 to reserve your piece of ground; the office is open seven days a week from 8 a.m. to 6 p.m. If you're not ready to make your reservations but have some general questions about the backcountry, call the park's rangers at ☎ 865-436-1297.

Where to Eat

The park doesn't have any restaurants, so you must head to one of the surrounding gateway communities for your meals. Gatlinburg, the main gateway town to the park, lays claim to the most restaurants and the greatest variety of food. You find quite a number of rib houses, but other options exist if they don't suit your palate.

Calhoun's

$–$$ Gatlinburg   AMERICAN

Okay, barbecue fans, this is your hangout. Start off with some fried green tomatoes or the hot beer cheese dip and then launch into one of the chef's specialities, such as hickory-smoked baby back ribs and smoked prime rib. For those of you not so keen on barbeque dishes, you can turn to steak, chicken, or trout. Eat inside or out back on the covered patio.

1004 Parkway. ☎ 865-436-4100. Main courses: $6.95–$18.95 all-day menu. AE, CB, DC, DISC, MC, V. Open: Mon–Thurs 11 a.m.–10:30 p.m., Fri–Sat 11 a.m.–11:30 p.m., Sun 11 a.m.–10 p.m.

Maxwell's Beef & Seafood

$$–$$$$ Gatlinburg   AMERICAN

Don't let "Max," the piranha drifting back and forth in the aquarium just inside the front door, fool you: You're here to eat, not to be eaten. And the food and setting in Maxwell's is among the best in Gatlinburg. In this land of barbecue and catfish, this chain drowns you with seafood, pastas, chicken, and beef dishes that you'd expect to find further north. Among the seafood specialities are pan-roasted sea scallops in a soy vinaigrette and pan-fried snapper or orange roughy. Pasta lovers choose between linguine primavera and linguine and shellfish, and meat eaters sate themselves with prime rib or filet mignon. But because you're in the Smoky Mountains, why not go with the Smoky Mountain Rainbow Trout, which is sauteed in butter and covered with toasted almonds. In spring, fall, or winter, ask for a table by the massive, four-sided fireplace.

1103 Parkway. ☎ 865-436-3738. Reservations not accepted, but you can call ahead to get your name on a list. Main courses: $11.95–$29.95. AE, DISC, MC, V. Open: Sun–Thurs 4:30–10 p.m., Fri–Sat 4–11 p.m.

The Park Grill
$$–$$$$ Gatlinburg   AMERICAN

Across the street from Maxwell's, this is another Gatlinburg restaurant where you really can't go wrong. True, the waiters and waitresses look a bit silly in outfits meant to resemble park ranger uniforms. (I thought our waitress was a girl scout.) But for both food and entertainment, the Park Grill is a reliable place. Inside this heavy log structure, you find a menu that ranges from big, hickory-smoked steaks and lamb chops to seafood, chicken, and vegetarian stir fries. If you really want to taste a local dish, try the "Moonshine Chicken," which features a skinless chicken breast marinated in orange juice, sweet lime, and real moonshine. On the porch during the summer season, between 6 and 8:30 p.m., storytellers, musicians, and even comedians entertain guests waiting for tables.

1100 Parkway. ☎ *865-436-2300. Reservations not accepted. Main courses: $12.95–$32. AE, DC, DISC, MC, V. Open: Sun–Fri 5–10 p.m., Sat 4:30–10 p.m.*

The Peddler Restaurant
$$$–$$$$$ Gatlinburg   AMERICAN

As with most restaurants, how much you pay for your steak dinner here depends on how much you eat. But unlike most restaurants, here your waiter slices your steak to order at your table, then hauls the cut back to the kitchen for cooking. The steaks start at set prices — $21.95 for a 10-ounce New York strip steak, for example — and then your waiter tacks on $2 for each additional ounce you order. Interesting concept, no? The seafood dishes — grilled salmon and charbroiled shrimp, for example — and chicken and chops have set fees with no "poundage" add-ons. A dinner here feels like you're back in the park in a log cabin. In fact, the restaurant is built around the homestead of C. Earl Ogle, one of the first settlers in Gatlinburg.

820 River Rd. ☎ *865-436-5794. Reservations not accepted, but you can call ahead to get your name on a list. Main courses: $15.95–$27.95. AE, CB, DC, DISC, MC, V. Open: Sun–Fri 5–10 p.m., Sat 4:30–10 p.m.*

Fast Facts: Great Smoky Mountains

Area Code
☎ 865.

ATMs
None in the park, but plenty in Gatlinburg's gas stations, groceries, and banks.

Emergency
☎ 911 or 865-436-1230.

Fees
This park has no entrance fee.

Fishing License
You can fish in the park with either a North Carolina or a Tennessee fishing license. Licenses are not sold in the park, but you can find them outside the park in sporting goods stores. A three-day nonresident

Tennessee license is $10.50; a three-day nonresident North Carolina license is $15.

Hospitals

The Gatlinburg Family and Urgent Care Clinic, 611 Oak St., Gatlinburg; ☎ 865-430-7369.

Information

Superintendent, Great Smoky Mountains National Park, 115 Park Headquarters Road, Gatlinburg, TN 37738; ☎ 865-436-1200 or 865-436-0120.

Lost and Found

☎ 865-436-1230.

Pharmacies

Mountain Pharmacy, 1455 Parkway, Gatlinburg; ☎ 865-436-6799; Parkway Pharmacy, 917 Parkway, Gatlinburg; ☎ 865-436-4240.

Post Office

1216 E. Parkway, Gatlinburg; ☎ 865-436-5464.

Road Conditions and Weather

☎ 865-436-1200.

Taxes

Gatlinburg: 11.5% lodging, 10% meals; Cherokee: 7% lodging and meal tax, plus $1 per night room fee or $.25 per night campsite fee.

Time Zone

Eastern standard time.

Web Site

www.nps.gov/grsm.

Chapter 16

Mammoth Cave National Park

· ·

In This Chapter

▶ Plunging into the world's longest cave

▶ Planning your trip

▶ Exploring below and above ground

▶ Finding the best hotels and restaurants

· ·

Americans are braggarts by nature. We proudly boast that we have the world's grandest canyon (the Grand Canyon), biggest trees (sequoias), and oldest national park (Yellowstone). Add to this list the world's longest cave.

Mammoth Cave, around which a national park is built, earns that distinction thanks to a spectacular series of wandering passages, towering rooms, and deep tubes that water has created by dissolving central Kentucky limestone underground over the course of millions of years.

Artifacts found in the caves indicate that the curious have been entering this subterranean labyrinth for roughly 4,000 years. In modern history, the cave supposedly was stumbled upon in the 1790s by a bear hunter named John Houchins, who, as the story goes, tracked a wounded bruin to the cave entrance. Whether this story is true continues to spawn debate. (Those who say it isn't contend that, if Houchins truly was a Kentucky hunter, he would have killed the bear with one shot — not wounded it.) Another continuing debate centers on the size of the cave system. In fact, we're still trying to get to the bottom of the cave today, something that's difficult — if not impossible — to accomplish due to the underground rivers that constantly bore through the limestone and create new passages. So far, more than 350 miles of passages have been explored in this national park, which requires an underground excursion to see its highlights.

Is Mammoth Cave a park you should visit? Some people assume that if they are claustrophobic, the answer is no. Indeed, some tour routes expose you to tiny crawl spaces, frightful ledges, and, not surprisingly, inky darkness. But many of the tour routes lead you through wide passages and rooms that are large, spacious chambers. You can choose the visit that suits your tastes — and phobias — and only spend time in

Mammoth Cave National Park

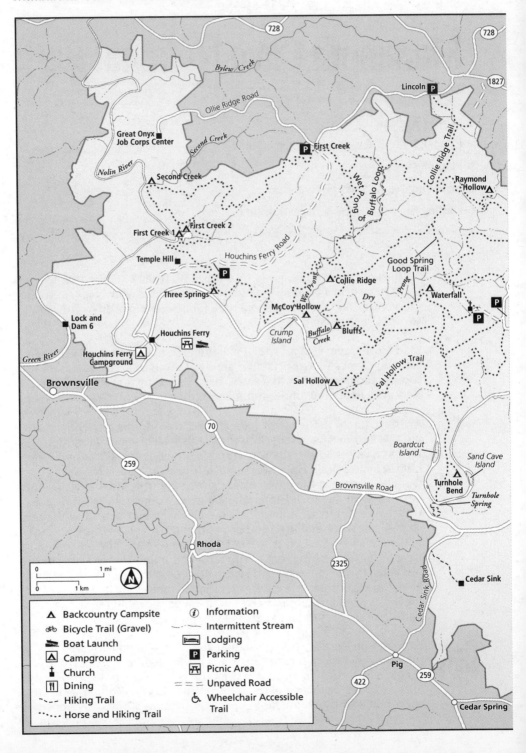

Map legend:

- ▲ Backcountry Campsite
- ⚲ Bicycle Trail (Gravel)
- 🚤 Boat Launch
- ◮ Campground
- ✝ Church
- 🍴 Dining
- - ‑ ‑ Hiking Trail
- •••••• Horse and Hiking Trail
- ⓘ Information
- – ‑ ‑ ‑ Intermittent Stream
- 🛏 Lodging
- 🅿 Parking
- 🧺 Picnic Area
- = = = Unpaved Road
- ♿ Wheelchair Accessible Trail

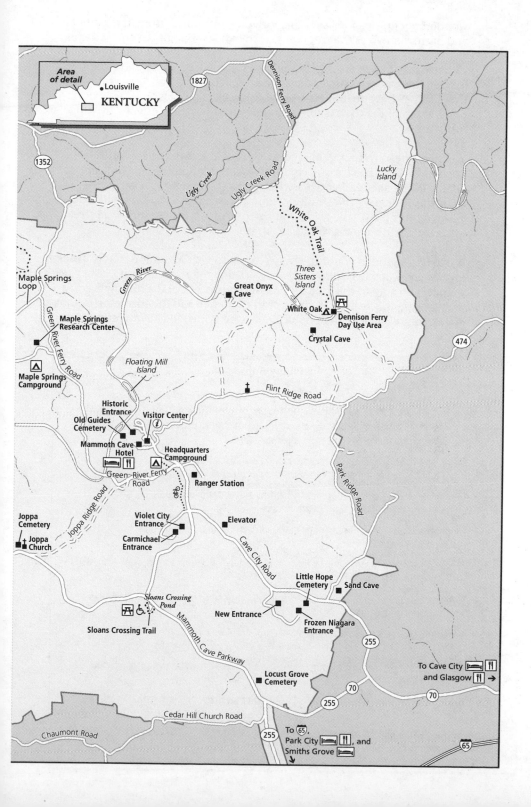

Area of detail

● Louisville

KENTUCKY

1827

Dennison Ferry Road

1352

Ugly Creek

Ugly Creek Road

Lucky Island

White Oak Trail

Green River

Great Onyx Cave

Three Sisters Island

White Oak

Dennison Ferry Day Use Area

Crystal Cave

474

Maple Springs Loop

Maple Springs Research Center

Green River Ferry Road

Floating Mill Island

Flint Ridge Road

Maple Springs Campground

Historic Entrance

Visitor Center

Old Guides Cemetery

Mammoth Cave Hotel

Headquarters Campground

Green River Ferry Road

Ranger Station

Park Ridge Road

Joppa Cemetery

Joppa Ridge Road

Joppa Church

Violet City Entrance

Elevator

Carmichael Entrance

Cave City Road

Little Hope Cemetery

Sand Cave

Sloans Crossing Pond

New Entrance

Frozen Niagara Entrance

Sloans Crossing Trail

Mammoth Cave Parkway

255

To Cave City and Glasgow

Locust Grove Cemetery

255

70

Cedar Hill Church Road

70

Chaumont Road

255

To 65, Park City, and Smiths Grove

65

wonderfully lit, spacious sections, or you can squirm through tight holes and narrow crevices that require you to exhale at points to continue on.

Unlike many caves, most of Mammoth Cave is dry. The waters that formed the passages have long since departed, moving lower into the Earth as they've funneled through cracks and dissolved new corridors. Much of the cave is dusty and dry without any actively growing formations.

You don't need to be a geologist to marvel at the cave's formations — such as Frozen Niagara, a 75-foot-tall formation that oozes from the ceiling in the section known as the cave's traveling rock corridor — or to be impressed by the Drapery Room, which seems to drip with rock. To enjoy this park, you only need a sense of adventure and an appreciation for Earth's underground artistry.

A trip underground is not the only reason to visit Mammoth Cave. Thick forests grow above ground, virtually erasing the rich cultural history of people who settled the area and carved farms out of the hollows. You can glimpse this history in preserved churches and tidy cemeteries that speak volumes about the people who lived above the cave system.

Cave talk

They say that the cave's walls are lined with "flowers" and "cave popcorn?" Before you get the wrong idea about what you'll find within Mammoth Cave, let me tell you what some of these descriptive terms mean.

- ✔ **Cave popcorn:** Clusters of cauliflower-like mineral deposits sprouting from cave walls and ceilings. Also known as "cave coral."

- ✔ **Draperies:** A cave decoration formed when water deposits harden in thin, often translucent, sheets that hang from a cave's ceiling.

- ✔ **Dripstone:** Mineral deposits (especially *stalactites* and *stalagmites*) formed by dripping or flowing water.

- ✔ **Flowstone:** Any mineral deposit formed in a cave by flowing water. Also known as "travertine."

- ✔ **Gypsum flowers:** Calcium sulfate formations that seemingly grow on the walls and ceilings of dry caves.

- ✔ **Rimstone:** Rings of calcium carbonate that form around pools of mineral-rich water.

- ✔ **Stalactites:** Formations of mineral deposits that grow downward from the cave's ceiling.

- ✔ **Stalagmites:** Formations of mineral deposits that grow upward from the cave's floor.

- ✔ **Travertine:** Also known as "flowstone," these deposits are created through precipitation of minerals carried in running water.

To best enjoy Mammoth Cave National Park, plan to spend a minimum of two days here. Underground, the atmosphere is pretty much the same day in and day out, so your choice of season won't affect your cave experience. The cave's darkness (outside of the artificially illuminated areas) remains constant, of course, and the temperature changes only slightly, staying right around 54 degrees. Humidity, however, varies; it can reach nearly 100% on some days, making the temperature inside the cave feel cooler.

As with most national parks, Mammoth Cave is busiest in summer, with July luring the year's largest crowds. If you're determined to avoid the hordes, try scheduling a visit in November, December, January, or February (outside of the holidays). However, keep in mind that most cave tours take place from May through early September.

Must-see Attractions

For the best of this park, you have to go underground. But with so much cave to explore, you're no doubt wondering what you should see on a guided tour. Not to worry. Here's a list of the must-see stops:

- ✔ **Cedar Sink:** Found on the southwestern edge of the park, you can hike down into this large, oblong sink hole to get an understanding of the Earth's plumbing in this part of the country.

- ✔ **The Drapery Room:** Most of Mammoth Cave's rooms and passageways are dry and, as a result, lack stalactites, stalagmites, and other dripstone formations, which is why you must visit the Drapery Room with its columns of stalactites and other travertine formations. You can view this formation on the Frozen Niagara or on the Travertine tours.

- ✔ **Frozen Niagara:** This 75-foot-tall travertine formation, found in the logically named Frozen Niagara section of the cave, is slowly and quietly growing as seeps continue to deposit calcium carbonate on the formation.

- ✔ **The Great Wall of China:** Although only 3-feet wide, this display of rimstone not far from Frozen Niagara is a beautiful work of art.

- ✔ **Register Hall:** Penmanship stands out in this section of Gothic Avenue, one of the cave's main passages, where 19th-century cave visitors recorded their names on the milky white ceiling with the sooty smoke from the candles they used to find their way. This is a great sight, but the Gothic Tour that passes through Register Hall is not always offered, so ask about it when you call for tickets. If not, you can see some name graffiti in the Snowball Room, which is used as a lunch room on the Grand Avenue tour.

Cave Formation 101

Mammoth Cave got its start about 350 million years ago when this part of the state was underwater. Lots of water. So much that it was considered an inland sea. As the shellfish and other critters that swam in this sea died, their shells and bones wound up on the ocean bottom. After even more time, these shells and bones mixed with sands and silts. The compressed mixture turned into limestone. Eventually, a layer of sandstone was deposited on top of the limestone.

About 25 million years ago, the forerunner of today's Green River started flowing, and in places, it slowly cut its riverbed through the sandstone layer. After cutting through this surface layer, the river's waters — turned into a weak solution of carbonic acid by picking up carbon dioxide from decaying plants and animals on the surface — quickly went to work dissolving parts of the limestone. As the river flowed through the cave, it occasionally dissolved a hole through the limestone that, like the drain in your kitchen sink, funneled the water down to the next level. Over the ensuing millions of years, the river and its tributaries produced the five distinct — and intricate — levels that make up Mammoth Cave.

But the cave has not stopped changing and growing. Rain and melting snow continue to funnel downward through the sandstone. The water's endless seeping, trickling, and dripping eat away at Mammoth Cave.

Getting There

You find Mammoth Cave National Park, an amoeba-like splotch of land located in west-central Kentucky, 35 miles north of Bowling Green and 90 miles south of Louisville.

Driving in

Running north-to-south just beyond the park's eastern border is Interstate 65, the major thoroughfare leading to the park. If you're southbound on I-65, get off at Cave City, exit 53, and head 10 miles west on Kentucky 70/255 to the park's visitor center. If you're northbound on the interstate, get off at Park City, exit 48, and follow Kentucky 255 for 9 miles west to the visitor center.

If you're coming in from eastern Kentucky, take the Cumberland Parkway or the Kentucky Parkway to I-65 and then go either north or south to the park. From the western side of the state, take the Western Kentucky Parkway to Kentucky 259, which runs 24 miles to Route 70 just east of Brownsville; you are less than a dozen miles to the park.

Flying in

Flying to the park is fairly easy because major airlines serve both Tennessee's **Nashville International Airport** (☎ 615-275-1600) and Kentucky's **Louisville International Airport** (☎ 502-368-6524). Whereas Nashville is 90 miles south of the park via I-65, Louisville is 90 miles north, also via I-65. The major rental car companies are represented at each airport; see the Appendix for their toll-free numbers.

Busing in

You can travel by bus most of the way to the park because Southeastern Greyhound (☎ 800-229-9424; Internet: www.greyhound.com) stops in Cave City. From here, take a taxi from **Howard's Taxi Service** (☎ 270-678-2700) to the park.

Planning Ahead

An advantage Mammoth Cave National Park has over most other parks is that you can reserve not only your lodgings months in advance but also your tickets on the underground tours. This section covers what you need to know about lodging, campsites, and packing before you visit the park.

For additional advance information, call **Mammoth Cave National Park** at ☎ 270-758- 2328 or check their Web site at www.nps.gov/maca.

Reserving a room or a campsite

Because this park is close to civilization, you don't need to make room reservations months ahead of schedule, unless you have a particular room or cabin in mind inside the park. In most cases, you can secure decent lodging a month before your visit. However, only one of the park's two campgrounds takes reservations, so either make them far in advance for that campground or be sure to nab a spot in the first-come, first-served campground in the morning before you head underground.

Making reservations for tours

I'm a big fan of reservations. They make your visit more relaxing because you don't have to worry about whether you're on the tour of your choice.

No matter what underground tour you plan to join, make a reservation (☎ 800-967-2283) before you leave home. You can make reservations up to five months before your visit, but you really don't need to plan that far ahead unless you plan to join the Wild Cave Tour, or you want to take a specific tour on a specific day at a specific time. Even during the busy summer months, for any tour except the Wild Cave Tour, you usually can call two weeks before your visit and reserve spots.

One tour in particular that requires advance planning is the Great Onyx Lantern Tour. This outing is offered only during the slow seasons outside of summer and accommodates only 40 people per trip.

See "Exploring the top attractions," later in this chapter, for my recommendations of the best underground tours.

Packing for cave tours

What should you bring for going underground? During any time of year, I suggest bringing a light jacket, sweater, or sweatshirt because of the cooler air in the cave. In winter, a heavier coat wouldn't be a bad idea, if only to keep you warm while taking the bus from the visitor center to some of the cave entrances and back, or during the short walk from the visitor center to the historic cave entrance. But if you go on the Wild Cave Tour during colder weather, I suggest leaving the heavy coat behind, because it won't endure the trek very well.

If you plan on attending the Wild Cave Tour, a good pair of jeans and a long-sleeved shirt are mandatory to minimize the scrapes and bumps you'll surely accumulate as you shimmy through some passageways. Also, you can't go on this trek without a sturdy pair of hiking shoes, ones that rise above your ankles and have a good tread for gripping the cave floor.

Guides offer Park Service–approved knee guards, which are handy while squirming through passages, but they're uncomfortable things made of hard rubber. Shower yourself with kindness before you visit the park and invest in kneepads and elbow pads, such as the pads used by basketball players and wrestlers. They're not critical, but you'll definitely appreciate them during your crawls. Don't worry about hard hats or headlamps, because the park provides these items. In fact, you get to keep your hardhat, complete with a Mammoth Cave National Park logo, as a memento. I took a fanny pack on my Wild Cave Tour to haul a water bottle, an extra shirt, and lunch, as well as my camera, wallet, and car keys. A small day pack can serve the same purpose. You don't need to pack a lunch, because you can buy something from the concessionaire in the Snowball Room.

Biggest and getting bigger

Mammoth Cave meanders for 350 miles, a slowly rising figure thanks to the ongoing surveys of the Cave Research Foundation. No other cave system in the world comes close to this kind of mileage. Second place in the longest cave competition is Optimisticeskaya Cave in the Ukraine, with a comparatively paltry 113¾ miles.

Learning the Lay of the Land

On the surface, Mammoth Cave National Park looks like another gorgeous piece of the gently rolling Kentucky countryside. Thick groves of beech trees, tulip poplars, sugar maple, and majestic old white and black oaks, as well as hickory trees cover the hills and sandstone ridges. A break in this setting occurs at park headquarters and around the Mammoth Cave hotel, where the lawns are closely cropped, much like a city park, and where you even find some tennis and shuffleboard courts.

Navigating this serene setting is simple because you don't have a lot of road options. In general, the roads that do exist lead to park headquarters, where you find the visitor center and Mammoth Cave Hotel. If you're heading south on Interstate 65 to the park, take Exit 53 at Cave City and head west on Route 70 and Kentucky 255 to the **Cave City Road** and park headquarters. If you're heading north on the interstate, take Exit 48 at Park City and take the **Mammoth Cave Parkway** to the headquarters.

Just south of park headquarters, the **Green River Ferry Road** leads to a ferry boat that can haul you and your car across the river. On the other side, you can resume travel on the **Green River Ferry Road,** which leads to the Maple Springs Campground and its assorted hiking trails before exiting the park and transforming into Kentucky 1352.

Arriving in the Park

Whether you enter the park from the west, east, or south, head for park headquarters, where you find the visitor center and rangers to answer any questions you may have. If you ignore my sage advice to reserve tour tickets in advance, this is the time and place to buy some.

Capturing the cave on film

Cameras and video cameras do work underground and are welcome. Some of the best underground shots are taken of the *flowstones* (mineral deposits formed by flowing water) in the Frozen Niagara Room. This "wet" portion of Mammoth Cave has dazzling formations that seem to drip from the cave's ceiling and walls. In addition to the *stalactites* (mineral deposits that grow downward from the ceiling), you can get good shots of *cave bacon* (thin strips of flowstone that look like, ahem, bacon).

For the best shots, use a fast film, at least 400 ASA, and get close to your rocky subject. A dozen feet away is good. Use a flash, too, especially if you have one of those disposable box cameras or an Instamatic. If you use a tripod, leave it behind as they are banned underground. Finally, be courteous to your other cave dwellers and try not to blind anyone with your flash.

Above ground, if you have a long lens, keep your eyes open for wild turkeys scratching for their meals in the grassy areas along the park's roads. Also, if you take a ride on the riverboat Miss Green River II, you may luck out and spot a great blue heron.

Finding information

The visitor center (☎ 270-758-2328) is adjacent to Mammoth Cave Hotel, off Mammoth Cave Parkway. Inside is the ticket office, an auditorium showing short orientation films, an information desk, and a selection of guidebooks for sale. The center is open from 7 a.m. to 7 p.m. during June, July, and August and from 8 a.m. to 5 p.m. during the other months of the year.

If you're taking a cave tour, you have to come to the visitor center to pick up your tickets and to board buses to the appropriate cave entrance.

Paying fees

Mammoth Cave National Park does not have an entrance fee; however, to tour the cave, you must join one of the ranger-led tours, which range in cost from $4 to $45.

Getting around

Although the primary mode of transportation while touring the park's biggest attraction is your feet — and maybe your hands, if you take the Wild Cave Tour — you need a car to get around above ground. The park doesn't provide a public transportation system.

Enjoying the Park

Mammoth Cave National Park offers three primary settings — the underground, the rivers, and the forests. All three offer something for park visitors from caving to hiking, biking, or paddling the Green River.

Exploring the top attractions

If you decide to visit Mammoth Cave National Park, you're probably interested in descending into the netherworld of rock passages, halls, and tunnels. With more than a dozen cave tours to choose from, you can explore as little or as much as you like, spending 30 minutes or 6 hours underground.

You have to come to the park's headquarters to pick up your tour tickets and board buses to the cave's entrances. If you have to wait before your tour begins, you may want to explore some of the 6 miles of trails nearby. The Heritage Trail is a good, short option with an interesting stop at the Old Guides Cemetery (see "If you have more time," later in this chapter).

If you take the Grand Avenue Tour, once inside the cave you can buy snacks in the Snowball Room, a large space with a small snack bar, picnic tables, and restrooms.

To get the most out of your underground voyage, keep the following in mind:

- ✔ **Know your limits.** Be honest with yourself when you plan a trip to Mammoth Cave. Don't let a gung-ho spelunker talk you into the six-hour-long Wild Cave Tour if you dislike tight squeezes. If the prospect of climbing down 500 steps and then back up again is unappealing, don't sign on for the Grand Avenue tour.

- ✔ **Make a reservation.** To go on a cave tour, make a reservation by phone at ☎ 800-967-2283 or online at http://reservations. nps.gov.

- ✔ **Be flexible.** Not all tours are available every day of the year, so have backup tours in mind in case your preferred tour isn't offered.

- ✔ **Watch the toddler transport.** Don't show up at the cave entrance with a stroller, as they are not allowed underground. If you have to put your toddler in a backpack, watch out for low ceilings.

What follows are my recommendations for the best cave tours.

Discovery Tour

This tour gives you a general introduction to Mammoth Cave National Park. The rangers lead you into one of the cave's largest spaces, discuss the saltpeter mining operations of the mid-1800s, and explain the geological workings of the cave system. This tour is a great introduction to the park, but too short if you've traveled a great distance to be here.

Distance: ¾ mile. Level: Moderate. Length: ½ hour. Cost: $4 adults, $2 ages 11 and under, $2 Golden Age or Gold Access cardholders.

Frozen Niagara Tour

Now you're getting serious about caving. Not only does this tour require you to work your way down a 300-step staircase and across some fairly steep terrain, but it also lets you view some of the cave's most elaborate dripstone formations. Frozen Niagara is the tour's crowning centerpiece, flowing 75 feet from the roof of the cave and reaching 50 feet in width. If you're claustrophobic or *acrophobic* (afraid of high places), this tour probably isn't the best one for you. But if you're fascinated by stalactites, stalagmites, rimstone, and draperies, sign up for this tour.

Distance: ¾ mile. Level: Strenuous. Length: 2 hours. Cost: $9 adults, $5 ages 6–11, $5 Golden Age or Gold Access cardholders, free ages 5 and under.

Grand Avenue Tour

If you've reserved a full morning or afternoon to go underground and you're intent on seeing as much cave — and as much variety — as possible in that timeframe, this tour is the one for you. After a bus ride to the Carmichael Entrance, you head into the cave and, over the next four hours, head up and down switchbacks and more than 500 stairs as you wind your way through avenues featuring four different types of cave formations. You also spend about 45 minutes in the Snowball Room for lunch: You can either tote your lunch in or buy one in the Snowball Room. This tour also includes portions of the Frozen Niagara and Travertine tours, so it's really like three tours in one.

Distance: 4 miles. Level: Very strenuous. Length: 4½ hours. Cost: $18 adults, $9 ages 6–11, $9 Golden Age or Golden Access cardholders. No children under 6 allowed.

Mobility Impaired Tour

Just because you face some physical limitation that makes getting around difficult doesn't mean that you can't explore the cave system. This tour begins with a van ride to the cave's elevator entrance. You then descend 267 feet via the elevator into a world of tubular passages with gypsum flowers growing along the walls. After you're underground, you visit the Snowball Room and roam the cave passages along Cleaveland and Boone avenues. Two wheelchairs are available, and the restrooms are wheelchair-accessible.

Distance: 1 mile. Level: Easy. Length: 1¼ hours. Cost: $10 adults, $5 ages 6–11, $5 Golden Age and Golden Access cardholders; free ages 5 and under.

Travertine Tour

This tour is the Cliffs Notes version of a visit to Mammoth Cave. You take a bus ride to the Frozen Niagara entrance, climb down just 18 steps (with another 98 optional), and see many of the same formations you would see if you opted for the more rigorous Frozen Niagara tour. If you have young kids or infants or if someone in your group can't handle long walks and staircases, this option is good.

Distance: ¼ mile. Level: Easy. Length: 1–1¼ hours. Cost: $8 adults, $4 ages 6–12, $4 Golden Age and Golden Access cardholders; free ages 5 and under.

Violet City Lantern Tour

Ahhh, the romance of caving by lantern. This seasonal tour, generally available in summer, is led by rangers carrying lanterns. Imagining that you've stepped back in time to the mid-1800s, when all tours were led this way isn't hard. During the tour, you see the ruins of saltpeter mining operations run during the War of 1812, stone huts built in 1842 for Dr. John Croghan's tuberculosis patients, and pictographs created an estimated 2,000 years ago by Native Americans. You also enter some of the largest rooms in the cave system open to the public. Your kids need to be at least six years old for this tour, and with no restroom facilities available, they have to be able to control their bladders for at least three hours.

Distance: 3 miles. Level: Strenuous. Length: 3 hours. Cost: $12 adults, $6 ages 6–12, $6 Golden Age and Golden Access cardholders. Children under 6 not allowed.

Wild Cave Tour

This is your kind of tour if you're an amateur spelunker, if you need some extra credit for that college geology course you're taking, or if you have an incredible aversion to sunlight. This tour heads off the beaten path, away from the staircases and down into holes and twisting passages, far from the glow of the artificial lighting that illuminates the public areas of Mammoth Cave. You're fitted with a hardhat and headlamp to light your way and kneepads for crawling on your belly through crevices — some aptly named the Key Hole, the Mole Hole, and even the Birth Canal. In some places, you even have to exhale to squeeze through. What more can you ask for? These tours are highly popular. Participants, upon returning to the visitor center, proudly show off the dirt and grime they picked up while slithering around underground.

Due to the this tour's popularity, you must pick up your tickets at the Will Call desk at the visitor center at least 30 minutes before your scheduled tour, or they'll be sold. Because of tight passages, your chest size must be no bigger than 42 inches.

Distance: 5½ miles. Level: Extremely strenuous. Length: 6–6½ hours. Cost: $45 adults, $23 Golden Age and Golden Access cardholders. You must be at least 16 years old to go on this tour.

Out-of-bounds underground

Although Mammoth Cave has more than 350 miles of passages, only about 14 miles have developed trails, and only 10 miles of these trails are open to the public. Why? Because these 14 miles represent everything you would see throughout the entire known cave system, expanding the public sections isn't necessary. Instead, the bulk of the passages are preserved, both for scientific research and to keep them pristine, because millions of people walking through passages kick up a lot of dirt and dust that blankets the normally white gypsum deposits found in some sections of the cave.

Taking a hike

This park boasts 73 miles of designated hiking trails. Sixty-plus miles of trail lie north of the Green River, which cuts across the park; the rest lie south of the river. Some trails require backtracking to complete a loop, although if you study the park's trail map (available at the visitor center), you can easily piece together a loop trail that keeps new territory in front of you.

Cedar Sink

This short, easy trail for the whole family provides an excellent example of how sinkholes drain surface water underground into the cave system. The trail leads to Cedar Sink, which is roughly a ¼-mile wide. From the lip of the sinkhole, a steep set of stairs leads you inside for a good view of how sinkholes work.

Distance: 2 miles round-trip. Level: Easy. Access: Cedar Sink Trailhead off Cedar Sink Road.

First Creek Hollow Trail

Not far from the park's western border, this trail roams along a sandstone bluff before descending to the banks of the Nolin River. Along the way, the trail passes First Creek Lake, the park's only lake. Other highlights inlude several old homesteads and three campsites.

Distance: 6¾ miles one-way. Level: Eash. Access: Temple Hill Trailhead.

Sal Hollow Trail

This trail is open to hikers, mountain bikers, and equestrians. If you want to travel by foot, you may want to consider another trail. What makes this hike good? Well, some neat homesites are along the way, as well as a waterfall, sinkholes, and caves. In general, you get a good field trip through the area's unique natural features. Overnight hikers can bed down at Sal Hollow campsite, which stands atop a ridge 7½ miles from the trailhead. Campers have another option: they can continue on another 1½ miles to the Bluffs campsite, accessed by the Good Spring Loop Trail, which begins at the end of the Sal Hollow Trail. (Take a left onto the Good Spring Loop Tail from Sal Hollow Trail.) Also on the loop trail, almost 2½ miles from the trailhead, is Good Spring Church, an interesting old church worth a visit.

Distance: 8¾ miles one-way. Level: Moderate due to twists and turns. Access: Maple Springs Road.

White Oak

This route through the northeastern corner of the park follows the old Dennison Ferry Road to the White Oak backcountry campsite. The walking is wonderfully easy on the way in. Starting at an elevation of 840 feet, you encounter an enjoyable downhill that begins just past the midway point in the hike and continues to the end, where the elevation is 458 feet. The trail passes the site of the White Oak School and several old homesites. You get some good views of the entrance to Cathedral Cave, as well as of Pike Spring, one of the park's major springs.

Distance: 2¾ miles one-way. Level: Easy on the way in, a bit tougher as the return route is uphill. Access: Ugly Creek Road.

One-day wonder

Ever think that you could spend a day shuttling from the netherworld to the woods and finally onto the water for a riverboat trip? With a good bit of stamina and some careful planning, you can pull off such an adventure in this park. The key is to start early and to keep on going, as I describe in this section. (Unless otherwise noted, see "Exploring the top attractions," earlier in this chapter, for information on the tours mentioned.)

Start planning your one-day wonder before you leave home by calling ahead (☎ 800-967-2283) to make reservations for one of the morning trips on the Violet City Lantern Tour and for an afternoon trip on the Frozen Niagara Tour. These two tours offer the best of the cave — a historical journey back in time and a look at nature's artistry.

Begin the day with the **Violet City Tour,** which enters the cave through the "historic entrance" behind the Mammoth Cave Hotel. Exploring the cave by lamplight on this tour duplicates what a mid-1800s Mammoth Cave tour must have been like.

After you exit the cave and return to the visitor center by bus, purchase tickets for an evening riverboat cruise on the Miss Green River II and then grab some lunch at the **Mammoth Cave Hotel.** (See "Where to Eat" later in this chapter.)

After lunch, join the **Frozen Niagara Tour.** Although shorter than the Violet City tour by both an hour and about a mile, this stroll takes you past some intricate artwork created by thousands of years of dripping, mineral-laden water.

After the tour, head a ½-mile down the Mammoth Cave Parkway from the visitor center to the Green River Ferry Road, which takes you to the riverfront and a parking lot for the **Miss Green River II boat ride** (☎ 270-758-2243. The hour-long cruise ($7 for adults, $4 for kids ages 11 and under) covers 7 miles and is a great way to see wildlife; you can often spot deer, ducks, great blue herons, kingfishers, and beaver. After your underground exploits, this float along the lazy river is a wonderfully relaxing way to wind up your day. If you're into power naps, this ride is a great place to take one.

If, somehow, you have any energy left when you get back to the dock, head to the visitor center and hike down the ⅓-mile-long Heritage Trail. This pleasant trail through the hardwood forest roams past the historic cave entrance, loops around the Old Guides Cemetery (see the next section for more on this site), and leads to a bench for viewing Sunset Point.

If you have more time

Before Mammoth Cave was declared a national park in 1941, the river bottoms and mountain hollows cradled dozens of communities. Valleys (now retaken by forest) once sprouted with about 700 tiny farms and 30 communities that climbed the steep hillsides to the ridge tops. Today, most traces of these homesteads are long gone. One solemn reminder, though, are the cemeteries. Contained within the park are more than 70 of them. Some are little more than family plots holding only five or six graves marked by simple headstones. However, more formal and well-kept cemeteries are along the park's roads or trails. These quiet, poignant clearings in the park's forest hold countless stories of the area's former settlers.

If history interests you, touring some of these cemeteries is a great way to spend a half-day or more. Here are some to check out:

- ✔ **Old Guides Cemetery,** found along the Heritage Trail by Mammoth Cave Hotel, is the only cemetery within the park spanning the early days of Mammoth Cave's historical exploration. Buried here is Stephen Bishop, a slave who explored much of the cave and began leading tours in 1838. His gravestone carries the message, "Stephen Bishop, First Guide and Explorer of Mammoth Cave." Also laid to rest here are three of Dr. John Croghan's tuberculosis patients — Charles Marshall, Margaret Barnes, and Oliver Blair — who died while living in the cave with hopes of being cured by its dry air. Other graves in the cemetery are thought to be the final resting places of other guides.

- ✔ **Joppa Cemetery,** located along the Brownsville Road just over 5 miles from the visitor center, holds the remains of Shorty Coats. A member of the Civil Conservation Corps that built some of the trails inside Mammoth Cave in the 1930s, Shorty later went on to become a guide. Next to the cemetery is the Joppa Missionary Baptist Church that was built in 1862. Outfitted simply with wooden pews, a pulpit, and a potbelly stove (outhouses are out back), the church still draws a crowd on the Fourth of July for a homecoming of former park residents.

- ✔ **Locust Grove Cemetery,** located on Mammoth Cave Parkway 5¼ miles from the visitor center, holds some plots marked by simple stones and others marked by more elaborate gravestones. Some graves contain the remains of people who died at the end of long lives, but others point to untimely deaths of children, some who died in childbirth or soon thereafter from disease or accident. A somewhat more recent grave holds Warner Peter Hanson, a World War II soldier killed in action on May 26, 1943.

- ✔ **Little Hope Cemetery,** located 3½ miles from the visitor center along the Cave City Road, just may be the park's oldest, as evidenced by the graves of James Adair and James Robinson. Both War of 1812 veterans, Adair was born in 1787 and died in 1857, whereas Robinson was born in 1777 and died in 1858. Members of the Doyel and Houchins clans, names found in the park on overlooks, roads, and valleys, also rest here.

Ranger programs

A visit to Mammoth Cave is one continual ranger-led activity. Rangers lead you through the cave while recounting history and legends, and they even dress up in 19th-century attire for campfire programs about the early days of the cave's human history. They also offer talks and show films in the visitor center's auditorium.

I recommend two programs: **Myths and Mysteries of the Underworld** (which reveals the facts and fables behind Mammoth Cave) and the ranger-led hikes to the **Old Guides Cemetery.**

If you have kids, check out the **Trog Tour.** These 2½-hour tours, which explore inside and outside of the cave, are designed for kids between the ages of 8 and 12. (You may have to show proof of their age, so be prepared.) You're expected to spend the first 15 minutes of the tour with your kids so they don't get too spooked and decide to bail. But after that, they're on their own. During their cave tour, which costs $8.50 and is limited to a dozen kids per tour, your kids are outfitted with helmets and headlights to help find their way.

Getting to know the park's critters

When you're walking in the dark through the cave, and you place your hand on a rock and feel something try to wiggle away, do you really want to know what it is? Frankly, the critter can be one of a dozen different things. Most are harmless. Really.

Four major classifications of life call Mammoth Cave home. You have your basic **troglobites,** which literally means "cave dwellers." These guys live their entire lives in the damp darkness of the cave. Some examples are flatworms, amphipods, eyeless cave shrimp, cave crayfish, and cave beetles. The *amblyopsis spelaea* is the cave's blind fish. Not only is this fish blind, but its body is translucent.

Then you have your **troglophiles,** which are "cave lovers." These fellas need cool, dark, moist areas to survive, and you can find them either inside or outside the cave. Examples are worms, snails, spiders, and millipedes — even salamanders.

Your third group of critters are **trogloxenes,** or "cave guests." These species can't live their entire lives in the cave but stop by from time to time. Some examples are crickets, bats, pack rats, and flies. Among the trogloxenes are 12 bat species that call Mammoth Cave home. Although you wouldn't want a bat to get tangled up in your hair, they do a great job controlling insects. Little brown bats, which are common in the cave, can eat 600 mosquitoes per hour.

Finally, you have your incidentals, guys that come into caves only occasionally. You are a great example of an incidental. Another would be a raccoon or frog.

Outside the cave, you find quite a bit of life in the park. The forests are home to **deer, fox, raccoons, opossums,** and other forest dwellers, including **wild turkeys** that were brought back to the park in 1983. Frankly, your best opportunity for spotting wildlife is to keep your eyes open while driving along the park's roads. I've spotted turkeys early in the morning pecking at insects along the roads, whereas deer come out in late afternoon to browse the grass along the roads.

The Green and Nolin rivers that flow through the park grounds are great fisheries. Take some time to try your luck with a fishing pole and you come across **bass, crappie, walleye, Sauger, muskellunge,** and **northern pike,** not to mention **bluegill** and **catfish.** (You don't need a Kentucky fishing license to fish in the park.)

If your kids get bitten by the spelunking bug (that's an interest in caving, not some deadly parasite), sign them up for the **Introduction to Caving class.** This 3- to 3½-hour activity for kids 10 and older teaches them the basics of caving. (Kids between the ages of 10 and 15 must be accompanied by a parent or guardian.) They learn about being responsible inside caves, both in terms of their personal safety and in terms of protecting the cave. You supply tough jeans, kneepads (those soft, basketball versions, not those hard plastic beasts used for inline skating), durable hiking shoes, and the kids, and the park supplies the hard hats, headlamps, and leadership — all for just $18.

For the latest ranger program itinerary and schedule, check the television monitors in the visitor center.

Keeping active

Caving is not the only reason to visit Mammoth Cave, although it's probably the best. If you spend any time on top of the ground, you soon discover that the national park is also a good place for hiking, canoeing, and biking. For hiking suggestions, see "Taking a hike," earlier in this chapter. For canoeing and biking suggestions, read on.

Canoeing

With 25 miles of the Green River to explore, the park is great for paddling. With a free backcountry permit (obtained at the visitor center), you can shove off at one end of the park and work your way to the other, with a few stops for camping along the way.

Two good launching points for your boat are on the eastern end of the park at the Dennison Ferry Day Use Area and in the middle at the Green River Ferry. (A boat launch is near the park's western border at Houchins Ferry, but the location is near a lock and dam that must be portaged around. Because of this hazard, staying away from this end of the river is recommended.) The river flows east to west, so your best bet would be to launch at Dennison Ferry and travel the 7½ miles to Green River Ferry and perhaps another 12 miles to Houchins Ferry.

 If you paddle through the park and continue down the Green River, be aware of the Green River Lock and Dam #6 that's located just beyond the park's western boundary. This dam, 3 miles from Houchins Ferry, isn't marked with warning signs, and you can run into trouble if you don't get off the river in time.

 As far as camping during your canoe trip, just about anywhere is fair game, as far as the park is concerned. If you opt to camp on one of the islands, though, and the weather turns bad, you should head for higher ground in case heavy rains upstream send a flood down.

If you want to paddle but don't have a boat, don't fret. Three concessionaires can outfit you: **Green River Canoeing** (☎ **800-651-9909** or 270-597-2031; Internet: www.mammothcavecanoe.com), **Barren River Canoe Rentals** (☎ **888-680-6580** or 270-796-1979; Internet: www.premiernet.net/~canoe) or **Mammoth Cave Canoe and Kayak** (☎ **270-773-3366**; Internet: www.mammothcavecanoe-k.com). All three offer daily rentals down the Green, ranging from $45 to $50 per canoe, including paddles, life jackets, and shuttles. Multiday rentals also are possible, with Barren River offering the best deal of $50 for a two-day rental. Time-wise, the trip from Dennison Ferry to Green River Ferry takes about four hours, whereas the trip from Green River Ferry to

Houchins Ferry takes between five and six hours, depending on the river current and your paddling prowess.

Biking

Although requiring a bit more energy than canoeing, cycling is another good way to spend your time outside the cave. Park officials, realizing the popularity of mountain bikes, have made an effort to accommodate them. You find three backcountry trails open for mountain biking: The 3½-mile-long Buffalo Trail, the 3½-mile-long Turnhole Bend Trail just south of the Buffalo Trail, and the almost 9-mile-long Sal Hollow Trail. You can even stitch together two loops from these three, one running about 5½ miles in length, the other just over 12 miles long.

Just learning how to mountain bike? Stick to the easier grades of the Buffalo Trail and the Turnhole Bend Trail. After you head past the intersection to the Turnhole Bend campsite, the trail gets a wee bit steep — too steep for beginners and families. The Sal Hollow Trail, however, is gnarly enough to give a few thrills to advanced riders. Some sections exceed 20% in grade.

All three trails are also open to hikers and horseback riders, so keep your eyes open. (In case you forget the trail courtesy rules, hikers need to yield to horses; bikers need to yield to both hikers and horses.) Also, the park doesn't want kids mountain biking by themselves.

Where to Stay

If you plan to stay inside Mammoth Cave National Park and don't want to camp, your choices are the Mammoth Cave Hotel and surrounding cottages. (A third option is the Sunset Point Motor Lodge near Mammoth Cave Hotel, but it's pretty uninspiring, so I don't include it in this section.) You may actually want to stay outside the park in Cave City or Park City because of the commercial cave operations in the area as well as the more plentiful dining options outside the park.

Lodging in the park

Mammoth Cave Hotel
$–$$ Near the East Entrance

You won't find stately national park elegance. What you do find is quick access to Mammoth Cave, however, because the hotel connects to the visitor center via an arched concrete bridge. The rooms in the two-story hotel, which from the outside lacks any semblance of Southern hospitality, are motelish, with brick walls offset by wood paneling. The companion Sunset Point Motor Lodge also lacks national park stateliness, but at least it's inside the park. Your best option (and best value) in the park are the free-standing Hotel Cottages, renovated in 1999. With double beds, television, air-conditioning, pine writing desk and dresser, and nice views into the woods, they're nicer than the hotel rooms and offer more privacy. Their only drawback is that they lack phones. If your budget is tight, look into the Rustic Cottages, which are cheaper but have less ambience and no air-conditioning.

Off East Entrance Road. ☎ *270-758-2225 for reservations. Fax: 270-758-2301. 62 rooms, 10 hotel cottages, 21 rustic cottages. A/C TV TEL in rooms, A/C TV in hotel cottages. Rack rates: $45–$75 double; $59 hotel cottages; $45–$48 rustic cottages. AE, DISC, MC, V.*

Top lodging outside the park

Best Western Kentucky Inn
$–$$ Cave City

You won't find quaint or unusual here, just a reliable motel with clean rooms and a nice pool to splash in after your day in the park 6 miles away. Also, a short drive away is an 18-hole golf course, if you insist on packing your clubs, as well as a miniature golf course for the kiddies. Meals at the Country Kitchen are a 5-minute walk from your room.

1009 Doyle Ave. (I-65 at Cave City). ☎ *270-773-3161 or 800-528-1234 for reservations. Fax 270-773-5494. 50 rooms. A/C TV TEL. Rack rate: $29–$99 double. AE, DC, DISC, MC, V.*

Cave Spring Farm Bed & Breakfast
$$ Smiths Grove

The extra 10- to 15-minute drive to Mammoth Cave National Park is worth it for this antebellum experience. The 13-room bed-and-breakfast is located within an 1858 manse that's listed on the National Register of Historic Places. On the surrounding 17 acres are a formal flower garden with picturesque gazebo, a 5-acre bird sanctuary, and a nature trail. One of the guest cabins is a converted one-room schoolhouse. The rooms? Inside the main house, they boast 12-foot ceilings. The Lincoln Room suite offers a private sunroom and bath, while the Lee Room offers a great view of the farm. Breakfast may feature crepes, waffles, or country ham and biscuits. In the fall and winter months, you dine before a roaring fire.

On Rocky Hill Road. ☎ *270-563-6941 for reservations. 2 rooms, 1 cottage. A/C TV. Rack rates: $85 double. MC, V. No children under 12.*

Park View Motel

$–$$ Cave City

It's nothing to write home about, but this motel is clean, tidy, and close to the park, just 2½ miles from the East Entrance. And you can't beat the price, particularly when you toss in a small outdoor pool for escaping summer's humidity. With picnic tables and grills on the grounds, you can even save a few more bucks by cooking your own dinners. Or rent the efficiency cabin, which has a kitchenette.

3906 Mammoth Cave Rd. ☎ *270-773-3463. 877-482-2262. Internet:* www.parkview motel.com. *16 rooms, 1 efficiency cabin. A/C TV. Rack rate: $48–$65 double; $65–$90 efficiency. DISC, MC, V.*

Rose Manor Bed & Breakfast

$$–$$$ Cave City

Located in the heart of Cave City, this Victorian manor features four spacious rooms that are named after precious stones, and one named after the pearl. The Sapphire Room, the only room on the main floor, is the biggest, featuring not only a king-size bed but also a Jacuzzi. You also find a Jacuzzi in the Amethyst Room, but the other three rooms make do with ordinary private baths. The place also has a den with television, VCR, and a good collection of movies, and most rooms have CD players. Relaxing on the covered porch with a cool drink after a long day is wonderful. If you're traveling with kids, you can stick them in the Pearl Room, which has two twin beds. Breakfasts may include pancakes with apples, cheese omelets, country ham, or French toast. Massages are available.

204 Duke St. ☎ *270-773-4402. Internet:* www.mammothcave.com/rose.htm. *5 rooms. A/C TV TEL. Rack rates: $90–$110 double.*

The Wayfarer Bed and Breakfast

$$–$$$ Cave City

Just outside the park's east entrance, this bed-and-breakfast with its five rooms and cottage is not only conveniently located but offers some caving history with its Floyd Collins Museum. The guest rooms are decorated with a mix of antiques and newer furniture. The Hanson Cottage, perfect for larger groups, sleeps up to six and offers a kitchen, dining room, sunroom, and a deck with a grill.

1240 Old Mammoth Cave Rd. ☎ *270-773-3366. 5 rooms, 1 cottage. A/C. Rack rates: $75–$125. AE, DISC, MC, V.*

Runner-up lodgings

Caveland Motel

$ Cave City   Five minutes from the park, this motel is clean and comfortable. Highlights include an outdoor pool and a "community canteen" where you can fix your own meals. *415 N. Dixie Hwy.* ☎ **270-773-2321**. *Internet:* http://mammothcave.com/caveland.htm.

Quality Inn

$–$$ Cave City   You find chain reliability at this motel, which has mini-suites with microwaves and refrigerators. Kids appreciate the game room and heated outdoor pool. *I-65 and Highway 90.* ☎ **270-773-3101**.

Ramada Limited

$–$$ Cave City   Just off the interstate, this property offers a free Continental breakfast, has a heated outdoor pool, and is within walking distance of a number of restaurants. I-65 and KY 70. ☎ **800-264-1514** *or 270-773-3121. Internet:* http://mammothcave.com/ramadacc.htm.

Travel Inn

$ Cave City   Ten miles from the park, this motel is popular with families thanks to its low rates. Pets are welcome, if you can't leave yours at home. *1224 N. Dixie Hwy.* ☎ **888-872-8552** *or 270-773-2138. Internet:* http://mammothcave.com/travlinn.htm.

Campgrounds

You probably didn't figure a park based around a cave would have a place to pitch your tent or park your RV, now did you? Well, Mammoth Cave National Park does offer three campgrounds, totaling 130 sites.

The **Headquarters Campground** (☎ **270-758-2212**) is the park's biggest with 109 sites. It's the only campground that accepts RVs and the only one with a dump station, a camp store, shower facilities (which you pay for), and flush toilets. Oh yeah, it's also the only one with a laundry facility. The combination of these amenities and the location — just a ¼ mile from the visitor center — make this the park's most popular campground. You don't need a reservation, but they're recommended. The fee is $15 a night, and the campground is open from March through November.

Maple Springs Campground (☎ **800-365-CAMP**) is where you want to head if you're traveling in a large group (up to 25). Located 6 miles from the visitor center and 3 miles north of the Green River Ferry, this campground runs $25 per night per site. Reservations are required. The easiest way to reach the campground is to cross the Green River on the ferry (accessed by the Green River Ferry Road), a proposition that can be time-consuming because the ferry can haul only 8 tons and because high or low water levels in the river can cause problems. If you can't use the ferry for some reason, your only option is to make a 35-mile trip along state and county roads. This campground is open from March through November.

Your last option is the **Houchins Ferry Campground** (no phone), which is 15 miles from the visitor center on the south bank of the Green River. The dozen sites go for $11 per night on a first-come, first-served basis. All sites come with a picnic table and a fire grate. You find fresh water, but the restrooms are limited to two chemical toilets. This campground is open year-round.

If you dislike developed campgrounds, by all means, head off into the Kentucky hills, but make sure that you pick up a backcountry permit first at the visitor center. The park has a dozen free **backcountry campsites** that each hold eight people. The best sites are at Raymer Hollow, McCoy Hollow, and the Bluffs. All the sites, except McCoy Hollow, have a nearby water source. The Raymer Hollow site sits atop a nice *bench* (a narrow shelf of ground) over a perennial stream, so water is especially convenient. Plus, you get a nice view of the countryside from the bench. Although McCoy doesn't have a convenient water source, the location sits about 250 to 300 feet above the Green River, and when the leaves are off the trees in the fall, you have a nice view up and down the stream. The Bluffs site, meanwhile, is located beneath a prominent rock formation that creates a natural shelter for your tent. Wherever you pitch your tent, be sure to treat the water before drinking. For information on backcountry sites, call the park information number, ☎ 270-758-2328. Backcountry permits are available at the visitor center.

Where to Eat

You can find a dining room and coffee shop at the Mammoth Cave Hotel, or you can head a few minutes outside the park to Cave City, Park City, or Glasgow for your meals.

If you prefer alcoholic refreshment with your meals, you're in the wrong part of the state. Most of central and western Kentucky is "dry," so pack your own and enjoy your drink before or after your meal.

Restaurants in the park

Mammoth Cave Hotel
$–$$ Near the East Entrance   AMERICAN

You won't break your budget here, but you won't find any culinary treasures, either. And if you dislike fried foods, plan on heading into Cave City for a wider variety. The house specials are fried chicken and butterflied prawns, both hand-coated in batter and fried. For lunch, you find a decent selection of sandwiches and burgers. Breakfasts are buffet style and revolve around scrambled eggs, cold cereals, and griddle items. If you're in a hurry, try the fast-food operation, serving fries and burgers, that the hotel runs from the Fourth of July through Labor Day.

Just off South Entrance Rd. ☎ *270-758-2225. Reservations not accepted. Main courses: $3.50–$6.95 breakfast; $3.25–$6.50 lunch; $6.95–$15.95 dinner. AE, DISC, MC, V. Open: Daily 7–1 a.m., 11:30 a.m.–2 p.m., 4:30–7:30 p.m.*

Restaurants outside the park

Bolton's Landing
$–$$ Glasgow   AMERICAN

In a sea of Southern-fried this and that, Bolton's offers a more upscale menu of fish, beef, chicken, and pasta dishes. Still, two of the dishes most in demand are local favorites, fried catfish and pan-fried pork tenderloin. Angel biscuits, a cross between a roll and a biscuit, disappear quickly from the table. You don't need to order these, because they're included in every meal. If fried foods don't appeal to you, try one of the seafood dishes or one of the steaks.

Route 31E South. ☎ *270-651-8008. Reservations only for parties of 6 or more. Main courses: $5.50–$6.95 lunch; $7.50–$16.95 dinner. AE, DC, DISC, MC, V. Open: Mon–Fri 11 a.m.–2 p.m.; Mon–Thurs 4:30–8:30 p.m., Fri–Sat 4:30–9 p.m.*

Hickory Villa
$–$$ Cave City   SOUTHERN

With a four-meat barbecue buffet offered every night of the summer, you know the sauce has to be good, and for 100 years, the recipe has been the same. You can order off the menu, but why would you want to if the buffet is just $10.95 per person, $8.50 on Sundays? Along with the meats, you find baked beans and your choice of potato salad or cole slaw and hot rolls or corn cakes on the buffet table. You also get a choice of mild, regular, or hot sauce. For those who shun barbeque, the menu also includes a 21-piece shrimp dinner, steaks, or chicken dishes.

806 Sanders Ln. (I-65, Exit 53). ☎ *270-773-3033. Reservations not accepted weekends or holidays. Main courses: $5.25–$19.99 lunch and dinner. AE, DISC, MC, V. Open: Wed–Sun 10 a.m.– 9:30 p.m.*

The Sahara Steak House
$$–$$$$ Cave City   AMERICAN

The name is campy, but don't let it prompt you to bypass this place. This decent steak house is a short drive from the heart of the park. Certified

Black Angus steaks — New York strips, ribeyes, and filet mignon — dominate the menu, but you also find chicken teriyaki, country ham, and even seafood, such as shrimp, halibut, and lobster. The soup and salad bar is included with your dinner, too. The atmosphere is nothing elaborate — little more than neatly tended tables and booths — but the locals show up regularly, which is a good sign. Plus, the service is quick and friendly.

413 Happy Valley Rd. ☎ **270-773-3450.** *Main courses: $ 4.95–$9.95 lunch; $9.95–$28.95 dinner. AE, DISC, MC, V. Open: Daily 11 a.m.– 9 p.m.*

Fast Facts: Mammoth Cave

Area Code
☎ 270.

ATMs
Inside the Mammoth Cave Hotel lobby.

Emergency
☎ 911.

Fees
No entrance fee.

Fishing License
No license needed, but you do need to follow Kentucky fishing regulations, which are available at the visitor center.

Hospitals
None in the park. Caverna Memorial Hospital, 1501 S. Dixie Hwy., Horse Cave, KY; ☎ 270-786-2191.

Information
Superintendent, Mammoth Cave National Park, P.O. Box 7, Mammoth Cave, KY 42259; ☎ 270-758-2328.

Lost and Found
☎ 270-758-2328.

Pharmacies
Branstetter Discount Pharmacy, 141 E. Main St., Horse Cave, ☎ 270-786-2466; Cave City Prescription Center, 101 S. Dixie Hwy., Cave City, ☎ 270-773-2252.

Post Office
At the gas station next to the Headquarters Campground, ☎ 270-758-2311.

Road Conditions and Weather
☎ 270-758-2328.

Taxes
Lodging 7%; meals 1%.

Time Zone
Central standard time.

Web Site
www.nps.gov/maca.

Chapter 17

Mount Rainier National Park

· ·

In This Chapter

▶ Discovering a real volcano

▶ Planning your trip

▶ Exploring the mountain and glaciers

▶ Finding the best rooms and meals

· ·

*I*n a state with more than its share of heady alpine vistas and dense evergreen forests, Mount Rainier is the relative new kid on the block. Whereas most of the mountains that comprise the Cascade Range are 12 million years old, Rainier is a geologic youngster at an age of about 1 million years. Rainier certainly has packed a lot into its short life, though, not only standing as Washington's tallest peak but also harboring the greatest concentration of glaciers of any single mountain in the Lower 48.

Gazing at the peak, you wouldn't guess that Mount Rainier is an active volcano. No steam vents are obvious to the naked eye, and you don't find jagged lava beds, such as those at Craters of the Moon National Monument in Idaho. What you do see are patches of white that represent 25 major glaciers that slowly, but steadily, are slipping down from the mountain's 14,410-foot summit. Roughly 36 square miles of the mountain's surface consist of glacial ice and perennial snowfields that hide Mount Rainier's lava underpinnings.

Not surprisingly, folks come to Mount Rainier National Park simply to gawk at the mountain and glaciers. But the more adventurous also frolic in snowfields or vanish into the woods along the mountain's hundreds of miles of trails.

No matter where you find yourself in the park, you're never very far from a view of the summit. As an added bonus, the mountain itself provides decent views of some of the Cascade Range's other volcanic peaks, all charter members of the Ring of Fire, a lava-spitting fraternity that rims the Pacific Ocean. From an overlook near the Sunrise area on the mountain's northeastern flanks, for example, you can see the Hood, Baker, and Adams mounts. Not visible, but 165 miles to the south, stand the crumpled remains of Mount St. Helens, a ring member that blew its top in 1980.

To stand on the flanks or in the shadow of beautiful Mount Rainier is an awesome experience. Where the dazzling glaciers and snowfields melt away, towering old-growth forests of Alaska yellow cedar, hemlocks, and red cedar blanket the terrain. In the northwest corner of the park near the Carbon River Valley, you even find a section of temperate rain forest much like that found in nearby Olympic National Park.

Plan to spend at least two days in Mount Rainier National Park. If you're into long hikes or want to visit the Carbon River Valley, set aside at least three days. No matter when you choose to visit, you always have something to do in this park, whether it's climbing, skiing, hiking, or simply watching the mountain. But don't forget that you're in the Pacific Northwest, one of the wetter places in the United States, so snow, rain, and clouds come with the territory. July and August can be exceptions, though. During these two months, rain is infrequent and temperatures enjoyable, with highs in the 70s. However, if you abhor crowds, you may want to avoid the park during the summer months, when the majority of Mount Rainier's 2 million annual visitors show up. If you do come at this time, avoid the full brunt of the summer's crowds by visiting at midweek.

If you're like me and enjoy crisp nights and cool days that make for great hiking, fall is the best time to visit Rainier. Barring an early-season snowstorm, trails are in top-notch condition, the park's few hardwood tree species (red alder, Pacific dogwood, and three species of maple) toss bursts of color into the coniferous forests, crowds are diminished, and rotting huckleberries add an interesting pungent smell to the air. But keep in mind that the likelihood of rain increases in September and October, and heavy snows are possible beginning in November.

Must-see Attractions

Okay, you found the park. (How could you not, with the way it towers above the surrounding landscape?) So now what? Well, only one main road runs through the park, so you need to head down it. Here's where you should stop along the way between points A (Longmire) and B (Sunrise):

- **Longmire:** The park's oldest developed area is here, just 7 miles inside the Nisqually Entrance. You can also find a good park museum, too, as well as the National Park Inn and Wilderness Information Center for planning backcountry treks.

- **Narada Falls:** These beautiful falls plummet 168 feet through a lush, green forest. The water cascades over a wall of lava left over from one of Rainier's periodic eruptions.

Mount Rainier National Park

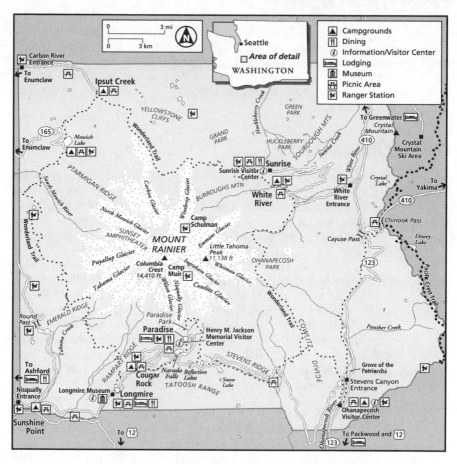

✔ **Paradise:** The setting surrounding this historic inn, known as Paradise, on the southern flanks of Rainier is gorgeous enough, but the sweeping fields of wild flowers that arise as the snows melt take your breath away. A short hike leads to an overlook of the Nisqually Glacier, the most accessible of the park's glaciers.

✔ **Reflection Lakes:** On clear days, these lakes, located south of Paradise on the road to Ohanapecosh, do what their name implies. For the best photo of Rainier and her reflection, head to the east end of the lake parking area.

✔ **Sunrise:** This is the highest point in the park that you can reach by car. From this 6,400-foot base camp meander more than a dozen hiking trails, including a link to the Wonderland Trail that winds 93 miles around the mountain.

Getting There

Off the beaten path, but not too far, Mount Rainier is somewhat close to Seattle and Tacoma. Most folks head for the Nisqually Entrance because of its proximity to Longmire and Paradise. Plus, Nisqually is the only entrance open year-round. As you may imagine, waits can be long here, but you can usually beat the traffic if you enter the park by 10:00 a.m.

Driving in

The Nisqually Entrance is about 87 miles from Seattle via Interstate 5 and State Routes 7 and 706. Tacoma is about 55 miles from Nisqually via State Routes 7 and 706. The White River Entrance Station, the closest to Sunrise, is 85 miles from Seattle via routes Interstate 5, Interstate 405, Washington 169 south to Enumclaw, and then Washington 410 to the park.

From Portland, Oregon, 136 miles from the Nisqually Entrance, follow Interstate 5 north to Exit 68 and turn right on U.S. Route 12 to Morton, where you head north on Highway 7 to Elbe and then east on State Route 706 past Ashford to the park. You can head for Mount Rainier's northwestern corner and the Carbon River Entrance via Washington 165, but you can't reach Sunrise, Paradise, or Longmire from here because Carbon River Road dead-ends after 6 miles. You can, however, reach a trailhead that leads to the base of Carbon Glacier.

Your only other options are to arrive through the Stevens Canyon Entrance in the southeastern corner via Washington 123 or, during the summer, from the east via Washington 410 and Chinook Pass. This option gives you a choice of heading north to the White River Entrance and Sunrise or south to the Stevens Canyon Entrance.

Most park roads are closed due to snow from October or early November through middle or late May. The only exception is the Nisqually Entrance Road, which has restricted hours in winter. See "Learning the Lay of the Land," later in the chapter for more details.

Flying in

The closest airport is the Seattle Tacoma International Airport (☎ 800-544-1965 or 206-431-4444), often referred to as "Sea-Tac." Most of the major airlines and car-rental agencies are here; see the Appendix for their toll-free numbers.

Three companies provide shuttle service from the airport to the park: **Rainier Overland Transportation Company** (☎ 360-569-0851),

Rainier Shuttle (☎ 360-569-2331), and **Ashford Mountain Center Shuttle** (☎ 360-569-2604).

Planning Ahead

For information in advance of your trip, write Superintendent, Mount Rainier National Park, Ashford, WA 98304-9751; call ☎ **360-569-2211** or 360-569-2177 (TTD); or check the park's Web site at www.nps.gov/mora.

Reserving a room

As with a visit to any national park, the key to a Rainier trip is making lodging plans early. If you don't, you may spend most of your trip driving to the park from far away. Paradise Inn and the National Park Inn are the only two hotels in the park, and they're very popular. Call about six months in advance for a room at the Paradise Inn and even earlier for a summer stay at the National Park Inn, which has only 25 rooms.

Packing for the park

Having rain gear here isn't quite as important as it is in Olympic National Park, but you won't regret having some when the weather turns wet. Keep in mind that spring and fall tend to be wetter than summer. In general, always be prepared for inclement weather, as Mount Rainier makes its own. For tips on what to pack for your vacation, see Chapter 8.

Paradise is a great place in winter for slipping and sliding on the snow. So if you're heading to the park in winter with kids, don't forget an inner tube or plastic sled or saucer; wood toboggans and sleds with metal runners are prohibited to protect sliders during collisions. No need to inflate the tube before you leave; the Jackson Visitor Center makes available a compressed air hose on weekends.

Learning the Lay of the Land

In general, you can get just about anywhere in Mount Rainier National Park, but not always easily. You have to earn your views, either by foot or by persevering down a long and winding road.

State Route 706 runs along the southern edge of the park. Between Nisqually Entrance and Paradise, State Route 706 is known locally as the **Longmire to Paradise Road**; between Paradise and Ohanapecosh, it's known locally as **Stevens Canyon Road**; going north from Ohanapecosh, it's known as **Highway 123** until Cayuse Pass, at which point it becomes

Washington 410 or **Mather Memorial Parkway** until it runs out of the park. Off of Washington 410 is the access road to Sunrise, which passes the White River Entrance station and the White River campground.

A few short roads wind along the park's western side. The **Westside Road** begins a mile inside the Nisqually Entrance. At one time, this road ran 13 miles north, passing several creeks and hiking trails. But floods along Fish Creek forced the closure of the road about 3 miles north of Nisqually. Two other spurs access the park's northwest corner: **Washington 165,** running 27 miles from Enumclaw to Mowich Lake and its campground, and **Carbon River Road,** jogging off 165 just after you cross the Carbon River south of Wilkeson and running into the park through the Carbon River Entrance. All three roads are seasonal.

Rainier has three main visitor areas: **Longmire,** located not far from the Nisqually Entrance; **Paradise,** east of Longmire, on the south flank of the mountain; and **Sunrise,** on the eastern shoulder of the mountain. Although you travel only 7 miles from the Nisqually Entrance to Longmire, the historic heart of the park, you have to go another 12 miles to Paradise and another 50 miles to Sunrise. Visitor centers are in Paradise, Sunrise, and Ohanapecosh (see "Finding information," later in this chapter). Longmire, Paradise, and Sunrise all have something to offer tourists (see "Exploring the top attractions," later in this chapter); Ohanapecosh has an interesting name, but not much else in terms of facilities. Ohanapecosh does sit amid a beautiful old-growth forest, though, and several popular trails start here, including the Hot Springs Nature Trail and the Silver Falls Trail.

Trying to squeeze in stops and walks at the main visitor areas makes for a very long day — not only because of the abundance of things to do but also because heavy traffic can jam the limited road system in summer. Still, if you stay at Paradise and get on the road early in the morning, you can visit Sunrise and Longmire and return to Paradise in time to stroll past the Nisqually Glacier.

If you enter the park through the Nisqually Entrance late in the morning on a summer day, watch for a sign on the right side of the road indicating that the Paradise parking lot is full. If this happens, you'll have to head someplace else or walk at least a mile up the road to the inn. This situation happens frequently on weekends and especially on holiday weekends when the weather is nice. Enter the park by 10 a.m., though, and you should be all right.

All is not lost if you do encounter this illuminated sign. You can head through the park to Sunrise and hit Paradise on your way back. Or, take a hike around Reflection Lakes and hope the crowds ease by the time you're ready to head over to Paradise.

Come winter with its heavy snows, getting around is tough. Most park roads are closed due to snow from October or early November through middle or late May. The only exception is the Nisqually Entrance Road, which has restricted hours. When snow falls, plows are out by 6 a.m. to open this road from the Nisqually Entrance to Longmire, and the road from Longmire to Paradise usually is open by 10 a.m.

Arriving in the Park

You'll probably head to the year-round Nisqually Entrance in the southwestern corner. Of all the points of entry, Nisqually is closest to the park's visitor centers and lodgings.

Finding information

The park has four visitor centers:

- ✔ **Henry M. Jackson Memorial Visitor Center** (☎ 360-569-2211, ext. 2328): This center is a must-stop for anyone heading to Paradise. Inside are exhibits tracing the park's natural and cultural history, as well as telescopes you can use free of charge to search the mountain for climbers heading up or down. This center is open daily from mid-April into October and then only on weekends and holidays from October through April.

- ✔ **Ohanapecosh Visitor Center** (☎ 360-569-2211, ext. 2352): Open daily from late May into October.

- ✔ **Sunrise Visitor Center** (☎ 360-569-2211, ext. 2357): This center focuses on Rainier's geologic history and future. As with the Paradise center, you can also use free telescopes here to scan the mountain activity, human or volcanic, although if you see the latter, you're not in a very good place. Open daily from late June into September.

- ✔ **Longmire Museum** (☎ 360-569-2211, ext. 3314). Inside this museum located at Longmire, you find the park's only year-round visitor center, open daily. In addition to dispensing park-wide information, the museum's exhibits tell the park's human history, as well as some natural history.

Paying fees

The fees for entering Mount Rainier National Park are $10 per vehicle for seven days or $5 per person (on foot, motorcycle, or bicycle) for seven days. A $30 annual pass covers entrance fees to the park for one year from the month of purchase. Of course, if you have a parks pass, you don't need to pay the entrance fee; see Chapter 8 for information on the National Park Pass and Chapter 4 for the lowdown on Golden Age and Golden Access Passports.

You don't pay a charge for backcountry use, but you must pay a fee to climb the mountain ($15 per person per climb or $25 per person annually) or to stay in one of the backcountry sites ($20 per party for 1–14 nights), which require reservations. You can obtain information and permits from the **Longmire Wilderness Information Center** (☎ 360-569-HIKE) or the **White River Wilderness Information Center** (☎ 360-663-2273, ext. 222) located at the White River Entrance. If you plan to climb in the park, you can get a permit at the ranger station in Paradise. Permits also can be obtained at the **Wilkeson Wilderness Information Center** (☎ 360-829-5127) outside the northwest corner of the park in downtown Wilkeson.

Getting around

Unless you're walking or can fly, the only way to tour Mount Rainier National Park is to take the roads that skirt the flanks of this magnificent mountain. No road neatly and completely circumnavigates Rainier. The park doesn't have a public transportation system; you need a car to get around.

Remembering Safety

If you visit in winter, be prepared for winter driving conditions. You need snow tires or all-season radials on your rig to manage the snowy and icy roads. State law also requires that you carry chains when traveling in mountainous terrain, and a shovel wouldn't be a bad idea, either, if you're determined to reach Paradise.

Remember that Mount Rainier is a living and breathing volcano. You may not see it exhaling from where you're standing, but on some parts of the mountain steam vents come through the earth's surface. Chances are that you won't ever see Rainier blow its top during your lifetime. But just the same, you may want to keep the following in mind:

- ✔ **Avalanches:** With so much snow and glacial ice in the park, avalanches happen. They are hard to predict, but you should be okay if you stay off steep slopes following heavy snowstorms.

- ✔ **Glacial outbursts:** If you're walking along a river and see a noticeable rise in the water level or if you hear a roaring sound like a locomotive, head to higher ground immediately. A glacial outburst may have unleashed a wall of water, mud, and rocks that can be heading your way.

- ✔ **Volcanic eruptions:** An earthquake is usually a precursor to a volcanic eruption. Another signal can be jets of steam venting from the mountain's flanks. In either case, seismic monitoring would indicate increased volcanic activity and rangers will provide you with plenty of advance notice if that's the case.

Before you lose any sleep over the possibility of a volcanic eruption, allow me to toss some perspective your way. Although at least two minor eruptions occurred on Mount Rainier in the 1800s, the last significant eruption occurred about 500 years ago. Plus, the volcano likely will give off some signals that a major eruption is on the way. In the case of Mount St. Helens, a sister volcano that erupted in 1980, scientists noted warnings two months before the actual eruption.

For additional tips on how to ensure a safe park visit, see Chapter 8.

Enjoying the Park

Sure, Mount Rainier is an active (albeit soundly sleeping) volcano, but much more than just a volcano awaits you here. The park has incredible glaciers and wonderfully thick forests for hiking and camping. And if you look around, you find some really cool waterfalls (particularly in late spring and early summer during the height of the snowmelt) and historically significant structures.

Exploring the top attractions

Carbon Glacier

It's big, it's bad, it's white, and it's right in front of you. No, not Moby Dick. I'm talking about the Carbon Glacier. This river of ice (at 700 feet thick) is accepted as the thickest glacier in the Lower 48, as well as the country's lowest elevation glacier — its snout creeps down to just about 3,600 feet above sea level. Best of all, a relatively short, 4-mile hike from the Ipsut Creek Campground in the park's northwestern corner leads you right to it. (See Carbon Glacier Trail, under "Taking a hike," later in this chapter.)

For a two- or three-night trip, hike up to the Carbon Glacier, over to Mowich Lake via the Spray Park Trail, and back to your starting point at the Ipsut Creek Campground via the Wonderland Trail.

Before you set out on the drive to the Carbon River Entrance, check with a ranger to see whether the road beyond the entrance is open, because the river frequently washes it out.

The Ipsut Creek Campground is 5 miles from the Carbon River Entrance (from Wilkeson on Washington 165 northwest of the park, drive Carbon River Road 13 miles to the entrance).

Longmire

This community was named after James Longmire, who, in 1883, went in search of his horse and stumbled upon the nearby mineral springs. Knowing a veritable gold mine when he saw one, Longmire built a resort of sorts around the springs. The resort is now gone, but you can follow the Trail of Shadows to the still active, but relatively cool, hot springs. This easy, ½-mile trail features interpretive panels on the Longmire family and the occasional Park Service employee dressed in period garb pretending to be James Longmire.

Here you also find the 25-room National Park Inn, the Wilderness Information Center, and the **Longmire Museum.** Open daily from 9 a.m. to 4 p.m., the museum is free and features exhibits on wildlife, climbers, and Native Americans, as well as fascinating photographs that show the ebb and flow of some of the mountain's glaciers. You can pick up a map for a self-guided tour of the area's Historic Landmark District, designated in 1997; the tour, which isn't long, reveals some interesting tidbits about Longmire's past.

Longmire is 7 miles east of the Nisqually Entrance on the park's main road.

Narada Falls

The Paradise River falls 168 feet at Narada Falls over hard andesite lava, a substance that provides a glimpse of the mountain's volcanic underpinnings. For a good (and dry) camera angle of the falls, hike down to the base of the falls and go a bit farther along the trail beyond the observation point. The parking lot above the falls has several picnic tables, making this area a good place to stop for lunch.

Narada Falls is 4 miles west of Paradise on the park's main road.

Paradise

No place in the park packages a Rainier summer vacation quite like Paradise, which has glaciers to gaze at, an active volcano, hundreds of miles of trails, spectacular subalpine wildflower meadows, and a ranger station and visitor center. To explore the area, follow the Nisqually Vista Trail (see the following "Taking a hike" section) to the glacier of the same name or hike to Alta Vista, a 1¾-mile trek that pays off with a great view of the Tatoosh Range to the south.

Also on the site is the historic Paradise Inn, dating from 1917 when a group of Tacoma businessmen realized that they could make money off the mountain. This inn is a marvel of rustic woodwork and ingenuity. Alaska yellow cedars that survived a fire in the Silver Forest below Paradise were used for its construction. You may scratch your head looking at the cedar beams and rafters holding up the roof that were put in place without nails; the notched pieces are held in place by weight. (See "Where to Stay," later in the chapter, for information on the inn.)

Paradise is 18 miles east of the Nisqually Entrance on the park's main road.

Reflection Lakes

If the skies are clear and the winds calm, this area provides a great photo opportunity. A 2½-mile hike wraps around the lakes, leading through lush meadows that explode with wildflowers in the summer. I've also seen black bears near here, so keep your eyes open and camera ready.

The lakes are 3½ miles east of Paradise on the park's main road, known locally as the Stevens Canyon Road.

Sunrise

At 6,400 feet, Sunrise is the highest point in the park that you can reach by car. Although this piece of trivia may be forgettable, the in-your-face view of the Emmons Glacier, the largest ice flow on the mountain, is not.

Once upon a time, Sunrise was a thriving summer community of rental cabins. Now the spot serves as a kind of environmentally sensitive way station for backcountry travelers and day hikers. You won't find any rooms for rent in the Sunrise lodge, which is reserved for concession employees, and the snack bar is overpriced and struggles to keep up with summer's crowds. But the view of Mount Rainier from Sunrise is stunning, and hiking possibilities abound, with trails for both novices and long-distance warriors. You can take a self-guided, 1½-mile walk along Sourdough Ridge that introduces you to the environment and perhaps provides a glimpse of some of the park's mountain goats. Other options include the hike to Frozen Lake and the Mount Fremont Lookout Station; long-distance hikers can jump onto the Wonderland Trail. (See information on the Mount Freemount Lookout Station and the Wonderland Trail in the "Taking a hike" section.)

The road to Sunrise is open only from July to late September.

Sunrise is 16 miles from the Mather Memorial Parkway (also know as Highway 410) in the northeast corner of the park.

Taking a hike

Mount Rainier National Park has almost 250 miles of maintained trails, including half-day hikes, treks for long-distance warriors, and family-friendly walks that interest, but not exhaust, youngsters. This section includes just a small sampling of the trails that Rainier offers.

Snow still covers many of the trails in June. July and August are the driest and warmest months in the park, although you can see snow on trails as late as mid-July. Late July through early September is the most reliable time of year for hiking, ensuring little snow on trails and decent weather.

A hike in the Carbon River section of the park is cool, literally, because you walk through dense temperate rain forest. The Carbon River Rain Forest Nature Trail, which makes a short loop through the forest, is perfect for younger kids.

Carbon Glacier Trail

You can get so close to the Carbon Glacier along this trail that it's scary. In fact, rangers warn you not to get too close because rock and ice fall off the glacier's snout fairly regularly. But if you want to see a glacier up close, this hike is a must, and one that's relatively short in light of the payoff. From this trail, you also can move on past the glacier and continue deep into Mount Rainier's backcountry.

Distance: 7 miles round-trip. Level: Moderate; the elevation gain to Carbon Glacier is 1,200 feet and to Moraine Park is 3,300 feet. Access: Ipsut Creek Campground, 5 miles inside the park's northeast entrance.

Glacier Basin Trail

This interesting hike mixes natural and cultural attractions. During the early stretch, watch for rusting remains of a mining operation that rooted into the mountain's flanks in the late 1800s. The trail follows an old road up past the headwaters of the White River. After 1 mile, veer to the left onto 1-mile Emmons Moraine Trail that leads to an overlook with beautiful views of the Emmons Glacier. Just past the junction of the main trail with the Buroughs Mountain Trail, you arrive at Glacier Basin Camp. From the camp, it's not far to Camp Schurman in the crook of the Emmons and Winthrop glaciers, where you may be able to spot some climbers heading up Mount Rainier or perhaps some mountain goats.

Distance: 7 miles round-trip. Level: Moderate to difficult. Access: At the far end of the White River Campground in Loop D.

Mount Fremont Lookout Station

Thanks to its southern exposure, this trail is one of the first to lose its snow in the summer. In early to mid-July, you may encounter some small snowfields on the way to Frozen Lake, but past the lake, the trail is usually clear. Mount Rainier is a constant companion over your left shoulder as you head to the lookout tower. Keep your eyes on the slopes above and below you for wildlife; if you're lucky, you may spot some of the park's mountain goats. You can't enter the lookout tower, which was built in the 1930s, but you can climb up onto its deck, although doing so isn't necessary for a beautiful view. To the north, Grand Park sprawls below you, and way off toward the horizon rises the North Cascade Range. Far off to the west are the snow-capped peaks of Olympic National Park.

Distance: 5½ miles round-trip. Level: Moderate. Access: North side of the Sunrise parking lot.

Nisqually Vista Trail

This loop trail delights kids young and old with its great views of the snout of the Nisqually Glacier. You may spot pocket gophers rooting through the meadow vegetation. In late summer, you can snack on the blueberry and huckleberry bushes — as long as you can reach the berries without leaving the paved trail. From the trail, you can see the entire length of the glacier, as well as the pile of boulders being pushed downhill by it. Pick up a self-guiding brochure for the trail at the Paradise Visitor Center or at the trailhead.

Distance: 1¼ miles round-trip. Level: Easy. Access: Just north of the Henry M. Jackson Memorial Visitor Center at Paradise.

Wonderland Trail

This hike is time-consuming; many trekkers spend 10 to 14 days on this trail, which wraps around the base of Mount Rainier. You need to approach this hike carefully because of the time and logistics it requires. Some hikers even cache food at various points along the trail before they head down the path. On the way to completing the circle this trail creates, you pass through subalpine meadows, ford or cross over glacial streams, funnel through mountain passes, and walk through towering forests. If you don't have two weeks to spare, you can use connecting trails to create a shorter trek. Historically, rangers used this route to patrol the park. Some of the original ranger cabins still remain along the trail. If you're determined to make the entire circuit, contact one of the park's Wilderness Information Centers for details on caching food along the way.

Vegetation and soil in subalpine meadows are easily damaged. To protect these fragile resources, hike only on trails and don't take shortcuts.

Distance: 93 miles round-trip. Level: Strenuous; 7,000-foot elevation gain. Access: Longmire, Paradise, Sunrise, Mowich Lake, or Carbon River.

One-day wonder

Thanks to its gorgeous setting on the flanks of Mount Rainier, the **Paradise Inn** should be your base camp for a park stay (see "Where to Stay" later in this chapter). After you've checked in, though, where do you go? What follows is my recommendation for a one-day itinerary. Unless otherwise mentioned, see "Exploring the top attractions," earlier in the chapter, for information on the various sights.

Capturing the park on film

Keep a photographic record of your visit to Mount Rainier, and your family and friends may think you visited several different national parks. At Paradise, you can get some great, brilliantly white close-up shots of snow-shrouded Rainier itself. Head a few miles west of Paradise to Narada Falls and capture a wonderful water-fall in action. Head a few miles east of Paradise for a stop at Reflection Lakes, and you can snap a shimmering reflection of Rainier in the water. Journey to the park's northwestern corner along the Carbon River and find a lush example of temperate rain forest, much as you would see in nearby Olympic National Park. At Longmire, you can capture the historic log architecture. Early summer is a particularly good time for photography because the runoff from melting snow nourishes acre after acre of wildflowers and generates cascading waterfalls throughout the park. Thanks to the diversity of the landscape, you need different film speeds — slow to capture the low-light forest settings and fast for the bright snowfields.

Stepping off trails onto fragile wildflower meadows won't get you a better picture, but it could get you a lecture and possibly a ticket from a park ranger!

Plan on getting an early start, preferably by starting with the breakfast buffet in the **Paradise Inn** dining room by 7 a.m. (While ordering break-fast, you may want to also order a picnic lunch — a much cheaper alternative to the lunch counter at Sunrise.) After breakfast, if you're a caffeine addict, snatch one more cup of coffee from the mezzanine coffee table on your way out.

First, head east on the park road to **Reflection Lakes.** The scenery here is picture-perfect. If the weather is clear, you can get a great picture of Rainier's reflection on one of the lakes. Walk along the lakes' edges to glimpse some wildflowers, but because you have plenty of time for flower-gazing down the road, don't dally too long.

Next stop: **Sunrise,** the crossroads of many hiking trails. You can jump onto the Wonderland Trail, take a self-guided walk along Sourdough Ridge, or head off in several other directions. I recommend the trail to the Mount Fremont Lookout (see "Taking a hike" earlier in the chap-ter). If you start your hike by 9 a.m., you can easily return to Sunrise by noon. If you were wise and ordered a picnic lunch back at Paradise, dig into it upon returning. If you didn't, your only option is the overpriced snack bar.

After lunch, head back south in the general direction of Paradise but stop at the **Grove of the Patriarchs** just north of the Stevens Canyon Entrance Station. The flat, 1½-mile round-trip hike through the grove takes no more than an hour and leads you past towering stands of Douglas fir and western red cedar trees nearing 1,000 years in age. You find the park's biggest red cedar tree on an island in the Ohanapecosh

River; a trail reaches the island by a suspension bridge. The milder, moister climate in this corner of the park is responsible for the moss-covered forest floor and its sword fern, salmonberry, and oak fern.

From the grove, head south toward the Stevens Canyon Entrance and leave the park on Washington 123. When you reach U.S. 12, 5 miles from the entrance station, turn right and head to Packwood, where, after stopping for some ice cream, you want to head west on Skate Creek Road, which is a 25-mile shortcut back to the Nisqually Entrance. Why do I suggest that you leave the park to return to the park? Because Skate Creek Road offers a much quicker return to Nisqually than staying inside the park and retracing your morning's winding tracks. Skate Creek Road delivers you back to Washington 706, just outside the Nisqually Entrance.

After you reenter the park, head 7 miles to **Longmire** for a quick walk through the historic district. If you think that you may want to come back to Rainier for a backpacking trip, check into the Wilderness Information Center, located in the old administration building, for information and a wilderness trip planner. The museum here is particularly good.

From Longmire, you have a 12-mile drive back to Paradise, where you should arrive in time for a tour of the **Henry M. Jackson Memorial Visitor Center** or a stroll along the **Nisqually Vista Trail**, a relaxing dinner at the inn, and a gorgeous sunset (on a clear day).

Ranger programs

With the bulk of Mount Rainier's visitors arriving during summer, and with so many hiking trails winding through the park's forests and sub-alpine and alpine regions, you won't be surprised that most ranger-led activities happen in summer and involve walks. The programs are always changing, so check the park's newspaper for offerings and schedules.

I recommend the ranger-led walk to Nisqually Vista. This 90-minute hike takes you to a strategic overlook of the glacier — something kids get a kick out of. The ranger discusses the mountain's volcanology and explains the difference between glacial ice and regular ice.

Another glacier-gawking program that I recommend is the two-hour ranger-led hike from the Glacier Basin Trailhead at the White River Campground to the Emmons Glacier, the largest glacier in the Lower 48. Winter ranger programs are few; however, one good option is the snowshoe walk that originates at the Jackson Memorial Visitor Center. This 1¼-mile walk lasts about two hours and roams the landscape in the Paradise area. Offered twice daily between Christmas and New Year's Day, and then on weekends through mid-April, the walk is limited to 25 people, ages ten and older, and the cost is just $1 for snowshoe rental. Have your own snowshoes? The stroll is free.

Spotting the local wildlife

You can never predict where you'll see Mount Rainier's animals. Heading down the road to Sunrise one morning, just past Reflection Lakes, I saw a **black bear** just off the road munching on vegetation. The bear couldn't be bothered by us sitting in our car, not 10 feet away. He contentedly ate as I unpacked my 300mm lens and captured some photos.

Although you, too, may spot one of the park's black bears this way, a more reliable place to look for them in late summer is near Bench and Snow lakes just east of Louise Lake. A 1¼-mile-long trail runs from the road to the lakes.

Nothing quite compares to the sight of a **mountain goat** nimbly hopping along a steep rocky cliff. Unfortunately, you're not likely to see any goats during your visit, at least not up close, because they are highly elusive and shy creatures. If you want to try, Rampart Ridge is a good place to search for mountain goats. You can access the ridge from a trail near the Trail of the Shadows at Longmire. Van Trump Park and Comet Falls, which you reach via a trail found near Christine Falls, are two other good areas to look for goats in late June and early July.

Elk also roam the park. They're not the native Olympic species but rather imports from Yellowstone. After hunters killed the region's native elk, a trainload of Yellowstone elk arrived near the park in 1912 for a restocking project. Another batch from Wyoming, taken from an elk refuge near Jackson, arrived in 1933.

Cougars, which rely on the park's elk and mule deer populations for sustenance, are more secretive than the mountain goats. About the only time you hear of the big cats is when they come down to the lowlands, and the campgrounds are temporarily closed until they leave the area.

No doubt, when you reach the park's subalpine and alpine zones around Paradise and Sunrise, you'll spot the **hoary marmots** that claim the meadows as their own. Somewhat used to people, these critters let you get surprisingly close before lumbering off. Sharing the meadows and rocky slopes with the marmots are **pikas** (a small relative of rabbits) and the ubiquitous **chipmunks** and **squirrels.**

A strange, and usually out-of-sight, park creature is the **sooty,** or **blue, grouse.** These birds are cousins to sage grouse found in Grand Teton National Park. Males have a distinctive mating call that they combine with a dance during which they fan their tails and puff up yellow neck sacks to court females.

A fun bird to watch is the **American Dipper,** which forages for food on stream bottoms. You often can spot them perched on rocks in mid-stream, gazing into the water for a bite to eat. When they spy something, they dive in. Most of the time, they appear to be swimming upstream after a meal, although sometimes they manage to walk on the stream bottoms if the current isn't too swift.

Although exceptions exist, you find most nonwalking programs in Paradise. One such example is the video *Perilous Beauty*, which you can view at the Jackson Visitor Center. This interesting, potentially scary video explains how the mountain can unleash a massive mudslide down its flanks without any warning or eruption. I highly recommend this intriguing video if you want to gain an understanding not only of the park but also of volcanics in general.

If you're not in Paradise, either put on your hiking shoes or wait for the weekend when rangers offer programs at the amphitheaters at Ohanapecosh and Cougar Rock and the campfire circle at the White River Campground. During the summer, rangers also present nightly programs at 9 p.m. at Longmire, Paradise, and Ohanapecosh; check the park's newspaper or bulletin boards for topics.

If you have kids, pick up information on the Junior Ranger Program (see Chapter 4) at the visitor centers.

Keeping active

In addition to hiking, Mount Rainier National Park is a great place for cross-country skiing and mountain climbing.

Cross-country skiing

The park has several cross-country trails. If you're new to the sport, test your balance on Barn Flats, which has a ¾-mile route. Intermediate skiers often head to the Nisqually Vista Loop, which runs 1¼ miles and offers great views of the mountain and Nisqually Glacier. Also marked for intermediates is the 3¼-mile round-trip from Paradise to Narada Falls. Veteran skiers enjoy the Skyline Loop (6 miles) and the Camp Muir Trail (9 miles), although both are unmarked and not suitable for skate-skiing or lightweight classic skis. You can rent skis in Longmire at the **National Park Inn** (☎ **360-569-2411**).

Mountain climbing

Think you want to try to summit 14,410-foot Mount Rainier? Call Rainier Mountaineering, one of the country's most respected climbing companies. Just be sure that you're in shape before you pursue this adventure. To attempt a summit climb, you must participate in a one-day climbing school that exposes you to the fundamentals of traveling over snow and using an ice axe to stop yourself from sliding down the mountain, an incredibly helpful skill. If the guides feel that you can handle yourself well on the snow and that you're in good physical shape, you're allowed to join a group aiming for the top. For details and an application form, contact **Rainier Mountaineering**, 535 Dock St., Suite 209, Tacoma, WA 98402 (☎ **235-627-6242**), during the months of October through April, or at Rainier Mountaineering at the Guide House at Paradise (☎ **360-569-2227**) during the summer months. For east side climbs, try **Alpine Ascents International** (☎ 206-378-1927), **American Alpine Institute** (☎ 360-671-1505), **Cascade Alpine Guides** (☎ 800-981-0381), or **Mount Rainier Alpine Guides** (☎ 360-569-2889).

Where to Stay

The park has only two lodges, which together offer fewer than 200 rooms. As a result, competition for a night's lodging is pretty steep. Fortunately, plenty of rooms are available just outside the park, with most in the area of Ashford, Washington.

If a winter visit appeals to you, reserve a room at the National Park Inn at Longmire. This inn is the only in-park lodging available during winter, and from the front doors, you don't have to go far for great cross-country skiing or snowshoeing. Hardier folks can try snow camping, which is allowed throughout most of the park after a thick blanket of snow has accumulated to protect plants.

Lodging in the park

National Park Inn
$$–$$$ Longmire

This great little getaway is a good base of operations for winter trips to the park. Located at Longmire just 7 miles from the Nisqually Entrance, this inn is all that remains of the original 16-cottage, 17-room National Park Inn that burned down in 1929. Fully renovated in 1990, the inn has 25 rooms open year-round. From the inn's front porch, you have a nice view of Mount Rainier. The small guest lounge is a welcoming spot to relax with a book, board game, or refreshment in front of the river rock fireplace. The rooms vary in size, but all come with rustic furniture, wall-to-wall carpeting, and coffeemakers. In the winter, you can rent cross-country skis or snowshoes. The inn's restaurant offers something for everyone.

Off State Route 706. ☎ *360-569-2275 reservations only, or 360-569-2211. Fax: 360-569-2770. Internet:* www.guestservices.com/rainier. *25 rooms, 18 with bath. Rack rates: $78 double without bath, $110–$150 double with bath. AE, DC, DISC, MC, V.*

Paradise Inn
$$–$$$$ Paradise

This rustic lodge, opened with just 33 rooms in 1917 and built from Alaska yellow cedar taken from within the park, offers sweeping views of Mount Rainier and the Nisqually Glacier. Miles of trails and meadows dappled with wildflowers in mid-summer make this spot perfect to base a Mount Rainier vacation. Cedar-shake siding, huge exposed beams, cathedral ceilings, and oversized rock fireplaces combine to create an idyllic mountain retreat. The guest rooms vary in size and amenities, so be sure to specify exactly what you want when making reservations. The inn's dining room is anchored by a large fireplace, and the windows with alpine views fill the long walls. The Glacier Lounge is the perfect spot to relax after a long day on the trail.

Just east of the Henry M. Jackson Memorial Visitor Center. ☎ *360-569-2275. Fax: 360-569-2770. 118 rooms, 98 with bath; 2 suites. Rack rates: $77 double without bath, $115–$146 double with bath; $161 suite. AE, DC, DISC, MC, V. Closed early Oct to mid-May.*

Lodging outside the park

Alexander's Country Inn
$$$ Ashford

This turn-of-the-20th century inn has long welcomed visitors to the park. After a long day of hiking, you can return here for a hearty meal and a dip in the hot tub. Not only does Alexander's have the best accommodations in the area, but also the best dinners. The dining room and a small gift shop consume the first floor, and a large sitting room with a fireplace is on the second. The best guest room is the tower suite, located in a turret with plenty of windows for surveying the surrounding woods. On the grounds are two guest houses that sleep up to eight and feature kitchens.

37515 State Route 706 East. ☎ *800-654-7615 or 360-569-2300. Fax: 360-569-2323. Internet:*www.alexanderscountryinn.com. *TV TEL in guest houses. 7 rooms, 5 suites, 2 guest houses. Rack rates: May–Oct $110 double, $140 suite, $195 guest house; Nov–Apr $89 double, $110 suite, $145 guest house. Rates include full breakfast. MC, V.*

Alta Crystal Resort at Mt. Rainier
$$$$–$$$$$ Greenwater

This is the closest lodging to the northeast park entrance and the Sunrise area. Although this condominium resort with wooded grounds is most popular in the winter when skiers flock to nearby Crystal Mountain, you can find plenty to do in the summer, with a heated outdoor pool and nearby hiking trails. A hot tub is set in the woods. Accommodations are in 1-bedroom and loft chalets. The former can handle two adults and two young children (under 12), and the latter have bed space for up to six people. All condos feature a full kitchen and fireplace.

68317 Washington 410 East. ☎ *800-277-6475 or 360-663-2500. Fax: 360-663-2556. 24 units. TV TEL. Rack rates: June–Sept $160–$220 (1–4 people). Non-smoking. AE, MC, V.*

Cedar Creek Treehouse
$$$$ Ashford

Swaying 50 feet up amid the limbs of a towering cedar tree, this treehouse offers some of the best views in the area. I mean, how many other lodgings can guarantee you a view of Mount Rainier from your bed? You don't lose track of the tree, either, because the trunk runs up through the kitchen of this treehouse, which features a sleeping loft with two double beds, dining room, observation room, and bathroom. The space is not sprawling, just 16 feet by 16 feet, but it's incredibly unique. Plus, you get the whole place to yourself; the treehouse is not staffed.

State Route 706 East (10 miles from the park). ☎ *360-569-2991. Internet:* www. cedar zcreektreehouse.com. *Sleeps five. Rack rates: $200 for two; $25 each additional person. Non-smoking. Open: Mar–Oct.*

The Nisqually Lodge
$$ Ashford

There's nothing fancy about this chalet-style motel, but its large, clean rooms come with air-conditioning, telephones, and TV. You can relax in the hot tub outside or in a small sitting area with a fireplace just off the registration desk. An annex added in the fall of 1999 provides meeting rooms and a laundry.

31609 State Route 706 East. ☎ *888-674-3554 or 360-569-8804. Fax: 360-569-2435. 24 rooms. A/C TV TEL. Rack rate: $60–$80 double. Rates include Continental breakfast. AE, MC, V.*

Wellspring Spa and Log Cabins
$$–$$$$$ Ashford

Rustic and eclectic sum up this relaxing hideaway in the woods. And the spa does a good job of pampering you, too. The accommodations are a fanciful mix. You have your modern log cabins, which are tucked up against the edge of the forest and feature feather beds, woodstoves, and vaulted ceilings. If you're more adventuresome, request "the Nest," where you find a queen-size bed suspended by ropes under a skylight. If that's a bit too much, settle into the Three Bears Cottage, which has rustic log furniture and a full kitchen. Another option is the Treehouse, a wooden structure, about the size of a tent, suspended in a tree with a TV/VCR and fold-out futon. For bigger groups, the Tatoosh Lodge features a large stone fireplace, a whirlpool tub, a waterfall shower, and room for 14. Want to sleep in a greenhouse with a cedar hot tub and wood-fired sauna? You can, but you have to wait until 9 p.m. to have the room to yourself (the hot tub and sauna are available for rental until that hour). Several of the rooms and the cabins come with a breakfast basket. Hot tubs and saunas are an additional $5 per person per hour for guests, $10 per hour for visitors. This New Age retreat isn't for everyone, but it's certainly the most unique accommodation in the area.

54922 Kernahan Rd. ☎ *360-569-2514. 4 rooms, 4 log cabins, 3 tent cabins, 1 cottage, 1 treehouse, 1 lodge that sleeps 14. TV in treehouse. Rack rates: $79–$369 double. MC, V.*

Runner-up lodgings

Inn of Packwood

$$–$$$ **Packwood**   Just south of the park's Stevens Canyon Entrance, the inn has standard motel rooms as well as kitchen units, plus a heated indoor pool. *13032 U.S. Route 12.* ☎ *877-496-9666 or 360-494-5500. Internet:* www. innofpackwood.com.

Mountain Meadows Inn

$$$ **Ashford**   This bed-and-breakfast on 11 acres offers 6 rooms and an outdoor spa just 6 miles outside the Nisqually Entrance. You can enjoy evenings on the wrap-around porch or in the outdoor hot tub. *28912 State Route 706 East.* ☎ *360-569-2788. Internet:* www.mnt-meadows-mt-rainier. com.

Mounthaven Resort

$$–$$$$ **Ashford**   The eleven cabins sleep from two to nine people and offer amenities ranging from kitchenettes to full kitchens and fireplaces. The convenient location is a ½-mile from the Nisqually Entrance. *38210 State Route 706 East.* ☎ *800-456-9380 or 360-569-2594. Internet:* www.mount haven.com.

Storm King Spa at Mount Rainier

$$–$$$$ **Ashord**   Whether you want the privacy of a cabin or the coziness of a B&B, this property can meet your needs. The B&B is housed in a historic home that dates to the early 1890s and is surrounded by 10 acres. *37311 State Route 706 East.* ☎ *360-569-2964 or 360-569-2964. Internet:* www. stormkingspa.com.

Campgrounds

Mount Rainier has six campgrounds with nearly 600 sites accessible by car. These range from the 18-site Sunshine Point Campground along the Nisqually River in the southwestern corner of the park to the 188-site Ohanapecosh Campground in the southeastern corner.

Reservations (☎ **800-365-CAMP**; Internet: http://reservations. nps.gov) must be made for the Ohanapecosh and Cougar Rock Campgrounds for stays between the last Monday in June through Labor Day. You can make reservations up to five months in advance. With this one exception, all campgrounds operate on a first-come, first-serve basis.

None of the campgrounds offers showers or RV hookups, although you can find showers at Paradise in the basement of the visitor center. All campgrounds except Ipsut Creek and Mowich Lake have potable water.

✔ **Cougar Rock Campground:** This spot, just over 2¼ miles northeast of Longmire in the park's southwestern corner, is one of the more popular campgrounds thanks to its location between Longmire and Paradise. You find 173 sites, including five group sites that you can reserve (☎ **360-569-2211,** ext. 3301) up to 90 days in advance. Fees are $15 a night during the summer, $12 after September 6. Amenities include flush toilets and a dump station for RVs. You can pass evenings by attending ranger talks in the campground's amphitheater. The campground is open from Memorial Day weekend through mid-October.

✔ **Ipsut Creek Campground:** Its 29 free sites are technically open year-round, but heavy snows and road closures can restrict access to this area 5 miles east of the Carbon River Entrance. The campground has pit toilets only. You find a ranger station and amphitheater here, and weekends feature campfire programs. *Note:* You need a high-clearance vehicle to get here.

✔ **Mowich Lake Campground:** Near the park's biggest and deepest lake, this campround is located just beyond the end of Washington 165 in the park's northwestern corner. You have to walk a bit from your car — about 100 yards from the parking area — to reach the camping area, which holds 30 tents. Campsites are free, but amenities are nonexistent, because of a lack of potable water. Only pit toilets are available. However, the lakeside setting and relative isolation is beautiful. You also can jump onto the Wonderland Trail. The campground is open late June through mid-October.

✔ **Ohanapecosh Campground:** Eleven miles north of Packwood, this 188-site campground is located in a gorgeous stand of old-growth forest. The tall forest canopy mutes the sunlight and creates a mostly shady atmosphere, which is refreshing during August's hot weather. Fees are $14 per site during the summer, $12 after September 6. The campground has flush toilets, drinking water, and a dump station for RVs. It's open from Memorial Day weekend through mid-October.

✔ **Sunshine Point Campground:** A ¼-mile inside the Nisqually Entrance, this one is more open than Ohanapecosh, and the melodic gurgling of the nearby Nisqually River is hypnotic when the time comes to call it a night. Each of the 18 sites cost $10 a night. This campground has drinking water, but only pit toilets. Open year-round.

✔ **White River Campground:** This is a great base if you like to hike. Located 5 miles west of the White River Entrance, the campground and its 112 sites are close to the Wonderland Trail, and the trails to Glacier Basin and Emmons Moraine start here. The campground has flush toilets and drinking water. Sites cost $10 a night. White River is open from late June through September.

Where to Eat

Formal dining in the park is limited: National Park Inn at Longmire and the Paradise Inn at Paradise are the only options. Expensive snack bars with limited offerings can be found at Sunrise and in the Henry M. Jackson Memorial Visitor Center at Paradise. Outside the park, your options increase extensively.

Restaurants in the park

National Park Inn

$–$$ **Longmire AMERICAN**

The dining room at this historic inn, just inside the park's Nisqually Entrance, is smaller and cozier than the one at Paradise Inn, even though it seats 90 people. Menus change each year, if not each season, but you usually can order pancakes, French toast, or even biscuits and gravy for breakfast. Lunches are built around burgers and sandwiches. You find New York steaks, trout, salmon, and pasta dishes on the dinner menu.

Just off State Route 706. ☎ *360-569-2275 reservations only, or 360-569- 2411. Reservations suggested for dinner. Main courses: $6–$8 breakfast; $ 7–$9 lunch; $13–$19 dinner. AE, DISC, DC, MC, V. Open: Daily 7 a.m.–8 p.m. in summer and until 7 p.m. in winter.*

Paradise Inn

$–$$$ **Paradise AMERICAN**

This dining room is the park's most picturesque. The long, rectangular space has windows lining both walls and a massive stone fireplace that dominates one end of the room. The Paradise buffet — featuring breakfast fare such as fresh fruits, pastries, cereals, muffins, and scrambled eggs — is the best deal in the morning at $9.50. If you prefer, you can order omelets made to order, French toast with hazelnuts and blackberry sauce, or oatmeal pancakes. One of the more interesting dinner dishes is Bourbon Buffalo Meatloaf, a hearty main course made from ground sirloin buffalo and served with a sauce made with Jack Daniels' bourbon whiskey and leek mashed potatoes. A buffalo stew also appears on the lunch menu.

Reservations are not accepted for the 200-seat dining room, so you may end up waiting a bit for a table. If you do, relax in the Glacier Lounge or on the lobby's second-floor mezzanine.

Located just east of the Henry M. Jackson Memorial Visitor Center. ☎ *360-569-2275. Reservations not accepted. Main courses: $6.25–$9.50 breakfast; $8–$12 lunch; $10–$23 dinner. AE, DC, DISC, MC, V. Open: 7–9:30 a.m., noon to 2 p.m., 5:30–8 p.m. (until 8:30 p.m. between mid-June to Labor Day).*

Restaurants outside the park

Alexander's Country Inn
$–$$$ Ashford   AMERICAN

Although this inn's main business comes from overnight guests, the dining room is open to the public and draws heavily with its varied menu that features steak, seafood, and pasta. The trout is as fresh as can be, having come from the trout pond out back, and the pan-roasted New York steak satisfies any empty stomach. If you like smoked salmon, be sure to try the smoked salmon dip appetizer.

37515 State Rt. 706 E. ☎ 800-654-7615 or 360-569-2300. Reservations suggested. Main courses: $3.95–$8.95 breakfast; $5.95–$9.95 lunch; $8.95–$20.95 dinner. MC, V. Open: Summer 8 a.m.–9 p.m. In winter open to inn guests during the week; open to the public on weekends.

Rainier Overland Restaurant and Lounge
$–$$$ Ashford   AMERICAN

Just outside the Nisqually entrance, this cozy restaurant and adjoining bar offer family dining popular with the locals. The atmosphere is relaxed, the menu of steaks, kid-friendly burgers, sandwiches, chicken, and seafood priced reasonably, and the food filling. If you're undecided on what to have, try the salmon with bay shrimp scampi served over linguini. In the lounge, you find some of the Northwest's tastiest microbrews.

31811 State Route 706 East. ☎ 360-569-0851. Main courses: $6.95–$21.95 dinner. DISC, MC, V. Open daily 4 p.m.–8 p.m. Closed Nov–March.

Fast Facts: Mount Rainier

Area Code

☎ 360.

ATMs

None in the park. Look for them in grocery stores in Ashford, Packwood, and Enumclaw.

Emergency

☎ 911.

Fees

$10 per vehicle per week; $5 for walk-ins per week.

Fishing License

Not required, although some streams are off-limits. For details, pick up a brochure at a visitor center or check the park's Web site.

Hospitals

None in the park. The closest is Morton General Hospital, 521 Adams Ave., Morton, WA; ☎ 360-496-5112.

Information

Superintendent, Mount Rainier National Park, Ashford, WA 98304-9751; ☎ 360-569-2211 or 360-569-2177 (TTY).

Lost and Found

Call the park headquarters (☎ 360-569-2211, ext. 2334) between 8 a.m.–4:30 p.m.

Pharmacies

Morton, Eatonville, and Enumclaw have phamacies.

Post Office

Year-round at National Park Inn at Longmire; late May to early October at Paradise Inn (when the inn is open).

Road Conditions and Weather

☎ 360-569-2211.

Taxes

In-park lodging 15%, meals 10%. Tax rates vary in towns outside the park.

Time Zone

Pacific standard time.

Web Site

www.nps.gov/mora.

Chapter 18

Olympic National Park

· ·

In This Chapter

▶ Introducing three parks in one

▶ Planning your trip

▶ Exploring mountains, beaches, and rain forests

▶ Finding the best hotels and restaurants

· ·

*O*lympic National Park is the answer for people who can't decide where to head on vacation. "Should I go to the beach this year or should I head to the mountains?" A trip to Olympic solves such dilemmas. Within its 922,653 acres, the park offers three totally different experiences. The only problem you face is packing for three different vacations.

Interested in mountains and glaciers? Olympic is capped by a range of sky-scraping, snow-capped mountains that support the lowest-elevation glacier system in the Lower 48. In roughly 40 miles, the park's terrain runs from sea level to peaks nearly 8,000 feet high. Topped by 7,965-foot-tall Mount Olympus, the park's roof features alpine and subalpine communities you can hike through in summer on multi-day backpacking treks or kick-and-glide through in winter on cross-country skis.

Love to roam wave-pounded beaches? Olympic boasts 63 miles of some of the most scenic coastline anywhere, thanks to towering *sea stacks* — rock monoliths left behind when the coastline receded under the relentless pounding of the waves — that rise above the foaming surf. Thick coniferous forests run up to the edge of the sand-and-cobble beaches, hiding them from the roads and lending some solitude. Although this stretch of Pacific Ocean probably is too cold to enjoy anything but a brief swim on a dare, the water teems with marine life ranging from whales and sea lions to colorful sea stars (starfish). If that's not enough, on clear days you're guaranteed spectacular sunsets thanks to the surf and sea stacks.

Thankfully, you won't find any beachfront homes or seaside burger joints along the park's coast, which is one of the largest sections of wilderness coast in the continental United States.

Olympic National Park

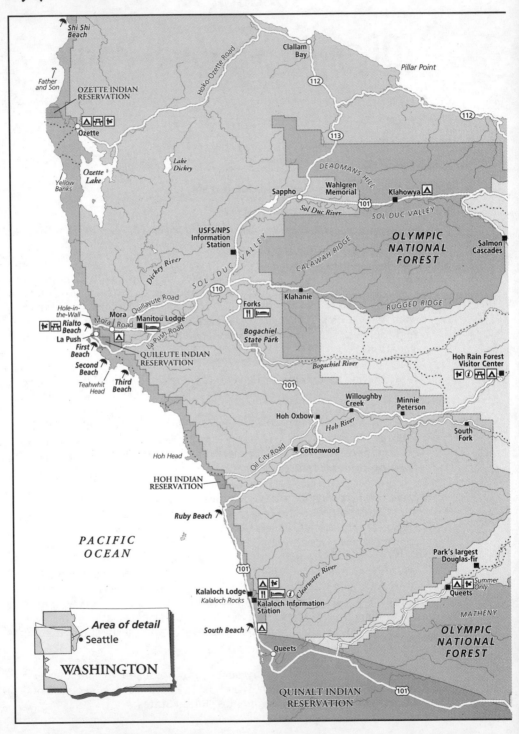

Shi Shi Beach

Father and Son

OZETTE INDIAN RESERVATION

Ozette

Lake Dickey

Ozette Lake

Yellow Banks

Hoko-Ozette Road

Clallam Bay

Pillar Point

112

113

DEADMANS HILL

Wahlgren Memorial

Sappho

Klahowya

Sol Duc River

SOL DUC VALLEY

Salmon Cascades

OLYMPIC NATIONAL FOREST

USFS/NPS Information Station

CALAWAH RIDGE

RUGGED RIDGE

Dickey River

SOL DUC VALLEY

110

Forks

Klahanie

Quillayute Road

Mora

Manitou Lodge

Mora Road

Hole-in-the-Wall

Rialto Beach

La Push

First Beach

La Push Road

QUILEUTE INDIAN RESERVATION

Bogachiel State Park

Bogachiel River

Hoh Rain Forest Visitor Center

Second Beach

Teahwhit Head

Third Beach

101

Willoughby Creek

Minnie Peterson

Hoh Oxbow

Hoh River

South Fork

Hoh Head

Oil City Road

Cottonwood

HOH INDIAN RESERVATION

PACIFIC OCEAN

Ruby Beach

Clearwater River

Park's largest Douglas-fir

Summer Only

Queets

101

Kalaloch Lodge

Kalaloch Rocks

Kalaloch Information Station

MATHENY

OLYMPIC NATIONAL FOREST

South Beach

Queets

Area of detail

• Seattle

WASHINGTON

QUINALT INDIAN RESERVATION

101

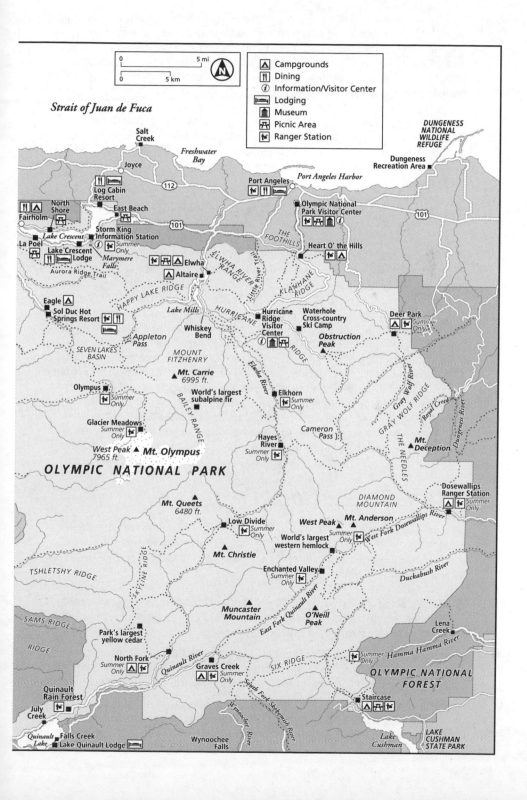

Strait of Juan de Fuca

Legend:
- △ Campgrounds
- ⑪ Dining
- ⓘ Information/Visitor Center
- 🛏 Lodging
- 🏛 Museum
- ⌘ Picnic Area
- ⚑ Ranger Station

Salt Creek

Joyce

Freshwater Bay

Port Angeles Harbor

DUNGENESS NATIONAL WILDLIFE REFUGE

Dungeness Recreation Area

Log Cabin Resort

Port Angeles

North Shore

Fairholm

East Beach

Olympic National Park Visitor Center

Storm King Information Station

Lake Crescent

La Poel

Lake Crescent Lodge

Marymere Falls

Aurora Ridge Trail

THE FOOTHILLS

Heart O' the Hills

Elwha

Altaire

ELWHA RANGE

Little River Trail

ELWHA RIVER Trail

KLAHHANE RIDGE

HAPPY LAKE RIDGE

Eagle

Sol Duc Hot Springs Resort

Appleton Pass

SEVEN LAKES BASIN

Lake Mills

Whiskey Bend

HURRICANE RIDGE

Hurricane Ridge Visitor Center

Waterhole Cross-country Ski Camp

Obstruction Peak

Deer Park
Summer Only

MOUNT FITZHENRY

Mt. Carrie
6995 ft.

Elwha River

Olympus
Summer Only

BAILEY RANGE

World's largest subalpine fir

Elkhorn
Summer Only

Gray Wolf River

GRAY WOLF RIDGE

Royal Creek

Dungeness River

THE NEEDLES

Glacier Meadows
Summer Only

Cameron Pass

West Peak
7965 ft.

Mt. Olympus

Hayes River
Summer Only

Mt. Deception

OLYMPIC NATIONAL PARK

Mt. Queets
6480 ft.

Low Divide
Summer Only

West Peak

Mt. Anderson

DIAMOND MOUNTAIN

Dosewallips Ranger Station
Summer Only

World's largest western hemlock
Summer Only

West Fork Dosewallips River

TSHLETSHY RIDGE

SKYLINE RIDGE

Mt. Christie

Enchanted Valley
Summer Only

Duckabush River

SAMS RIDGE

RIDGE

Muncaster Mountain

East Fork Quinault River

O'Neill Peak

Lena Creek

Park's largest yellow cedar

SIX RIDGE

Hamma Hamma River

Summer Only

OLYMPIC NATIONAL FOREST

North Fork
Summer Only

Quinault River

Graves Creek
Summer Only

South Fork Skokomish River

Staircase

Quinault Rain Forest

Wynoochee River

Lake Cushman

LAKE CUSHMAN STATE PARK

July Creek

Quinault Lake

Falls Creek

Lake Quinault Lodge

Wynoochee Falls

If neither snow-capped peaks nor surf-swept beaches sound appealing, head into the Northwest's largest remaining undisturbed old-growth and temperate rain forests. The park's muggy forests, soaked by 12 to 14 feet of rain a year and often cloaked in low-lying clouds or drizzle, wrap around you with thick, mossy-green walls of vegetation. You can almost feel the forest growing.

In addition to rugged mountains, wilderness beaches, and lush rain forests, you also find meadows strewn with wildflowers, deep valleys, shimmering lakes, soothing hot springs, and cascading waterfalls tossed in between the coastline and the peaks. Three unique choices — one park, one trip.

You need at least three days to explore Olympic National Park. Frankly, your choice of when to visit boils down to how much you like wet weather. Spring can be on the raw side and wet, but it does have its own magic. For starters, the wetness enhances the emerald color of the rain forests. And you often see gray whales cavorting along the coastline while they migrate north. Summers can't be beat. July and August are the driest months in the park, and September can be quite nice, too. The threat of the forests growing moldy disappears because rain is relatively minimal this time of year. Fog banks often roll inland from the Pacific in the mornings, but the mist usually burns off by midday to reveal mostly blue skies. Like spring, fall can also be wet and raw, but this season has its high points, too. The rain forests become extra lush, and in early fall, you can often spot sea lions lounging along the coast. Crowds are sparse in Olympic during winter, the onset of the rainy season — the year's heaviest rains fall in December and January. At this time, the park's upper elevations become buried in snow — on average, the park's high country receives 15+ feet of snow each winter.

Must-see Attractions

Where to go, where to go, where to go? That's the dilemma with a park of Olympic's diversity. So let me give you some suggestions for a wonderful sampling of all the different landscapes — and seascapes — that this national park has to offer:

- **Hoh Rain Forest:** This pocket of humidity, with its moss-covered trees, bushy ferns, and slimy banana slugs, is a perfect example of the world's temperate rain forests.

- **Hurricane Ridge:** The highest point in the park you can easily reach by car, its views of the Strait of Juan de Fuca and Mount Olympus and the rest of the Olympic mountains are riveting.

- **Lake Crescent:** Anglers appreciate this glacier-carved lake for its rare Beardslee and Crescenti trout species, whereas romantics are happy just to pull up a lakefront chair at Lake Crescent Lodge.

✔ **Marymere Falls:** This 90-foot waterfall that cascades out of the forest nourishes a moss community that blankets the cliffside and the boulders at the falls' base.

✔ **Ruby Beach:** Sea stacks — rocky outposts that are remnants of a coastline long knocked down by Pacific storms — make this nook of the park a favorite with photographers, rock hounds, and kids who've never seen sea stars or anemones (small, colorful, spineless creatures with tentacles) revealed in a tidal pool during low tide.

✔ **Sol Duc Hot Springs:** Most parks have a commercial side, and this spot is Olympic's. But its pools are kid magnets and wonderful for us older folk to ease into, too, after a long day on the trail.

Getting There

Reaching Olympic National Park is easy, thanks to the international airport near Seattle, which is a relatively short car ride — or shuttle flight — from the park. Heck, you can even reach the park from the sea, thanks to the docks at Port Angeles and the ferries that arrive there from Victoria, British Columbia

Driving in

Seattle is the closest major gateway to Olympic National Park, which anchors Washington State's peninsula in the Pacific. From the city, you can reach the park either by taking a ferry across Puget Sound or by heading south on Interstate 5 to Tacoma, and then Washington 16 north to Bremerton and Washington 3 north to U.S. 101 to reach the east side of the park, or drive west from Olympia on Washington 8 to Aberdeen and then north on U.S. 101 along the park's western side.

If you take the ferry across the sound from Seattle, you find park entrances along U.S. 101 at Port Angeles, Hurricane Ridge, Elwha, Lake Crescent, and Sol Duc.

Traveling up U.S. 101 from Aberdeen, you have the choice of entering the park in the Quinault or Queets valleys, or at Kalaloch Beach, the Hoh Rain Forest, or Mora. You reach Ozette in the northwestern corner via a road off Washington 112. From spur roads off U.S. 101 on the east side of the park, you can reach Staircase and the park's entrance at Dosewallips. You find an entrance to Hurricane Ridge on the southern border of Port Angeles, and you can reach Deer Park via a road that heads south off U.S. 101 just east of Port Angeles.

Some of these entrances may close in the winter, so check with the park visitor center at ☎ 360-565-3130 before setting out for Olympic.

For Puget Sound ferry schedules, contact **Washington State Ferries** (☎ **206-464-6400**). For ferries arriving in Port Angeles from Victoria, British Columbia, contact **Black Ball Transportation** (☎ **360-457-4491**) in Port Angeles. **Victoria Express** (☎ **800-633-1589** or 360-452-8088), meanwhile, offers seasonal, walk-on ferry service.

Flying in

If you want to fly to the park, **Horizon Air** provides service to **Fairchild International Airport** (☎ **360-457- 8527**) in Port Angeles from Seattle Tacoma International Airport and Victoria, British Columbia. **Budget Rent-A-Car** has an outlet at Fairchild. (See the Appendix for the toll-free number for Horizon and Budget.)

The closest major airport is the **Seattle Tacoma International Airport** (☎ **800-544-1965** or 206-431-4444), known as Sea-Tac, located 15 miles south of Seattle on Interstate 5. Most of the major airlines and car-rental agencies are here; see the Appendix for their toll-free numbers. For bus service from the airport, see the next section, "Busing in."

Busing in

Olympic Bus Lines (☎ **360-417-0700**) offers twice daily service from Seattle and Seattle Tacoma International Airport to Port Angeles. **Pennco Transportation** (☎ **360-582-3736**) makes nine trips daily to the airport from Port Angeles. Other bus companies on the peninsula include **Clallam Transit** (☎ **800-858-3747** or 360-452-4511), which operates Monday through Saturday within Port Angeles with commuter services to Sequim, Joyce, Lake Crescent, Forks, Neah Bay, and La Push; **Jefferson Transit** (☎ **360-385-4777**), which is based in Port Angeles and serves Brinnon and connects with Clallam Transit in Sequim; **Grays Harbor Transit** (☎ **800-562-9730** or 360-532-2770), which operates from Olympia and Aberdeen with service to Lake Quinault; and **Mason County Transit** (☎ **800-374-3747** or 360-427-5033), which runs between Shelton, Olympia, Bremerton, and Brinnon.

On the peninsula, **Olympic Tours** (☎ **360-457-3545**) offers park tours for groups as large as 30 people and can shuttle you to or from trailheads for backpacking treks.

Planning Ahead

For information in advance of your trip, write Superintendent, 600 East Park Avenue, Port Angeles, WA 98362; call ☎ **360-565-3130**; or check the park's Web site at www.nps.gov/olym.

Reserving a room or a campsite

A lead time of several weeks to a month is usually sufficient for reserving a room at many of the motels and hotels found in the Port Angeles area, but several months would be more appropriate for such resort locations as Lake Crescent and Quinault Lake.

Due to the park's popularity with backpackers, some backcountry sites — Ozette Coast, Grand and Badger valleys, Royal Basin, Lake Constance, Flapjack Lakes, and the Sol Duc/Seven Lakes Basin — operate under a quota system. You can reserve one of the designated sites in these areas for trips between May and September by calling the **Wilderness Information Center** (☎ **360-565-3100**) up to 30 days before your trip.

Packing for the park

Don't forget your rain gear when packing for Olympic National Park. You may be able to sneak in a multi-day trip in summer without needing it, but better to have it and not need it than need it and not have it, right? Trust me, rain gear almost always comes in handy.

If you're going to be camping, make sure that your tent has a good rain fly. For more tips on how to pack for your national park vacation, see Chapter 4.

Learning the Lay of the Land

Olympic National Park is a veritable island of wilderness in the heart of the Olympic Peninsula. In fact, 95% of the park is officially designated wilderness. Surrounded on three sides by water — the Pacific Ocean to the west, the Strait of Juan De Fuca to the north, and the Hood Canal to the east — the park offers sanctuary to a rich animal kingdom and an escape from humanity for those who visit.

No roads loop through the park. Instead, **U.S. 101** hooks and crawls around the park's west, north, and east sides. A few roads make relatively short forays into the park from the highway. None of these is longer than 17 miles, which usually means a quick trip to your destination.

The one destination that is difficult to reach is **Ozette.** Getting there requires a 40-mile side trip from Sappho, near the park's western border, down Washington **Highways 113** and **112** that lead you through the Olympic National Forest to the coast.

Park headquarters and the biggest (and best) visitor center are both located on the north side of the park in **Port Angeles.** From the visitor center, **Hurricane Ridge** — with its smaller visitor center, picnic area, hiking trails, and panoramic views of the Olympics with their glaciers and the Strait of Juan de Fuca — lies 17 miles south via the aptly named **Hurricane Ridge Road.** Stemming off from this road are hiking trails and a dirt road leading to Obstruction Peak.

Other side roads that dash into the park include the following:

- **Elwha Valley Road** leads to Altaire Campground, Elwha picnic area, and Lake Mills just below the northern edge of the park.

- **Sol Duc Road** leads to the Sol Duc campground, Sol Duc Hot Springs Resort, and several popular trailheads in the park's northwestern corner.

- **Hoh River Rain Forest Road** leads to the Hoh Rain Forest and its visitor center and campground in the west side of the park.

- **Queets Valley Road** leads to the Queets campground near the park's southwestern corner.

- **North Shore Road** runs along the north side of Quinault Lake to the Quinault Rain Forest and the North Fork and Graves Creek campgrounds on the southern tip.

- **South Shore Road** runs along the south side of Quinault Lake to the North Fork and Graves Creek campgrounds.

- **Staircase Road** in the park's southeastern corner runs to the Staircase campground and several trailheads that lead you to breathtaking alpine vistas and thick forests.

- **Deer Park Road** leads to the Deer Park campground on the northeastern corner.

Although physically separated from the alpine heart of the park, the 63 miles of **coastline** are indeed part of Olympic. This rugged stretch of sand and rock runs from Kalaloch Beach just above the Quinault Indian Reservation all the way north to Shi Shi Beach that borders the Makah Indian Reservation. **U.S. 101** runs 10 miles along the coast between South Beach and Ruby Beach, and **Washington 110** runs to Rialto Beach and La Push midway along the coastline. The only other coastal access in the park is via the **Hoko-Ozette Road,** which runs about 20 miles from Washington 112 to Ozette Lake.

When exploring the park, remember to be patient. Like other park road systems, Olympic's is nothing like a freeway system. U.S. 101 has a few straight stretches, but for the most part it winds and bends and creeps over and around the mountainous landscape. After you leave this main road for one of the spur roads, the number of bends and turns seems to double.

Arriving in the Park

When you enter the park, you are handed a copy of the park's newspaper, *Bugler,* a great source for discovering what's happening during your visit. For more information, head to one of the visitor centers or ranger stations.

Finding information

The park has three visitor centers that offer exhibits, maps, guides, and information, plus smaller ranger and information stations (open only in summer) located at popular trailheads.

Olympic National Park Visitor Center (☎ 360-565-3130), on the southern edge of Port Angeles, is the park's largest visitor center and offers great exhibits on Olympic's Native American history and wildlife, as well as a good selection of park books, posters, videotapes, and postcards. The center is open year-round; hours vary by season.

A 45-minute drive from the main visitor center brings you to one of the most popular spots in the park, the **Hurricane Ridge Visitor Center.** Here you find free telescopes for spying on distant peaks and glaciers, as well as a snack bar, interpretive exhibits, and trails. The center is open daily from 10 a.m. to 5 p.m.

The **Hoh Rain Forest Visitor Center,** on the west side of the main part of the park, is some 15 miles down a turnoff from U.S. 101. This tiny center offers a good explanation of rain forests and their climate, as well as a primer on glaciers. You can pick up wilderness trip permits here if you plan to take the Hoh River Trail 18½ miles to Glacier Meadows. The center is open daily; hours vary seasonally. Smaller information centers include the **Storm King Information Station,** on Lake Crescent in the northern section of the park, and the **Kalaloch Information Station,** on the south end of the beach section of the park. You can get food and some supplies near the **Sol Duc Ranger Station** at the Hot Springs Resort.

For maps and updated trail conditions, stop at the nearest ranger station or at the **Wilderness Information Center** (☎ 360-565-3100), located just behind the main visitor center in Port Angeles.

Paying fees

Entrance into the park for up to a week costs $10 per vehicle, or $5 per individual hiking or biking. Annual passes cost $30. If you have a park pass, you don't need to pay the entrance fee; see Chapter 8 for information on the National Park Pass and Chapter 4 for the lowdown on Golden Age and Golden Access passports.

Parking at Ozette costs $1 per day.

All overnight hiking trips require a $5 permit registration fee that is good for two weeks and covers up to a dozen people, as well as an individual nightly fee of $2 per person for every night out. (Hikers 16 and younger are exempt from the nightly fee.) Permits are available at the **Wilderness Information Center** (☎ **360-565-3100**) in Port Angeles.

Getting around

To get around Olympic National Park, you need a car. The park does not have a public transportation system.

Remembering Safety

If you plan to head off into the park's backcountry, keep in mind these pointers to ensure a safe trip:

- ✔ **Hypothermia:** A real danger with Olympic's generally wet, cool climate. Protect yourself by having rain gear with you and by dressing in layers of synthetic clothing, which dries much more quickly than cotton clothing.

- ✔ **Cougars:** They roam the park's backcountry, and although you most likely won't spot one, if you do, don't turn your back on it or try to run away. These actions can encourage the cougar to attack. If the big cat seems aggressive and begins to stalk you, try to scare it off by waving your arms and shouting or by throwing rocks or sticks at it.

- ✔ **Black bears:** These animals also call the park home and are much more visible than cougars. If you see a bear down the trail, either give it a wide berth or backtrack until it leaves. If a bear comes into your camp, make some noise to scare it off. Also, be sure to hang your food high above the ground from a bear wire, where available, or store the food in an animal-resistant food container, which are available for a $3 per trip donation from the **Wilderness Information Center** (☎ **360-565-3100**) and any staffed ranger station.

If you plan to make a trip to the beach, keep the following in mind:

- ✔ **Coastal hiking:** This activity can be dangerous because tides can trap you. Never hike around headlands unless you know how high tides can get and when they come in. Detailed maps, showing safe routes around headlands, as well as tide tables, are available from visitor centers, the Wilderness Information Center (☎ 360-565-3100), and staffed ranger stations.

✔ **Swimming:** Along the coast, swimming can be hazardous because of logs in the surf. Felled by storms and washed into the ocean by streams, they can easily knock a swimmer unconscious. Also, the cold water and strong currents make swimming a risky proposition along the coast.

✔ **Raccoons:** Believe it or not, these critters can be troublesome for campers on the beach near Ozette. Park officials suggest that you store your food in animal-resistant food containers to thwart these masked marauders.

For additional tips on how to ensure a safe visit to the park, see Chapter 8.

Enjoying the Park

Although the vast majority of Olympic National Park is rugged back-country that you need a horse or a pair of hiking boots to reach, you can get a strong impression of the park from several readily and easily accessible areas.

Exploring the top attractions

Beaches

Although sea stacks make Ruby Beach the favorite spot among photographers and kids alike (see the listing, later in this section), the coastline has other notable stretches.

Rialto Beach is the most accessible beach in the park, because the Mora Road runs to a parking lot just above it. The beach makes a good starting point for hikes along the park's coastline and is a great place for kids who like to search for wave-polished stones or peer into tide pools in search of sealife. One-and-a-half miles north of the parking lot lies Hole-in-the-Wall, a jutting piece of headland through which the surging surf has chiseled a tunnel that you can explore during low tide. You find a picnic area at the beach and camping nearby at Mora.

Although not as accessible, **La Push,** just below Rialto Beach, has a larger collection of sea stacks than Ruby Beach.

If you're worried about running into crowds at Rialto or Ruby beaches, try one of the six beaches along the coast between Ruby Beach and South Beach. Known simply as **Beach 1, Beach 2, Beach 3,** and so on, you reach these beaches via footpaths across from small pullouts on U.S. 101. Some of these beaches have tide pools to explore; others are great for beach-combing or clamming during the season. (Clamming season varies depending on the beach and type of clam. For more details, check with the nearest ranger station.)

Before you walk out across the rocks during low tide, make sure to check the tide table for the day and keep an eye on the incoming water or you can quickly find yourself stranded.

The rules of most national parks state that taking anything out of the park is illegal, but in Olympic you're allowed to collect a handful of stones or empty shells from the beaches. So you don't have to look nervously over your shoulder as you pocket a few.

Rialto Beach is at the end of Mora Road off Washington 110. La Push is at the end of Washington 110. The beaches on the coast between Ruby and South Beach are along U.S. 101.

Hoh Rain Forest

Overload your senses here. Your nose fills with the rich scent of the earth that nurtures the forest while your eyes try to decipher the varying hues of green that tint this emerald cathedral. Sitka spruce trees 8 feet thick climb skyward for 200 to 300 feet, mossy curtains droop from vines and big-leaf maples, and blankets of Oregon oxalis and waist-high Sword ferns cover the forest floor.

As you walk the forest's trails, be careful not to squish the Banana and European Black slugs, which are oversized snails traveling without their shells. These slimy critters come in various sizes and colors. The Banana Slug is the biggest (up to a foot long) and the most colorful, coming in greens, browns, and yellows. While looking for the slugs, you may spot large tracks left by the elk that live in the forest.

For my recommended hikes in the rain forest, see Hall of Mosses Trail and Spruce Nature Trail in "Taking a hike," later in this chapter.

The rain forest is at the end of Hoh River Rain Forest Road, which is roughly 10 miles south of Forks off U.S. 101.

Hurricane Ridge

If you visit Hurricane Ridge during any season but winter, you won't find much solitude. The ridge is immensely popular, and the drive there during warm-weather months often is done in convoy. But where else can you stand in one place and see both the ocean and a nearly 8,000-foot-tall peak covered with snow and glaciers?

On the 17-mile drive up to the ridge along Hurricane Ridge Road, you're quickly pulled out of the muggy lowlands and deposited near the roof of this corner of the world. On a clear day, from the trails that scamper across the ridge, you can gaze north to the Strait of Juan de Fuca and beyond to Canada. (See High Ridge and Alpine Hills, in "Taking a hike," later in this chapter.) To the south, snowy Mount Olympus and her sister peaks, which are home to 60 glaciers, tear at the horizon. As you stand on Hurricane Ridge under the summer sun, you may find yourself longing for a little shade.

If you abhor crowds, plan either an early-morning or late-afternoon trip to the ridge top.

For similar views and fewer people, go to nearby Deer Park, located at the end of a serpentine 15-mile-long road that begins outside the park just east of Port Angeles. What's the catch? The steep gravel road is off-limits to recreational vehicles and rigs hauling trailers. Plus, negotiating this road takes a lot longer than the paved Hurricane Ridge Road.

Hurricane Ridge is 17 miles south of Port Angeles on Hurricane Ridge Road.

Lake Crescent

You may think that you've been transported to New York's Adirondack region when you reach Lake Crescent on the north end of the park. Dense forests surround this glacial lake, and the shorefront Lake Crescent Lodge features the same dark paneling and stone fireplace that you would find in an Adirondack lodge. You can even settle into a lawn chair with a view of the lake.

Lake Crescent is a great place to rent a canoe or rowboat to ply the waters in search of the Beardslee or Crescenti trout that lurk far beneath the surface. This is a "catch and release" fishery, so pack your camera to record your catch. See "Keeping active," later in this chapter, for details on boating.

Near the Lake Crescent Lodge are the Storm King Ranger Station and a 1¼-mile trail that leads to **Marymere Falls,** a beautiful and feathery 90-foot waterfall. Along the trail, mosses, lichens, and ferns clutter the forest floor and climb up into the canopy. Narrow, single-log bridges twice cross Barnes Creek just before the falls. (These bridges are not difficult to cross, unless they're wet and slippery.) Just after you begin a steep climb up the hillside toward the top of the falls, a shortcut breaks off to the left and follows a more level, less strenuous path to an overlook opposite the falls. At the most, plan on a 90-minute round-trip, but if you're in a hurry, you can visit the falls and get back to your car in half that time.

Lake Crescent is roughly 21 miles west of Port Angeles on U.S. 101.

Ruby Beach

Having grown up in New Jersey, I'm a sucker for beaches. But Ruby Beach is nothing like the smooth, sandy beaches of my childhood. Towering stacks of basalt stand at the mouth of Cedar Creek that pours into the ocean here. The stacks are remnants of cliffs that were slowly, but steadily, pounded into sand by the waves.

A short trail winds down from the parking lot to the beach and offers a great photo op of these stacks. But don't immediately turn around and head back to your car after snapping a few pictures. This beach is a beachcomber's dream, with polished agates, tangles of drift logs, and other flotsam tossed up by the waves. Pockets of water on the beach are alive with marine life; spend some time searching in the small pools for green anemones, sea urchins, shellfish, and brightly colored sea stars, also known as starfish.

 Most people congregate near the stacks at the creek mouth; if you walk 10 minutes north or south along the beach, you leave most of humanity behind. The best time to visit Ruby Beach is at low tide, because the dropping water level reveals more water pockets full of marine life.

 If you're determined (and foolhardy enough) to dash into the surf for a dip, watch for rogue logs that were washed out to sea by rivers after being toppled by storms. Waves toss these around like toothpicks, and you can't win a collision with them.

Ruby Beach is along U.S. 101 almost 8 miles north of the Kalaloch Information Station.

 ### Sol Duc Hot Springs

Although the Sol Duc area has hot, spring-fed swimming pools, the reason to visit is not for the pools — although the watery diversion is good for controlling any troublesome kids in your car. The real reason is for the roughly 1½-mile round-trip hike to Sol Duc Falls (see the description under "Taking a hike," later in this chapter). Although less than half as tall as Marymere Falls, these falls offer more water volume and plunge into a rectangular flume that the Sol Duc River has cut through the bedrock. A wooden bridge just below the falls is a great spot for photographs.

The trail to the falls also provides access into the backcountry. From it you can hike to the High Divide for stunning views of the Hoh Valley and Mount Olympus, explore the Seven Lakes Basin, or trek to the headwaters of the Bogachiel River.

Sol Duc Hot Springs is 40 miles west of Port Angeles via U.S. 101 and the Sol Duc Road.

Capturing Olympic on film

Make sure your camera bag is well stocked for a trip to Olympic National Park. Along with having a wide range of films — slow-speed films for rain forest settings and fast-speed films for shots of crashing surf and those bright snowfields near Hurricane Ridge — you'll definitely appreciate a good tripod.

For the ultimate rain-forest shot, spend time in the Hoh Rain Forest. If you can't find something there to suit your needs, you're not a very good photographer. The hike to Marymere Falls provides more opportunities for lush, emerald-green old growth-forest photographs, although the best subject in this end of the park is the beautiful waterfall. If you're a fan of waterfalls, another good one to frame with your lens is Sol Duc Falls, which you find about a mile down the trail from the trailhead at the end of the Sol Duc Road just beyond the Sol Duc Hot Springs Resort.

Timing is a prerequisite for a good shot of the waves smashing into the sea stacks along the park's coastline. In my humble opinion, late afternoon is the time to photograph here, because the setting sun's rays wonderfully backlight the crashing waves.

Hurricane Ridge is perhaps the best spot you can reach — without hiking — to capture the park's alpine personality. And if you tire of taking pictures of Mount Olympus and her fellow snow-shrouded peaks, turn around and take a picture of the Strait of Juan de Fuca to the north.

Taking a hike

With its coastlines, dense rain forests, and alpine terrain, Olympic offers too many hiking opportunities for you to drive through this park and stay in your room. You have beaches to comb, rain forests to explore, and high country trails to cruise along. In all, more than 600 miles of marked trails and 955 designated campsites exist in the park. Following are just some of the hiking possibilities.

See "Arriving in the park," earlier in this chapter, for information on backcountry hiking and fees.

Bogachiel River

Your energy level determines how far you can hike on this trail, which features a rain forest setting similar to that of the Hoh Rain Forest but without the crowds. The trail runs about 21½ miles from the park boundary to the junction of the Mink Lake and Little Divide trails. The first few miles wind through thick rain forest with towering Douglas firs, Sitka spruce, Western cedar, and big-leaf maples, all wearing mosses. Along the way are several stream crossings. The Bogachiel Shelter, 6 miles from the trailhead, is a good destination for an overnight, round-trip hike. Of course, heartier hikers may want to go further.

Got goats?

Mountain goats arrived on the peninsula in the 1920s when a dozen of them from Alaska and British Columbia were imported to the region. Unfortunately, the goats did tremendously well in the climate, and by the early 1980s, their population had surpassed 1,000. Their proliferation created problems for the park's subalpine meadows because the goats heavily browsed the vegetation and also created dusty wallows by rolling on the ground. A live-capture program in the late 1980s managed to trim the population, but it was discontinued out of concern for the safety of the rangers involved who needed helicopters to reach the goats. These days, several hundred goats still live in the park, and officials are debating how best to deal with them.

Distance: 43¼ miles round-trip. Level: Easy to moderate in the lowlands, steeper as you head inland. Access: 5 miles south of Forks, turn onto Undie Road and drive 5 miles to the trailhead.

Cape Alava/Sand Point Loop

This great three-legged loop trail offers ocean views, beach camping, *petroglyphs* (prehistoric rock art), and an easy round-trip back to your car. The trail begins on a cedar-plank boardwalk that winds about 3 miles through coastal marsh and grasslands to the beach and Cape Alava, the westernmost point in the Lower 48. As you make your way 3 miles south on the beach, be sure to look for the petroglyphs on the rocks along the shore next to the high-tide mark. The end of this leg is marked by the Sand Point Trail, another boardwalk stretch that runs 3 miles back to the ranger station at Ozette.

Before you embark on this trek, check the tide charts posted at the trailhead. Take care on the boardwalks, which can get slippery when wet.

Distance: 9¼ miles round-trip. Level: Easy. Access: Ozette Ranger Station.

Glacier Meadows

This is one of the routes taken by climbers heading to Mount Olympus. Early on, the hiking is easy and captivating as you pass through the rain forest with its dense vegetation and towering trees. If you're alert, you may be able to spot the Roosevelt elk that live in the area. The trail's first 12 miles follow the Hoh River Valley and are easy to walk. Beyond the intersection with the Hoh Lake Trail, you enter a deep gorge past Elk Lake and on to Glacier Meadows and the toe of Blue Glacier on Mount Olympus. Plan this hike carefully. Snowmelt from the glaciers picks up in late July and can make travel tricky. Hiking this trail round-trip can take several days; most people take four days.

Distance: 37 miles round-trip. Level: Easy early on, then moderate as you begin to climb into the high country and encounter stream crossings, most over foot logs or bridges. Access: Hoh Rain Forest.

Hall of Mosses Trail

If you have time for only one hike in the Hoh Rain Forest, this is it. Hiking the loop takes about 40 minutes. The trail winds through a green kingdom of lush vegetation. It's not steamy, like a tropical rain forest, but you can feel the humidity. Along the trail, *epiphytes* — plants that grow on other plants — in the form of spongy club mosses, mosses, lichens, liverworts, and licorice ferns scramble across tree trunks and limbs and up into the leafy canopy where they manage to block most of the sun's rays from reaching the floor. Scattered here and there on the ground are toppled trees and rotting stumps that serve as nurseries for the next generation of trees. Shallow, crystal clear creeks flow through the forest.

Distance: ¾ miles. Level: Easy. Access: Hoh Rain Forest Visitor Center.

High Ridge and Alpine Hills

The short, paved, 1-mile High Ridge Route is great for kids: It's short enough so it won't tire them out, offers great views of Mount Olympus and her sister peaks to the south, and contains interpretive exhibits to teach them something. If you're up for more, follow the unpaved trail to Sunrise Ridge, which, on clear days, serves up sweeping views of the Strait of Juan de Fuca and Port Angeles to the north.

Distance: 1–8 miles round-trip. Level: Easy to moderate. Access: Hurricane Ridge Visitor Center.

Sol Duc Falls

Although short, this picturesque forest hike offers great photo opportunities, a refreshing waterfall, and kid-friendly hiking. Streams jumping through moss-covered boulders, the dense emerald forest, and the cascading waterfall along the Sol Duc River are perfect photo backgrounds. Just below the falls, you find a bridge across the river that provides a great vantage point to see how the river has cut a channel through the bedrock.

Distance: 1½ miles round-trip. Level: Easy. Access: Near Sol Duc Ranger Station.

Spruce Nature Trail

This trail through the Hoh Rain Forest takes about an hour to negotiate. Because this section of forest is younger, the route is not as densely packed with vegetation as the Hall of Mosses Trail. A highlight, however, includes a side trail to the Hoh River where you can see *glacial flour,* finely ground sediment that the Hoh Glacier scraped from the bedrock as it inched its way down below the snowfields beneath Middle and East peaks. The flour gives the Hoh River its milky appearance.

Distance: 1¼ miles. Level: Easy. Access: Hoh Rain Forest Visitor Center.

One-day wonder

The only way to cross Olympic National Park is on foot. Although U.S. 101 does wrap around three sides of the park, its route runs through the Olympic National Forest, not the park. To get into the park, you need to shoot down spur roads that can run up to 17 miles in length. As a result, if you're determined to see as much of the park as possible, you're going to have to drive quite a bit and pack and unpack your bags every day.

But don't despair. You can get a surprisingly good feel for the park in one day. It'll be a long day, for sure, but you'll come away having sampled its three main environments. (Unless otherwise mentioned, see "Exploring the top attractions," earlier in this chapter, for information on the attractions mentioned in this itinerary.)

The best place to start this journey is in **Port Angeles.** After rising early and eating a good breakfast, if weather allows leave for **Hurricane Ridge** in time to get there by 8 a.m. On a clear day, you'll be rewarded with eye-popping views of Mount Olympus and the Strait of Juan de Fuca.

A good, quick hike on Hurricane Ridge is the High Ridge route. After an initial 1-mile walk along a paved trail that offers good interpretive panels, you can continue to Sunrise Ridge, with its killer views of the strait to the north and the glacier-coated peaks to the south.

By 10 a.m. you should be ready to head back down to Port Angeles and the **Olympic National Park Visitor Center.** Here you can load up on any brochures or additional guidebooks that strike your fancy and also get grounded in the region's cultures and natural history.

Your next stop is the **Hoh Rain Forest,** 91 miles and roughly two hours away by car. It'll probably be approaching midafternoon by the time you near the rain forest, so stop at the **Hard Rain Café and Mercantile** for lunch (see "Where to Dine," later in this chapter). The two-beef-patty Mount Olympus Burger and an order of fries will keep you going for the rest of the afternoon.

After lunch, continue to the rain forest, where a hike through **Hall of Mosses** (see the "Taking a hike" section) is mandatory. The hike won't take long, but the route does lead you through some of the park's best rain forest. Following the hike, you can either continue down the nearby Spruce Nature Trail, which leads along the fringe of the rain forest and out to the Hoh River, or spend some time in the visitor center's tiny museum with its solid primer on rain forests.

If you manage to stay fairly on schedule, you can make it from the Hoh Rain Forest to **Ruby Beach,** roughly 30 miles away, in time to enjoy a stroll along the beach and get some great sunset photographs. Take a short stroll whether it's a clear day or raining — walking through mists can be just as interesting as walking in sunshine, plus you can get some beautiful photographs of the sea stacks laced with fog.

A great way to end your day is with dinner and a room at the **Lake Quinault Lodge,** which is 40 miles from Ruby Beach, just outside the park's southwestern corner (see "Where to Stay," later in this chapter). This gorgeous, lakefront, log lodge was visited by President Franklin Delano Roosevelt in October 1937 during a trip he conducted to determine whether a national park should be established here.

If you have more time

Although not as big as Yellowstone and some other sprawling Western parks, Olympic National Park requires more than a day or two if you're determined to see it all. (Well, seeing it all can take years.)

If you do have a few extra days, consider a trip to **Lake Ozette** on the coast. Although the lake is popular, a visit is well worth your time. The focal point of this area is the 7,787-acre freshwater lake, but you're also close to the coast with its tide pools, old-growth coastal rain forest, and, if you look hard enough, petroglyphs. (Hint: You can find them on Wedding Rocks found halfway between Cape Alava and Sand Point.) The lake's campground has only 14 sites, so if you're lucky enough to get one, you can enjoy relative solitude at night. The area also has backcountry lake sites that you reach by boat, and more backcountry sites along the coast.

For a hike in the area, see Cape Alava/Sand Point Loop under "Taking a hike," earlier in this chapter. The 9¾-mile hike from Cape Alava to Shi Shi Beach is another good option, if you don't mind getting wet. The trail crosses the Ozette River, which can be waist deep at times.

Ranger programs

Campfire talks, guided walks through the rainforest or subalpine meadows, and beachcombing are the hallmarks of ranger-led activities in the park.

Definitely plan to accompany one of the rangers on the tidepool beach walks that they lead daily during the summer months from Mora and Kalaloch. Kids and adults alike love these 2½-hour hikes, which investigate the marine life of tide pools. Meeting times vary according to the tides. Check the *Bugler,* the newspaper that you receive upon entering the park, or park bulletin boards, for exact times.

Another great family outing is stargazing atop Hurricane Ridge. With much of the light pollution left behind in Port Angeles, the inky black skies above the ridge come alive on clear nights with flickering stars and planets. Rangers occasionally lead stargazing parties, so consult the park's newspaper for dates.

Although you can guide yourself along the trails through the Hoh Rain Forest, ranger-led hikes held daily provide background on the forest's plant and animal dynamics, as well as on the nearby Hoh River.

For families with small children, the ubiquitous campfire talks are held regularly at various locations around the park; check the *Bugler* for dates and times. You can also pick up information on the Junior Ranger Program at the main park visitor center in Port Angeles (see Chapter 4 for information on this program).

Keeping active

In addition to hiking, Olympic National Park offers several opportunities for outdoor fun.

Boating

Although large and often windy, glacier-carved Lake Crescent is a beautiful place to do a little paddling. Lush, green forests rise straight up from the shores of this 624-foot deep lake. You can find boat ramps on U.S. 101 at Storm King (near the middle of the lake) and at Fairholm (at the west end of the lake). The Log Cabin Resort, on East Beach Road on the lake's northeast shore, has a private boat ramp.

You can rent canoes at **Fairholm General Store and Cafe** (☎ **360-928-3325**) at the west end of the lake or at the **Log Cabin Resort,** 3138 E. Beach Rd. (☎ **360-928-3325**), on the lake's northeast shore. Lake Crescent Lodge rents rowboats (☎ **360-928-3211**).

If you're paddling, be careful not to stray too far out from shore because midday winds can quickly whip up the lake.

Fishing

If you love to fish, you've come to the right park. However, most fish caught in the park's freshwater streams and lakes must be released. Because fishing regulations can change from year-to-year, to keep track of what you can and can't take home, pick up a copy of the fishing regulations from any ranger station or visitor center.

Spotting the local wildlife

With its vast array of wildlife, Olympic National Park offers incredible opportunities for seeing animals in their natural habitats. Where else can you see both whales and black bears on the same day? Even more fascinating is that the glaciations that once isolated the peninsula from the rest of the continent led to the evolution of at least 18 unique types of animals, including the **Olympic snow mole**, the **Olympic short-tailed weasel**, and the **Olympic marmot**.

Tidepools along the coast are the best places to spot a variety of the park's wildlife in one place. In these shallow pools, you usually can find **green anemones** (small, colorful, spineless creatures) with their tentacles floating in the water. If you stick your finger into the middle of them, or if one snares food with its tentacles, the anemone pulls its tentacles inward. You may also spot **sea stars** (starfish) and **hermit crabs** in these pools, as well as a variety of **mussels**.

While you're searching tide pools, from time to time remember to take a look out at the ocean. If you're lucky, you may spot a **California sea lion** or perhaps a **harbor seal.** These furry critters enjoy sunning themselves on off-shore rocks when they're not frolicking in the water. A good time to look for them is in late summer and early fall when they migrate up the coastline toward the Strait of Juan de Fuca and Puget Sound. Harder to spot are **Northern fur seals,** which prefer the waters off Cape Flaherty on the peninsula's northwestern tip.

East Coasters usually need to board a boat to spot whales, but in Olympic National Park all you need to do is be on the right beach at the right time of year. If you visit in the spring or fall, head to the coast to look for waterspouts made by passing **gray whales.** These guys like to feed just off the beaches where the Hoh and Quillayute rivers pour into the Pacific. Another good place to look for them is from the bluffs of Beach 6 along U.S. 101 north of Kalaloch Lodge. Rangers at the **Kalaloch Ranger Station** (☎ 360-962-2283) can provide information on the whale migrations.

Moving inland, you may cross paths with **Roosevelt elk.** Slightly bigger than their Rocky Mountain cousins, the park almost was named after them. They're easiest to spot in the early morning or evening browsing in old clearcuts in the Olympic National Forest that surrounds the park. The Hoh and the Quinault valleys are also good places to look for elk. Just as visible are **Columbia black-tailed deer,** which prefer Hurricane Ridge during the early morning or late-afternoon.

Black bears are not so easily spotted, but they're out there. In early summer along Hurricane Hill, you may see them munching on the lush vegetation.

If you head into the high country, you may spot a **mountain goat** clattering along a rocky ridge. These animals are not native to the park. (See the "Got goats?" sidebar, earlier in the chapter.)

Harder to spot, but park residents just the same, are **cougars, bobcats, weasels, river and sea otters, beavers, marmots, flying squirrels, two varieties of skunk, coyotes,** and **black bears.** A former park resident that may one day return is the **gray wolf.** Early settlers wiped out the peninsula's native wolf population in the 1930s. A wildlife survey released in 1999 determined that the park's habitat and

(continued)

(continued)

prey base can support a population of 56 wolves, although no recovery plan has been prepared.

In the park's rivers and lakes and in the ocean off the coast are five types of **salmon,** four **trout** species (including the Beardslee and Crescenti trout species native to Lake Crescent), three kinds of **char,** as well as **whitefish, shiners, lampreys, bass, suckers, perch, Northern pikeminnow,** and **sculpin.**

If you're lucky, as I was, you may see a **bald eagle** hoisting one of these fish out of the park's waters. Dozens of bird species travel through Olympic at various times of the year, taking advantage of its fisheries and forests for food and shelter. Along with the more common **blackbirds, finches, ravens,** and **sparrows,** you can spot various **shorebirds, woodpeckers, pelicans,** and **loons.**

Perhaps the park's most comical-looking bird is the **tufted puffin.** Their bodies are covered with black feathers, and they have large, bright-orange bills and heads covered with white feathers that sweep back into yellowish tufts. Unfortunately, you probably won't spot any of them because they avoid people and spend most of their time on off-shore islands, although people who have visited Cape Flattery, which is outside the park's boundaries, have seen them.

You don't need a Washington state fishing license inside the park, but if you plan to go surf fishing in the ocean or clamming, you need to stop by a sporting goods store to get the requisite state licenses.

Snowshoeing and cross-country skiing

You can have a satisfying winter trek on any of the snow-covered roads leading into the mountains. However, if you want great views, head to Hurricane Ridge with the rest of the winter crowd and set out on any of the area's trails. Cross-country and downhill ski rentals and snowshoe rentals are available from the ski shop on the lower level of the **Hurricane Ridge Visitor Center** (no telephone).

White-water rafting

In and around the park, you can white-water raft, enjoy a scenic float, or go sea kayaking. Guided trips generally last a half-day, and canoe and kayak rentals are available. For details, contact **Olympic Raft & Kayak,** 123 Lake Aldwell Rd., Port Angeles (☎ **888-452-1443** or 360-452-1443; Internet: www.raftandkayak.com).

Escaping the rain

On a rainy day, a good place to take your kids is the visitor center at park headquarters in Port Angeles (see "Finding information," earlier in this chapter). Not only does this center have top-notch displays on

Native Americans and wildlife, but younger kids enjoy the Discovery Room, where they can play in a miniature log ranger station, learn about ecology, and build a totem pole with felt stick-on pieces. Older kids are kept busy in the main visitor center with the virtual scavenger hunt that requires them to study the exhibits so they can answer questions about the park.

Where to Stay

The park offers only a few options when it comes to putting a roof over your head. Two are at Lake Crescent, the third is just south of there, and the fourth is along the coast.

Winter offers the year's best lodging rates. You can usually find a bargain at Kalaloch Lodge during the winter months.

Lodging in the park

Kalaloch Lodge
$$–$$$ **North of South Beach**

The lure of this lodge and its huddled cabins is the sea-front location. But be careful when making reservations, because only some cabins feature ocean views (and wood-burning stoves). Although the cedar-shingled lodge and some of the cabins perch on a bluff above the mouth of Kalaloch Creek and the sandy coast, some cabins are across the highway and lack views. The cabins accommodate between four to seven people. Despite the coastal location here, you find more romantic accommodations at Lake Crescent Lodge and Lake Quinault Lodge, the latter just south of the park.

Still, this lodge is the only one on the coast within the park's boundaries. If you reserve a cabin with a kitchenette, you need to bring your own cookware and utensils. Although you would be wise to make a reservation at least four months ahead of your arrival, the lodge holds five rooms for walk-in business.

157151 U.S. 101 (North of South Beach). ☎ *360-962-2271. Fax: 360-962-3391. Internet:* www.visitkalaloch.com. *8 rooms, 2 suites, 44 cabins. Rack rates: $89–$135 double; $149–$244 suites; $115–$258 cabins, some with kitchenettes. Lower rates weekdays Nov–May. AE, MC, V.*

Lake Crescent Lodge
$–$$$$ **Lake Crescent**

A great, peaceful location on the park's north end, the lodge is just minutes from Marymere Falls and less than an hour from Hurricane Ridge.

Although the historic lodge is picturesque, I recommend the fireplace-equipped cabins. Located along the lakeshore, these cabins offer better views than the lodge rooms, have their own bathrooms (the lodge rooms don't), and are simply more comfortable. Motel-style rooms with their own bathrooms are also available, but only some of them have lake views.

416 Lake Crescent Rd. ☎ *360-928-3211. Internet:* www.lakecrescentlodge.com. *36 rooms, 20 cottages. Rack rate: $43–$72 double without bath, $65–$152 double with bath; $70–$205 cottage. Open late April to Oct. AE, CB, DC, DISC, MC, V.*

Log Cabin Resort
$$$ Lake Crescent

This turn-of-the-century resort on the north shore of Lake Crescent offers some of the cheapest lodging in the park. The four lodge rooms are the best deal, featuring lake and mountain views, a private bathroom, and a queen bed and a queen futon. The resort also has chalets on the shoreline with lake and mountain views. The chalets have bathrooms and showers and sleep up to six people. You also find an assorment of cabins, ranging from those with kitchenettes and bathrooms to simple cabins without indoor plumbing (and a communal bathroom is nearby). If you opt for a no-plumbing cabin, note that you need to supply your own bedding.

3183 E. Beach Rd. ☎ *360-928-3325. Fax: 360-928-2088. Internet:* www.logcabinresort.net. *4 rooms; 12 chalets; 3 kichenette cabins; 5 cabins with bath; 4 cabins without bath. Rack rates: $117 double; $142 chalet; $105 kitchenette cabin; $88 cabin with bath; $60 cabin without bath. DISC, MC, V. Cabins closed Oct–April.*

Sol Duc Hot Springs Resort
$$$ Port Angeles

These cabins are nothing fancy, but the hot springs are nearby, so if a good soak is all that matters, stay here. But if the heavy traffic of campers, day trippers, and other resort guests is likely to spoil your vacation, head elsewhere. If you want to handle your own meals, opt for the higher-end cabins, because they include kitchens. You won't find any phones, radios, or televisions in the cabins, but the lodge has payphones. The lodge also offers a decent restaurant, pool-side deli, espresso bar, and grocery. You can arrange a massage, but they're pretty pricy, starting at $45 for 30 minutes.

Sol Duc Road (near Eagle). ☎ *360-327-3583. Fax: 360-327-3593. Internet:* www.northolympic.com/solduc. *32 cabins. Rack rates: $110–$130 cabin for two. AE, DISC, MC, V.*

Top lodging outside the park

Best Western–Olympic Lodge
$$–$$$$$ **Port Angeles**

This location is a great vacation base camp, with views of both the Olympic Mountains and the Strait of Juan de Fuca. Adults who don't get enough exercise in the park can work out in the fitness room, and kids can head out to the heated pool. Rooms are spacious with king- or queen-sized beds and are equipped with coffee makers and dataport phones for those who can't leave their work behind. A golf course is next door.

140 Del Guzzi Dr. ☎ *800-600-2993 or 360-452-2993. Fax: 360-452-1497. Internet:* www.portangeleshotelmotel.com. *104 rooms, 1 suite. A/C, TV, TEL. Rack rates: $89–$299 double. AE, CB, DC, DISC, V.*

Lake Quinault Lodge
$$$–$$$$ **Quinault**

Just beyond the park's southern boundary, this lakeshore lodge is worth a stay because of its setting. Built in 1926 (after a fire destroyed the original log hotel on this site), Quinault Lodge exudes a backwoods elegance. The lobby boasts a huge fireplace and the grounds include a small beachfront where you can rent a boat for a paddle. The accommodations range from small rooms in the main lodge to modern rooms in outlying buildings with wicker furniture and little balconies. Some rooms have fireplaces. The annex rooms are least attractive and have distressingly thin walls and ceilings. None of the rooms has a TV or telephone. For information on the lodge's restaurant, see "Where to Eat" in the next section.

South Shore Road. ☎ *800-562-6672 or 360-288-2900. Internet:* www.visitlake quinault.com. *92 rooms, 1 suites. A/C. Rack rates: June–Sept $105–$180 double, $250 suite; Oct–May $68–$130 double, $195 suite. AE, MC, V.*

The Tudor Inn
$$–$$$ **Port Angeles**

This inn is a charming getaway winter or summer. Thanks to its setting in a residential area 13 blocks from the waterfront, this quaint inn offers a quieter setting than other downtown accommodations in Port Angeles. Pushing a century in age (it was built in 1910), the home was fully restored in 1995 to bring out the most of its Tudor charm. The bedrooms, located upstairs and featuring European antiques, are fairly simple, yet comfortable with private baths and king- or queen-size beds. Several rooms have views of the Olympic Mountains to the south; the best view is from the Tudor Room. The main-floor lounge and library have warming fireplaces. Outside is a large yard with beautiful gardens. The owners will arrange cross-country ski or snowshoe tours in winter.

1108 S. Oak St. ☎ *866-286-2224 or 360-452-3138. Internet:* www.tudorinn.com. *5 rooms. Rack rates: Late May to early Oct. $90–$145 double, mid-Oct to mid-May $85–$135. AE, DISC, MC, V. Rates include breakfast. No kids under 12 years old.*

Runner-up lodgings

The Forks Motel

$$–$$$ **Forks** You can find standard motel rooms as well as two-bedroom units with kitchens at this property on the park's west side. The Pacific Coast is just 20 minutes away, and the Hoh Rain Forest is a 40-minute drive. 351 S. Forks Ave. ☎ **800-544-3416.** Internet: www.forks motel.com.

Manitou Lodge

$$–$$$ **Near Rialto Beach** This lodge started its life as a hunting retreat but now offers seven rooms on 10 wooded acres just a few miles from Rialto Beach. Your room rate buys you a full breakfast as well as cookies, tea, coffee, and hot chocolate in the afternoon. Kilmer Road. (Call for directions.) ☎ **360-374-6295.** Internet: www.manitoulodge.com.

Olympic Suites

$$ **Forks** Not only can you inexpensively rent a one- or two-bedroom room with a full kitchen here, but the property is surrounded by thick forest and close to the coast and, if you're an angler, steelhead fishing. 800 Olympic Dr. ☎ **800-262-3433.** Internet: www.olympicsuitesinn.com.

Port Angeles Inn

$$–$$$ **Port Angeles** Just a block from the main drag and two blocks from the ferries, this inn offers rooms with a view of either the Strait of Juan de Fuca or the Olympic mountains. *111 E. Second St.* ☎ **800-421-0706** *or 360-452-9285. Internet:* www.portangelesinn.com.

Campgrounds

The camping options in the park are just as varied as the scenery, with both developed campground and primitive backcountry sites available in the rain forests, along the coast, and in the high country. Even with 15 campgrounds and more than 900 sites inside the park, lining up a spot to pitch your tent or park your camper can be tricky. The weather, lack of an all-inclusive reservation system, and restrictions against RVs and trailers can all conspire against you.

Campground reservations are restricted to the group sites at Kalaloch and Mora. Everywhere else is first-come, first-served. Lining up your campsite early in the day is always wise. This practice is mandatory on nice weekends when the weather lures more people to the park.

If you want to camp in the off-season, your only options are the campgrounds at Elwha, Heart o' the Hills, Hoh, Kalaloch, and Mora. Others are open seasonally or closed during low-use periods. Because weather can keep some campgrounds closed longer than you may expect, call **park headquarters** (☎ 360-565-3130) to see what's open before you make plans.

So, what are the tricks to landing a campsite? Simply put, knowing the territory and the trends. To enhance your odds and improve your selection, arrive early in the day and in mid-week, if possible.

Although Olympic's campgrounds are scattered around the park, the crowds are not. The Sol Duc and Kalaloch campgrounds usually fill first, followed by Hoh and Altaire. **Sol Duc Hot Springs,** with its 80 sites, is also popular because of the pools there.

Although **Lake Ozette** is remote, it's a favorite among many and can be crowded. Fifteen campsites are on the lake and accessible by car. More sites are available in the backcountry; you can reserve them by phone (☎ 360-565-3100). The Ericsons Bay site on the lake promises solitude because you can reach it only by boat — it's well worth the effort.

A not-so-crowded spot is the Deer Park campground. Close to Port Angeles, **Deer Park** has 18 sites accessible only by a narrow gravel road, which switchbacks its way from sea level to 5,400 feet. RVs and trailers are prohibited on the road.

The park offers many options for **backcountry camping.** Reservations are available in a few spots, too. All the sites on the Ozette Coastal Loop require advance reservations; other popular wilderness camp areas, including Grand Valley and the Seven Lakes Basin, also offer reservations. To make reservations and obtain camping permits for the park's backcountry wilderness, contact the park's **Wilderness Information Center** (☎ 360-565-3100).

Where to Eat

The park has few dining options, but you visit Olympic for the scenery, not the food, right? The dining rooms at Lake Crescent Lodge and the Log Cabin Resort, both on Lake Crescent, are open seasonally. Dining rooms at Kalaloch Lodge on the coast and in the Lake Quinault Lodge on the eastern shore of Lake Quinault are open year-round. On the northeastern end of the park, head into Port Angeles for a better variety of eateries.

Hark! What grows there?

From 200-foot-tall **Sitka spruce trees** to hard-to-find **calypso orchids**, the vegetative side of Olympic National Park can be just as dazzling as its wildlife. The rain forests are heavy with **spruce** and **big-leaf maples** draped in mosses and lichens, and the somewhat drier lowland forests feature **Douglas fir, Western hemlocks, Western red cedar, red alder**, and, in especially dry areas, **Pacific madrone**, a red-barked tree that peels its outer layers much like a tourist who has spent too much time in the sun.

In the high country of Hurricane Ridge and above are twisted and gnarled subalpine **fir trees** contorted by the winds and heavy snows, as well as dainty **white avalanche** and yellow **glacier lilies, marigolds, paintbrushes,** and **buttercups** that burst into color when the snows melt.

Throughout the park are a number of plant species unique to the peninsula, including Olympic Mountain Milkvetch, Piper's Bellflower, Flett's Fleabane, Olympic Mountain Rockmat, and Flett's Violet.

Top restaurants in the park

Kalaloch Lodge
$$–$$$ **North of South Beach   SEAFOOD**

With the ocean a stone's throw from the kitchen, it's no surprise that seafood dominates the dinner menu. Delectable choices may include a grilled salmon filet served with lemon-dill butter or a full pound of peel-and-eat shrimp. You also find vegetarian dishes and chops on the menu. Near the front of the lodge is a coffee shop where you can order breakfast or a sandwich for lunch.

157151 U.S. 101. ☎ *360-962-2271. Reservations recommended. Main courses: $4.50–$9 breakfasts; $5–$10 lunch; $11–$20 dinner. AE, MC, V. Open: 7 a.m.–9 p.m.*

Lake Crescent Lodge
$$–$$$ **Lake Crescent   AMERICAN**

The picturesque view of the lake through this restaurant's two walls of windows lends great atmosphere to your meals. The dinner menu blends creative seafood dishes like "Triple Fins," an entree of salmon, mahi, and halibut, with pastas, and steaks, while seafood omelets, traditional egg dishes, fresh fruit crepes, and "Candy Apple French Toast" hold down the breakfast menu. A corner lounge in the lobby serves up drinks that you can enjoy in front of the fireplace or on the veranda.

416 Lake Crescent Rd. ☎ 360-928-3211. Reservations required for dinner. Main courses: $4.50–$7.95 breakfast; $5.95–$10.95 lunch; $9.95–$22 dinner. AE, DC, DISC, MC, V. Open: Late April to Oct 7:30–10 a.m., noon to 2:30p.m., 6–9 p.m.

Log Cabin Resort

$–$$$$ Lake Crescent   AMERICAN

The dinner menu is built around seafood caught locally, although you can get steak and chicken, too.

3183 E. Beach Rd. ☎ 360-928-3325. Reservations required for dinner. Main courses: $4.50–$13.95 breakfast; $3.95–$13.95 lunch; $8.75–$35 dinner. DISC, MC, V. Open: Mid-May to Sept 8–10:30 a.m., 11 a.m.–8 p.m.

Top restaurants outside the park

Bella Italia

$$–$$$ Port Angeles   ITALIAN

If you're hungry when you pass through Port Angeles, stop for some of western Washington's best Italian food. This street-level restaurant starts you out with a basket of bread with an olive oil, balsamic vinegar, garlic, and herb dipping sauce. Along with the traditional Italian dishes, the menu includes salmon ravioli, a smoked salmon fettuccine, and steamed clams and mussels. Nightly specialities creatively blend seafood with local vegetables. Brunch is available on Sunday.

118 E. First St. ☎ 360-457-5442. Reservations recommended. Main courses: $12–$24. AE, DISC, MC, V. Open: Sun–Thurs 4–9 p.m., Fri–Sat 4–10 p.m.

Hard Rain Cafe and Mercantile

$ Forks   AMERICAN

You can pick up postcards, local artworks, souvenirs, and a noontime meal at this funky cafe that doubles as a mini-grocery. This restaurant is a great place to stop for a bite either on the way to or from the Hoh Rain Forest. You can take your meal with you or sit out on the porch and enjoy the sunshine.

5763 Upper Hoh Rd. ☎ 360-374-9288. Main courses: $6.50–$9.50 lunch. MC, V. Open: Daily summer 8 a.m.–8 p.m., winter 9 a.m.– 7.p.m.

Lake Quinault Lodge

$$–$$$ Quinault   AMERICAN

This lodge is a sister to Kalaloch, and the menu is just as inspiring. You can start with a bowl of homemade clam chowder and move on to a seafood pasta dish with halibut, salmon, Chilean shrimp, and clams sauteed with mushrooms and red onions. Or you can sate yourself with the Cajun Chicken Pasta. The dining room fronts the lake and offers wonderful sunsets.

South Shore Rd. ☎ **360-288-2900** *or 800-562-6672 in Washington and Oregon. Reservations recommended. Main courses: $4–$14 breakfast; $7–$14 lunch; $15–$28 dinner. AE, MC, V. Open: Daily 7 a.m.–9 p.m.*

Fast Facts: Olympic

Area Code
☎ 360.

ATM
None in the park, but you can find them in Port Angeles or Forks.

Emergency
☎ 911

Fees
$10 per vehicle per week; $5 for walk-ins.

Fishing License
Not required within the park, but stop by ranger and visitor centers for regulations.

Hospitals
Olympic Memorial Hospital, 939 Caroline Street, Port Angeles, WA (☎ 360-417-7000); and Forks Community Hospital, 530 Bogachiel Way, Forks, WA (☎ 360-374-6271).

Information
Olympic National Park, Visitor Center, 600 East Park Avenue, Port Angeles, WA 98362; ☎ 360-565-3130.

Lost and Found
☎ 360-565-3000

Pharmacies
Rite Aid Pharmacies, 110 Plaza St., Port Angeles (☎ 360-457-3456); and Safeway 110 E. 3rd St., Port Angeles (☎ 360-457-0788).

Post Office
424 E. First St., Port Angeles; and E. Division St., Forks.

Road Conditions and Weather
☎ 360-565-3131 (recorded) or ☎ 360-565-3132 (visitor center).

Taxes
Lodging and meal rates vary depending on location.

Time Zone
Pacific standard time.

Web Site
www.nps.gov/olym.

Chapter 19

Sequoia and Kings Canyon National Parks

. . . .

In This Chapter

▶ Discovering tall trees, rugged canyons, and cool caves

▶ Planning your trip

▶ Exploring above ground and below

▶ Finding the best beds and meals

. . . .

Some people say that Congress doesn't always act rationally. As evidence, these naysayers can point to Sequoia and Kings Canyon national parks — two parks in Northern California that exist where one would suffice. They share a common border and management, and they encompass much of the same fantastic High Sierra backcountry.

The parks' aesthetic and natural beauty profits from the lesson the National Park Service learned from nearby Yosemite, which is overrun by visitors during the summer months: Easy access and ample amenities threaten the park's very nature. As a result, Kings Canyon and Sequoia have few man-made attractions and are best experienced on foot.

Kings Canyon is far off the beaten path at the end of a long, circuitous, and steep road. The brakes on your car may hate you for venturing down the steep and twisting stretch of California 180 that leads here (as will any passengers who are afraid of heights). But after you reach the cobbled banks of the raging South Fork of the Kings River, you'll know the trip was worth it.

Kings Canyon National Park needs no frills to augment nature's beauty. A day spent watching the river seethe and roil as it plunges wildly downhill through its riverbed of boulders can nurture your soul. The thrill of hooking one of the trout that lurk in the stream's eddies isn't such a bad thing, either. The park has meadows for strolls (as long as you're well-lathered with bug repellent during the height of summer) and short hikes that serve as samplers for longer forays into the high country. Plus, the scenery is incredible — the park is a miniature Yosemite. Surrounding the Cedar Grove area, towering cliffs of granite similar to those that made Yosemite famous rise above the meadows. But Kings Canyon feels wilder than Yosemite because of a fortunate lack of crowds and development.

Sequoia, meanwhile, also is relatively off the beaten path and minimally developed. The only accommodations, at Wuksachi Lodge, are subdued and don't overwhelm the wonderfully forested setting. A day's drive takes you past the park's major attractions — magnificent stands of sequoia trees. However, you need to get out into the backcountry to savor the High Sierra with its craggy, snow-swept peaks.

From Ash Mountain at 1,700 feet to the 14,494-foot crown of Mount Whitney, the 865,257 combined acres of Sequoia and Kings Canyon national parks offer the greatest range in elevation of any protected area in the Lower 48.

The limited access to the High Sierra is both a blessing and a curse. Few folks venture into the high country, so the blessing is the solitude you find there. It becomes a curse, though, if you're short on time and can't embark on a long hike to explore it.

For those who do have the time, these parks deliver the unexpected — granite domes (which most people associate with Yosemite), a sparkling crystalline cavern hidden beneath a landscape of big trees, and majestic alpine settings. Plan to spend at least three days: one day in Sequoia, one day in Kings Canyon, and one day to travel and explore between the two.

Whether you visit these parks in spring, summer, or fall depends on your preference for colorful spring wildflowers or fall leaves (as well as your ability to endure bugs, which plague the lower elevations in June and higher elevations in July). Seasonal crowds are not a factor in choosing when to visit. You can avoid most crowds, even in the most popular areas. (I tell you how to avoid the masses in the "Exploring the top attractions" section.) For all practical purposes, Kings Canyon is closed in winter, specifically from late November to early April. Only the Grant Grove section of Kings Canyon has year-round road access. But Sequoia is wonderful to visit in winter as you can cross-country ski into the forest with only your shadow as your companion.

Must-see Attractions

The big, bigger, and biggest trees can be found in these parks, but that's not all that merits a trip to Sequoia/Kings Canyon. You also find great granite outcrops (some that you can scale) and even a dark hole in the ground worth venturing into. The highlights include:

Sequoia and Kings Canyon National Parks

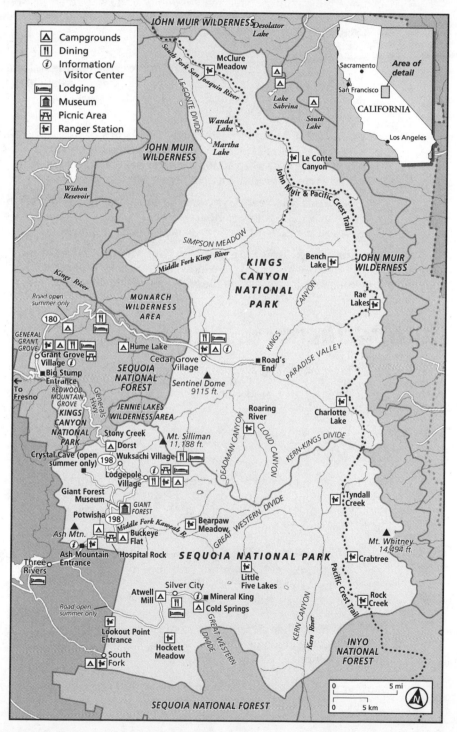

Legend:
- △ Campgrounds
- 🍴 Dining
- ⓘ Information/Visitor Center
- 🛏 Lodging
- 🏛 Museum
- 🎋 Picnic Area
- 🛖 Ranger Station

JOHN MUIR WILDERNESS

Desolator Lake

McClure Meadow

South Fork San Joaquin River

LE CONTE DIVIDE

Lake Sabrina

South Lake

Wanda Lake

Martha Lake

JOHN MUIR WILDERNESS

Le Conte Canyon

John Muir & Pacific Crest Trail

Wishon Reservoir

SIMPSON MEADOW

Middle Fork Kings River

KINGS CANYON NATIONAL PARK

Bench Lake

JOHN MUIR WILDERNESS

Kings River

Road open summer only

180

GENERAL GRANT GROVE

MONARCH WILDERNESS AREA

KINGS CANYON

Rae Lakes

PARADISE VALLEY

Grant Grove Village

Hume Lake

Cedar Grove Village

Road's End

Big Stump Entrance

SEQUOIA NATIONAL FOREST

Sentinel Dome 9115 ft.

To Fresno

REDWOOD MOUNTAIN GROVE

KINGS CANYON NATIONAL PARK

JENNIE LAKES WILDERNESS AREA

Roaring River

Charlotte Lake

DEADMAN CANYON

CLOUD CANYON

KERN-KINGS DIVIDE

Stony Creek

Mt. Silliman 11,188 ft.

Generals Hwy

Dorst

Crystal Cave (open summer only)

198

Wuksachi Village

Lodgepole Village

Tyndall Creek

Giant Forest Museum

GIANT FOREST

GREAT WESTERN DIVIDE

Potwisha

198

Middle Fork Kaweah R.

Mt. Whitney 14,494 ft.

Ash Mtn.

Buckeye Flat

SEQUOIA NATIONAL PARK

Crabtree

Ash Mountain Entrance

Hospital Rock

Little Five Lakes

Pacific Crest Trail

Three Rivers

Atwell Mill

Silver City

Mineral King

Rock Creek

KERN CANYON

Cold Springs

Road open summer only

Lookout Point Entrance

GREAT WESTERN DIVIDE

Kern River

INYO NATIONAL FOREST

Hockett Meadow

South Fork

0   5 mi
0   5 km

SEQUOIA NATIONAL FOREST

Area of detail

Sacramento

San Francisco

CALIFORNIA

Los Angeles

- **Crystal Cave:** In Sequoia, a park dedicated to big trees, a trip underground into a cave is an anomaly. You swap towering forests and sunshine for humidity, cool darkness, and crystalline formations. The Discovery Tours are especially fun.

- **General Grant Grove:** A stroll through this grove of sequoias leaves you feeling like an ant walking through a cornfield. Here grows the General Grant Tree, which is the third-largest living tree in the world, as well as the Fallen Monarch, a storm-toppled sequoia you can walk through.

- **Giant Forest:** Meandering through the world's best-known stand of sequoias is hard because your head is constantly tilted back. Among the forest's attractions are the General Sherman Tree, which is considered the largest living thing in the world.

- **Moro Rock:** On clear days from the top of this large granite dome, you can see the rocky rampart of the Great Western Divide to the east and the edge of the San Joaquin Valley to the west.

- **Tunnel Log:** Okay, it's a bit hokey, but when you drive your rig through the hole cut in this downed sequoia, you gain some appreciation for how big these trees really are.

Getting There

Sequoia and Kings Canyon are relatively easy to reach. That said, don't forget that these parks are mountainous, and the roads that wind through them are twisted, hilly, and narrow. As a result, you have to travel a bit slower than usual.

Driving in

The High Sierra blocks you from entering these adjoining parks from the east, leaving you no choice but to enter Sequoia from the southwest or west and Kings Canyon from the west via an incredibly long, steep, and winding road.

One way to reach Sequoia is by driving 36 miles along California 198 from Visalia to the **Ash Mountain Entrance** in the park's southwestern corner. From Ash Mountain, it's 16 miles and about 60 minutes to one of the park's main attractions, **Giant Forest.** Along the way are 130 curves and 12 switchbacks. Don't take my word for it — count them. If your rig is more than 22 feet long, save yourself some aggravation (the switchbacks are steep and tight) and skip this entrance in favor of the one at Big Stump.

Another option is to come in from the west via Fresno (53 miles away) on California 180 to the **Big Stump Entrance** of Kings Canyon National Park and then head south on the Generals Highway into Sequoia.

To enter Sequoia through the **Lookout Point Entrance** that leads to **Mineral King,** turn right off California 198 and onto the Mineral King Road 3 miles west of the Ash Mountain Entrance. Eleven miles later you arrive at the Lookout Point Entrance, and another 14 miles delivers you to Mineral King. However, this steep and winding road (698 curves from start to finish) is only open in the summer, and visitors with trailers and RVs should avoid it.

If you're headed to Kings Canyon, unless you're already in Sequoia National Park, your only choice is to travel 53 miles down California 180 from Fresno and enter at the Big Stump Entrance. That's the easy part. After you pass the Grant Grove, go 31 miles down a steep, winding two-lane highway through the Sequoia National Forest and into the lower stretch of Kings Canyon to re-enter the park and arrive at **Cedar Grove.** Due to the road's gnarly nature, the section between Yucca Point and Cedar Grove is open from late April to mid-November.

Flying in

The nearest major airport is the **Fresno–Yosemite International Airport** (☎ **559-498-4095**), 53 miles from the Big Stump Entrance to Kings Canyon. **American Airlines, American Eagle, Skywest, United Airlines, United Express,** and **US Airways** all fly here. You can connect into Fresno from both San Francisco and Los Angeles. At the airport, you can rent a car from **Avis, Budget, Dollar, Hertz,** or **National.** (See the Appendix for the airlines' and car agencies' toll-free numbers.)

Visalia Municipal Airport (☎ 559-559-713-4201), a tiny airstrip 36 miles from the Ash Mountain Entrance, is served by **United Express** and has a **Hertz** car-rental agency.

Busing or training in

Bus service is limited, with **Greyhound** (☎ 800-229-9424; Internet: www.greyhound.com) and **Trailways** (☎ 800-343-9999; Internet: www.trailways.com) traveling only as far as Visalia and Fresno. Ditto with train service. **Amtrak** (☎ 800-USA-RAIL; Internet: www.amtrak.com) goes as far as Hanford, where you have to take a bus approximately 30 miles to Visalia or Fresno and then rent a car. For car rentals in both cities, see "Flying in."

Planning Ahead

For advance information, write Sequoia and Kings Canyon National Parks, 47050 Generals Hwy., Three Rivers, CA 93271-9700, or check the parks' Web site at www.nps.gov/seki. You can also call ☎ **559-565-3341** for 24-hour recorded information on road/weather conditions (updated daily), camping, lodging, and activities or to reach a ranger.

Reserving a room or a campsite

Accommodations in these two parks are very limited, so you definitely need to plan far ahead for your vacation. Cedar Grove Lodge in the heart of Kings Canyon has just 22 rooms, and the John Muir Lodge at Grant Grove Village has only 30 rooms. In addition, 52 tent and wood cabins are available in Grant Grove. In Sequoia, Wuksachi has 102 rooms, and that's it for the park.

So what do you do? Call early and often. See "Where to Stay," later in this chapter, for telephone numbers and information on each place. Or, you can pack the tent and prepare to jockey for a campsite. Most of the campgrounds in the two parks fill on a first-come, first-served basis. The exceptions are the highly popular **Lodgepole and Dorst campgrounds** in Sequoia. Both campgrounds operate on a reservation system; Lodgepole between Memorial Day and mid-October and Dorst between Memorial Day and Labor Day.

Going into the backcountry

Backcountry permits are required for all overnight camping outside designated campgrounds. The free permits are not required for day hikes, with the exception of those in the Mt. Whitney area. You can obtain them from the ranger station closest to your trailhead.

Quotas limit the number of people who can obtain a permit on a single day for a certain trailhead. Some popular trailheads fill during summer. For a $10 fee, you can reserve a backcountry permit for a trip between mid-May and September. The park accepts reservations for the current year no earlier than March 1 and no later than three weeks before the start of your trip. All reservation requests must be sent to the Wilderness Office by fax (559-565-4239) or mail (Wilderness Permit Reservations, HCR 89 Box 60, Three Rivers, CA 93271). Fax requests must include payment by Visa or MasterCard. Mail requests must include payment by Visa, MasterCard, money order, or check, payable to the National Park Service. For more information call the **Wilderness Office** (☎ **559-565-3708**).

Learning the Lay of the Land

From lowland foothills to mid-elevation forests and alpine crags, Sequoia and Kings Canyon throw tantalizing possibilities at you in terms of what to do and see. Unfortunately, the lack of easy access limits what you can enjoy on one visit, particularly if it's a short one.

Kings Canyon National Park

Kings Canyon is split in two. The bulk of the park, which contains Cedar Grove, the destination for motorized visitors, rests to the north of Sequoia. A separate, smaller section, called Grant Grove, shares a border with Sequoia National Park and is linked to Kings Canyon only by the rambling umbilical cord of California 180.

I can't suggest any shortcuts through Kings Canyon, because only one road, **California 180,** goes into the heart of the river canyon that leads to Cedar Grove. (Because the canyon is accessible only by this one route, you encounter fewer people in Kings Canyon than in Sequoia.)

As national park developments go, **Cedar Grove** is spartan. The lodge is old and small, with just 22 rooms, although it does have a well-stocked camp store. You also find three campgrounds, with a total of 314 sites.

Due to the adventuresome nature of the road to Cedar Grove, plan to stay at least one night, either at the Cedar Grove Lodge or in a tent. To creep into the park, spend half a day hiking or fishing, and then backtrack out would be much too stressful to qualify as a vacation.

By comparison to Cedar Grove, **Grant Grove** is Grand Central Station. You find three sprawling campgrounds with nearly 400 sites, a 30-room lodge, grocery, visitor center, picnic grounds, and stables. California 180 passes right through the heart of this complex before tying into the Generals Highway that continues into Sequoia.

Sequoia National Park

Sequoia also has only one road, **Generals Highway,** which winds into the developed part of the park and passes the gigantic trees that gave the park its name. From Grant Grove in Kings Canyon National Park, the Generals Highway negotiates a short stretch of the Giant Sequoia National Monument in Sequoia National Forest before entering Sequoia National Park just north of the Dorst Campground. The road continues to **Wuksachi Village,** home of the Wuksachi Lodge, and then on to **Lodgepole Village,** which has a small visitor center, grocery, short-order grill, showers, laundry facilities, and campground.

From Lodgepole, the highway heads south through the **Giant Forest** section, passing spur roads to the Wolverton picnic grounds with its network of trails, the Giant Forest Museum, Moro Rock, and Crystal Cave. Next, the road passes Buckeye Flat and Potwisha campgrounds before reaching the Foothills Visitor Center and the Ash Mountain Entrance.

Just inside Sequoia's southern border lies the primitive **Mineral King.** Once eyed by ski resort developers, this scenic area is dotted by lakes and laced with trails heading into the high country. In the heart of the basin are two campgrounds — one not far from the Atwell Grove (the highest elevation grove of sequoia trees), the other at Cold Springs — the privately owned Silver City Resort with its rental cabins and general store, and the park's Mineral King information station. The dirt road that leads to Lookout Point Entrance and Mineral King is found off California 198 between Three Rivers and the Ash Mountain Entrance; it's open from Memorial Day weekend through October.

Arriving in the Parks

Unless you're on horseback or hiking, you must use one of two main entrances — the Big Stump Entrance on California 180 or the Ash Mountain or Lookout Point entrances on California 198. After you arrive in either park, you're never far from a visitor center.

Finding information

The parks have four visitor centers. The biggest is the **Lodgepole Visitor Center** (☎ 559-565-3782), north of Giant Forest in Sequoia National Park on Generals Highway, which features exhibits on geology, wildlife, air quality, and park history. Although hours of operation can fluctuate from year to year, in general the center is open mid-June through Labor Day from 8 a.m. to 6 p.m., September from 9 a.m. to 6 p.m., October through mid-April Saturday and Sunday from 9 a.m. to 4:30 p.m., and mid-April until mid-June from 8 a.m. to 5 p.m.

The **Foothills Visitor Center** (☎ 559-565-3135), on California 198 just inside Sequoia's Ash Mountain Entrance, includes exhibits on the region's ecosystem. The center is open daily, mid-April through October from 8 a.m. to 5 p.m., and November through mid-April from 8 a.m. to 4:30 p.m.

The **Giant Forest Museum** (☎ 559-565-4480), on the Generals Highway in Sequoia National Park, includes exhibits on sequoia ecology. The center is open year-round, daily, with hours of operation similar to the Lodgepole Visitor Center.

The **Grant Grove Visitor Center** (☎ 559-565-4307), on California 180 in Kings Canyon National Park, includes exhibits on logging and the role of fire in the forests. It's also open year-round, daily, from approximately 8 a.m. to 5 p.m., except from November until mid-April when the hours are 9 a.m. to 4:30 p.m.

Paying fees

A fee of $10 per vehicle or $5 per individual (on foot, motorcycle, or bicycle) provides access to both parks for seven days. A $20 annual pass covers entrance fees to the parks for one year. If you have a park passport, you don't need to pay the entrance fee; see Chapter 8 for information on the National Park Pass and Chapter 4 for the lowdown on Golden Age and Golden Access passports.

Although backcountry permits are required for all overnight camping outside designated campgrounds, the permits are free . . . but there is a $10 fee to make permit reservations. For reservations on certain trails, see the earlier section, "Planning Ahead."

Getting around

The parks are not linked by a public transportation system. Unless you plan a very long hike, you need a car to travel from one park to the next. While a free shuttle bus system once operated between Giant Forest, Lodgepole, and Wuksachi, the service has been discontinued.

Remembering Safety

If you plan to head down California 180 into Kings Canyon, double-check your rig's brake system. Also, because no gas stations operate inside the parks, make sure to top off your tank before you pass through one of the entrance stations. Kings Canyon Lodge on California 180 in Sequoia National Forest has a gas station, but expect prices much higher than you would find in the small communities just west of the parks.

See the "Spotting the local wildlife" sidebar, later in the chapter, for important information about black bears, mountain lions, and rattlesnakes.

For additional tips on how to ensure a safe park visit, see Chapter 8.

Enjoying the Parks

Just as you may expect from two parks connected like Siamese twins, Sequoia and Kings Canyon offer a lot to see and do. Your biggest problem may be deciding what to see and where to go. To help you make your choices, let me give you a concise rundown of what you should try to pencil into your itinerary.

The only congested spots in these parks are the General Sherman and General Grant areas; however, you can flee these crowds by following the longer, less popular trails.

Exploring the top attractions

Crystal Cave
Sequoia National Park

With only 3 miles of explored passages, Crystal Cave can't compare to Mammoth Cave or Carlsbad Caverns. But in this land of big trees, going underground for an hour is a nice change of scenery. One of an estimated 200 caves in the park, Crystal Cave is the most beautiful with its crystalline formations, *cave bacon* (thin strips of flowstone that look like bacon), *soda straws* (long, thin formations that look like, well, straws), stalactites, and stalagmites. Two park employees out on a fishing expedition discovered the cave in 1918. Initially, the underground space was off-limits to the public because park officials feared that vandals would damage the formations.

Today you have to pass through a gate in the shape of a spider web to enter the cave. Once underground, you wind through about ½ mile of paved and lighted trails, stopping in the Dome Room, the Junction Room, the Organ Room, and the Marble Room so your guide can impart some cave history and science. In the Marble Room, the largest room in the cave's explored sections, the guide turns out the lights for a few minutes to let you experience total darkness. The gurgling and dripping water, which continues to carve the cave, can be eerie in the dark, but most visitors get a kick out of it.

If you want to tour the cave, purchase your tickets at the Lodgepole or Foothills visitor centers, because none are sold at the cave itself.

Because the 7-mile road leading to the cave from Generals Highway weaves through the forest and is followed by a 15-minute hike to the cave entrance, head for the cave 1½ or even 2 hours before your scheduled tour.

This attraction is open only from mid-May through late September.

Crystal cave is 7 miles down a paved side road (open seasonally), about 14 miles north of Foothills Visitor Center, off Generals Highway. Admission: $8 adults, $6 seniors, and $4 ages 6 to 12; 5 and under free. Open: Mid-May to late Sept.

General Grant Grove
Kings Canyon National Park

Grant Grove started out as a national park of its own, called General Grant National Park. When Kings Canyon was established as a national park in 1940, General Grant National Park was incorporated into it.

The towering sequoias in the Grant Grove annex of Kings Canyon National Park explain why this nook once was a national park in its own right. Located in the Grant Tree section of the grove, which is a mile northwest of the visitor center, is the 267.4-foot **General Grant Tree,** recognized as the world's third-largest living tree. It also doubles as the Nation's Christmas Tree, a designation bestowed by President Coolidge in 1926. Every December, a yuletide celebration is held in front of the 2,000-year-old tree. On the second Sunday of that month, a high school choir sings carols in front of it, and rangers place a wreath at its base. The tree also serves as a National Shrine, the only living memorial to Americans who have died at war. President Eisenhower extended that designation in 1956.

A ⅓-mile, paved trail in General Grant Grove takes you past the General Grant Tree and to the **Fallen Monarch.** In the untold years since this humongous sequoia was toppled, the tree has served as a homesteader's cabin, a bar, and a stable for the U.S. Cavalry. Take a walk through this big old log and imagine what it must have been like to seek shelter inside of it.

To escape some of the crowds that clog the path, head down the North Grove Loop trail, which roams for 1½ miles through a section of sequoias, past meadows, and into a mixed-conifer forest. The trailhead is in the Grant Tree parking area.

General Grant Grove is on California 180 just north of the Big Stump Entrance to the parks.

Giant Forest
Sequoia National Park

Just south of Lodgepole Village is the heart of the Giant Forest, the largest collection of sequoias in the park. Four of the world's five largest sequoias grow here. (The fifth is the General Grant Tree in General Grant Grove.) Walking among these ancient and towering trees, you feel as if you've entered a wilderness cathedral, a place of reverence. The 2-mile Congress Trail weaves past the **General Sherman Tree,** the largest living tree in the world, as well as the "House" and "Senate" groups of large sequoias. You also come upon the President, Chief Sequoyah, General Lee, and McKinley trees. Trail access is available from the Sherman Tree parking area in Giant Forest.

Two miles south of Lodgepole Village on Generals Highway, Crescent Meadow Road leads first to **Moro Rock** (see the listing in this section) and then to **Tunnel Log,** a downed sequoia through which a hole that can swallow a car was cut back in 1938. Kids get a kick out of driving through the tree; just make sure to take the bikes off the roof rack first.

A parking lot 1¼ miles beyond Tunnel Log marks the western terminus of the High Sierra Trail. This is where you leave your car if you're heading into the high country along this route. But you don't have to hike the entire 71 miles to Mount Whitney to savor the gorgeous High Sierra countryside. You can just go 200 yards to the southern edge of **Crescent Meadow,** a dazzling place for spring wildflower photos.

You can also hike a mile from the parking lot to **Tharp's Log,** which is on the edge of Log Meadow. Talk about a real log cabin; Hale Tharp lived in this hollowed out sequoia during summers from 1861 to 1890 when he would bring his cows up to graze in Huckleberry, Crescent, and Log meadows. Judging from the wooden bunk inside, I don't think his nights were entirely comfy, but he was no doubt dry when the rains came.

From Tharp's Log, you can head around the northern tip of Log Meadow and hook into the **Trail of the Sequoias**, or you can head west on a path that leads to **Chimney Tree.** This towering tree trunk was gutted by fire; you can crawl into it and look out through the sheared off top. The Crescent/Log Meadow Loop Trail then loops back to Crescent Meadow, passing dozens of sequoia and small forest openings which blaze with color when the flowers bloom.

Giant Forest is on Generals Highway between Lodgepole Village and Giant Forest Musem.

Mineral King
Sequoia National Park

Unfortunately (because it's time-consuming), or fortunately (because not many people do it), you have to temporarily leave Sequoia National Park to reach Mineral King. Most families intent on seeing the big trees in the park won't make the 90-minute drive to reach this glacially carved valley. As a result, although backpackers use Mineral King as a starting point for the High Sierras, this is a good place to head to avoid crowds.

The valley is breathtaking, with thick stands of conifers and outcrops of red and orange shale offset by white marble and black metamorphic shale and granite. Towering over the basin is Sawtooth Peak, which stands 12,343 feet tall and holds snowfields throughout the year. If you make the drive, spend a night in one of the campgrounds or at the Silver City Resort (see "Where to Stay" later in this chapter) and follow a trail into the mountains.

The basin is accessible by car only during the summer months.

Mineral King is on a mostly unpaved road that leads from the Lookout Point Entrance.

Capturing the parks on film

These two parks offer a wonderfully diverse array of photographic subjects, from the frothy Kings River to the stately sequoia trees and pillars of granite. Roam the Giant Forest and Grants Grove and discover countless subjects standing tall for their pictures to be taken. Just remember, though, that these trees are so big your pictures will benefit from a wide angle lens. I find that young kids perched on gnarled roots of a towering sequoia are particularly photogenic because of the scale they lend. You can obtain another intriguing photo by standing near the foot of a sequoia and pointing your camera up into the forest canopy. If you find yourself passing through the Big Stump Entrance to Kings Canyon National Park, take time to make the short hike down into Big Stump Basin. The huge tree stumps, left behind from the days when this area was logged, are worth a picture or two.

Because of relatively low light in the sequoia forests, your best pictures will be captured with a fast film. If you have slow film, be sure to use a tripod to steady the camera for the relatively long exposures the film will require. In the Cedar Grove section of Kings Canyon, you find soaring towers of granite for worthy pictures. For an interesting shot, try capturing the reflection of North Dome in the South Fork of the Kings River.

Moro Rock
Sequoia National Park

Moro Rock is a big granite dome jutting into the deep canyon cut by the Middle Fork of the Kaweah River. On days when the air pollution isn't too bad, this bulbous rock offers breathtaking views of the canyon below, the snow-capped peaks that form the Great Western Divide to the east, and the San Joaquin Valley far off to the west. If you keep track of such things, it's 370 steps to the rock's top from its base. Although the trail is steep in places and passes through some slots and keyholes, it's all worth it when you're standing on top, 4,000 feet above the river. If you need some inspiration on the way up, look for lizards scurrying over the rock face; they'll encourage your progress by performing some pushups for you.

From the top, look for the serpentine Generals Highway as it snakes up from the Ash Mountain Entrance. You may feel sorry for the road crews that had to hack the road out of the forests and mountainsides.

This place is great for sunset photos. If you're an early riser, get to the top by 8 a.m. during the week and you may have the place to yourself for some peaceful meditation and inspiration.

A few warnings: If thunderstorms threaten, don't turn yourself into a lightning rod by climbing to the top. Keep a tight grip on little tykes who could easily slip through the railings. Don't kick or toss stones into the great beyond because climbers may be below you. Finally, don't try to scale the rock if ice and snow cover the steps.

Moro Rock is on Crescent Meadow Road (not plowed in winter), which is by the Giant Forest Museum on Generals Highway.

Taking a hike

With so much fantastic backcountry, not answering the call to head into the mountains is hard. Unfortunately, time doesn't always allow for extended hikes. Luckily, both Kings Canyon and Sequoia have a variety of short- and medium-length hikes to sate your hunger for a walk in the out-of-doors. Of course, they may also convince you to return again to go farther into the High Sierra. For information on permits for back-country hikes, see "Planning Ahead," earlier in this chapter.

Alta Peak
Sequoia National Park

This hike is one of the most strenuous on the western side of Sequoia because of steepness and altitude. (Alta Peak tops out at 11,204 feet!) If you're not in good shape or acclimated to higher elevations, take the hike to Tokopah Falls instead (described later in this section). You start out on the Lakes Trail for this jaunt, but turn right on the Panther Gap Trail rather than left. After you pass through the 8,400-foot gap, turn left onto the Alta Trail and go past the junction with Seven-Mile Hill Trail. When you hit the junction for the Alta Peak Trail, turn left and get ready to grunt. The final 2 miles include a 2,000-foot increase in elevation. Once atop the peak, though, you find great views in all directions. If the sky is clear, you can see past the Great Western Divide to Mount Whitney.

Distance: 13¾ miles round-trip. Level: Strenuous. Access: The southeastern end of the parking area at Wolverton picnic area, off Generals Highway.

Bubbs Creek Trail
Kings Canyon National Park

This hike treats you to views of Paradise Valley, Cedar Grove, and a large emerald pool filled by a waterfall. The start isn't encouraging, though, because you cross Copper Creek twice in the early going. This area once was an Indian village, and you may spot some shards of *obsidian* (dark volcanic glass) in the area. After the first mile, you enter a swampy area popular with wildlife. Here the trail closes in on the river, where deer and bear often drink. Two miles from the trailhead is a junction; the trail to the left heads to Paradise Valley, whereas the hike to Bubbs Creek veers right and crosses Baily Bridge over the South Fork of the Kings River.

You cross four more bridges back and forth over Bubbs Creek, and then begin climbing on the creek's north side. The switchbacks offer good views up Paradise Canyon and down to Cedar Grove. Three miles from the trailhead, you come upon the emerald pool and its waterfall. Far up on the mountainside is the Sphinx, a rock formation John Muir named for its likeness to the sphinxes in Egypt. One more mile brings you to Sphinx Creek, which is a nice place to spend the day. If you plan to camp, you need to pick up a backcountry permit before leaving the valley.

Distance: 8 miles round-trip. Level: Moderate to strenuous. Access: The east end of the parking area at Road's End.

Lakes Trail
Sequoia National Park

Unless you're a marathon hiker, this trip is best started early in the morning so you're not stumbling your way back in the dark. This hike's payoff is a series of lakes cradled in glacier-scooped basins. Head east from the trailhead, making sure to follow signs that help you stay on the Lakes Trail and avoid the Long Meadow Trail. You soon climb up a ridge and hike above Wolverton Creek, which cuts through a meadow lush with wildflowers in season. When you reach the junction with the Panther Gap Trail, head left toward Heather Lake. At the next junction, choose between going right up the Hump Trail, which is aptly named for its steepness, or head left along the Watchtower Trail, which leads along a granite ledge blasted in the rock with dynamite. If you don't have the constitution of a mountain goat, you may want to forsake this vertigo-inducing section by taking the Hump Trail. Both lead to Heather Lake, and a bit farther down the trail, Emerald and Pear lakes (5¾ miles and 6¾ miles, respectively, from the trailhead).

Distance: 13½ miles round-trip. Level: Moderate to strenuous. Access: The eastern end of the parking area at Wolverton picnic area off Generals Highway.

River Trail
Kings Canyon National Park

This trail hugs the Kings River and offers several hikes of different lengths. From the parking lot, you can make the up-and-back trip to Roaring River Falls for a total of a ½ mile, or follow the trail in the other direction to Zumwalt Meadow and back for a total of 3 miles. If you continue to follow the path along the river from Zumwalt Meadow, you come to Zumwalt Bridge. Cross here, and you're a ¼ mile from the Zumwalt Meadow parking lot. If you don't cross but continue down the trail, you come to the meadow's edge in another ¼ mile. If you continue, you face another footbridge in about a mile. Cross it and you're a ½ mile from the Road's End parking area.

Distance: 5½ miles round-trip. Level: Easy. Access: From the Cedar Grove Ranger Station, drive 3 miles to the Roaring River Falls Parking area.

Tokopah Falls

This short trail is fairly level. The payoff is Tokopah Falls, which tumble 1,200 feet down smooth granite cliffs. Once there, you can make your way to the river at the falls' base or pull up a rock and catch some rays.

Distance: 3½ miles round-trip. Level: Easy. Access: Lodgepole Campground on the north side of Log Bridge.

One-day wonder

Sequoia and Kings Canyon don't have many roads that delve into all the parks' various nooks and crannies, so you're fairly restricted as to what you can do and see in a limited amount of time. If you have only one day, you can make the most of your time if you concentrate on the more user-friendly Sequoia.

The following is my recommendation for a one-day itinerary of Sequoia National Park. Unless otherwise indicated, see the "Exploring the top attractions" section for information on the attractions.

Most visitors to Sequoia tend to sleep in. As a result, if you start your day early, you almost get the feeling that you're in your very own national park. So spend the night at **Wuksachi Lodge** (see "Where to Stay" later in this chapter) and get an early start in the morning. After breakfast at the lodge, head over to the **Lodgepole Visitor Center** or the **Giant Forest Museum** (see "Finding information" earlier in this chapter) to pick up any self-guiding trail brochures you may be interested in or to buy postcards to document your journey. Then drive down to **Moro Rock** and climb to the top. In summer, watch for the hummingbirds that feast on the nectar from the flowers growing on the granite.

From Moro Rock, continue east on the Crescent Meadow Road, passing through **Tunnel Log** and heading for the parking lot at the end of the road. From there, hike to **Crescent Meadow**, to **Tharp's Log,** and onto either the **Trail of the Sequoias** or the trail that leads to **Chimney Tree** — both are worthwhile.

By now you should be ready for lunch. Just down the road towards Lodgepole, you find **Wolverton** with its pleasant picnic area. (Here you also find marked cross-country ski trails in the winter, so keep it in mind when you're wondering where to go in mid-February.)

After lunch, stop at the **Giant Forest Museum.** This museum in a historic building that once housed a grocery, provides a primer on the life and times of sequoia trees. Make sure to visit the nearby Big Trees Trail, which goes around Round Meadow, or drive to the **General Sherman Tree** and hike portions of the 2-mile Congress Trail.

A great way to spend the rest of the afternoon is to hike, and the trail to **Tokopah Falls** is great for kids and adults (see "Taking a hike" earlier in the chapter). The 1¾-mile trail (3½ miles round-trip) ends at a towering waterfall cascading out of the high country. Afterward, head back to your room and clean up for dinner. You're sure to be hungry again!

If you have more time

When passing through Grant Grove, check out **Big Stump Basin,** just south of Grant Grove Village along California 180. A 1-mile loop through the basin takes you past the stumps of sequoias that fell to loggers' saws in the 1890s. The forest is steadily coming back, but when you look at the size of the stumps you sadly realize that it'll be 500 to 600 years before they are dwarfed by living sequoias.

Ranger programs

Your best (and only) bet for finding out about ranger programs is to keep a close eye on bulletin boards in campgrounds and visitor centers. The parks have a few amphitheaters so you can expect a talk or two during your stay. Most of the programs get under way late in June. For ranger-led snowshoe hikes, see the following section, "Keeping active."

If you have little ones with you, pick up materials for the Junior Ranger Program at any visitor center (see "Finding information" earlier in the chapter). To find out about this program, see Chapter 4.

Keeping active

These two parks offer numerous ways to get a workout. In addition to hiking (see the "Taking a hike" section), you have several other options:

- ✔ **Cross-country skiing: Sequoia Ski Touring** (☎ 559-565-3435) operates at Wuksachi, just north of Giant Forest. They offer rentals, instruction, and trail maps for 35 miles of marked backcountry trails.

- ✔ **Fishing:** Easily accessed waters are limited to Kings and Kaweah rivers, and fishing permits and California state fishing licenses (available at most park grocery stores) are required. High-country lakes have a few nonnative trout.

✔ **Snowshoeing:** On winter weekends, rangers lead introductory snowshoe hikes in General Grant Grove (☎ 559-565-4307) and the Lodgepole/Giant Forest area (☎ 559-565-3782). Showshoes are provided, but a $1 donation is requested.

✔ **White-water rafting:** If you want a thrill, try white-water rafting. **Whitewater Voyages** (☎ 800-400-RAFT; Internet: www.white watervoyages.com) is a local outfit that runs class III, IV, and V trips for beginners and intermediate paddlers. Trips usually last five hours, although longer ones can be arranged. Trips take place from April through August with costs up to $170 per person. **Kaweah White Water Adventures** (☎ 800-229-8658 or 559-561-1000) also runs trips down the Kings and Kaweah Rivers.

Spotting the local wildlife

One of the most visible animals in these parks is the **mule deer.** These guys have grown accustomed to having humans around and will usually go about their browsing unless you get too close.

Also visible are **black bears,** which humans have managed to spoil with our sloppy ways when it comes to food. When you pull into the Lodgepole Campground, notice a sign that keeps a tally of the number of cars that bears have broken into during the year. At the Lodgepole Campground, you also notice the large number of bear-proof storage bins scattered about. Use them. And make sure that you empty your car of all foods, including apple cores and chips. The park's bruins can smell these tasty treats and are strong enough to peel your car open like a can of sardines to get to them. The rangers have pictures to show you exactly how much damage bears can exact on your rig.

If you have good eyes and are lucky, you may spot a **gray fox** in a meadow or darting across a road in the evenings. Also present are **coyotes, bobcats, badgers,** and **ringtail cats.**

Mountain lions also live in the parks — definitely watch out for them. Although your coming across one of these big cats is unlikely, if you do, be prepared to face it. Don't flee. Mountain lions view people and their pets as prey. If you try to run, they switch into attack mode. Your best defense is stand up tall and shout at the cat. You may even try pelting the animal with rocks or sticks if it begins to act aggressively.

In the parks' foothills, you're likely to spot **turkey vultures** as well as **red-tailed hawks** overhead. In campgrounds at higher elevations, the raucous and begging **Steller's jays** will find you.

While walking in the foothill areas of the parks, watch out for **rattlesnakes.** They won't come looking for you, but if you're not careful where you put your feet and hands, you may inadvertently find one.

Escaping the rain

Even though the odds are against daylong rains during a summer visit to these parks, it can happen. So what do you do? Go underground with a visit to **Crystal Cave.** You won't get rained on while you're underground, but you may see the aftermath of the rain in the form of increased water flows in the cave.

The **Giant Forest Museum** is a great place to avoid rain while gaining a better understanding of the ecology of sequoia groves. Of course, if the rain's not coming down too hard, and you have rain gear, don't let the weather stop you from seeing the parks. A walk through misty sequoia groves can be entrancing, and if you stop at Tharp's Log near Crescent Meadow, you can take in the same view that Mr. Tharp did on rainy days.

Where to Stay

The arrival of Wuksachi Lodge at Sequoia National Park and John Muir Lodge at Grant Grove Village in Kings Canyon National Park in the summer of 1999 brought two much-needed lodging options to the parks, but, overall, your choices are still pretty limited. (The parks do not have a "signature" lodge to take your breath away.) Call as early as possible for a reservation at any of the parks' hotels.

Lodging in the parks

Cedar Grove Lodge

$$–$$$ Kings Canyon National Park

This lodge, situated along the banks of the South Fork of the Kings River, isn't the Grand Hotel, but it's the only place in the park where you can have a roof over your head and a cafe downstairs. The modest rooms that line a central hallway are comfortable, but you won't find a telephone or TV in them. You find communal decks off the first and second floors, a small picnic grounds squeezed between the lodge and the river, and a cafe serving three meals a day that, while not exactly sumptuous, gets the job done.

California 180, Cedar Grove. ☎ *559-335-5500. 22 rooms. Rack rate: $99–$110 double. AE, DISC, MC, V. Closed in winter.*

John Muir Lodge

$$–$$$ Kings Canyon National Park

This lodge's opening in the summer of 1999 brought a badly needed flourish to accommodations in Grant Grove Village, which previously had been limited to woefully rustic cabins and tent cabins. The rooms offer two queen beds and feature handmade hickory log furniture. You find a large rock fireplace in the lodge's great room; the log mantle over the fireplace was cut in the Giant Forest in the late 1800s. If you plan a summer stay here, book your room at least two months in advance. During the off-season, a week ahead usually is good enough.

California 180, Grant Grove Village. ☎ *559-335-5500. 24 rooms, 6 suites. TEL. Rack rates: $99–$140 double; $189–$240 suite. DISC, MC, V.*

Silver City Resort
$$–$$$$$ **Sequoia National Park**

This private resort is popular and books quickly. The 13 cabins are fairly well dispersed across eight acres. All have kitchens (with dishes, pots, and pans) and decks with barbeque grills; some have wood-burning stoves. Less expensive cabins sleep two to five guests, and some require users to head to centrally located showers and restrooms. The more expensive chalet-style cabins sleep six to eight people and have a living area and private bathrooms. For high-season rentals, folks should call at least six months ahead (reservations are accepted up to a year in advance); for low seasons, a month in advance usually works.

Mineral King Road (off California 198; the resort is about halfway between Lookout Point and Mineral King). ☎ *559-561-3223. In winter, call 805-528-2730. Internet:* www.silvercityresort.com. *13 cabins; 4 with private bath, 3 with shared bath, the rest use a bathhouse. Rack rates: $70–$250 double; 25% less from June 1–15 and Sept 17–Oct 1. MC, V. Open: Early June to mid-fall.*

The Tent Cabins at Grant Grove
$–$$$ **Kings Canyon National Park**

A rustic feel pervades these cabins. Only nine have indoor plumbing and private baths. Fourteen have electricity. The rest feature battery-powered lamps for illumination, propane- or wood-burning stoves for heat, and communal bathrooms. Oh yeah, some of the cabins are wooden, and others are canvas. Just make sure you break the news to your family before arriving.

California 180, Grant Grove Village. ☎ *559-335-5500. 52 cabins, 9 with private bath. Rack rates: $45–$105 double. AE, MC, V.*

Wuksachi Lodge
$$–$$$$$ **Sequoia National Park**

Opened in 1999, this lodge has three detached buildings with rooms and a separate lodge holding a great room with wood stove, dining room, small lounge, and meeting rooms. Although the guestrooms are spacious and complete with TVs, phones, and phone dataport (if you just can't leave work at home), they are motelish and lack the elegance of a top-of-the-line park lodge. They're also hard to get into, literally, as the doors into each building are on the back side and require you to negotiate a paved walkway from the parking lot. That said, these are the best rooms in the park — comfortable and in a gorgeous setting.

Generals Highway, Wuksachi Village. ☎ *888-252-5757. 102 rooms. TV TEL. $86–$219 double. AE, DISC, DC, MC, V.*

Lodging outside the parks

Stony Creek Lodge

$$$ Giant Sequoia National Monument

Located along the General's Highway between General Grant Grove in Kings Canyon National Park and Giant Forest in Sequoia National Park, this river rock and timber lodge is a perfect middleground from which to base your explorations. With just 11 rooms, the lodge operates much like a bed and breakfast. The spacious lobby has a stone fireplace to relax in front of after a day in the parks. Rooms come with televisions and dataport phones, and the lodge has a cyber room if you left your laptop at home.

Generals Highway (between General Grant Grove and Wuksachi Village. ☎ *559-565-3909. 11 rooms. Rack rates: $125 double occupancy. Rates include Cointinental breakfast. AE, DISC, MC, V. Open: Late May to Oct.*

Runner-up lodgings

Best Western Holiday Lodge

$$–$$$ Three Rivers   This hotel along the banks of the Kaweah River offers standard rooms as well as suites with fireplaces. A pool is on the property, and you can bring your pets if you can't travel without them. 40105 Sierra Dr. ☎ *800-528-1234* or 559-561-4119.

Buckeye Tree Lodge

$$–$$$$ Three Rivers   Just ¼ mile west of Sequoia National Park, this lodge offers motel rooms and a cottage that sleeps five. A pool and a creek for fishing are on the grounds. 46000 Sierra Dr. ☎ *559-561-5900.* Internet: www.buckeyetree.com.

Montecito-Sequoia Resort

$$–$$$$$ Sequoia National Forest   A great family retreat for week-long summer vacations, this lodge just southeast of Grant Grove also rents rooms by the night on summer weekends and for two nights at a time in winter. 8000 Generals Hwy. ☎ *800-227-9900* or 559-565-3388. Internet: www.montecitosequoia.com.

Sequoia Village Inn

$$–$$$$$ **Three Rivers**   Just outside Sequoia National Park's south entrance, this operation offers a collection of cottages and chalets perfect for a night or a week. 45971 Sierra Dr. ☎ *559-561-0410* or 559-561-3652.

Campgrounds

Scattered throughout the parks are 14 campgrounds offering a variety of amenities. They all offer tables, fire grills, garbage cans, and pit or flush toilets. All but South Fork have drinking water. Most also have bear-proof storage bins that you must use. Rates range from $8 to $16 per night.

Lodgepole and **Dorst campgrounds** in Sequoia get the most action. They are the only places that accept reservations (☎ 800-365-2267), and then only for the busy summer season between Memorial Day and mid-October. You can call five months in advance of your trip. Dorst, which is open from Memorial Day through Labor Day, also has group sites.

To arrange group campsites at **Grant** and **Cedar Groves,** call ☎ 559-565-4341 or write either Sunset Group Sites at Grant Grove or Canyon View Group Sites at Cedar Grove, both at P.O. Box 926, Kings Canyon National Park, CA 93633.

Many of the parks' higher elevation campgrounds close in late fall. There is a limit of one vehicle and six people per campsite. You can get your trailer into 11 of the 14 campgrounds, but none of the campgrounds has hookups.

In Sequoia National Park

For getting away from it all and escaping the crowds, go to **Atwell Mill Campground** (☎ 559-565-3341). Located along Mineral King Road, 20 miles east of California 198, the campground has just 21 sites along the East Fork of the Kaweah River. Mineral King Road is not recommended if you are hauling a trailer or driving an RV.

Much the same description befits **Cold Springs** (☎ 559-565-3341), closer to Mineral King, 5 miles to the east of Atwell Mill. At 7,500 feet, this campground (which has 40 sites) is the highest you can reach with your car in the park. Popular on summer weekends, the sites often fill up on Friday afternoons on holiday weekends. Come early if you want a spot. During mid-week, you shouldn't have any problem finding a site.

If you really want to flee the crowds, head for the **South Fork Campground** (☎ 559-565-3341) in the park's southern tip. To reach this secluded spot and its 10 sites, take the South Fork Road turnoff from California 198 and drive 13 miles. The setting along the South Fork of the Kaweah River is nice. The campground is busy in spring and fall, but in summer the heat keeps the crowds away. You can self-register here for a backcountry trek, but if you need maps or have questions, go to the Foothills Visitor Center near the Ash Mountain Entrance.

If your idea of camping is pitching your tent next to 204 others, then the **Lodgepole Campground** (☎ 800-365-2267) is for you. Despite the awesome setting in Marble Fork Canyon, I'm not a fan of this place because of the crowds. Still, amenities are plentiful, with a grocery, showers, restaurant, dump station, gift shop, and stables nearby. Plus, ranger talks are held most evenings in the summer.

Dorst Campground (☎ 800-365-2267) also is an experience in communal camping with its 201 sites. The location isn't bad, just 14 miles northwest of the Giant Forest on the Generals Highway. Like Lodgepole, its selling points are facilities: Grocery, dump station, and laundry.

If it's near sundown as you pass through the Ash Mountain Entrance, the **Potwisha Campground** (☎ 559-565-3341) is just 3 miles up the road. This somewhat small campground has 42 sites. The setting amidst oak trees and along the Marble Fork of the Kaweah River is pretty, but it can be hot in the summer.

Buckeye Flat Campground (☎ 559-565-3341) also is close to the Ash Mountain Entrance. About 6 miles inside the park, you see the Hospital Rock Ranger Station. From here, follow the signs to the campground with its 28 sites, which are a few miles further down a narrow, windy road. Like Potwisha, the pretty riverside setting is nice, but it can get awfully hot in the summer.

In Kings Canyon National Park

Kings Canyon has six campgrounds, all of them fairly large.

The best settings, in terms of facilities and atmosphere, are the three campgrounds in Grant Grove. The tall trees are nearby, and all three have evening ranger programs. You also find a grocery, showers, and stables within walking distance. **Crystal Springs Campground** (☎ 559-565-3341) is the park's smallest facility with 63 sites. Nearby is **Sunset Campground** (☎ 559-565-3341) with 200 sites and **Azalea Campground** (☎ 559-565-3341) with 113 sites. These places don't usually fill during the middle of the week, but they can quickly do so on weekends.

The four other campgrounds are in the vicinity of Cedar Grove, which offers a grocery, laundry, bicycle rentals, and stables, in addition to a small cafe at the Cedar Grove Lodge. **Sentinel Campground** (☎ 559-565-3341) fills surprisingly fast even though it has 83 sites. The other nearby choices are **Sheep Creek Campground** (☎ 559-565-3341) with 111 sites or **Moraine Campground** (☎ 559-565-3341), which opens its 120 sites only when the other two campgrounds are full — something that doesn't happen too often. **Canyon View Campground** (☎ 559-565-3341) has 37 sites for tents only.

Where to Eat

With few lodging options inside the parks, you shouldn't be surprised that dining options are limited, too, outside of the snack bars at Lodgepole, Grant Grove, and Cedar Grove villages. In Sequoia, the only true sit-down dinner is at Wuksachi Lodge; Lodgepole has a fast-food grill. In Kings Canyon, your choices are the Family Dining Restaurant at Grant Grove Village and the Cedar Grove Lodge. The meals aren't terribly creative, but then, this isn't San Francisco. Breakfast options are predictable: Eggs, pancakes, French toast, and cereal. Lunches revolve around burgers and sandwiches, and dinners mainly include beef, pasta, chicken, and fish.

Restaurants in the parks

Cedar Grove Café

$–$$ **Kings Canyon National Park** **SHORT-ORDER GRILL**

This place is your only option in the bottom of Kings Canyon National Park. The food is basic but affordable, ranging from pasta dishes to nightly specials such as chicken fried steak. Breakfasts range from eggs and bacon to French toast, and lunch is mostly burgers and sandwiches. You can eat in a small dining area or take your food outside to the deck or even to a picnic area by the river, if the bugs aren't biting.

California 180, Cedar Grove Village. ☎ **559-565-0100.** *Main courses: $3.95–$6.25 breakfast; $3.95–$7.95 lunch; $3.95–$15 dinner. AE, DISC, MC, V. Open: Daily 8 a.m.–8 p.m. Closed Oct–May.*

Family Dining Restaurant

$–$$ **Kings Canyon National Park** **AMERICAN**

You won't be dazzled by the ambience — but then, you're here for food, not photo ops. The menu fits the restaurant's name and appeals to entire families. Breakfasts run the gamut from short-order grill items like pancakes and French toast to biscuits and gravy and cheese omelets. A selection of fresh fruit is usually offered, too. Sandwiches and burgers dominate the lunch menu, and dinners reflect the West: Steaks, BBQ ribs, and trout dishes, with a few pasta options.

California 180, Grant Grove Village. ☎ *559-335-5500. Main courses: $3.95–$7.95 breakfast; $6–$ 7.95 lunch; $11.95–$18.95 dinner. AE, MC, V. Open: May–Sept 7 a.m.–9 p.m.; Oct–April 7 a.m.–7 p.m; hours may vary.*

Lodgepole Deli and Pizza

$$ Sequoia National Park   SHORT-ORDER GRILL

There's nothing fancy about this short-order grill, but it's quick and inexpensive. If your meal doesn't fill you, visit the grocery next door.

Generals Highway, Lodgepole Village. No phone. Main courses: $2–$7 breakfast; $3.75–$9.95 lunch; $3.25–$9.95 dinner. AE, DISC, DC, MC, V. Open: Daily 8 a.m.–8 p.m.

Silver City Restaurant

$–$$ Sequoia National Park   AMERICAN

It's not fancy by any means, but you find home-cooked meals at this restaurant if you can't be bothered with cooking for yourself in your cabin. Silver City is open for three meals a day Thursday through Monday; on Tuesdays and Wednesdays the cook heads to town to restock, although you can still get breakfast here. The restaurant offers a cold breakfast buffet with cereals, baked goods, and instant oatmeal. The lunch menu features grill items such as burgers, hot sandwiches, and French fries. Dinners mirror the lunch menu, with the addition of a weekly special such as lasagna, a lemon chicken dish, or tri-tip roast.

Mineral King Road, Mineral King (off Hwy. 198; the resort is about halfway between Lookout Point and Mineral King). ☎ *559-561-3223. Main courses: $3.50–$6 breakfast; $5–$6 lunch; $4–$13 dinner. MC, V. Open: Early June to mid-fall Thurs–Mon 8 a.m.–8 p.m; Tue–Wed breakfast buffet 8 a.m.–5 p.m.*

Wuksachi Lodge

$–$$$ Sequoia National Park   AMERICAN

Beams and rock-work lend a rustic elegance to this lodge, which features a small lounge and 130-seat dining room. The views of 11,188-foot Mount Silliman from the dining room are gorgeous, particularly as the sun is setting. The food is filling, ranging from a simple fettuccine dish with apple-wood bacon and wild mushrooms to herb-crusted pork tenderloin.

Generals Highway, Wuksachi Village. ☎ *888-252-5757. Reservations recommended. Main courses: $1.75–$13.50 breakfast; $6.50–$9 lunch; $6.75–$24.50 dinner. AE, DISC, DC, MC, V. Open: 7 a.m.–4:30 p.m., 5:30–9 p.m.*

Restaurants outside the parks

Kings Canyon Lodge Bar and Grill

$$ Sequoia National Forest   DINER/BARBECUE

Found at the bottom of the mountain as you head to Cedar Grove, this waystation is good for a quick bite or a cool drink before you continue to the park. The restaurant offers short-order dishes for breakfast and burgers, soups, and salads for lunch and dinner. The atmosphere is interesting, because meals are served inside a well-aged bar.

California 180 (between Grant Grove and Cedar Grove Villages). ☎ *559-335-2405. Reservations not needed. Main courses: $3.95–$5.95 breakfast; $4.95–$7.50 lunch and dinner. MC, V. Open: Daily 8 a.m.–8 p.m. Closed mid-Nov to April.*

Fast Facts: Sequoia and Kings Canyon

Area Code
☎ 559.

ATM
You can find ATMs at Grant Grove and Lodgepole Villages.

Emergency
☎ 911.

Fees
$10 per vehicle per week; $5 on foot, bicycle, or motorcycle.

Fishing License
California license required, available at most park grocery stores. Get a copy of park fishing regulations at any visitor center.

Hospitals
Exeter Memorial Hospital, 215 N. Crespi Ave. in Exeter; ☎ 559-592-2151.

Information
Sequoia & Kings Canyon National Parks, 47050 Generals Hwy., Three Rivers, CA 93271-9651; ☎ 559-565-3341.

Lost and Found
Contact nearest visitor center.

Pharmacies
Three Rivers Drug Store, 40893 Sierra Drive in Three Rivers; ☎ 559-561-4217.

Post Office
Lodgepole Market Center, Sequoia National Park, 559-565-3468; Grant Grove, Kings Canyon National Park, ☎ 559-335-2499.

Road Conditions and Weather
☎ 559-565-3341.

Taxes
12% for lodgings, 9.25% for meals.

Time Zone
Pacific standard time.

Web Site
www.nps.gov/seki.

Chapter 20

Yellowstone National Park

• •

In This Chapter

▶ Introducing my favorite park

▶ Planning your trip

▶ Exploring geysers, hot springs, canyons, and lakes

▶ Finding lodging and restaurants around the park

• •

*W*hich park in America is my favorite? Yellowstone National Park, hands down. Nowhere else can you find the diversity that this park offers. From the world's greatest collection of geysers and hot springs to sparkling alpine lakes, rugged peaks, and an incredible array of wildlife, Yellowstone packs more into its boundaries than any other park. Early explorers called it "Wonderland."

With more than 10,000 geothermal features in all shapes, sizes, temperaments, and temperatures, Yellowstone is geyser central. Old Faithful is just one of roughly 150 geysers in the park's Upper Geyser Basin. In the Midway Geyser Basin simmers Grand Prismatic Spring — an azure-hued hot spring ringed by yellow and orange algae as well as the park's largest spring with its 370-foot diameter. At Mammoth Hot Springs, centuries of cascading, mineral-laden hot water have stacked brilliantly white terraces one upon another. These and the rest of Yellowstone's thermal features are constantly changing. Some die out, others get feistier, and new ones spit, claw, and fume into existence through rifts in the earth.

Not upstaged by these waterworks is Yellowstone's animal world. This park has the market cornered when it comes to big furry poster animals suitable for environmental issues. With the reintroduction of wolves in the mid-1990s, the park's wild kingdom has been returned to its original state for the first time since government hunters wiped wolves out of Yellowstone in the 1950s. The more than 100 wolves that now lope about Yellowstone share the park with elk, bison, coyotes, bears, and the occasional moose. The animals give Yellowstone a wild, sometimes scary, edge. On spring and fall nights you may hear the baleful howling of wolves. If your timing is right, you may see grizzly bears and wolves tussling over elk and bison carcasses in the Lamar Valley. In the Hayden Valley, you may have to stop your car to make way for bison, which can weigh nearly a ton and have horn-topped heads.

Yellowstone National Park

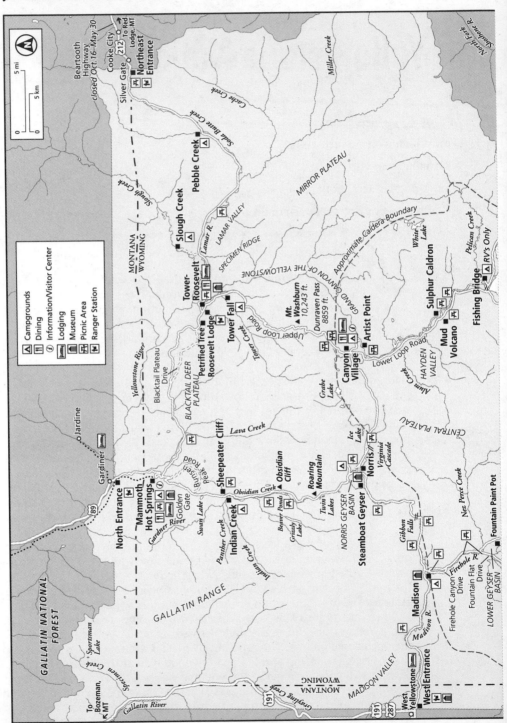

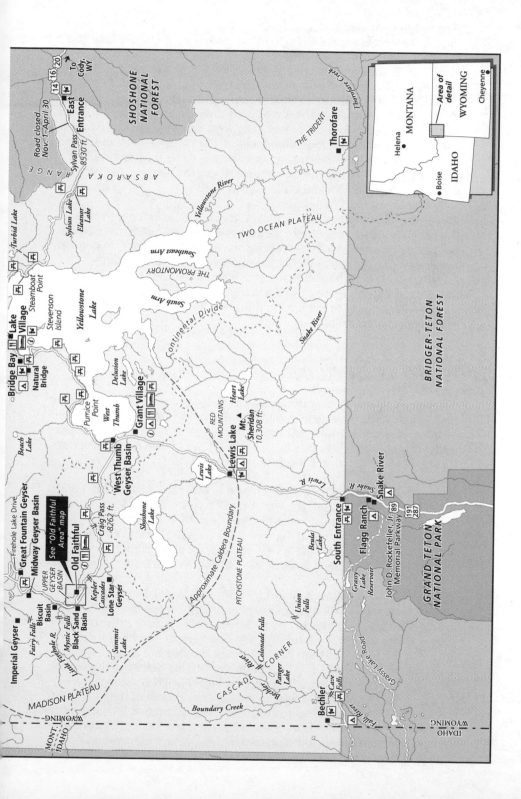

Also unforgettable is Yellowstone Lake. Glassy and serene during the early mornings and evenings on calm summer days, the lake can quickly be whipped into a choppy inland ocean with 6-foot waves. Dotted by islands and rimmed by dense lodgepole forests, the lake nurtures rich fisheries that lure anglers from around the world. Draining the lake, the Yellowstone River flows serenely to the Grand Canyon of the Yellowstone, where it roars over two towering waterfalls. Standing on the brink of 308-foot-tall Lower Falls, you may feel a passing wave of vertigo, but you'll also understand why 19th-century landscape artists, such as Thomas Moran, were so taken by the setting. After crashing to the canyon floor, the river continues to cut the canyon deeper and deeper through yellow- and buff-colored walls.

If you can visit only one national park, make it Yellowstone. Granted, the park's immense popularity generates stifling summertime masses, but in this chapter, I share secrets for avoiding the throngs. In general, remember that, although the front country can get frustratingly crowded during the height of summer when most of the park's 3 million annual visitors arrive, the backcountry provides solitude, serenity, and the same image of the Rocky Mountain West that confronted 19th-century mountain men.

Choosing a Season

You should spend at least three days in Yellowstone. When should you visit? Most visitors come in summer and avoid winter, although the weather is unpredictable year-round. Snow can fall any day of the year, and midwinter *chinooks* (warm, dry winds) can spawn spring-like days. Fickleness aside, the park has four distinct seasons.

Spring doesn't really show up in earnest before mid-May. In fact, I find April and early May about the worst times to visit Yellowstone. Sure, you won't encounter many crowds. But the mud, the harsh bite of a late-season snowstorm, and the weather's overall rawness can be trying. But one positive side is that you can get a bargain on lodging this time of year — imagine a room at the Old Faithful Inn for $25 a night!

Summer begins to show its hand by mid-June as red, blue, purple, orange, and yellow wildflowers erupt in bloom across the park's lower reaches, a ritual that slowly creeps into the high country throughout July and into August. By late June, the first serious waves of tourists arrive in the park, and their cars, at times choking the roads, begin to crawl along the Grand Loop (the main road). This height of the season is a paradox, capturing the best and the worst of Yellowstone. Comfortable temperatures and long days offer plenty of time for sightseeing. But hotels and lodges are booked, campgrounds fill early in the day, and the narrow roads overflow with cars, trucks, and lumbering motor homes. You'll appreciate having made your room reservations well in advance and heeding my advice for avoiding crowds.

Fall consists of the few weeks of decent weather between Labor Day and the return of winter. If you're not bound by school vacations, early fall — from mid-September to mid-October — is the best time to visit Yellowstone. Crowds are generally tolerable, animals return to the river bottoms to fortify themselves against the onslaught of winter, and the weather is typically reliable. Not to be ignored are the occasional bargain prices — savings of 30% and greater! — to be found at the lodges in the fall as closing day approaches.

Winter is Yellowstone's longest season, and it certainly isn't bashful. Winter can settle in as early as October and stay through April. Heavy snows and freezing temperatures (which can plunge far below zero at night and hover around zero during the day) hamper life, both human and animal. Most park roads are closed to automobile traffic between November and May. Only the route from Mammoth Hot Springs to the Northeast Entrance remains plowed through the winter, so the gateway communities of Silvergate and Cooke City, Montana, aren't detached from the world. But cross-country skis, snow coaches, and snowshoes provide a fun mode of travel elsewhere in the snowbound park.

Must-see Attractions

Should you look for geysers? Bison? Wolves? Glassy lakes? Which direction should you head when you arrive in Yellowstone? These questions are always tough for me, because the park has so many wonderful places to go and things to look for. I'm sure that you'll quickly develop your own favorites, but until then, here's a cheat sheet to get you started:

- ✔ **Artist Point:** One of several overlooks below the Yellowstone River's Lower Falls, this vantage point has inspired artists for more than a century.

- ✔ **Lake Yellowstone Hotel:** This Colonial Revival–style hotel, with an interior that may remind you of *The Great Gatsby,* offers the park's most luxurious accommodations. Its Sun Room, just off the lobby, features 1891 wicker furniture and live music nightly.

- ✔ **The Lamar Valley:** This rolling valley in the park's northeast corner comes to life in late spring when elk, bison, grizzly bears, and wolves all converge for nourishment.

- ✔ **Mammoth Hot Springs:** Located just inside the North Entrance, Mammoth Hot Springs is home to park headquarters and, in the Albright Visitor Center, one of the park's best museums. You also find buildings dating to Fort Yellowstone, which was the military outpost when the cavalry administered the park before the National Park Service took over.

You'll fall for these!

Often overlooked because of the park's geothermal features and wildlife are Yellowstone's more than 100 major waterfalls. Among them are the well-known Lower Falls in the Grand Canyon of the Yellowstone and the overlooked 30-foot-tall Moose Falls found less than 1 mile inside the park's South Entrance. The extreme southwestern corner of the park has so many waterfalls that it's known as Cascade Corner, where you find Dunanda Falls (150 feet), Ouzel Falls (235 feet), Colonnade Falls (a "double" waterfall that has a 35-foot upper fall and a 67-foot lower fall), and Union Falls (250 feet). But you can only see the falls in Cascade Corner if you plan a multiday backcountry trip; none of them is close to a road.

✔ **Mud Volcano:** The sulphurous, sputtering machinations of mud pots and hot springs found at this attraction are amazing. Because the springs are heavy with muds and clays, their fizzling, bubbling, and plopping is different from what you see at the other geyser basins.

✔ **The Norris Geyser Basin:** The park's hottest, and oldest, geyser basin has more than 2 miles of trails that navigate through the geysers and hot springs. The area contains Steamboat, the world's tallest active geyser, which blasts 300 to 400 feet into the sky. While spectacular, Steamboat is utterly unpredictable. Eruptions often are many years apart; this geyser last erupted in May 2000, and before that in October 1991.

✔ **The Upper Geyser Basin:** One of five basins in the park's front country where thermal features are concentrated, this area is home to Old Faithful, the world's most famous geyser, and the historic Old Faithful Inn.

Getting There

Yellowstone seems terribly far away, because it's located almost entirely in Wyoming's northwestern corner with some spillover into Idaho and Montana. The park is accessible by state and national highways from all three states, as well as via bus service year-round from Bozeman, Montana, to West Yellowstone. Unless you live nearby or enjoy long drives, fly into one of the nearby airports, rent a rig, and drive to the park.

Flying in

Commercial air service can get you close to the park, with the nearest airports being in Bozeman, Montana, and West Yellowstone. Bozeman's

Gallatin Field (☎ 406-388-6632) is served daily by **Delta, Northwest,** and **United,** along with regional airlines **Horizon** and **Skywest.** Car rentals are available on-site from **Avis, Hertz, Budget,** and **National.** Off-site rentals include **Enterprise, Thrifty, Rentawreck,** and **Dollar.** (See the Appendix for the toll-free numbers of all the airlines and car-rental agencies mentioned throughout this section.)

Skywest, which is affiliated with Delta and United, serves **West Yellowstone Airport** (☎ 406-646-7631) from May through September. **Avis** and **Budget** provide car rentals. The airport closes in winter.

Farther away is Billings, Montana, a 129-mile drive from the park's Northeast Entrance that easily takes more than three hours. Billings' **Logan International** (☎ 406-238-3420 or 406-657-8495) has service from **Big Sky, Delta, Horizon, Northwest,** and **United.** Car rentals are available from **Avis, Budget, Hertz,** and **National.**

South of Yellowstone, the **Jackson Hole Airport** (☎ 307-733-7682) lies within Grand Teton National Park. **American, Delta, Northwest, Skywest,** and **United Express** serve this airport, which is 56 miles from Yellowstone's South Entrance. Car rentals are available from **Alamo, Avis, Budget,** and **Hertz.**

In Cody, Wyoming, **Yellowstone Regional Airport** (☎ 307-587-5096), located 52 miles from the East Entrance, offers year-round service via **Skywest** and **United Express** and car rentals from **Hertz, Avis,** and **Thrifty.**

Driving in

If you drive to Yellowstone from Cody, Wyoming, follow U.S. 14/20/16 west to the park's East Entrance. From Jackson, Wyoming, take U.S. 191/89/287 north to the park's South Entrance. From Idaho, U.S. 20 north from Island Park leads 29 miles to West Yellowstone and the West Entrance. In Montana, U.S. 191 leads 91 miles south from Bozeman to West Yellowstone. From Bozeman, U.S. 89 leads 79 miles east to the North Entrance at Gardiner, Montana.

Because winter weather closes most park roads, if you're planning an early spring or late fall trip, check road conditions with the park (☎ 307-344-7381) before heading out. Whereas the road from Mammoth Hot Springs to the Northeast Entrance communities of Silvergate and Cooke City is open year-round, weather and road conditions permitting, the West Entrance Road typically closes to automobile traffic from the first Sunday in November through the third Friday in April. The South and East Entrance Roads usually close the first Sunday in November and reopen to auto traffic on the first Friday in May. As soon as snow cover allows — generally the third Wednesday in December — these roads, and the West Entrance Road, reopen to over-the-snow vehicles.

The Beartooth Highway, which climbs through the Absaroka Range on a 69-mile journey from Red Lodge, Montana, to the park's Northeast Entrance, is one of the most scenic routes in America. But its precipitous curves can generate vertigo, and winter weather usually keeps it closed from the day after Columbus Day to Memorial Day weekend. The Chief Joseph Highway from Cody to the Northeast Entrance is also spectacular, with sprawling views of the Sunlight Basin, but its many switchbacks aren't designed for speed.

Busing in

During the summer months, you can take **Greyhound Bus Lines** (☎ **800-229-9424** or 406-587-3110; Internet: www.greyhound.com) from downtown Bozeman, Montana, to West Yellowstone.

Yellowstone Alpen Guides (☎ **800-858-3502** or 406-646-9374; Internet: www.yellowstoneguides.com) offers private park tours for families and small groups, as well as winter snow coach tours.

Planning Ahead

Fame carries its burdens, and in Yellowstone, a big one is a lack of lodging and campsites. Fail to plan ahead by at least several months, and you have a hard time finding any accommodations, even in the fall when crowds drop off. And if you don't start working on reservations at least six months ahead, you won't be able to stay exactly where you want to, or when.

All lodging, as well as the Madison, Grant Village, Bridge Bay, and Canyon campgrounds and the Fishing Bridge RV Park, is managed by **Xanterra Parks & Resorts** (☎ **307-344-7311**; Internet: www.xanterra. com.). You can make reservations a year in advance for both hotels and campgrounds through their phone number or Web site. (You also can make dinner reservations months in advance at restaurants inside the park lodges.)

If you want to head into the backcountry, you need to obtain a $15 backcountry permit from the park's **Central Backcountry Office** (P.O. Box 168, Yellowstone National Park, WY 82190; ☎ **307-344-2160** or 307-344-2163). On April 1, the park begins booking reservations for backcountry campsites. All reservation requests received by that date are randomly prioritized by computer and processed in that order. After April 1, reservations are made as requests are received. If you have specific dates and campsites in mind for your trip, I suggest that you apply before the April 1 date. Otherwise, you chance not getting what you want, although you may still be able to choose from a limited selection. For information on this process, and for details on backcountry campsites, contact the backcountry office.

Learning the Lay of the Land

Yellowstone is bigger than Rhode Island and Delaware combined. Most of the park's 3,472 square miles are rugged wilderness — canyons cut deep by rushing rivers, mountains thrust above 11,000 feet by volcanics and earthquakes, and alpine lakes gleam under an endless sky. Weaving through the heart and soul of this wilderness is the **Grand Loop,** a lazy, figure-eight, two-lane road that crawls past the major attractions. You won't travel fast on this road (which is broken into the Upper and Lower Loops), because portions of it are continually under repair. Cut from the wilderness as a narrow stagecoach route in the 19th century, the base of the loop roads struggles with ponderous motor homes, with underlying thermal heat that weakens some spots of the road surface, and with brutal freeze-thaw episodes that buckle the asphalt.

Upper Loop Road

From **Mammoth Hot Springs,** the 70-mile **Upper Loop Road** runs to the way stations of **Norris, Canyon Village,** and **Tower-Roosevelt** before heading back to Mammoth Hot Springs.

Mammoth Hot Springs is home to park headquarters, as well as a hotel, some restaurants, a grocery, a gas station, and other facilities. Norris has a campground, small visitor center, and ranger museum, but no hotel accommodations or restaurants. Canyon Village has lodging, restaurants, a gas station, and a visitor center. Tower-Roosevelt has a lodge/restaurant, surrounding cabins, as well as a small grocery and a gas station.

Two miles south of Tower-Roosevelt is the **Tower Fall** complex, which has a convenience store, gift shop, campground, and a nice hike to one of the park's most accessible (and most dramatic) waterfalls.

Firestorm central

From Norris, the Upper Loop road runs east passing the tip of a 22-mile-long stretch of flattened forest known simply as the Norris-Canyon Blowdown. The trees here were toppled by a 1984 windstorm and were bone dry when the 1988 wildfires swept the park. As a result, this area burned particularly hot. Today, even though thousands of young pines root in the ash-rich soil, you can see charred reminders of the historic fires. Stopping at the lookout point not only gives you a sense of nature's wind and fire power, but the army of young trees shows how forests mend themselves.

Old Faithful Area

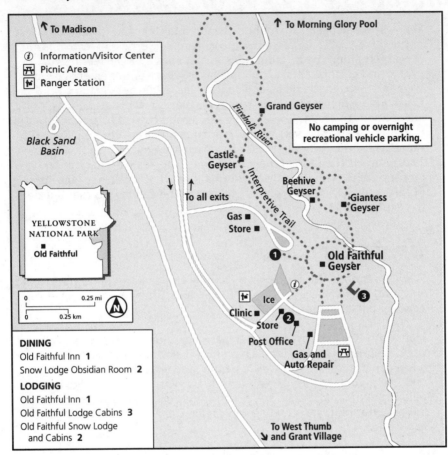

Finding information

The park has five major visitor and information centers. The **Albright Visitor Center** (☎ 307-344-2263) at Mammoth Hot Springs is the largest. It provides visitor information and publications about the park, exhibits depicting park history from prehistory through the creation of the National Park Service, and features a wildlife display.

The **Old Faithful Visitor Center** (☎ 307-545-2750) is another large facility. An excellent short film describing the geysers is shown throughout the day. You can also load up on guidebooks and maps and get a schedule for the day's predicted geyser eruptions.

The **Canyon Visitor Center** (☎ 307-242-2550) in Canyon Village is the place to go for books and an informative display about bison in the park.

Running to the east of Tower-Roosevelt is the **Lamar Valley Road** that leads through the wildlife-rich Lamar Valley on its way to the park's Northeast Entrance at Silvergate, Montana.

Lower Loop Road

I haven't seen any studies, but my guess is that the 96-mile Lower Loop Road, which ties together Madison, Old Faithful, West Thumb, Bridge Bay, Lake Village, Fishing Bridge, Canyon Village, and Norris, is the busiest drag in Yellowstone. The best of Yellowstone's geothermal features are along this road — in the Upper Geyser Basin, West Thumb, Norris, Mud Volcano, and the Lower and Midway Geyser basins.

The **West Entrance Road** ties into Lower Loop Road at Madison, which has a campground, museum, and picnic area. Just south of Madison is **Firehole Canyon Drive,** a 2-mile road that follows the Firehole River upstream and passes 800-foot-high lava cliffs. (This stretch of river is popular with swimmers, although there are no lifeguards, and diving from the cliffs is prohibited.)

Farther south, Lower Loop Road passes through **Old Faithful,** a great base camp. Here you find three places to stay, plus a few restaurants, a visitor center, gift shops, a grocery, a service station, and a medical center. See the Old Faithful Area map in this chapter for locations.

The **South Entrance Road** meets the Lower Loop Road at **West Thumb,** which has boardwalk trails running through a geyser basin and a small visitor center. From here, moving northeast, Lower Loop Road continues along the western shore of **Yellowstone Lake.** Along this shore, you find a campground and marina at **Bridge Bay** and the gracious **Lake Yellowstone Hotel** and laid-back **Lake Lodge** in Lake Village, which also has a hospital, convenience store, and ranger station.

The **East Entrance Road** winds from Cody, Wyoming, over 8,530-foot Sylvan Pass and along the northern shore of Yellowstone Lake to connect with the Lower Loop Road near **Fishing Bridge.** Then Lower Loop Road travels northward to **Canyon Village** through the undulating **Hayden Valley** and past short roads leading to lookout points at **Grand Canyon of the Yellowstone.**

Arriving in the Park

Thanks to its remote location, by the time you reach Yellowstone, you'll be ready to get out, stretch your legs, and gain your bearings. Let me tell you how to do that.

The **Fishing Bridge Visitor Center** (☎ 307-242-2450) near Fishing Bridge has an excellent wildlife display. You can get information and publications here as well.

The **Grant Village Visitor Center** (☎ 307-242-2650) has information, publications, a slide program, and a fascinating exhibit that examines the effects of fire in Yellowstone.

Other sources of park information are at the Madison Information Station; the Museum of the National Park Ranger and the Norris Geyser Basin Museum, both at Norris; and the West Thumb Information Station.

Paying fees

A pass to enter Yellowstone is $20 per vehicle for a seven-day period (no matter the number of occupants), and covers Yellowstone and nearby Grand Teton National Park. Entering on a motorcycle costs $15 for seven days, and if you enter the park on bicycle, skis, or foot, you pay $10. If you expect to visit Yellowstone or Grand Teton more than once in a year, buy an annual pass for $40. With a park pass, you don't have to pay the entrance fee; see Chapter 8 for information on the National Park Pass and Chapter 4 for the lowdown on Golden Age and Golden Access passports.

You must have a backcountry permit for any overnight trip (see "Planning Ahead," earlier in this chapter).

Getting around

Inside Yellowstone, you're left to get around by your own means, because the park does not have public transportation.

Concessionaires provide **summer bus tours** and **snow coach tours** in winter, but these don't allow for much lingering, and they have a traveling-with-the-pack feel. If that's okay with you, contact **Xanterra Parks & Resorts** (☎ 307-344-7311; Internet: www.xanterra.com) about their summer bus tours of the Lower Loop, the Upper Loop, and the Grand Loop. A ticket for the Upper Loop tour, known as the Washburn Expedition, runs $34 per adult (except if you're picked up at Canyon Village, where the fee is $28) and $16 for kids ages 12 to 16. Children 11 and under are free. The Lower Loop tour, known as the Circle of Fire, costs $38 for adults and $17 for kids ages 12 to 16. Children 11 and under are free. The Grand Loop tour, tabbed "Yellowstone in a Day," costs $42 for adults and $20 for those ages 12 to 16; kids 11 and under are free.

In winter, Xanterra's snow coach tours travel round-trip from Mammoth Hot Springs to Old Faithful ($48.50 per person each way);

West Yellowstone to Old Faithful ($46 per person each way); Flagg Ranch to Old Faithful ($51 per person each way); Mammoth Hot Springs to Canyon Village ($97 per person round-trip; one-way service is not available); and Old Faithful to Canyon Village ($97 per person round-trip; one-way service is not available). These all-day trips are expensive if you're taking your family, but a great way to explore the park in winter.

Road work in Yellowstone is as common as elk and bison. As a result, you need to expect delays. For instance, construction along the Madison-to-Norris road could generate 30-minute delays in 2003. More substantial is the planned rebuilding of the Grand Loop Road between Tower Junction and Fishing Bridge, which is scheduled to begin in 2003, with some portions not completed until 2008.

Remembering Safety

Although relaxing in a hot tub after a long day is great, Yellowstone's thermal features are definitely not suited for this activity. They're called *hot springs* for a reason. Temperatures of some springs, stoked by molten rock miles underground, measure well above the boiling point. (Parents, be particularly mindful of your youngsters around these features.) Even if you could survive a dip in a spring, swimming in them can damage their plumbing, so this activity is illegal in the park.

Boardwalks and fencing are not available to keep you a safe distance from thermal features in the backcountry. As a result, be very careful when hiking near these areas. At the Shoshone Lake Geyser Basin, for example, you can walk right up to the edge of the hot springs, but fight the urge to do so. The Earth's crust near these features is often very thin and breakable. Sadly, some hikers have fallen in and died as a result of the water's high temperatures.

Yellowstone's lakes, while picturesque, also can be quite deadly. Their waters are bitterly cold, and if you capsize a canoe or kayak you could be overcome by hypothermia in a short time. Sadly, there are many stories of drownings on Yellowstone Lake and Shoshone Lake

Another safety issue to keep in mind when you're in the backcountry is the wildlife. Grizzlies and black bears both have a good sense of smell, so you need to keep a clean campsite to keep them away. Also, even though moose may look ungainly, they are amazingly quick and won't hesitate to run you down if you threaten their space.

For more tips on how to ensure a safe visit to the park, see Chapter 8.

Enjoying the Park

The park's geographic diversity has led to its division into five districts. **Mammoth Country** covers the northwestern corner, a region of delicate limestone terraces, broad valleys, and dense forests flanking the mountains. In the park's northeastern corner, **Roosevelt Country** embraces the Lamar Valley with its rolling plains that rim the Lamar River. Just to the south is **Canyon Country,** which claims the Grand Canyon of the Yellowstone, with its two towering waterfalls, and the Hayden Valley. **Lake Country** encompasses the park's southeastern corner, including Yellowstone and Heart lakes. The southwestern corner is **Geyser Country,** where you find the bulk of Yellowstone's 10,000 plus geothermal features.

Because these five districts are linked by the Grand Loop, you can split the park in half during visits if you don't have much time. Although you can zoom around the Grand Loop in one day and try to see all the major attractions, I don't recommend it. With unplanned wildlife sightings, the long list of worthwhile sights, and the inevitable meal breaks, you just can't do it all in 24 hours. However, if one day is all the time you have, see "One-day wonder," later in this chapter, for my suggested itinerary.

Exploring the top attractions

Grand Canyon of the Yellowstone

This canyon is an eyeful. But don't let its name confuse you with that other park farther south in Arizona; they're two wonderfully distinct and unique places. Yellowstone's Grand Canyon was colored yellow, tan, red, and buff by thermal water reacting on the park's volcanic underbelly. (*Note:* For trivia fans, the name Yellowstone River was bestowed by French trappers who coined it not because of this canyon, but because of the yellowish banks of the river much farther north in Montana.) Take some time here, and you find numerous overlooks from which to view the canyon and the Yellowstone River. Located on the canyon's south rim, **Artist Point,** which is less crowded than the north-rim overlooks closer to Canyon Village, offers a better view of Lower Falls, and is handicapped-accessible. For a great, off-the-beaten-path view of the canyon, take the Specimen Ridge Trail (see "Taking a hike," later in this chapter).

Watch your step on staircases that lead to canyon overlooks, particularly in spring and fall when snow and ice can make them slippery.

You reach Grand Canyon of the Yellowstone by side roads running east from the Upper and Lower Loop roads as they pass Canyon Village.

Hayden Valley

The Yellowstone River flows serenely through the valley bottom, luring not only pelicans, osprey, and eagles that seek its fish but also attracting teeming bison herds and grizzly bears that come for a drink while rooting through the hillsides and meadows for meals.

The valley is on Lower Loop Road between Canyon Village and Fishing Bridge.

Lamar Valley

Running through the park's northeastern corner, this valley is one of the most reliable places for seeing wildlife during the spring and fall months. If you have a spotting scope or pair of binoculars, definitely pack them so you can spot grizzlies, bison, and even wolves in this sprawling valley. The area has some nice campgrounds and some great hikes, too.

The Lamar Valley is cut by the Northeast Entrance Road that runs 29 miles from Tower-Roosevelt to Silvergate, Montana.

Mammoth Hot Springs

History and geology converge at Mammoth Hot Springs, which in March 2002 was listed on the National Register of Historic Places. In the late 19th century, the U.S. Army set up camp here so soldiers could patrol the park and protect it from poachers and souvenir hunters. Today, this area is the park's headquarters, and many of the Army buildings house park offices as well as the park's best museum in the Albright Visitor Center.

You also find Minerva Terrace, a natural artwork of cascading pools fueled by hot springs. See the Lower Terrace Interpretive Trail under "Taking a hike," later in this chapter, for a short walk around the area.

Mammoth Hot Springs is at the junction of U.S. 89 and the Upper Loop Road.

Capturing Old Faithful on film

For that memorable shot of Old Faithful, rise early in the morning to capture a sunrise photo without the crowds. The softer light at this time also makes for a better image. If you have a decent zoom lens, hike the ½-mile to Observation Point just southeast of the geyser. This vantage point 200 feet above the geyser gives you a sweeping view of most of the Upper Geyser Basin. (This spot is good any time of day for escaping the crowds.) The early morning is best for photography because you can capture the steam wafting from the basin's geysers and hot springs.

Not an early riser? Then sleep in and get your Old Faithful picture at sundown, when most folks are eating dinner.

Mud Volcano

What makes the hot springs in the Mud Volcano area different from the hot springs elsewhere in the park? For starters, the soil-laden waters give rise to this area's fuming mud pots. Moreover, the waters are highly acidic, which lends to their pungent smell. At Dragon's Mouth Spring, muddy water from an underground cavern is spit forth by escaping steam and sulfurous gases to the surface where the waters color the earth in shades of orange and green. Farther up the path, the actual Mud Volcano spring is a simmering pond of mud, fueled by escaping sulfurous gases and steam.

Although all the park's geyser basins are kid-friendly — kids get a kick out of eruptions — young visitors find Mud Volcano particularly fun because of the plopping and fizzing of the mud pots.

Mud Volcano is on Lower Loop Road between Fishing Bridge and Canyon Village.

Norris Geyser Basin

This kid-pleasing attraction is the park's oldest basin with a history of thermal activity that goes back more than 115,000 years. This basin is also the hottest, with a temperature of 459 degrees measured 1,087 feet below the surface. The basin holds 2 miles of trails, which lead to such thermal stalwarts as Steamboat and Echinus geysers. Steamboat is the world's tallest active geyser, with gushers of 300 to 400 feet, but honestly, its eruptions are so infrequent that the odds of witnessing the spectacle are incredibly slim. Echinus, meanwhile, erupts 40 to 60 feet once or twice an hour. (For an orientation of this basin, see the Old Faithful Area map in this chapter.)

Norris is also home to Porcelain Basin, where you can find multihued hot springs. The basin's name comes from the underlying minerals and clays that, depending on the resident minerals, turn the roiling waters pearly with milky or orangish tints.

At the trailhead to the geyser basin is a small geology-oriented museum, one of the park's original trailside museums. Another larger museum, the nearby Museum of the National Park Ranger, showcases the history of rangerdom. Both museums are free; hours vary depending on season and staffing.

The Norris Basin is at the junction of the Upper and Lower Loop roads.

Upper Geyser Basin

No geothermal area in the world rivals the Upper Geyser Basin, another kid-friendly attraction, which packs 150 geysers and hot springs into 1 square mile alone. Five of the six geysers whose eruptions are predicted by the park staff are located here: Castle, Grand, Daisy, Riverside, and the famous Old Faithful. (The sixth is Great Fountain in the Lower Geyser Basin.)

The Old Faithful Geyser clearly is the park's greatest single drawing card, and its location on a wide gray geyserite mound sets it apart from the rest of the basin and enhances its nobility. Rimmed by a boardwalk that's covered with benches, the geyser performs about every 92 minutes. But frankly, one Old Faithful performance is enough, because its eruptions draw thousands of gawking tourists and turn the performance into something of a sideshow. Other spectacular geysers offer incredible displays but don't lure the crowds: Riverside is one, and another is Lone Star (found at the end of the Lone Star Geyser Trail — see "Taking a hike").

Parents, don't forget, be sure to keep a tight rein on your young children while visiting geyser basins.

Upper Geyser Basin is also the location of the historic Old Faithful Inn. A seat before the fireplace in the log inn's cavernous lobby is almost as awe-inspiring as watching Old Faithful bluster, sputter, and fume into being. (See "Where to Stay" for more on this hotel.)

Upper Geyser Basin is on Lower Loop Road near Old Faithful.

West Thumb Geyser Basin

Much smaller than the Lower, Midway, and Upper Geyser basins, West Thumb is almost intimate. You don't find towering geysers here, but you see sputtering, multicolored paint pots and fuming, deep blue hot springs. Off the shore of adjacent Yellowstone Lake is Fishing Cone, a hot spring where anglers cooked their fish by dipping them in the cone. (No need to tote your fishing pole, though, as fishing at the geyser basin is prohibited).

West Thumb is at the junction of Lower Loop Road and South Entrance Road.

Yellowstone Lake

This lake is home to North America's largest population of cutthroat trout. Lower Loop Road has several turnoffs for awesome views of the lake. With a length of 20 miles and a width of 14 miles, Yellowstone is the largest natural freshwater lake situated above 7,000 feet in the United States. (Its elevation is 7,733 feet.)

The lake drains into Yellowstone River at Fishing Bridge, on the lake's north end. Anglers years ago would crowd the bridge with hopes of hooking one of the river's cutthroat trout, but today, fishing is banned from the span. But you still can walk across the bridge and, if your timing is right, see osprey, eagles, and pelicans pluck trout from the river. The area also has an excellent museum focusing largely on the lake's aquatic life and a campground specifically for hard-shelled trailers and recreation vehicles.

Lower Loop Road hugs the lake between West Thumb and Fishing Bridge.

Taking a hike

You can't experience the essence of Yellowstone inside a car or bus. Get out and walk through the geyser basins, along the lakeshores, and into the forests. You don't have to stray far from your car if you don't want to. Boardwalks roam through the Upper, Midway, Lower, and Norris Geyser basins, as well as through the Mud Volcano area. Near the start of these boardwalks, you can buy a pamphlet, for a nominal charge, that guides you through the features.

If you go on a day hike, carry water, watch the weather, and pack rain gear. Take extra caution around thermal features, because no fences or boardwalks define a safe distance, and keep an eye out for wildlife.

In the following section, I list just a handful of day and overnight hikes (remember to get a backcountry permit for all overnight trips). You can find guidebooks that outline the bulk of the park's hiking trails at any of the visitor centers. If you prefer not to hike alone, the Yellowstone Association Institute and Yellowstone National Park Lodges (☎ 307-344-5566) offers a package that mixes naturalist-led hikes with lodging.

Lone Star Geyser Trail

An easy walk along a paved trail that follows the Firehole River leads to a backcountry wonder worth a visit. The geyser, alone in a clearing, rifles a stream of water 20 to 40 feet into the air above its tall geyserite cone. The geyser erupts about every three hours; a nearby log tracks the eruptions. Bicycles are permitted on the trail, which is paved almost all the way to the geyser. A bonus of this hike is the view near the trailhead of Kepler Cascades, which plunges 125 feet. This trail is also an invigorating ski in the winter.

Distance: 5 miles round-trip. Level: Easy. Access: South of the Old Faithful complex, the trailhead is at the parking lot opposite Kepler Cascades.

Lower Terrace Interpretive Trail

This easy, self-guided path winds up through the *travertine* (mineral deposits formed by flowing water) terraces laid down over the centuries. The trail offers up-close views of thermal plumbing and a nice panorama of Mammoth.

Distance: 1½ miles round-trip. Level: Easy. Access: Trailhead is located just south of Mammoth Hot Springs on the road to Norris.

Mount Washburn Trail

If you can only take one hike at Yellowstone, take this one. The rises are fairly gradual, and they're interspersed with long, fairly level stretches. At this elevation, however, you still need to pace yourself, which not only saves energy, but also provides time to appreciate the eastern views of the Absaroka Mountains, the southern views of Yellowstone Lake, and the western views of the Gallatin Range. Odds are good that you'll see mountain sheep, because Mount Washurn is a popular summer grazing area for them, as well as yellow-bellied marmots and the wily red fox. The hike to the summit, where you find a fire lookout, is an easy 90-minute walk at a steady pace, or 2 hours with breaks. At this elevation, where weather changes quickly, dress in layers and carry water. Fortunately, a warming hut, complete with viewing scopes and rest rooms, is at the base of the lookout.

Distance: 6 miles round-trip. Level: Moderate. Access: The trailhead is at the end of the Old Chittenden Road and at Dunraven Pass.

Shoshone Lake Trail

This is my favorite hike in the park. Not only does the trail lead to the country's largest backcountry lake, one you can't reach by auto, but it crosses the Firehole River, into a beautiful lodgepole pine forest, and arrives at a sprawling geyser basin, which appears the same today as it did to explorers in the 1800s. From Lone Star Geyser, the trail crosses the Firehole River before climbing about 300 feet to cross the Continental Divide through Grants Pass and then dropping down to the lake where campsites dot the shoreline. (The campsites must be reserved — see "Planning Ahead," earlier in the chapter.) A spur trail runs to the Shoshone Geyser Basin. Be careful in the basin, though, because at least one backcountry traveler has died from a fall into the hot water. Hikers can either retrace their steps back to the trailhead after a multinight stay at the lake, or continue around the lake to the Lewis Lake Trailhead, a one-way trip of about 22 miles from the Lone Star Trailhead.

Distance: 17 miles round-trip via Lonestar Geyser. Level: Moderate. Access: Use the Lone Star Geyser Trailhead.

Specimen Ridge Trail

This kid-friendly trail is another of my favorites because it offers sweeping views of the Lamar Valley, leads you to the world's largest collection of petrified trees, and can be extended to the rim of the Grand Canyon of the Yellowstone depending on how much time you have. Roughly 2 miles from the trailhead, you pass a "grove" of petrified trees, which also offers excellent samples of petrified leaf impressions, but you have to look hard to find them. (Keep in mind that taking anything, including fossils, from the park is a federal crime.) Although you can turn back after viewing the fossilized trees, the open country that roams along the ridge invites exploring. When you reach the ridgetop, head west over the open ground to the rim of the Grand Canyon of the Yellowstone for a magnificent view of this abyss.

Distance: 4 miles round-trip. Level: Moderate. Access: Lamar River Bridge east of Tower Junction.

One-day wonder

You want to visit Yellowstone but can only squeeze in a day. Can you see all the sights? No. But you can see some of the park's most famous features. The key, obviously, is to keep moving and be flexible. Yellowstone is a big park and its attractions, far-flung. To see as much as possible in one day, you need to get up early and keep going until sundown. For information on the attractions in this section, see "Exploring the top attractions," earlier in this chapter, unless otherwise noted.

Plan to stay in the **Old Faithful** area and concentrate on touring the attractions along Lower Loop Road. Not only do you get to see the park's famous geothermal features, but you can also encounter lots of wildlife, particularly in the Hayden Valley.

Because the **Old Faithful Visitor Center** (see "Finding information," earlier in this chapter) doesn't open until 9 a.m., stop by the night before to see if they've posted a schedule of predicted geyser eruptions for the next day. If you're lucky, Old Faithful will be ready to go right after you finish breakfast, and you can see the show and cross it off your to-do list.

Next, head north on the Lower Loop Road toward Norris, stopping at the **Midway Geyser Basin** to view Grand Prismatic Spring.

Move on to **Norris Geyser Basin,** roughly 30 miles north of Old Faithful. Take the trail leading south from the parking lot to Emerald Spring, Steamboat Geyser, and on to Echinus Geyser. You probably won't see Steamboat erupt, but take the short walk down the trail to Echinus Geyser, whose eruptions occur every one to four hours. A crowd of people surrounding it means an eruption is in the offing. If you don't see a crowd, head down the boardwalk to see Arch Steam Vent and Green Dragon Spring before returning to Echinus, which might now be ready to erupt.

After Echinus's show, instead of making the entire Back Basin loop, backtrack to the Norris Museum and the trail leading down into Porcelain Basin. Follow the boardwalk counterclockwise, passing Ledge Geyser, Whirligig Geyser, Whale's Mouth, and Crackling Lake before ending up back near the start across from the Black Growler Steam Vent.

When you feel that you've seen enough at Norris, head 12 miles east to **Canyon Village** for a quick lunch at the Canyon Glacier Pit Snack Bar or the Canyon Lodge Cafeteria. Afterward, visit the **Grand Canyon of**

the Yellowstone by heading along North Rim Drive for a stop at Inspiration Point and then on to the Brink of the Falls Trail to make the 1½-mile round-trip down to the lip of the falls and back.

Back in your car, finish the North Rim Drive, turn left, and head south toward Lake Village, 17 miles away. Along the way, you bisect the **Hayden Valley** with its bison herds before arriving at **Mud Volcano** and **Sulphur Caldron,** which are across the road from one another. You don't need to hike the ⅔-mile, Mud Volcano trail system unless you want to. Just getting out to peer into Dragon's Mouth Spring gives you an indication of the geothermal activity in this corner of the park.

From Mud Volcano, stop at the **Lake Yellowstone Hotel** (see "Where to Stay") to either relax with a refreshment in the Sun Room or head out to the shore for a short walk along the beach. After this, return to Old Faithful and take a final walk on the boardwalk before or after dinner.

If you have more time

If you visited the Norris and Upper Geyser basins and still haven't had your fill of gurgling and steamy water, head to the Lower and Middle Geyser basins. Both are located on Lower Loop Road between Madison and Old Faithful.

Even though the **Midway Geyser Basin** is minuscule compared to the Upper Geyser Basin, it packs a lot into a small area. An awesome sight is the Excelsior Geyser, a 200- by 300-foot crater that dumps more than 4,000 gallons of water into the Firehole River every minute of every day. Grand Prismatic Spring, the park's largest spring at 370 feet wide and 121 feet deep, is believed to be the third largest in the world, behind two in New Zealand. The yellow-and-orange rimmed pool, with its deep blue waters, is definitely worth some pictures. This area has boardwalks through small sections of hot springs and geysers.

The main attraction of the **Lower Geyser Basin** is the 3-mile Firehole Lake Drive, which leads to terraces fed by the twice-a-day eruptions of Great Fountain. Boardwalks roam through small sections of hot springs and geysers. Check with the rangers at the Old Faithful Visitor Center for estimated eruption times.

Ranger programs

Yellowstone ranger programs typically begin in early June and run through August. Walks, talks, and hikes top the list of ranger-led activities at Mammoth Hot Springs, Norris, Madison, Old Faithful, Grant Village, Lake Village, Canyon Village, and Tower-Roosevelt. The offerings change from season to season and year to year, so check the park newspaper (you receive one upon entering the park) or visitor center bulletin boards for topics and times.

Spotting the local wildlife

Because the park boasts the richest, most diverse wildlife community in the Lower 48, you can spend hours debating whether Yellowstone's wildlife takes a backseat to its geological wonders.

Sometimes called America's Serengeti, the park's northern range is where you should focus your search for animals in late spring, early summer, and fall. You can spot most of the animals mentioned here in the Lamar and Hayden valleys. Because the animals — particularly bears and wolves — will be small dots on the far side of the valleys, you'll want binoculars or a spotting scope to bring them into focus.

When park officials reintroduced **wolves** to the park in the 1990s, Yellowstone's wild kingdom became whole, completely representative of the animals that roamed the park a century earlier. Ten packs of wolves have restored order to the park's kingdom after they had been absent from Yellowstone for more than 60 years. **Coyote** populations, which erupted after wolf packs were exterminated in the 1920s in the name of predator control (although there were reports of lone wolves in the park in the 1930s), have been reduced by the wolves. **Elk** herds, too, are expected to experience a decline in population, because the wolves came from a region of Canada where they preyed primarily on elk.

Bison, which along with elk are the park's most visible species, are not as vulnerable to the wolves because of their bulk and generally irascible demeanor when confronted. These shaggy guys prefer nothing more than hanging out in meadows and on the plains to graze on grasses and wildflowers. What too many visitors somehow overlook is that these critters are wild and unpredictable, not hand-fed poster animals for the National Park Service. Although they make great photo ops, every year several people end up becoming too familiar with the sharp horns of an 1,800-pound bison that proved surprisingly quick on its hooves. Watch yourself and your kids closely.

Until the wolves returned, bears were number one on vacationers' want-to-see list. **Grizzly bears** are usually seen from a distance, and that's a good thing. Long gone are the days when Yellowstone's garbage pits were surrounded by bleachers so you could watch grizzlies chow down on whatever you didn't finish for breakfast. Now, grizzlies seldom frequent the front country, preferring to browse distant hillsides and the backcountry for grubs, berries, rodents, and, in the spring, newborn elk and bison calves. You can usually spot grizzlies in the Lamar and Hayden Valleys in the spring, when their mischievous side comes out. Yearlings have been spotted sliding down waning snow fields.

Black bears, on the other hand, don't seem to mind sharing the front country with humans. You may see them browsing hillsides just feet from the Grand Loop as you approach Roosevelt from the south.

The programs tend to showcase and study the features of their locations. For example, at Old Faithful, most programs focus on the park's geologic machinations. Among the favorites is a walking tour of Geyser

Hill that gives you a thorough understanding of the geothermal plumbing that fuels Yellowstone's hot springs and geysers. At Mammoth Hot Springs, American history surfaces, because this area is where the U.S. Army was based (at Fort Yellowstone) when it patrolled the park before the National Park Service was created. Many of the park offices are housed in the fort's buildings, and just walking past them is a treat as you can imagine soldiers coming and going. At Grant Village, the programs tend to revolve around wildlife. You often can sign on for tours at Canyon Village that lead into the Hayden Valley, and rangers usually offer walks along the rim of the Grand Canyon of the Yellowstone. You can also enjoy half-day backcountry hikes led by rangers. The Ranger Adventure Hiking Series charges a fee, though, to help the Park Service pay for the staff and supplies for these hikes. Still, at $15 for adults and $7 for kids ages 7 to 15, that's a pretty good bargain for a half-day of focused interpretation in Yellowstone's backcountry.

One of the more unusual programs in the Lake Village area especially appeals to kids. Along the Elephant Back Trail just south of Fishing Bridge, a park ranger dressed in period garb talks about the life and times of mountain men in Yellowstone. Check at the Fishing Bridge Visitor Center for the schedule. The Junior Ranger Program is another kid favorite. Materials for this activity are available at any visitor center. (See Chapter 4 for information about the Junior Ranger Program.)

Keeping active

Yellowstone can keep you on the go year-round. If you want to snowshoe or cross-country ski in winter, **Xanterra** (☎ **307-344-7311;** Internet: www.xanterra.com) offers package trips as well as shuttle service to various areas of the park, such as Tower Fall and Indian Creek from Mammoth Hot Springs and Fairy Falls, and to the Continental Divide from Old Faithful. You can also arrange guided tours, year-round, to the Grand Canyon of the Yellowstone and the backcountry around Old Faithful.

Temperatures can be bitterly cold in winter. That's why the park has warming huts at Canyon Village, Fishing Bridge, Indian Creek, Madison, Old Faithful, and West Thumb. With the exception of the Old Faithful hut, which is open only during the day, all huts are open 24 hours.

The following activities guarantee to get your heart pumping summer and winter:

✔ **Boating:** The best place to enjoy boating in Yellowstone is on Yellowstone Lake, which has easy access and beautiful, panoramic views. The lake is also one of the few areas where powerboats are allowed. You can rent rowboats and outboard motorboats at **Bridge Bay Marina** (☎ **307-344-7381**). You can use motorboats, canoes, and kayaks on Lewis Lake, too. Wherever you float in the park, you're required to have Coast Guard-approved life vests.

If you want to launch your own boat at Bridge Bay, you must obtain a permit. Permit fees are $20 per season or $10 for seven days for a motorized craft; $10 per season or $5 for seven days for a nonmotorized craft.

✔ **Cross-country skiing:** Gliding through the park on a bright winter day is a wonderful way to experience Yellowstone's beauty. All the park's trails are open to skiers. The Lamar Valley is a particularly good spot. Another good starting point is Tower Junction, where you can slip past a gate that blocks cars from heading south, and you can ski 2 miles down the road to Tower Fall. Then you can hike a ½-mile trail down to the base of the waterfall, which can be ice-encrusted from around December through February, the park's coldest months. Ski rentals ($9.25 for a half-day; $14.25 all day) are available through **Xanterra** (☎ 307-344-7311) at Mammoth Hot Springs and Old Faithful.

✔ **Fishing:** Yellowstone, Shoshone, and Lewis lakes are good places to drop a line, whereas many sections of the park's rivers are perfect for fly-fishing. The Madison, Firehole, and Yellowstone rivers are famous for their brown, brook, and cutthroat trout fisheries. If you plan to fish, stop at a ranger station, a visitor center, or Yellowstone General Stores to pick up a permit and pamphlet of regulations. Some park streams are closed to fishing, some are catch-and-release only, and number and size limits vary by species, so you definitely need a copy of the regulations. You don't need a Wyoming fishing license, but anglers 16 years and older must pay $10 for a 10-day park permit or $20 for a season-long permit. Kids ages 12 to 15 need a nonfee permit, and kids 11 and younger don't need one as long as an adult supervises them.

✔ **Ice skating:** If you stay at Mammoth Hot Springs, take time to skate on the rink behind the hotel. Rentals run $1 an hour or $4 for the day.

✔ **Snowshoeing:** If you seek a slower, quieter pace, snowshoe packages are available through **Xanterra** (☎ 307-344-7311) at Mammoth Hot Springs and Old Faithful ($8 for a half-day; $11 all day). All hiking trails are open to snowshoers, although I recommend those in the Lamar Valley.

Where to Stay

Don't make a last-minute decision to visit Yellowstone. Lining up a warm place to sleep requires months of planning. With that in mind, your lodging choices run the gamut from rustic cabins at Roosevelt (which have only woodstoves for heat and a communal bathhouse a short walk away) to a presidential suite at the Lake Yellowstone Hotel. As expected, prices vary, too — from $40 for a spartan cabin to almost $400 for the suite. For a real bargain, try camping. The park has many campground sites where you can pitch your tent ($10–$15) or park your RV ($29).

The timing of your visit determines your number of lodging options. For example, the Old Faithful Inn is open from early May until mid-October, and the Old Faithful Lodge cabins are available from mid-May to mid-September. The Old Faithful Snow Lodge does business from mid-May to mid-October, then reopens from mid-December through mid-March for the winter season. The Mammoth Hot Springs Hotel and cabins follow this same schedule. Lake Yellowstone Hotel is open from mid-May through September; the Lake Lodge cabins are available from mid-June to mid-September; Grant Village Lodge is open from mid-May to mid-September; and the Canyon Lodge and its cabins, as well as the Roosevelt Lodge cabins, are open from early June through August.

The listings in this section for the park hotels don't include individual phone numbers or addresses. All lodging is managed by **Xanterra Parks & Resorts.** One phone number (☎ 307-344-7311), Web site (www.xanterra.com), and address (P.O. Box 165, Yellowstone National Park, WY 82190) is good for all properties. Don't worry about not being able to find your hotel. When you enter the park, you'll receive a map pinpointing the location of each one.

Lodging in Lake Village

Removed, yet elegant. That fairly well defines this north-shore community on Yellowstone Lake. Although you're not in the middle of a geyser basin, you're close to Mud Volcano and the West Thumb Geyser Basin. Plus, the sweeping Hayden Valley with its bison herds is not far off, either. You can choose from plush accommodations in the elegant Lake Yellowstone Hotel; clean, comfortable, and simple Lake Lodge cabins; or a more rustic experience in aged cabins. Along with a variety of dining options, you find a ranger station, gift shops, a small hospital, a grocery, and boating and hiking options.

Lake Yellowstone Hotel and Cabins
$$–$$$$ Lake Village

Lake Yellowstone Hotel (commonly known as "Lake Hotel") is the Grand Dame of Yellowstone's lodges. Erected in 1891 and painstakingly restored in 1989, the hotel is the perfect place for spoiling yourself. There's no roughing it here, thanks to the Sun Room that fronts the lake, a prim dining room, and 194 carpeted guest rooms. Not five minutes from the lobby is the lakeshore, perfect for an after-dinner stroll. You find the park's nicest (and most expensive) rooms in the hotel. But you can avoid the hefty $100 plus per night charge and still enjoy the atmosphere by staying in one of the less expensive, and stark, Lake Hotel Annex rooms or one of the simple Lake Hotel Frontier cabins (with beds, showers, toilets, and sinks) and walking over to the hotel for its ambience and amenities. Neither the annex rooms nor the cabins offer much character, but the walls in the annex are a bit thicker and bathrooms more complete than those in the cabins.

As with Old Faithful Inn, dinner reservations in the hotel are precious, so book early.

193 rooms; 102 cabins; 1 presidential suite. TEL. Rack rates: $157–$167 double; $83 cabin; $392 presidential suite. AE, DC, DISC, MC, V. Open: Mid-May to early Oct.

Lake Lodge Cabins
$$–$$$ Lake Village

A third option at Lake Village is to check into one of these cabins and walk the ¼-mile to the hotel for meals and atmosphere. These cabins come in two flavors: An older, more economical Pioneer version with one double bed, shower, toilet, and sink, and the motel-style Western cabin, which is a bit more spacious and contains two double beds and a bathroom with tub and shower. The log lodge offers a small lounge and nondescript cafeteria, so any money you save by staying in one of the cabins will likely be spent on the food and ambience over at the hotel.

186 cabins. Rack rates: $51–$112 double. AE, DC, DISC, MC, V. Open: June–Sept.

Lodging in Mammoth Hot Springs

This community offers it all — a range of accommodations from historic hotel to campground, fine dining, the park's best visitor center, and limestone terraces built up over the millennia. The historic Fort Yellowstone, restaurants, gift shops, a convenience store, and a service station complete the package. On the downside, even though the Mammoth Hot Springs Terraces are just a short walk from the hotel, you're far removed from the mainstays of the park's geothermal attractions. In the winter, though, this place is a good base camp, thanks to the hotel, skating rink, and proximity to the Lamar Valley for snowshoeing and wildlife spotting.

Mammoth Hot Springs Hotel and Cabins
$$–$$$ Mammoth Hot Springs

Somewhere between the high-brow Lake Yellowstone Hotel and the low-rent Roosevelt Lodge cabins is Mammoth Hot Springs Hotel. The hotel is a turn-of-the-20th-century creation 5 miles inside the North Entrance, and its rooms are not elaborate. Most offer comfortable beds and functional bathrooms; if you don't reserve early enough, though, you may need to walk down the hall to the communal bathroom. The hotel has two plush suites. The cottage-style cabins are an economical alternative, and four actually have their own hot tubs. Again, book early because not all cabins feature bathrooms.

The hotel lobby has a woodstove that you can cozy up to in winter and a wood floor maintained to a high luster. Off the lobby is the sprawling Map Room — a high-ceilinged, rectangular room filled with overstuffed sofas, writing desks, and huge windows through which, in spring, summer, and fall, you can count the dozens of elk lured to the sweet grass lawns surrounding the park headquarters. The room's name stems from a large wooden map, made from 15 different woods from nine countries, that hangs on one wall.

If Old Faithful is your destination, pass on staying here, which is 51 miles away from Upper Geyser Basin along twisting roads.

95 rooms; 115 cabins; 2 suites. Rack rate: $65–$90 double; $54–$125 cabin; $261 suite. AE, DC, DISC, MC, V. Open: Early May to early Oct, Dec–March.

Lodging in the Old Faithful area

Sure, this area is crowded, but it's surrounded by the world's greatest collection of geysers and hot springs. Plus, the Old Faithful Inn has the most rustic charm of any of the park's accommodations. And as a bonus, a variety of dining options, from short-order grill to multi-course, sit-down restaurants, are nearby. Come winter, the pace eases a bit while the ambience is heightened thanks to the snow and cold. The Old Faithful complex includes a convenience store, gift shops, a visitor center, a medical clinic, and a service station. (See the Old Faithful Area map in this chapter.)

Old Faithful Inn
$$–$$$$ Old Faithful area

If you loved Lincoln Logs as a kid and want the true Yellowstone experience, stay here. Located near the apron of the Old Faithful Geyser, the inn was crafted from trees pulled from the surrounding forests and rock quarried from the nearby Black Sand Basin. Probably the biggest log cabin you'll ever see, this inn oozes rustic charm, from the gnarled lodgepole limbs used as decorative braces to accent the interior to the Mission-style library desks on the second-floor balcony.

When foul weather arrives, squirrel yourself away with a book or a deck of cards in a corner of the second- or third-story balconies. (On clear days, the second-story deck offers nice views of Old Faithful and much of Geyser Hill.) Reservations fill up quickly for dinner at the inn, so make yours before heading into the park for the day. Also, make sure to visit the Bear Pit Lounge to see the whimsically etched glass panels.

Like no other place in the park, the inn and its rooms meld modern comforts and wilderness. Some of the rooms lack baths, so if trudging down the hall in your robe and slippers bothers you, you have even more reason to start planning your trip early.

Reservations ☎ 307-344-7311. 327 rooms. Rack rates: $69–$164 double; $334 suite. AE, DC, DISC, MC, V. Open: Mid-May to mid-Oct.

Old Faithful Lodge Cabins
$–$$ Old Faithful area

The lodge houses a cafeteria, snack bar, and gift shop. Several cabin options are available depending on how rustic you're willing to go. Whereas the Frontier cabins offer you a private bathroom, the Pioneer units have toilets and sinks but no baths. The bargain-basement Budget units constitute the Upper Geyser Basin's low-rent district. They come with beds, sinks, and a short walk to a communal bathhouse. A tent offers more atmosphere than these claustrophobic and rundown Budget shacks, so definitely call far enough in advance to get a Frontier or Pioneer unit.

96 cabins (some without baths). Rack rates: $40–$65 double. AE, DC, DISC, MC, V. Open: May–Oct.

Old Faithful Snow Lodge and Cabins
$$–$$$ Old Faithful area

Dedicated in May 1999, the Snow Lodge is the newest accommodation at Old Faithful. The $20 million rock-and-timber structure replaced an ancient structure originally built as a dormitory for employees. The lodge offers 100 rooms, a restaurant and lounge, a fast-food grill, and a ski-rental shop. The rooms' personality is infused with animal motifs carved into the lamps and the furniture. The lobby with its fireplace is handsome and comfortable, and the inn has a nice lounge and attractive dining room. As the only winter lodging available at Old Faithful, competition is keen for reservations. Thirty-four year-round cabins are also associated with the Snow Lodge. They are motel-like and charmless, but clean and comfortable.

100 rooms, 34 1-bedroom cabins. Rack rates: $134 double; $68–$112 cabin. AE, DC, DISC, MC, V. Open: Early May to mid-Oct., mid-Dec to early March.

Lodging in Tower-Roosevelt

The log lodge and its surrounding cabins are near the spot where President Roosevelt camped during a 1903 trip to the park. The cabins are not luxurious by any stretch of the imagination, but the lodge, although not huge, is rustic and cozy and serves up decent meals. You don't need to be an overnight guest to sample the tasty cornbread or to spend time in one of the front porch's rocking chairs with a view into the Lamar Valley.

The cabins are as close to roughing it in Yellowstone as it gets without having a tent or the open sky overhead at night. Whereas the lodge's Frontier and Economy cabins offer various degrees of plumbing, Roughriders don't even feature sinks. Communal bathhouses are nearby, though, so you don't have to go to bed grimy. If you've come to Yellowstone to look for wildlife, this is the place to be in the late spring and early summer.

Roosevelt Lodge and Cabins

$–$$ **Tower-Roosevelt**

It seems like you don't get much when you reserve the Frontier, Economy, or Roughrider cabins that surround the Roosevelt Lodge. And you don't. Heated by woodstoves, the few Frontier cabins feature showers, toilets, and sinks, an undistinguished claim to fame in the present. But it's an impressive claim when compared to the Roughrider units, which have stoves but not running water; the communal bathhouse is a short walk away. The Economy cabins fall in between: They include a toilet and sink, but no shower facilities. These cabins are very similar to the old models at Old Faithful. Still, I find that this location, with its lodgepole forest, the Lamar Valley falling away to the east, and the log lodge for meals and drinks in front of a roaring fire, nurtures a decidedly rustic charm absent from the park's other offerings.

80 cabins. Rack rates: $48–$86 double. AE, DC, DISC, MC, V. Open: Early June to early Sept.

Runner-up lodgings

Park lodging is also available in Canyon and Grant villages. If you wait too long to book reservations in the park, you don't need to postpone your Yellowstone trip. Just across the park's northern and western borders are a number of motels and lodges in the Gardiner (Chamber of Commerce, ☎ **406-848-7971**) and West Yellowstone (Chamber of Commerce, ☎ **406-646-7701**) areas. I list the best of these accommodations here.

Absaroka Lodge

$–$$ **Gardiner**   Set high on the banks of the Yellowstone River where you can fish for a trout dinner, the lodge is just a two-block walk from the park's north entrance. *South U.S. 89 (at Yellowstone River Bridge).* ☎ *800-755-7414 or 406-848-7414. Internet:* www.yellowstonemotel.com.

Canyon Lodge

$$–$$$ **Canyon Village**   This national park lodge lacks ambience and has a motel-like feel. However, the location, a ½ mile from the Grand Canyon of the Yellowstone, is a plus. Cabins also are available. ☎ *307-344-7311.*

Grant Village Lodge

$$–$$$ **Grant Village**   This national park lodge offers accommodations in six plain buildings, stacked two stories high, along the edge of Yellowstone Lake. ☎ *307-344-7311.*

Stagecoach Inn

$–$$$ **West Yellowstone** This hotel, if you can't tell from its name, has a Western flavor. Stuffed animals hang on the lobby's wood-paneled walls, and in the rooms, you find elk-antler lamps and bedspreads and drapes with patterns of elk, bison, moose, and bears. *209 Madison (at Dunraven).* ☎ *800-842-2882 or 406-646-7381. Internet:* www.yellowstone inn.com.

Campgrounds

Yellowstone has a dozen campgrounds: seven overseen by the National Park Service (NPS) and five by **Xanterra.** The differences among them? You can reserve a spot to fling your tent or park your RV in one of the Xanterra campgrounds months ahead of your arrival, but the NPS sites fill up quickly on a first-come, first-served basis. Nightly rates at both Xanterra and NPS locations range from $10 to $15, except at the Fishing Bridge Campground, where sites are restricted to RVs and hard-shell campers (due to grizzly bears in the area) and cost $29 per night.

None of these campgrounds provides the wilderness experience so readily available with a hike into the backcountry. Instead, you have a mass group setting, where you're surrounded by other happy campers — sometimes hundreds of them.

If you don't want to get away from it all, stay at the Tower Fall, Mammoth, Bridge Bay, Fishing Bridge, Canyon Village, or Grant Village locations. These campgrounds are the closest to restaurants and gift shops. But if you're looking for a semblance of peace, some solitude, and the chance to spot animals, the Slough Creek and Pebble Creek campgrounds are the smallest (29 and 32 sites, respectively) and lie within the home ranges of two wolf packs.

Xanterra campgrounds

The Xanterra campgrounds are at **Fishing Bridge, Bridge Bay, Canyon Village, Madison,** and **Grant Village.** Because of grizzly bears drawn to the Yellowstone River and its cutthroat trout, the Fishing Bridge site caters only to hard-sided vehicles. You also can find room for your RV at the other Xanterra campgrounds; although they don't have utility hookups, they do have sanitary dump stations.

To make reservations, call ☎ **307-344-7311,** or write to Xanterra Parks & Resorts, P.O. Box 165, Yellowstone National Park, WY 82190. You can reserve a space, but a specific site is not assigned until your arrival.

 Campgrounds generally are open from early May through October. Weather, however, can force campgrounds to open later or close earlier in the season. If you make an early- or late-season reservation with Xanterra, call shortly before your arrival to find out if the campground is open.

National Park Service campgrounds

The NPS-operated campgrounds are at **Indian Creek, Lewis Lake, Mammoth Hot Springs, Norris, Pebble Creek, Slough Creek,** and **Tower Fall.**

Camping is allowed only in designated areas and is limited to a maximum stay of 14 days between June 15 and September 15 (30 days the rest of the year). Checkout time for all campgrounds is 10 a.m., and quiet hours (8 p.m. to 8 a.m.) are strictly enforced. No generators, radios, or other loud noises are allowed during these hours.

Backcountry sites

If you want solitude, Yellowstone's backcountry offers more than 1,200 miles of marked trails that enable you to escape the multitudes. I like to flee to Shoshone Lake, the park's second largest lake. Located 8½ miles south of Old Faithful via the Lonestar Geyser Trail or 3 miles south of Lower Loop Road via the DeLacy Creek Trail, the lake offers waterfront campsites. Here you can try to land some trout, capture a few great sunset and sunrise photos, or explore the Shoshone Geyser Basin on the lake's west shore. Unfortunately, the lake's popularity over the years has forced officials to ban wood fires to protect the forest, so bring your propane stove.

You must obtain a permit for backcountry hiking. See "Planning Ahead," earlier in this chapter, for information. The park service also makes sure that you learn the dos and don'ts of backcountry hiking before you set out. They give you a handout and require that you watch a short video on hiking in bear country.

Where to Eat

Whether you're in search of linen tablecloths, silverware, and fine china, or a quick burger, you can find it in Yellowstone. All major hotels — Mammoth Hot Springs Hotel, Old Faithful Inn, and Lake Yellowstone Hotel — feature elegant dining rooms with excellent meals. How you dress is up to you. People dining at the Old Faithful Inn come in more comfortable attire, as if they just returned from a hike. However, finding some Lake Yellowstone Hotel diners in semiformal wear is not unusual. Menus run the gamut, from beef to trout.

Roosevelt Lodge offers a decidedly more relaxed setting, and although the meals are not as fancy as the meals at Old Faithful Inn, Lake Yellowstone Hotel, or Mammoth Hot Springs Hotel, the food is hearty.

A rung down the culinary ladder are less-expensive meals available in cafeterias, delis, or fast-food grills at Old Faithful, Mammoth Hot Springs, Canyon Village, Grant Village, Lake Village, and Lake Lodge. Assuming that you'll work up a hearty appetite in the park, the chefs don't skimp on the portions.

The dining rooms at Grant Village, Lake Yellowstone Hotel, and the Old Faithful Inn require reservations. You can actually make them when you call to make your lodging reservations. To do so, call the dining rooms directly at the numbers given or try the central reservations office at ☎ 307-344-7311.

Dining in Grant Village

Grant Village Lake House
$–$$ Grant Village AMERICAN

The proverbial stone's throw from Yellowstone Lake, this restaurant features buffet breakfasts and pizzas and a pasta bar for dinners. The lake view through the restaurant's windows makes this a great place to enjoy a sunset meal.

☎ *307-344-3419. Main courses: $4.95–$7.75 breakfast; $5.95–$8.25 lunch; $8.75–$19.75 dinner. AE, DC, DISC, MC, V. Open: Late May to early Oct 7–10:30 a.m., 5:30–9 p.m.*

Dining in Lake Village

Lake Yellowstone Hotel
$–$$$$$ Lake Village AMERICAN

This restaurant is the best in the park, hands down. The service generally is highly attentive, the meals creative and well-prepared, and the atmosphere definitely elegant in the high-ceiling dining room with windows that allow you to gaze out at Yellowstone Lake. Dinner entrees include beef in various forms, pastas, duck breast, quail, salmon, trout dishes, as well as nightly specials such as fettucine with scallops and roasted shiitake mushrooms. I recommend the lavish breakfast buffet, although you can also order à la carte from the menu. For lunch, hot sandwiches, burgers, and chicken curry dishes dominate the choices.

On the north shore of Yellowstone Lake. ☎ 307-242-3899. Dinner reservations required. Main courses: $3.50–$7.75 breakfast; $4.95–$29 lunch; $11.95–$29 dinner. AE, DC, DISC, MC, V. Open: Mid-May to early Oct 6:30–10:30 a.m., 11:30 a.m.–2:30 p.m., 5–10 p.m.

Dining in Mammoth Hot Springs

Mammoth Hot Springs Hotel Dining Room
$$–$$$ Mammoth Hot Springs AMERICAN

After the Lake Yellowstone Hotel, this spot probably has the best meals. The setting is elegant, with linen-covered tables, china, and etched-glass windows. Don't pass on the bargain, all-you-can-eat breakfast buffet, featuring scrambled eggs, French toast, bacon, sausage, hot and cold cereals, pastries, fresh fruit, and yogurt. Lunch fare focuses on burgers, hot and cold sandwiches, and such specialties as fish and chips or trout. Dinners — beef, fish, chicken, or pasta — aren't gourmet, but they're appetizing and filling. Don't forget to ask about the "daily plates," which vary from day to day ranging from porterhouse pork chops to fettucine with mussels.

☎ *307-344-5314. Dinner reservations required. Main courses: $4.25–$7.75 breakfast; $5.50–$17.50 lunch; $8.95–$19.75 dinner. AE, DC, DISC, MC, V. Open: Early May to early Oct and Dec–March, daily 6:30–10 a.m., 11:30 a.m.–2:30 p.m., 5–10 p.m.*

Terrace Grill

$–$$ Mammoth Hot Springs   FAST FOOD

This hectic, kid-friendly cafeteria always seems crowded. It's about as close to fast food as you get in the park. Burgers, hot dogs, soups, and sandwiches are the fare, and if you're in a rush to get on down the road, this is a good place for a quick bite. Nothing gourmet, that's for sure, but the food will tide you over until your next meal.

☎ *307-344-7901. Main courses: $2.50–$4 breakfast; $3–$6.50 lunch and dinner. Open: Early May 10 a.m.–5:30 p.m.; late May to early Sept 7–10:30 a.m., 11 a.m.– 9 p.m.; mid-Sept to early-Oct 10 a.m.–9 p.m.; early Oct to mid-Oct 11 a.m.–5 p.m.*

Dining in the Old Faithful area

Old Faithful Inn

$$$–$$$$ Old Faithful area   AMERICAN

After Lake Yellowstone Hotel, this is my favorite spot to dine, probably because of the setting in the log-walled dining room. Toward the end of summer, the service can be spotty, however, because the college kids are losing their focus and tired of dealing with tourists. The dinner menu is lined with beef, pasta, and poultry dishes, usually with a fish special tossed in daily. The breakfast buffet is king. Lunches include hot and cold sandwiches, burgers, and trout.

Near Old Faithful geyser. ☎ *307-545-4999. Dinner reservations required. Main courses: $4.25–$7.75 breakfast; $5.50–$10.25 lunch; $8.25–$22.75 dinner. AE, DC, DISC, MC, V. Open: Mid-May to mid-Oct 6:30–10 a.m., 11:30 a.m.–2 p.m., 5:30–10 p.m.*

Snow Lodge Obsidian Room

$$–$$$ Old Faithful area   AMERICAN

Featuring large windows and wrought iron trim, this Snow Lodge, which opened for business for the 1999 season, is a vast improvement over its predecessor. The meals aren't bad, either, although your choices for lunch and dinner aren't extensive. Eggs, pancakes, French toast, and hot and cold cereals are the heart of the breakfast menu. The lunch and dinner menus are essentially identical, featuring burgers, sandwiches, chicken, cornish game hen, pasta, and trout. The dinner menu also includes prime rib and nightly specials, such as New Zealand Red Deer Medallions.

Near Old Faithful geyser. ☎ 307-545-4800, ext. 4010. Dinner reservations required. Main courses: $3.50–$6.75 breakfast; $5.75–$11.95 lunch; $8.95–$29 dinner. AE, DC, DISC, MC, V. Open: Early May to mid-Oct and mid-Dec to early March 6:30–10 a.m., 11:30 a.m.–10 p.m.

Dining in Tower-Roosevelt

Roosevelt Lodge

$$–$$$$ Tower-Roosevelt   AMERICAN

This is my third favorite place to eat in the park, after Lake Yellowstone Hotel and the Old Faithful Inn. It's not elegant or stately, but cozy, like a backwoods diner that dishes up hearty, heavy meals. You don't find a breakfast buffet, but you can order eggs, pancakes, oatmeal, cereals, and biscuits and gravy off the menu. Lunch focuses on sandwiches, chili, soup and salad, and trout, whereas dinner features delicious barbecued ribs and chicken as well as steak and trout. For a unique experience and a treat for your kids, sign on for one of the chuckwagon dinners. Diners travel by horse-drawn wagon to a nearby meadow for a Western barbecue of steaks, baked beans, potato salad, corn, watermelon, and apple crisp. Your little 'pokes will enjoy the storytelling, music, and horses.

No phone. Reservations not accepted. Main courses: $4.25–$6.75 breakfast; $5.25–$17.95 lunch; $12.95–$19.50 dinner. AE, DC, DISC, MC, V. Open: Early June to early Sept 7–10:30 a.m., 11:30 a.m.–4 p.m., 5–9 p.m.

Fast Facts: Yellowstone

Area Code
☎ 307.

ATM
Available at Fishing Bridge General Store, Grant Village General Store, Lake Yellowstone Hotel, Mammoth General Store, Mammoth Hot Springs Hotel, Old Faithful Inn, Old Faithful Snow Lodge, Old Faithful Upper Store, Canyon General Store, and Canyon Lodge.

Emergency
☎ 911.

Fees
$20 per vehicle per week; $10 on foot, bicycle, or skis.

Fishing License
Park permit needed for anglers 16 and older: $10 for ten days, $20 for the season. Ages 12 to 15 also need a permit, but they're free. Permits and fishing regulations available at

ranger stations, visitor centers, and Yellowstone General Stores.

Hospitals

Lake Clinic, Pharmacy and Hospital is open from late May to mid-September; ☎ 307-242-7241. Mammoth Clinic is open year-round; ☎ 307-344-7965. Old Faithful Clinic is open from mid-May to mid-October; ☎ 307-545-7325.

Information

Yellowstone National Park, P.O. Box 168, Yellowstone National Park, WY 82190; ☎ 307-344-7381.

Lost and Found

☎ 307-344-7381.

Pharmacies

Lake Clinic, Pharmacy and Hospital is open from late May to mid-September; ☎ 307-242-7241.

Post Office

You find post offices at Mammoth Hot Springs (open year-round; ☎ 307-344-7764), Old Faithful (open mid-May to early Oct and mid-Dec to mid-March; ☎ 307-545-7252), Grant Village (open mid-May to mid-Sept; ☎ 307-242-7338), Lake Village (open mid-May to mid-Sept; ☎ 307-242-7383), and Canyon Village (open early May to late October; ☎ 307-242-7323).

Road Conditions and Weather

☎ 307-344-7381.

Taxes

Vary depending on the county. Old Faithful area: 6% lodging and meals.

Time Zone

Mountain standard time.

Web Site

www.nps.gov/yell.

Chapter 21

Yosemite National Park

• •

In This Chapter

▶ Introducing a picture-perfect park

▶ Planning your trip

▶ Exploring Yosemite Valley, the High Sierra, and beyond

▶ Finding the best lodging and meals

• •

Born of water and ice that cut a fantastic landscape, Yosemite National Park is a storybook fairyland. How else to explain the wispy, 2,425-foot stream of Yosemite Falls that spills into the Yosemite Valley, or the massive granitic mound known as Half Dome (which looks like a monument to a loaf of bread). On the valley floor the tranquil, tree-lined Merced River traces lazy oxbow bends, whereas the palatial The Ahwahnee hotel has comforted queens and presidents, actors and athletes.

Take the time to climb up and out of this peaceful notch in California's High Sierra landscape, and you enter a boundless backcountry of granite and pine where you can lose yourself down a trail or savor some solitude on the shore of a lake.

If you're in search of breathtaking scenery, choose to visit Yosemite, a park overly endowed with natural beauty. Arrive any summer day via California 41 from Fish Camp, a town just south of the park, and you can marvel at the scenery as soon as you pop out of the Wawona Tunnel. To your right is Bridalveil Fall, an impressive 620-foot drop, which serves as a modest opening act for Yosemite Falls just down the road. On your left is El Capitan, one of the world's tallest chunks of exposed rock, which rises 3,593 feet above the valley floor. Dead ahead is the bulging Half Dome.

Meandering through the middle of this paradise is the Merced River, which literally dives into the valley via Nevada and Vernal falls. Adding contrast to the gray granite and the foaming white falls in spring and summer are showy displays of lilies and columbines and stands of evergreens.

Yosemite National Park

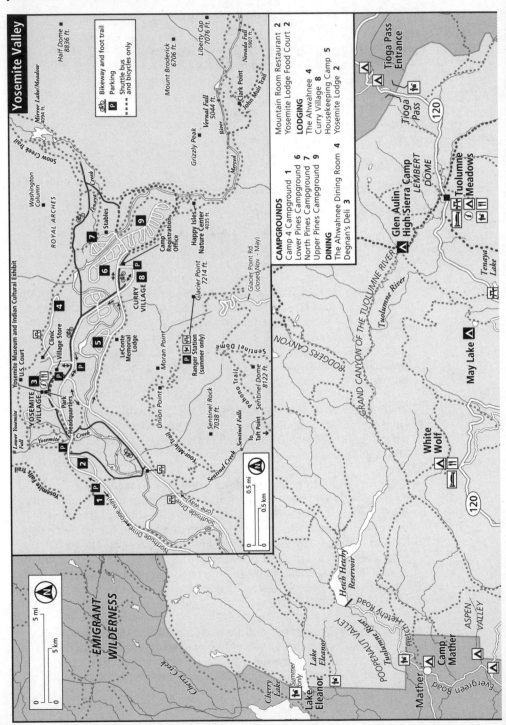

Yosemite Valley

Bikeway and foot trail
P Parking
Shuttle bus and bicycles only

CAMPGROUNDS
Camp 4 Campground 1
Lower Pines Campground 6
North Pines Campground 7
Upper Pines Campground 9

DINING
The Ahwahnee Dining Room 4
Degnan's Deli 3

Mountain Room Restaurant 2
Yosemite Lodge Food Court 2

LODGING
The Ahwahnee 4
Curry Village 8
Housekeeping Camp 5
Yosemite Lodge 2

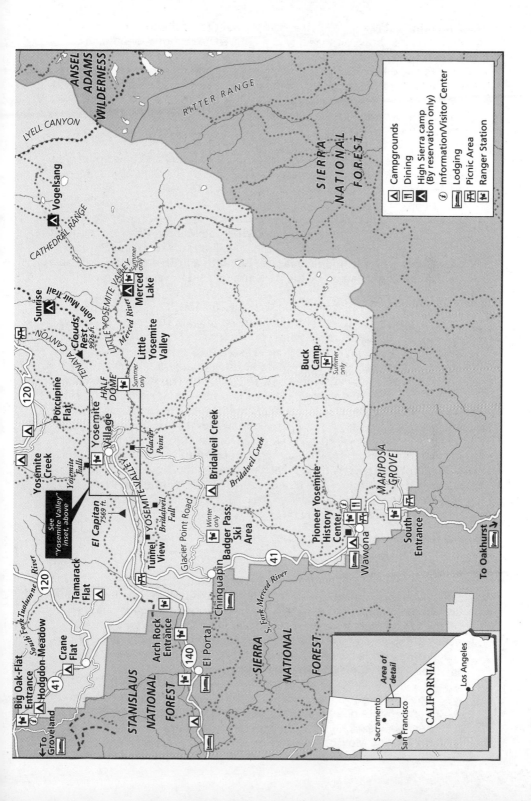

Legend:
- Campgrounds
- Dining
- High Sierra camp (By reservation only)
- Information/Visitor Center
- Lodging
- Picnic Area
- Ranger Station

ANSEL ADAMS WILDERNESS

RITTER RANGE

LYELL CANYON

Vogelsang

CATHEDRAL RANGE

SIERRA NATIONAL FOREST

John Muir Trail

Sunrise

Merced River

Summer only

Merced Lake

TENAYA CANYON

Clouds Rest 9926 ft.

LITTLE YOSEMITE VALLEY

Little Yosemite Valley

Buck Camp

Summer only

120

Porcupine Flat

HALF DOME

Summer only

Yosemite Creek

Yosemite Village

Glacier Point

Bridalveil Creek

Bridalveil Creek

MARIPOSA GROVE

Yosemite Falls

YOSEMITE VALLEY

See "Yosemite Valley" inset, above

El Capitan 7569 ft.

Bridalveil Fall

Tunnel View

Winter only

Pioneer Yosemite History Center

South Entrance

Badger Pass Ski Area

Glacier Point Road

41

Wawona

Tamarack Flat

120

Chinquapin

S. Fork Merced River

South Fork Tuolumne River

Crane Flat

Arch Rock Entrance

El Portal

140

SIERRA NATIONAL FOREST

To Oakhurst

Big Oak Flat Entrance

41

Hodgdon Meadow

STANISLAUS NATIONAL FOREST

←To Groveland

Inset map (California):

Sacramento

San Francisco

Area of detail

CALIFORNIA

Los Angeles

What other park offers such a visible feast of water and rock? None. But don't just stay in the valley and ignore the rest of Yosemite. In summer, the ride to Tuolumne Meadows winds first through deep pine forest before breaking into alpine meadows and massive granite outcrops. White Wolf Lodge is a popular base camp for day hikers, and eating family-style at Tuolumne Lodge (a misnomer in that there is no lodge, only tent cabins) is an excellent way to make friends and gain insights into the park.

In the park's southwestern corner, you find not only a sky-scraping forest of giant sequoia trees, but also the stately Wawona Hotel, a National Historic Landmark that dates to the 1850s.

All this beauty naturally generates crowds — big ones, particularly during the height of summer. That's when the Merced River bogs down with convoys of rubber rafts and the Mist Trail to Vernal and Nevada falls swells with the midday masses. But with a little patience, and careful planning, you can enjoy the park almost as if it were your own.

Although you can visit Yosemite Valley in one long day, you need at least two days if you also want to head up toward Tuolumne Meadows. When you visit depends on what you want to see or do. If you want to avoid crowds, summer is not your season — more people descend on Yosemite between May and September than at any other time of year. But if you follow my advice on how to cope with the masses, summer can be a wonderful time thanks to warm temperatures and accessibility throughout Yosemite. If waterfalls are first and foremost on your must-see list, late spring and early summer are the best times for you. If hiking is your passion, fall is your season. In comparison to summer, fall generates fewer crowds, has more comfortable temperatures, and is definitely more striking. If great skiing and solitude are what you seek, winter is for you. The lack of crowds in the winter months — outside of the holidays — also makes a Yosemite trip more affordable at this time because lodging rates dip.

Must-see Attractions

Wispy waterfalls, towers of granite, breathtaking High Sierra landscape, stately national park lodging — Yosemite National Park has much to offer. This big park takes time to navigate due to attractions in the valley and high country. Thankfully, appreciating Yosemite doesn't take much time — this park makes an immediate impression. Here is a list of stops to get you started on your explorations:

✔ **The Ahwahnee:** This blue-blood hotel, opened in 1927, is built from granite blocks and concrete stained to resemble redwood beams. A National Historic Landmark, its name means "Place of the Gaping Mouth." You may do some gaping when you stand in the doorway to the cavernous dining room.

✔ **Ansel Adams Gallery:** Yes, this is a retail shop. The gallery pays homage to the renowned landscape photographer whose black-and-white masterpieces from 50 years ago still resonate today. Look at his work. Maybe buy some. You won't be sorry.

✔ **Curry Village:** Cooled by the afternoon shadow of Glacier Point, this tent camp marked its centennial in 1999. The camp is a bit rustic for some tastes, but other people enjoy its flavor. Even if you don't stay here, the adjoining village is a good place to go for ice cream or pizza. The Yosemite Mountaineering School and mountain shop are located here.

✔ **El Capitan:** The road into Yosemite Valley passes this ridiculously tall chunk of rock, so you won't miss it.

✔ **Glacier Point:** You can drive to this overlook, which offers sweeping views of the valley floor, Yosemite Falls, the Merced River, The Ahwahnee, Half Dome, Vernal and Nevada falls, and the peak of Clouds Rest looming far off to the northeast.

✔ **The Mist Trail:** A wonderfully wet hike on a hot day, this trail follows the Merced River upstream from the valley floor to 317-foot Vernal Fall (which provides a drenching with misty spray during spring and early summer months) and 594-foot Nevada Fall.

✔ **Tenaya Lake:** Named after the chief of the last Indian tribe to live in the Yosemite Valley, this high-country lake is rimmed by granite domes and offers picnic grounds on the northeast and southwest ends.

✔ **Tunnel View:** Carrying a camera with you? If so, pull over here, try to squeeze El Capitan, Bridalveil Fall, and Half Dome into your viewfinder, and press the shutter release.

Getting There

Yosemite is easily accessible. If you live outside of California, a morning flight to either Fresno or Merced can be followed by an afternoon in the park. What you need to decide before you head to Yosemite, though, is whether you want to go straight to the high country, visit the park's sequoia groves, or make a beeline for the valley floor. This prioritizing helps you determine which entrance to take into the park.

Driving in

You can get into Yosemite by car in four ways, and all but the Tioga Pass Entrance (10 miles west of Lee Vining, California) are open year-round.

The South Entrance, with access to Wawona and the Mariposa Grove of sequoia trees, is 64 miles north of Fresno via California 41. Coming from the west, your options are the 75-mile drive along California 140 from Merced to the Arch Rock Entrance and into the valley floor, or the 88-mile drive along California 120 from Manteca to the Big Oak-Flat Entrance. The park's northwestern corner is accessed through the Hetch Hetchy Entrance, which lies about 9 miles north from the park's Big Oak-Flat Entrance on Evergreen Road.

Tioga Pass Entrance typically closes to all but cross-country ski traffic when the first big snowstorm of the season hits in November and doesn't reopen until late May or early June. The 39-mile-long Tioga Road, which runs between Tuolumne Meadows and Crane Flat, also closes.

Flying in

You can fly into **Fresno-Yosemite International** (☎ 559-498-4095), 90 miles from the South Entrance at Wawona. **American Airlines, American Eagle, America West Express, Delta Connection, Horizon, United Express, US Airlines,** and **U.S. Airways Express** fly into this airport. Most of the major car-rental companies are here. See the Appendix for the toll-free numbers.

The **Merced Airport** (☎ 209-385-6873), 73 miles southwest of the Arch Rock Entrance, is served from Las Vegas by **Scenic Airlines** (☎ 800-634-6801). Two rental car agencies are within 1½ miles of the airport: **Aide Rental Car,** 1530 W. 16th St. (☎ 209-722-8084 or 800-717-8084), and **Enterprise,** 1334 W. Main St.

Planning Ahead

To obtain information in advance of your trip, write Superintendent, Yosemite National Park, CA 95389-0577, or check the park's Web site at www.nps.gov/yose. You can purchase publications about the park by contacting **Yosemite Association,** Box 230, El Portal, CA 95318; ☎ 209-379-2648; Internet: www.yosemite.org.

If you have computer access, you should also check out **Yosemite Area Traveler Information** on the Web at www.yosemite.com. The site has information on the 11,000-square-mile area surrounding the park, with information on lodging, road conditions, the weather, activities, and just about everything else under the sun. Another good source of information is the park's concessionaire, **Yosemite Concession Services** (☎ 559-252-4848; Internet: www.yosemitepark.com).

Reserving a room or a campsite

It's late June and you're thinking that spending the Fourth of July weekend at The Ahwahnee would be really cool. And you're right, it would.

But if you don't already have reservations, start thinking about next year's Fourth of July weekend, because you certainly won't find a room this summer. In fact, even if you were willing to delay your trip until Labor Day weekend, you probably wouldn't find a room in the lodge.

That's how popular Yosemite is. When it comes to booking lodging in national parks, few parks pose the problems Yosemite does. Even though you can book a room 366 days before your visit, almost within minutes of the opening of the reservation office at **Yosemite Concession Services** (☎ **559-252-4848**), rooms at the Ahwahnee, Yosemite Lodge, and Wawona Hotel sell out for weekends, holiday periods, and every day between May and September.

So how do you get a room in one of these popular lodges? Trying to book early is a good suggestion. A better one is to visit during November, early December, January, February, and March. Not only are you more likely to get the room of your choice, but rates are down 25% from the high season. Another angle, if you can leave on a moment's notice, is to call and ask about cancellations. You can also take part in special events — wine appreciation, cooking events, and ski packages — offered during these months. Call Yosemite Concession Services (☎ **559-252-4848**) for information and reservations.

To get into the park during the high season, consider lowering your comfort level and staying in a canvas tent cabin at Curry Village, Tuolumne Meadows, or White Wolf Lodge. Complete with wood floors, canvas walls and ceilings, cots, woodstoves, and a communal bath-house down a short path, these cabins definitely are not plush. But they are far cheaper than lodge rooms and offer a rustic flavor. Often you can snag one of these cabins by calling only two weeks prior to your visit. If you reserve one reluctantly, when you arrive to check in, ask whether any cancellations created an opening in one of the other lodges. It's unlikely, but asking is worth five minutes of your time. Even better, check with the reservations desk 30 days before your arrival and again 10 days out and 3 days out — the most likely times when other people will cancel their reservations.

When trying to make a reservation, call on a Sunday, which is the day of the week that the fewest calls are made to the reservation desks, so you'll have a better chance of getting through. You can also try to book online at www.yosemitepark.com.

Going into the backcountry

Heading into Yosemite's backcountry is one of my favorite ways of enjoying the park. Not only do you flee the crowds, but you also see some awesome country. Backcountry wilderness permits are required for all overnight trips, year-round. Reservations are available, and encouraged, for dates from May through September. Reservations can be made as early as 24 weeks in advance and as late as two days before your trip. Permits are not needed for day hikes. You can obtain your permit by writing to **Wilderness Permits,** P.O. Box 545, Yosemite, CA 95389 or by calling ☎ **209-372-0740.** Although the backcountry permit itself is free, you must pay a $5 per person processing fee for reservations.

Reservations are not available for dates from October through April. Rangers allow a specific number of backcountry hikers at each trailhead. At least 40% of a specific trailhead's hiker quota is available on a first-come, first-served basis on any given day. These last-minute permits are available at the Wilderness Permit Station nearest your departure trailhead.

Learning the Lay of the Land

You can be in one of two places when you visit Yosemite: In the valley or out of it. The two areas are very different.

The **Yosemite Valley** floor is tourist central. At Yosemite Village, on the north side of the Merced River, you find shops and restaurants, as well as the valley's only medical clinic and a grocery. The village is also home to park headquarters, Yosemite Concession Services offices, and Yosemite's largest visitor center, the Valley Visitor Center. All are located within short walking distance of each other. For the locations of the valley's attractions and services see the map in this chapter.

 Getting into and out of the valley isn't hard, but travel here takes a little time so you need to be patient. Due to the large amount of backcountry (704,624 of the park's 747,956 acres are official wilderness), Yosemite has few roads. Those that do exist are narrow, wind around mountains, and often clog with traffic.

Big Oak-Flat Road (California 120) from Big Oak-Flat Entrance, **El Portal Road** (California 140) from Arch Rock Entrance, and **Wawona Road** (California 41) from South Entrance all converge near the west end of Yosemite Valley, so you won't have a hard time finding the valley floor. Once there you must take one of two one-way roads: **Southside Drive,** which snakes east to Curry Village, or **Northside Drive,** which runs west from Curry Village back out of the valley. A few bridges cross the Merced River on the valley floor to help you alternate between these one-way ribbons, but if you miss these bridges when you're trying to change your direction of travel, you have to make a lap of the Southside-Northside loop.

Fleeing the valley is easy when it comes to directions, but the actual trip can be harrowing during the height of summer because of traffic. To get down to **Wawona** and **Mariposa Grove,** take Northside Drive to the junction with Wawona Road and then head south for 36 miles. The trip takes about an hour.

Fourteen miles south of the valley, Wawona Road meets **Glacier Point Road,** at Chinquapin junction, which leads to Glacier Point. Although the trip is only 30 miles from the valley floor, the drive takes about an hour depending on traffic.

To reach **Tioga Road** (which runs to White Wolf Lodge and campgrounds at Yosemite Creek, Porcupine Creek, and Tuolumne Meadows), follow Northside Drive out of the valley to Big Oak Flat Road and turn right at the Crane Flat intersection onto the Tioga Road. From Crane Flat, the Tioga Road travels about 14 miles to White Wolf Lodge, 30 miles to Tenaya Lake, and 39 miles to the Tuolumne Meadows, a miniature village with a gas station, ranger station, another visitor center, a campground, and the Tuolumne Lodge and tent cabins. From Tuolumne Meadows, the **Tioga Pass Entrance** is another 7½ miles. Tioga Road is open only during the summer months.

Keep in mind when planning a late fall, winter, or early spring trip that Tioga Road usually closes from November to early May because of snow.

The Big Oak-Flat Entrance, accessed via Big Oak-Flat Road (California 120), is just a bit more than 6 miles away from Crane Flat and the Tioga Road junction. You can reach Hetch Hetchy Reservoir, north of the Big Oak-Flat Entrance, by heading 6 miles north from Big Oak-Flat on the **Evergreen Road** to Mather, where you pick up the **Hetch Hetchy Road** that runs 7½ miles to the reservoir.

Arriving in the Park

When you arrive in Yosemite National Park, you'll want to gawk at the landscape rather than worry about picky details. While checking out the scenery, here are a few orientation tips to keep in mind.

Finding information

Two park newspapers, the *Yosemite Guide* and *Yosemite Today,* are available at entrance stations and visitor centers. They provide up-to-date park information and activity schedules.

The park's best and biggest visitor center is the **Valley Visitor Center in Yosemite Village** (☎ **209-372-0299**), which is open daily year-round from 8:30 a.m. to 5 p.m. The center provides information about tours, daily ranger programs, lodging, and restaurants. The rangers are helpful, insightful, and knowledgeable. Inside, information boards update road conditions and campsite availability, and they also serve as message boards. You can buy maps, books, and videos, and check out exhibits on the park, its geologic history, and the surrounding area. Be sure to orient yourself to the park by watching the film, *Spirit of Yosemite,* in the center's theater.

Also in Yosemite Village is the Yosemite Valley Wilderness Center, a small building with high country maps, information on necessary equipment, and trail information. A ranger at the desk can answer all your questions, issue permits, and offer advice about the high country.

Elsewhere, the **Wawona Information Station** (☎ **209-375-9501**) and **Big Oak Flat Information Station** (☎ **209-379-1899**) provide general park information. In the high country, the Tuolumne Meadows Visitor Center (☎ **209-372-0263**) is helpful. These centers are open only in summer.

Paying fees

The park fee is $20 per car per week, or $10 per person per week if you arrive on bike or foot. If you have a park passport, you don't need to pay the entrance fee; see Chapter 8 for information on the National Park Pass and Chapter 4 for the lowdown on Golden Age and Golden Access passports.

Getting around

With the park's free shuttle bus system, you don't really need your own car to move around the east end of Yosemite Valley, so help reduce congestion and pollution by parking your vehicle. The buses operate year-round, stopping at lodging properties, restaurants, trailheads, and attractions. The park newspaper carries a map of the shuttle routes. Additionally, in summer, free shuttle buses run from Wawona to the Mariposa Grove and from Tioga Pass to Tenaya Lake. Large day-use parking lots are in the east end of the valley near Curry Village and Yosemite Village where you can park your car and board shuttles.

For a fee, hikers' buses run daily to Glacier Point from late spring through autumn and to Tuolumne Meadows late June through Labor Day. For fees, schedules, and reservations, call ☎ **209-372-1240** or visit any tour desk.

Yosemite Concession Services offers a variety of guided tours for those who want to be led around the park. Choices range from two-hour valley floor tours (which take you past the must-see attractions of El Capitan, The Ahwahnee, Yosemite Falls, and Bridalveil Fall) to six-hour trips to the Mariposa Grove of big trees near the park's southern border. Prices range from $18.50 to $55, depending on the tour. For details and other tour options, check with **The Ahwahnee** (☎ **209-372-1406**), **Curry Village** (☎ **209-372-8323**; summer only), **Yosemite Lodge Tour Desk** (☎ **209-372-1240**), and **Yosemite Village Kiosk** (☎ **209-272-1268**; spring–fall).

Remembering Safety

Parts of Yosemite may look like a nicely tended city park, but don't let that impression fool you. The park can be dangerous in places. Waterfalls are beautiful to view, but if you take a hiking trail that passes near one, watch out for slippery footing. And if you climb to the top of Nevada Fall, definitely be careful not to stroll too near the lip of the falls, because it's a long way down if you slip. If you watch climbers scale some of the valley's prominent outcrops, stay a good distance from the cliff base out of the way of falling rocks or dropped climbing gear. Finally, keep alert while driving because of congestion in Yosemite Valley and the conditions of high country roads, which are steep and twisting and often icy in spring or early fall. Plus, wildlife can dart across a park road at any time.

The park's wildlife is a whole 'nother issue; see the "Yosemite's birds and beasts" sidebar, later in this chapter, for my tips on how to behave wisely around these park inhabitants.

For additional tips on how to ensure a safe park visit, see Chapter 8.

Enjoying the Park

Enjoying Yosemite National Park can be as simple as sitting on a bench watching a cascading waterfall or as complicated as backpacking across the park. This section introduces these options, as well as several in between these extremes.

Be prepared to encounter other human beings who share your mission of escaping other human beings. Can you escape the crowds in Yosemite? To a degree. Obviously, in the height of summer your chances of finding solitude in the park are not as good as in the middle of March. But you can minimize your contact with others during summer months by getting out into the park as early as possible and by staying out late in the afternoon. Although your odds of avoiding others on hiking trails that begin on the valley floor are not as good, you can, literally, walk away from many of them. If you hike the Mist Trail, for example, push on past the top of Vernal Fall to the top of Nevada Fall, because not all folks go the extra mile.

Exploring the top attractions

Ansel Adams Gallery
Yosemite Village

If you admire landscape photography (or simply need another roll of film), stop by here. The gallery showcases the life and times of photographer

Ansel Adams, America's pre-eminent landscape photographer. You find books and videotapes on him as well as copies of his works — ranging in size from postcards to wall posters — for sale. Contemporary artists' works also are displayed, and revolving exhibitions come through each year.

Near the Valley Visitor Center. Admission: Free. Open: Daily 9 a.m.–9 p.m.

High Sierra

North of, and above, the Yosemite Valley is a wonderfully picturesque stretch of rock, forest, and water that is the most accessible piece of backcountry in the park. The Tioga Road slices through this part of the park and offers access to numerous hiking trails (such as the one to Clouds Rest, described in "Taking a hike," later in this chapter) as well as to **Tenaya, May,** and **Dog lakes.** As with the valley floor, you really don't need to get out of your car to admire the High Sierra scenery this road travels through, but why miss an opportunity to hike across some of the granitic mounds or to picnic along one of the lakeshores?

Before you leave the Yosemite Valley for the High Sierra, stop at the visitor center and snag a copy of *The Yosemite Road Guide*, which notes points of interest along the Tioga Road. If you need munchies, try the Yosemite Valley Store or Degnan's Deli for supplies.

You also can pick up picnic supplies at the Crane Flat store at the intersection of Big Oak Flat Road and the Tioga Road.

Tioga Road runs through this area from Crane Flat in the west to the Tioga Pass Entrance Station in the east.

Yosemite Museum and Indian Cultural Exhibit
Yosemite Village

This attraction traces the park's cultural history. The Indian Cultural Exhibit explains the lives of the Ahwahneeche, Miwok, and Paiute tribes that once lived in the area. You occasionally find Native Americans speaking here or giving demonstrations of long-forgotten arts, such as basket weaving. A replica of an Ahwahneeche village is behind the museum. Its exhibits guide you through the tribe's transformation in the years after whites discovered the valley. A ceremonial roundhouse, which is still used, is also on site.

Near the Valley Visitor Center. Admission: Free. Open: Daily 9 a.m.–4:30 p.m.

Yosemite Pioneer Cemetery
Yosemite Village

This cemetery is the final resting place of some of the valley's homesteaders. It's worth a visit, if for no other reason than to examine the headstones, some of which bear rudimentary or fading writing to identify the grave. On your way over to the cemetery, stop at the Valley Visitor Center to pick up a copy of the *Guide to the Yosemite Cemetery*. Among the souls buried here is James Lamon, an early settler considered to be the first white man to winter in the valley, back in 1862 to 1863. He also lived here year-round and planted apple trees, which still bear fruit.

Near the Valley Visitor Center.

Yosemite Valley

If you're primarily interested in Yosemite's waterfalls and granitic domes, spend the bulk of your trip (if not all of it) on the valley floor, which runs 7 miles west-to-east and barely a mile wide at its broadest point. Here you see Yosemite's main attractions — **Bridalveil Fall, El Capitan, Yosemite Falls, and Half Dome** — simply by driving into the valley. But you really need to get out and do a little exploring. Perspective is a funny thing. Although viewing Yosemite Falls from a distance is captivating, you have a vastly different experience when you stand near its base and feel the thundering waters crashing down.

Yosemite Valley's best vantage point is from atop **Glacier Point,** which juts out 3,200 feet above the valley floor. Sure, any trail that gains some elevation provides stunning valley views, but none of them are like those from this outlook. An easy 30-mile drive from the valley floor, the overlook offers stellar views of **Half Dome, Vernal and Nevada falls, Yosemite Falls,** and the lazy meanders of the **Merced River.** You can even see 9,926-foot-tall **Clouds Rest** far off to the northeast.

A great way to combine a hike and a visit to Glacier Point is to take one of the hikers' shuttles to the point and then hike down to the valley via the Panorama Trail. (Call ☎ **209-372-1240** for information on the shuttle.) This 8½-mile trail provides views of three waterfalls: Vernal, Nevada, and Illilouette. Other hiking trails in the valley include Bridalveil Fall, Half Dome, The Mist Trail to Nevada Fall, The Mist Trail to Vernal Fall, and Upper Yosemite Fall Trail. See "Taking a hike," later in this chapter, for descriptions of these.

For a bit of human history in the valley, see the listings in this section for the Ansel Adams Gallery, the Yosemite Pioneer Cemetery, and the Yosemite Museum and Indian Cultural Exhibit.

When you arrive in the valley, park your car and walk to the places you want to see, or ride the free shuttle buses that go just about everywhere on the eastern end of the valley floor.

Take Big Oak-Flat Road, El Portal Road, or Wawona Road to Southside Drive, which runs into the valley.

Taking a hike

Waterfalls are great from a distance, but they're even more mesmerizing when you're standing close enough for the spray to wash over you. With waterfalls in every direction you look in the valley, and 840 miles of hiking trails throughout the park, you would be silly if you didn't spend at least a little time getting up close to the scenery. Sometimes you only need to go a quarter-mile to get close to a waterfall. Backcountry treks, on the other hand, can cover dozens of miles over numerous days.

Bridalveil Fall

This short hike takes only 10 minutes from the time you leave your car to the time you're snapping pictures. You see the fall when you drive into the Yosemite Valley, so you may as well get up close — and wet — too.

Distance: ½ mile round-trip. Level: Easy. Access: Bridalveil Fall Parking Area 3 miles west of Yosemite Village.

Cathedral Lakes

This trail quickly leaves the Tioga Road and gets you into a spectacular backcountry setting of granite domes, conifer forests, and shimmering lakes. From the trailhead, you encounter a gentle, but steady, climb that rises 1,000 feet en route to Upper Cathedral Lake. Before you reach the upper lake, a half-mile spur drops to the southwest and Lower Cathedral Lake, which is surrounded by the soaring granite walls of Cathedral and Tresidder peaks. The work of glaciers long-since melted can be found in highly polished patches of granite along the lake shores and the U-shaped valley.

Distance: 7 miles round-trip. Level: Easy to moderate. Access: Cathedral Lakes Trailhead just west of Tuolumne Meadows complex. Shuttles are available from Tuolumne Meadows.

LeConte Memorial

In 1870, Joseph LeConte became one of the first geologists to support John Muir's theory that the Yosemite Valley had been carved out by repeated glaciations. LeConte died of natural causes in July 1901 during a visit to Yosemite. In 1903 the Sierra Club built a memorial to him on the south side of the Merced River across from the Housekeeping Camp. The building actually served as the park's first visitor center. Today the LeConte Memorial Lodge (☎ 209-372-4542) has a library, with a children's corner, and a variety of evening programs. See "If you have more time," later in this chapter, for information on programming.

Clouds Rest

The trail starts off with a short downhill stretch to Sunrise Lake. From there, you head up out of Tenaya Canyon. At the junction, bear right. Killer views abound, and with 9,926-foot-tall Clouds Rest filling the horizon, losing your way is hard. The final push to the summit tests your mettle, thanks to the precipitous dropoffs on either side. That's the Yosemite River on your right and the Little Yosemite Valley on your left.

Distance: 14 miles round-trip. Level: Moderate. Access: Take Tioga Road to Tenaya Lake. The trailhead is at a parking lot down a closed road that crosses an outlet of the lake.

Half Dome

Mounting this dome makes for a long day but offers a view almost as breathtaking as the one from Glacier Point; the difference is you don't get to see Half Dome in the background. Along the way to the top, you pass Vernal and Nevada falls and cross the Little Yosemite Valley. Make sure you pack plenty of water, just in case you miss the spring located just off the Half Dome Trail. You're assisted along the final 600 feet to the top by cable railings.

Distance: 16½ miles round-trip. Level: Moderate to strenuous. Access: Mist Trail trailhead near Happy Isles Nature Center. Shuttle bus stop #16.

The Mist Trail

This kid-friendly trail is one of the valley's classic, must-do hikes. Why? If you follow it to the top, a 7-mile round-trip, you get great views of the Yosemite Valley and the spot where the Merced River leaves the Little Yosemite Valley and tumbles out of the high country. Plus, on hot, sultry summer days, you get a wonderfully cool drenching from the falls' spray. The first half of this hike leads to Vernal Fall. The trail up to the footbridge that crosses the Merced River below the falls is paved, and it turns into an expressway during the high season. Trust me, though, the experience — if you continue on to the top of Nevada Fall — is worth facing the crowds. At the footbridge, after snapping a few pictures up- and downstream, you can choose between turning back and going forward, first to the top of Vernal Fall and then on to the top of Nevada Fall. Which choice you make determines whether you get wet.

Choose to continue upward, and after you leave the footbridge over the Merced River, things get interesting. The asphalt is gone and the trail takes on a decidedly uphill nature. Before too long, you're huffing up a series of granite steps. If you're wise, you brought a raincoat to deflect the sheets of mist and spray coming from 317-foot Vernal Fall. Be careful — the steps can be incredibly slick and you should hold onto any small children in your party. Just below the lip of the falls, where you gain protection from the mist, is a great place to take pictures of the rainbows that form in the canyon below you.

Capturing Yosemite on film

Yosemite, with its waterfalls and bulbous rock mounds, is one big photograph waiting to be taken. Springtime is the best time to capture Yosemite Valley's waterfalls, because they're often raging with snowmelt and surrounded by wildflowers. Colorful sunrises and sunsets likewise make for wonderful pictures in the valley, because the gray granite provides a wonderful contrast to the reds, oranges, and yellows in the sky.

When in the park's high country, make sure your camera is loaded with film and accessible. You never know when a bear or some other wildlife will come into view. Along that line, a good telephoto or zoom lens comes in handy, too. Finally, don't be bashful about experimenting with black-and-white film. Some guy named Adams made quite a name for himself with black-and-white park portraits.

The Ansel Adams Gallery offers a 90-minute photography walk and class. These classes are limited to 15, so make sure you sign up in advance at the gallery. The Yosemite Concession Services also offers 90-minute photography walks, which start from The Ahwahnee hotel or Yosemite Lodge. For more information and to register for these classes, which are limited to 35, check at the front desk of either lodge.

A few more steps lead to the brink of Vernal Fall. From here the trail heads upstream for a short period before crossing a bridge to the north side of the river and then ascending to the top of Nevada Fall. Although the Merced River certainly looks refreshing, be careful and watch your footing. Hikers have slipped on algae-covered rocks and been swept over the 594-foot falls.

Distance: 3 miles round-trip to Vernal Fall; 7 miles round-trip to Nevada Fall. Level: Strenuous. Access: Happy Isles Nature Center, shuttle stop #16.

Upper Yosemite Fall Trail

Standing in the valley gazing at Yosemite Falls, you may be tempted to make this hike. You can do it — just plan accordingly. The hike takes between six and eight hours, round-trip. The 2,700-foot elevation gain sucks the life from your legs, but after you're on top, the views, and the pictures, make the trip worthwhile. As with any long, steep hike, the key is to pace yourself. This isn't a race to the top. Walk a little, rest a little, and walk a little more. One mile into the hike, you reach Columbia Point, which offers a decent view of the valley. The rest of the way doesn't have as many good views because the trail bobs and weaves. The last quarter-mile is the real gut-buster, because you're faced with what seems like an endless series of switchbacks. But after you get to the top, I'm sure you'll agree that the trek was worth it.

Distance: 7¼ miles round-trip. Level: Strenuous. Access: Camp 4 Campground, shuttle stop #8.

One-day wonder

To get the most out of Yosemite in one day, you need to change your focus as often as possible, moving from the valley to the high-country lakes. But that would be a very full day and you're on vacation, right? In this section, I suggest a more leisurely approach that focuses on the valley's highlights.

If money is no object, spend the previous night at **The Ahwahnee.** If you're budget-minded, choose **Yosemite Lodge** or even a **Curry Village** tent cabin, a good choice if you're traveling with kids. (See "Where to Stay," later in this chapter, for information on all three options.)

Be sure to start your day early. If possible, sit down to breakfast by 7:30 a.m. so you can be on your way before 9 a.m. Make your first stop the **Mist Trail** (see "Taking a hike"). Early morning is the best time of day to take this popular hike because most folks are still lingering over breakfast while the sun generates rainbows in the mist as it climbs into the sky. To reach the trail, either park your car at the Curry Village day-parking area and walk to the trailhead at the Happy Isles Nature Center, or take a shuttle bus to stop #16 near the nature center.

When you finish the hike, it'll no doubt be time for lunch, so either head to **Curry Village, Yosemite Lodge,** or **The Ahwahnee** for a well-deserved meal (see "Where to Eat," later in this chapter). If you're not staying at The Ahwahnee, make sure to pay a visit before, after, or during lunch. To reach the hotel, you can walk, drive, or take a shuttle bus to stop #3. A walk through the imposing hotel gives you a hint of what park life was like in the 1920s when rich Easterners made summer-long excursions to national parks and stayed in opulent structures such as this.

After lunch, why not spend time boning up on the park's history? Stop by the **Yosemite Pioneer Cemetery** and the **Yosemite Museum and Indian Cultural Exhibit** (see "Exploring the top attractions," earlier in this chapter).

Next, it's time to make a decision about how to spend the rest of the day. If you don't mind heights and are determined to coax the most out of your day, plan on having an early dinner and then heading up to **Glacier Point.** Not only does this towering promontory offer an incomparable panorama of Yosemite Valley, but it's also a wonderful spot for some sunset photographs of Half Dome. If a full moon is scheduled to rise, you can get shots of it rising and some of soft light bathing the valley below. Plus, the moonlight highlighting Half Dome is priceless. If the moon doesn't rise, well, you can gaze at a few billion stars overhead. Whatever the case, rest assured, you'll have a perfect ending to an incredible day.

If you aren't interested in sunset photos, head up to Glacier Point after you've toured the cemetery and then return to the valley floor for a relaxing dinner.

If you have more time

If you really want to see giant sequoias, stop by **Mariposa Grove,** near the park's South Entrance. Divided into the Upper and Lower groves, Mariposa holds 500 sequoias, some as old as 3,000 years. They stretch almost 300 feet tall into the air, are 50 feet in circumference, and weigh an average of 2 million pounds. You can walk or take a tram (for a fee) through the groves.

Don't drive out of your way to visit Mariposa Grove — driving back and forth from the Yosemite Valley consumes 2½ to 3 hours. If you want to stop here, organize your trip so that you exit or enter the park from the South Entrance. (However, if you really want to experience sequoias, my advice is to visit Sequoia National Park [Chapter 19] on your next vacation, because it has many, many more sequoias than Yosemite.)

The valley's **LeConte Memorial Lodge** (☎ 209-372-4542), open Wednesday through Sunday during summer months, has a variety of free evening programs run by the Sierra Club. Throughout the summer on Friday, Saturday, and Sunday evenings at 8 p.m., you usually find poets, environmentalists, and writers making presentations. If you're bringing kids to the park, you may want to check out the center's free family events, which range from 90-minute programs that delve into the park's bears (and include time in the field searching for signs of the bruins) to twilight "discovery walks" at Mirror Lake discussing topics such as the Ice Age or Native Americans. For current schedules, call the lodge or check out the activities boards at the campgrounds, the lodge, the Valley Visitor Center, or the post office. Yosemite Concession Services also offers free evening programs at The Ahwahnee, Yosemite Lodge, and Curry Village.

Yosemite's birds and beasts

Okay, Yosemite's bear problems are famous among national park goers, and you may already know the story, so let's get through this quickly. Yes, **black bears** live in Yosemite. These guys are easy to spot because they unfortunately have figured out that where people congregate, they can usually find a meal. During my stay at Tuolumne Lodge, one of the bruins trotted determinedly out of the woods shortly before our dinner and inspected each and every bear locker in search of one that wasn't closed properly. Fortunately, even though the park's bears can smell a jelly donut from a good distance, they still haven't figured out how to get into the bear lockers, so use them during your stay. Bears are adept, though, at peeling open your car like a can of tuna, so do not store any food — not even a pack of gum — in your rig. In 1998 alone more than 1,100 vehicles were broken into by bears in Yosemite.

By the way, black bears come in various shades. Whether brown, cinnamon, blond, or just black, they're all black bears. Once upon a time, grizzlies were in the region, too, but the last one spotted *in the entire state of California* was in 1922 near today's King's Canyon National Park. The last known grizzly in Yosemite was killed near Crescent Lake east of Wawona in 1895.

Mountain lions also call this park home, but you probably won't see them because of their small numbers and natural reclusiveness. Although their numbers have been on the upswing, these big cats are usually hard to spot. If you spy one trotting through a meadow or stalking some mule deer, consider yourself extremely fortunate, because it's a sight few people ever see. To keep from encountering mountain lions, don't leave any pets outside and unattended, because they seem like menu items to the lions. Also, when you go on a hike, go in a group, if possible, and don't let your children get too far ahead or behind.

In the unlikely event that you do find yourself face-to-face with a mountain lion, don't even think about running. You can't win this footrace. Instead, extend your arms over your head, preferably while holding a pack, to make the lion think you're a pretty big dude not worth messing with. If this still doesn't faze the cat and it begins to stalk you, throw rocks and sticks at it and shout. The message you're trying to convey is that not only aren't you food, but you can be pretty dangerous, too.

Another reclusive animal that makes its home in the park is the **bighorn sheep.** Yosemite's mountains and alpine meadows once hosted hundreds of them. Over the years, however, poaching, disease, and competition for food by domestic sheep wiped out the park's bighorn population. Fortunately, transplant efforts started in 1986 by the park service, U.S. Forest Service, the California Department of Fish and Game, and the Yosemite Fund, have built a herd of roughly 40 bighorn sheep in the park. Your best shot at spotting one of these nimble creatures is in the rocky slopes along California 120 just outside the park's east entrance.

Coyotes are a very commonly seen park critter. You sometimes hear them howling and yipping at night, or spot them pouncing on mice and *voles* (small rodents) in meadows. Like the bears, these guys know that people pack food. Please don't feed the beggars.

Although timid, **mule deer** are frequently spotted in the park's meadows. Don't be fooled by their Bambi-ish looks. Over the years, deer have attacked people more often than bears have. Their antlers are sharp, as are their hooves. As with all the other creatures, don't tempt deer with handouts.

Yosemite is home to a few **peregrine falcons.** These dive-bombing birds love to nest on high ledges and prey on white-throated swifts that dart about the granite domes. Look for peregrine falcons near El Capitan and Glacier Point.

Other birds you may spot in the park include **prairie falcons, kestrels,** and **merlin falcons,** as well as **golden eagles** and **great gray owls.** Always looking for handouts are dark-blue colored birds known as **Steller's jays.** These characters aren't bashful about landing on your picnic table in search of a crumb or two.

Ranger programs

Throughout the summer, rangers lead walks throughout Yosemite to explain aspects of the park's natural and cultural history. These programs, offered at various times throughout the day, touch on geology, forest ecology, wildlife, waterfalls, human history, or current park management issues. Programs on Yosemite's bear population — "The Bear Problem: Theirs or Ours?" and "Everything You Wanted to Know About Bears But Were Afraid to Ask Them" — are particularly informative and interest many young minds.

In winter, rangers on snowshoes lead hikes into the forests surrounding the Badger Pass Ski Area.

You don't need to look too far for something to do at night. The Park Service, Yosemite Concession Services, Sierra Club, and Ansel Adams Gallery all offer hour-long programs that may include talks, film and slide presentations, storytelling, and music. Rangers also lead stargazing programs atop Glacier Point during summer months.

For information on all the programs mentioned here, check the park newspapers as well as bulletin boards at visitor centers.

If you have kids, pick up information on the Junior Ranger Program (see Chapter 4) at the visitor center. The program is active in Yosemite from late June through August.

Keeping active

Yosemite offers numerous opportunities for outdoor fun. In addition to hiking (see "Taking a hike," earlier in the chapter), you can bike, ski, rock climb, fish, and even golf. Here's what you need to know for each sport:

- ✔ **Biking:** You can rent bikes by the hour ($5.50) or the day ($21) at Curry Village or Yosemite Lodge. Both shops are open from 8 a.m. to 7 p.m. daily in summer, but the one at Curry Village closes in winter. Hours may vary slightly depending on weather and season. For information, call ☎ **209-372-8319.** Helmets are required for riders under age 18 and are provided to riders of all ages free of charge. Cyclists have access to special bikeways in the eastern end of Yosemite Valley, as well as shuttle bus roads and thoroughfares for general traffic. Biking is prohibited on all trails.

- ✔ **Cross-country skiing:** Excursions are led from the Badger Pass Ski Area to Glacier Point. For information, call ☎ **209-372-8444.** You can rent skis at Badger Pass. Heartier mountaineers can journey into the backcountry.

- ✔ **Fishing:** Yosemite's stream fishing season runs from the last Saturday in April to mid-November, although you can fish in lakes and reservoirs throughout the year. Anglers ages 16 and older need a California fishing license. For information on where to obtain these licenses, and park-specific fishing regulations, stop at one of the visitor centers.

✔ **Golf:** Wawona sports a 9-hole golf course; call ☎ 209-375-6572 to book a tee time.

✔ **Horseback riding:** Yosemite offers two-hour and full-day rides from stables in Yosemite Valley and Wawona from spring through fall, weather permitting. In summer, rides also depart from Tuolumne Meadows. Call ☎ 209-372-8348 for information or reservations. Prices range from $40 for a few hours to $900 for a six-day guided trip into the backcountry. Backcountry trips are available only with advanced reservations from May to September. These lead to Yosemite's High Sierra camps, and trips include meals.

✔ **Ice skating:** The ice rink at Curry Village is open from early November to March, weather permitting. One 2½-hour session costs $5.25 for adults and $4.75 for children. Skate rental is another $2.25. There are four sessions daily.

✔ **Rock climbing:** If you've been bitten by the climbing bug, Yosemite is the place to be. It's one of the world's premier playgounds for experienced climbers. The **Yosemite Mountain School (☎ 209-372-8344)** provides experienced instruction for beginning, intermediate, and advanced climbers in the valley and Tuolumne Meadows from April through October. Classes last anywhere from a day to a week.

✔ **Skiing:** Yosemite's Badger Pass Ski Area (☎ 209-372-8430) is open from mid-December through Easter Sunday with alpine and nordic skiing, snowboarding, and tubing. Lessons for all skill levels are available and prices are reasonable: A half-day beginner's lesson with all equipment and all-day lift ticket runs about $50. Snow boarders are welcome on the slopes; boards and boots are also available for rent.

Where to Stay

Are you a blue blood or a frontiersman? Are you adamant about getting cozy each night in a king-sized bed with thick comforter, or are you willing to stoke the woodstove and pile into a cot with two wool blankets? You can have either experience in Yosemite, or choose from a variety of accommodations in between.

At one extreme is a room at The Ahwahnee, a National Historic Landmark with great halls, a cavernous dining room, gracious rooms, and stellar views. You pay dearly for a night here. At the other extreme (not counting backcountry camping under the stars) is a tent cabin at Curry Village,

White Wolf Lodge, or Tuolumne Meadows. No more than canvas tossed over a frame set on a wood or concrete floor (with bathrooms and showers in a communal bathhouse), these cabins recreate what camping was like in the 1920s. And, frankly, sleeping in one of these with woodstoves is fun. For only $54 to $59 a night, they're also a deal.

Yosemite Concession Services (YCS) oversees all lodging in the park — except some private homes at Wawona. You can make reservations by telephone (☎ **559-252-4848**), online (www.yosemitepark.com), or writing to Yosemite Reservations, 5410 E. Howe Ave, Fresno, CA 93727. Although the Wawona Hotel is operated by YCS, the dozen private homes available for rent nearby are handled through **Redwood Guest Cottages** (☎ **209-375-6666**). Addresses are not included in the listings below for the park hotels. Upon entering the park, you receive a map that pinpoints the location of each one.

Lodging in the park

The Ahwahnee
$$$$$ **Yosemite Valley**

The Ahwahnee is one of the crown jewels of the park system. The guest list is formidable: Queen Elizabeth, President Kennedy, 49ers quarterback Steve Young, and Clint Eastwood. You can add your name, too, if you're willing to pay the price, which can get quite steep for multiple-day stays. This elegant hotel, which marked its 75th anniversary in 2002, is the place to come for a pampering experience in the wilderness. Walk into the Great Lounge, a 77-foot-by-51-foot reading room with a 24-foot-high ceiling, and you find not only overstuffed couches and armchairs but back-to-back fireplaces big enough to walk into. The monstrous dining room has a 34-foot-high ceiling, is 130 feet by 51 feet, and seats 450 people. Light streams in through the 11 full-length windows for breakfast and lunch, but at dinner, tapers set in wrought iron holders illuminate the tables. You also find a small swimming pool outside the bar.

The rooms are among the best in the national park system. Suites feature two rooms, whereas regular rooms provide either two double beds or one king-sized bed, a couch, plush towels, and wonderful comforters. Stencils that rim the walls date to 1927 when the hotel was built.

Rooms can be very difficult to get during peak seasons. Try calling as early as a year in advance to reserve one for the summer or a holiday weekend. For more on making reservations, see "Planning Ahead," earlier in this chapter.

95 rooms, 4 suites, 24 cottages. A/C TEL. Rack rates: $366 double and cottages, additional charge for extra adults, specials during off-season; up to $1,079 for suites. DC, DISC, MC, V. Rates include coffee and pastries for breakfast. Parking available or take the shuttle bus to stop # 3.

Curry Village
$–$$ Yosemite Valley

This tent and cabin village, which marked its centennial in 1999, was designed to offer an economical lodging alternative to the now-defunct Sentinel Hotel. The accommodations in each tent cabin aren't much — a couple of cots, dressers, and warm blankets with the restrooms and showers a short walk away. Some of the wooden cabins have baths; the rest use communal facilities. Curry Village can be overrun with kids, it's noisy (the tent walls do little to muffle sounds from other tents and the nearby parking lot), and its bath houses aren't cleaned often enough. Still, the accommodations are inexpensive and the location is close to the village's pizza parlor, cocktail lounge, taco stand, coffee corner, sports shop, general store, overpriced cafeteria, ice cream stand, swimming pool, and sundeck.

183 wooden cabins, 427 canvas cabins, 18 hotel rooms. Rack rates: $49 tent cabin; $77 wooden cabin without bath; $92 wooden cabin with bath; $112 hotel room; all cabin rates are double occupancy, extra charge for additional adults. Lower rates off-season. DC, DISC, MC, V. Parking is available or take the shuttle to stops #1, #13, or #14.

Housekeeping Camp
$ Yosemite Valley

These interesting units are concrete and canvas — three walls and the floor are concrete, and the roof is a double layer of canvas. A canvas wall in the units separates the sleeping quarters from a cooking/dining area that centers around a picnic table. Tents have electric lights and outlets, so I guess you're a rung up from those folks staying in a tent cabin in Curry Village. A laundromat is nearby, as are communal restroom and shower facilities.

266 units. Rack rates: $56 per site for 1–4 people; $4 for each additional person. DC, DISC, MC, V. Open: Mid-April to mid-Oct. Parking is available or take the shuttle to stop #12.

Tuolumne Meadows Lodge
$$ Tuolumne Meadows

Although spartan, these tent cabins provide a memorable and highly affordable lodging option for adventurous visitors. Beds are simple bunks with reasonable mattresses covered by wool blankets. Woodstoves furnish the heat on cool nights and mornings, and a table stands ready for a game of cards. A short trail leads to a nearby communal bathhouse/restroom. Meals at the lodge are served family style, ensuring that you get to know your fellow travelers. The lodge also has a tour desk and dining room.

This place is similar to White Wolf Lodge, although a bit more crowded.

Tioga Road (California 120). 69 canvas tent cabins. Rack rate: $59 double, with additional charge of $8.25 per extra adult or $4 per child. DC, DISC, MC, V. Open: Mid-June to mid-Sept.

Wawona Hotel
$$–$$$ **Wawona**

Next to The Ahwahnee, this lodge is the most elegant in the park. The rooms are housed in a cluster of six Victorian-style buildings set in a forest clearing. You can relax on wide porches or play tennis or golf. Like The Ahwahnee, the hotel is a National Historic Landmark. Rooms are comfortable and quaint and come with a choice of a double and twin bed, a king bed, or a double bed. Fifty rooms have private baths; those without have access to a communal facility. All rooms open onto wide porches and overlook sprawling green lawns. A pianist plays in the downstairs lobby of the main hotel each night.

Wawona Road (California 41). 104 rooms. Rack rates: $101 double without bath, $161 double with bath; additional charge for extra adults. DC, DISC, MC, V.

White Wolf Lodge
$$ **White Wolf**

Not only does this small area offer a welcome escape from the valley crowds, but it's a bargain, too. The tent cabins are typically cleaner than those in Curry Village, and the wood-burning stoves and candles for light add a dash of charm on cool nights. You find a small general store and restaurant here. The location is popular with hikers and those seeking a weekend getaway. The canvas cabins share communal restroom and shower facilities, but the wooden cabins have their own bathrooms and small porches with chairs to plop into. Things really get quiet here at 11 p.m., when the generator is turned off. Those staying in tent cabins must stash their food in bear-proof lockers.

Tioga Road (California 120). 24 canvas tent cabins, 4 wooden cabins. Rack rates: $55 double without bath, $88 with bath; additional charge of $8.25 for extra adults and $4 per child. DC, DISC, MC, V. Open: Late June to early Sept.

Yosemite Lodge
$$–$$$ **Yosemite Valley**

Dating to 1915, this lodge has become a mishmash of accommodations over the years. You can't beat the location, at the base of Yosemite Falls, but the elegance of The Ahwahnee has not rubbed off. However, neither have The Ahwahnee's prices — this place is much more reasonable. The accommodations range from cabins and motel-style rooms to suites. Some offer views of the waterfalls, some have patios, others balconies. The lodge also has helpful services — a post office, bicycle rental stand, gift shops, and swimming pool. The amphitheater in the middle of the lodge is handy for attending ranger programs and slide presentations.

245 motel rooms and suites. Some with A/C TEL. Rack rates: $113–$138 double, with additional charge for extra adults. Lower rates off-season. DC, DISC, MC, V. Parking available or take the shuttle to stop #8.

Lodging outside the park

Yosemite West Cottages
$$–$$$$$ Sierra National Forest

Although these accommodations aren't in Yosemite, you have to drive through the park to get to them. These private homes range in size and accommodate families as well as couples. All cabins come with kitchenettes, whereas homes have full kitchens, and most have fireplaces or wood-burning stoves. Homes are equipped with oversize beds. From here the distance is 10 miles to the Yosemite Valley floor and just 8 miles to Badger Pass, making this spot the best if you're planning a winter ski trip in the park.

Off Wawona Road (California 41), 12 miles north of Wawona, near Chinquapin. ☎ *559-642-2211. Internet:* www.yosemitewestreservations.com. *A fluctuating number of cabins and private homes are available throughout the year. TV. Rack rates: $85–$215 and up. No credit cards.*

Runner-up lodgings

Best Western Yosemite Way Station
$$ Mariposa   Clean, comfortable, and kid-friendly thanks to the outdoor pool, this chain motel includes continental breakfast in its rates. *4999 Hwy. 140.* ☎ *888-742-4371 or 209-966-7545. Internet:* www.yosemite-motels.com/ymbwyws.html.

Cedar Lodge
$$–$$$ El Portal   Just 8 miles west of Yosemite's Arch Rock Entrance, this lodge is set on 27 mostly wooded acres, offers standard motel rooms as well as suites, and has a pizza parlor and lounge on the property. *9966 Hwy. 140.* ☎ *888-742-4371 or 209-379-2612. Internet:* www.yosemite-motels.com/ymcedar.html.

Comfort Inn of Oakhurst
$$ Oakhurst   Located 15 miles south of Yosemite's South Entrance, this chain property offers a pool, Jacuzzi, and Continental breakfast, and is near a golf course. *40489 Hwy. 41.* ☎ *888-742-4371 or 559-683-8282. Internet:* www.yosemite-motels.com/ymcio.html.

Groveland Hotel

$$$–$$$$$ **Groveland** Twenty-three miles west of Yosemite's Big Oak Flat Entrance, this gracious two-story hotel dates to 1849 and names most of its 17 rooms after women of the Sierra. Not exactly kid-friendly, but adults admire the antiques and candlelit dining room. *18767 Hwy. 120.* ☎ *800-273-3314 or 209-962-4000. Internet:* www.groveland.com.

Campgrounds

In Yosemite you can choose from the park's 13 front country campgrounds and 5 High Sierra camps, the latter offering a somewhat pampered backcountry experience. Read on for details on these options.

Camping in the front country

Yosemite has 13 campgrounds — a baker's dozen, or is that a camper's dozen? Anyway, the one you choose depends on where you want to be in the park, and whether or not you want to arrive with a reservation or jockey for one of the first-come, first-served sites.

To reserve a site at any campground — later I tell you which places accept reservations — call ☎ **800-436-7275** between 7 a.m. and 7 p.m. Pacific Standard Time. Computer-literate readers can place their reservations online by visiting http://reservations.nps.gov. You can make reservations up to five months in advance of your trip, starting on the 15th of each month.

For road warriors traveling by RV, none of the 13 campgrounds has a utility hookup, although sanitary dump stations are available in Yosemite Valley, Wawona, and Tuolumne Meadows (summer only).

The campgrounds have most of the amenities of home . . . within walking distance. All valley campgrounds offer showers and flush toilets nearby, as well as laundry facilities, groceries, swimming, fishing, and even horseback riding. Head out of the valley, though, and the amenities begin to dwindle. For example, only campers at White Wolf or Tuolumne Meadows enjoy nearby showers, and only those at Wawona, Crane Flat, and Tuolumne Meadows have a grocery nearby. For details on a specific campground, call ☎ **209-372-8502.**

If the valley floor and its attractions are the focus of your trip, find a spot in either the **Upper Pines Campground,** open year-round; the **Lower Pines Campground,** open from March through October; or the **North Pines Campground,** open from April through October. Reservations are required at these popular sites, so you can guarantee yourself a spot if you plan properly. The three campgrounds have comparable settings, but if you like to fall asleep to the sound of rippling waters, aim for a site in the North Pines campground, located along the Merced River.

If you fail to land a spot in these three campgrounds, your only other option in the valley floor is the **Camp 4 Campground** located west of Yosemite Lodge along Northside Drive. However, this walk-in campground is very popular with climbers and backpackers and can be on the rambunctious side. This facility operates on a first-come, first-served basis, and often fills before 9 a.m. each day May through September.

Outside the valley, only the **Wawona and Hodgdon Meadows campgrounds** are open year-round. Both campgrounds are quiet and more secluded than those on the valley floor. Reservations for these sites are required from May through September; the rest of the year they go on a first-come, first-served basis.

The **Tuolumne Meadows Campground** is open July through September. Half the sites are filled by reservation and the other half by walk-up traffic.

Reservations are always required at the **Crane Flat Campground,** which is open from June to September.

Sites at the **Bridalveil Creek, Tamarack Flat, White Wolf, Porcupine Creek, and Yosemite Creek campgrounds,** which are open during the summer months, are filled on a first-come, first-served basis. If you want a more out-of-the-way spot, **Yosemite Creek Campground,** which is located at the end of a steep, 5-mile unpaved road just east of White Wolf, fits the bill.

Camping in the backcountry

If a pampered backcountry experience is what you want, consider spending a few nights at one of Yosemite's five **High Sierra camps.** Unlike your usual backcountry treks, here you can sleep on a reasonably soft mattress in a tent cabin and relish great meals that *someone else* prepares. The five camps are Merced Lake, Vogelsang, Glen Aulin, May Lake, and Sunrise. The dormitory-style canvas cabins can sleep between 32 and 60 people. You get more than just a soft place to bed down, too, because each camp is complete with restroom and shower facilities.

The price for this camping experience may seem steep — $109 per adult per night, $76 per child — but when you consider the high-country setting and the meals included in the price (filet mignon, chicken dishes, pork loin, fish, or pasta for dinner, and pancakes, eggs and bacon, Danish, and cereals for breakfast), it doesn't seem so bad, now does it? These accommodations, available late June to Labor Day, are popular. For this reason, a lottery determines who lands a bed. Camp applications are accepted between October 15 and November 30; winners are notified the following March. If you have questions or want an application, call the **High Sierra Desk** at ☎ 559-253-5674.

If a more traditional backcountry experience is what you seek, see "Planning Ahead," earlier in this chapter for information on obtaining a mandatory wilderness permit.

Where to Eat

When you're wondering what to pack for your trip, rest assured that if you toss your tux or cocktail dress into your suitcase, you'll have a place to wear it. Being overdressed for dinner at The Ahwahnee hotel is impossible, although you probably want to leave the tux behind if you're dining on beer and pizza over at Curry Village.

You find plenty of dining options in Yosemite Valley, although they narrow considerably when you head to the high country of Tuolumne Meadows and White Wolf Lodge. Although menu prices throughout the park may raise your eyebrows, you'll be satisfied when you push away from the table.

I don't include all the park's dining options in the listings below. You also find inexpensive cafeterias, grills, and pizza places at Curry Village and Yosemite Village. The Yosemite Lodge has a recently renovated cafeteria.

The Ahwahnee Dining Room
$$$$–$$$$$ Yosemite Valley   AMERICAN

Don't be surprised if it takes you a little while to get around to reading the menu after you're seated. This cavernous hall deserves a once- or twice-over. National park stateliness can be defined by this room, with its 34-foot-tall beamed ceiling, its candelabra chandeliers, and the thin tapers that dress your table. The menu is equally impressive, with dinner entrees ranging from salmon Ahwahnee with Dungeness crab to rack of lamb with rosemary polenta. For breakfasts, they roll out the crepe pan and fresh fruit if you're not in the mood for omelettes or French toast. Pasta salads and a variety of sandwiches hold down the lunch menus. Gentlemen (and boys over 12) are required to don jackets, preferably with ties, and slacks for dinner.

In The Ahwahnee. ☎ *209-372-1489. Dinner reservations required. Main courses: $3.50–$15.50 breakfast; $11–$14.50 lunch; $19.30–$29.20 dinner. DC, DISC, MC, V. Open: Daily 7–10:30 a.m., 11:30 a.m.–3 p.m., 5:30–9 p.m. Shuttle bus stop #4.*

Degnan's Deli
$$ Yosemite Valley   DELI SANDWICHES

Ah yes, your typical deli. Not a complete New York deli, but Degnan's has a good selection of sandwiches that will keep you going through the afternoon. The lines can get long at the height of the lunch hour, but they move pretty quickly, so don't despair. You also find plenty of premade salads, sandwiches, and snacks in general to toss into your pack for that meal somewhere down the trail. They have a decent wine and beer selection, too. If you still have room after you're meal, you can head next door for ice cream.

Yosemite Village. No phone. Main courses: $4–$7 breakfast, lunch, and dinner. DC, DISC, MC, V. Open: Daily 7:30 a.m.–5 p.m. Shuttle bus stops #2, #4 and #10.

Degnan's Loft
$$–$$$ Yosemite Valley   ITALIAN

This pizza place is a great place to take your family. The atmosphere is light and cheery, and the food is filling. The bread sticks, salads, and desserts are all made daily. This place is good for a quick, reliable meal. While waiting for your meal, cozy up to the fireplace that anchors the center of the restaurant.

Yosemite Village. No phone. Main courses: $7–$14 lunch and dinner. DC, DISC, MC, V. Open: mid-April to Oct, Mon–Fri, noon to 9 p.m. Shuttle bus stops #2, #4 and #10.

Mountain Room Restaurant
$$$$ Yosemite Valley   AMERICAN

Suffering from Ahwahnee taste but a Wal-Mart budget? This place is the one for you. You don't enjoy the sprawling opulence of The Ahwahnee's dining room, but you get fantastic views of Yosemite Falls through the restaurant's floor-to-ceiling windows. The prices are much more tolerable than at The Ahwahnee, and the menu is good, ranging from traditional steaks to untraditional California Thai Chicken, which is served with a tangy chilled peanut sauce. Your dinner includes an entree and choice of vegetables and sourdough bread, but you have to dig a bit deeper into your budget if you want soup or salad.

In Yosemite Lodge. ☎ 209-372-1281. Main courses: $15.70–$21 dinner. DC, DISC, MC, V. Open: Daily 5:30–9 p.m. Shuttle bus stop #8.

Tuolumne Meadows Lodge
$$$–$$$$ Tuolumne Meadows   AMERICAN

The food here is surprisingly good, considering how far from civilization you are. One night I ordered the lamb chops and they ran out, so instead I got tenderloin of lamb. Talk about roughing it. But that brings up a key point — sometimes they run out of dishes, so make an early dinner reservation. Seating is family style, so you never know who may end up at your table.

Tioga Road (California 120). ☎ 209-372-8413. Reservations required for dinner. Main courses: $4.15–$8 breakfast; $9.15–$20 dinner. DC, DISC, MC, V. Open: Mid-June to mid-Sept, 7–9 a.m. and 6–8 p.m.

Wawona Hotel Dining Room
$$$-$$$$$ Wawona   AMERICAN

For a laid-back, relaxing, and dignified dining experience, come here. The dining room, like the rest of the hotel, is wide open with lots of windows and sunlight. The menu is not only affordable but delectable, with combination meals for breakfast (French toast or pancakes with eggs and bacon); lunches that feature everything from cheeseburgers to ratatouille; and dinners of thick slabs of prime rib, grilled salmon, or sauteed chicken breast seasoned with a cream sauce of roasted red bell pepper and basil. On Sundays, schedule your day around brunch. You have a choice of two seatings: one ($10.35) from 7:30 to 10:30 a.m., and another ($16.60) from 10:30 a.m. to 1:30 p.m. Both give you a wide choice of egg dishes, fresh fruit, fruit breads, juices, blintzes, and meats, whereas the second adds pan-fried trout and a carving station with roast beef, turkey, and pork roast.

Wawona Road (California 41). ☎ 209-375-1425. Reservations recommended. Main courses: $2.15–$7.95 breakfast; $6.95–$10.35 lunch; $11.50–$26.25 dinner; $9.95 and $16.95 Sun brunch. DC, DISC, MC, V. Open: Easter week to early Oct, daily; late-Oct to Thanksgiving, weekends only; Christmas to New Years Day, daily; Jan–March weekends; Mon–Sat 7:30–10 a.m., noon–1:30 p.m., and 5:30–8:30 p.m.; Sun brunch seatings 7:30 and 10:30 a.m., Sun dinner 5:30–8:30 p.m.

White Wolf Lodge
$$-$$$ White Wolf   AMERICAN

By now you probably have breakfast menus memorized: pancakes or French toast, cereals and eggs, biscuits and gravy. Dinners are also pretty predictable at most national park restaurants, and this place is no exception. The menu always has a beef, chicken, fish, pasta, and vegetarian offering. Thankfully, after a long day on the trail, the portions are large, and the staff is fun and enthusiastic. You can't sit down to lunch here, but the lodge has a store where you can buy food.

Tioga Road (California 120). ☎ 209-372-8416. Reservations required for dinner. Main courses: $3.60–$6.70 breakfast; $5.95–$16.20 dinner. DC, DISC, MC, V. Open: Late June to early Sept, daily 7–9 a.m. and 6–8:30 p.m.

Yosemite Lodge Food Court
$$$ Yosemite Valley   PIZZA/DELI/GRILL

This recently remodeled cafeteria offers the option of enjoying a sit-down meal or grabbing a quick bite before heading out into the park. Hot and cold food stations offer a varied selection ranging from a pasta station; pizza station; deli station with salads, and cheese and fruit plates; wrap and deli sandwiches; and a grill serving burgers, hot dogs, fries, and chicken and fish sandwiches. You also can choose vegetarian or meat-based entrees. Breakfast fare ranges from grilled items to cereals. Prepackaged picnic items are also available.

In Yosemite Lodge. No phone. Main courses: $8.50–$12.35 breakfast, lunch, and dinner. DC, MC, V. Open: Daily 6:30 a.m.–8 p.m. Shuttle bus stop #8.

Fast Facts: Yosemite

Area Code

☎ 209 and 559.

ATM

Available at Yosemite Village (just south of and inside of the Village Store), in Yosemite Lodge, and inside the gift shop in Curry Village.

Emergency

☎ 911; from a hotel room, ☎ 9-911.

Fees

$20 per vehicle per week; $10 per week on foot, bicycle, or motorcycle.

Fishing License

California license needed for ages 16 and older. Regulations available at visitor centers.

Hospitals

Yosemite Medical Clinic (Ahwahnee Drive); ☎ 209-372-4637. Dental services adjacent to medical clinic; ☎ 209-372-4200 or 209-372-4637.

Information

Yosemite National Park, P.O. Box 577, Yosemite, CA 95389; ☎ 209-372-0200.

Lost and Found

☎ 209-372-4357 for items lost in Yosemite's restaurants, hotels, lounges, shuttle buses, or tour services; ☎ 209-379-1001 for items lost in the park.

Pharmacies

Yosemite Medical Clinic (Ahwahnee Drive) has a limited pharmacy; ☎ 209-372-4637.

Post Offices

Yosemite Village, Yosemite Lodge, Curry Village, Wawona, and Tuolumne Meadows.

Road Conditions and Weather

☎ 209-372-0200.

Taxes

10% lodging, 7.75% meals.

Time Zone

Pacific standard time.

Web Site

www.nps.gov/yose.

Chapter 22

Zion National Park

● ●

In This Chapter

▶ Going into the redrock canyon

▶ Planning your trip

▶ Hiking the trails to high peaks and lush pools

▶ Finding the best beds and meals

● ●

Southern Utah's canyon-riddled redrock country is so fantastic that one national park alone can't capture its beauty, which is why you find five national parks and two national monuments displaying its marvelous and rugged landscape. But squeezing in stops at all seven during a typical, weeklong vacation is impossible if you want to do them all justice.

That's where Zion National Park comes in. More than any of the other Utah parks, Zion offers an intoxicating primer on redrock country. Whereas one part of the park is a stark, high-desert landscape, the other teems with lush oases that erupt with blooms of wildflowers in the spring.

What strikes you first as you enter the heart of the park, via Zion Canyon Drive, are towering cliffs cut by deep side canyons. The rugged landscape doesn't seem very nurturing. But take a little time to explore this maze-like park and you discover flourishing hanging gardens fed by cascading streams, narrow slot canyons with sandstone walls fluted by thousands of years of rushing waters, and glimmering emerald green pools stepping their way down mountainsides.

Although Zion doesn't boast the incredible number and diversity of rock arches that define Arches National Park (see Chapter 10), its Kolob Arch is one of the world's largest freestanding arches. And even though nearby Bryce Canyon National Park is the world champion when it comes to sheer numbers of rocky spires, pinnacles, and hoodoos, spend some time on Zion's eastern flanks, and you find plenty of mushroom-shaped hoodoos to sate your curiosity about these intriguing rock outcrops. Utah's Capitol Reef National Park may boast ship-sized rock formations, but Zion counters with the Great White Throne and the Watchman, two of the biggest sandstone monoliths known on Earth. Although Zion can't compete with Canyonlands National Park when it comes to sprawling canyons that swallow the landscape, trek through Zion's Narrows, a narrow and towering slot canyon, and you'll come away with a life-long memory of a 24-foot-wide, 1,000-foot-deep crack in the earth.

Zion crams into one place all the highlights of redrock country, and the park is compact enough to easily navigate, particularly if you're short on time. You can see some of the park's best attractions in just a day; however, plan for two days if you want to hike the Narrows or visit the Kolob Canyons in the northwest section.

When should you visit Zion? The park is generally overrun by tourists during the summer months and largely deserted during the winter months, but each season has its pros and cons. Although spring can be wet, it's my second favorite time in the park thanks to warm days and May wildflowers. Summer is fairly comfortable, although it can get hot, with highs routinely approaching 100 degrees. My favorite season in Zion is fall because water levels in the canyons are low, making for easy hiking into the slots; crowds are manageable; and lodging is easy to find. Plus, autumn's crispness is perfect for hiking. Even though some snow falls in the park in winter, storms usually don't dump many inches; however, ice can make some park roads and trails difficult to negotiate, and some trails might even be closed.

Must-see Attractions

As soon as you enter Zion Canyon, your head is going to tilt back. That's the only way you can take in all the incredible slickrock scenery that frames this canyon cut by the Virgin River. But after you venture inside, where should you aim your sights? Let me give you some ideas:

✔ **Angels Landing:** King of the Hill, anyone? Stand atop this outcrop, and you've won that title. Below you, the park falls away in all directions. Off in the distance, you can see Cathedral Mountain, Observation Point, Cable Mountain, and the Great White Throne. Of course, to get to this summit, you have to negotiate a trail that, at points, is quite precipitous and not for everyone. But hey, you want to experience Zion, right?

✔ **Emerald Pools Trail:** In a land as arid as Utah, just about any water is worth a visit. Hike this trail and you'll return home talking about towering waterfalls that leap-frog down the mountainside, creating a series of pools and lush, hanging gardens.

✔ **Great White Throne:** This is Zion's version of Yosemite's El Capitan (see Chapter 21). A large rectangular block of sandstone set on end, the throne rises 2,344 feet above the Zion Canyon floor and is thought to be one of the largest upright masses of sandstone in the world. You find this monolith about 3 miles upriver from the Zion Canyon Visitor Center.

Zion National Park

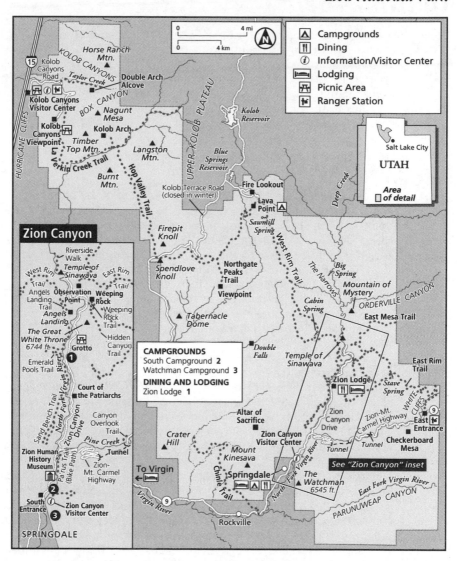

The Watchman: This sandstone monolith stands guard over the park's south entrance like a stony sentinel. It climbs 2,555 feet above the road.

Weeping Rock: This rock grotto is a wonderful place to cool off during the height of summer, and the lush, colorful hanging gardens that drape the cliffside with Zion columbines, shooting stars, and scarlet gilia make it hard to believe you're in the middle of a desert.

Getting There

Zion is located near the bottom of Utah in the state's southwestern corner where canyon country runs far and wide. The park could have been made much larger — that's how much spectacular countryside there is in this part of the state. In fact, Bryce Canyon National Park is just 85 miles to the northeast, Cedar Breaks National Monument is 80 miles to the north, and the Grand Staircase-Escalante National Monument is only 60 miles to the east.

Driving in

Thanks to Interstate 15, just 25 or 31 miles west of the park's South Entrance (depending on whether you're coming from the north or south), getting to Zion is easy. If you're heading north from St. George, take Exit 16 and drive 11 miles north on Utah 9 to La Verkin, where you turn right and continue to Springdale. If you're coming from Salt Lake City, 325 miles to the north, get off at Exit 27 and head 5 miles east along Utah 17 to La Verkin. Then turn left onto Utah 9 and continue 20 miles to Springdale and the South Entrance. (If you're coming from the north, you can't use the Northwest Entrance to get to Zion Canyon. This entrance leads to a dead-end road.)

The roads between I-15 and the park don't take you through the most scenic approach to Zion (an experience that is reserved for those who travel Utah 9 from U.S. 89 to the East Entrance), but they do offer the most expedient route. If you use the South Entrance, you avoid delays that often occur at the East Entrance, where traffic enters through the Zion-Mt. Carmel Tunnel. Plus, if you can't find a room inside the park, the town of Springdale near the South Entrance offers several possibilities.

The ride to the park's East Entrance runs 24 miles from the Mt. Carmel Junction on Utah 9. The canyon country along this route is spectacular thanks to the aptly named Checkerboard Mesa (a sandstone mountain that is crisscrossed with grooves) and beautiful views into canyons that fall away from the road. The road tests your brakes a bit, because it drops 2,400 feet, slips through the mile-long Zion-Mt. Carmel Tunnel, and negotiates six switchbacks. If you're driving a particularly large rig — one at least 11 feet, 4 inches tall or 7 feet, 10 inches wide — entering the park via this route costs $10 extra because you need an escort through the tunnel. (Tall vehicles have to drive down the middle of the tunnel to keep from running into its arched walls.)

Flying in

The nearest airports are in **St. George, Utah** (☎ 435- 634-3830), 45 miles away from the South Entrance, and **Cedar City, Utah** (☎ 435-586-3033),

15 miles from the Kolob Entrance and 59 miles from the South Entrance. Both airports are on the small side, but you can get service to them on **Delta-Skywest Airlines.** (See the Appendix for the toll-free numbers of all airlines and car-rental agencies mentioned in this section.)

Car-rental agencies with offices in St. George include **ABC** (148 W. St. George Blvd.; ☎ **435-628-7355**), **Avis** (St. George Municipal Airport; ☎ **435- 627-2002**), **Budget** (176 W. St. George Blvd., ☎ **435-673-4293;** St. George Municipal Airport, ☎ **435-673-6825**), **Dollar** (1175 S. 150 E.; ☎ **435-628-6549**), and **National** (St. George Municipal Airport; ☎ **435-673-5098**). **Avis** and **National** provide car rentals at the Cedar City airport.

The closest major airport is **McCarran International Airport** (☎ **702-261-5743**) in Las Vegas, which is about 110 miles southwest of St. George via I-15. Most major airlines fly into McCarran, and most major car rental agencies have outlets at the airport. The **St. George Shuttle** (☎ **435-628-8320**; Internet: www.stgshuttle.com) provides daily service between St. George and Las Vegas.

Planning Ahead

You have to plan well in advance to secure a room in Zion. Although the park may not be as popular as Yellowstone or Yosemite, or let alone next-door-neighbor Grand Canyon, Zion's rooms fill up quickly because there just aren't many of them. The same is true for campsites in the developed campgrounds. As a result, if you're planning a mid-summer visit, when most tourists head to Zion, make room reservations at least six months ahead of your arrival. As for campground space, sites in both the Lava Point and South campgrounds are doled out on a first-come, first-served basis. You can reserve sites at the Watchman Campground by calling ☎ **800-365-CAMP.**

For general information in advance of your trip, write Superintendent, Zion National Park, Springdale, UT 84767 or call ☎ **435-772-3256.** You can also check the park Web site at www.nps.gov/zion.

Learning the Lay of the Land

Zion National Park, sprawled across nearly 150,000 acres, is shaped like a block, except for a small peninsula off the park's northwestern corner. The heart and soul of the park is in and around Zion Canyon, which is traversed by the 7-mile-long **Zion Canyon Drive.** Paralleling the drive is the North Fork of the Virgin River. Located in the canyon are several trailheads, cascading streams, and the Zion Lodge, the only lodge inside the park.

Unless you have a reservation at the Zion Lodge, you cannot drive along Zion Canyon Drive during high season, approximately April through October. Instead, you must park your car in Springdale or at Zion Canyon Visitor Center, on the south end of the park. You can then take a seat in one of the free, propane-powered **shuttle buses** that run all the way to the Temple of Sinawava, a canyon surrounded by rock walls located at the north end of the canyon floor. See "Getting around," later in this chapter, for information on the shuttle.

Enter the park via the East Entrance along **Zion-Mount Carmel Highway** and you encounter the intriguing Checkerboard Mesa with its slashed and grooved sandstone face dotted with ponderosa pines. Horizontal grooves in Navajo sandstone are common, but the vertical ones on this mountain are thought to have been cut by freezing and thawing processes and enlarged by erosion.

Just beyond Checkerboard Mesa, you pass through a colorful garden of red, orange, tan, and white rock formations in all shapes and sizes before entering two narrow tunnels. On the east end of the second tunnel is a pullout for the mile-long Canyon Overlook Trail that offers a great view into Zion Canyon. Exiting the second tunnel, you quickly exchange a landscape of rugged mountains for the broad and deep Zion Canyon with its abrupt cliffs.

After negotiating a series of switchbacks that lower you to the valley floor, you arrive at the junction of Zion-Mount Carmel Highway and Zion Canyon Drive. You can turn right if you have a room at Zion Lodge. If not, a left turn takes you to the **Zion Canyon Visitor Center.** Less than a mile south of the visitor center is the **South Entrance,** and just beyond that is **Springdale** with its dozens of restaurants and lodging options.

Roughly 45 minutes away from the Zion Canyon Visitor Center via Interstate 15 is the park's **Northwest Entrance** station, where you find the **Kolob Canyons Visitor Center** and realize that you left most of the park's crowds back in Zion Canyon. This marks the start of **Kolob Canyons Road,** which creeps 5 miles into the park to several overlooks that show off the park's red- and orange-rock landscape with canyons 1,500-feet deep. The small visitor center offers many of the services found at the main visitor center back in Zion Valley. Before ending at an overlook, Kolob Canyons Road leads you past viewpoints of Horse Ranch Mountain, which, at 8,726 feet, is the park's highest point; of the deep and narrow Box Canyon through which the South Fork of Taylor Creek flows; and of Timber Top Mountain, which, as its name implies, is capped by a stand of fir and ponderosa pine. Also along this short stretch of pavement is Rockfall Overlook, which shows off a large scar gashed into the mountainside in July 1983, when a 1,000-foot chunk of stone came tumbling down.

Between Zion Canyon and Kolob Canyons lies the park's other road, **Kolob Terrace Road.** This route, which closes in winter, heads north off

Utah 9 from the village of Virgin, about 15 miles west of the park's South Entrance. The road leads to two reservoirs just beyond the park's northern border, as well as to the primitive Lava Point Campground.

Arriving in the Park

Most visitors, unless they're planning a backcountry journey into one of the park's remote corners, enter Zion at Springdale. Unless you have a room at Zion Lodge, you must park your car in this gateway town and ride a free shuttle bus into Zion Canyon. You can't get around this restriction by entering the park at the East Entrance, because you'll be directed to the South Entrance to park your car in Springdale and board a shuttle. Don't worry about getting an orientation to the park; you'll get one when the shuttle stops at the main visitor center.

Finding information

The park has two visitor centers. The **Zion Canyon Visitor Center and Transportation Hub** (☎ **435-772-7616**), near the South Entrance, has outdoor exhibits that provide an introduction to the park. Rangers here can answer questions and provide backcountry permits. You can also buy books, maps, videos, postcards, and posters, and pick up free brochures. The center is open from 8 a.m. to 7 p.m. daily in summer with shorter hours the remainder of the year; it's closed December 25. The **Kolob Canyons Visitor Center** (☎ **435-586-9548**), in the northwest corner of the park off I-15, provides information, permits, books, and maps. The center is open from 8 a.m. to 7 p.m. daily in summer with shorter hours the remainder of the year; it's closed Thanksgiving and December 25.

Paying fees

Entry into the park (for up to seven days) includes unlimited use of the shuttle buses and costs $20 per private vehicle and $10 per individual on motorcycle, bicycle, or foot. If you have a park pass, you don't need to pay the entrance fee; see Chapter 8 for information on the National Park Pass and Chapter 4 for the lowdown on Golden Age and Golden Access passports.

In addition to the entrance fee, drivers of oversized vehicles (see "Learning the Lay of the Land") must pay $10 to pass through the Zion-Mount Carmel Tunnel on the stretch of highway from the East Entrance to the Zion Canyon Drive.

Permits are required for all overnight hikes in the park and for all slot canyon routes. They cost $5 per person per night and are available at the visitor centers.

Getting around

Unless you have a reservation at the Zion Lodge, you won't be able to drive along Zion Canyon Drive from approximately April through October. Instead, you must park your car at the **Zion Canyon Visitor Center and Transportation Hub** near the South Entrance, or in Springdale, and take the **Zion Canyon Shuttle.**

Being hauled like a herd of cattle into a national park may sound like a hassle to you, but in reality, taking the shuttle makes your visit much more enjoyable. During the peak of the summer season, from late May to early September, the buses run from 5:45 a.m. to 11 p.m. every day. Inside the park, they stop about every 1½ miles, so you're never very far from where you want to be. And with shuttles coming by every six minutes or so during the busiest part of the day, and about every half-hour at night, you won't wait long for a ride. (Times and frequency are reduced in the earlier and later parts of the season.)

Remembering Safety

If you're coming from a low elevation, keep in mind that Zion is located at 4,000 feet and higher, so you may feel a bit winded your first or second day. You may even get a headache or experience insomnia. Combat these maladies by taking it easy your first day and by making sure to drink plenty of water.

Remember, too, that Zion is in the desert. During summer's heat, you can easily and quickly become dehydrated, particularly if you're hiking, so continue to drink water; a gallon a day isn't too much. If you haven't been to the desert before, comprehending the heat, dryness, and intensity of the sun can be difficult. If you're prone to dry skin, moisturizing lotion is a must; even if you're not, you'll probably end up using it.

It's bright in the park thanks to the general lack of trees and the wide open expanses, so use sunblock, a hat, and sunglasses with full ultraviolet protection.

State health officials also warn outdoor enthusiasts to take precautions against Hantavirus, a rare but often fatal respiratory disease first recognized in 1993. About half of the country's confirmed cases have been reported in the Four Corners states of Colorado, New Mexico, Arizona, and Utah. The disease is usually spread by the urine and droppings of rodents. Health officials recommend that campers and hikers avoid areas with signs of rodent occupations. Symptoms of Hantavirus are similar to flu, and lead to breathing difficulties and shock.

For more tips on how to ensure a safe park visit, see Chapter 8.

Capturing Zion on film

Desert landscapes provide wonderful images to capture on film — the starkness of the land, sparse vegetation, wide open places with solitary focal points, such as buttes, lone trees, or cacti. Zion National Park has all these features, plus towering sandstone cliffs with hidden pockets of lush vegetation nourished by the occasional downpour. (Weeping Rock is a great place to find hanging gardens.) You never run out of things to photograph during a visit to this park.

Because of the towering cliffs that rim Zion Canyon Drive, a wide-angle lens comes in handy for capturing the immensity of this part of the park. Just don't forget to add a person to the foreground to give the cliffs some perspective. Also, a zoom lens is great for bringing arches and cliffs closer. And if you're a student of botany, a macro lens is a nice tool to have for capturing cactus blooms up close. Don't forget your tripod, either, because your hand may not be steady enough for low-light conditions in some of the park's recesses. As with a trip to any park, keeping a range of films in your bag is wise — ISO100 films for bright conditions and ISO400 for dimly lit settings.

Enjoying the Park

Most Zion visitors spend all their time on the floor of Zion Canyon. And that's okay, because the canyon has enough attractions to fill your entire stay in the park, whether it's one day or several days. However, to reach some of the best sights — such as Emerald Pools, Angels Landing, and Weeping Rock — you must hit the trails. That's why this section begins with "Taking a hike."

Although crowds descend on Zion in summer, you can avoid them. First, don't sleep in. (If you do, you miss seeing the park in one of its prettiest settings, with the rays of the slowly rising sun casting wonderful shadows and dazzling highlights across the redrock.) Because most people do sleep in, or simply have a hard time energizing themselves, if you get out in the park at least by 8 a.m., you won't have to jostle with others to enjoy the overlooks. Plus, hikers who hit the trail right around sunrise increase their odds of seeing wildlife before the animals bed down for the day. The next best way to avoid the crowds is to flee them. Head down a trail, not merely 50 yards, but a mile or more.

Taking a hike

If you've never hiked through a narrow slot canyon with walls towering 100, 200, 300, or more feet above you, put this activity at the top of your to-do list. Sculpted by countless years of water erosion, slot canyons are cool, dark, and even haunting as they twist and turn through the landscape. They're also beautiful, thanks to the colorful fluting erosion imparted on the sandstone.

Slot canyons can also be dangerous because you never hear the approaching thunderstorms that can generate flash floods through the canyon you're navigating. Also, many of the slots require technical equipment and practiced skills to negotiate. But then, driving a car or walking across a street can be dangerous, too. The key to safety is to employ common sense. If you're not sure of your ability, seek out an experienced guide.

Before you start down a slot canyon trail, check the region's weather forecast (posted at the Zion Canyon Visitor Center) and chat with a ranger. After you're inside a slot canyon, if there's a stream running through it, pay attention to the water. If the water level suddenly starts rising, you need to start rising, too, to higher ground. If you see clouds building overhead or hear thunder rumbling off in the distance, and if you're not far from one end of the canyon, get out as quickly as you can. A flash flood may not result, but if one does, you'll be glad you're out of the canyon. If you're too far from one of the entrances to leave the canyon, search for high ground.

No matter what type of hike you take, carry water with you. A hiking staff is a good idea, too, especially if you're going to wade through streams. And don't forget to pick up a backcountry permit at a visitor center for any overnight or slot canyon hikes.

Zion has a variety of hikes, from those that wind through tight slot canyons to others that run along canyon rims. Stop by a visitor center to find out about all the park's hiking opportunities. This section includes my recommendations.

Angels Landing Trail

If you like a challenging hike, one that tests your fear of heights, this is it. The trail climbs 1,488 feet to a summit with incredible views of Zion Canyon. But be prepared: The final ½-mile to the top crawls along a narrow, knife-edge trail where footing can be dicey under even the best of conditions. To help you along this section, the park has mercifully added chains that you can cling to. But the view from the top is worth the work. You can gaze in all directions, taking in the Virgin River sweeping through the bottom of the canyon, the Great White Throne, Red Arch Mountain to the southeast, and the entrance to the Narrows beyond the Temple of Sinawava to the north.

Think twice about hiking to Angels Landing if you have young children or if you dislike heights. The last ½-mile of the trail is particularly harrowing due to its precipitous nature.

Distance: 5 miles round-trip. Level: Difficult. Access: Grotto Picnic Area along Zion Canyon Drive.

Chinle Trail

The first few miles of this quiet desert trail are fairly easy walking along a wide sandy path. Ahead you have views of Mount Kinesava and the Three Marys formation. To the south behind you, and outside the park, rises a series of peaks known as the Eagle Crags. A gradual 150-foot incline brings you to the petrified forest denoting the top of the Chinle Formation, a sedimentary rock layer. While inspecting the rock-like logs, don't forget that removing anything from the national park is illegal; leave the lovely pieces of petrified wood as you find them. After crossing Huber Wash, the trail heads for Scoggins Wash through more desert terrain, which is dotted by juniper, pinyon, and sagebrush. To the northwest, you can see Cougar Mountain, and looking east allows views of the Towers of the Virgin, the West Temple, and the Sundial — all craggy rock formations. After you're on the mesa beyond Scoggins Wash, the trail heads for three *knolls* (mounds), passing through several small *saddles* (ridges between two peaks), traversing a meadow, and crossing the Old Scoggins Stock Trail, built by the area's early pioneers. Continuing west, the trail passes between two knolls and bends to the north, where you'll have no trouble finding an attractive campsite. The final descent into Coalpits Wash brings Cougar Mountain, Smith Mesa, and Lambs Knoll into view, and at the bottom you find a pretty waterfall a bit upstream from Coalpits Spring — the end of the trail.

This hike can be uncomfortably hot in summer but is an absolute delight from November to May (blankets of wildflowers delight the eye in spring). The elevation gain of this hike is a gradual 550 feet over the first 5 miles, after which you drop about 250 feet over the last 3 miles.

Distance: 16¼ miles round-trip. Level: Easy to moderate. Access: From the South Entrance to the park, drive west on Utah 9 for 3½ miles to a parking area on the right side of the road. From here, a four-wheel-drive road heads north 1½ miles to the park boundary and the trailhead. Close all gates behind you.

Emerald Pools Trail System

You get to decide how much of a workout you want on this route. You can enjoy a leisurely one-hour walk or a somewhat strenuous two-hour hike. The first ⁶⁄₁₀ mile of this trail is paved and suitable for people in wheelchairs, with some assistance. This stretch leads from the trailhead through a forest of oak, maple, fir, and cottonwood to several waterfalls, a hanging garden, and the dazzling Lower Emerald Pool. From here, a steeper, rocky trail continues for a ¼-mile to Middle Emerald Pool and then climbs another ⅓-mile past cactus, yucca, and juniper to Upper Emerald Pool, with still another waterfall. After you see the pools, you'll understand how they were named. Elevation gains are 69 feet to the Lower Emerald Pool, 150 feet to the Middle Pool, and 400 feet to the Upper Pool.

If you do embark on this wonderful hike, leave your swimsuit behind; swimming and wading in the pools are strictly prohibited. Look east from this trail for great views of Red Arch Mountain and the Great White Throne.

Distance: 1¼-2½ miles round-trip. Level: Easy to moderate. Access: Trailhead across from Zion Lodge.

Weeping Rock

This hike is short, but beautiful. Along the way to the rock grotto, you pass interpretive signs explaining the natural history of the area. The path leads you through a mixed forest to a rock alcove with lush hanging gardens of ferns and wildflowers. The mist that sprays from the Weeping Rock will please everyone in your group on a hot day. In the fall, the colorful vegetation along the trail is striking.

Distance: ½-mile round-trip. Level: Easy. Access: Weeping Rock parking lot on Zion Canyon Drive.

West Rim Trail

If you're interested in getting away from the crowds, head down this trail, which runs across the Horse Pasture Plateau (offering wonderfully panoramic views) before dropping down into Zion Canyon. The good news is that this trail drops 3,560 feet on the way from the trailhead to the Grotto Picnic Area. The bad news is that you have to climb 3,560 feet up and out if you're on a round-trip hike. (Most folks just go one way.)

You need to arrange transportation to the Lava Point Trailhead. The names of various shuttle companies are available at the park's main visitor center. At the Grotto Picnic Area at the end of the trail, you can catch the shuttle back to your car.

Distance: 28½ miles round-trip. Level: difficult for round-trippers, moderate for one-way. Access: Lava Point Trailhead.

Zion Narrows

Backcountry trekkers familiar with Zion talk almost reverently about the Narrows. The "trail" actually is the North Fork of the Virgin River, which flows through a 1,000-foot deep chasm that is a confining 24 feet wide in places. As you work your way downstream, you pass through fancifully sculpted sandstone arches, hanging gardens, and waterfalls. It's a magical place, but you must be in good shape for the hike, not just for its distance but to cope with strong currents that you may encounter.

The entire Narrows experience can be had in one long day, or you can break it up with an overnight in the backcountry. Before your trip, check at the visitor center for information on arranging a shuttle both to the trailhead and from the Temple of Sinawava, where you leave the canyon. Before you head out, make sure to pick up a $5 permit (required for slot canyon hiking) from the Zion Canyon Visitor Center and, if you plan an overnight trip, receive a campsite assignment.

Spotting the local wildlife

If you like numbers, here are some facts for you: Zion's borders contain 75 species of mammals, 271 bird species, 36 species of reptiles and amphibians, and 8 kinds of fish.

This means that if you're hoping to see some wildlife during your visit to the park, don't worry — you will. If you're specifically hoping to see one of the park's **mountain lions,** also known as cougars, don't get your hopes up. Yes, a few of these cats prowl Zion's backcountry, but because they're reclusive creatures, your chances of spotting one are slim. You can try to enhance the odds by sticking to the east side of the park beyond the Zion-Mount Carmel Tunnel, but I'm not guaranteeing anything when it comes to mountain lions. They are known to lurk around the backcountry in the park's northwestern corner near Kolob Terraces Road, so if you strike out on the eastern side and are determined to search for one of the big cats, try up there. Naturally, where you find mountain lions, you also find **mule deer,** probably the most visible large animals in the park.

Zion also is home to a number of **desert bighorn sheep,** and as with mountain lions, your best chances of spotting one of these critters is to pan your binoculars around the east side of the park.

Among the smaller animals that roam the park are **gray fox, desert cottontail rabbits, coyotes,** and even **beaver,** which ply the smooth waters of the Virgin River. One of the more unusual park critters — unusual if you're from the East or West coasts or the northern tier of states — is the **ringtail cat.** These skittish cousins to raccoons lurk around the park after dark, looking for campsites or backpacks they can raid for munchies. Although seeing these long, bushy-tailed cats working their way through a bag of pretzels or chips may be cute, their getting into your food cache is not good, so do your best to maintain a clean campsite.

Overhead, you may catch a glimpse of a speedy **peregrine falcon.** Once thought to be on their way to extinction, these swift raptors are making a comeback around the country. In Zion, at least 15 pairs of peregrine falcons have been seen nesting. You stand a chance of spotting one of these birds along the Angels Landing and Cable Mountain trails and in the area around the Great White Throne. Bald Eagles also have been spotted in the park, but usually only during the winter, so if you're planning a spring, summer, or fall trip, you're probably out of luck.

Red-tailed hawks are very common in the park; you usually can spot them high overhead drifting on the wind currents. Among the dozens of other birds that pass through the park are **American kestrels, doves, great horned owls, ravens, pinyon, Steller's jays,** and even **American robins.** You may also spot **great blue herons** along the Virgin River. If you're a dedicated birder, you may want to plan a year-end trip to Zion and participate in the park's Christmas bird count.

Being canyon country, Zion is also home to creepy-crawly critters like the **great basin rattlesnake, tarantulas,** and even **scorpions.** The park also has quite a good selection of **amphibians,** including the **Arizona tiger salamander** and **red-spotted toad,** and reptiles, such as the **chuckwalla lizard,** which, with a mature size of 20 inches, is the park's largest lizard.

A side trip to Bryce Canyon National Park

If you want to explore more of southern Utah, check out **Bryce Canyon** (☎ **435-834-5322,** Internet: www.nps.gov/brca), just 85 miles from Zion National Park's East Entrance. Although a fraction the size of Zion, Bryce with its 35,835 acres is just as spectacular with its rock gardens. Cream- and orange-colored spires, hoodoos and goblins jut out of the main canyon. Your options here include hiking down below the canyon rim and through the rock gardens, or staying atop the rim and gazing down into the maze of pinnacles. If you have the time, go down below and into the deep amphitheaters with their cliffs, windows, and arches. The Navajo Loop Trail is a great, and short (1½ miles round-trip), way to experience Bryce Canyon. From the Rim at Sunset Point, the trail runs 521 feet to the canyon floor and loops back up. Along the way you get great views of Wall Street, the Twin Bridges, and Thor's Hammer, a precariously balanced rock.

When you first start hiking from the trailhead at Chamberlain's Ranch, the hike appears nothing like its name suggests. From the trailhead, on private land, you ford the river and follow a dirt road downstream. Please remain on the road and leave all gates as you find them. The road ends a short distance beyond an old cabin, and then you hike either along or in the river, which has cut a deep V into the Navajo sandstone. Occasionally, you may spy a lone conifer dangling out from the cliffside at some bizarre angle. When you come up against a 12-foot waterfall, the path circumnavigates this natural barrier by leading you through a slot in the rock.

After you pass the waterfall, you're within the park, and in another 1½ miles, you arrive at the confluence with Deep Creek, where the canyon opens up a bit to swallow this stream of water. In the next 2 miles lie the designated (and assigned) campsites. The current here is faster due to the increased flow of water, and the rocks underfoot are slippery, so step carefully and, if you brought one, use your hiking staff. Kolob Creek is the next tributary you see, although it flows only when waters are released from Kolob Reservoir for downstream irrigation. Then comes Goose Creek, which leads to a deepening of the water and, in some places, requires waist-deep wading. Soon you see Big Springs pouring over moss-covered stone on the right wall of the canyon, which signifies the beginning of the Narrows.

For the next 3 miles, there is no place to climb out of the water in the event of a flood. There is also practically no vegetation to grab onto, as any small seedling is periodically ripped from the walls by the raging waters. The river spreads from wall to wall, forcing you to wade in a deep canyon with little light. The water has even undercut the walls near the confluence with Orderville Canyon. Runoff from above oozes from the canyon walls, providing moisture for hanging gardens and habitat for the teeny Zion snail, which is found nowhere else in the world. About a mile farther where the canyon opens up, a narrow ribbon of water slips out of Mystery Canyon above and skims down the rounded canyon wall. Just beyond, you can finally climb out of the water onto the paved Riverside Walk that takes you to the Temple of Sinawava and the end of the hike.

If you don't have time for a full day, or overnight, hike, consider hiking into the Narrows from the Riverside Walk. The access is at the Temple of Sinawava, and you can hike as few as 2 miles (round-trip). The walk is paved all the way to the Narrows. When you reach the Narrows, how far up you walk is up to you. Just remember to pay attention to the water level and the weather forecast.

When preparing for this hike, you may want to slip a pair of sneakers or sturdier boots with good ankle support into your backpack. You can wear these in the water and keep your hiking boots dry. To keep your balance in swift currents, you may also want to bring along a hiking stick.

Distance: Up to 16 miles one-way. Level: Moderate to difficult. Access: Chamberlain's Ranch (outside the park) or via the Riverside Walk.

One-day wonder

The bulk of Zion's highlights are captured within the confines of Zion Canyon, which makes seeing the park in one day a pretty easy experience. To come away with the best impression, start the day early with a picnic lunch in your daypack, a good hiking staff and boots, plenty of water, and lots of film. For descriptions of the trails I mention in this section, see the previous section.

Make your starting point the Zion Lodge or the Zion Canyon Visitor Center and take a shuttle bus to the **Temple of Sinawava** at the northern end of Zion Canyon Drive. Follow the **Riverside Walk** a mile into the southern gateway of the Narrows, the park's most famous slot canyon. You don't need to hike all the way through this slot, but at least take some time to travel into it to get the feel of being surrounded by towering rock walls. The experience is unforgettable.

After returning to the shuttle stop, ride back down Zion Canyon Drive to the **Weeping Rock Trail.** Follow this short, easy trail that quickly delivers you to a memorable rock alcove where, in spring and summer, lush hanging gardens thrive on the drenching they receive from the water draining out of the high country.

Continue to work your way back down canyon on the shuttle to the Zion Lodge. Check out the lodge if you're not staying there; then cross the Virgin River and spend a couple hours working your way up the **Emerald Pools Trail,** a 2½-mile round-trip hike. The three shimmering pools of water that give the trail its name are gorgeous and worth some film. The Upper Pool, although reached via the steepest stretch of the trail, is a good place to rest and enjoy a picnic lunch amid the maples.

After lunch, hike back down to the shuttle stop and, if you're feeling good and have a party of strong hikers, catch the shuttle back north to the Grotto picnic area for a hike up the **Angels Landing Trail.** (If you're not up for this hike, catch the shuttle bus back to the visitor center, where you can view exhibits or tackle the 2-mile-round-trip Watchman Trail, an overlooked trail that offers nice views of the lower end of Zion Canyon and the town of Springdale.)

By the time you return from this hike, you'll most likely be ready to return to your room for a shower and a quick "power nap" before heading out to dinner.

If you have more time

Most tourists confine their visit to the highlights of Zion Canyon, while those with a bit more ambition also see **Kolob Arch,** one of the world's longest freestanding arches with a span of 310 feet. You can hike to the arch and back in one long day on the La Verkin Creek Trail, a 14-mile round-trip hike from Lee Pass along Kolob Canyons Road in the park's northwestern extension.

Another good hike in this area leads to **Double Arch,** unique in that an arched alcove is topped overhead by an arch in the cliff. You reach the formation on the Creek Trail, a 5½-mile round-trip hike that crosses the Middle Fork of Taylor Creek and passes two log cabins before arriving at a viewpoint of the arch. You can access the trailhead from Kolob Canyons Road.

Should you add Kolob Arch, or even Double Arch, to your itinerary? If you enjoy backcountry hiking, the answer is probably yes. But if you've been to Arches National Park, or plan to go there, then these two sights are not a must-see.

Ranger programs

Zion has rangers, of course, but you won't find as many ranger-led activities here as you do in Yosemite or Cape Cod National Seashore, for example. Still, Zion's rangers lead short, 1- to 2-mile hikes most mornings and afternoons. Also on afternoons, you usually find rangers on the Zion Canyon Visitor Center patio, the Zion Human History Museum patio, and the Zion Lodge lawn, talking about the various aspects of the park. You can figure on finding an evening slide show or talk at the campground amphitheaters as well as in Zion Lodge. If that's not enough, a guided shuttle tour, requiring free tickets, is conducted each morning from Memorial Day weekend through mid-September.

The best way to find out what's going on during your stay is to look for the weekly schedules posted at the visitor centers and on bulletin boards throughout the park. These notices tell you when ranger-led activities are scheduled, what they're about, and whether you need to make a reservation to attend.

To keep your kids interested in the park, enroll them in the Junior Ranger Program at the Zion Nature Center. For program details, see Chapter 4.

Keeping active

In addition to hiking, Zion offers opportunities for the following out-door fun:

- **Biking:** You can't ride your bike outside of designated trails in the national parks, and biking is prohibited from many Zion trails. Despite this fact, Zion is one of the most bike-friendly parks in the Western U.S. The Pa'rus Trail runs a little under 2 miles along the Virgin River, from the South Entrance as far north as the Zion Mount-Carmel Highway. This trail crosses the river and several creeks and provides good views of the Watchman, West Temple, the Sentinel, and other lower canyon formations. Cyclists can also ride on the park's main roads, although not through the Zion-Mount Carmel Tunnel.

- **Horseback riding:** Guided rides in the park are available March through October from **Canyon Trail Rides** (☎ **435-679-8665;** Internet: www.canyonrides.com). Ticket sales and information are available at the horse corrals across from Zion Lodge. A one-hour ride along the Virgin River costs $20 and a half-day ride on the Sand Beanh Trail costs $45. Riders must weigh no more than 220 pounds, and children must be at least seven years old for the one-hour ride and eight years old for the half-day ride. Reservations are advised.

- **Rock climbing:** Expert technical rock climbers love the tall sand-stone cliffs in Zion Canyon, although rangers warn that much of the rock is loose, or "rotten," and climbing equipment and tech-niques suitable for granite are often less effective here. Five-dollar permits are required for overnight climbs, and because some routes may be closed at times, such as during peregrine falcon nesting from early spring through July, climbers should check at the visitor center before setting out.

Escaping the rain

Where do you head when rains fall on Zion? Well, if they come during the height of summer, you just may want to stay outdoors and enjoy the refreshing drenching. But if the cloudburst turns torrential, con-sider heading to **Zion Canyon Theatre** (145 Zion Park Blvd.; ☎ **888-256-3456** or 435-772-2400) in Springdale to get out of the rain for an hour or so. This 60 x 82-foot big-screen theater shows movies about the park. The film *Zion Canyon: Treasure of the Gods,* for example, not only captures much of the park's physical beauty but also delves into its Native American legends. The theater is open from May through November daily from 11 a.m. to 8 p.m., and the rest of the year from 11 a.m. to 7 p.m. Admission is $7.50 for ages 12 and older and $4.50 for ages 3 through 11.

Another option is the **Zion Human History Museum,** which debuted during the summer of 2002. The museum, located in the old visitor center along the park's shuttle bus route, in part chronicles the park's human activity. You find displays on wildlife, geology, and plants and how the environment has affected Native Americans, settlers, and visitors. A small bookstore with maps, videos, postcards, and posters is on the premises. Summer hours are from 8 a.m. to 7 p.m., with shorter hours the rest of the year.

Where to Stay

If you're determined to stay inside the park with a roof over your head and a comfortable bed under your back, plan far in advance because the park has only one lodge. Zion Lodge is worth the extra effort, though, because it's centrally located in Zion Canyon and surrounded by forest and 2,000-foot-tall cliffs that shimmer in the sunlight. If you can't get into the lodge, you find a wide range of bed-and-breakfast options, motels, and inns outside the park's South Entrance.

Lodging in the park

Zion Lodge
$$$ Zion Canyon

Sadly, this is not the original Zion Lodge that was designed by Gilbert Stanley Underwood in the 1920s. That building, which featured rustic design and charm, was destroyed by fire in 1966. Although it was rebuilt later that year in just 100 days, the reincarnation didn't completely capture Underwood's original vision. In 1990, the lodge's exterior was remodeled to reflect its original appearance. You can't beat the location. The Virgin River is right across the road, and a trail from the lodge leads to the West Rim Trail with its many possibilities.

Because this is the only lodging option inside the park, plan to call far in advance if you want a room during the busy summer season. If you call early enough, you can choose between the lodge's motel-style rooms and its charming cabins. Opt for the cabins, because there's nothing quite like returning from a day in the park and starting a fire in the fireplace to ward off the evening chill. The fireplaces are gas-powered, so you don't have to mess with firewood. The cabins feature two double beds, log beams, and private porches for relaxing before you call it a day.

The rooms inside the two-story lodge are nothing to turn your nose up at, but they lack the charm and privacy of the cabins. They come with two queen-size beds and a private balcony or porch. The suites are large, feature a king-size bed, a separate sitting room with a queen-size hide-a-bed, and a refrigerator.

On Zion Canyon Drive. ☎ *435-772-3213. Internet:* www.zionlodge.com. *For reservations, contact Xanterra Parks & Resorts* ☎ *307-344-7311; Internet:* www.xanterra.com. *75 rooms, 40 cabins, 6 suites. A/C TEL. Rack rates: $107 double, $5 extra per person; $135 suites; $116 cabins, $5 extra per person. AE, DISC, MC, V, CB.*

Lodging outside the park

Best Western Zion Park Inn
$$–$$$ **Springdale**

This sprawling complex sits less than 2 miles beyond the park's south entrance and offers tremendous views of 7,285-foot Mount Kinosava. Just about everything you need for a park visit can be found here: lodging, a restaurant, gift shop, state liquor store, even Internet access. There's also an outdoor pool to fight off the summer's oven-like heat, a hot tub, and rooms complete with dataport connections.

1215 Zion Park Blvd. ☎ *435-772-3200 or 800-934-7275. Fax: 435-772-2449. 118 rooms, 2 suites. A/C TEL TV. Rack rates: $70–$105 double; $100–$150 suites. AE, DISC, MC V.*

Flanigan's Inn
$$–$$$ **Springdale**

This gorgeous inn just beyond Zion's South Entrance features rustic beams and natural rock-work surrounded by decks and terraced lawns and gardens. Although parts of the inn date to 1947, all the rooms were renovated in the early 1990s and feature a Southwest decor. Some of the rooms feature whirlpool tubs and bidets. Kitchenettes are available, but if you want a fireplace, call early because only one room has this feature. You also find a pool and nature trail on the grounds, as well as a wonderful restaurant that sports a greenhouse/garden atmosphere.

428 Zion Park Blvd. ☎ *800-765-7787 or 435-772-3244. Fax: 435-772-3396. Internet:* www.flanigans.com. *39 units. A/C TV TEL. Rack rates: Mid-March to Nov $79–$209 double; Dec to mid-March $49–$139 double. AE, DISC, MC, V. Rates include Continental breakfast.*

Under the Eaves
$$ Springdale

This B&B boasts "the best front porch in Utah," and even though it may not be the best, it does offer great views of redrock country. Inside, this beautiful 1929 cottage displays antiques and local artworks, creating an inn that is both attractive and comfortable. The main floor has two guest rooms, decorated in early-20th-century style. Each features a double bed and private sink, although the two rooms share a bath (shower only). If sharing a bath doesn't appeal to you, consider the huge (1,200 square feet) upstairs suite, which features vaulted ceilings, a cathedral window through which you can view the terraced gardens, a kitchenette, a claw-foot tub with shower, a sitting room, and a wood-burning stove. Another option is the Garden Cottage, a small cottage built in the 1920s inside the park, which was relocated behind the B&B in 1989. The cottage has three guest rooms, each with a private entrance, bathroom, and shower. Breakfasts usually include freshly baked goods, fresh fruit, and main dishes such as omelets or pancakes. Children ages 8 and older are welcome.

980 Zion Park Blvd. ☎ *435-772-3457. Fax: 435-772-3324. Internet:* www.under theeaves.com. *5 rooms (2 with shared bath), 1 suite. A/C. Rack rates: $55–$85 double; $100–$130 suite, $10 extra per person. AE, DISC, MC, V. Rates include full breakfast.*

Runner-up lodgings

Driftwood Lodge
$$ Springdale   Large rooms decorated with Southwestern art, an outdoor pool, and complimentary Continental breakfast make this a popular place to stay. *1515 Zion Park Blvd.* ☎ *435-772-3262. Internet:* www.driftwoodlodge.net.

Harvest House Bed & Breakfast
$$ Springdale   Each of the inn's four rooms comes with a private bath. Those with balconies have great views of the park. *29 Canyon View Dr.* ☎ *435-772-3880. Internet:* www.harvesthouse.net.

Novel House Inn
$$–$$$ Springdale   Each of the ten rooms in this inn is dedicated to a famous writer; downstairs you find some of their works in the library. *73 Paradise Rd.* ☎ *800-711-8400 or 435-772-3650. Internet:* www.novelhouse.com.

Pioneer Lodge
$–$$$$ Springdale   On the shuttle bus route to the park, this motel offers comfortable rooms and two apartments for longer stays, as well as a pool and hot tub. *838 Zion Park Blvd.* ☎ *888-772-3233. Internet:* www.pioneerlodge.com.

Campgrounds

Two developed campgrounds are available if you want to pitch your tent or park your RV in Zion. Both **Watchman** and **South campgrounds,** located near the South Entrance, are spacious and have trees, restrooms with flush toilets, drinking water, picnic tables, fire grates, and dump stations.

South Campground and its 126 sites are open only from April through September, and the 231 sites at Watchman Campground are available year-round. Individual sites at both parks go for $10 a night ($5 if you have a Golden Age or Golden Access passport) or $14 if you want one with electricity. South is first-come, first-served. If you like to plan ahead, reserve one of the Watchman sites by calling ☎ **800-365-2267** or by logging on to the park's reservation system at http://reservations. nps.gov. During the summer months these campgrounds can fill quickly, but in general, if you arrive before noon, you should be able to find a space.

The one primitive campground (without water or flush toilets), **Lava Point,** is 20 miles down Kolob Terrace Road in the northern end of Zion. Just six sites are here, and the campground is open only from June through November.

Another option is just about a ½-mile outside the park's South Entrance. The **Zion Canyon Campground & RV Park** (P.O. Box 99, Springdale, UT 84767; ☎ **435-772-3237;** Fax: 435-772-3844; Internet: www.zioncanyon campground.com) gets crowded during the summer months, but it's clean and well maintained and offers some nice shady sites and grassy tent sites.

Where to Eat

Although you have only one real option for dining inside the park, aside from a snack bar at the Zion Lodge, if you backtrack to Springdale just beyond the South Entrance, you find a wide array of dining options, from quick burger joints to high-end eateries with all the trimmings. Menus range from Southwestern and Mexican dishes to traditional American and pizza.

Restaurants in the park

Zion Lodge Dining Room
$$$–$$$$ **Zion Canyon**   **AMERICAN**

Looking out through the dining room's large windows at the park's towering rock formations makes concentrating on your meal difficult. Among the lodge's specialities are slow-roasted prime rib, New York strip steak, and Southwestern grilled chicken. You also find fish and vegetarian items on the menu, so making everyone in your party happy shouldn't be a problem. For dessert, try the cheesecake sampler plate — just remember to leave a good amount of room for it.

For lunch, the kitchen serves up burgers, sandwiches, and several salads. Breakfast offerings are typical, ranging from hot and cold cereals to egg dishes, fresh fruits, and bagels. The kitchen also prepares sack lunches for hikers; place your order at least one hour in advance for these.

In the Zion Lodge. ☎ 435-772-3213. Dinner reservations recommended in summer. Main courses: $1.95–$7.25 breakfast; $4.95–$6.95 lunch; $12.95–$22.95 dinner. AE, DC, DISC, MC, V. Open: Daily 6:30–10 a.m., 11:30 a.m.–3:30 p.m., 5:30–9 p.m.

Restaurants outside the park

Bit & Spur Restaurant and Saloon
$$ Springdale   MEXICAN/SOUTHWESTERN

Rough wood-and-stone walls and an exposed beam ceiling give this restaurant the look of an Old West saloon, but it's an unusually clean saloon that also features a family dining room, patio dining, original oil paintings from regional artists, and live entertainment. The food is also a notch or two above what you may expect, closer to what you would find in a good Santa Fe restaurant. The menu ranges from Mexican standards — such as burritos, flautas, chile rellenos, and a traditional chile stew with pork — to more unusual creations such as pollo relleno (grilled chicken breast stuffed with cilantro pesto and goat cheese and served with smoked pineapple chutney) and smoky chicken (a smoked, charbroiled game hen with sourdough stuffing and chipotle sauce).

1212 Zion Park Blvd. ☎ 435-772-3498. Reservations recommended. Main courses: $10–$20. DISC, MC, V. Open: March–Oct daily 5–10 p.m. (bar open until midnight); Nov–Feb Thurs–Mon 5– 9 p.m. Closed: Dec.

Flanigan's Inn
$$–$$$$ Springdale   AMERICAN/REGIONAL

Flanigan's Inn feels like an escape from the high desert to a lush oasis. This award-winning restaurant has a greenhouse/garden atmosphere that's refreshing after a day in the park's dry air. You can still see the area's incredible scenery through the large windows, though. Flanigan's uses fresh local ingredients and herbs from the inn's garden whenever possible. The dinner menu ranges from simple fare, such as burgers, a chicken breast sandwich, and a grilled vegetable burrito to more creative entrees, such as Tournadoe of Beef Tenderloin with smoked tomato chutney and vegetable parfait and broiled fresh Atlantic salmon with melted dill butter. A menu staple is the Utah red trout. To refresh your palate, try one of the region's fine microbrews or sample the inn's 2,000-bottle wine celler.

428 Zion Park Blvd. ☎ **435-772-3244**. *Reservations recommended. Main courses: $5–$10 breakfast; $12–$21 dinner. AE, DISC, MC, V. Open: Daily summer 5–10 p.m.; winter hours shorter.*

Switchback Grill

$–$$$$ Springdale   AMERICAN/ITALIAN

Step into the Switchback Grill and you find a menu as diverse as the park's landscape. Spit-roasted chicken, steaks, and hickory-smoked ribs contrast with French-influenced and Italian dishes. You can eat heavy with a USDA prime filet or go light with pecan-encrusted Utah trout or perhaps a pizza or salad. The atmosphere is just as delicious as the menu, thanks to heavy timbers, vaulted ceilings, and a wall of glass that lets diners gaze their eyes on the park's southern ramparts.

1149 Zion Park Blvd. ☎ **435-772-3700** *or 877-948-8080. Reservations recommended. Main courses: $4–$7 breakfast and lunch; $10–$28 dinner. AE, DISC, MC, V. Open: May–Oct daily 7–11 a.m., 11:30 a.m.–2:30 p.m., 5–10 p.m.; Nov–April hours shorter.*

Zion Pizza & Noodle

$$$ Springdale   PIZZA/PASTA

Sometimes you just want to kick back with a pizza or some pasta and a cold brew. Your kids may feel that way, too — although you'll swap that brew for a soda. At this place, the whole family can be happy. Located in an old Mormon Church built in 1930, the setting is decidedly informal, with small, closely spaced tables and black-and-white photos on the walls. You order at the counter, grab a non-alcoholic drink at the beverage bar, and sit back and relax until your meal is delivered.

The gourmet pizzas, with wonderfully chewy crusts, are baked in a slate stone oven and come with a variety of unusual toppings. You can have a barbecued chicken pizza with red onion, cilantro, and gouda and mozzarella cheeses; a six-cheese pizza with asiago, Parmesan, mozzarella, feta, romano, and cheddar cheeses; or even a Thai chicken pizza with fresh-grilled chicken. Oh yeah, the menu also includes your run-of-the-mill cheese pizzas — a kid favorite. On the pasta side of the menu are fettucines, stromboli, and manicotti marinara. For lunch, the menu expands to make room for garlic and veggie burgers as well as brauts. Some of Utah's finer microbews are also on the menu, and you can enjoy them in the shaded beer garden out back.

868 Zion Park Blvd. ☎ **435-772-3815**. *Internet:* www.zionpizzanoodle.com. *Reservations not accepted. Main courses: $3.95–$11.95 lunch; $7.95–$11.95 dinner. No credit cards. Open: March to Thanksgiving, daily, noon to 10 p.m.; late Nov to Dec shorter hours. Closed: Jan–Feb.*

Fast Facts: Zion

Area Code
☎ 435.

ATM
None in the park. Located in Springdale at banks and at the Zion Canyon Theater.

Emergency
☎ 911.

Fees
$20 per vehicle per week; $10 on foot, motorcycle, or bike.

Fishing License
Utah license required, available at Ace Hardware, 489 W. State St., in Hurricane; ☎ 435-635-4449.

Hospitals/Clinic
Zion Canyon Medical Clinic in Springdale; ☎ 435-772-3226.

Information
Zion National Park, Springdale, UT 84767; ☎ 435-772-3256.

Lost and Found
☎ 435-772-3256.

Pharmacies
Zion Drug, 72 S. 700 W., in Hurricane; ☎ 435-635-4456.

Post Office
624 Zion Park Blvd. in Springdale; ☎ 435-772-3950.

Road Conditions and Weather
☎ 800-492-2400.

Taxes
Springdale: lodging 11.5%, meals 7%.

Time Zone
Mountain standard time.

Web Site
www.nps.gov/zion.

Part IV
The Part of Tens

The 5th Wave   By Rich Tennant

"The guests are getting hungry. You'd better push over another garbage dumpster."

In this part . . .

So many parks, so many vistas, so many places to stay. As you make the rounds of the park system, you'll surely develop your favorites. (I know I have, to the detriment of parks that haven't yet made it on to my to-do list.) But if you're a national parks newbie, where do you begin? This part gives you the bottom line on great park vistas, why a national park vacation beats visiting a theme park hands down, and how you can get the most out of the national parks without taking out a second mortgage. Best of all, this part is organized in a quick, easy-to-read, top-ten format.

Chapter 23

Ten Incredible National Park Vistas

By their very nature, national parks are incredibly scenic places. The old saying "beauty is in the eye of the beholder" doesn't seem to apply. You get a beautiful view just about everywhere you look. Sunsets? Parks virtually have a monopoly on the breathtaking ones. Purple mountains majesties? Got 'em by the truckload. Forests by the Brothers Grimm? Yep, you find these, too. The parks have so many wonderful views that you don't even need to get out of your car to enjoy them — but do pull over and get out. Take a short walk, pull up a rock or downed tree trunk, and look around. You can thank me later.

If you want to capture these incredible vistas on film, but are a bit unsure of your camera skills, check out *Photography For Dummies,* by Russell Hart (Wiley), for the lowdown on how to become an expert shutterbug.

Badwater, Death Valley National Park

Imagine Badwater in August: The sun's glare off the dazzlingly white salt pan pains your eyes, and while you peer upward at a sign on a cliff indicating sea level 282 feet *above* you, the 120-degree Fahrenheit temperature slowly bakes your body. Pretty intense, eh? This spot is great for photographers any time of year. Just as the temperatures are unusual on the bottom floor of North America in summer, so are the lighting conditions year-round. Early mornings and late afternoons are perfect for experimenting with the play of light across the salt pan's jigsaw puzzle construction. (And it's a heckuva lot cooler at these times than at high noon, too!) Even if you're not a shutterbug, the chance to inspect the ornate fractures that riddle the salt pan and to gaze up at 11,049-foot Telescope Peak is worth a stop. See Chapter 12.

Clingmans Dome, Great Smoky Mountains National Park

Somehow, a view of mountains retreating into the distance seems to sum up the outdoors, and no place stacks mountains one after another better than Great Smoky Mountains National Park. From atop the observation tower on Clingmans Dome, you can gaze across these many-tiered mountains and into seven states (if the skies are clear). Even on overcast days, the view is impressive. Adding to the beauty, misty clouds swirling about the mountains, opening and closing vistas while the winds push the vapor around. Year-round, the trees (stunted by powerful winds and short growing seasons) conjure the magical forests that the Brothers Grimm created for their fairy tales. Come winter, snows coat the trees, creating yet another intriguing landscape. See Chapter 15.

Giant Forest, Sequoia National Park

Big, bigger, and biggest. That pretty much sums up the trees in this corner of Sequoia National Park. How do you measure up in comparison? Not even the word *dwarf* accurately describes your diminutive size when you stand next to these trees that soar more than 300 feet and have waist lines measured in tens of feet, not inches. Want even more perspective? Compare your own age to the age of one of these wooden giants, which can live to be 3,200 years old. You won't find just one mighty sequoia in the Giant Forest, but nearly 9,000 of them standing tall over 1,800 acres. See Chapter 19.

Glacier Point, Yosemite National Park

The drive from the Yosemite Valley floor to the top of Glacier Point is long, and the hike is even longer, but the view is awesome. To the east, the thin ropes of white that seem to dangle from a cliff are Nevada and Vernal falls. Just a bit north of them stands the rock structure known as Half Dome, which resembles a huge loaf of bread. A few thousand feet below your toes is the valley floor, which is not-so-neatly divided by the Merced River, The Ahwahnee hotel, and Curry Village. Keep scanning the horizon, and you find Yosemite Falls and, way off to the northeast in Yosemite's backcountry, the mountain called Clouds Rest. If you want some isolation, check out the view in the winter, when cross-country skies or snowshoes are about the only means of travel to the overlook. See Chapter 21.

Grand Canyon of the Yellowstone, Yellowstone National Park

Whether you stand on the lip of one of the two waterfalls in the Grand Canyon of the Yellowstone or simply view this majestic crack in the earth from one of the numerous observation points, you experience a thing of beauty. When the sun shines, it tints the mist of the falls with rainbows. In winter, the icy setting is enchanting (and dangerous, so watch your footing!). Any time of year, add the falls' frothy might to the yellows, buffs, oranges, chalky whites, and tans of the deep and rugged canyon, and you get an incredible setting. Most visitors get their initial view of the canyon from North Rim Drive (found near Canyon Village), but a more-spectacular view is from Artist Point on South Rim Drive. And don't be shy about walking beyond Artist Point on the South Rim Trail, because most folks usually return to their cars after snapping some pictures from the point's overlook. By taking a short walk, you can enjoy the canyon with a bit more solitude. See Chapter 20.

Hoh Rain Forest, Olympic National Park

The Hoh Rain Forest may not have hobgoblins or fairies, but you may think that they're watching your every move from a hiding spot in this densely vegetated realm. Lush, dark, and green, this corner of Olympic National Park is North America's largest undisturbed temperate rain forest. Each year, 12 to 14 feet of rain drench the forest, producing trees of astounding size. How does a 300-foot-tall hemlock sound? And blankets of vegetation not only coat the forest floor but also hang like veils from the canopy high overhead. Spongy mosses, rope-like vines, and delicate ferns add to the dazzling scenery. See Chapter 18.

Oxbow Bend, Grand Teton National Park

A beer commercial was filmed at Oxbow Bend, so you know the setting has to be stupendous. Snow-capped Tetons are off in the distance, and thick forest is all around, but to me, the view of wildlife is the big attraction. Moose, bald eagles, osprey, trumpeter swans, white pelicans, playful river otters, and oodles of ducks crowd this stretch of the Snake River that meanders below Jackson Lake Dam. Plenty of overlooks allow you to pull over in your car and take in the setting, although the best view is from a raft or canoe drifting slowly downstream. Photographers will want a long lens to best capture the river corridor's critters (especially the eagles hauling fat trout out of the river) on film. See Chapter 14.

Paradise, Mount Rainier National Park

Paradise is not lost in Mount Rainier National Park, where a nicely paved road leads to the Paradise Inn. If you agree that a rustic inn backed up to a snow- and ice-covered mountain has something special, you'll understand what makes this place one of the most gorgeous settings in the park system. Paradise is also beautiful in late spring, when wildflowers blossom in the meadows surrounding the inn, or in fall, when the forest blazes with orange and red leaves. (Summer is pretty, too, but with all the people milling about, the natural beauty is difficult to fully appreciate.) See Chapter 17.

Point Sublime, Grand Canyon National Park

My high school track coach often told me that nothing worthwhile is ever easily attained. That's definitely the case with Point Sublime, located off the beaten path, so you won't run into throngs of camera-toting tourists. The view south and southwest into the many-colored gorge of the Grand Canyon is unforgettable, particularly when far-off thunderstorms are rocking and rolling over some distant corner of the canyon. The sunsets imprint themselves on your memory (in case you forget your film). See Chapter 13.

Zion Canyon Narrows, Zion National Park

There are slot canyons and then there are *slot* canyons. Zion Canyon Narrows is one of a kind. Walking even a little way into this rock-lined passage is sort of like entering the bowels of a mountain; in some areas, the sandstone walls tower 2,000 feet overhead, and the passage is only 20 feet wide. What created these dramatic slots? Lots of water and time. Over the course of centuries, the Virgin River cut through the Navajo sandstone and into the Kayenta sandstone. In some places, the polished sandstone was delicately fluted. And the river hasn't finished its job. The water nourishes beautiful hanging gardens and continues to carve away the canyon walls. To truly appreciate the entire slot, you need to make a 16-mile trek through the canyon. But if you're pressed for time, you can see stunning vistas on a short, 2-mile round-trip walk into the slot from the Temple of Sinawava. See Chapter 22.

Chapter 24

Ten Reasons Why a National Park Is Better Than a Theme Park

National park or theme park? How will you spend your vacation? If you're having difficulty deciding between the two, listen up: I can give you ten reasons why a national park visit beats a trip to a theme park — hands down.

Stretching Your Dollar

For $20 (or $10 in some parks and nothing in a select few), you and everyone in your car can enjoy a national park for a week. When was the last time you encountered that kind of fee at a theme park? Let me answer for you — never. Heck, most high-tech entertainment centers cost at least $40 per person, per day. In the national park system, 20 bucks (tops) gets you the grandest canyon in the world, the greatest collection of thermal features on Earth, animals that aren't detained behind bars, and rivers wild. And that's just for starters.

Expanding Your Mind

Unlike theme parks, national parks can enlighten you about the world. Pay attention to the park surroundings, and you're likely to find out information about conservation, environmentalism, and zoology. In Yellowstone, the Wolf Recovery Program is an excellent example of species conservation and ecosystem preservation, whereas the Grand

Canyon is one of the world's largest geologic classrooms. Great Smoky Mountains, along with harboring one of the most diverse forests in the country, is also rich in Appalachian cultural history. Best of all, these lessons reach the young as well as the old. Most kids learn best when they don't realize that they're in a learning environment. And in national parks, they're too busy having fun to realize that they're exercising their minds as well as their muscles.

Touring a Real Wild Kingdom

You won't find anything artificial about the wild kingdoms in national parks. The animals aren't contained by bars (which is not always a good thing, so beware), no trainers make them beg for food or make them do tricks, and the parks don't have cages to hose down. Yellowstone, for example, hosts vast herds of bison, numerous black and grizzly bears, and elk, wolves, and other animals — all at home in their natural settings. At Acadia and Olympic, you may even spot a seal or whale cavorting in the waters off the parks' shores.

Staying Open after 9:00 p.m.

Theme parks have closing times; national parks don't. A ranger will not kick you out at closing time because the park doesn't have a closing time. If you didn't need to sleep, you could roam a park 24 hours a day, 7 days a week, 365 days a year. The parks have been managing themselves pretty darn well for the last few thousand years, so they don't need to be shut down each day so the custodial crews can clean 'em up.

Avoiding Lines

Yes, some park attractions attract crowds. Old Faithful in Yellowstone and the Mist Trail in Yosemite are two good examples, but you probably won't stand in line for over a half-hour for anything. And if you don't want to commune with the masses, you can leave them behind by taking a hike, a nap, or a lunch break in a secluded spot.

Spending the Night

When was the last time you stayed overnight in an amusement park (unless you were stranded on a broken-down ride)? Most parks provide lodges and campgrounds inside their borders where you can bed down at the end of a day. And if you feel like getting up in the middle of the night to make sure that everything is hunky-dory outside, that's okay, too.

Enjoying Vendor-Free Zones

Is anything worse than having a little kid stand in line next to you getting his cotton candy on your clothes? This won't happen in a national park, 'cuz parks don't have cotton candy vendors (or lines, remember?). You also won't find candy apple hawkers, popcorn peddlers, or even midway barkers — thank goodness.

Weathering Any Storm

Neither rain, nor snow, nor dark of night can shut down a national park's attractions because weather conditions are part of the package. If an earthquake changes the dynamics of Yellowstone's geysers, or a dry summer idles Yosemite's waterfalls, or high runoff makes some backcountry trails inaccessible, well, that's part of life in the natural world. Sometimes, Mother Nature's whims can make a park's natural setting even more interesting, and no one will ask you to pay more money for the privilege of seeing the spectacle.

Picking Your Pace

Is it just me, or do theme parks generate most of their "amusement" by scaring folks with rides that defy gravity or whip you upside-down at speeds of 60 miles per hour or more? National parks take a gentler approach: Natural beauty is the main entertainment ingredient, and you can enjoy it at your own pace. If you're a thrill-seeker, climb the Grand Teton, raft the Colorado River through the Grand Canyon, or go on a wild cave tour in Mammoth Cave. If you're not adventurous, you can take a nap beneath a sequoia or stroll an easy trail to a waterfall.

Encouraging Exercise

National parks are good for your physical well-being. Why? Because they encourage you to leave your couch-potato ways at home to explore the park on foot. At Yellowstone, you'll want to walk along the boardwalks that wind through the geyser basins. In Yosemite, you'll feel the urge to stroll the Mist Trail. In Acadia, your feet will guide you to the top of a mountain or along a sandy beach. And while you walk, your body will feel healthier with every step, and you won't pass a single booth selling greasy or fattening foods.

Chapter 25

Ten Incredibly Cheap Ways to Enjoy a National Park

. . . .

In This Chapter

▶ Watching the sky — sunrise, sunset, and stars

▶ Getting active — hiking, camping, climbing, and fishing

▶ Expanding your mind — ranger talks, kids' activities, and more

. . . .

*W*ay back in the front of the book, I mention that national parks are a bargain. If you doubt me, check out this top-ten list of cheap thrills. I guarantee this list will convince you that a national park is the best buy around. And just in case you forgot, or if you skipped the introductory chapters, keep in mind that one small fee (no more than $20!) gets you and your entire family into a park. You won't pay extra for parking, and tickets aren't required for hiking the trails.

Watching the Sun Rise

Along with sunsets and mountains, sunrises are free. In Acadia National Park, you can enjoy the sun and the mountains at the same time. Get up before dawn between October and early March in Acadia and drive or hike to the top of Cadillac Mountain. From the summit, you can catch the first rays of the sun to reach the United States. If Acadia isn't your park pick, check with the visitor center for the exact time of the sun's rise. Then simply get up early in whichever park you're visiting, drive to a picturesque location, sit back, and enjoy the show. You won't be disappointed.

Hiking Down a Trail

One of the best ways to unwind is to hike a trail, preferably one that leads over a ridge and around a few bends. You can't completely experience a national park through a windshield. You need to get out on the ground, walk through the forests, climb a ridge, and dip your toes in a stream.

Watching Wildlife

In many ways, parks are open-air zoos. Some parks, such as Yellowstone, are teeming with animals. Others, such as Death Valley, make you spend a little time looking for the locals. But the critters are out there, and occasionally, they reveal a comical side. Doubt me? Bears fresh out of hibernation like to have a little fun in between scavenging for meals. Head to Yellowstone's Lamar Valley in spring and, with a good pair of binoculars or a spotting scope, you just might see grizzlies whiling away an hour or so sliding down a snowfield. You can watch wildlife in all national parks throughout the year. You can spot seals off the coast of Olympic or Acadia national parks, black bears in Great Smoky Mountains, moose in Grand Teton, or burros in Death Valley.

Going Camping

For a small fee, usually less than $20, you can head off into a park's backcountry, pitch your tent in a grove of trees, on a sandy beach, or in a sandstone alcove, and just relax. Leave radios, television, phones, and wake-up calls behind. Most likely an incredible setting will surround your campsite. You can enjoy some peace and quiet as you see stars sparkling at night like you've never seen before and spot animals in their natural environments. And, you don't have to worry about checking out with a gargantuan hotel bill.

Involving Your Kids

Why spend $50 on some hand-held computer game when you can entertain your kids with a contest of who can spot the most animals, or the most types of animals, or the most birds? Not only is this type of fun cheap, but it's educational, too. Think about the essays your kids can write when their teachers ask them what they did during their summer vacation. Who knows, they may also be inspired to pursue great careers as park rangers, wildlife biologists, or nature writers.

Climbing a Mountain

Mountains are free to climb. And you don't have to climb Grand Teton or Mount Rainier to have a great experience. The parks have plenty of smaller, more assailable, mountains with incredibly awesome scenery. Not only will you be rewarded with wonderful vistas, but you'll get some exercise, too!

Listening to a Ranger

Before criminals started coming to parks to see what loot they could score from naive tourists, rangers actually spent most of their time talking to park visitors. Even though law enforcement is a disappointingly high priority in parks these days (see Chapter 7), rangers still organize hikes and gather around campfires to share their knowledge of the parks — for free. Rangers tell you about interesting things, such as the geothermal machinations of Yellowstone, how Yosemite's Half Dome rock formation got its unusual shape, and how Acadia's Somes Sound was carved. The talks are almost like college seminars (without the fear of follow-up quizzes!).

Going Fishing

As a young boy, I spent quite a few days fishing in the lakes, rivers, and oceans of the national parks. Plenty of adults continue to spend their days this way — and I'm one of them. Many parks have wonderful fisheries, and licenses are free or cost only a small fee. (See the individual park chapters for information on obtaining licenses.) If you're a successful angler, dinner gets less expensive, too.

Counting Stars

Ever try to count stars in a city? You can't see them very well because of all the light pollution. That's not a problem in national parks, which usually are far from urban areas and generate only a minimum amount of light. As a result, the Milky Way sparkles overhead on moonless nights. In some northern parks, such as Yellowstone, you can occasionally spot the Northern Lights dancing across the sky in winter.

Watching a Sunset

Sunsets are free. Always have been, probably always will be. Watching the sun go down behind a mountain, beneath the ocean, or below a desert is not only beautiful but is also a great way to reconnect with simple pleasures.

Appendix

Quick Concierge

Fast Facts

American Automobile Association (AAA)

For emergency road service, call ☎ 800-AAA-HELP (800-222-4357). To locate the AAA office nearest the park you're visiting, log on to www.aaa.com.

American Express

For cardholder services, call ☎ 800-528-4800; for lost or stolen travelers checks, call ☎ 800-221-7282.

ATMs

Most national parks have ATMs within their borders. For parks that don't, you can usually find an ATM in a gateway community. Call ☎ 800-424-7787 or 800-4CIRRUS for Cirrus, and ☎ 800-843-7587 for Plus.

Business Hours

Parks are open all the time. The front desks of lodges are usually open around-the-clock, and restaurants typically open by 7 a.m. and close by 11 p.m., if not a bit earlier. Grocery stores and gift shops often stay open until 9 p.m.

Credit Cards

MasterCard's general information number is ☎ 800-307-7309. For Visa, call ☎ 800-847-2911.

Drug Stores

You won't find a drug store inside a national park. Gift shops often have a very small collection of over-the-counter remedies (aspirin, antacids, and sunscreens), whereas in-park groceries or camp stores have a somewhat larger selection.

Emergencies

Call ☎ **911** to report a fire, contact a ranger, or get an ambulance in all but Acadia National Park. For Acadia, call ☎ **207-288-3369**. In some parks, you may need to dial a prefix before the emergency number. If time is of the essence, just call ☎ **0** and have the operator connect you. Additionally, the park newspaper you receive when you enter a park contains a phone list for medical services in the park.

Health

I can't emphasize this too much: Wear sunscreen and drink lots of water when traveling in a national park. The sun can be surprisingly strong — because you're outside all day at a higher elevation where the thinner air lets through more rays or because you're near water that reflects the rays. Before you know it, you can get sunburned and dehydrated. Some of the bigger parks — Yellowstone, Yosemite, and Grand Canyon, for example — have well-stocked and staffed medical clinics within their borders, but in most cases, you have to reach a gateway community for medical facilities.

Liquor Laws

Liquor laws for the individual parks are determined by their location. Depending on the prevailing state law, convenience stores may carry beer and hard liquor, or just beer.

Mail

You can find mail drops in most lodges, visitor centers, and park headquarters.

Maps

Upon entering each park, you receive a free copy of a National Park Service map. National Geographic's *Trails Illustrated* publishes incredible maps with all sorts of information, such as hiking trails, mountain bike routes, scenic points, and more. If you need driving directions to a park, AAA members can get excellent maps in advance at their local AAA office. Free of charge, Mapquest (Internet: www.mapquest.com) will plot a route from point A to point B for you, if you know your exact points of departure and arrival.

Newspapers/Magazines

Park gift shops carry a decent selection of magazines as well as newspapers. Each park also publishes its own newspaper, which usually comes out seasonally and is given to you when you enter the park.

Photography

National parks offer a widely varied range of photographic conditions — such as the bright light of Death Valley, the low light of Olympic National Park's rain forests, and the near blackness of Mammoth Cave. Brighter conditions require slower films — that is, films with a low ASA, or ISO, number — to produce sharper pictures. In general, an ASA of 100 or 200 is good for most daytime situations, whereas early morning or late

afternoon and evening settings demand a faster film, say an ASA of 400. Serious shutterbugs with more than point-and-shoot cameras may also want to invest in a *polarizer,* which reduces contrast, deepens colors, and eliminates glare.

Film is heat sensitive. Never leave your camera or film in a car in the sun because your images can be damaged. In Yellowstone, be vigilant around geysers, hot springs, and other thermal features by quickly wiping spray or steam from your lens. This moisture is mineral-rich and can leave lasting marks behind if you don't remove it quickly.

Safety

You need to take the usual common-sense precautions for your personal safety and your belongings. See Chapter 7 for information about what to do if your money gets lost or stolen, and see Chapter 8 for tips on safely sharing the parks with wildlife.

Smoking

Lodges in more and more parks are becoming smoke free, although some lodges do have a small number of rooms for smokers.

Taxes

The national parks do not have uniform tax rates. See the "Fast Facts" section in each park chapter for individual tax rates.

Tipping

Tipping in national parks is no different than tipping in your favorite restaurant. See Chapter 3 for details.

Weather Updates

Although TVs are few and far between in national parks, most lodges usually post three-day forecasts near their front desks. If you're staying in a gateway community, your accommodation's cable TV service probably offers a weather channel — either *the* Weather Channel or a local station.

Toll-Free Numbers and Web Sites

Airline carriers

Air Canada
☎ 888-247-2262
www.aircanada.ca

Alaska Airlines
☎ 800-426-0333
www.alaska-air.com

American Airlines (American Eagle)
☎ 800-433-7300
www.aa.com

American Trans Air
☎ 800-225-2995
www.ata.com

America West Airlines (America West Express)
☎ 800-235-9292
www.americawest.com

Continental Airlines (Continental Express)
☎ 800-525-0280
www.continental.com

Delta Air Lines
☎ 800-221-1212
www.delta.com

Frontier Airlines
☎ 800-432-1359
www.frontierairlines.com

Horizon Airlines
☎ 800-547-9308
www.horizonair.com

Midwest Express
☎ 800-452-2022
www.midwestexpress.com

Northwest Airlines
☎ 800-225-2525
www.nwa.com

SkyWest
☎ 800-221-1212 (Delta Connection flights)
☎ 800-241-6522 (United Express flights)
www.skywest.com

Southwest Airlines
☎ 800-435-9792
www.southwest.com

Sun Country
☎ 800-359-6786
www.suncountry.com

Sunrise Airlines
☎ 877-978-6747
www.sunriseair.net

United Airlines (United Express)
☎ 800-241-6522
www.united.com

US Airways (US Airways Express)
☎ 800-428-4322
www.usairways.com

Car-rental agencies

Advantage
☎ 800-777-5500
www.advantagerentacar.com

Alamo
☎ 800-327-9633
www.goalamo.com

Avis
☎ 800-331-1212
☎ 800-TRY-AVIS in Canada
www.avis.com

Budget
☎ 800-527-0700
www.budgetrentacar.com

Dollar
☎ 800-800-4000
www.dollar.com

Enterprise
☎ 800-325-8007
www.enterprise.com

Hertz
☎ 800-654-3131
www.hertz.com

National
☎ 800-CAR-RENT
www.nationalcar.com

Payless
☎ 800-PAYLESS
www.paylesscarrental.com

Rent-A-Wreck
☎ 800-535-1391
www.rentawreck.com,

Thrifty
☎ 800-367-2277
www.thrifty.com

Concessionaires
Aramark Parks
Olympic National Park
www.aramarkparks.com

Delaware North
Yosemite and Sequoia/Kings
Canyon national parks
www.visitsequoia.com
www.yosemitepark.com

Grand Teton Lodge Company
Grand Teton National Park
www.gtlc.com

Guest Services Company
Mount Rainier National Park
www.guestservices.com

National Park Concessions
Mammoth Cave National Park
www.mammothcavehotel.com

Xanterra Parks & Resorts
Death Valley, Grand Canyon,
Yellowstone, and Zion national parks
www.xanterra.com

Hotel and motel chains
Best Western International
☎ 800-528-1234
www.bestwestern.com

Clarion Hotels
☎ 800-CLARION
www.clarionhotel.com

Comfort Inns
☎ 800-228-5150
www.comfortinn.com

Courtyard by Marriott
☎ 800-321-2211
www.courtyard.com

Days Inn
☎ 800-325-2525
www.daysinn.com

Doubletree Hotels
☎ 800-222-TREE
www.doubletree.com

Econo Lodges
☎ 800-55-ECONO
www.hotelchoice.com

Fairfield Inn by Marriott
☎ 800-228-2800
www.marriott.com

Hampton Inn
☎ 800-HAMPTON
www.hampton-inn.com

Hilton Hotels
☎ 800-HILTONS
www.hilton.com

Holiday Inn
☎ 800-HOLIDAY
www.basshotels.com

Howard Johnson
☎ 800-654-2000
www.hojo.com

Hyatt Hotels & Resorts
☎ 800-228-9000
www.hyatt.com

La Quinta Motor Inns
☎ 800-531-5900
www.laquinta.com

Marriott Hotels
☎ 800-228-9290
www.marriott.com

Motel 6
☎ 800-4-MOTEL6 (800-466-8536)
www.motel6.com

Quality Inns
☎ 800-228-5151
www.hotelchoice.com

Radisson Hotels International
☎ 800-333-3333
www.radisson.com

Ramada Inns
☎ 800-2-RAMADA
www.ramada.com

Red Roof Inns
☎ 800-843-7663
www.redroof.com

Residence Inn by Marriott
☎ 800-331-3131
www.marriott.com

Ritz-Carlton
☎ 800-241-3333
www.ritzcarlton.com

Rodeway Inns
☎ 800-228-2000
www.hotelchoice.com

Sheraton Hotels & Resorts
☎ 800-325-3535
www.sheraton.com

Super 8 Motels
☎ 800-800-8000
www.super8.com

Travelodge
☎ 800-255-3050
www.travelodge.com

Westin Hotels & Resorts
☎ 800-937-8461
www.westin.com

Wyndham Hotels & Resorts
☎ 800-822-4200
www.wyndham.com

Where to Get More Information

If you're like me, when you decide to go someplace, you want to do as much research as possible so you're somewhat familiar with your destination before you arrive. After all, that's why you bought this book, right?

Well, thanks to computers, rounding up information on national parks is a snap (or is that a click?). The place to start — after reading this book, of course — is at the **National Park Service** Web site, www.nps.gov. Log on, and the park system becomes an open book. You can find Web sites for each park, make your lodging and campground reservations online, delve into the park system's cultural and natural history, and even see what jobs are available.

After you've emptied the site of its information, check out the **American Park Network** (www.americanparknetwork.com). These folks print many of the small, glossy, park guidebooks you receive for free at the parks. At this site, you can pull up an electronic version of these guides for some of the more popular parks. You find, among other things, information on the park's lodgings, sites worth visiting, hiking suggestions, and history. You won't find every unit of the national park system represented, but most of the major ones are here, and you can build on the information you gained at the National Park Service site and in this book.

If you haven't yet mastered the computer age, write to the National Park Service, Office of Public Inquiries, 1849 C Street, NW, Room 1013, Washington, D.C., 20240, and request general information on the park system as well as brochures about a specific park. If you don't like waiting on the mail system, call the office at ☎ 202-208-4747 Monday through Friday from 9 a.m. to 3 p.m. and place your request.

Two more good publications can help you get a feel for the national park landscape. The first is *National Parks Visitor Facilities & Services.* This booklet can be purchased for $5.50 from **The National Park Hospitality Association,** 3701 Court House Dr., Ellicott City, MD, 21043 (☎ **410-480-2240;** Internet: www.nphassn.org). The second source is *The Complete Guide to America's National Parks,* published by the **National Park Foundation,** 11 Dupont Circle, NW, Sixth Floor, Washington, D.C., 20036 (☎ **202-238-4200**). This guide, which costs about $16, can often be found in bookstores as well.

Making Dollars and Sense of It

Expense	Daily cost	x	Number of days	=	Total
Airfare					
Local transportation					
Car rental					
Park Fee					
Lodging (with tax)					
Parking					
Breakfast					
Lunch					
Dinner					
Snacks					
Activities					
Babysitting					
Attractions					
Gifts & souvenirs					
Tips					
Other					
Grand Total					

Fare Game: Choosing an Airline

When looking for the best airfare, you should cover all your bases — 1) consult a trusted travel agent; 2) contact the airline directly, via the airline's toll-free number and/or Web site; 3) check out one of the travel-planning Web sites, such as www.frommers.com.

Travel Agency_____ Phone_____
   Agent's Name_____ Quoted fare_____

Airline 1_____ Quoted fare_____
   Toll-free number/Internet_____

Airline 2_____ Quoted fare_____
   Toll-free number/Internet_____

Web site 1_____ Quoted fare_____

Web site 2_____ Quoted fare_____

Departure Schedule & Flight Information

Airline_____ Flight #_____ Confirmation #_____

Departs_____ Date_____ Time_____ a.m./p.m.

Arrives_____ Date_____ Time_____ a.m./p.m.

Connecting Flight (if any)

Amount of time between flights_____ hours/mins

Airline_____ Flight #_____ Confirmation #_____

Departs_____ Date_____ Time_____ a.m./p.m.

Arrives_____ Date_____ Time_____ a.m./p.m.

Return Trip Schedule & Flight Information

Airline_____ Flight #_____ Confirmation #_____

Departs_____ Date_____ Time_____ a.m./p.m.

Arrives_____ Date_____ Time_____ a.m./p.m.

Connecting Flight (if any)

Amount of time between flights_____ hours/mins

Airline_____ Flight #_____ Confirmation #_____

Departs_____ Date_____ Time_____ a.m./p.m.

Arrives_____ Date_____ Time_____ a.m./p.m.

Sweet Dreams: Choosing Your Hotel Or Campground

Enter the hotels where you'd prefer to stay based on location and price. Then use the worksheet below to plan your itinerary.

Hotel/Campground	Location	Price per night

Sights to See, Hikes to Take, Things to Do

Enter the attractions you would most like to see. Then use the worksheet below to plan your itinerary.

Attractions/Activities	Amount of time you expect to spend there	Best day and time to go

Index

South Kaibab Trail (Grand Canyon), 204
South Rim (Grand Canyon), 193, 195
Southeastern Greyhound bus service, 289
Southwest Harbor (Acadia), 91, 98
Specimen Ridge Trail (Yellowstone), 409
spelunking. *See* Mammoth Cave National Park (Kentucky)
spiders. *See* bites and stings
Spring Creek Ranch (Grand Teton), 249
spring, visiting during, 27. *See also individual parks'* when to visit
Spruce Nature Trail (Olympic), 351–352
Stagecoach Inn (Yellowstone), 420
Stony Creek Lodge (Giant Sequoia), 385
Storm King Information Station (Olympic), 343
Storm King Spa at Mount Rainier, 329
storytelling hikes (Acadia), 103
Stovepipe Wells (Death Valley), 164
Stovepipe Wells Village (Death Valley), 162, 167, 180, 181, 183
String Lake (Grand Teton), 240
String Lake Stroll (Grand Teton), 243
Sugarlands Visitor Center (Smoky Mtns), 262, 264, 271
Sulphur Caldron (Yellowstone), 411
summer vacations, 27, 71. *See also individual parks,* when to visit
sunburn, 142, 168, 201–202, 497
Sunflower Hill Bed & Breakfast Inn (Arches), 129
Sunrise (Mt. Rainier), 311, 319, 322
Sunrise Visitor Center (Mt. Rainier), 315
sunrises, 493
Sunset Campground (Death Valley), 181

Sunset Campground (Kings Canyon), 387
sunsets, 495
Sunshine Point Campground (Mt. Rainier), 330
Sweetwater Restaurant (Grand Teton), 255
swimming
Acadia, 104
Grand Teton, 234, 241
Olympic, 345
Switchback Grill (Zion), 481

• *T* •

taxes, 35, 498. *See also individual parks,* basic/emergency information
teenagers, activities for, 40
Telescope Peak Trail (Death Valley), 173–174
Temple of Sinawava (Zion), 473
Tenaya Lake (Yosemite), 431
Tennessee Ridge Inn (Smoky Mtns), 276
Tent Cabins at Grant Grove (Kings Canyon), 384
Terrace Grill (Yellowstone), 423
Teton Park Road, 231
Teton Range, 225
Teton Village KOA, 252
Texas Spring Campground (Death Valley), 165, 181
Tharp's Log (Sequoia), 376, 380
theft, handling, 69–70. *See also* safety tips
theme parks, versus national parks, 489–491
thermal features, safety tips, 84
Thorndike Campground (Death Valley), 182
Thunder Hole (Acadia), 89, 96, 101
Thunderbird & Kachina Lodges (Grand Canyon), 214–215
ticks, deer, 80–81
tide pooling (Acadia), 97, 103
tides, safety tips, 83

time zones. *See individual parks,* basic/emergency information
tipping, 35–36, 498
Tokopah Falls (Sequoia), 381
Tony Andrews Farm (Cape Cod), 151
Toroweap Valley (Grand Canyon), 195, 206
tourist information. *See* visitor information
tours. *See* guided tours; organized tours, escorted and package
Tower Arch (Arches), 125
Tower Fall complex (Yellowstone), 399
traffic jams
Cape Cod, 133, 136
Grand Canyon, 194
Great Smoky Mountains, 262–263
Trail of the Sequoias (Sequoia), 376
Trailer Village (Grand Canyon), 218
trails. *See* bicycling, bike tours; hiking, walking trails
Trailways bus service, 369
train travel
to Arches, 114
to Grand Canyon, 190
to Sequoia/Kings Canyon, 369
Trans-Canyon Shuttle (Grand Canyon), 196
transportation costs, estimating, 32
Trapper Inn (Grand Teton), 250
Travac Tours & Charters Web site, 55
travel agents, 49–50
travel, arranging, 49–55
Travel Companion Exchange, 44–45
Travel Guard International, 75
Travel Inn (Mammoth Cave), 305
Travel Insured International, 75
Travel With Your Children (Family Travel Times newletter), 40
traveler's checks, 68

Notes

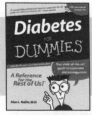

FOR DUMMIES

A world of resources to help you grow

HOME & BUSINESS COMPUTER BASICS

0-7645-0838-5

0-7645-1663-9

0-7645-1548-9

Also available:

Excel 2002 All-in-One Desk Reference For Dummies
(0-7645-1794-5)

Office XP 9-in-1 Desk Reference For Dummies
(0-7645-0819-9)

PCs All-in-One Desk Reference For Dummies
(0-7645-0791-5)

Troubleshooting Your PC For Dummies
(0-7645-1669-8)

Upgrading & Fixing PCs For Dummies
(0-7645-1665-5)

Windows XP For Dummies
(0-7645-0893-8)

Windows XP For Dummies Quick Reference
(0-7645-0897-0)

Word 2002 For Dummies
(0-7645-0839-3)

INTERNET & DIGITAL MEDIA

0-7645-0894-6

0-7645-1642-6

0-7645-1664-7

Also available:

CD and DVD Recording For Dummies
(0-7645-1627-2)

Digital Photography All-in-One Desk Reference For Dummies
(0-7645-1800-3)

eBay For Dummies
(0-7645-1642-6)

Genealogy Online For Dummies
(0-7645-0807-5)

Internet All-in-One Desk Reference For Dummies
(0-7645-1659-0)

Internet For Dummies Quick Reference
(0-7645-1645-0)

Internet Privacy For Dummies
(0-7645-0846-6)

Paint Shop Pro For Dummies
(0-7645-2440-2)

Photo Retouching & Restoration For Dummies
(0-7645-1662-0)

Photoshop Elements For Dummies
(0-7645-1675-2)

Scanners For Dummies
(0-7645-0783-4)

Get smart! Visit www.dummies.com

- **Find listings of even more Dummies titles**

- **Browse online articles, excerpts, and how-to's**

- **Sign up for daily or weekly e-mail tips**

- **Check out Dummies fitness videos and other products**

- **Order from our online bookstore**

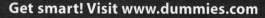

Available wherever books are sold. Go to www.dummies.com or call 1-877-762-2974 to order direct

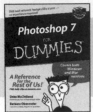